Seeing Things John's Way

Westminster John Knox Press is committed to preserving ancient forests and natural resources. We elected to print this title on 30% post consumer recycled paper, processed chlorine free. As a result, for this printing, we have saved:

13 Trees (40' tall and 6-8" diameter)
5 Million BTUs of Total Energy
92 Pounds of Greenhouse Gases
5,791 Gallons of Wastewater
196 Pounds of Solid Waste

Westminster John Knox Press made this paper choice because our printer, Thomson-Shore, Inc., is a member of Green Press Initiative, a nonprofit program dedicated to supporting authors, publishers, and suppliers in their efforts to reduce their use of fiber obtained from endangered forests.

For more information, visit www.greenpressinitiative.org

Environmental impact estimates were made using the Environmental Defense Paper Calculator. For more information visit: www.edf.org/papercalculator

Seeing Things John's Way

The Rhetoric of the Book of Revelation

David A. deSilva

WESTMINSTER
JOHN KNOX PRESS
LOUISVILLE · KENTUCKY

© 2009 David A. deSilva

First edition
Published by Westminster John Knox Press
Louisville, Kentucky

09 10 11 12 13 14 15 16 17 18—10 9 8 7 6 5 4 3 2 1

All rights reserved. No part of this book may be reproduced or transmitted in any form or by any means, electronic or mechanical, including photocopying, recording, or by any information storage or retrieval system, without permission in writing from the publisher. For information, address Westminster John Knox Press, 100 Witherspoon Street, Louisville, Kentucky 40202-1396. Or contact us online at www.wjkbooks.com.

Unless otherwise indicated, Scripture quotations are by the author. Those marked NRSV are from the New Revised Standard Version of the Bible, copyright © 1989 by the Division of Christian Education of the National Council of the Churches of Christ in the U.S.A., and are used by permission.

Book design by Sharon Adams
Cover design by Mark Abrams
Cover art: St. John Eating the Book, no. 28 from "The Apocalypse of Angers,"
1373–87 (tapestry) by Nicolas Bataille

Library of Congress Cataloging-in-Publication Data
deSilva, David Arthur.
  Seeing things John's way : the rhetoric of the book of Revelation / David A. deSilva.
    p. cm.
  Includes bibliographical references and index.
  ISBN 978-0-664-22449-3 (alk. paper)
  1. Bible. N.T. Revelation—Criticism, interpretation, etc. I. Title.
  BS2825.52.D48   2009
  228'.066—dc22
                                                                              2009001902

PRINTED IN THE UNITED STATES OF AMERICA

∞ The paper used in this publication meets the minimum requirements
of the American National Standard for Information Sciences—Permanence of Paper
for Printed Library Materials, ANSI Z39.48-1992.

Westminster John Knox Press advocates the responsible use of our natural resources.
The text paper of this book is made from at least 30% postconsumer waste.

*In honor of my parents,
Dr. J. Arthur de Silva and Mrs. Dorothy A. de Silva,
on the fiftieth anniversary of their wedding,*

*and my grandmother,
Mrs. Dorothy Strout Snethkamp,
on her ninetieth birthday*

Contents

Preface	ix
Acknowledgments	xi
Abbreviations	xiii

1. "Favored Are Those Who Read": Orientations to Revelation in the History of Interpretation — 1

2. The Rhetorical Setting of Revelation: Seven Congregations in the Roman Province of Asia — 29

3. What Does John Really Want? The Rhetorical Goals of Revelation — 65

4. "What Is and What Will Be Hereafter": The Cosmos according to John — 93

5. Why Should We Listen to John? The Construction of Ethos in Revelation — 117

6. *Stealing* Authority? John's Use of the Hebrew Bible — 147

7. The Strategic Arousal of Emotions in the Oracles to the Seven Churches — 175

8. "I Saw a Monster Rising Up!" Appeals to Pathos in the Visions of Revelation — 193

9. Appeals to Rational Argument (Logos) in Revelation: The Seven Oracles — 229

10. Argumentation in John's Visions: Revelation 14:6–13 as Focal Summary of Main Points — 257

11. Literary Logic in Revelation: Rational Argument
    through Narrative and Intertexture   285

12. John's Vision beyond the Roman World:
    What Might the Spirit Continue to Say
    to the Churches?   313

Bibliography   351
Index of Ancient Texts   365
Index of Modern Authors   381
Index of Subjects   385

Preface

This study constructs an argument for a rhetorical reading of Revelation. It begins by locating a classical rhetorical-critical approach within the history of interpretation and by stating the guiding questions that rhetorical criticism brings to a text like Revelation (chap. 1). It moves thence into the historical situation of Revelation from a rhetorical point of view. That is, it inquires into those features of the actual historical situation that John strategically selects as focal points for attention and, in many cases, problematizes for his audience (chap. 2). This leads, in turn, to an assessment of John's rhetorical goals for Revelation in regard to the features of the audience's situation that he does highlight (chap. 3).

The next eight chapters seek to display the rhetorical strategies that John employs as means of attaining those goals. John's choice of apocalypse as the principal genre of Revelation brings along with it strategies essential to John's interests in displacing Roman imperial ideology, and these are explored in chapter 4. Chapters 5 and 6 examine John's textual construction of his own authority and deconstruction of the authority of rival voices since such appeals to ethos are indispensable to a speaker's success. The emotionally evocative power of Revelation has often been noted and even experienced by interpreters, but never systematically explored. This is the goal of chapters 7 and 8. Finally, although interpreters rarely look for "logic" in John's bizarre visions, John does have a case to make. The study thus moves forward to analyze John's appeals to reason, both in the form of enthymematic-argumentative elaboration (chapters 9 and 10) and in the form of narrative elaboration of underlying premises (chapter 11). A concluding chapter examines arguments against continuing to hear Revelation as an authoritative word, and then explores what formative impact John's rhetorical strategies and John's ideological program might beneficially have on those who are inclined to engage Revelation as authoritative Scripture.

The reader who progresses through the book in order, therefore, will experience the unfolding argument most fully. However, I recognize that most readers—whether pastors in the course of preaching and teaching, or students in a class on "Exegesis of Revelation," or instructors preparing for the same—do not come to a book on Revelation primarily because they are interested in that book's argument, but rather are interested in working through the text of Revelation. The order of material in this book can be readily adapted for such readers. In a classroom setting, where one usually finds a number of introductory topics and portions of Revelation distributed over a set number of class meetings, I recommend something like the following distribution of the material, with parentheses indicating alternative placement of chapters:

Topic	Material in this volume
Orientation to interpretation	chapter 1
Historical Setting	chapters 2 and 3
Genre	(chapter 4)
Use of the Jewish Scriptures	chapter 6
Revelation 1	chapter 5 (chapter 6)
Revelation 2–3	chapters 7 and 9
Revelation 4–5	chapter 4 (chapter 8)
Revelation 12–13	chapter 8
Revelation 14–16	chapters 10 and 11
Revelation 17:1–19:10	(chapters 8 and 10)
Interpretation and Application	chapter 12

Sections within chapters could be appropriately read alongside still other sections of text. The section on "Fear and Confidence in the Visions" in chapter 8, for example, focuses on Revelation 6–9, while the section on "Emulation" in chapter 8 focuses on the vision of the two witnesses in Revelation 11. The introductory chapter provides enough grounding in classical rhetoric and a sufficient road map of the book's landscape to allow for broad latitude in the order in which the material is read.

Acknowledgments

The major portion of the research for this book, along with several chapters, was completed during a year's research leave spent at the Institut für antikes Judentum und hellenistische Religionsgeschichte of the Eberhard-Karls-Universität Tübingen, supported by the Alexander von Humboldt Foundation. I am deeply grateful to the foundation for this opportunity, to the gracious hospitality of my academic sponsor and his wife, Herr Prof. Dr. Martin Hengel (emeritus) and Frau Marianne Hengel, and to Herr Prof. Dr. Hermann Lichtenberger and Frau Marietta Hämmerle as well, both of whom provided invaluable assistance in many practical matters throughout the course of the year. I wish to express my gratitude also to my home institution, Ashland Theological Seminary, and its Board of Trustees and administration, for amending the faculty handbook to allow for full-year research leaves, and for additional support during the year abroad.

It was singularly appropriate to study Revelation while living as a foreigner in a land not my own, and while acquiring a perspective on the policies and practices of my native land that would not have been possible living within its border. Although Tübingen was a foreign city to me and my family, we found it a truly friendly one. Many couples welcomed us with open hearts and open doors, and we will forever treasure them for their gift of friendship: Herr Alexander and Frau Berit Teltscher, Herr Dr. Gottfried and Frau Linda Kiefner, Herr Dr. Walter and Frau Dr. Annegret Klaiber, Pfarrer Martin and Frau Ellie Jäger, Herr. Dr. Dieter and Frau Isolde Belschner, and the congregation of the Friedenskirche in Tübingen.

Several chapters of this book have previously appeared in academic journals. Chapter 7 was published in slightly longer form as "The Strategic Arousal of Emotions in the Apocalypse of John: A Rhetorical-critical Investigation of the Oracles to the Seven Churches," *New Testament Studies* 54 (2008): 90–114. Chapter 8 appeared as "The Strategic Arousal of Emotions in John's Visions of Roman Imperialism: A Rhetorical-critical Investigation of Revelation 4–22," *Neotestamentica* 42 (2008): 1–34. Chapter 9 was released as "Out of Our Minds? Appeals to Reason (*Logos*) in the Seven Oracles of Revelation 2–3," *Journal for the Study of the New Testament* 31 (2008): 123–55. Chapter 11 incorporates some material previously published as "Final Topics: The Rhetorical Functions of Intertexture in Revelation 14:14–16:21," pages 215–41 in *The Intertexture of Apocalyptic Discourse in the New Testament,* edited by D. F. Watson, Symposium Series (Atlanta, Ga.: Society of Biblical Literature, 2002). I am grateful to the publishers for permission to present this material again in the context of an integrated rhetorical-critical study of Revelation.

In the final stages of preparation, I enjoyed the help of several people, to whom I extend my thanks: Ms. Lori Shire, Mrs. Donna Jean deSilva, and Mr. Benjamin Gemmel, who assisted me in the preparation of the indexes; Ms. Shire again, who proofread the entire manuscript; and Dr. Russell Marton, who proofread several chapters.

Finally, I name with gratitude my maternal grandmother, Mrs. Dorothy Strout Snethkamp, with whom I first read Revelation nearly thirty years ago, and my parents, Dr. J. Arthur F. de Silva and Mrs. Dorothy Alberta de Silva, with whom I first sang its wondrous songs in the liturgy and choral program of our home church, St. Andrew and Holy Communion Episcopal, South Orange, New Jersey, at about the same time. Some things *do* stick with one's children. It is to them that I dedicate this volume in honor of two very special landmarks: to my parents, in honor of their fiftieth wedding anniversary, and to my grandmother, in honor of her ninetieth birthday.

David A. deSilva
All Saints' Day 2008

Abbreviations

AB	Anchor Bible Commentary
AUSS	*Andrews University Seminary Studies*
BDAG	Bauer, W., F. W. Danker, W. F. Arndt, and F. W. Gingrich. *Greek-English Lexicon of the New Testament and Other Early Christian Literature*. 3rd ed. Chicago: University of Chicago Press, 2000.
BDF	Blass, F., A. Debrunner, and R. W. Funk. *A Greek Grammar of the New Testament and Other Early Christian Literature*. Chicago: University of Chicago, 1961.
BR	*Biblical Research*
E	English Bible versification
HNT	Handbuch zum Neuen Testament
HTR	*Harvard Theological Review*
I. Eph.	*Die Inschriften von Ephesos*. Edited by H. Wankel et al. 8 vols. in 11. Bonn: Rodolf Habelt, 1979–84.
JBL	*Journal of Biblical Literature*
JSNT	*Journal for the Study of the New Testament*
JSNTsup	Journal for the Study of the New Testament Supplement Series
LCL	Loeb Classical Library
LXX	Septuagint
NICNT	New International Commentary on the New Testament
NovT	*Novum Testamentum*
NTS	*New Testament Studies*
QJS	*Quarterly Journal of Speech*
RB	*Revue biblique*
SBL	Society of Biblical Literature

SBLDS	Society of Biblical Literature Dissertation Series
SBLSP	Society of Biblical Literature Seminar Papers
TDNT	*Theological Dictionary of the New Testament.* Edited by G. Kittel and G. Friedrich. Translated by G. W. Bromiley. 10 vols. Grand Rapids: Eerdmans, 1964–1976
WBC	Word Biblical Commentary
WUNT	Wissenschaftliche Untersuchungen zum Neuen Testament

Chapter 1

"Favored Are Those Who Read"
Orientations to Revelation in the History of Interpretation

When we open up a Bible to the book of Revelation, if we open up a Bible to that book at all, we open ourselves up to a strange world indeed. We are greeted by a fiery, glowing Jesus who looks nothing like the man we knew from the stories in the Gospels (even the shining Jesus of the transfiguration is tame by comparison). We hear him confront seven communities with limited praise and spirited censure, issuing commands and warnings, making extravagant promises and threats. We enter into scenes of heavenly worship involving fantastic heavenly hybrid creatures and stretching out through hosts of angels to all of creation, all surrounding a seven-eyed Lamb, slaughtered but standing, and all this to-do over some sealed scroll.

And that's the *easy* part of the book. Then come the devastations of the seals, the army of white-robed martyrs, seven trumpets unleashing unnatural disasters and armies of unnatural creatures. When we encounter a colossus with pillars of fire for legs, we actually breathe a sigh of relief before being plunged again into a world where a dragon has it in for some star-crowned woman and her offspring, sending in his clone and a second monstrous henchthing to ferret them out and kill them (since her true progeny would never worship an image), but where this is all right, since they become the army of the slain-but-standing Lamb. A third series of seven devastations makes the first two series look like target practice, after which we pause to look a little more closely at some great city, which shows up now as a gaudy prostitute offering us a cup full of blood and God-knows-what-else, and then watch her be stripped and eaten up by the dragon's clone before she becomes a city again, going up in smoke. The heavenly beings celebrate this event, and then we're off to the arranged marriage of the Lamb with some woman we haven't met yet, but not before the Lamb, who's now bipedal and riding a horse through the air (but nothing strikes us as odd by this point), throws the dragon's chieftains into a fiery lake and serves up their armies to the birds of the air. The dragon is bound in the abyss while the dead followers of the Lamb enjoy a thousand-year reign with him, after which the dragon is teased with having one last crack at overthrowing God and God's Anointed, which lands him in the fiery lake as well. Then comes the final judgment, sorting out humanity into their eternal destinies, and the bride appears at last—as a city, the new Jerusalem, descending from a new heaven to the new earth, where God's kingdom is realized at last in an urbanized garden of Eden.

Having opened up this book—a veritable Pandora's box (also giving Hope as its final gift)— its world and its inhabitants rush out into our world, invading our normal reality. We don't know quite how to put the two worlds together, and we start looking for the beast, or the prostitute, or the beast's mark, or the falling star "Wormwood" in the world around us. Where *did* that beast go? Can you see it raising its head(s) somewhere out there? How do we open up this book, this Pandora's box, in a way that makes sense to us living in *our* world?

FOUR MAJOR INTERPRETIVE KEYS

Interpreters intuited that they needed a key to open up *this* book. In 1627 a teacher named Joseph Mede wrote a treatise called *Clavis apocalyptica* (The Key to the Apocalypse). This was followed by another book by Samuel Hartlib and John Drury, with a much longer title: *Clavis apocalyptica, or, the revelation revealed in which the great mysteries in the Revelation of St. John and the prophet Daniel are opened: it being made apparent that the prophetical numbers come to an end with the year of our Lord 1655*, that is to say, four years after the book was published.[1] Revelation was less to be read and more to be decoded. To understand Revelation, you just needed the right decoder. For the majority of interpreters, this decoding proceeded on the basis of one foundational premise: Revelation was a book of predictions awaiting fulfillment. The title of the second book reveals a foundational concern behind the decoding enterprise: Where are *we* in this line of predictions?

Surveys of the landscape of interpretation of Revelation often identify four basic schools of interpretation: the preterist, historicist, futurist, and idealist

---

1. Mede 1627; Hartlib and Drury 1651.

approaches.[2] The first three of these schools, however, share the single premise articulated above: Revelation contains prophecies that must be fulfilled at some point in history. Those three schools differ only in terms of the time frame of that fulfillment.

The historicist approach reads Revelation as a prediction of events spanning the time between the book's composition and the establishment of the new heavens and new earth.[3] It is, perhaps, the most intuitive approach in this regard. After all, the book starts with messages addressing seven churches at the end of the first century and ends with visions of Christ's return, the Last Judgment, and the breaking in of God's eternal kingdom. The visions falling in between must then represent the course of history from John's time to Christ's end-time return. The events portrayed in Revelation become "milestones which are able to give the traveler some reasonably clear indication of how far has been traveled and how much further there is yet to go."[4]

Joachim of Fiore, a thirteenth-century priest, brought this reading to new prominence. Joachim read Revelation as a prediction of events down to his own day, naming the Holy Roman Emperor Henry IV and Saladin among the successions of "heads" of the beast. Joachim located his generation near the end of the sequence, giving fresh impetus to expectations that the millennium would soon begin.[5] Martin Luther also pursued a historicist reading of Revelation, once he overcame his initial doubts about the book and recognized its usefulness for antipapal propaganda.[6] Historicism remained popular into the nineteenth century, and the application of the "year-day" principle derived from Ezekiel 4:4–6 (with a "day" in a prophetic text indicating the passing of a "year" in everyday life) became an important means by which to span the growing gap between John's time and the interpreter's.[7] Historicist readings, however, are highly Eurocentric. Rarely if ever does a historicist reading take the church in Asia or the southern hemisphere into account, except perhaps as the object of Western missions.[8]

2. Gregg 1997 and Mounce 1977, 24–29 adopt this schema.
3. See the fuller discussion in Wainwright 1993, 49–61; Newport 2000, 6–11.
4. Newport 2000, 7.
5. Wainwright 1993, 49–52; Barr 2003, 3.
6. Koester 2001, 11–12.
7. Gregg 1997, 34–35; Newport 2000, 8–10.
8. Gregg 1997, 37. The reading of the seven oracles as seven epochs of church history, an element of historicism that appears in futurist readings as well, exemplifies this Eurocentric and, more particularly, Protestant-centered reading quite starkly. The focus of attention moves from the apostolic age (Ephesus), through the period of persecution from Nero through Diocletian and Maximian (Smyrna), and through the period of legalization under Constantine (Pergamum). At this point the Western church moves into center stage to the exclusion of Christianity elsewhere. The oracle to Thyatira characterizes (caricatures) the period of the papacy, the oracle to Sardis speaks of the Western post-Enlightenment church, the oracle to Philadelphia the great awakening and missionary endeavors of England and the United States, and finally, Laodicea the lukewarm state of the modern church (again, in the West).

Aside from the gross oversimplification this imposes even upon the Western church, the scheme completely neglects the state of the church in the southern hemisphere and the Middle and Far East. The scheme presumes that God, in revealing this information, is really only concerned with the

A second approach to Revelation as predictive prophecy to be decoded is the futurist view. Futuristic readings understand some of Revelation to pertain to events contemporary with its author ("the things that are," Rev. 1:19), often reading the seven oracles as a means of bridging the distance between John and the present generation, but then look to the future for the fulfillment of the vast majority of Revelation's material ("the things about to happen," 1:19). This approach was renewed in the modern age as one Catholic response to antipapal applications of the historicist approach, which often claimed that a particular pope or the papacy represented the fulfillment of prophecies concerning the beast or the whore.[9] It became an important component of dispensationalism as articulated by John N. Darby in the early nineteenth century, was widely disseminated in the West through C. I. Scofield's annotations to the Bible and Charles C. Ryrie's *Study Bible*, and was more recently popularized in Hal Lindsey's *The Late Great Planet Earth* and the Left Behind series by Tim LaHaye and Jerry Jenkins. The futurist reading allows for the highest degree of literalism, for example, the expectation that a third of earth's trees and grass will perish. Since this has never actually happened, the historicist reading must temper the literal sense somehow in order to connect the sounding of that first trumpet (8:7) with some past event, while the futurist reading is free to imagine the scene of destruction more literally.[10]

Futurist readings face some serious obstacles, however. They render most of Revelation irrelevant to the first audience, save perhaps for the assurance that God would eventually triumph over evil. The distance created between the first hearers and the fulfillment of Revelation's visions stands in stark contrast to the consistent emphasis throughout Revelation that "the time is near" (1:3; 22:10) and that the visions are imminently relevant (coming to pass *quickly*: 1:1; 3:11; 22:7, 12, 20). Particularly problematic is the claim by "prophecy experts" that the message of Revelation is finally being revealed in current events, when John himself regarded the message of Revelation to stand "unsealed," open to be understood by his immediate readers (22:10; contrast Dan. 12:9). Furthermore, when a futurist reading is combined with dispensationalism—particularly in regard to a "Rapture" of the faithful prior to the events narrated after Revelation 4:1—it renders most of Revelation irrelevant to Christian readers in every age,[11] except

---

Western church up through the Reformation, and thereafter with the Protestant churches, largely in America. If the oracle to Laodicea is meant to characterize the church of the present day, the glorified Christ would be giving no notice to the millions of faithful Christians in the developing world whose fidelity to God under great pressure, and whose enthusiasm for evangelism, far more closely resemble the conditions in Smyrna and Philadelphia than Laodicea.

Since Revelation itself articulates an explicitly global view of the church (a kingdom drawn out for God "from every tribe and language group and people and nation," 5:9; 7:9) and of the scope of God's concern (as in 14:6–7), it would be perverse to maintain the suggestion that Rev. 2–3 preserves a message chiefly concerned with the Western (and eventually, Protestant) churches for the sake of preserving a historicist (sequential) interpretation of these oracles.

9. Wainwright 1993, 61–63. This antipapal reading survives to this day in some nonmainline Protestant readings of Revelation.
10. Gregg 1997, 40.
11. Gregg 1997, 42.

perhaps as an exercise in prophetic voyeurism of the horrendous fate of unbelievers and the tribulation of those converted only after the Rapture (and thus, more positively, as an incentive to remain faithful and to engage in evangelism).[12]

Preterism, the third of these related approaches, also emerged afresh in the modern age as a Catholic response to antipapal readings of Revelation.[13] Preterists suggest that the predictions of Revelation, save for a few pertaining to the end time, were fulfilled in the distant past. Some preterists read Revelation as a prediction of events from John's time to the establishment of the Christian state under Constantine, with the millennium representing the age of the church following its legalization and ascendancy.[14] More radically, some preterists read virtually all of Revelation as a prediction of events culminating in the destruction of Jerusalem (represented, in this reading, by Babylon) in 70 CE, which is equated with the second coming of Christ.

The fourth approach in this common schema is the idealist interpretation, which could also be called the "spiritual," "allegorical," or even "archetypal" reading. This approach does not share the premise that Revelation is primarily a collection of predictions. Rather, Revelation uses symbol, vivid imagery, and dramatic action to express transcendent truths that are valid in every generation. It provides "a general commentary on the struggle between good and evil,"[15] a kind of philosophy of history. Origen, for example, rejected a literal fulfillment of the promises about the saints enjoying earthly wealth, power, and abundance in the new Jerusalem, preferring a spiritual interpretation of those details more in keeping with the spiritual nature of the resurrection body described by Paul (1 Cor. 15:44, 50).[16] Augustine also read Revelation spiritually as an allegory of the soul's journey from the city of this world to the city of God.[17]

A purely idealist approach, however, runs afoul of John's own perspective on the imminence, and therefore special relevance, of the material for his immediate audience. A timeless style of reading also passes over the close and obvious correlation of Revelation's primary symbols with the politico-economic realities that characterized Roman Asia Minor with a stunning degree of particularity and "timeliness."[18] It does have the advantage, however, of not reducing Revelation to

---

12. Futurist readings looking for a correspondence between contemporary events or figures and the symbols and scenes of Revelation on a one-to-one basis often allow fundamentalist Christians to promote imperialist agendas—a use diametrically opposed to John's own agenda in writing Revelation. See further Schüssler Fiorenza 1991, 9, critiquing Walvoord 1991, which enjoyed tremendous popularity during the First Persian Gulf War.

13. Wainwright 1993, 63–66; see also Newport 2000, 15–16.

14. Augustine championed the view that the millennium began with Constantine's decree of toleration, though Augustine himself held most closely to the fourth interpretive approach (Wainwright 1993, 33–48).

15. Newport 2000, 15.

16. Augustine, *De principiis* 2.11.2–5.

17. Barr 2003, 3. See Augustine, *City of God* 20.

18. Mounce (1977, 29) insightfully calls these varying approaches "an accident of history. The author himself could without contradiction be preterist, historicist, futurist, and idealist. . . . The interpretive problem grows out of the fact that the End did not arrive on schedule."

a series of "steno-symbols,"[19] symbols that have only one referent and so relate to some reality on a one-to-one basis and then have nothing more to say. An idealist approach is more conducive to reading Revelation as a matrix of "tensive symbols," which "can evoke a whole range of meanings and can never be exhausted or adequately expressed by one referent."[20]

A FIFTH INTERPRETIVE KEY

Alongside the three modes of interpretation that read Revelation as a collection of predictions in search of fulfillment and the fourth mode that reads Revelation as an allegory communicating timeless truths stands a fifth approach, sometimes called the "contemporary-historical" approach.[21] The foundational premise guiding this approach is the modest affirmation that "the Apocalypse was written specially for the benefit of certain people who were living at that time, and for the purpose of being understood by them."[22] Reading from this perspective produces several principal questions: "How would a Christian in Ephesus (or Pergamum or Thyatira, etc.) have understood John's Revelation?" "What referents would *they* have associated with John's symbolic language, and how would those associations have motivated them to respond?"

This interpretive key requires readers to immerse themselves in the political, social, cultural, and economic landscape of Roman Asia Minor (and the larger Mediterranean arena, insofar as it impinged on the lives of its inhabitants) in the hope that, by so doing, many of Revelation's images and claims will also become less unfamiliar, even immediately recognizable. The contemporary-historical approach regards the creative speculations of futurist interpreters in regard to the significance of the beasts, the image, the mark, and the prostitute as the result not of our *closer* proximity to the fulfillment of Revelation's predictions in our near future. Rather, these speculations are the result of our greater *distance* from obvious, everyday realities in the landscape of first-century Roman Asia Minor to which John draws attention—and about which he makes revelatory comments—by means of such images.[23] This approach assumes that John cared most about the readers he actually addressed, and that he wrote Revelation for them rather than any future generations of readers.

19. Schüssler Fiorenza 1985, 183.
20. Schüssler Fiorenza 1985, 183.
21. Hemer 1986, 20.
22. Wettstein 1752, 2:893 (as quoted in Wainwright 1993, 138). Wainwright (1993, 107–58) provides a concise overview of the rise of critical scholarship from early third-century discussions of authorship of Revelation based on stylistic and lexical differences between Revelation and the Fourth Gospel through the twentieth century, with the rise of source-critical, "contemporary-historical," tradition-critical, and social-scientific analyses of Revelation.
23. See the affirmation by Mounce (1977, 29) that Revelation's symbols "are not esoteric and enigmatic references to some future culture totally foreign to first-century readers (e.g., hydrogen bombs, satellite television, and the European Common Market)."

Although congenial with preterist approaches, this strategy is not strictly the same thing. Preterists also often interpret Revelation with a view to how it would have made sense to the seven congregations addressed in Asia Minor, yet "contemporary-historical" interpreters tend not to regard Revelation as essentially predictive prophecy, nor expect to find a one-to-one correspondence between its images and the unfolding course of history in the apostolic, post-apostolic, or ante-Nicene periods.[24] It is also not a type of idealist approach, since it seeks not the *timeless* meaning of Revelation, but the very *timely* message and challenge Revelation posed to the congregations of the Roman province of Asia Minor, deriving any ongoing meaning from this starting point.[25] Contemporary-historical interpreters approach Revelation essentially as they approach Amos, Galatians, or any other such situation-specific call for faithfulness to the God of the covenant.[26]

Interpreters of Revelation working from a contemporary-historical paradigm are not a homogeneous lot, nor do they produce readings of solely antiquarian interest. Some are as deeply interested in the present as futurists who expect Revelation's seals to begin to be opened next month. This is particularly true of several streams of ideological interpretation—interpretations generated by readers deeply aware of, and engaged with, their own social locations of reading.

Liberationist readings represent a very important strategy that considers the contemporary-historical approach as its home base, though with a very specific goal for engaging this approach. Such readers understand "the oppressive powers of the present in light of the past and the future in light of God's liberating action" and motivate "the reader to engage in resistance and struggle for change."[27] Allen Boesak's *Comfort and Protest: The Apocalypse from a South African Perspective* is a singular achievement in this regard. Rooted in a contemporary-historical reading of Revelation, Boesak moves forward into the situation of apartheid South Africa, using John's interpretation of Roman imperialism as a resource for interpreting and challenging the apartheid state that existed at the end of a long history of colonialism in South Africa. Boesak works from analogy, in keeping with John's own practice: "Just as the author of Revelation has used . . . the Exodus of Israel or the eschatological vision of Ezekiel for giving a prophetic interpretation of his

---

24. The charge that this approach shows "no respect whatever for the Apocalypse as an inspired writing" (Pieters 1937, 42) confuses the commitment to read Revelation as predictive prophecy with the commitment to hear the text as word of God. Reading Revelation as an unveiling of how the realities of first-century Asia Minor under the shadow of Roman imperialism look from God's point of view is not a denial of its inspiration and continuing challenge, but the result of a different understanding of the book's purpose and genre.

25. Gregg (1997, 43) includes "all approaches that do not look for individual or specific fulfillment of the prophecies of Revelation in the natural sense, but which believe only that spiritual lessons and principles (which may find recurrent expression in history) are depicted symbolically in the visions" under this category.

26. Walvoord (1966, 18) sees "contemporary liberal works" working with a combination of a preterist approach that dates the book to Domitian's reign and an idealist approach that then extrapolates meaning. But such an approach is not more preterist and idealist than our interpretation of a text like Galatians. Walvoord misapplies the categories and misunderstands the hermeneutic.

27. Schüssler Fiorenza 1991, 10–11.

own sociopolitical situation, so liberation theologians utilize Revelation for the theological interpretation of their own historical situation."[28]

Feminist interpretations sifting Revelation for its potential to speak a liberating word to people coming out of the domination system of patriarchy form another group of ideological readings within the contemporary-historical approach. Elisabeth Schüssler Fiorenza, Tina Pippin, and Susan Hylen have produced important readings, wrestling specifically with the gendered images and language of Revelation, asking whether or not any reading of Revelation can still be liberating for women.[29] No hard and fast lines should be drawn between feminist and (other) liberationist readings. Schüssler Fiorenza refuses to separate reading for gender from the larger matrix of "the Western classical patriarchal system and its interlocking structures of racism, classicism, colonialism, and sexism."[30]

In this book I seek to contribute to opening up Revelation's composition, construction, meaning, and significance using this fifth key. In particular, it will do so by giving close attention to John's *rhetoric*, both in terms of the rhetorical strategies and effects resulting from John's choice of the genres in which to communicate to his hearers and in terms of the ways John fulfills general expectations, current in the first century, of a public act of communication geared toward persuading. Like liberationist readings, this reading will explore how Revelation holds the practice of modern churches within a particular range of social locations under a critical yet healthful lens, offers a critical perspective on the domination systems within which we live and with which we cooperate, and challenges us to respond in ways that renew the prophetic witness that John exemplified and to which he called his own congregations. In other words, "application" will proceed neither by extracting timeless principles nor by playing the matching game between prediction and fulfillment, but by recontextualization.

In the next section we will consider the reading cues that John gives his audience in the opening lines of Revelation and how these cues orient the attentive hearer/reader to the work. Following this, we will consider how the discipline of rhetorical criticism equips us to pursue—in concert with historical research on Revelation and first-century Asia Minor, studies on John's use of sacred traditions, and the like—a fresh contribution to contemporary-historical interpretation.

---

28. Schüssler Fiorenza 1991, 11. See Boesak 1987 and, more recently, Blount 2005, another reading strongly rooted in contemporary-historical exegesis for the purpose of inquiring into Revelation's word for readers from a particular social location. Both authors remain remarkably relevant without ever asserting a one-to-one correspondence between John's images and their modern situations.

29. Schüssler Fiorenza 1985; Pippin 1992; Hylen 2003.

30. Schüssler Fiorenza 1991, 15. Not every contemporary-historical interpreter is interested in Revelation's ongoing "word" to the churches. D. H. Lawrence (1931), for example, seems ready to discard Revelation on account of its exclusivism, violence, and authoritarianism. See further Carey 2001, 169.

REVELATION'S READING CUES

John gives his readers at least three distinct yet complementary reading cues, signaling three literary genres in which his work participates. Such signals evoke expectations on the part of an attentive audience in regard to how they should engage the content. Discerning genre is basic to communication. Many times each day people make decisions about genre. These decisions affect how they experience and engage the communications they encounter, whether oral or written. We would instinctively recognize the genre of the newspaper article, the commercial, the joke, the letter, the exegesis paper, the test, the shopping list, the sitcom, the bedtime story.

Recognizing "genre" extends even more broadly to other human interactions. When I (as ordained minister) enter the room of a parishioner in a hospital, I enact a kind of script (a set of expectations on my part), and the parishioner also recognizes my entrance as signaling the start of an interaction belonging to the genre of pastoral visit. The course of our interaction is not thereby straightjacketed, but certain expectations are raised, certain allowances and freedoms are given (the parishioner can more freely raise faith questions and spiritual issues pertaining to the hospital stay than in conversations with nurses or doctors). In human interactions and human communications, appropriately discerning the genre helps us negotiate the form, entertain proper expectations, and discern the purpose of the exchange.

Revelation as Letter

John gives a clear signal that Revelation is to be read as a letter, specifically a pastoral letter. After an introductory paragraph in which John does not speak in his own voice, but in the impersonal voice of other introductions to biblical prophecies (cf. Rev. 1:1–3 with Isa. 1:1; Jer. 1:1–3), John sounds his own voice in a manner recalling the opening of other early Christian letters: "John to the seven churches that are in Asia: Grace to you and peace" (Rev. 1:4). The standard formula with which letters began ("sender to addressees, greeting") is clearly present. More particularly, John uses Paul's earlier modification of the same— "Grace to you and peace" (χάρις ὑμῖν καὶ εἰρήνη)—rather than the standard "Greeting" (χαίρειν). Also like Paul, John announces several key themes in this opening greeting (Rev. 1:4–8) that will dominate the whole work.

One crucial "reading cue," then, is that John writes a letter addressed explicitly to seven real communities of Christians in the Roman province of Asia Minor (now western Turkey). John therefore intended his letter to be understood by *them*, shape *their* perceptions of *their* everyday realities, and motivate a particular response to *their* circumstances. The pervasive use of the number "seven" in Revelation suggests that the seven churches are, in some way, representative of the achievements and challenges facing churches across the Mediterranean in the first century and across the globe now, such that the words addressed to them speak to churches beyond this circle.³¹ Nevertheless, these seven churches are seven real churches facing particular difficulties and situations, whose response to their world John wanted to affect profoundly. A grounded and responsible reading of Revelation begins as it does for every other New Testament letter: with an understanding of the historical situation of these seven churches and the problems besetting them, and the ways in which Revelation interacts with and reorients the first-century addressees toward that situation. This will provide a secure place from which to hear the challenge of Revelation for the churches today.

Revelation as Early Christian Prophecy

The first beatitude (or macarism, from the Greek word μακάριος, which begins each beautitude), spoken in a voice other than John's own (since it speaks also of John in the third person), names a second "reading cue": "Privileged is the one who is reading out loud, and those who are listening to, the words of *this prophecy*, and who are keeping the things written in it" (Rev. 1:3; see also 22:7, 10, 18, 19). Prophecy is both a literary and a lived phenomenon in the early church, whose adherents believed themselves to have experienced a fresh outpouring of God's prophetic spirit.³²

"Prophecy" is often used synonymously with "prediction," as in the prophecies of Nostradamus or Edgar Cayce. Although Jewish and early Christian prophecy could include a predictive element, it was also (perhaps primarily) a declaration of God's action in the present or of God's evaluative perspective on the present actions of God's people. When a prophet speaks of the future, it usually involves the immediate rather than a distant future, and that, again, in terms of the positive or negative consequences that would follow the people's fidelity or infidelity in living out the covenant.³³ John remains within this range, seen in his emphasis on the "imminence" of the confrontations and events he narrates (Rev. 1:3b, 19; 22:6b, 7, 10, 12, 20).

Prophecy presents a "word of the Lord" for the Lord's people who need guidance, encouragement, or a call to repentance and recommitment in their situation. The seven oracles (2:1–3:22) offer prime examples of early Christian prophecy.³⁴ The glorified Christ speaks a word to the churches through the prophet John, affirming their strengths, diagnosing their weaknesses, call-

---

31. Regarding each church as representative of the whole church in a particular era grossly caricatures the periods of church history so described. Moreover, there has hardly ever been an era in which the diversity of the churches addressed by Revelation—and greater diversity besides—failed to be represented. I find it more prudent to regard the seven churches together as typical of the church in every age, rather than each one as typical of the entire church in any one period.

32. See Acts 2:14–21; 1 Cor 12:4–11; 14:1–40; *Didache* 10.7; 11.3–13.7.

33. A significant exception to this rule is Agabus's prophecy concerning Paul's fate (Acts 21:10–14), meant both to forewarn *and* forearm the apostle for the hardships ahead (still facilitating his fidelity in the midst of trying circumstances to come).

34. I reject the tradition of calling these "letters" since, after the command to "write" down the words (addressed to John), each utterance actually begins in a manner recalling the prophetic "Thus says the Lord" (e.g., "These are the words of the Son of God," Rev. 2:18).

ing them to faithful action, threatening judgment upon the recalcitrant, and promising favor for the penitent and faithful. They accomplish precisely what the Hebrew prophets sought to do for the communities of Israel and Judah. The visions of Revelation support this prophetic word, providing the picture of reality and the interpretation of the believers' world (particularly Rome, her agencies, and her politico-economic system) that will motivate and legitimate the response of faithful witness and protest.

The "prophecy expert" holds that everything presented in the Bible as a forecast of some future event must be fulfilled at some point. If the "prophecies" of Revelation did not match historical events or figures during the first or second century, they must at some point have such a match. This tenet, however, ignores the primary purpose of prophecy, which is not to give hard-and-fast statements about an unchangeable future, but to evoke faithful response. Jonah proclaimed that "forty days more, and Nineveh shall be overthrown" (Jonah 3:4). In response to this vision of the future, the city's inhabitants repented and turned to God, with the result that God spared the city (3:10). Jonah, like the prophecy expert, was still watching, however, "to see what would become of the city" (4:5); he was bitterly disappointed that the prediction was not to be fulfilled. God's purposes for the prophetic word, however, were fulfilled: the repentance of an entire population. Like Jonah's word, Revelation, as prophecy, seeks mainly to stimulate faithful response among John's audience, not to provide an absolute blueprint for an uncertain future.

Revelation as Apocalypse

The first reading cue offered to the audience of Revelation appears in the opening words of the book: a "revelation [an *apokalypsis,* Ἀποκάλυψις] of Jesus Christ" (Rev. 1:1). An "apocalypse" is also a lived experience in the early church. One member has an ecstatic experience and then allows other members to access its import as the ecstatic recounts the experience in narrative form. Revelation opens with a string of words found in one other New Testament text. In Galatians, Paul asserts that his own apostolic commission and his grasp of the message that he would preach came not through human communication, but "through a revelation of Jesus Christ" (δι' ἀποκαλύψεως Ἰησοῦ Χριστοῦ, Gal 1:12). Paul refers here to his encounter with the glorified Christ, about which he does not give many details (Gal. 1:15–16; 1 Cor. 15:8). But Paul had other ecstatic experiences, calling these "visions and revelations of the Lord" (ἀποκαλύψεις κυρίου, 2 Cor. 12:1) as well. At least one involved an otherworldly journey into the third heaven and the hearing of heavenly secrets that are neither able nor permissible to be shared with others through words (2 Cor. 12:4). Nor did Paul expect ecstatic experiences to be limited to himself or other apostles. When Christians gather for worship, he expects someone routinely to come with "a revelation" (ἀποκάλυψις might here include the phenomenon of prophecy, an ecstatic expression promoted throughout 1 Corinthians 14) alongside others coming with psalms, teachings, utterances in tongues, and interpretations of tongues (1 Cor. 14:26). The lector presenting John's text as "a revelation of Jesus Christ" invites the audience to hear it as a narration of an experience of heavenly mysteries, a journey into heaven to see and hear what transpires there that has significant precedent in Pauline Christianity.

It is precisely as a *narration* of such an experience that the term "apocalypse" comes to be used (rightly, if somewhat anachronistically) to denote a literary genre comparable to the letter and the prophecy (the latter also being both experienced live in the early church as well as being read). Strictly translated, the word *apokalypsis* (ἀποκάλυψις) would denote the "lifting off of a veil." But precisely what does Revelation unveil? The more we familiarize ourselves with a larger sampling of apocalypses, the more informed our expectations in this regard. For many readers of the Protestant Bible, Revelation is unique, with no basis for comparison except for significant sections of its Old Testament precedent, Daniel. Scores of texts similar to both Daniel and Revelation, however, were composed during the second century BCE and onward into the first century CE, and these can inform our reading of Revelation. Two of these books were extremely influential. *First Enoch*, a composite text written over a period of about two centuries, was authoritative at Qumran and is quoted as an authoritative text in Jude. *Fourth Ezra*, a Jewish response to the destruction of Jerusalem in 70 CE, was so highly regarded in the early church that anonymous Christians wrote both a prologue and epilogue to the work (the form in which it appears in modern editions of the Apocrypha).[35] Other important examples include *2 Enoch, 2 Baruch, Apocalypse of Abraham,* the *Testament of Levi,* and the *Sibylline Oracles.*

Recognizing the similarities among these works, a group of scholars worked to codify their generic features and to clarify the expectations these apocalypses generated. Common features include the following: the revelation of insight and information through visions and through pronouncements of divine or angelic mediators; otherworldly journeys that allowed the reader to peer into the invisible regions surrounding the everyday world, such as God's throne room and the abyss, and to observe the beings that inhabit them; narrations of the larger "history" that brackets normal, lived experience, such as creation and primeval events or judgment and consummation.

Revelation shares much in common with these apocalypses. The book presents its message in the form of visionary experiences: the author "sees" into the invisible realm and witnesses the proceedings there. He "hears" what is spoken and converses with a number of heavenly beings. He undertakes something like an otherworldly journey, viewing the activity around the throne of God, the abyss, the lake of fire, and the new Jerusalem. His account focuses on time and history beyond the present. While it may not look back to the events of prehistory, such as creation, life in Eden, and the giants, Revelation does look back upon cosmic conflict between the dragon and God's angels and forward to the

---

35. See, further, deSilva 2002a, 323–51.

judgment and renewal of all things. It shares in a dualistic view of humanity, sharply divided between those sealed by God and those marked by the beast, envisages the eschatological judgment, which will sort out the wheat from the chaff, and ends with a vision of cosmic transformation as new heavens and new earth replace the fallen cosmos. In all of this, it shares a basic grammar with other apocalypses of the period.[36]

Compiling these common features, J. J. Collins has provided a comprehensive definition of "apocalypse" as a literary genre:

> "Apocalypse" is a genre of revelatory literature with a narrative framework, in which a revelation is mediated by an otherworldly being to a human recipient, disclosing a transcendent reality which is both temporal, insofar as it envisages eschatological salvation, and spatial, insofar as it envisages another, supernatural world.[37]

The definition highlights several features of apocalypses that are essential to their rhetorical strategy and effect. Apocalypses open up vistas beyond normal, lived experience, setting the audience's space within the context of a larger, invisible world. They also open up the time, both prior and subsequent, beyond normal lived experience, placing the audience's time in the context of a sacred history of God's activity and carefully defined plan. Apocalypses construct, and invite hearers into, the larger context, the "bigger picture" that provides an interpretive framework for lived experience. By painting the cosmic backdrop of an audience's everyday realities, apocalypses place those realities under the interpretive light of that cosmic backdrop. In most cases, the seers look squarely at specific features of the audience's lived experience in light of these larger contexts and in the interpretive light of the sacred tradition from which the images and their valuations are derived.

An apocalypse, therefore, puts an everyday situation in perspective by looking at the larger context (the cosmos of faith) that should interpret that situation. From this an apocalypse derives its power to comfort those who are discouraged or marginalized, admonish those whose responses in their situation are not in line with their religious values, and provide the necessary motivation to take whatever action the seer recommends. Specimens of the genre allow the recipients to examine their behavior, whether "to continue to pursue, or if necessary to modify" it, in light of "a transcendent, usually eschatological, perspective on human experiences and values."[38] The genre allows the seer to legitimate his

---

36. One notable difference is the lack of a pseudonym. Most apocalypses claim to come from a venerable figure from the past (like Enoch or Ezra). John, however, writes in his own name and was probably known personally to the first audiences. This distinctive practice aligns with the Christian conviction that the gift of prophecy, conferred by the Spirit poured out upon believers, was again being manifested in the Christian communities. Such a conviction stands in stark contrast with the common perception within Judaism that the prophetic voice had ceased (see 1 Macc. 4:46; 14:41; Pr. Azar. 1:15), though the expectation that prophecy would revive is also well attested.
37. J. Collins 1979, 9.
38. Aune 1997, lxxxii.

message and the values and behaviors it seeks to nurture by inviting the audience into an experience of the transcendent realities in which that message is grounded. In effect, the audience is enabled to "see" the otherworldly and "converse" with supernatural beings through the mediation of the apocalypse.[39]

These three reading cues support the pursuit of a contemporary-historical reading of Revelation since this reading aligns more closely with the ways in which the text itself asks to be read and understood. As a letter, Revelation is anchored firmly in the historical situation of the seven churches it addresses. As we would read Galatians with reference to the specific situation and challenges of Gentile Christians in the Roman province of Galatia and seek to understand how it reshapes their perspective on, and response to, that situation, so it needs to be with Revelation. As prophecy, Revelation purports to bring a word from the Lord into a specific situation for specific people. The audience would expect it to reveal God's perspective on their behaviors and on the challenges around them, alerting them to the course they must take to remain in, or return to, favor with God and to avoid judgment. As an apocalypse, Revelation spreads before the eyes of the Christians in Asia Minor that larger canopy of space and time that puts their mundane reality, along with its challenges and options, in its "true" light and proper perspective. Their world will look different when seen in the light of the endless worship that surrounds God's throne, the reality and ferocity of God's judgments upon idolaters, and the rewards of faithfulness. More than seeking to *be interpreted*, Revelation seeks to *interpret* the reality of the audience, showing them the true character of features of that landscape, identifying the true struggle that they must engage, naming the true stakes of the choices before the hearers.

As John lifts the veil under which everyday realities parade as all-important and ultimate, he shows them to be of secondary importance to the call of God. He thus enables the Christians in Asia Minor to reconsider how they will act in the world, freeing them from responding to the demands of a political and economic system as if these were the ultimate forces to be reckoned with and enabling them to respond instead to the invisible, but truly ultimate, God. While Revelation may appear, then, to lift the veil from future events, Revelation's ultimate goal is to lift the veil from contemporary actors, events, and options.

A RHETORICAL ANALYSIS OF REVELATION

The study of rhetoric is, essentially, the study of available means of persuasion.[40] Applied to a particular text as "rhetorical criticism," this involves the analysis of how a particular author or group of authors has mobilized particular means of persuasion to a particular end or ends. Rhetorical criticism is thus highly congenial to the contemporary-historical approach, since it immerses the interpreter

---

39. Aune 1997, lxxxii.
40. Kennedy's definition of rhetoric as "that quality in discourse by which a speaker or writer seeks to accomplish his purposes" (1984, 3) provides the starting point for this study.

"Favored Are Those Who Read" 15

in the historical setting of the first audiences and the particular challenges they faced (or that the author wished them to face), while analyzing the text as the means by which the author positions the hearers to identify the challenges and respond to them in a particular way.

While rhetorical criticism has been vigorously applied to the study of other New Testament letters and speeches, Revelation has largely passed under the radar of rhetorical critics. This was partly due to the obvious distance between John's Revelation and the material upon which classical rhetorical theory was itself developed and systematized (that is, straightforward rational speeches delivered in political, civic, or juristic settings), as well as the distance between John's Revelation and other New Testament texts that seemed to share more with Dio Chrysostom's *Orations* than the ravings of apocalyptic visionaries.[41]

Elisabeth Schüssler Fiorenza presided over the first fruitful wedding of rhetorical criticism and the interpretation of Revelation.[42] Her work provides a prototype for investigating "how arguments are constructed and how power is inscribed" in Revelation, as well as "how interpretive discourse affects the social formation of which it is a part."[43] The classical rhetorical critic uses the ancient handbooks on rhetorical practice dating from the fourth century BCE (Aristotle's *Art of Rhetoric*) through the late first century CE (Quintilian's *Institutio oratoria*) as "tools for analyzing the persuasive power of a text," while seeking to avoid the trap of viewing them as "definitive prescriptive structures."[44] The latter is of vital importance, not only because methods must never become Procrustean beds that obscure and distort the text they are meant to illumine, but all the more because of Revelation's particular distance from the kinds of communication analyzed by these classical theorists. Schüssler Fiorenza makes the following as a programmatic statement:

> A critical rhetorical analysis of Revelation seeks to trace its ideological practices and persuasive goals and to identify the literary means by which they are achieved.... It must therefore concern itself with reconstructing both

---

41. Consider several statements found in Stamps 2001: "There is little if any discernible correspondence between Graeco-Roman rhetorical practice and the discourse of Revelation" (2001, 631); "The distinctive literary nature of Revelation in relation to Hellenistic literature ... distances the work from the probable influence of the Graeco-Roman rhetorical tradition" (2001, 630). The solid observations in regard to John's distinctive means of expression lead to premature and ultimately untenable judgments concerning John's participation in the larger cultural conventions in regard to the art of persuasion: "It is unlikely one will find distinct aspects of rhetorical conventions in terms of arrangement, invention and style" (2001, 630). Although one must concede the point in regard to arrangement, rhetorical critics have even found John to utilize many figures of speech and figures of diction also employed in classical orations (see Longenecker 2001; Moore 1983; Nikolakopoulos 2001), to engage in forms of argumentation and invoke many of the argumentative topics outlined in the *progymnasmata* (elementary rhetorical exercises) and classical rhetorical handbooks (see Rossing 1999; deSilva 1998a; 1999a; 2002b), to utilize many of the topics and strategies for appealing to the emotions codified by Aristotle (deSilva 2008a), and to pay a great deal of attention to questions of ethos, or rhetorical credibility (Carey 1998; 1999b; Duff 2001). See the review of research in deSilva 2008b.
42. Schüssler Fiorenza 1985, 181–204; 1991.
43. Schüssler Fiorenza 1991, 21.
44. Schüssler Fiorenza 1991, 22.

Revelation's rhetorical world of vision and the rhetorical and sociopolitical situations in which this imagery can be understood to have developed as an active and fitting response.[45]

Classical rhetorical criticism and contemporary-historical interpretation exhibit a close correlation, such that the former can function as a species of the latter. But it is an active and dynamic species, inviting us into John's inventive and boldly ideological engagement with the "sociopolitical situations" of the seven churches, and into the ways in which the unfolding text draws the hearers closer and closer to John's desired outcomes for them.

Rhetorical criticism is not limited to investigating the ways in which a text persuades at its first utterance.[46] Indeed, precisely because of Revelation's perennial power to persuade people—or rather, because authors and speakers find in Revelation an ever-ready rhetorical resource for persuading people—rhetorical critics also exhibit interest in analyzing the rhetoric of the interpretation of Revelation in new settings, down to the present day.[47] Revelation still imprints a vision of the cosmos and its destiny on the worldview of millions of American Christians. Its power to create hard-and-fast divisions between the sealed of God and the servants of the beast continues to reinforce group boundaries and motivate particular social responses (sometimes quite dramatically and tragically, as in the case of the Branch Davidians).

Entering into the rhetoric of Revelation as a text addressing challenges faced by Christians contemporary with the author both facilitates our analysis of new attempts to harness Revelation's rhetoric *and* provides the means by which to critique such attempts on the basis of a common appeal to Revelation's authority. Are modern applications of Revelation or uses of its rhetoric consonant with John's goals for shaping Christian witness and orientation to the world? Do these modern interpreters reliably use Revelation as a diagnostic tool for unveiling the challenges to faithful discipleship in their new setting? Or do they harness Revelation's powerful rhetoric to draw their hearers in directions that run counter to its historical trajectory? It may also help to answer particularly pressing questions about Revelation's perennial appeal: Why do Christians keep reading this book? Why do so many continue to find it a compelling vision of the world and a compelling story about their world, past and future?

The present study relies heavily on the discussions of the art of persuasion found in Greek and Latin rhetorical handbooks, particularly Aristotle's *Art*

---

45. Schüssler Fiorenza 1991, 22.
46. Schüssler Fiorenza (1991, 21) drew attention not only to the rhetorical practices of John, but also to "how interpretive discourse affects the social formation of which it is a part," that is, how interpretations of Revelation are rhetorical productions and performances influencing the behavior of those who share in such discourse.
47. See O'Leary 1993; 1994; Reid 1983. Newport (2000, 3) calls for more attention to be given to analysis of popular interpretation of Revelation, "for it is primarily in this setting and not in a critical one that texts have the most significant impact." Although not writing from a rhetorical-critical approach, Arthur Wainwright (1993, 161–230) provides an excellent analysis of the history of Revelation's impact in the spheres of politics, culture, worship, spirituality, and social reform.

of Rhetoric (fourth c. BCE), the near-contemporary *Rhetorica ad Alexandrum* (by Anaximenes), the *Rhetorica ad Herennium* (first century BCE, once attributed to the contemporary Cicero), Cicero's rhetorical treatises (particularly *De inventione rhetorica*), Quintilian's *Institutio oratoria* (late first c. CE), and the elementary exercises in rhetoric (the *progymnasmata*) of Aelius Theon of Alexandria (second–third c. CE) and Hermogenes of Tarsus (second c. CE). No presumption is made here that John ever had direct access to any one of these resources.[48] Rather, these handbooks provide snapshots of a range of rhetorical *practices* to which New Testament authors and audiences would potentially have been exposed, and thus of the practices they might have expected to engage when composing and listening to discourses intended to persuade.[49]

Aristotle's *Art of Rhetoric*, for example, gives modern critics direct access to the conventions of Greek oratory in the fourth century BCE, which are otherwise available only inductively through the study of the extant corpus of orations—the very work that Aristotle undertook as he composed his descriptive treatise. These conventions of Greek oratory, granting four centuries of development and some degree of variation between and within Greek and Latin oratory, contributed to some degree to the shaping of any particular work by a particular orator (e.g., Galatians, Hebrews, or even Revelation). Moreover, these handbooks provide a language for speaking about the text's persuasive strategy and its effects upon its audience that is contemporary with, and culturally proximate to, the work in question.[50]

The rhetorical handbooks indicate the essential tasks to which orators attended, inviting us to explore how *John* has attended to these tasks, to the extent that he did. Thus the handbooks provide a framework for exploring how John (1) constructs and deconstructs credibility (appeals to *ethos*); (2) engages the feelings of the hearers (appeals to *pathos*); and (3) formulates arguments leading the audience toward the decision that the author favors (appeals to *logos*). They help us to be on the lookout for specific rhetorical topics, helping us analyze how

---

48. David E. Aune (2003, 306–7) argues that Aristotle's *Rhetoric* enjoyed very limited circulation in antiquity. Its influence emerges in Rome in Cicero's *De oratione* and Dionysius of Halicarnassus's *1–2 Epistulae ad Ammaeum* and then largely disappears until the 1200s. However, few if any rhetorical critics of the NT assume that Paul or John or even the author of Hebrews had ever read or studied Aristotle's *Art of Rhetoric* firsthand.

49. My working premise is that early Christian authors, to the extent that they learned the "art of persuasion," learned it inductively through observing and hearing public speakers, itinerant philosophers, and even synagogue preachers in the cities in which they dwelled (whether in the cities of Judea and Galilee or the cities of Syria and Asia Minor), although a few (like the authors of Hebrews and Luke-Acts) possess such a facility in the art of argumentation, reproduce known patterns from the *progymnasmata*, and attend to matters of style to such a degree as suggests some formal training. "We should be cautious in assuming too much formal rhetorical knowledge, . . . but we should not sell them too short as uncultured and uneducated" (Royalty 1997, 600; see also Johns 1998, 763; Diefenbach 1994).

50. Classical rhetorical handbooks provide "a vocabulary for discussing the rhetoric of Revelation that corresponds to the vocabulary of Greco-Roman antiquity for discussing public discourse. The Greek of Revelation may not be up to Attic standards, but the text lends itself to analysis in terms of rhetorical invention, arrangement, and style" (Royalty 1997, 601).

each topic might contribute to these three major rhetorical tasks. They provide a framework for theorizing about John's goals—namely, to what extent he wishes to influence the values held by the hearers, promote or avert particular courses of action, or incite a verdict of innocence or guilt—on the basis of the topics evoked, and to distinguish between primary and ancillary ends. They also raise questions concerning the strategic arrangement of the material encountered in Revelation as well as questions about stylistic concerns (for example, what diction and idiom would best contribute to achieving the desired results).

The authors of these rhetorical handbooks place conveniently at our disposal many resources that we *might* find John using to accomplish these tasks, while inviting us also to be alert to resources peculiar to John's tradition, his chosen genre, and his cultural-ideological location as a prophet within the early Christian movement. Careful rhetorical analysis seeks to uncover the persuasive strategies that inhere within a particular text, using all near-contemporary works on the art of persuasion *heuristically* to get at the "literary means by which" John's "ideological practices and persuasive goals . . . are achieved."[51] Significant facets of classical rhetorical theory are simply inapplicable to Revelation, notably the discussions of arrangement of material (save perhaps for some observations about beginnings and endings of speeches). Nevertheless classical rhetorical theory alerts us to inquire into the rhetorical effects of the arrangement John has constructed, even though it does not correspond with the actual patterns discussed in the handbooks. Significant facets of Revelation are also not contemplated within classical rhetorical theory. The aim of this study is not to force correlations in order to demonstrate Revelation's alignment with classical rhetoric, but to use the latter as a near-contemporary heuristic device insofar as it is helpful. At many points we will need to look beyond the rhetorical handbooks (for example, to sociology of religion in chap. 4, or to the resources of the Hebrew Bible and other traditions sacred to John and his hearers in chaps. 6 and 11) to examine the distinctive ways in which Revelation attends to the principal tasks in the art of persuasion.

EXCURSUS: A BRIEF INTRODUCTION TO CLASSICAL RHETORICAL CRITICISM

Readers who are not already familiar with the basic contours of Greco-Roman rhetorical theory and the use of this theory in New Testament interpretation may find the following discussion helpful.[52] The principal sourcebooks on rhetoric in the Greek, Hellenistic, and Roman periods are Aristotle's *Art of Rhetoric*; Anaximenes' *Rhetorica ad Alexandrum* (once attributed to Aristotle); the *Rhetorica ad Herennium* (once attributed to Cicero); Cicero's *On Invention, On the Orator,*

---

51. Schüssler Fiorenza 1991, 22.
52. For more detailed introductions, see Mack 1990; Kennedy 1984; Watson 1988a.

Partitions of Oratory, Brutus, The Orator, and *Topics*; and Quintilian's *Institutio oratoria.* These books represent systematizations of the process of creating effective oratory from gathering possible arguments and topics to the delivery of the polished speech. The handbooks reveal how orators and leaders could successfully persuade an audience to choose a particular course of action, to embody a certain value, or to render a certain verdict. They inform us about the place of appeals to the mind, the emotions, and the trust of the audience in effective oratory. Classical rhetorical theory helps us to become more adept at discerning when an early Christian author is trying to arouse a certain emotion in his hearers, and to what end, or to analyze the logical argument of a passage, or to see how the author is trying to affirm his own credibility while seeking to undermine the credibility of others who might urge a different course of action. Because these rhetorical handbooks reflect contemporary and near-contemporary persuasive practices, they help us know what to look for in these texts as we consider how the author was orchestrating argument and exhortation to produce a faithful response.

The Three Genres of Oratory

Oratory grew out of the practical needs of the Greek city and its institutions: the council chamber, lawcourt, and public forum. Enrolled citizens gathered in the council chamber to determine what course of action the city should take to meet some particular need. Inevitably a variety of options emerged, and citizens could speak in favor of one or another, weighing advantages and disadvantages, comparing one available course with another. This was the native home of deliberative rhetoric, speeches promoting a certain course of action or dissuading the citizenry from taking a certain course of action. Those promoting a course would seek to demonstrate that it was right (in keeping with the culture's core values, like courage, prudence, justice, or generosity), expedient (tending to preserve existing goods, gain other advantages, or ward off ills), feasible (the resources to undertake the course being available), honorable (embodying virtues, tending toward the praiseworthy), and the like.[53] Speakers would often employ topics of amplification, showing the favored course to be more noble, more just, more expedient than others. The opposite topics would be used to dissuade the assembly from some course of action.

People living together under a body of laws never do so flawlessly, hence the need for the lawcourt. Here citizens would gather to assess the guilt or innocence of those accused of wrongdoing. This was the home of forensic (or judicial) rhetoric, in which the orators (a prosecutor and an advocate) would try to affix blame or establish innocence concerning some past action. Oaths, witnesses, material proofs, and logical probabilities were the chief tools in reconstructing the past event and assigning guilt.

---

53. For a fuller discussion of these topics, see *Rhet. Alex.* 1421b.21–1423a.12; *Rhet. Her.* 3.2.2–3.4.9.

Finally, citizens and noncitizens would gather in the public forum to commemorate the life or lives of the honored dead, with speeches reciting the virtues and achievements of the deceased. This was the birthplace of epideictic rhetoric, speeches which praised the virtuous and censured the vicious, and which, in so doing, reminded the gathered audience of the values that sustained their culture and society. Honoring the departed aroused emulation in the audience, stirring up their desires for acquiring the same honor by embodying the same virtues exhibited, and achievements attained, by the departed.[54] Funeral orations generally lifted up the external advantages enjoyed by the departed (native city, parentage or ancestry, education, friends, wealth, offices held, kind of death), physical excellence (strength, beauty, health), and moral excellence (virtues, praiseworthy habits, behaviors, and achievements manifesting interior virtues, attitudes in performing those actions).

While the three basic genres of oratory (for council chamber, lawcourt, public forum) developed in these everyday settings, they did not remain bound to them. Deliberative topics and strategies were employed wherever some group needed to make a decision about a future course of action. It was a small step from the political assembly to the assembly in the synagogue, the church, or any other voluntary association. Paul uses deliberative strategies and topics extensively in his letter to the Galatian Christians, as he advises them against a course of action (undergoing circumcision). Forensic rhetoric could be employed outside a formal court wherever issues of blame or innocence were involved. Forensic topics are prominent in 2 Corinthians 1 and 2, where Paul must first answer "charges" about his sincerity and truthfulness and prove that he did not in fact injure the believers, before they can move forward in their relationship together.[55] Epideictic rhetoric moved beyond the public forum very early: praise or censure of a living person already played a part in judicial and deliberative speeches by Aristotle's time. The prosecutor frequently censured the defendant and his defender in order to undermine their credibility, while an orator in the council chamber frequently praised the figures who previously pursued a course of action like the one he was promoting.

This observation brings us to an important point. Already Aristotle had recognized that a speech was rarely a pure example of a single genre.[56] A delibera-

---

54. In Thucydides, *History*, Pericles gives a eulogy for the fallen Athenian soldiers, at the end of which he fosters the hearers' feeling of emulation by direct exhortation and application: "It is for you to try to be like them. Make up your minds that happiness depends on being free, and freedom depends on being courageous" (2.44). See also 4 Macc. 18:1–2; Dio Chrysostom, *Or.* 29.21. The primary goal of such addresses was the reinforcement of cultural values.

55. See further deSilva 1996a.

56. Aristotle, *Rhet.* 1.3.5: "The end [goal] of the deliberative speaker is the expedient or harmful; for he who exhorts recommends a course of action as better, and he who dissuades advises against it as worse; *all other considerations, such as justice and injustice, honour and disgrace, are included as accessory in reference to this*" (emphasis added). See also *Rhet. Alex.* 1427b.31–35; *Rhet. Her.* 3.8.15. A similar phenomenon appears in the discussions of types or categories of letters in the ancient theorists of epistolography (see Pseudo-Libanius, *Epistolary Styles* 46, 92; text, translation, and introduction in Malherbe 1977).

tive speech, for example, could employ both epideictic and forensic topics along the way. A nuanced rhetorical analysis does not merely try to decide that the speech is deliberative, but to discern the ways in which epideictic and forensic topics, if present, support the overarching deliberative goal.

The Five Stages of Speechmaking

Composing and delivering a speech involved five basic steps: invention, arrangement, style, memory, and delivery. Orators began the task by considering all the possible avenues of advancing their case, laying out the proofs and appeals at their disposal. The orators would consider what prejudices and arguments existed against them or their case, and how to answer these obstructions. This was the task of invention.[57] Then orators would consider how best to arrange the material to make the strongest impression on the hearers. As a general rule, prejudice against the speaker and the case had to be removed up front, and prejudice against opponents aroused at the end of a speech. The strongest proofs were presented at the beginning and ending of the argument, making a strong first impression and a strong denouement.[58] Orators then attended to stylistic considerations: when to use the grand style, suitable for rousing attention and emotion; when to use the plain style, suited to rational argumentation; where to use ornaments and figures of diction to dress up the way the speech falls upon the ears of the hearers. Once the text of the speech was set, the orator would memorize the speech and go on to consider how best to use physical presence and gestures in the delivery of the speech.

Since we have only the texts themselves and not their performance, the material on memory and delivery plays almost no role in New Testament interpretation. It is not likely that the reader memorized the letter before sharing its contents, so memory simply would not apply. Emissaries may have been coached concerning how to deliver the contents to the gathering, or have taken thought themselves on how to make the delivery most effective through varying tone of voice, use of physical gestures, and the like, but such matters are irretrievable. Invention, arrangement, and style are the focal points of most rhetorical-critical studies, and of these, the material in the rhetorical handbooks treating the first two is the most helpful in getting at the meaning of a text.

Invention: The Three Kinds of Proof

Classical orators understood that people were not persuaded by appeals to the mind alone. They would be influenced by their emotions as well as their assessment of the speaker. Thus rhetorical handbooks routinely refer to three kinds of appeals or proofs that must be woven together into the successful speech: the

---

57. Most of Aristotle's *Rhetoric* is devoted to invention (1.4–2.26).
58. *Rhet. Her.* 3.10.18.

appeal to *logos* (the reason of the hearer), *pathos* (the emotions of the hearer), and *ethos* (the hearer's perception of the speaker).[59]

Aristotle calls the appeal to ethos the most important form of proof (*Rhet.* 1.2.4). A speaker must show himself or herself to be virtuous, expert, and benevolently disposed toward the hearers.[60] The combination of these qualities made the speaker credible and disposed the audience to trust and follow the speaker. Any prejudice against the speaker must be eliminated before the speaker can get to the subject matter of the speech.[61] The audience must never be alienated from the speaker: if he blames them harshly, he must also palliate them so as to assure them of his goodwill. On the other hand, it is advantageous to a speaker to cast doubt on the sincerity, reliability, and goodwill of opposing speakers.

Aristotle recognized that people make different decisions when they are angry, calm, afraid, or confident, and that orators would frequently arouse particular emotions in the hearers to their advantage (1.2.5; 2.1.2, 4, 8). An orator seeking a verdict of guilt would seek to rouse indignation or anger against the defendant; an orator wishing to persuade the audience to take a certain course of action would perhaps strive to make them feel confident that they could achieve the goal, or afraid or ashamed not to try, and so forth. Aristotle provides a long list of topics and situations that arouse eleven different emotions, helping the modern reader to learn sensitivity to this aspect of oratory and to detect where an author may be trying to make the audience feel pity, fear, confidence, emulation, and the like (2.2–11).

Finally, there is the appeal to the hearer's reason. An orator will tend to establish one's case by both deductive and inductive means. Deductive proofs include the syllogism and the enthymeme (EN-thih-meem). Aristotle described an enthymeme as, in effect, a statement or maxim supported by a rationale, which adds the "why and wherefore" (2.21.2). Thus the statement "No one is truly free" is a maxim. When it is joined to an explanation, it becomes an enthymeme: "No one is truly free, for one is the slave of either wealth or fortune" (2.21.2). Other enthymematic forms treated by other classical rhetoricians will be discussed in chapter 7.[62]

---

59. See Aristotle, *Rhet.* 1.2.3: "Now the proofs furnished by the speech are of three kinds. The first depends upon the moral character of the speaker, the second upon putting the hearer into a certain frame of mind, the third upon the speech itself, in so far as it proves or seems to prove."

60. See Aristotle, *Rhet.* 2.1.3: "It makes a great difference with regard to producing conviction . . . that the speaker should show himself to be possessed of certain qualities and that his hearers should think that he is disposed in a certain way towards them; and further, that they themselves should be disposed in a certain way towards him"; *Rhet.* 2.1.5: "For the orator to produce conviction three qualities are necessary. . . . These qualities are good sense, virtue, and goodwill (φρόνησις, ἀρετή, εὔνοια)." See also Quintilian, *Inst.* 3.8.13.

61. See especially *Rhet. Her.* 1.9 on the elimination of prejudice through the "subtle approach."

62. Aune (2003) helpfully critiques this limited definition of the enthymeme, drawing attention to the multiple argumentative forms referred to within the category of "enthymeme" across the field of classical rhetorical theory, as well as emphasizing the critical difference between logical and rhetorical syllogisms: the former required certainty while the latter only required probability. Aune's treatment of the enthymeme will guide our own investigations of the same in Revelation (see chaps. 7 and 8, below).

The orator's goal is to lead the hearer from established premises (facts that the audience would take for granted and not question) to probable conclusions.[63] Syllogisms involve at least two premises and a conclusion; for example:

All patrons deserve gratitude.

Erastus has benefited our community.

Therefore, we must honor Erastus.

An enthymeme typically presupposes a syllogism or, at least, a fuller deductive process, but does not rehearse the whole deductive process since the orator will assume that the audience can supply the missing steps: "We ought to honor Erastus, for he has benefited our community," or "Let us honor Erastus, for all patrons deserve gratitude." Aristotle preferred the form of the enthymeme as less pedantic and more effective in persuading. Enthymemes are built around a variety of topics like the possible and impossible, opposites or contraries, the lesser and the greater, projected consequences of an action, analogy, cause and effect, and the like.[64] The topics special to each genre of oratory also provide the raw material of enthymemes (for a deliberative speech, for example, the considerations of what is just, expedient, feasible, and honorable). The example given above employs a topic of justice (benefactors deserve gratitude).

Inductive proofs allow the audience to draw conclusions by considering examples (which can be historical precedents or fictional stories) or analogies.[65] An orator who wishes one's city to declare war may tell the story of those who, in similar circumstances, forestalled disaster and achieved greatness by taking the initiative in military conflict. Recalling historical precedents was especially effective, since the audience could, in effect, "see" in the past the outcome of the course they are contemplating for the future.[66] Dio Chrysostom, urging his fellow citizens not to parade their internal quarrels when the new governor first arrived in their province, used analogies drawn from the animal world to support his case (the harmony shown by bees, *Or.* 48.15–16).

Maxims, legal precedents, and authoritative texts also furnish the raw material of appeals to *logos*. Maxims or proverbs are statements of common knowledge or opinion, and so are likely to add credibility to the conclusions based on them.[67] Similarly, authoritative texts (like Homer and Hesiod for a non-Christian, or the Septuagint for Christians and Diaspora Jews) lie at the core of group identity and lend their authority freely to the points derived from them. The respect accorded the ancient text, in effect, bleeds over into the new text.

---

63. See Aristotle, *Rhet.* 2.22; *Rhet. Alex.* 1430a.27–34.
64. Aristotle provides a host of examples of such topics in *Rhet.* 2.18–19, 23–26.
65. Aristotle, *Rhet.* 2.20; *Rhet. Alex.* 1429a.25–28.
66. See Aristotle, *Rhet.* 1.9.40; *Rhet. Alex.* 1428b.12–17; 1429a.25–28; Quintilian, *Inst.* 3.8.36.
67. Aristotle, *Rhet.* 2.21; *Rhet. Alex.* 1430a.40–1430b.7.

Arrangement: The Outline of a Classical Speech

The typical deliberative or forensic oration consisted of four (following Aristotle) or five (following the Roman rhetoricians) sections, each of which had a particular set of functions.[68] The speech opened with (1) an exordium, providing the theme of the speech while also establishing the credibility and authority of the speaker (Aristotle, *Rhet.* 3.14). The opening should render the hearers "receptive, well-disposed, and attentive" (*Rhet. Her.* 1.4.7). If prejudice existed against the speaker, the exordium would be the place to dismantle it. Especially in forensic speeches, this introduction would be followed by (2) a narration of the events under dispute. The narration is not merely a "statement of facts," but a strategically shaped and colored rehearsal of events. A defender would tell the story in such a way as would put the defendant in the most favorable light, while the accuser would do the opposite. (3) The proposition, the main point to be demonstrated, would follow, introducing (4) the *probatio*. Here was the heart of the speech in terms of marshaling proofs in favor of the speaker's position. The orator would close with (5) a peroration, in which the main points could be summarized, concluding exhortations made, appeals to emotion (particularly in legal cases) played up, and parting shots taken at the opposing speakers and their cases. (On the role of the peroration, see Aristotle, *Rhet.* 3.19.)

Rhetorical critics have most frequently and most justifiably come under fire when trying to apply this framework to individual New Testament writings.[69] Galatians fits this pattern exceptionally well,[70] but other texts resist being divided neatly into the four or five parts of the Greco-Roman speech.[71] At this point it seems more prudent to use the rhetorical handbooks only as strictly or as loosely as the text under investigation suggests, rather than forcing the text into a mold that it may not fit.

Classical discussions of arrangement offer little for the analysis of Revelation, "with its complicated patterns of interlocking, interwoven, and intercalated visions,"[72] and more generally, with the narrative mode that dominates Revelation 4:1–22:5. Notably, the technique of *synkrisis*, the "comparison" of two figures or cities often found in specimens of epideictic rhetoric, is also very important in Revelation, with its contrastive juxtaposition of well-developed image sequences (the worship around God and the Lamb vs. the worship centered on the beast and his image, orchestrated by his henchthing; the character

---

68. Eulogies and encomia (epideictic speeches) followed a different outline: external advantages, physical qualities, and moral qualities typically would be handled in turn, although a fair amount of freedom could be expected in the arrangement.

69. See, e.g., Gordon Fee's criticisms (1997, 15–16) of the cogent but irreconcilable attempts to analyze Philippians according to this five-part scheme by Duane Watson (1988b) and Gregory Bloomquist (1993, 84–96, 119–38).

70. See Betz 1979.

71. Ben Witherington III (1995) avoids this pitfall by recognizing that a single letter can contain several discrete arguments, each with its own proposition and proofs.

72. Royalty 1997, 603.

and fate of Babylon vs. New Jerusalem).[73] Additionally, the classical discussions of what exordia and perorations are expected to accomplish help to orient us toward the "framing" sections of Revelation (i.e., 1:1–20; 22:6–22). The aim of employing our firsthand knowledge of classical rhetoric is always to lay bare the persuasive techniques and strategies of the author, never to force the text to wear false or misleading labels for the sake of preserving some textbook scheme. The heuristic, rather than normative, quality of the rhetorical handbooks should never be compromised.

GUIDING QUESTIONS FOR A RHETORICAL INTERPRETATION OF REVELATION

While I was a student in learning exegesis, nothing was more helpful than having sets of questions to bring to a text. Some of the resources to which I still return are pages of questions that give me an orientation to a biblical text and set me on a path of investigation that will open up that text in fresh ways.[74] The present study has been guided by a series of specific questions that, I hope, result in a solidly *rhetorical* investigation of this text, and that I foreground here both as a means of laying out the plan for the book and for the sake of other students who practice exegesis best when they have clear questions before them to guide their explorations of a text and their assessment of the data they uncover. These questions may, for example, be of use to the student writing an exegetical paper on Revelation, supplying a dimension of rhetorical analysis to the fuller panoply of exegetical skills with which previous classes have supplied the student, whether or not one chooses to use *classical* rhetorical resources as fully as I do to answer them.

>Chapter 1: Questions concerning "Location" in the History of Investigation
>How have people read, and how do people continue to read, Revelation? How will *we* approach reading Revelation? Where does our angle of reading fit in with the history of interpretation, that larger conversation about reading Revelation?
>
>Chapter 2: Questions concerning Rhetorical Focus
>Out of all the possible features available, to what features of the hearers' situation does John call their attention? What is of concern to him, that he wants also to be of concern to his hearers? How does he problematize particular features of the hearers' situation that might not otherwise be problematic (or significant) to others, and normalize features of the hearers' situation that might be problematic to others?
>
>Chapter 3: Questions concerning Rhetorical Goals
>What does John want to see happen in regard to those features of the situations that he brings to attention? What other agendas are potentially at

---

73. See Schüssler Fiorenza 1991, 33; Royalty 1997, 604; Rossing 1999.
74. E.g., Elliott 1993, 72–74 (1990, xxv–xxvi); Kee 1989, 65–69.

work in those situations, particularly in regard to those features? How does John's agenda line up with (or against) these other agendas?

Chapter 4: Questions concerning Rhetorical Presentation
How does John present those local features and concerns to which he draws the hearers' attention? What evaluations does he seek to evoke in regard to these features by his description of them? What resources or techniques does John employ to accomplish the evocation of these evaluations? How does the presentation serve his rhetorical goals (including diminishing the appeal of competing agendas)? How does John's presentation of the "larger picture" of the cosmos reinforce the evaluations and responses he seeks to evoke? These questions grow out of our acknowledgment of the specific rhetorical potential of apocalypse, the primary genre John employs to communicate his message.

Chapters 5 and 6: Questions concerning Construction of Authority (Ethos)
How does John establish credibility and authority for his message? How does he diminish the credibility of voices that present an alternative view of the churches' situations and support alternative responses? What resources and strategies (like labeling) does he employ, and how do these resources advance his authority over rival speakers' authority?

Chapters 7 and 8: Questions concerning Engaging Emotions (Pathos)
What emotions does John seek to elicit from the hearers in regard to particular figures, features, and situations? On what basis in the text can we support our identification of these emotional appeals? Can we discern larger patterns in his isolated appeals to emotions? Where do we detect conflicting or complementary emotional appeals? How do these appeals to emotion in regard to particular entities or responses move the hearers closer to John's goals for them in their situations?

Chapters 9, 10, and 11: Questions concerning Argumentation (Logos)
Where does John exhibit patterns of rational argumentation? How would we analyze John's deductive or inductive processes in those passages? What argumentative topics does he employ (a question of argumentative content)? What argumentative strategies does he use (a question of argumentative form, e.g., arguments from the contrary, from analogy, or from historical example)? How do nondiscursive elements of Revelation (e.g., plot, intertexture [the incorporation of material from, or references to, other texts or traditions], and the like) contribute to the development of argument? What premises would the hearers have to share in order to find John's argumentation persuasive?

Chapter 12: Questions concerning Application to New Rhetorical Situations
What is our assessment of John's agenda and of the means by which he promotes it? What problems do we identify (e.g., the use of violence to bring about God's ends, the implications of the roles assigned to feminine figures in the story), and how do we adjudicate these? What does Revelation contribute to our own identification of problematic features in our situations, our assessment and interpretation of these features, our discernment of a response that signals faithfulness to the tradition in which we may stand, and our witness concerning these features?

This list of questions may not produce a *full* rhetorical analysis, but should still empower a fully *rhetorical* analysis. Some aspects of rhetorical criticism are omitted here. Incomplete attention is given to identifying and analyzing John's use of figures of diction and figures of speech. Discussion of rhetorical "arrangement" is subsumed chiefly under discussions of plot in chapter 4 (in part due to Revelation's defiance in regard to fitting into the typical patterns of public discourse contemplated by classical theorists). Nevertheless, pursuing the avenues of investigation outlined here will open up a distinctly rhetorical analysis of the traditional issues of historical setting and genre, as well as take us deep into John's engagement of rhetorical invention and thus the literary means by which he so effectively and powerfully engages his audience.

Chapter 2

The Rhetorical Setting of Revelation
Seven Congregations in the Roman Province of Asia

A contemporary-historical approach to Revelation requires that we look closely at the historical setting within which it was written and which it was to address. The rhetorical-critical mode that this book embraces requires further that we look at the historical landscape reflected within the text with a certain awareness of how the author's viewpoint and agenda have shaped that view of the landscape. Rather than attempt a description of the "historical situation" here, then, we will pursue a description of the "rhetorical situation."[1] Lloyd F. Bitzer defined the "rhetorical situation" as "a complex of persons, events, objects, and relations presenting an actual or potential exigence which can be completely or partially removed if discourse, introduced into the situation, can so constrain human decision or action as to bring about the significant modification of the exigence."[2] It is "rhetorical"

---

1. Both are also to be distinguished from the rhetorical situation inscribed within the text, namely, the situation of the glorified Christ addressing the prophet John on Patmos. There may be significant differences between "the actual historical-rhetorical situation" and the "*textual* rhetorical situation" (Schüssler Fiorenza 1991, 118). The distance between the two is especially clear, e.g., in discussions of the nature of the persecution experienced among the seven churches and the persecution described within Revelation's visions.
2. Bitzer 1968, 6.

insofar as it is determined by the interests and attention of the author, outlining those features of the "historical" situation to which, in the author's opinion, some particular response is warranted.

To what features of the first-century landscape does John draw the audience's attention? An author is *always* selective in this regard. A text seeking to persuade will direct us to look at what the author wants us to look at. Often this selectivity is strategic. The author who seeks to promote cooperation with, and accommodation to, the surrounding culture might strategically focus the audience's attention more fully on the goods to be enjoyed and the benefits to be derived from such a behavioral shift. Thus an author might draw our attention to pressing needs (e.g., of our children, whose future will be more stable as we amass greater wealth and build stronger social networks) that would be thereby alleviated. Authors are also *always* interpretive in regard to the features of the landscape to which they draw attention. We see those features as the author *wants* us to see them.

Uncovering the rhetoric of Revelation requires recovering alternative angles of vision on the features of the historical landscape to which John draws attention, so that we can see more clearly both that feature and his *interpretation* of that feature. We need to recover, as Elisabeth Schüssler Fiorenza stresses, not only the author's voice, but also "the other voices which [John] engages and which the discourse of [his] text submerges or represses."[3] Indeed, the recovery of the latter facilitates recovery of the former, allowing us to discern the counterintuitive ways in which John problematizes peaceful coexistence with, even prosperity within, the surrounding society, or in which he normalizes marginalization, poverty, even the experience of violent death. Once we gain clarity concerning the rhetorical situation and John's goals within that situation, we will be better able to trace how Revelation is constructed to bring about those goals through the various angles of investigation pursued in this study.

The seven oracles to the churches (Rev. 2–3) are customarily read as primary sources for issues of concern to John, and thus for the reconstruction of the historical and rhetorical setting. This approach has certain advantages. These chapters are the most transparent and explicit in terms of referring to local conditions and challenges.[4] Addressed to each individual congregation, we anticipate that they will give us the most detailed view of each particular situation. However, relying on the seven oracles has the disadvantage, if left without supplement, of highlighting particular local challenges to the neglect of challenges that all seven congregations share in common, which are accordingly treated in the visions addressed to all the congregations together.

The paucity of references to imperial cult in the seven oracles, for example, must be weighed against the fact that references to this cult dominate the second half of the visions. Does John defer treatment of the imperial cult, which

---

3. Schüssler Fiorenza 1991, 118.
4. See the extensive analyses in Ramsay 1909 and Hemer 1986.

enjoyed a significant presence in each of the seven cities, to the visions of Revelation because it was *not* a concern locally, or because it was a concern shared in *all* or *most* localities? The visions, moreover, will also place the local conditions and challenges (and potential responses to the same) against the backdrop of the larger conditions and concerns. For example, as John draws attention to the larger realities of Roman imperial economy (at least the facets he wants his hearers to "see" and in the colors in which he wishes them to see them), the Laodiceans look at their own wealth and local economy differently.

After a brief treatment of authorship and date, we will explore the features of the local and empirewide landscape to which John draws attention. We will try to look behind or around John's rhetoric in order to glimpse such features from a different perspective and to understand better the variety of responses to the features legitimately available to the Christians in Asia Minor, and thus understand better the significance of John's taking issue with those features in the way he did. This will be followed in chapter 3 by an attempt to discern what John really wants, that is, the reinforcements or changes in behavioral, cognitive, and affective response that John seeks to achieve by sending his "Revelation" to these audiences.

JOHN WHO?

The author identifies himself as John. There is little reason to suspect pseudepigraphy, especially since the author includes no biographical reminiscences or other details that could be seen to bolster the authority of the work by tying it more closely and manifestly to an important "John" from the recent past (contrast 2 Pet. 1:16–18).[5] This same observation, however, also means that we have little hope of certainty about the author's identity, save that his name was John.

There were several prominent figures named John in the first century (John the Baptist, John Mark, John the apostle, John the elder). Traditionally, the author of Revelation is identified with John the son of Zebedee; he and his brother James were apostles of Jesus.[6] Both Justin Martyr (*Dial.* 81.4) and Irenaeus (*Haer.* 4.14.1; 5.26.1) name *this* John as the author of Revelation. The latter carries some weight since, as a young man, Irenaeus knew Polycarp, who had in turn known John. The widespread acceptance of this view probably accounts for Revelation's eventual inclusion in the New Testament canon.[7] On the other hand, Dionysius of Alexandria was already questioning this tradition in the mid-third century on the grounds of differences in style and vocabulary between Revelation and the Gospels and Epistles also ascribed to John the apostle. Gaius, a late second-century Roman presbyter, also disputed Johannine authorship, claiming

---

5. Lipinski 1969 provides one of the very few attempts to argue in favor of pseudonymous authorship.
6. Mounce (1977, 31) argues in favor of this position.
7. Lohse 1981, 229.

(without supporting evidence) that the protognostic Cerinthus wrote Revelation pseudonymously to discredit John (see Eusebius, *Hist. eccl.* 3.28.1–2). Both Dionysius and Gaius were engaged in theological debate with opponents using Revelation as authoritative support for their positions. They sought to undermine these opponents' positions by distancing Revelation from any apostolic authority. Both the early proponents and critics of the traditional view of authorship remind us, therefore, that attributions of authorship are closely tied to—perhaps even ciphers for—commitments to the authority of a text and the role it should play in the life of the church.

Internal evidence is far from conclusive. John refers to himself as a "brother" and "partner" of the believers in the congregations (1:9); he is identified by others as one "slave" among many (1:1–2) or one "prophet" among others who stand on a par with him as his "brothers" (22:9). He seems to look upon the circle of apostles from the outside (21:14), even as he stands outside the circle of the twelve patriarchs (21:12). Relying primarily on internal evidence, we see John primarily as a prophet. He may have exercised a prophetic ministry in one of the seven churches alongside other prophets in that church and in the other churches of Asia. He may have exercised this ministry throughout the seven churches he addresses. While the number "seven" is indeed prominent throughout Revelation, giving some credence to viewing these seven congregations as representative churches, their particular geographic distribution, arranged in a horseshoe circuit and each no more than a two-days' journey from the next, would have been quite conducive to the ministry of an itinerant prophet.

The itinerant charismatist or prophet was a familiar figure in the early church. Such charismatists lurked behind Paul's troubles in the Corinthian church in the later stages of that conflict (2 Cor. 10–13). Those teachers clearly grounded their authority in both their natural and supernatural giftings, a topic that Paul in turn will harness indirectly and ironically to support his own authority (2 Cor. 12:1–10). The *Didache* witnesses to the activity of prophets and itinerant charismatists in the churches of its region, giving disproportionate space to the treatment of such persons in such a brief manual of church order and teaching (11–13). Revelation itself bears witness to the phenomenon. "False apostles" came to Ephesus from outside and failed to gain a hearing within that church (2:2). A female teacher in Thyatira ("Jezebel") is challenged as a person claiming (falsely, in John's opinion) the ministry of a "prophet" (2:20). There are also a number of other prophets active among the churches to whom John takes no objection (Rev. 22:9).[8]

---

8. Aune (1989) argues that Revelation addresses first a circle of prophets, who constitute the "you [plural]" in Rev. 22:16: "I, Jesus, sent my angel to bear witness to you [plural] concerning these things for [ἐπί] the churches." In this scenario, "Revelation has been entrusted by John to prophetic colleagues and envoys for distribution and presentation to the seven churches." The strange preface (Rev. 1:1–3) prior to the direct opening of the text (1:4) "functions to legitimate the fact that the revelation which John has received and written is in possession of prophetic envoys charged with its dissemination" (Aune 1989, 110).

These observations do not conclusively tell against authorship by John the apostle, any more than observations from external attestation cement it. But they do raise interesting questions about how John conceives of his own authority and how he communicates that authority in his work, since he presents himself unambiguously in the role of a Christian prophet. These questions are of paramount importance to rhetorical analysis, since appeals to ethos—the attempt to establish and reinforce one's credibility—were essential for persuasion. We will explore these questions in chapters 5 and 6.

John writes from Patmos, a small island lying about thirty-seven miles southwest of Asia Minor. It is not entirely clear how John came to be on this island, or what the circumstances of his stay were. From the text itself, we have only the indication that John came to be on that island "on account of [διά] the word of God and the testimony of Jesus" (1:9), in the close context of speaking of himself as a fellow sharer in the "tribulation" and "patient endurance" (as well as the "kingdom") involved in being a witness to this Jesus. Leonard Thompson argues that John went to Patmos voluntarily for the sake of preaching the Gospel there, taking the preposition διά as indicative of purpose rather than cause.[9] A purposive sense, however, is not within the established range of meanings for διά, which looks backward, never forward.[10] Thus John was on Patmos "on account of" prior activity connected with the Word of God and testimony of Jesus.

Eusebius read this in line with the tradition that John was exiled to Patmos during the reign of Domitian as a result of his activity in the churches (*Hist. eccl.* 2.20). The sentences of *relegatio* and *deportatio ad insulam* could be used to remove a potentially dangerous person from his or her sphere of influence to a sufficiently distant and isolated island. Confronted with John's stance toward Roman imperialism and outspoken critique (evidenced in Revelation itself), a local official (if not Domitian) might well have seen relegation to an island like Patmos as a politic solution.[11] What is surprising here is that the sentence was

---

Both Aune (1989, 111) and Schüssler Fiorenza (1985, 146) speak of these prophets as a prophetic "school" analogous to the circle gathered around Elisha. Aune invokes 1 Cor. 14:29–33 as evidence for early Christian prophetic "schools." While it is true that "a group of prophets functioned in a special way in the Corinthian church" (1989, 111), the text itself does not suggest that they were an organized, static group like a "school." Paul envisions, much more simply, individuals gifted in a given worship service with prophetic inspiration who, in effect, are able to put a check on each other's inspired utterances. Beyond the assumption that the prophets around John formed a discrete circle or school is the further assumption that John is their *leader* (Schüssler Fiorenza 1985, 146), a claim that he himself does not make, rather than a peer, a claim that he does consistently make. I would agree with Kraybill (1996, 39 n. 52) that it "may overstate the case to speak of [prophetic] 'schools.'"

9. L. Thompson 1990, 172.
10. A. Collins 1984, 55; BDAG, 225–26.
11. Saffrey 1975, 391. So also Hemer 1986, 26–27 and Kraybill 1996, 32–33. Saffrey (1975) and L. Thompson (1990, 143) point out that, far from being a barren rock, Patmos appears to have been home to a military garrison, an Artemis cult, and two *gymnasia*. Hemer (1986, 27) also questions the presence of mines on the island, where prisoners would have lived out their sentence in forced labor. A military installation rather than a penal colony, Patmos remains a fitting place to situate a dissident whom it would have been more problematic to execute.

exile rather than execution, a fact that has suggested to some that John was in fact a member of the elite (whether in Asia Minor or, more likely, in Palestine, whence he came). If this is correct, we could no longer explain John's criticisms as stemming from a sense of personal deprivation (or more basely, envy). Rather, "John's willingness to trade his privileged social location in Roman society for life among the struggling *ekklēsiai* represents John's 'coming out' of the 'great city Babylon.'"[12]

WHEN?

Knowing *when* a work was written can help get at *why* a work was written, or at least help define the circumstances to which the work was a response. Scholars generally date Revelation either to the "Year of the Four Emperors" (68–69 CE) or to the end of the reign of Domitian, emperor from 81 to 96 CE.[13] Sometimes a third possibility is advanced, the middle-to-later years of the reign of Trajan, emperor from 98 to 117 CE.[14] Discussions of the date are hampered by a recurring logical fallacy in the conversation, the claim that Revelation had to be written in connection with a period of intense persecution. Proponents of the earlier date often support their position by pointing out that there was no empirewide persecution of Christians under Domitian—but since there was fierce persecution under Nero, and the memory of this would be quite fresh, the earlier date is more plausible.[15] Or since the first official prosecutions against Christians *as* Christians in the eastern part of the empire occurred under Pliny the Younger during his governorship of Bithynia (a province in northern Asia Minor), a date under Trajan—thus under the shadow of these legal proceedings—is necessitated.[16] These arguments are grounded in the assumption that apocalypses respond to desperate social situations, consoling the oppressed by envisioning the punishment and overthrow of their oppressors and promising otherworldly compensation. Apocalypses, however, can afflict the comfortable just as much as comfort the afflicted. Careful analysis of the references to persecution and oppression in Revelation creates a very different picture, and therefore a different social function for the book, with John issuing a call to leave a comfortable and even prospering relationship with the surrounding society as its underside is more fully revealed.[17]

---

12. Howard-Brook and Gwyther 1999, xxvii; Witherington 2003, 9.
13. Arguments in favor of the earlier date include Bell 1978; Rowland 1982, 403–13; J. C. Wilson 1993; and van Kooten 2007. Proponents of the Domitianic date include A. Collins 1984, 54–83; Roloff 1993, 16–19; Hemer 1986, 2–5. Aune (1997, lvi–lxx) offers a review of the various positions along with a mediating position connected with his hypothesis of a multiple-stage composition. See also Beale 1999, 4–27; deSilva 1992a, 273–81; 2004, 896–98.
14. Downing 1988.
15. See Robinson 1976, 221–53; Bell 1978.
16. Downing 1988, 113.
17. See deSilva 1991; 1992a; 1992b.

Discussions of Revelation's date also tend to focus on identifying the seven heads (and sometimes the ten horns) of the beast from the sea. The heads are identified as kings, five of which have fallen, one of which "is" at the implied time of writing, and one of which is yet to come (followed by an eighth; 17:9–10). Most scholars understand these kings to be sequential, leading to two points of debate: where to start the sequence, and what to do with the interregnum emperors: Galba, Otho, and Vitellius (all of whom "reigned" during the space of a single year, but whose governments never became secure). Beginning with Julius Caesar leads to Nero as the sixth head; beginning with Augustus leads to Galba.[18] If the head count is a reliable indicator of date, and if the starting point is correct, this would point to 68 CE. Nero's suicide becomes thereby the mortal wound from which the beast recovers.

I find two difficulties with pressing this case. John did not identify "seven" as the number of these heads purely because the number corresponded with a discrete sequence of emperors starting with Julius or Augustus, the founders of the new order, as did the author of *4 Ezra* when choosing the number of wings and heads for his monstrous eagle.[19] Rather, the number seven results from John's earlier decision to portray the Roman Empire as the unholy amalgamation of the four beasts of Daniel 7 (which, together, had seven heads). A. J. P. Garrow would object that "seven kings which are purely symbolic sit uncomfortably alongside the adjacent reference to the symbolic and literal seven hills of Rome (17.9)."[20] But on the contrary, it might seem a sufficiently fortunate coincidence that John can draw a correspondence between the seven-headed hybrid and the famed number of Rome's hills. It is probably too much to ask that they correspond also to a discrete sequence of seven specific emperors.[21] The most significant feature of these emperors is that, at the implied time of writing, John and his audience stand under the penultimate one, near the end of the beast's wild ride. We cannot speak with certainty, however, concerning where the series begins, since John has not chosen the number seven because it corresponds with his location in Suetonius's list of the twelve Caesars. It came with Daniel 7 as part of the package.

A second difficulty involves the fluidity of John's own language. He speaks of one of the beast's heads receiving a death-blow (13:3), which might indeed recall Nero's suicide, but then speaks of the beast *itself* being wounded with the sword and yet surviving (13:12, 14). The latter image could encompass not

---

18. Lipinski 1969, 226; Engels 1964, 340.
19. Ulrichsen (1985) argues that the heads of the beast ought to begin with Caligula, the first emperor after Christ's resurrection and thus the first to come to power in the new age (thus directly opposing the reign of the newly ascended heavenly regent). Beyond any of his predecessors, Caligula impressed the underside of Rome and her emperors on the Jewish mind, particularly in his misguided attempt to give the Jews an image of their god—himself—to stand in their temple. Taking Caligula as the first head, Ulrichsen argues, Domitian is the sixth if the heads tally only the major emperors; the horns represent every official regent (thus including the interregnum emperors), leading again from Caligula to Domitian as the ninth. In both cases, Domitian is the presently reigning emperor, leaving the count open for a coming ruler under whom the crisis will come to a head.
20. Garrow 1997, 72.
21. See Downing 1988, 119.

merely the death of Nero, but also the civil wars that followed, when the beast—the imperial enterprise—as a whole (and not merely one of its heads) was in danger of faltering.[22] How would John have seen Galba, Otho, and Vitellius? The image of the beast itself being mortally wounded but recovering suggests that John looks back upon the civil wars as a whole, for only with the rise of Vespasian is the "mortal wound," opened up by Nero's suicide but not closed during the short-lived rise of Galba, healed. The resurgence of worship and awe directed toward the principate after the healing of this mortal wound, moreover, aligns with the revival of interest in the imperial cult in Asia under the Flavian dynasty—a revival due in part to the locals' desire to see this new dynasty's government fully and solidly planted, lest the prosperity and safety of the empire be threatened yet again by further civil war.

Another body of data involves the echoes of Nero and Nero-related traditions throughout the Apocalypse. The best solution for the number of the beast, which represents a gematria for the number of a person's name (13:18), remains Nero Caesar, whether as נרון קסר, which adds up to 666, or in a variant form lacking the second nûn, נרו קסר, which yields the occasional variant 616. There are clear echoes of the Nero redivivus or Nero rediturus myth, the fear (or hope, depending on one's view) that Nero was not really dead, but would return one day at the head of a great army to reclaim his throne. These echoes are often taken as support that Revelation was composed during the civil wars, when the expectation of Nero's return might be thought to be most vibrant, but this need not be the case.[23] A returning "Nero" still plays a part in rebellions in

---

22. Van Kooten (2007, 206) justifiably emphasizes the importance of the civil wars of 68–69 for those who lived through what threatened to be "for the state almost the end" (Tacitus, *Hist.* 1.11 [LCL]). Josephus also speaks of "the very hegemony of the Romans being shaken" by these events (*J.W.* 4.502, my trans.) and the outcome remaining uncertain until Vespasian established a new dynasty, a situation also reflected in *4 Ezra* 12:17–18.

23. Van Kooten presents new considerations for dating Revelation to 69 CE. He identifies Nero's *Domus Aureus* (his palace) with its colossal statue of Nero, erected in Rome after the great fire of 64 CE cleared the necessary space, as John's focus (2007, 221). He argues that "if John were concerned about the Roman imperial cult in one particular province, that of Asia, it would be very artificial if he were to speak only of one particular image," going on to assume that this would have to be an image of Nero (2007, 232–33). "Most importantly, however, there is no evidence of any imperial temple or shrine devoted to Nero which might have explained the prominence of Nero's image particularly in Revelation" (2007, 233). However, an image of the beast is not an image merely of one of its heads, that is, of a single emperor. If the beast represents the collective principate, that greater power of which each head is a manifestation, then the "image of the beast" is already a figurative expression denoting the iconic representation of imperial rule, necessarily a multiplicity of cult statues of particular emperors and other members of the imperial family.

Van Kooten (2007, 231) presents Otho and Vitellius as the two-horned second beast, persuading the people to erect a cult statue to Nero. However, Nero was *himself* the one who erected his Colossus prior to his own death; Otho and Vitellius may have erected other honorary images of Nero, but van Kooten has been arguing that Nero's Colossus is really the image of the beast in view. Thus his historical allegory falters here.

Other details also do not line up within van Kooten's theory. He writes, e.g., of "the exemplary victory of the Neronian martyrs standing beside the heavenly sea of glass, '*those who have been victorious* against the beast and his image'" (2007, 238, referring to Rev. 15:2). However, the Neronian martyrs achieved no victory over the beast's *image*, if we accept van Kooten's focus on Nero's Colossus in Rome, since they were killed prior to the erection of the *Domus Aureus*.

88 CE.[24] The identification of the beast with Nero in some sense is a claim not about date, but about the character of the principate. John could quite appropriately assert this identification even under the Flavians, when Christians might be tempted to forget the "true" character of the system under which they live.

Finally, the passage in 11:1–2 concerning the measuring of the temple, only the *outer* courts of which are given over to the Gentiles to trample for forty-two months, is often read as a prophecy stemming from the siege of Jerusalem but belied by the later events of 70 CE. Every other reference to a temple in Revelation, however, has the celestial temple in mind rather than the edifice in Jerusalem (cf. 6:9–11; 8:1–5; 14:15, 17; 15:5, 6, 8; 16:1), including one reference integrally related to this passage (11:19). John does not indicate that his focus has shifted away from this heavenly or cosmic temple in 11:1–2, making this passage less helpful for dating.

On balance, though I would be reluctant to accept a Domitianic date primarily on the basis of Irenaeus's late second-century testimony,[25] the prominence of the imperial cult in Revelation—particularly as a response to the complete closure of the wound that threatened the beast—matches well the increased excitement surrounding this cult in the Flavian period. Other factors, such as the appearance of churches in cities of which no mention is made in Christian writings from the period before 70 CE, the increasing focus on participation in the traditional and imperial cult as the point of conflict between the church and society (as actually erupts under Trajan in 110 CE), and the echoes of the economic crisis that an edict of Domitian sought to help correct—all point to a setting during the later Flavian period.[26]

MANIFESTATIONS OF ROMAN IMPERIALISM AND ITS LEGITIMATION

A number of powerful, well-developed figures—the dragon, the beast from the sea, the beast from the land, and "Babylon the Great" (both as luxuriating harlot and urban seat of world empire)—dominate the terrestrial landscape of Revelation's visions. Throughout the centuries popular interpretations of Revelation have exerted a great deal of energy in trying to identify these figures in their own context. There is little reason to suspect that John's own hearers had to reach very far to identify these figures.

24. See Suetonius, *Nero* 57.2; Dio Cassius (*Rom. Hist.* 66.19.3) recounts the exploits of another false "Nero" active from the Euphrates to Asia Minor in 80 CE. See Aune 1998a, 737–40; H.-J. Klauck 2001; van Kooten 2005.

25. Irenaeus, *Adversus haereses* 5.30.3; see also van Kooten 2007, 208.

26. According to Hemer (1986, 4), "Rev 6.6 alludes to an edict issued by Domitian in AD 92 to restrict the growing of vines in the provinces (Suet. *Dom.* 7.2; 14.2)"; so also Brent 1999, 165–66. Yet Rev. 6:6 refers to the *conditions* that gave rise to Domitian's policy, not to the actual edict. Domitian's edict was intended to limit the space allotted to export crops like olive oil and wine in favor of grain and thus tried to remedy the problem represented by the third horseman's ride.

A "great city" sitting "upon seven hills" and having "authority over the kings of the earth" (17:9, 18) resonates immediately with the hearers' experience. The seven hills of Rome were celebrated in literature and coinage.[27] A yearly festival commemorated Rome's expansion to enclose the seven hills within the city limits.[28] On this basis, both Christian hearers and outsiders would immediately connect Babylon with Rome. Despite people's awareness of other nations that were not (yet) under Roman dominion—that, indeed, often posed a threat to Rome's dominion in some sectors—"authority over the kings of the earth" was regularly attributed to Rome. Virgil celebrates Zeus's promise that the Romans would "rule the sea and all the lands about it" (*Aeneid* 1.236–37), referring to the *orbis terrarum*, the "circle of the lands" around the Mediterranean constituting the civilized world, the world that counted. Zeus declares Rome's destiny to be to "bring the whole world under law's dominion" (*Aen.* 4.232). Indeed, as the Roman eagle overshadowed more and more of the Mediterranean basin, it exercised "authority over every tribe and people and language and nation" (Rev. 13:7). Minucius Felix, a second-century Christian, would write of the Romans that "their power and authority has occupied the circuit of the whole world [again the concept of the *orbis terrarum*]: thus it [Rome] has propagated its empire beyond the paths of the sun, and the bounds of the ocean itself" (*Octavius* 6).

Neither would the economic picture of Revelation 18, especially the flow of goods into this city, have strained credulity. A near contemporary of John, Aelius Aristides, paints a similar picture in his panegyric on Rome:

> Around lie the continents far and wide, pouring an endless flow of goods to Rome. There is brought from every land and sea whatever is brought forth by the seasons and is produced by all countries, rivers, lakes, and the skills of Greeks and foreigners. . . . Anyone who wants to behold all these products must either journey through the whole world to see them or else come to this city. . . . One can see so many cargoes from India or if you wish from Arabia . . . that one may surmise that the trees there have been left permanently bare, and that those people must come here to beg for their own goods whenever they need anything! (*To Rome* 11–13)

The disciples in the seven churches would have had strong cause to surmise that John was subjecting Rome and her imperialist political and economic practices to trenchant critique.[29]

---

27. Virgil, *Aeneid* 6.782; Cicero, *Ad Atticum* 6.5; Martial, *Epigrams* 4.64; Aelius Aristides, *Or.* 26.3. See also the discussion of the *Dea Roma* coin, showing the goddess Roma reclining against seven mountains, in Aune 1998b, 920–22, and the classical references gathered in Aune 1998a, 944–45, 959; Strecker and Schnelle 1996 at 17:18.

28. Suetonius, *Dom.* 4; Witherington 2003, 223.

29. On the beast and whore as Roman emperors and as Rome, see Bousset 1906, 358–65, 418–26. Jörg Frey (2006, 236) helpfully orients readers to this view of Revelation: "Many elements of the visionary sequence do refer to the world of the addressees—and not to a distant future—in order to reveal the true character of the challenges the readers have to face." "The visionary images reveal the deeper, the true character of the ruling powers, . . . and they develop an overwhelming

Similarly, when John uses Daniel's images for world empires to speak of a "beast" (Rev. 13:1–2; see Dan. 7:3–7), fatally wounded but healed (Rev. 13:3), worshiped by "the inhabitants of the earth" in a manner involving a cult image (13:4, 8, 14), exercising authority over a multiethnic, multilingual, multinational empire (13:7), the Roman emperors were immediately available to John's hearers as plausible referents.[30] Contemporary writers remember the suicide of Nero and the civil wars that followed as a blow that nearly brought this particular imperial power down. Most telling, the ubiquity of imperial cult, particularly in the eastern Mediterranean, would make the Roman emperor (or more properly, the collective emperors, the *Sebastoi* [= Latin *Augusti*, the "venerable, revered ones"]) and the imperial cult the obvious point of connection in their situation.

John selected these "landmarks" from the landscape of first-century Roman Asia for special examination through his apocalyptic lens. We need to enter into those interpretive, subversive visions with a clear sense of what Rome, her emperors, and their cult represented for people living in and around the province of Asia Minor, and in what ways these realities were represented to them by voices other than John's.

Two rather distinct pictures of the Roman imperial presence and economy emerge from near-contemporary sources. Elite sources paint a picture of a world power that brings tremendous benefits to humankind: an end to civil strife, protection from invasion, improvement of means of travel by land (through expert road construction) and by sea (through expansion of ports and harbors), as well as the dramatic reduction of brigandage and piracy. Trade is facilitated, steady distribution of grain and relief in times of shortfall improved, and the rule of law maintained. The "media" of the period (inscriptions, panegyrics, coin mintings) celebrate this side of Roman rule. Plutarch, a near-contemporary of John, spoke thus of Rome's rise and unification of the Mediterranean: "Rome developed and grew strong, and attached to herself not only nations and peoples but [also] foreign kingdoms beyond the sea; and then at last the world found stability and security, when the controlling power entered into a single, unwavering cycle and world order of peace" ("On the Fortune of the Romans" 2 [*Moralia* 317]). And according to Virgil, Rome's gifts and graces were "to pacify, to impose the rule of law, to spare the conquered, and battle down the proud" (*Aen.* 6.851–53).

Plutarch and Virgil both bear witness (and contribute) to the public discourse about Rome as the city chosen by the gods for the special destiny of bringing stability, rule of law, peace, and temporal prosperity as signs of divine favor. Adding the epithet *Aeterna* to *Roma* advances the bold claim that this destiny was unchanging and everlasting. Plutarch reflects this when he affirms that

---

argument for the conviction that the final victory is with God and Christ. . . . Thus, the visions also give deeper reasons for the admonitions of the seven letters. Only from the visionary part does it become clear why the readers should 'leave Babylon' (Rev 18:4)" (2006, 246).

30. Other Jewish authors draw upon Daniel to speak of Rome, though usually identifying Rome as Daniel's fourth beast/kingdom and not as a new hybrid of all four (see *4 Ezra* 12:11–12; *2 Bar.* 39:5–7 refers to Rome as the "fourth kingdom" without depicting it as a beast).

Rome provides a "secure mooring cable" for the world, using adjectives such as "unwavering" to describe her rule. Many of the positive claims about Roman rule (the nontheological claims, at least) enjoy sufficient evidence to be accepted as historical fact. Moreover, individual emperors gave significant benefits to cities in Asia Minor, reinforcing the "public discourse" with tangible demonstrations of its truth. Tiberius provided financial assistance to several cities after an earthquake in 17 CE. Nero dredged the harbor of Ephesus, restoring the city's most important economic asset. Domitian provided Laodicea with a stadium and Smyrna with an aqueduct.[31]

Rome's symbolic representations were striking and ubiquitous. The goddess *Roma* was the visible representation of the "order," the "rule of law," the "peace" and "stability" brought by imperial expansion. Local manifestations of the cult of Roma represented the ultimate legitimation of Roman power. She was often featured on the reverse of coins minted under Nero and Vespasian. She is more prominently visible in the cult statues throughout the Mediterranean. Smyrna established a temple to "Rome" as early as 195 BCE. Augustus refused to allow any temple to be consecrated to himself unless Roma were also included. In 29 BCE, Pergamum erected such a temple to Augustus and Roma. In the same year Ephesus rededicated part of its celebrated temple of Artemis to the deified Julius and Roma. Imperial cult thus also reinforced the belief that Rome was divinely chosen to rule the world, to subdue all nations, and to lead them into a golden age of lasting peace and well-being, united under her banner.[32]

Divine Providence worked in Rome's rise and reign, and particularly in the rise and reign of Augustus and his successors. Here our focus temporarily shifts from Rome to her leaders, the other prominent feature caricatured in Revelation's terrestrial landscape. Rome was an empire long before Augustus: the Roman Republic already controlled most of the lands around the Mediterranean. But the Republic offered power-hungry senators too much opportunity for factionalism and, ultimately, civil war. The Mediterranean was twice subjected to the horrors of civil war prior to 31 BCE, when Octavian, soon to be renamed Augustus, finally emerged from the strife victorious. He quickly forgave the armies of his rivals, uniting their power to his own, and ushered in the Pax Augusti, the Augustan Peace. "By universal consent"—and this phrase is vitally important to the legitimation of his rule—he accepted perpetual powers in the Republic. Government became stable, and provinces flourished again.

An inscription at Priene, a coastal city in Asia Minor halfway between Ephesus and Miletus, captures the spirit of this new age. The provincial council (the *Koinon Asias*, which functioned as an important local force promoting imperial cult) decreed that Augustus's birthday would mark the start of the new year, since his birth was the "beginning of the good news" for the world ("good news" here translates εὐαγγέλιον, the same word often translated "gospel" in the New

---

31. Kraybill 1996, 79.
32. See Mellor 1975.

Testament). This inscription lauded Augustus as Providence's provision for the people's "highest good," a ruler whom Providence "filled with excellence for the benefit of humanity," and hailed him as "savior." This laudatory declaration was inscribed in temples to Caesar across the province, making its language available to the citizens of the seven cities.[33] Similar acclamations of the emperor reverberate to the very end of the first century CE. Concerning Domitian, Statius writes: "Behold! He is a god! At Jupiter's command he rules the happy world on his behalf" (*Via Domitiani,* in *Silvae* 4.3.128–29). By the standards of Christian rhetoric, acclamations of the emperor were no less than messianic.

Temples to Augustus rose across the eastern Mediterranean, whose inhabitants were accustomed to treating their rulers and exceptional benefactors as gods. Nicolaus of Damascus, a friend of Herod the Great, explained the phenomenon in the opening of his *Life of Augustus*: "All people address him [as Augustus] in accordance with their estimation of his honor, revering him with temples and sacrifices across islands and continents, organized in cities and provinces, matching the greatness of his virtue and repaying his benefactions towards them." Roman power was represented in the seven cities in many ways, but perhaps the most prominent was the imperial cult: the temples, shrines, altars, and cult images dedicated to Augustus, to members of his household, and to all who succeeded to the imperial office.

This cult was not imposed on the provinces; it was locally motivated, the response of provincial populations to the tremendous power of the emperor, perceived as truly godlike, and to the benefits that the emperor's rule brought to the provinces. Since his gifts matched those sought from gods, it was deemed fitting that the expressions of gratitude and loyalty should take the form of worship. Such displays of loyalty and gratitude ensured both that the empire would remain strong (averting the disasters of civil war and foreign invasion, ensuring continued peace and prosperity) and that the emperor would remain well-disposed toward the province when it needed imperial aid. Elites who held priesthoods in the imperial cult were strategically chosen to serve as the province's ambassadors to the emperor, suggesting that the cult served both to represent the emperor to the province *and* the province to the emperor.[34]

By the end of the first century CE, thirty-five cities in Asia Minor held the honorific title of "temple warden" (νεωκόρος, *neōkoros*) of an imperial cult site.[35] All seven cities addressed by John had cultic sites: six (all but Thyatira) had imperial temples; five (all but Philadelphia and Laodicea) had imperial altars and priests. Pergamum was a center for imperial cult, the first in the province

---

33. Barnett 1989, 118; Witherington 2003, 192.
34. Thompson 1990, 158. On imperial cult as an expression of loyalty and gratitude, see deSilva 1991, 187–93. Howard-Brook and Gwyther (1999, 95) stress that competition for the honor of erecting new temples to an emperor reflected a competition to show one's own city (or one's own province, when the *Koinon Asias* united their respective cities in some new imperial cult venture) to be the most grateful and loyal toward the imperial house, and thus most deserving of imperial patronage.
35. Price 1984, 66–67.

to honor Augustus with a temple to Rome together with her new emperor (29 BCE), as was Ephesus, which made room for the worship of the deified Julius and Roma in the Artemision that same year. These two cities competed for the title of *neōkoros* of the imperial cult. Toward the end of the first century, Ephesus undertook a new initiative: the Flavian temple in the heart of downtown, honoring the living emperor, Domitian, with a colossal statue and cult, erected alongside the older temple to Rome and Julius Caesar and the portico dedicated to Artemis, Augustus, and Tiberius.[36]

But the imperial cult was not merely a matter of stone temples, lifeless statues, and voiceless inscriptions passively waiting to be noticed. Priests and celebrants regularly brought these sites and their ideology to life, following a calendar of imperial celebrations, including the monthly commemoration of the reigning emperor's birthday.

> Imperial temples and sanctuaries were wreathed with flowers. Animals were sacrificed at various altars throughout the main locations of the city, for example, the council house, temples of other deities, theatres, the main squares, stadiums, and gymnasiums. These political, religious, and public buildings were linked together by processions and dignitaries, garlanded animals being led to slaughter, and bearers of icons and symbols of the emperor. As the procession passed by, householders would sacrifice on small altars outside their homes. The whole city thus had opportunity to join in the celebration.[37]

The air would be filled with the sound of hymns chanted to the emperor and to the gods on behalf of the emperor, as by the choral association in Pergamum "whose sole function was to sing hymns to Augustus as a god in the temple precincts."[38] Scenes of worship centered upon the image of the beast were both elaborate and commonplace in the experience of John and his audience.

The prominence of the beasts from sea and land, the "image of the beast," and the worship of the same throughout the visions of Revelation suggests that John wanted to highlight the imperial cult as a significant feature of the landscape of the rhetorical situation.[39] His selection of *these* landmarks as a focal point for Christian self-differentiation from, and opposition to, the non-Christian society would prove quite significant for the church's future. Participation in the cults of the emperor and Roma demonstrated, in the eyes of the local citizenry and elites, appropriate gratitude to the emperor and the Roman order for maintaining the peaceful conditions that facilitated stability, even prosperity. It evidenced the

---

36. Brent 1999, 176–77; see also Hemer 1986, 55. Friesen (2001, 23–131) provides a comprehensive survey of available imperial cult sites.

37. L. Thompson 1990, 162.

38. See *I. Eph.* 18d.11–14; Kraybill 1996, 62; Brent 1999, 194–95.

39. See the judgment of Jörg Frey (2006, 241): "In view of these observations, it would be unwise to underestimate the cultic dimension as a whole, the issue of true and false worship for the addressees of Revelation, or to deny the imperial cult's relevance for the communities addressed in the seven letters."

piety and sense of duty (*pietas*, εὐσέβεια) that assured one's neighbors of one's commitment to do one's part to support that order on which the well-being of the local community depended. By promoting withdrawal and distance from the cult, John would heighten the Christians' neighbors' suspicion that the Christian communities were pockets of dissent and, potentially, sedition.

While John foregrounds imperial cult activity in his landscape, he also draws attention to the broader phenomenon of idolatrous worship of the Greco-Roman pantheon across that landscape. This reflects the tendency of the public discourse to ground imperial cult in the worship of the sacred pantheon, often in spatial arrangements (for example, the erection of imperial statues or altars within the sacred spaces of the traditional gods) as well as in verbal articulations of imperial ideology (as in Virgil's *Aeneid*, where Zeus exercises his rule through the rise of Rome and her rulers). Traditional idolatrous worship appears most visibly in Revelation at the conclusion of the judgments unleashed by the first six trumpets:

> The rest of humankind, who were not killed by these blows, neither repented from the works of their hands, so as not to worship the demons and the idols, the gold and silver and bronze and stone and wooden things which can neither see nor hear nor walk about, nor did they repent of their murders or their sorceries or their sexually immoral acts or their thefts. (9:20–21)

The link between the worship of idols as lifeless representations and the worship of demons as spiritual forces infusing these idols appears elsewhere in Jewish and Jewish-Christian texts (e.g., Bar. 4:6–7; 1 Cor. 10:14–21). John draws on this connection further when he connects the worship of the emperor with the worship of the demons' chief: "All the earth marveled after the beast, and they worshiped the dragon, because he gave authority to the beast, and they worshiped the beast" (Rev. 13:3b–4a).

With such language, John draws attention to the worship of Zeus and to the ways in which the oversight of divine "Providence" acting through the principate is given expression in the seven cities. The local reference to "the throne of Satan" in the city of Pergamum is probably part of this matrix. While notable scholars have read this as a reference to Pergamum's temple of *Roma et Augusti*,[40] the city's most distinctive landmark was the great altar of Zeus, set atop a mountain, from which it dominated the city (and indeed had the appearance of a great throne). The identification of Satan as the spiritual force *behind* the principate (the many-headed sea-beast) throughout the visions strongly suggests that the throne of Satan would reflect some landmark or practice associated more closely with the traditional gods, especially the chief god, Zeus.[41] Scholars

---

40. Schüssler Fiorenza 1991, 54; A. Collins 1983, 733–34; Frey 2006, 244–45; Hemer 1986, 82–85.

41. Writing of this thronelike altar, Hemer (1986, 85) observes that "the obsessive serpent motif of its sculptures and the title 'Soter'" would signal to John deliberate parody of Christ and the cult's being in league with Satan.

disagree whether Christians experienced more hostility and pressure in regard to their nonparticipation in the imperial cult or in the cults of the traditional gods.[42] Quantifying such matters, however, is less important than observing that John focuses attention on both in his survey of the features of the landscape that ought to cause concern for his readers (given the subversive way in which John presents these cults).[43]

The cults of Roma and the emperors, then, together with the complex of topics and media that constituted "public discourse" about Roman imperial rule, affirmed that rule's legitimacy, greeting it as a welcome presence into the local scene. But there is another side.

Not every people group came under the *imperium* voluntarily, as did Asia Minor. Some were "taken" by military force, not "received" through diplomatic relations.[44] Threats to the Roman peace were brutally neutralized. John's scenes of blood filling valleys and endless flocks of carrion birds gathering to feast upon the flesh of kings and soldiers are not products of apocalyptic imagination. They were available to be seen throughout John's lifetime (e.g., in the First Jewish Revolt or the suppression of smaller revolts throughout the East). Most criminals deemed seditious died by crucifixion, one of the most economical and cruel forms of punishment ever devised—economical because it required only some reusable wood and nails, but lasting for days as a deterrent to others who might disturb the Roman peace. The bloodbath in Rome under Nero, especially targeting Christians, showed the fragility of the protection afforded by law and long remained a traumatic blot on the memory of Roman rule among conscientious Christians. Even a man as highly placed as Tacitus could see what Rome looked like "from the outside," as his German chieftain comments on the advancing Roman army: "to violence, rapine, and plunder they give the name, 'government'; they make a desert, and call it 'peace'" (*Agricola* 30).

The Roman peace was not only built upon violence, but also built and maintained upon the backs of slaves, humans sufficiently dehumanized to be spoken of as "bodies" or, in Aristotle's infamous phrase, "living tools" (*Politics* 1.4 [1253b27–33]). Though slaves lived under conditions that ran the gamut from unconscionable to lavish, they shared this basic definition and the precariousness it implied for their identity and security as persons. John draws attention to this facet of the Roman economy—indeed, its bedrock—by listing "bodies, that

---

42. For the former position, see Biguzzi 1998; Brent 1999, 164–209; for the latter, Aune 1997, lxiv; L. Thompson 1990, 164.

43. The Christians' withdrawal from all forms of idolatry contributed to their neighbors' sense of "alienation" from them (ξενίζονται, 1 Pet. 4:3–4), while applying legal pressure upon those denounced as Christians had, for Pliny the Younger, the winsome effect of renewing local interest and participation in the cults of the traditional gods (*Ep.* 10.96).

44. Coins bearing the inscription *Asia Recepta* commemorate Asia's peaceful submission to Roman rule. This stands in stark contrast to coins celebrating the "taking" of Egypt and Armenia, or the (re)taking of Judea: *Aegypto Capta*, a minting featured under Octavian in 28 BCE; *Armenia Capta*, another minting under Augustus; *Judea Capta*, from multiple mintings commemorating the suppression of the First Jewish Revolt.

is, human lives" in the inventory of the cargo that streams toward Rome from every quadrant of the *orbis terrarum*.[45] In this list of twenty-eight items (Rev. 18:11–13), John has given "bodies" the climactic position by placing it last and heightened emphasis by providing this brief gloss.

The Roman economy itself is a feature of the landscape that John selects for concerted attention. The wealth (luxury) of Rome figures prominently in the description—and indictment!—of Babylon in Revelation 17–18.[46] Close study of John's use of Hebrew prophecy reveals that he both selects earlier prophetic indictments of imperialist economies *and* increases the concentration of language and imagery concerned with wealth as he applies these older traditions to "the Great City."[47]

Several ancient observers comment on the conspicuous consumption and ostentatious display that characterize Rome and Roman elites, substantiating John's accusations of Rome's intemperate "luxury" (στρῆνος, 18:3; στρηνιάω, 18:7, 9). Lucian's *Nigrinus*, for example, castigates Rome as a "symbol of not only excessive wealth and vice but [also] the excessive, even ostentatious, display of wealth, power, purple, and gold."[48] We have also already encountered Aelius Aristides's "celebration" of Rome's stripping the provinces bare to satisfy the tastes and cravings of its elites. Tax incentives reinforced Rome's priority in the global market: an inscription at Ephesus exempts merchants from paying customs on goods carried "on behalf of the people of Rome."[49]

Global trade with this ultimate, luxuriating consumer brought several significant economic consequences. First, such trade allowed local provincials to increase their wealth and thereby their status. While "aristocratic Greeks and Romans held commerce in low esteem," many, including Jews and Christians (for whom the path of military service, with its oaths and rites, was even more problematic), found commerce to be their only path to upward mobility.[50] There

---

45. On σῶμα as a synonym for δοῦλος, see Glancy (2002, 10–11), who also suggests that John "may be emphasizing the bitterness of the slave trade" in Rev. 18:13.

46. "The ample space allotted to economic sins in the lament portion of the chapter gives them special emphasis" (Hylen 2003, 213).

47. Royalty 1998, 79. Royalty (1998, 208) rightly observes the importance of Ezek. 26–27 as a resource for Rev. 17–18, though we need to refine his point that John selects only kings and those engaged in commerce from Ezekiel's long string of characters in his invective. Within his larger prophetic announcement of destruction addressed directly to Tyre, Ezekiel had himself foregrounded a lament spoken by "the princes of the sea" who perform acts of mourning (26:16–18), placing an additional lament on the lips of the "mariners and all the pilots of the sea" (27:32b–36). Kings and merchants are prominently named near the end of this lament (27:35–36). John has had to do less selective editing of Ezek. 26–27 to achieve this desired focus on economic exploitation than Royalty suggests.

48. Royalty 1998, 123. Royalty's assertion that "this rhetoric of blame would have been familiar to Asian audiences when they heard John's attack on Rome in Revelation," however, cannot be sustained in light of the fact that Royalty had only produced mid-second-century evidence of the same.

49. Engelmann and Knibbe, 1989, par. 1–9, 25. Cited in Kraybill 1996, 66.

50. Kraybill 1996, 83–93, esp. 83. Kraybill (1996, 102–41) provides an extensive discussion of the commercial shipping industry, shipping guilds, privileges for shippers, and the wealth to be made through maritime trade during the principate.

It is unlikely that either John or his audience shared the aristocratic disdain for wealth gained through commerce, not being aristocratic Greeks and Romans themselves (contra Royalty 1998,

were probably many Christians among the seafarers and merchants transporting goods to Rome and other important urban centers, seeking thus to improve their lot and the lot of their children.[51] Many Christians prospered under Roman rule, as the oracle to Laodicea suggests by drawing attention to the wealth and the claims to have "grown rich" within the congregation (3:17–18).

A second consequence is inflation or deprivation in the provinces where the goods are produced. Toward the end of the inventory of cargoes, John lists the "wine and oil and fine flour and grain" streaming toward Rome (18:13). Grain was, in fact, the mainstay of maritime trade, supplying the daily free distribution of grain for Rome's 200,000 families on the "dole."[52] Although Rome purchased this grain inexpensively (with the money supplied, in part, from the tribute of client states), the residents of the provinces where this grain was produced often paid high prices for their grain, and in times of shortage they went without.[53] This was exacerbated by local landowners' interest in producing crops that brought in a better financial yield per arable acre. Market demands made the production of oil and wine far more attractive, often leading to scarcity in the essentials of wheat and barley in the provinces.[54] Revelation 6:5–6 reflects a situation in which the prices of staples are grossly inflated, while production of oil and wine proceeds unabated.[55] John calls attention to the parasitic side of the Roman imperial economy, in which only shippers and merchants profit. Here he speaks in concert with other voices expressing resentment as wealth flowed out of the province.[56]

---

186). A principal thesis of Royalty's work is that John promotes the acquisition of heaven's wealth as high-status wealth that confers status as well as material, over against Babylon's wealth, which is disparaged as the "low" wealth of trade commerce (1998, 96–97, 111). But alleging snobbery substitutes an attitude toward commerce extrinsic to Revelation for the explicit rationales John advances for avoiding entanglement with Babylon's wealth, which center on the unjust practices that undergird and maintain its global economic system. The pressing issue of Rome's wealth is not that it is low-status wealth, but that it is built upon violence and exploitation, all whitewashed with politico-religious propaganda.

51. Kraybill 1996, 101; see further Bauckham 1993a, 338–83.
52. Kraybill 1996, 107.
53. Kraybill 1996, 107. So much grain was exported to Rome to meet the city's demands that Asia Minor even had to import grain from Egypt or the Black Sea, at added expense, to provide for local needs (Kraybill 1996, 66).
54. Howard-Brook and Gwyther 1999, 98.
55. Howard-Brook and Gwyther 1998, 98; Wengst 1987, 224; Kraybill 1996, 66.
56. Bauckham (1993a, 379, 382) recites two important witnesses from the *Sibylline Oracles*:

> However much wealth Rome received from tribute-bearing Asia,
> Asia will receive three times that much again
> from Rome and will repay her deadly arrogance to her.
> (3.350–352)

> Great wealth will come to Asia, which Rome itself
> once plundered and deposited in her house of many possessions.
> She will then pay back twice as much and more
> to Asia, and then there will be a surfeit of war.
> (4.145–148)

The latter text dates from the late first century CE and appears in connection with the anticipation of a return of Nero (4.137–139), here seen as the hero of the East.

A third consequence is the undermining of resistance among non-Roman populations through cultivating the desire for what Rome has and can provide. John may have these consequences in mind as he speaks of the great whore seducing the inhabitants and kings of the earth. Tacitus attested to the fact that growing fond of and accustomed to the luxury goods and entertainments introduced with the Roman presence undermined resistance to Roman rule. With customary perspicuity, he has his general Civilis in Batavia exhort his people: "Away with those pleasures which give the Romans more power over their subjects than their arms bestow!" (*Hist.* 4.64.3). In places where there was resistance, Romans introduced luxury and offered the "privilege" of Greek and Roman education for the children of local elites in order to achieve what force could not as efficiently (Plutarch, *Sertorius* 13–14).[57]

The wealth to be enjoyed by participating in the larger global economy was, as far as John was concerned, a dangerous lure toward sharing in the violence and political injustice that created the sociopolitical context that maintained such an economy, as well as sharing in the economic injustice that allowed the resources and produce of the provinces to be siphoned off to satisfy the immoderate cravings of Rome's inhabitants and worldwide elite. Long before the prophets of postcolonialism, John understood that a person cannot share in the profits of domination without also sharing in its crimes.

But the arrangements of the economic system also involved the participant in entanglements with idolatrous religion.[58] Harbors, the centers of the maritime trade, also gave prominent place to cultic sites of both the traditional gods and the emperor. In Alexandria, the *Sebasteum*, a temple to the *Augusti*, faced the harbor. The harbor of Cenchreae near Corinth featured temples or statues to Aphrodite, Poseidon, Asclepius, and Isis. The harbor at Ostia similarly sported cult images and shrines both to emperors and traditional gods. Religious ceremonies opened the sailing season, with pious seafarers and merchants invoking the gods' favor.[59] The temple of Diana in Ephesus was both a celebrated cultic site and the principal bank of the province of Asia.[60] Business associations in Asia Minor took oaths of loyalty to the emperor as an assurance that their assemblies were not conducted for any subversive political purposes.[61] Similarly, imperial cult ceremonies were conducted in the guilds at Ostia. Membership among the *Augustales*, a guild of freedmen promoting the imperial cult, facilitated advancement in business and trade.[62] John himself points to the connection between

---

57. Howard-Brook and Gwyther 1999, 96.
58. John was "not against commerce and trade in themselves, as if they were intrinsically evil. Rather, *John warned Christians to sever or to avoid economic and political ties with Rome because institutions and structures of the Roman Empire were saturated with unholy allegiance to an Emperor who claimed to be divine (or was treated as such)*" (Kraybill 1996, 17, emphasis orig.).
59. Kraybill 1996, 123–27.
60. Howard-Brook and Gwyther 1999, 103.
61. Kraybill 1996, 78–79.
62. Kraybill 1996, 128–31.

commerce and participation in the imperial cult (Rev. 13:15–17), so closely interwoven were idolatrous cults and participating in trade.[63]

> Loyalty to Jesus Christ was a total commitment that left no room for a "divine" Emperor. Yet veneration of a deified ruler pervaded harbors, trade venues, and commercial rituals of the late first-century Roman Empire. Even coins of the realm, without which trade was almost impossible, made blasphemous claims about the house of Caesar.[64]

Roman imperialism, with its seductive economy and blasphemous imperial cult, is the main challenge John identifies in Revelation 4–22. John raises his voice alongside those of other protestors like the authors of *4 Ezra* and *2 Baruch*. John was not a solitary, raving lunatic. The asylum was full of people who just couldn't "see things" in line with the official picture. The multiplicity of voices calling out against Rome's injustices at the close of the first century, of which John's voice was one, helps us see that Jews and Christians in Asia Minor were not only concerned about local affairs, internecine strife, or throwing stones at the church or synagogue across the way. The "system," together with all its local manifestations, was also a major problem.

Uniting the practice of exerting control and maintaining peace through violent suppression of dissent, the promotion of an economy arranged for the great benefit of the few, and the prominent use of religious language and ritual to claim sacral legitimation for these arrangements—uniting these is both the genius of Rome and the heap of her sins for which John excoriates her.[65] Focus can easily be overdrawn on one facet of this system (e.g., the imperial cult, though its stark offensiveness for monotheists makes it a striking feature of the landscape) to the detriment of other facets (e.g., economic exploitation or the use of violence),[66] but it is a far greater mistake to read Revelation as if John were only concerned about interlopers in his churches and local power struggles with other prophets.

LOCAL CONCERNS UNDERSCORED IN THE RHETORICAL SITUATION OF THE SEVEN ORACLES

Having explored the landmarks of the larger landscape to which John draws the hearers' attention, we have also already indirectly encountered local landmarks that Revelation would evoke in the hearers' imaginations. The "image of the

---

63. Duff (2001, 68) underscores John's assumption that "doing business in the empire requires the collaboration of Satan."

64. Kraybill 1996, 139. Kraybill understands the mark of the beast to encompass the "ubiquity of the imperial cult" (1996, 136), though he notes the special resonances of this phrase with the coin of the realm (where "image" and "mark" are terms used to describe the imprint on the coin faces; Kraybill 1996, 138, citing E. Janzen 1994, 650). John's passion is very much akin to the Zealots' attitude toward images on coins and in plastic representations (see Hengel 1989, 193) and their emphasis on the recognition of "One God, One Lord above all others."

65. See also Bauckham 1993a, 349.

66. So rightly Howard-Brook and Gwyther 1999, 116.

beast" takes the hearer not only to the imperial cult in general, but also to specific, local manifestations of the same (e.g., the temple to Domitian in Ephesus or the temple to *Roma et Augusti* in Pergamum). References in the visions to idolatry in general invite the hearers to imagine local sites where such worship is offered, as in the renowned temple of Diana in Ephesus, the altar of Zeus in Pergamum, and the many temples to the gods in each locale. This larger landscape impinges upon, and provides an interpretive context for, many of the local landmarks to which John draws specific attention in the seven oracles. This interaction between local concerns identified in the seven oracles and the more global challenges facing disciples in the Roman world depicted in the visions is an important feature of the rhetorical strategy of Revelation as apocalypse, drawing attention to the "bigger picture" that shows local phenomena in their "true" light (in terms of the Jewish-Christian tradition), inviting a response to these phenomena that might otherwise seem counterintuitive.

In the seven oracles, John raises a variety of pastoral concerns regarding the situation of each congregation. John draws attention to several external factors, one of which is the hostility of the surrounding society. In Pergamum, John recalls the violent death of Antipas, identified as Jesus' "witness" and "faithful one," a death under circumstances that might have led other Pergamene Christians to have denied their association with Jesus (2:13). In the oracles to Ephesus and Thyatira, John speaks of the "endurance" the believers demonstrated there, "bearing up" specifically "on account of [Christ's] name" (2:3, 19) or persevering rather than denying Christ's name (cf. 3:8, 10). There is sufficient tension between church and society that John expects credibly to predict imprisonment and even execution as forthcoming realities in Smyrna (2:10). This cumulative textual data suggests that social pressure in varying kinds and degrees is an important element of the rhetorical situation of several congregations.

Two oracles make specific reference to a distinct social body that John labels "a synagogue of Satan" (συναγωγὴ τοῦ Σατανᾶ, 2:9; 3:9), people who "claim to be Jews, and are not, but they are lying" (3:9; cf. 2:9). This group appears to be the source of "slander" (βλασφημία, 2:9), more likely directed against local Christians rather than "blasphemy" in the traditional sense of speech against Deity, and may provide some impetus to the hostility forecasted for Smyrna. Most scholars read these passages as references to the activity of local Jewish communities in Smyrna and Philadelphia, another minority culture trying to survive in a situation of colonialism and domination (in the uncomfortable wake of a failed revolt against domination!).

John also calls attention to conditions and entities *within* the Christian communities. In the oracle to Ephesus, he speaks of the disciples there testing "those calling themselves apostles" and discerning that they are, in fact, not authentic teachers (2:2), as well as rejecting "the deeds of the Nicolaitans" (2:6).[67] The

---

67. Schüssler Fiorenza (1985, 144) identifies the "false apostles" with the Nicolaitans, reading 2:2b and 2:6 as parallel or equivalent statements; see also Duff 2001, 37. If this is not the case, John does not give us enough information to say anything about the character and message of the "false apostles."

Nicolaitans appear on John's radar screen again in the oracle to Pergamum, where their activity is described as analogous to that of Balaam, "who taught Balak to throw a stumbling block in front of the children of Israel, to eat things sacrificed to idols and to have illicit sexual relations" (2:14–15). In the oracle to Thyatira, John relates the glorified Christ's denunciation of a female Christian prophet—a status that she claims but John denies—for similarly leading some members of that community astray. John thus devotes significant space to the phenomenon of other Christian teachers, providing significant (if highly colored) detail about their activity, suggesting their importance within the rhetorical situation he addresses.

Finally, John calls attention to the poverty of the Smyrnaean Christians and the wealth of the Laodicean Christians (2:9; 3:17), claiming that the poverty of the former is not poverty at all, while denying the claim of the latter to be rich, much as John denies "Jezebel's" claim to be a prophetess and the synagogue's claim to be the genuine people of God. The economic situation of these congregations is explicitly raised as a topic of concern, and in a world in which commerce and religion were so closely intertwined, economic concerns may also provide the impetus for Christian prophets to find a way to justify "eating things sacrificed to idols" (2:14, 20). Nelson Kraybill suggests that the Christians in these cities "probably experienced more internal *desire* to conform to pagan society than external *pressure* in the way of persecution,"[68] a suggestion that may identify an important aspect of the rhetorical situation, and thus part of the rhetorical problem John must overcome.

We should not lose sight of the full range of pastoral concerns evidenced in these oracles, avoiding the temptation to elevate one as the primary concern or reduce the complexities of these real-life situations to one dimension.[69] In the following sections, we will take up each feature of the local landscape in turn, seeking to discern the situation behind the text to which John draws such allusive and interpretive notice. We will be inquiring, for example, into how the activity of the synagogue or "Jezebel" might look to those not disposed to see them in precisely the way that John does. This will help us gain a more sympathetic understanding of the pressures and alternatives facing the congregations, and thus also of John's rhetorical achievement, as we grasp more fully the mental, affective, and volitional distances across which he must move these audiences to win their assent to his program.

A SITUATION OF PERSECUTION?

Revelation is commonly assumed to address Christians facing severe persecution. This has become the typical thumbnail sketch of the historical setting

---

68. Kraybill 1996, 196.
69. A. Collins (1984, 4–7) demonstrates this balance well; see also deSilva 1992a, 286–96; 1998a, 82–87. John's concern includes, but is not limited to, the internal tensions between rival prophets and the direction the church would take following one over another prophet (deSilva 1992a, 292–95; contrast Duff 2001 and Royalty 2004, which focus exclusively on the "power play" between rival teachers).

found in brief introductions to Revelation in Bibles or liturgical reading. This view accepts the portrayal of Domitian as a "second Nero" in his cruel repression of the Christian movement found in some second-century sources. Obsessed with his own divinity, Domitian mercilessly cut down any who refused him the worship he believed to be his due.[70] In addition to the more modest indications of hostility against Christians found in the seven oracles, the descriptions of persecution in the visions of Revelation are seen to reflect the readers' present circumstances, rather than either past or future anti-Christian actions, creating a scenario in which Christians would find themselves daily in danger of denunciation and execution.

The received view has been helpfully challenged in recent decades.[71] Leonard Thompson subjected the traditional portrait of Domitian to thorough critique, arguing that the senatorial class's hatred of Domitian resulted from his favorable attitude toward the provinces and commitment to curtail the senators' exploitation of the same. He observes that the standard Latin sources for Domitian's reign were written shortly after his death, during Trajan's reign.[72] The odium expressed against Domitian in Pliny's *Panegyricus* or Suetonius's *Lives of the Caesars* served as a rhetorical foil for the praiseworthy, reigning emperor, Trajan (who was not of the Flavian household, and thus whose reign would benefit from denigrating that household's last incumbent).[73] While several writers do address Domitian as a god during his lifetime, Thompson argues this is more a sign of the flattery used to address an emperor "from below" rather than evidence of Domitian's own insistence on the use of such language.[74] Images of persecution and calls to endurance are prominent in Revelation only because they are stock topics of the apocalyptic genre that John employs rather than indications of the circumstances of John's audiences.[75]

Such critique has invited fresh explorations of the evidence within Revelation, though, as with so many correctives of deeply entrenched scholarly dogmas, Thompson has overstated the case in Domitian's favor and understated the degree of hostility experienced by Christians. First, while apocalypses typically inscribe a situation of high tension between the group that produced and read it and some larger, more powerful body, it does not follow that the inscribed situation fails to reflect the real situation. Would a writer choose a genre so ill-suited to the author's own situation? Does a person write a lament psalm when nothing is wrong, or does a person's decision to write a lament psalm, with all of its generic topics, rather reveal something about the writer's situation? Most of the persecution described

---

70. Brent (1999, 164) revives this traditional portrait, reasserting that Revelation addresses Christians facing serious persecution as a present, and not forthcoming, reality. See also Schüssler Fiorenza 1985, 6–8. For ancient Christian evidence concerning Domitian as a persecutor, see Melito of Sardis (preserved in Eusebius, *Hist. eccl.* 4.26.5–11); Tertullian, *Apol.* 5.3–4; Eusebius, *Hist. eccl.* 3.18.1–4.
71. See esp. L. Thompson 1990; A. Collins 1984.
72. L. Thompson 1990, 95–115.
73. L. Thompson 1990, 111–15.
74. L. Thompson 1990, 106.
75. L. Thompson 1990, 191–92.

in Revelation belongs to John's vision for the *future*, but we should not dismiss the evidence of conflict and crisis in the seven oracles as generic topics having no bearing on the realities faced by their audiences, nor dismiss John's portraits of emperors and Rome as not reflective of deep ideological conflict between the dominant culture and (certain sectors of) the Christian culture.[76]

Second, though Thompson correctly observes that authors writing under Trajan could find it advantageous to create positive contrasts between the present regime and the Flavian dynasty, he does not give due weight to the more virulent rhetorical exigence of writing in such a way as to please a current emperor, which explains the dearth of criticism of Domitian coming from writers during his reign. Thompson's position has also not won broad acceptance among modern historians, who continue to place more weight on the ancient historians' evaluation of Domitian's rule,[77] as well as recorded reactions against Domitian's reign (*damnatio memoriae*, smashing of statues, and the like), unprecedented save in the case of Caligula—a far from exonerating parallel.

On balance, Domitian's attitude toward his own divinity is less relevant than the enthusiasm of the local elites in Asia Minor to demonstrate their loyalty— and make bids for the attention and favor of the imperial house—by means of offering cult to the Flavian household. Domitian may have encouraged such enthusiasm, but the *Koinon Asias* and the assemblies of Asia's individual cities had a track record that showed little need for further encouragement. As for the nature of the persecution faced by the readers of Revelation, a close reading of the text provides a sufficiently nuanced picture to account for the historical complexities to which Thompson and others have drawn attention.

Within the seven oracles, John brings to remembrance the violent death of Antipas in connection with his identification as a Christian.[78] He is the only named martyr in the seven oracles.[79] John is not writing within a situation of

---

76. It is important to reject the fallacy, however, that apocalypses presuppose a situation of oppression or persecution. An apocalypse is a powerful tool of ideological warfare in any social setting, not merely a means by which to comfort the afflicted (see deSilva 1991, 200–201; 1992a, 301–2; 1992b, 375–78, 393–94).

77. See Griffin 2000, 81–82; Witherington 2003, 5–6; deSilva 1991, 198–200.

78. Attempting to highlight the work of rival prophets as the one and only issue giving rise to Revelation, Duff (2001, 37–38) offers a list of "conceivable" scenarios for Antipas's death that do not involve an anti-Christian act. He claims that John does not *show* that Antipas's death occurred on account of his identity as a Christian, but "*wants* the reader to believe that Antipas was martyred" (Duff 2001, 38). John, however, refers to an event in the living memory of the Pergamene church and speaks of it as an occasion that might have reasonably motivated other Christians to renounce their affiliation with this Jesus. John would be taking a needless risk if he were to suggest an unwarranted connection between Antipas's death and hostility against the local Christian community, since the audience's own memory would produce the contrary evidence needed to discredit him as a spokesperson for the glorified Christ.

79. The exhortation in the oracle to Sardis to "strengthen *those things* that remain (τὰ λοιπά), but are at the point of death" (3:2) is not a reflection of persecution and martyrdom. Witherington (2003, 105), following Aune (1997, 219), proposes the translation, "Strengthen *those who* remain but are at the point of death." Reading the *neuter* substantive τὰ λοιπά as "those who remain," however, certainly cuts against the grain of the natural reading, though Aune cites 1 Cor. 1:26–27 (rightly) and Heb. 7:7 (problematically) as parallel cases where a *neuter* substantive is used to repre-

empirewide persecution spearheaded by Domitian, nor even locally motivated persecution. This was an isolated act, whether accomplished through official channels or in the dark alleys.[80] On the other hand, Antipas's death shows Christians just how precarious their position is, and why muting their Christian witness rather than trumpeting their allegiance to Jesus might be the more advantageous course. The glorified Christ praises Ephesus and Thyatira for displaying "endurance"(2:3, 19) and Philadelphia for not "denying my name" (3:8), recalling the situation of hostility in Pergamum, where this is also a lively option (2:13). In Smyrna, sufficient tension with society exists to render plausible the prediction of forthcoming imprisonment (2:10).[81] Every reference to the outside world in the seven oracles involves hostility, antagonism, or social tension.[82]

The visions teem with references to martyrdom. The fifth seal showcases "the souls of those who had been slain on account of the word of God and on account of the testimony which they had" (6:9), whose number remains ominously incomplete (6:11), forecasting further martyrdoms on the near horizon (4:1; cf. 1:1). The story of the two witnesses tells of martyrdom on account of bearing testimony to the One God (11:7–10). The expulsion of Satan from heaven is a victory in which those who bore testimony and "loved not their lives unto death" participate (12:10–11). John paints a scenario in which refusal to worship the beast's image results in economic marginalization and execution (13:15–17). Babylon the Great already totters about, "drunk from the blood of the holy ones and from the blood of the witnesses of Jesus" (17:6), necessitating the city's downfall (18:24). The souls under the altar and the hosts of heaven celebrate the justice of punishing Rome and its citizens for their violent acts against the saints (6:9; 19:2; cf. 16:5–6). In the new order, the "souls of those who had been beheaded on account of the testimony of Jesus and on account of the word of God" rule alongside the Lamb (20:4–6).

The distance between the oracles and the visions suggests that John's visions of martyrdom belong not to the present, but to the past and the future. By the

---

sent a class of people. More problematic is the interpretation of the depiction of these "remainders" or "remaining people at the point of death" as a sign of "the real possibility of martyrdom" (Witherington 2003, 105). There is little justification for reading "on the point of death" independently here from the "dead name" that clings to the Christian community as a whole—surely not a sign of martyrdom in the community, which would be a mark of a "living name" and "praiseworthy reputation" in John's eyes. The received interpretation, "take stock of what signs of faithful discipleship still remain in your midst and devote yourself to building these back up," remains the more exegetically sound.

80. Knight 2001, 477; Kraybill 1996, 37.

81. Duff (2001, 45–46) again downplays evidence of external threats in this oracle. While the prediction of imprisonment refers to some future act, to be plausible it must grow out of some present scenario. Duff claims that "we are given no reason to suppose that there is any sound basis for that prediction," but it is equally risky to assume, as he does, that there is *no* sound basis for John's foreseeing escalating trouble for his friends in Smyrna—especially when Duff *consistently* chooses in favor of such an assumption against a reading that takes the evidence of external pressure or threat seriously. The "slander" of the synagogue is likely to carry more weight and threat than "two rival groups taking 'pot shots' at each other."

82. Slater 1998, 241.

time John writes, it is already appropriate to speak of Rome as "intoxicated" with the blood of Jesus' witnesses (17:6). Rome could and did act violently against Christians with impunity throughout the first century, although not in any widespread or systematic fashion. The execution of Jesus by the Romans sounded an inauspicious prelude for Roman-Christian relations. The trials and probable execution of Peter and Paul added to the tally. The stunningly brutal anti-Christian acts in Rome under Nero still claimed the attention of Tacitus and Suetonius fifty years later and etched their memory deep on John's own consciousness, since he sees the principate through the lens of Nero throughout the Apocalypse, as if Nero showed the principate's true colors. There were many souls indeed to gather beneath the altar and cry out for vindication (6:9–11). John draws attention to this story of Rome's hostility against Christians, all the way up to the recent episode of Antipas, as an element in the rhetorical situation not to be passed over in favor of the story of Rome's (so-called) benefits to the province.

John also foresees that witness-bearing would become increasingly costly. In Antipas, John saw the shape of things to come. The kinds of harassment that *some* of the Christians currently experienced might have been limited to verbal assaults ("slander," βλασφημία; 2:9), economic hardship ("poverty," 2:9), and other indignities to be "endured" (2:3, 19).[83] Insults, physical abuse, and disenfranchisement were the common lot of many Christians throughout the Eastern Mediterranean (see 1 Thess. 3:1–6; 2 Thess. 1:3–9; Heb. 10:32–34; 13:3; 1 Pet. 2:11–12, 18–25; 3:13–17; 4:1–4, 12–19).[84] Such harassment communicated a message: it was a social act calling deviants back into conformity with the values and behaviors considered important for the larger society's well-being. In the Christians' case, it was a call to return to the traditional piety upon which all other social values were founded, and to the solidarity and civic unity that such piety expressed and facilitated.[85] It was a call to show oneself aligned with the larger group's loyalty to the emperors as the fount of patronage and good wishes for Rome's continued strength that ensured the peace and security of the *orbis*

---

83. It is vitally important not to overgeneralize when making statements about the conditions faced by the "audience" of Revelation, since this "audience" is by no means a homogeneous group, but rather a collection of seven different congregations in different locations facing different challenges. Moreover, particular congregations were not homogeneous bodies. There is no evidence of hostility or pressure being brought to bear on the congregation in Sardis, and even less in Laodicea. Indeed, a primary challenge facing the latter, according to John, is that they blend in *too well* in their city and experience far too little hostility or rejection by their neighbors. Hostility is most pressing in Smyrna, whose (current) affliction Jesus acknowledges.

84. Thus also Slater 1998, 254. On shaming as a deviancy-control technique applied to Christians in the first century CE, see deSilva 1995, 146–64; 2000a, 44–50.

85. The episode of Paul in Ephesus (Acts 19) is instructive. Hostility against the intrusion of a novel religious movement is motivated by the economic concerns of a guild of silversmiths whose trade is intimately connected with the worship of Artemis. Hostility against Paul, moreover, takes the form of affirmations of the greatness of Ephesian Artemis, the reference point in regard to which all else must be judged in Ephesus. If the narrative reflects a historical episode, it suggests that Christianity's incompatibility with traditional religion was *immediately* apparent in Ephesus, a city whose inhabitants equated civic pride with the veneration of Artemis (Not merely "Great is Diana!" but "Great is Ephesian Diana!") and whose elites were also at the forefront of the promotion of the imperial cult.

The Rhetorical Setting of Revelation 55

terrarum. This call, no doubt, weighed heavily on the minds of many Christians, moving them to deliberate about how to balance the human drive to enjoy a serene and secure life with their religious commitments to the God of Israel and his Messiah. John, who had clear views on this subject, also knew that continued resistance to their neighbors' summons—especially if the believers' critique of the Roman imperial system and its religious legitimation became more vocal— would eventuate in sharper deviancy-control techniques, filling up of the tally of the martyrs (6:11; 13:15–17). John had no illusions about the consequences of his preferred course of action.

HOSTILITY BETWEEN SYNAGOGUE AND CHURCH?

In the oracles to the churches in Smyrna and Philadelphia, John calls attention to another social body distinct both from the Christian assemblies and from the majority culture, which he labels "a synagogue of Satan" (συναγωγὴ τοῦ Σατανᾶ, 2:9; 3:9), people who "claim to be Jews, and are not, but they are lying" (3:9; cf. 2:9). Since ethnic Jews use "synagogue" self-referentially, many interpreters read these references as an indication of tension between the Christian assemblies and the Jewish synagogues.[86] John provides little evidence to justify such a harsh denunciation on his part, save that they are the source of "slander" (βλασφημία, 2:9) directed, most likely, against the Christians in Smyrna.

This is not the first time that a Jewish author has spoken of closely related opponents as the spawn of Satan. In the Fourth Gospel, Jesus denounces opposing Jewish leaders as belonging to their father, the devil (John 8:44). The elder divides humanity into children of God and children of the devil (1 John 3:8– 10), the latter including the secessionists from his own congregations, whom he also labels antichrists (2:18). The authors of the Dead Sea Scrolls call fellow Jews who are not part of the Qumran covenant community the "congregation of Beliar" (1QH 2 [10].22; 1QM 4.9).

The label "synagogue of Satan," however, may reflect more than a stock slur. In Revelation, Satan is the force behind the principate and the imperial cult. The worship and authority of the emperor is grounded in the worship and authority of Satan, who has his seat in Pergamum. When John's audience looks for Satan in their context, John leads them to look toward Zeus or the less personal *Providentia*—the divine force supporting the rule of Rome through her emperors in the dominant cultural ideology.

The Jewish ruling class navigated with difficulty the narrow channel between Rome's expectations and the zeal of Judeans for the One God and for political independence. Zealots regarded the brilliant compromise of offering sacrifices in the Jerusalem temple *on behalf of* Caesar as courting the godless Gentile power too closely. The cessation of those sacrifices was the symbolic act in which Judea

---

86. See Hemer 1986, 66–68; Aune 1997, 160–65; Keener 2000, 114–16; Beale 1999, 239–41.

declared its independence.[87] After the temple's destruction in 70 CE, however, a new sign of loyalty was imposed upon Judeans. The temple tax (see Matt. 17:24), formerly paid by every adult Jew for the support of the daily sacrifices and maintenance of the Jerusalem temple, would now be collected on behalf of the temple of Jupiter Capitolinus in Rome (Josephus, *Jewish War* 7.6.6, §218). The price of toleration was an annual contribution to a pagan cult—indeed, *the* pagan cult—taking literally what belonged to God and giving it to Caesar.[88] This practice allowed local Jewish communities to continue to flourish in the Roman economy. Judea remained well placed for international commerce, with cargoes from the East or from Arabia tending to move, at least in part, through its seaports.[89] Jews continued to participate in Roman imperial politics and economics, some even attaining equestrian status.[90] Archaeological, epigraphic, and literary evidence suggest that Jews were well integrated in the cities of Asia Minor, even to the point of holding municipal offices.[91]

Nelson Kraybill plausibly suggests that "such a *modus vivendi* between diaspora Jews and Rome could have helped generate John's caustic comment about a 'synagogue of Satan' (Rev. 2.9; 3.9)."[92] Why were the synagogues throughout the Diaspora and the Holy Land now willing to do what even Jews deeply sympathetic to the hellenizing policies of the apostate high priest Jason in 175–172 BCE had scruples against doing? When Jason designated a gift of money for sacrifices to Hercules at the games in Tyre, his envoys diverted it toward the construction of ships as a public benefaction for that city (2 Macc. 4:18–20). Now *all* Jews were sending money to support pagan cult. For John, the continued collection of the *fiscus Judaicus* could suggest that the synagogues were now in league with Satan, paying the tribute due to the One True God to the central religious site of the Roman anti-God.

Economic contacts between Jews and Gentiles, and the potential for commerce to lead Jews to compromise loyalty to the One God, were a concern to the rabbis as well, who forbade contact with Gentiles during the latter's religious festivals (*b. 'Abod. Zar.* 1.8a), advised merchants to conduct trade outside of cities that contained idols (1.11b), and prohibited providing Gentiles with items that would be used in idolarous rites (1.13b, 14b).[93] Rome generally showed indulgence toward Jewish scruples. Jewish merchants could excuse themselves from overtly compromising situations on the basis of this long-standing toleration, coupled with the official toleration now purchased by the *fiscus Judaicus*.[94] John, therefore, would likely have regarded his fellow Jews as having compromised their witness and loyalty to the One God by their willingness to pay a

---

87. Josephus, *J. W.* 2.197, 409. See also Hayes and Mandell 1998, 184.
88. See Smallwood 1976, 345; Hemer 1986, 8; Kraybill 1996, 183.
89. Kraybill 1996, 185; see further Applebaum 1976.
90. Kraybill 1996, 175, citing Josephus, *J.W.* 2.14.9, 305–8.
91. Schüssler Fiorenza 1991, 136.
92. Kraybill 1996, 184.
93. Kraybill 1996, 191.
94. Kraybill 1996, 192–93.

subvention to the cult of Jupiter Capitolinus and by their continued participation in an economic system built upon violence, exploitation, and suppression of dissent. He would see the synagogue as having already done what some parties within the church are pushing for.

The synagogue's slander of the Christians is intelligible against the backdrop of the concerns of Jewish communities living in the situation post–70 CE. Christian claims about the Hebrew Scriptures, the constituency of the people of God, the role of the Torah in regulating human behavior—these were always problematic for other Jews. The response to Stephen, Paul's persecution of the churches in Judea, and the persecution that dogged Paul after his conversion are cases in point (Acts 7:54–8:3; 9:1–2; 12:1–3; 13:48–52; 14:19–20; Gal. 1:22–24; 1 Thess. 2:13–16; etc.). After the suppression of the First Jewish Revolt (66–70/73 CE), however, the Christian movement became even more of an embarrassment to the Jewish community. First, the Christian gospel was revolutionary since Jesus' disciples awaited the return of their crucified leader, who would usher in a new kingly reign (see, e.g., 1 Thess. 1:10). The Jewish community was hard pressed now, however, to demonstrate their acceptance of Roman rule and to distance itself from the revolutionary impulses responsible for the sedition in Judea.[95] Monitoring boundaries closely, pointing out that Christians were not Jews, would be both politically and economically advantageous for the Jews in Asia Minor, who would thus maintain good relations with both officials and their own business associates. The Christian movement's success in converting Gentiles might also help to motivate this distancing. When the Jewish community was seen to draw too many Gentiles away from traditional religion (e.g., in the conversion of noble Gentiles to Judaism during Tiberius's reign), repressive action could be taken against the Jews.[96] With the Christian movement drawing significant numbers of Gentiles away from "piety," it would be a protective measure to say, "They're not Jews; *we* didn't convert those Gentiles!" The "slander" of the synagogue need have consisted of nothing more than statements such as this reasonable measure of self-defense against anti-Jewish and antirevolutionary sentiments.[97]

Most scholars infer a causal connection between the slander against the Christians and the forthcoming imprisonment and, quite probably, executions forecast for the believers in Smyrna.[98] Was the "slander" more formal, perhaps

---

95. This apologetic runs throughout Josephus's own retelling of the history in *Jewish War*.
96. See Leon 1995, 17–20.
97. Schüssler Fiorenza 1991, 136; Carey 1999b, 19–21. Robert Royalty limits the hostility between the synagogue and church to divergent interpretations of the Hebrew Bible rather than anything resembling denunciation of Christians to outsiders, but this undervalues the evidence (the attention drawn to "slander" and the link, whether implied or merely inferred, between this "slander" and the future dangers to which the congregants in Smyrna will be exposed).
98. In the Roman judicial system, imprisonment was not a form of punishment. Rather, it was used to detain defendants awaiting trial, to gain the cooperation of recalcitrant parties, and to hold those sentenced to be executed (Hemer 1986, 68; Ramsay 1909, 273–74; Aune 1997, 166). Jesus' self-identification as one who passed through death into life, the promise of the crown of life for those who endure to the end of this trial, and the promise of exemption from suffering the second death (2:8, 10–11) cumulatively suggest that the third situation appertained.

taking the form of denunciations, informing local magistrates of a group that met to practice a religion that was not formally tolerated (not a *religio licita*)? A number of noteworthy scholars find the hypothesis persuasive that local Jewish communities were cooperating with the local government "to repress the Christian minority."[99]

> Individual Jews may have informed against Christians, or the synagogues may have provided on occasion lists of bona fide members of their congregations. The authorities, primarily concerned with tax-avoidance [of the *fiscus Iudaicus*], may thus have had forced on their attention a powerful movement which appeared to defy the emperor under the guise of a Judaism which the official Jews repudiated.[100]

By informing against Christians, the synagogue set in motion an investigation that would expose the disciples as a potentially subversive group that, when examined, would be subjected to penal action.

Admittedly, no such causal connection is explicit in the oracle itself.[101] By drawing attention to the "slander" of the Jewish community, however, John evokes awareness of situational elements that could plausibly lead to increasing vulnerability for the Christians. It is also important to bear in mind that the Jewish community could draw unwanted attention to the Christians' marginal legal status without acting as informers in any official capacity. Even if the Jewish community's intentions did not extend beyond protecting their own reputation in the eyes of the local and Roman powers, the effects could be considerably more far-reaching and deleterious for the Christians.

IMPETUS TO COMPROMISE

John was deeply concerned about the Roman imperial economy, the ills that both maintained and devolved from it, and the significance of Christian par-

---

99. Keener 2000, 115; Beale 1999, 240; Witherington (2003, 100–101) points out that such action was hardly unprecedented: "We have the independent testimonies of both Paul's letters and Acts that Jews sometimes brought Christians before the Roman authorities (see Acts 18 [esp. 18:12–17]), as did pagans." He also cites the *Martyrdom of Polycarp* (12.2; 13.1) as evidence for ongoing anti-Christian sentiments and activities among the Jews, who call for Polycarp's death and help gather wood for the fire (though the latter detail seems a bit grotesque, such that I would prefer to read it as a "narrative elaboration" of their anti-Christian sentiments rather than a detail of fact). See also Aune 1997, 162–63; Hemer 1986, 7–9.

100. Hemer 1986, 9–10. Hemer (1986, 152) appears to overstep the evidence when he suggests that "a majority of the church had gained acceptance in the synagogue at the cost of the implicit denial of the 'name' of Christ," whereas the faithful few had been expunged from the rolls (and thus were here assured that their names would *not* be expunged from the Book of Life; see also Brent 1999, 187). This promise, however, comes from the oracle to the church in Sardis (3:5), in which nothing is said about tension with the local synagogue. If the Jewish community was actively engaged in "outing" Christians, this activity is limited to Smyrna (possibly also Philadelphia) and not a universal challenge facing the churches.

101. Aune 1997, 166.

The Rhetorical Setting of Revelation   59

ticipation in it. It is not surprising, then, that John would draw attention to the poverty of the Smyrnaean Christians and the wealth of the Laodicean Christians (Rev. 2:9; 3:17), praising the former and problematizing the latter. In a system in which idolatry and commerce are so closely intertwined, "poverty" (Smyrna, 2:9) and lack of worldly clout (Philadelphia, 3:8b) are appropriate for monotheists unwilling to compromise with the idolatrous economic and political system,[102] the results of their "determination to resist assimilation into the larger culture at all costs."[103] John is not against wealth per se: the new Jerusalem is every bit as opulent as Babylon.[104] But John is deeply concerned about the compromises necessary to obtain wealth within the Roman imperial economic system—not just compromising with idolatry, but also with a self-glorifying, violently repressive, economically exploitative system.

The position advanced by the rival teachers that John calls the "Nicolaitans," one of whom he calls "Jezebel" (2:6, 14–15, 20–23), probably relates to these issues of poverty and wealth, at least in part.[105] John only says that they lead Christians "to eat things sacrificed to idols and to have illicit sexual relations" (2:14–15, 20).[106] Whatever this may mean, this much is clear: the rival teachers

---

102. Kraybill 1996, 171. Royalty (1998, 242–43) reads his emphasis on the power struggle between prophets into the oracle to Laodicea: "Christ censures and rebukes the Laodiceans, encouraging them to support John and his prophetic circle in the power struggles within the Christian churches." There is, however, no mention of a power struggle in the oracle to Laodicea, no discussion of false teachers, and nothing suggesting that "Christ's" agenda is rallying support for John—topics that John is hardly reticent to invoke where relevant. The issues have to do with rejecting an identity-formation forged on the basis of economic prosperity and adopting one on the basis of faithful response to Jesus (i.e., faithful response to the Hebrew Scriptures, the Jesus tradition, and the apostolic witness concerning discipleship—including, but not limited to, the vision of discipleship in Revelation). Royalty's elevation of the power struggle as the central issue, and his reading of this power struggle into the hot-and-cold imagery that could easily support other interpretations, shows his tendentiousness on this point, especially considering that the majority of Revelation's visions foreground the question of what stance a person takes in regard to idolatry and imperialism, not in regard to John's personal authority.

103. Duff 2001, 30.

104. Duff 2001, 63.

105. See deSilva 1992a, 292–96; Duff 2001, 47. Witherington (2003, 102) understands "Balaam" also to be a reference to an actual local Christian teacher, though not by his real name. Unlike "Jezebel," however, the reference to Balaam reads like a genuine allusion to a past historical figure, especially since this Balaam is elaborated with reference to a historical encounter known from the tradition (2:14b). Identifying Balaam as someone who interacted with Balak personally precludes seeing this as a reference to a contemporary figure in Pergamum. When John names his female rival in Thyatira "Jezebel," he does not muddy the time zones by elaborating upon her as one "who promoted the cult of Baal under Ahab" or the like. The Nicolaitans (2:15) are introduced as the true descendants of Balaam, the ancient and paradigmatic false prophet or "prophet for hire." Royalty (1998, 30) asserts that the Nicolaitans and those who "hold to the teaching of Balaam" are not the same group, despite the clear linguistic identification of the two (the choice of "Balaam" as a slanderous eponym and an approximate linguistic equivalent for Nicolaus), the rhetorical function of Balaam as a historical precedent for the activity (and fate) of the Nicolaitans, and the connecting conjunction οὕτως, "in this way," that identifies the Nicolaitan position as the manner in which Balaam's teaching is manifested in the contemporary Thyatiran situation.

106. Were these rival teachers libertines? Idolatry and sexual immorality were closely linked in Jewish anti-Gentile polemics (see Wis. 14:12; Rom. 1:18–32; see also *Testament of Reuben* 4:6; *Ep. Aristeas* 152; Duff 2001, 56), and no doubt also in actual practice (reflected, perhaps, in 1 Pet.

try to make room for Christians to interact more closely with their non-Christian neighbors where pagan rites are concerned.

Where would people eat food sacrificed to idols, and why would an inner-Christian movement seek to render such action defensible? Religious festivals were frequently occasions for social feasting. Important public festivals moved from lavish sacrifices to the gods to distributions of meat throughout the city, symbolizing—indeed, realizing—the ideals of civic unity and celebrating the solidarity enjoyed between citizenry and gods. The refusal to eat "things sacrificed to idols" (εἰδωλόθυτα), or from society's perspective, "*holy* offerings" (ἱερόθυτα), would cause offense.[107]

One would also encounter εἰδωλόθυτα at a private dinner party or at a dinner of clubs and associations (including "trade guilds").[108] Consistently absenting oneself from the acts of gratitude toward the association's or the host's patron deities, and picking only at the vegetable dishes all evening, would raise questions that could not be comfortably answered by the Christian who sought to belong to the social networks important for economic and political advancement. Paul encountered these complexities in the Corinthian congregation's situation, seeking to forge a middle way that would preserve the integrity of the church's witness against idolatry, the integrity of the conscience of the more scrupulous disciples, and the necessity of occasionally dining with non-Christians so as to preserve at least the minimum required business networks. Paul Duff plausibly suggests that Erastus of Corinth (Rom. 16:23), as a public

---

4:3–4). Nevertheless, discourse about sexual intercourse, about partnerships, whether with a whore or as a bride, and the like, is used throughout Revelation in ways that suggest a metaphorical significance. "Sexual immorality" functions as a label for all improper intercourse with Roman society and its gods; sexual purity or fidelity represents loyalty to the one God and God's Messiah. Improper sexual intercourse led the people of Israel into idolatry in the incident at Baal-Peor (Num. 25:1–2), a plan for apostasy masterminded by Balaam (31:16), such that these two actions are also linked in the tradition upon which John draws. Therefore, there are sufficient indications that "sexual immorality" may be regarded here as a "metaphorical reiteration of εἰδωλόθυτα" (Duff 2001, 56), or perhaps better, as an interpretation of the relational *significance* of εἰδωλόθυτα for one's connection with God. See also deSilva 1992a, 294; 2004, 904–5.

107. Duff 2001, 51–52.

108. Finley (1985, 138) warns us that the associations or *collegia* were largely social and benevolent confraternities, often united by some common occupation or characteristic (see also Hermansen 1981, 110). These were not "regulatory or protective agencies in their respective trades," which was "the *raison d'être* of the genuine guilds, medieval and modern" (Finley 1985, 138). Associations of persons sharing a common trade nevertheless provided important opportunities for networking, offered a stable circle of social relationships, and often formed something of a safety net in times of hardship (as when an association would provide for the burial of members in need). While membership in such an association may well not have been "essential" (as asserted in Horsley and Llewelyn 1981–92, 5:106–7), it would be sufficiently advantageous and desirable to make the idolatrous components of guild membership a pressing concern for the churches' reflection and decision.

All such associations required the emperor's approval (Kraybill 1996, 115). This would become a sticking point for the church, which could claim legitimacy neither as a Jewish body nor as an emperor-approved *collegium*. The meetings of associations involved rites paying honor to the patron god or goddess and increasingly to the emperor (Kraybill 1996, 117). The latter is especially understandable as an antidote to suspicion against such assemblies: Trajan writes, for example, that "men banded together for a common end will all the same become a political association before long" (Pliny the Younger, *Ep.* 10.34).

official, would have jeopardized his career by not dining with other civic bureaucrats, while Lydia of Philippi (Acts 16:14) "could hardly avoid dining with clients or potential suppliers. A refusal to share a meal could severely hinder such a person's livelihood."[109]

The Christian teachers labeled "Nicolaitans" and "Jezebel" would allow Christians to participate in those social, civic, and perhaps even religious contexts where food sacrificed to idols is ingested.[110] Such flexibility would alleviate the tension between the host society and the Christian movement (which would be seen as less of a threat to piety and civic solidarity) and would restore Christians to those social and economic networks that facilitated survival, even thriving.

John does not provide clues concerning the arguments that Jezebel or the Nicolaitans might have advanced in support of Christian participation in those social and civic settings.[111] The kind of reasoning found in Corinth and hinted at by Paul may provide a starting point. Forty years before John wrote Revelation, some disciples in Corinth argued that, since "an idol is nothing" and "there is no God but the One" (1 Cor. 8:4), ingesting meat that had been offered to an idol could not bring spiritual harm to the disciple. They might have remembered the saying of Jesus that "there is nothing outside a person that, by going in, is able to defile that person" (Mark 7:15). Why, then, should Christians—to their own hurt and impoverishment—provoke their neighbors unnecessarily by remaining absent from civic festivals and from dinners in the homes of their associates or the dining halls where their patrons and others would hold symposia?

The "strong" in Corinth and the Nicolaitans in Asia Minor were not the only ones advocating the performance of outward rites for the sake of social cohesion while remaining inwardly critical of the religious value of those rites.

109. Duff 2001, 55.
110. So also Schüssler Fiorenza 1985, 195; Hemer 1986, 128; Talbert 1994, 19; Ford 1975, 291; Mounce 1977, 81; LeGrys 1992, 76–80; Caird 1966, 39. Duff (2001, 54) suggests that Jezebel may simply have been "*allowing* Christians to eat sacrificial meats in certain circumstances (much as Paul had done several decades earlier)," tolerating rather than encouraging the practice (2001, 58). Whatever her own degree of enthusiasm for the practice, Jezebel's activity as a prophet legitimates a practice that is, for John, a clear and present danger to the integrity of the Christian community in Thyatira.
111. Royalty (2004, 287) suggests that the battle with Jezebel was over scriptural interpretation, since she is presented as also exerting a teaching ministry. However, the mere fact that Jezebel is a teacher does not say anything about the basis for her teaching. It is clear that John is reading the Scriptures and using them to counter the arguments and authority of opposing teachers, but there is no hint that Jezebel is doing the same. Indeed, no one who has reconstructed Jezebel's or the Nicolaitans' position has suggested that they offered *scriptural* arguments for eating food sacrificed to idols. Rather, commentators tend to find the most immediate precedent for her line of thinking in the position of the "strong" in Corinth (cf. Rom. 14:1–3; 15:1; in 1 Cor. 8:1–13 only the "weak" ones are mentioned), with whose position Paul concurs up to a point (but *only* up to a point; see Schüssler Fiorenza 1991, 133–34). Neither the "strong" nor Paul use Scripture to *support* eating εἰδωλόθυτα, though Paul (like John) does use Scripture to alert the "strong" to potential dangers and to limit their participation (1 Cor. 10:1–22). Royalty (2004, 297) seems to list further off course when he claims that Rev. 22:18–19 "focuses the battle with opposing teachers and prophets over the *interpretation of texts*, specifically this text" (i.e., Revelation). But Jezebel and the Nicolaitans would not be embroiled in any battle over the interpretation of Revelation with John. They would marginalize his voice with other arguments and authorities but not find it necessary to provide an alternative interpretation of his text.

The Epicureans, a notable, if not always respected, philosophical school, also promoted such a position. Those who participated in religious rites developed a reputation not only for piety but also for reliability in human and civic interactions: "Do honour to the divine power at all times, but especially on occasions of public worship; for thus you will have the reputation both of sacrificing to the gods and of abiding by the laws" (Isocrates, *Ad Demon.* 13). Plutarch expresses the negative side of this as he censures the lack of regard for the gods as a threat to the foundations of the social order (*Reply to Colotes* 31 [*Mor.* 1125D–E]). It is this connection between public worship and social approval, he avers, that leads Epicureans to participate in religious rites without sincerity:

> For out of fear of public opinion [the Epicurean] goes through a mummery of prayers and obeisances that he has no use for and pronounces words that run counter to his philosophy; when he sacrifices, the priest at his side who immolates the victim is to him a butcher; and when it is over he goes away with Menander's words on his lips: "I sacrifice to gods who heed me not." For this is the comedy that Epicurus thinks we should play, and not spoil the pleasure of the multitude or make ourselves unpopular with them by showing dislike ourselves for what others delight in doing. (Plutarch, *A Pleasant Life Impossible* 21 [*Mor.* 1102 C–D]; LCL)

There were strong precedents, strong motivations, and strong arguments for Christians to make room for religious rites that held no conviction for them for the sake of being neighborly.

John draws special attention, then, to competing voices within the churches that seek to steer the communities in different directions, with some leading toward the reduction of tension and lowering of group boundaries, but John advocating the sharpening of difference and, therefore, tension.[112] A pressing factor in the rhetorical situation is the promotion of a practice that makes room for participation in cultic meals and the social and economic associations that are nurtured by such participation, for it is to this element that John devotes perhaps the most space in the oracles and thus draws the most attention.[113] "At stake here was the question of assimilation: what pagan customs could

---

112. DeSilva 1992a, 292–96; 1991, 207–8; 1993, 55–57.
113. Thus Duff 2001, 13; Royalty 1998, 241. Duff elevates conflict with Jezebel, something that scholars have long perceived as one concern within the situation, as *the* principal concern of John. While this particular conflict is indeed important, Duff's emphasis leads to some questionable interpretive moves in his own reconstruction of the rhetorical situation. For example, he reads the accusation that the Christians in Ephesus have "forsaken their first love" (Rev. 2:4) as a sign that "the community had fragmented into factions" and "was no longer as receptive to John *because* it had fragmented into factions, not all of which were open to John's leadership" (Duff 2001, 37), despite the fact that the oracle otherwise gives unequivocal evidence of the congregation's resistance to competing teachers and the factionalism that would ensue if they had been received. Similarly, Royalty, who paints John as being chiefly concerned with augmenting the power and influence of his prophetic circle (1998, 245–46; 2004, 286) asserts that "Christ censures and rebukes the Laodiceans, encouraging them to support John and his prophetic circle in the power struggles within the Christian churches" (1998, 242–43), despite the absence of any mention of power struggle or inner-Christian conflict in that oracle. Monographs focused on John's appeals to ethos have tended

Christians adopt for the sake of economic survival, commercial gain, or simple sociability."[114] But also at stake was *witness*, a key word in Revelation, testimony to the world that "The LORD is God, and God alone!" (cf. Deut. 6:4)

SYNTHESIS

The rhetorical situation encompasses multiple voices, attractions, and pressures. Living within the matrix of Roman imperialism, the churches continually encounter reminders of the ideology of Rome and the rule of her emperors. These voices announce the divine favors granted through Roman imperialism, calling for gratitude and loyalty, inviting people into the prosperity and security to be enjoyed by the loyal and cooperative subject peoples. This invitation is very attractive. The Christians in Laodicea present living proof that the promise of prosperity is no myth. Local populations in several of the cities of Asia Minor (at least Pergamum, probaby Ephesus and Thyatira as well), pursuing the goods promised by these voices, exert pressure upon those in their midst whose behavior calls the dominant ideology and its hope into question. At the same time, the synagogue is using its voice in Smyrna and Philadelphia to speak against the Christian community, exerting its own kind of pressure upon them. Finally, other Christian prophets and their followers speak of a way of being Christian without sacrificing the promises of prosperity and security offered by the Roman economic system—and without calling for the sacrifices that would be incurred by continuing to alienate non-Christian neighbors. Such voices are particularly strong in Pergamum and Thyatira.

These voices, attractions, and pressures are not equal in the historical situation of each of the seven churches, which also show a wide range of response to these voices already. The believers in Ephesus, Smyrna, and Philadelphia, together with some part of the congregations in Pergamum, Thyatira, and Sardis, are inclined to respond to them as John would think appropriate, though some other exigencies exist in several of these situations. Some in Pergamum and Thyatira, the majority in Sardis, and, it would seem, virtually the whole congregation in Laodicea—such Christians have been responding more positively to these other voices. Part of the genius of Revelation is its ability to speak to the peculiar exigencies of each of these different situations, moving believers in each setting toward what John hopes will become the unified Christian interpretation of, witness within, and response to the more overarching challenges identified in the rhetorical situation.

---

to project their own focus on issues of authority in the text more forcefully and uncompromisingly onto their reconstruction of the rhetorical situation and John's intentions.
114. A. Collins 1983, 740–41; 1984, 88.

Chapter 3

What Does John Really Want?
The Rhetorical Goals of Revelation

What was John after when he interjected his Revelation into the lives of the Christians in Asia Minor? What was the presenting crisis that evoked so forceful a communication? Scholars are accustomed to asking such questions on analogy with New Testament epistolary literature. When Paul writes Galatians or the Corinthian Letters or Philippians, he is clearly responding to some issues facing the congregations he addresses (including developments in his relationship with the congregations he addresses), and is prompted to write in order to address those issues. What was the precipitating "crisis" that drove John to write Revelation?

Readers have answered this question in many ways. The most conservative readers would respond that John's motivation was a series of visionary encounters with the glorified Christ and the dominical command to "Write!" and "Send!" (1:11) these oracles and visions. That, however, begs the question: What was so dire about the churches' situations that the glorified Christ must appear and address them personally? The long-standing misconception that apocalypses arise out of situations of social deprivation and oppression has led to the hypothesis that elevated "persecution" was the principal crisis behind

Revelation.[1] John's goal for Revelation, like the goal for apocalypses in general, was to comfort the oppressed with visions of eventual triumph and otherworldly compensation.[2] Apocalypses like *4 Ezra*, however, seriously challenge the premise that specimens of this genre must arise from situations of persecution. There it is enough that the world is not working as the apocalyptist's tradition says it *should* be working.[3] We have also seen that the evidence of contemporary persecution in Revelation is rather limited (not all seven churches show signs of experiencing even moderate harassment), rather more ordinary (such as is the common experience of many Christian communities addressed by New Testament writings), and thus not somehow elevated in such a way as to constitute a precipitating crisis.

What, then, drives John to write (or the glorified Christ to communicate), and what does John hope to accomplish by sending this communication around to the seven churches? In other words, what does John really want?

JOHN WANTS POWER

Several recent authors, particularly those using rhetorical criticism as a methodological approach to Revelation,[4] focus on the activity and success of Jezebel and the Nicolaitans as the precipitating crisis that evokes John's response. John writes principally to maintain or expand his own prophetic influence among the churches, to consolidate his control over the congregations. Robert Royalty, for example, asserts that "the intra-Christian tension and the violent rhetoric of Revelation suggest that John and his disciples were part of a radical prophetic community seeking to expand their influence and authority within the Christian communities of Asia Minor."[5] The main crisis prompting Revelation is an inner-Christian struggle over "who should have authority within the Christian communities."[6] Paul Duff zeros in on the conflict with "Jezebel" as the focal point of John's concern, asserting that "John's followers [must] accept his leadership to the exclusion of any other person."[7]

Such a reading emerges from a "hermeneutic of suspicion," inquiring into the potentially self-serving motives for a religious communication. Several considerations, however, suggest that these scholars are overly suspicious of John's motivations—or, at least, overly fixated on one possible motive.

Perhaps the most important consideration is the multiplicity of presenting problems articulated within the oracles themselves. Royalty is not unaware of

---

1. See discussion in deSilva 1992b, 375–76; 1993, 58–59.
2. Berger 1967, 68–69; Gager 1975, 49–57, 64–65; Hanson 1976, 30; R. R. Wilson 1981.
3. See Longenecker 1995, 11–16; deSilva 2002a, 323–24, 332–34, 342–46.
4. See especially the work of scholars whose focus is on matters pertaining to rhetorical ethos: Duff 2001; Royalty 1998; Carey 1999b.
5. Royalty 2004, 286.
6. Royalty 1998, 28.
7. Duff 2001, 49.

these: "Several issues seem to have been at stake in this struggle: how to practice the Christian religion in relationship to the dominant Greco-Roman culture; philosophical speculation and the interpretation of Scripture; the role of women; and the role of prophecy within the emerging church structure."[8] Yet Royalty chooses to foreground a power struggle as the real crisis when he admits to so many other issues on the table, as if power itself and not the presenting issues are the real focal point of concern for John.

These authors deal with the multiplicity of issues named in the oracles either by downplaying the evidence for some of them or by reading other passages in the oracles as though they were integral to the power struggle, when a more natural reading suggests that they are, in fact, addressing unrelated issues. Such a focus puts them in a good position to develop a nuanced reading from Thyatira, but it is reductionist in terms of representing John's "real" interests or "complete" agenda for his work and its reception in the seven churches, leaving them ill-equipped to deal with the reading of Revelation from other congregations.

Duff, as we have seen, consistently downplays the evidence for external harassment, no matter how many oracles give some hint of this, as well as the importance of the imperial cult, despite its prevalence in the visions. In regard to Laodicea, Duff claims that there is "no significant elaboration of problems . . . and little, if any, encouragement," suggesting that John "sees little point in trying to persuade these communities to his point of view."[9] This is especially problematic, since 3:17–18 elaborates significantly on the problem of being "lukewarm" and the reversal of this condition. Moreover, the oracle to Laodicea includes extensive, even intimate encouragement: "Those whom I love I reprove and discipline"; "I stand at the door and knock" (3:19, 20). Duff has pigeonholed this oracle incorrectly alongside Sardis (an oracle that truly does *not* offer significant elaboration of the issue) because it does not fit his model of Revelation being occasioned primarily by conflict between prophets.

If Duff had applied his own methods of looking for "homologies" between the oracles and the visions, he would have seen that John painted the Laodicean community in hues that reappear in the portrait of Babylon. Especially pertinent is the represented speech of both (3:17a and 18:7b) and the self-deception inherent in this "self-talk" (exposed in 3:17b and 18:8). He would have discovered

---

8. Royalty (1998, 28) engages in an ideological ploy here when he names "the role of women" as an issue. John himself gives no indication that Jezebel (the *only* woman whose leadership role is questioned, alongside the leadership role of the Nicolaitans and the "false" apostles) should be removed from a position of authority as a teacher on the basis of her *gender* rather than her actual *message*. Schüssler Fiorenza observes that "the only text that vilifies an actual wo/man is Rev. 2:20–23, where John argues violently against a leading wo/man prophet whom he calls 'Jezebel,' but he does so not because she is a wo/man but because she and her followers are advocating adaptation to Roman society" (2007, 143 n. 101). While John will employ gender stereotypes to make Jezebel's activity look as odious as possible, this is not the same thing as saying *women* should not be teachers—only that *this woman* should not be allowed to teach. Nevertheless, by depicting the issue as "the role of women," Royalty subtly arouses prejudice against John and sympathy and even support for Jezebel, whose right to teach should not be impugned on account of her gender.

9. Duff 2001, 35–36.

the alignment of the contrast between Laodicea's Christians' false wealth and the better wealth that Christ offers with the contrast between Babylon's wealth and the better wealth of the new Jerusalem ("better," since given by God rather than acquired through participation in idolatrous and exploitative practices). This alignment in turn supports Christ's challenge to the Laodiceans to release their misplaced confidence in the former and gain the true wealth of the latter. In other words, Duff would have seen that John is every bit as concerned with the Laodiceans' relationship to the imperial economy as he was with Jezebel's influence in Thyatira, and every bit as hopeful about effecting a change in their situation.

Royalty, on the other hand, deals with the evidence in the oracle to Laodicea not by minimizing it, but by drawing it entirely into orbit around his emphasis on the power struggle between prophets: "Christ censures and rebukes the Laodiceans, encouraging them to support John and his prophetic circle in the power struggles within the Christian churches."[10] There is, however, no mention of a power struggle or false teachers in the oracle to Laodicea, and nothing suggesting that "Christ's" agenda is to rally support for John in a power struggle—topics that John is hardly reticent to invoke where relevant. The issues have to do with rejecting an identity formation forged on the basis of economic prosperity and adopting one on the basis of faithful response to Jesus (that is, faithful response to the Hebrew Scriptures, the Jesus tradition, and the apostolic witness concerning discipleship—including, but not limited to, the vision of discipleship in Revelation). Royalty's elevation of the power struggle as the central issue, and his reading of this power struggle into the hot-and-cold imagery that could easily support other interpretations, shows his tendentiousness on this point, especially considering that the majority of Revelation's visions hinge on the question of what stance a person takes in regard to idolatry and imperialism, not in regard to John's personal authority. The struggle between Jezebel and John is one significant rhetorical problem in one of the multiple audiences reading Revelation in Asia Minor.[11] Resolving that problem is, moreover, merely a means to an end: convincing the church in Thyatira as a whole to make an uncompromising stand against even the whiff of participation in idolatry.[12]

---

10. Royalty 1998, 242–43.

11. Kennedy (1984, 36) speaks of a "rhetorical problem" as an obstacle inherent in the subject matter, in the relationship between the speaker and the audience, or in the authority that the audience is willing to ascribe to the speaker, complicating the process by which one could hope to attain the rhetorical goal(s) for the discourse. In Thyatira, the activity of a rival prophet, who has won over some portion of the congregation to a position that is antithetical to the position John seeks to advance, constitutes a significant rhetorical problem.

12. Duff (2001, 127) provides an example of inverting primary and ancillary goals when he writes that "John mounts an anticommerce campaign . . . because 'Jezebel's' followers were intent on advancing in society both economically and socially, since her constituency was probably made up of freedpersons who were accumulating capital in order to improve the life of their children and grandchildren, a common situation at the time the Apocalypse was penned." But John does not oppose commerce because *Jezebel's* followers were social climbers; he opposes social climbing and the teaching that fosters social climbing through social networking around idol feasts because he sees cooperation with empire to be antithetical to faithfulness to God's kingdom.

Duff's claim that John is concerned to enjoy *sole* and unquestioned leadership in these churches is an assertion lacking textual evidence. Telling in this regard are John's references to other prophets whose leadership and influence he would affirm as legitimate (22:6, 9). The view that these prophets are members of a prophetic school—one that is under John's oversight—enjoys precious little supporting evidence.[13] On the other hand, these references could also be read as a sign that John was quite open to other prophetic voices, as long as those voices did not, in his opinion, call for the compromise of the group's core values and distinctive witness within the larger social arena, for example, the witness that there is only one God worthy of worship, to whom idolaters ought to pay more attention. Indeed, given the Christian culture of "testing" prophets, especially by other prophets, these verses might more naturally be understood as an anti-authoritarian acknowledgment on John's part, who submits his word to these other prophets for testing and verification (and if accepted as a word from the Lord, for help in disseminating).

At issue is not personal loyalty to John, but collective loyalty to the "commandments of God and the testimony of Jesus" (Rev 12:17). John would have no qualms about Jezebel's prophetic activity—her leadership among the congregations alongside his own, even eclipsing him in his exile—if she advocated a position more in line with the Jewish-Christian tradition that, in John's view, stands as an authority and a point of accountability over all prophets, himself included. Indeed, John believes that Christ has given this prophetess opportunity to come back in line with the larger tradition (2:21), attempting to *preserve* her place in active leadership. From the ideological location of many modern readers, according to which theological innovation and plurality of expressions of Christianity are valued, John may still look too oppressive even here, but at least we must admit that he is not merely interested in expanding his own power and eliminating the competition. Like Paul, he is quite content to share the limelight with other leaders, as long as discipleship is not thereby compromised. Our search for the rhetorical goal of Revelation, therefore, must take us beyond the supposition that John is merely out to hold on to, or increase, his power.

JOHN WANTS TO FOSTER CRITICAL DISTANCE AND PROPHETIC WITNESS

Focusing on John's alleged desire for power as the primary rhetorical goal for Revelation requires downplaying (1) the crisis faced in Smyrna and Philadelphia with regard to the hostility between church and synagogue; (2) the crisis of spiritual health in Ephesus, Sardis, and Laodicea, where, for example, economic success has become a source of spiritual self-deception; (3) the crisis of failing to maintain prophetic witness against the domination systems at work in Roman

---

13. See discussion (above) in chap. 2, n. 8; also A. Collins 1984, 46.

imperialism, confounding God's vision for a just and whole human community. It represents a misconception of the rhetorical situation similar to the elevation of persecution as the primary concern, and the encouragement of the persecuted as John's primary rhetorical goal. The rhetorical situations that John addresses are multiform and variegated.

Taking the data from all seven oracles into account, however, one could outline John's rhetorical goals more completely: (1) John is concerned that the Christians in Ephesus recover their embodiment of the core Christian virtue of love (ἀγάπη, 2:4–5);[14] (2) John is concerned that the congregations in Smyrna and Philadelphia continue to hold their course in the face of pressures from another minority group; (3) John wants to see the influence of the Nicolaitans and Jezebel decrease in the congregations in Pergamum and Thyatira, since their teaching seems to him to threaten another core Christian virtue: absolute fidelity to the One God; (4) John seeks to awaken the congregations in Sardis and Laodicea to the dangers of their spiritual condition, about which they have deceived themselves (and perhaps others) on account of their material prosperity, with the desired result that they divest themselves of their involvement in a corrupt economy.[15]

Each of these concerns represents a local manifestation of a larger, overarching rhetorical goal. John wants "conquerors." He wants his hearers to "overcome" the challenges to faithful discipleship and the forces, social and spiritual, that conspire to defeat disciples in their contest to keep the commandments of God and to keep faith with Jesus.[16] And for John, "overcoming" entails gaining critical distance from, and engaging in prophetic witness in the midst of, the domination systems of Roman Asia Minor.

The choice of apocalypse as the primary genre of this communication contributes directly to fostering critical distance. The genre provided the literary and conceptual resources required to impart to John's audiences a sense—an interpretation—of the "true" nature of the realities they encounter each day, doing so in a way that immediately exposes the distance between the understanding of those realities as communicated within the public discourse of Asia Minor and the understanding imparted from within the Jewish and Christian tradition (as interpreted by John). As an "unveiling," Revelation serves John's goal of opening the eyes of the Christians to the spiritual dimension of the world that surrounded them and the significance of their choices and allegiances within that world. "John did not write this book to manufacture a crisis for a people who had become complacent about the empire. Rather, he

---

14. The argumentative texture of this oracle revolves completely around this issue, elevating it as John's primary concern for that congregation. See discussion in chap. 9 (below).

15. The images of soiling or not soiling one's garment (3:4–5) and of acknowledging the spiritual impoverishment that has come about in connection with sharing in the prosperity that Babylon and the Roman "peace" make possible (3:17–18) point in this direction.

16. John uses the verb "to conquer" prominently to describe those who hold fast to the courses of action he promotes in each of the seven churches, as well as for Christians living under empire more generally (2:7b, 11b, 17b, 26–28; 3:5, 12, 21; 12:10–12; 15:2–4; 21:7).

tried to reveal that this complacency about Rome *was* the crisis, if only they had 'apocalyptic eyes.'"[17]

In particular, John wants to foster critical distance from the practices of idolatrous worship (including imperial cult) and from the imperial economic system by means of depicting these practices as they are seen through the lens of the Hebrew Scriptures, early Jewish literature, and the Jesus traditions. John seeks to demonstrate that the worship of God and the worship of idols are fundamentally incompatible, and that the person who engages in the latter cannot escape punishment for sharing God's honor with God's enemies. He regards the voices that make room for idolatrous practice in any form as especially great dangers to the churches, and dedicates much of his vision to rendering their position untenable. The issue of monolatry—the faithful witness that "the LORD is God, the LORD alone" (Deut. 6:4)—versus participation in idolatry was such a central one in the Hebrew Scriptures and the ongoing life of Judea that John justifiably regards this as a make-or-break issue for the churches' fidelity to the Jewish tradition that spawned the movement and remained, to a large extent, authoritative within it. He also seeks to fix in his hearers' minds the violence, the unjust economic practices, and the masking of the full truth that maintain the imperial economy into which the merchants and tradespeople of the cities of Asia are invited.[18] John seeks to topple the imperial ideology through his visions, showing believers the "true" nature of Rome and her emperors, warning them against accepting any share in or partnership with a system built on the violence, injustice, and arrogance that call down God's vengeance.

This critical distance is to be accompanied by prophetic witness *to* the One God and what that God values in human community, and witness *against* the abuses of that God and God's values in the practices of Roman imperialism. Bearing "witness" (μαρτυρία) and serving as a "witness" (μάρτυς) constitute a fundamental activity of John himself (1:2, 9), Jesus (1:5; 3:14), exemplary Christians whom Christ commends (2:13) or who play an important role in the execution of God's purposes for the nations (11:3–13), and God's holy ones in general (12:17; 19:10). John prepares the hearers for the cost of bearing witness (6:9; 17:6), but also insists that "witness" is the path to overcoming the Satanic powers of this age (12:11). Sharing in Christ's task of bearing testimony leads to sharing in Christ's messianic reign (20:4). The disciples are indeed called to "come out" from Babylon (18:4), yet from their liminal position still to call out to others through witness, extending to them the invitation to discover that critical distance.

---

17. Howard-Brook and Gwyther 1999, 116; so also Knight 2001, 475.
18. L. Snyder (2000, 409) captures with precision the rhetorical effects of Revelation in this regard: "John's narrative thus has dehortative purposes: he invites the readers to reject enticements from their enemies, especially temptations to cultural assimilation. . . . The listener wants to share the victory over [the harlot] and, in order to do so, must repudiate the tendencies of his or her own heart to be unfaithful through love of luxury. In this way, John's narrative of a future event shapes his audience's contemporary attitudes."

As John promotes unyielding allegiance to the One God and fidelity to God's commandments and to God's Messiah, John moves the churches toward a more sectarian stance vis-à-vis the host society as opposed to the more open, "denominationalizing" stance urged by Jezebel and the Nicolaitans. In so doing, he preserves not only the distinctiveness of Christian identity, preventing it from becoming another mystery cult existing peacefully and unobtrusively alongside the religious legitimating mechanisms of empire, but also the distinctiveness of the Christian voice, made known in speech and in lifestyle.[19] The sectarian course on which John set the churches, and the theological and liturgical resources John provided for the journey,[20] made it possible for the Christian critique of Rome and its world to continue to be heard, such that it remained a continual witness to other definitions of reality and other values throughout the next two centuries.[21]

DOES JOHN CARE ABOUT SOCIAL JUSTICE?

As we have previously observed, the authors who champion the position that John is primarily interested in securing his own power and influence support their claim by downplaying other possible interests or goals John might have.

---

19. See further deSilva 1992a, 296–302; 1991, 207–8; 1993, 55–57; Knight 2001, 480. Duff (2001, 98) observes that "John strenuously resists εἰδωλόθυτα, for defiling food entering the individual body articulates the fear of corruption entering the social body." While the anthropological theory behind this statement is sound, in this particular case the one ("defiling food entering the individual body") is not a symbol for the other (the corruption of "the social body"). The former directly effects the larger "corruption" that John fears. Eating food sacrificed to idols does not happen independently of sitting in a social setting of some kind where one's actions bear public witness to the acceptability of idolatrous worship, and hence a violation of a primary identity marker of the group (from John's perspective—and one might add, of the whole of the Hebrew scriptural witness).

20. John gives significant attention to crafting liturgical elements within his Revelation. Schüssler Fiorenza (1991, 103) asserts that John "does not seek to inculcate religious-cultic practices," but rather to move "the audience to political resistance," setting obeisance to God over against obeisance to "the dominion of Rome." While I agree with Schüssler Fiorenza's analysis of the sociopolitical effect of John's "liturgical rhetoric," the either/or dichotomizing appears to be unwarranted. John may *well* seek to influence Christian liturgy, energize participation, and make of the experience of worship a continual reinforcement of the ideological distance from Roman imperial ideology that will reinforce the "political resistance" he nurtures, and that indeed will foster long-term critique and witness. See also Ruiz 2001, 74.

· 21. In his conclusion, Duff (2001, 131) evaluates the positions of John and Jezebel in the light of contemporary and subsequent Roman-Christian relations. He concludes that John's position was less accurate than Jezebel's insofar as "objective historical evidence does not suggest, as John believed, that 'Babylon' was out to destroy Christianity at John's time." He counterposes, however, that "John was essentially correct in his understanding of Christianity's vulnerability, for later Roman action against Christians affirmed his story (albeit belatedly) and demonstrated that 'Jezebel's' program of assimilation was wrongheaded and futile." I find difficulties with both assertions. First, John does not claim that Babylon is out to destroy Christianity *at the present time*, though Babylon clearly has a lot of Christian blood on her hands already. John anticipates the escalation of hostility, specifically where Christians respond to his call to bear vocal witness to the injustice of idolatrous cult, Roman power, and imperial economics. Second, Rome's later violence against Christians does not show Jezebel's program to be "wrongheaded and futile." If her program *had been* widely accepted, Roman violence against Christians *would not* have escalated. Because John's stance was the more widely adopted, violence escalated—by all accounts, beginning in the nearby provinces of Bithynia and Pontus.

Paul Duff strongly opposes the claim that John is interested in social justice. As support, Duff argues that there is hardly any evidence for dissatisfaction with Roman rule among the poor, that one can actually find literary evidence that the opposite was the case.[22] Aside from the fact that the voice of the poor is generally the most difficult voice to uncover reliably from literary, epigraphic, and other remains, Duff fails to take into consideration the possibility that John saw connections between the provincial elite's cooperation with Rome and the exploitation of the poor that even the local "poor" in the cities of Asia did not see. The mechanisms of oppression often remain opaque to both oppressors and victims.

Reading Revelation 18, Duff claims further that the language of bloodshed, sorcery, fornication, and the like are just "stock accusations leveled at Israel's enemies throughout the Hebrew Scriptures," appearing in Revelation merely to "fulfill readers' expectations," leaving the condemnation of merchants enriching themselves as the only one of real import.[23] But the topoi that John selects to include from the much wider array of available apocalyptic topics probably have more relevance than "fulfilling readers' expectations." Here Duff's argument amounts to little more than special pleading, claiming that only those topics are relevant that align with the facets of the situation Duff seeks to highlight. Here we find another instance of eliminating some of the evidence from consideration so as to foreground what he wants to foreground—in this case the issue of merchants and John's subtle approach to merchants among the seven congregations—rather than engaging in a more finely nuanced and complex analysis.[24]

Royalty similarly chastens John for his "complete disregard for social justice."[25] Surveying texts from the Hebrew prophets, he correctly observes that "some of the most important Jewish texts dealing with economic morality have no parallel in John's Apocalypse. The more one reads Jewish literature with an eye for passages about wealth and trade, the more striking it is that nowhere in the Apocalypse is there any strong concern for social justice, the poor, the widowed, or the orphaned."[26] In his understanding, the God of the Apocalypse "shows no special concern for economic justice," punishing the poor along with the rich in 6:15; 13:16; 19:18.[27]

Granted, John does not call his hearers to "defend the orphan, plead for the widow" (Isa. 1:17), although he does commend and promote acts of love and

---

22. Duff 2001, 64.
23. Duff 2001, 67.
24. It also exhibits the fallacy of the criterion of dissimilarity, now applied to a literary genre, and is, as ever, self-confirming. The fact that *4 Ezra* and *2 Baruch* bear contemporary witness to concerns over Roman violence and exploitative practices is not recognized as a sign that Jewish apocalypticists, including John, were all engaged in sociopolitical critique and witness, but were rather all merely reinscribing the topics inherent in the genre.
25. Royalty 1998, 154.
26. Royalty 1998, 78.
27. Royalty 1998, 183. Royalty has listed Rev. 13:16 among the texts that show God punishing the poor alongside the rich, but this seems to be in error: that text refers to the second beast requiring that all, "the small and the great," receive the beast's mark in order to participate in the empire's commerce.

service (Rev. 2:4–5, 19), which would be heard in the Christian cultural context to promote showing care for the needs of one another and their neighbors. Moreover, John also cries out against the violent snuffing out of lives for the sake of maintaining imperial "peace." He cries out against political murders, the execution of the dissident voices like those of apostles, prophets, and holy ones. He cries out against an exploitative economy that has organized production and trade across the empire for the benefit of the elite few and the capital city's inhabitants, often endangering the provincials' access to affordable food.[28] John's placement of "slaves" in the climactic position of the list of cargoes streaming toward Babylon, both setting the term in the final position in the list and giving it heightened emphasis by means of a brief gloss ("bodies, that is, human souls," Rev. 18:13), underscores a pervasive imperial abuse and corrects public discourse about slaves as "bodies" rather than "human souls."[29] He calls for(th) a human community where the nations come together for healing and all dwell in true safety, where the gates are always open because there is no terror—and perhaps there is no terror because the bifurcations between nations and competing national interests, between those who prosper and those who labor without reward, have been overcome. These are *all* salient sociopolitical justice issues and surely qualify John to stand alongside Isaiah with the latter's concern for other aspects of social justice.[30] Royalty and Duff have drawn the perimeter of social justice around too confined a space if they do not include such concerns.

That God should punish the poor along with the strong ("the small and the great," 6:15; 19:18), moreover, does not mean that, in Revelation, "God shows no special concern for economic justice." It *does* mean that God shows no *bias* toward the poor. The issues of concern for John have to do with support of, or witness against, the Roman domination system, and the poor can actively support that system by participation in its self-legitimating cults as surely as can the rich. In a way, John affords the poor a certain dignity that is absent from a vision in which God holds only the rich accountable. The poor are also responsible actors, and their choices can make a difference in terms of the ability of the domination system to lie effectively to itself and to the world.

John is very much concerned about social justice, though he focuses his congregations' attention on different aspects of social justice than those articulated, for example, in Isaiah 1:17. He calls not only for acts of love and service for those in need, but also and chiefly for witness in speech and lifestyle against the system that ignored or created such victims and perpetrated far more evils besides. If divestment and the call to divest from South Africa sought to advance social justice, John's call to "come out" from Babylon, neither participating in

---

28. Revelation 6:7–8 is a reflection of the local effects of global economy.
29. Clarice Martin (2005, 86) recognizes this as she highlights John's critique of the "pervasive and baleful commodification and trafficking of human beings throughout the Roman Empire." See also Glancy 2002, 10–11.
30. See the extensive discussion in Howard-Brook and Gwyther 1999, 168–77.

nor profiting from the unjust system—and boldly bearing witness to the larger society about that system's injustices—did so no less.

WOULD WITNESS LEAD TO CONVERSION?

When we inquire into the question of the conversionist possibilities of Revelation, we are inquiring into John's heart for the world beyond the congregations. Did John's concern extend beyond his congregations (and the church more broadly) to those outside the Christian confession? Was he insular in this thinking, concerned with the preservation of boundaries as walls that would preserve the purity of insiders, or did he seek to strengthen those boundaries as thresholds over which outsiders would be invited to cross, to become sharers in the tribulation and the kingdom and the patient endurance that leads to the enjoyment of that new community formed around God and the Lamb? The question is important not only for settling the question of John's attitude, but more urgently for determining the attitudes and motivations he was seeking to nurture among his readers in their response to non-Christians.

The text of Revelation provides conflicting evidence. On the one hand, the punitive judgments that God sends upon idolaters and beast-worshipers do not effect a change of heart. After the sixth trumpet, "the rest of the people, who were not killed by these plagues, neither repented of the works of their hands, in order not to worship demons and idols, . . . nor repented of their murders nor their sorceries nor their sexually immoral deeds nor their thefts" (9:20–21). After the fourth and fifth bowls are poured out, "they bad-mouthed the name of the God who possessed the authority over these plagues and did not repent, to give him glory" (16:9) and "did not repent of their works" (16:11). Such a response to God's plagues recalls the tradition concerning the response of the Canaanites, who likewise did not repent and turn to God as God began to "drive them out little by little" (Wis. 12:8–11). Most strikingly, one of the final exhortations of the book is couched in language that calls explicitly for *no* change in the hearers' alignment in light of the proximity of the coming judgment: "Let the one practicing injustice practice injustice still and let the filthy person be filthy still, and let the just person practice justice still and let the holy person be holy still" (Rev. 22:11).

These passages can create the impression that no chance to repent is really given, since no positive response to God is shown.[31] This leads to the conclusion that John's thinking is entirely insular, that John's depictions of opponents, opposing powers, and outsiders are calculated to portray them entirely unsympathetically, so that John can "do whatever he wants with them" in the narrative.[32]

Such observations, however, are based on only half the evidence. Revelation 11 tells of the effective testimony of God's witnesses, whose faithfulness in their

---

31. Carey 1999b, 160.
32. Carey 1999b, 163.

witness unto death (and God's vindication of the same) moves nine-tenths of the population to "become afraid and give glory to the God of heaven" (11:13), the very thing that does *not* eventuate from the experiences of God's punitive judgments elsewhere.[33] This positive response is the very thing for which the first of three angels calls in 14:6–13, proclaiming the "eternal gospel," which is "the call to all nations to worship the One True God who is coming to judge the world and to establish his universal rule,"[34] the summons that had rung out long before in the Psalms: "Ascribe to the LORD, O families of the peoples, . . . ascribe to the LORD the honor due God's name" (Ps. 96:7–8).

The call of the three angels, summoning the nations to "fear God and give God honor," announcing Babylon's doom, and warning of the consequences of worshiping the beast (Rev. 14:6–13), interrupts two scenes connected by the imagery of the familiar agricultural cycles of "firstfruits" (14:1–5) and "harvest" (14:14–20). The scenes of judgment in 14:14–20, with its multiple harvest images (harvesting of wheat, trampling of grapes), speak not only of condemnation but also of the salutary gathering of the redeemed.[35] "Reaping is always a positive image of bringing people into the kingdom (Mark 4:29; John 4:35–38)," with Hos. 6:11 providing the only biblical exception, whereas "threshing" is the aspect of harvesting commonly used to indicate destructive judgment (as in Jer. 51:33; Mic. 4:12–13; Hab. 3:12; Matt 3:12; Luke 3:17).[36] The hope of the psalmist that "all the nations" made by God would "come and worship before" God and "glorify God's name" (Ps. 86:9) is proclaimed also by the redeemed beside the throne of God: "Who shall not fear you, Lord, and give honor to your name, . . . because all the nations will come and worship before you" (Rev. 15:4), and made real as the kings of the earth bring their glory into the new Jerusalem and the nations walk in the light of God and the Lamb that illumines the city (21:23). Notably, these people are *not* left outside among those excluded (21:8; 22:15). All of this suggests that "the conversion of the nations—not only whether it will take place but also how it will take place—is at the centre of the prophetic message of Revelation."[37]

---

33. On the basis of this episode, Schüssler Fiorenza (1991, 79) finds John to be essentially optimistic about the results of Christian witness: "Nine-tenths of the nations and citizens of the world will repent and 'give God honor.' . . . . It is crucial to recognize that Revelation's rhetoric of judgment expresses hope for the conversion of nine-tenths of the nations in response to Christian witness and preaching." The fraction "nine-tenths" comes from the detail that "one-tenth of the city fell" in the earthquake that followed the ascension of the witnesses, killing 7,000 people. John's scope is not limited to the inhabitants of any particular city here, ranging twice to "the dwellers upon the earth/land" (11:10). The literal-minded could argue that John envisions only 63,000 residents of a city repenting and giving God due honor, but the chief point is that far more are turned toward God by this witness than not.

34. Bauckham 1993a, 288.

35. Bauckham (1993a, 290–96) offers a helpful discussion of the contrasting images of gathering (to preserve) and destroying.

36. Bauckham 1993a, 296. The treading of the grapes in John's source text, Joel 3:13 LXX (4:13 MT), is a negative image, and Rev. 14:19–20 certainly moves in this direction (incorporating images from Isa. 63:1–3 and *1 Enoch* 100:3).

37. Bauckham 1993a, 238. See also Bauckham 1993b, 103.

Not all read these visions so benignly. Greg Carey, for example, claims that the hope that the nations will come to acknowledge God is a false one: "Nothing about coming and worshiping implies conversion or redemption."[38] Rather, the ensuing visions are all about vanquishing, not converting. Fearing God, giving honor to God's name, and worshiping God, however, are all behaviors and attitudes of the redeemed, or of God's people, throughout the Hebrew Scriptures.[39] This is the proper and just response to the Creator of all. When the psalmists invite the nations to fear God and worship him, the language does not imply conquest of the nations by the forces of the psalmists' nation: it implies the nations coming alongside Israel in its posture of worship before the One God—a vision that inspires Paul's gospel as well (see, e.g., Rom. 15:7–13). The recalcitrant, including the domination systems that orchestrate resistance to the One God and God's vision for human community, are vanquished; those who are receptive to the testimony of the witnesses, the summons of the angels, and so forth, are converted and invited into the community of the new Jerusalem.

How, then, would a rhetorical reading hold these two sets of texts—the one nurturing the expectation that witness will be effective, the other depicting outsiders as recalcitrant in the face of divine judgment, even to the point of exhorting "nonconversion"—together as part of a single strategy? Or are they irreconcilable strands? "Refusal to repent" is a topic linked with the future experience of God's judgments, events "that must soon take place" but have not yet. The summons to the unjust to be unjust still (22:11) is the most extreme expression of this topic, sandwiched between two affirmations of the proximity of God's judgments and Christ's coming (22:10, 12).

But the judgments of God "have been revealed" long before they will be enacted. Revelation makes known in the here and now what God will do in the then and there, thus creating the opportunity to repent, to fall in line, to respond to God with fear and reverence now so as to avoid being calcified among the recalcitrant later. A rhetorical analysis should not fail to take into account the rhetorical nature of these visions of judgment, which after all exist only on paper and, ostensibly, in the near future, and which, therefore, are spurs to action to all who hear them in the present, both those within the churches and those among the nations who hear the witness that is borne by those who are persuaded by Revelation. As John calls for witness, so witness calls for an audience, and an audience can be persuaded.

The prejudice that "'Jezebel' advocated engagement with the larger society (probably with an eye to reforming it from within)" while "John recommended withdrawal into the ghetto"[40] therefore needs to be challenged. To start with, the parenthetical claim regarding Jezebel's intentions in regard to reforming the larger society is completely speculative. The use of the word "probably" is here

---

38. Carey 1999b, 161–62.
39. See the discussion in deSilva 1999a, 88–90.
40. Duff 2001, 61; see also 2001, 131.

a rhetorical mask distracting the reader from the complete lack of evidence for such a claim. Indeed, the form of "engagement" with the larger society that "Jezebel's" teaching permits does not suggest the goal of reform, but rather the goal of securing economic advantage for upwardly mobile Christians while disturbing one's neighbors as little as possible with the reformative potential of the Christian gospel, especially its summons to forsake idolatry and participation in activities that help to legitimate the domination systems of empire. Further, the claim that John "recommended withdrawal into the ghetto" does not square with John's call to the congregations to bear witness, to put their claims "out there" so clearly and prominently that their neighbors could be expected to call for the death of the witnesses, governors could be expected to start granting their neighbors' requests for legal action as a result of the process,[41] and the nations could be brought to acknowledge the glory of this One God. It is John, not Jezebel, who advocates potentially reformative engagement with the larger society in the form of prophetic critique and bold witness to an alternative world order.

John's rhetorical goals, then, do not merely involve "erecting a wall between Christianity and the enemy culture" or maintaining "the boundaries between John's 'us' and 'them.'"[42] John indeed took issue with Jezebel's manner of crossing boundaries in regard to idolatrous settings not because it threatened the boundary, but because it threatened the core identity of Christians as adherents of the monotheistic creed of Israel and the covenant that, for him, still included not paying honor or even lip service to idols or any other gods. John's boundaries are also porous, but for him the movement must flow in the opposite direction. He calls Christians out from colluding with, and thus helping to perpetuate, the domination systems of Roman imperialism, including the religious legitimation machine, the economic machine, and the conspiracy of silence about the underside of Rome's rule. As his audiences respond to his call to draw themselves more clearly and nearly into orbit around the One God, he creates the opportunity for other "inhabitants of the earth" to take a second look at the empire around them and to gain liberating critical distance as they, too, move toward and across the boundary between Babylon and new Jerusalem.

JOHN'S GOALS AND THE RHETORICAL GENRE(S) OF REVELATION

An important step in a rhetorical analysis is to determine the rhetorical genre of the communication. Classical rhetorical theory identified three prominent genres of oratory: epideictic, deliberative, and forensic (or judicial) rhetoric, allowing that, in actual practice, an oration might combine elements of these

---

41. See the famous correspondence of Pliny and Trajan (Pliny the Younger, *Ep.* 10.96–97).
42. Duff 2001, 134.

genres. Determining whether a New Testament text is primarily "deliberative," "forensic," or "epideictic" is not merely a quest for a label. Rather, it is a way to discern what a particular author is trying to accomplish. It inquires into the fundamental issue or issues in the audience's situation selected by the author for attention and the principal goal or goals of the author for his readers or hearers in that situation. Does the author primarily seek to persuade the audience to pursue, avoid, or desist from a certain course of action in the immediate future? Does the author primarily seek a verdict of condemnation or acquittal in regard to actions that have already been committed? Does the author seek to win assent to a proposition, a celebration of some virtue, or a denunciation of vice? The answer to this question provides a focal point for the exposition of the whole text, inviting the interpreter to inquire how each passage contributes to advancing the author's goals for the hearers.

The threefold classification of rhetorical genre grew out of the practice of oratory in the Greek city and its institutions.[43] Public speech was essential to the functioning of the city in three primary settings: the council chamber, lawcourt, and the forum. Deliberative oratory occupied the council chamber, where citizens gathered to decide what course of action the city should take to meet some particular need. Citizens in favor of one course or another would speak in favor of their preferred course of action and against alternatives. Important strategies included alleging and weighing the consequences of the various courses of action, demonstrating that one's preferred course was ethically virtuous, expedient, feasible, honorable, and praiseworthy, and showing how alternative courses of action were lacking in these qualities.[44]

Forensic oratory belonged in the lawcourts, where citizens gathered to assess the guilt or innocence of those accused of wrongdoing. The goal of the orators (a defender and an accuser) here was to establish guilt or innocence in regard to some past action, and to secure a verdict from the jury. Orators relied on oaths, witnesses, material evidence, and deduction to provide support for their reconstructions of the events in question, on the basis of which guilt or innocence could be determined.[45]

The most prominent specimen of the third genre, epideictic oratory, was the funeral oration, delivered in the public forum to commemorate the life or lives

---

43. See Aristotle, *Rhet.* 1.3.1–6; *Rhet. Her.* 1.2.2; Quintilian, *Inst.* 3.4.1–16. Quintilian includes a lengthy discussion of alternative schema, showing how, in his opinion, each falls short of the tripartite schema of Aristotle developed on the basis of the "three kinds of hearers" (Aristotle, *Rhet.* 1.3.1; Quintilian, *Inst.* 3.4.6), by which is meant the three kinds of responses hearers would be expected to give, and toward which end the oration was framed.

44. See *Rhet. Alex.* 1421b.21–1423a.12; *Rhet. Her.* 3.2.2–3.4.9.

45. See, further, Aristotle, *Rhet.* 1.10; Quintilian, *Inst.* 3.9–11; *Rhet. Her.* 2.1.1–2.19.30. Aristotle discusses "inartificial proofs" that are particularly appropriate for forensic oratory in *Rhet.* 1.15, while his more fulsome discussion of "artificial proofs" (logical deduction and induction not directly supported by oaths, witnesses, physical evidence, and other such support that lies beyond the orator's "invention") in *Rhet.* 2.18–26 treats argumentative topics and strategies appropriate to all genres of oratory ("common topics") as well as those more particularly appropriate to one genre over the others ("special topics").

of the honored dead, elevating the deceased's virtues and achievements, and thus reminding the gathered audience of the values that sustained their society and culture. Epideictic rhetoric included the art of praising the living, as in Pliny the Younger's *Panegyricus* honoring the emperor Trajan, and the reverse art: vituperation, censuring those who have acted viciously, against the public interest. Alongside praise and censure, epideictic ("demonstrative," or "display") oratory included the demonstration of a philosophical or ethical thesis. The author of 4 Maccabees, for example, uses the cognate verb ἐπιδείκνυσθαι (*epideiknysthai*, to demonstrate) to describe his rhetorical goal, namely, to demonstrate the power that devout Torah observance gives the practitioner over the passions, emotions, and cravings (4 Macc 1:1; see also ἀποδείξαιμι, 1:8; ἀπόδειξις, 3:19), at the same time including the "praise" (ἔπαινος, 1:2) of virtue and those who have embodied virtue (1:10). Epideictic oratory sought to win assent to the praiseworthiness (or baseness) of the persons who were being lauded or censured, or to a proposition or thesis that was being advanced. Praise of another would typically arouse emulation in the audience, stirring them up to embody the same virtues in order to attain similar honor.[46]

Epideictic speeches had hortatory potential. The close relationship between epideictic and deliberative oratory was not lost on classical theorists. Aristotle wrote that "praise and counsel have a common aspect, for what you might suggest in counseling becomes encomium by a change in the phrase. . . . Accordingly, if you desire to praise, look what you would suggest; if you desire to suggest, look what you would praise" (*Rhet.* 1.9.35–36).[47] Anaximenes provides an identical list of topics for treatment in encomium and deliberation. The writers of an encomium will seek to develop "praiseworthy things," namely, those things "that are just, lawful, expedient, noble, pleasant, and easy to accomplish" (*Rhet. Alex.* 1425b.38–41). The writer of a protreptic speech (an exhortation to a course of action) "must prove that the courses to which he exhorts are just, lawful, expedient, honorable, pleasant, and easily practicable" (1421b.28–31). The primary difference lay in the rhetorical goal: the former sought, through praise, to uphold audience commitment to general values; the latter sought to promote a more particular course of action for adoption among the hearers.

The argumentative strategies, topics, and goals exhibited in civic discourse were not limited to those settings. Anaximenes spoke of "exhortation and dissuasion" (the two species of deliberative oratory) as "among the forms most employed in private conversation and in public deliberation" (1421b.18–20). Deliberative rhetoric pervaded real-life conversations in any setting where some group or someone needed to make a decision about a future course of action. The move from the council chamber to the synagogue, the church, or any

---

46. See chap. 1, n. 54. Perelman and Olbrichts-Tyteca (1969, 50) affirm this ethical function of epideictic oratory which, in their analysis, "strengthens the disposition toward action by increasing adherence to the values it lauds." Epideictic rhetoric could thereby assist the execution of the decisions and judgments made in response to a deliberative speech.

47. See also Quintilian, *Inst.* 3.7.28.

other voluntary association was a small one. Paul, for example, marshals deliberative topics and argumentative strategies in Galatians to advise an "assembly" (*ekklēsia*) against a course of action on the table for consideration (undergoing circumcision).

A speaker or writer could also employ topics and strategies of forensic rhetoric outside of a courtroom setting wherever issues of guilt or innocence might be involved. To take another example from Paul's letters, the apostle presents a full-scale "defense speech" in 2 Corinthians (1:15–2:4; 7:8–12) in regard to allegations made about his sincerity, truthfulness, and motives in writing a harsh letter. The charges may not belong in a court of law, but they might seriously damage the apostle's relationship with his congregation and so must be dealt with before Paul can move forward with the Corinthians.[48]

Epideictic rhetoric, similarly, was not confined to the forum or marketplace. Indeed, this genre of rhetoric was often used in conjunction with the other rhetorical genres to help advance a deliberative or a forensic goal. A prosecutor might develop a period of epideictic rhetoric within a larger forensic oration in order to censure the defendant or to undermine the credibility of the defending orator. A speaker advancing a particular course of action might find it useful to develop the praise of some figure from history who pursued a course of action similar to the one he was promoting and who thus arrived at an honorable and praiseworthy end. Aristotle had already observed that a speech was rarely a pure example of a single genre.[49] The task of a nuanced rhetorical analysis is not merely to decide that a particular speech is deliberative (or epideictic, or forensic), but to discern the ways in which epideictic and forensic topics, for example, support an overarching deliberative goal.

The structure of Revelation does not reflect the four or five divisions of an oration noted in classical rhetorical theory, placing severe limitations on any attempt to analyze it as a deliberative *speech* or forensic *oration*. Our inquiry here is more concerned to refine our understanding of the different kinds of topics and argumentative strategies John weaves into Revelation, and our analysis of how these topics work together within a larger rhetorical strategy to attain John's goals. Any discussion of Revelation as deliberative rhetoric, then, must not be confused with (futile) attempts to outline Revelation as a deliberative *speech*, forcing the contents of Revelation into a foreign mold.

The task is further complicated by the fact that John addresses not one audience (as would the author and performer of a typical deliberative, forensic, or epideictic address), but seven. The rhetorical situations of these congregations vary widely, and no single rhetorical situation is entirely homogeneous. Thus, we would expect John to have multiple rhetorical goals not only in regard to the seven congregations, but also in regard to each particular congregation. It is

---

48. See deSilva 1996a.
49. Aristotle, *Rhet.* 1.3.5; see also *Rhet. Alex.* 1427b.31–35 and esp., *Rhet. Her.* 3.8.15: "And if epideictic is only seldom employed by itself independently, still in judicial and deliberative causes extensive sections are often devoted to praise and censure."

highly unlikely that all of these goals will fall in line with one rhetorical genre, leading us to expect that Revelation will combine elements of multiple rhetorical genres in the service of a diverse set of rhetorical goals.

Revelation as Deliberative Discourse

The seven oracles provide an important starting point for rhetorical analysis since, in part, the speaker's goals for the discourse are here most transparent. In regard to their rhetorical genre, John Kirby writes: "The seven letters, in contrast with the book as a whole, may seem initially to have a judicial aspect insofar as they deal with evaluation of the justice of past action, but finally their thrust is deliberative, for each letter purports to stir its audience to a course of action."[50] In support of these calls to action, moreover, the oracles include "considerations of the consequences," a major deliberative topic, both as warnings concerning the negative consequences following failure to act as the oracle recommends and as assurances concerning the positive consequences following adoption of the recommended course of action (often in the form of divine promises concerning the reward awaiting those who "overcome").[51]

In the oracle to Ephesus, for example, John gives voice to the glorified Christ's advice in light of the critical needs he has diagnosed:

> Remember, then, whence you have fallen and repent and do the former works: But if not, I am coming to you, and I will remove your lampstand from its place, unless you repent. . . . To the one who overcomes, to that one I will grant to eat from the tree of life, which is in the paradise of God. (Rev. 2:5, 7b)

John calls the congregation at Ephesus to take action to recover the love they formerly displayed and find new ways to manifest such love in their setting (2:5), supporting both by an assertion of the negative consequences of failing to act and by an affirmation of the benefits that will follow adopting the recommended course. These consequences are not supported by arguments from historical precedent or analogy, but are based on the future actions of the Lord, who will judge his congregations. They remain, however, arguments from the consequences, and thus deliberative topics.

Most of the other oracles also promote particular courses of action in response to the challenges of each congregation's situation. In regard to the prognosis of increasing tension with, and hostile action on the part of, the civic authorities, the glorified Christ urges the Christians in Smyrna to "be faithful to the point of death" rather than pursue other available courses of action (e.g., seeking some compromise to reduce the tension, making peace with the synagogue by any

---

50. Kirby 1988, 200.
51. The author of *Rhet. Her.* (3.17.4) affirms that the focus of deliberative proofs is on the consequences that follow the possible courses of action being contemplated.

means necessary, or leaving the city to seek a more tolerant environment). This call is supported by the promise of positive consequences grounded in the future benefactions of the Lord toward those who display costly loyalty (2:10c, 11b). The Christians in Pergamum are called to "repent" of the presence and activity of the Nicolaitan party in their midst and are left to discern for themselves exactly what such repentance would look like in action (disavowal of and withdrawal from the Nicolaitans? expulsion of the teachers from their midst?). The call to action in the oracle to Thyatira is more subtle but still readily apparent. The glorified Christ declares: "See, I am throwing [Jezebel] upon a bed, and her adulterous partners into great distress, unless they repent of her works" (2:22). This announcement of the consequences of heeding Jezebel's teaching comes with an escape clause ("unless they repent"), which thereby indicates the advantageous course of action.

The oracle to Sardis is replete with imperatives calling for action in regard to Jesus' "diagnosis" of their condition. This congregation is urged to "become vigilant and strengthen the things that remain and are on the verge of dying," to "remember what you have received and heard, and keep [these things] and repent" (3:2–3a). They are not to continue in their present course but rather to alter it significantly so as to avoid untoward future consequences (3:3b). The positive model of the "few" in Sardis orients the rest of the congregation to "keeping one's clothes unsullied" as a component of this response they are called to make to their own advantage (3:4–5). Only the oracle to Philadelphia seems to lack a genuine call to action, save to "hold on" to what they have. The oracle to Laodicea returns to an overtly deliberative mode, with the glorified Christ even using the verb par excellence of deliberative oratory—"I advise you" (συμβουλεύω σοι, 3:18)[52]—to call the hearers to take some action in regard to their involvement with the wealth of the Roman imperial economy so as to acquire the lasting wealth that will provide honor and security beyond the present life. In every case the speaker uses topics drawn from the consequences to support the course of action promoted.

Revelation exhibits deliberative goals also in the visions of a future in which certain actions or alliances are shown to be advantageous and others disadvantageous.[53] In several instances the calls to action in the seven oracles will be clarified by means of the display throughout the visions of several possible courses of action and their consequences. These visions thus reinforce and extend the deliberations within the seven oracles.

The visions include straightforward exhortations to a particular course of action. The summons of the first of the three angels is a case in point: "Fear God and give honor to him, because the hour of his judgment came, and worship the one who made heaven and earth and sea and springs of waters" (14:7). The

---

52. In Greek rhetorical handbooks, deliberative rhetoric is referred to as συμβουλευτικόν, "symbouleutic rhetoric" (See Aristotle, *Rhet.* 1.3.3).
53. DeSilva 1998a, 79.

message promotes a particular course of action, invoking two deliberative topics in support: such a course leads to safety in regard to the judgment of God and embodies the just response to the God who, as Creator of all, is the universal benefactor.[54] The third angel follows this up with an announcement of the negative consequences that follow the contrary course of action, namely, worshiping the beast or its image and receiving its mark (14:9–11), painting a grisly picture of the pain and degradation that would result. Although they are overhearing these proclamations, as it were, the believers are led by the narrative to identify with the universal audience of these brief deliberative addresses (14:6) and thus to consider the import of these protreptic and apotreptic announcements in their own contexts. Another important instance occurs in 18:4: "Come out, my people, from [Babylon], in order that you may not become a partner with her in her sins, and in order that you may not receive a share of her punishments." The audience would identify themselves with the addressees (God's "people"), and so would be set on the path of seeking to discern what such "coming out" would look like. The call to action again uses topics drawn from the consequences: those who remain involved with Babylon become entangled in the sinful practices that render Babylon liable to God's judgment, and thus put themselves in jeopardy in regard to God's future intervention.[55]

But the more outstanding deliberative effect of Revelation's visions is not achieved through direct exhortation and supporting argument. By writing an apocalypse, with the possibility it provides of "narrating the future," John can exploit deliberative strategies peculiar to this genre, strategies inconceivable to Aristotle.[56] By displaying future events or circumstances befalling particular groups of people, John puts the audience in a position to trace out and correlate the various courses of action that lead to such consequences, forcing the ques-

---

54. Justice in the ancient world meant honoring one's obligations, giving to each person or entity (e.g., the state, the gods) what was due. The *Rhetorica ad Herennium* lists "the just" among deliberative topics, suggesting that "we shall be using the topics of Justice . . . if we show that it is proper to repay the well-deserving with gratitude; . . . if we urge that faith (*fidem*) ought zealously to be kept; . . . if we contend that alliances and friendships should scrupulously be honored; if we make it clear that the duty imposed by nature toward parents, gods, and the fatherland (*in parentes, deos, patriam*) must be religiously observed; if we maintain that ties of hospitality, clientage, kinship, and relationship by marriage must inviolably be cherished" (*Rhet. Her.* 3.3.4).

55. Royalty (1997, 602) objects to calling Revelation deliberative rhetoric since "the few calls for action in the text are vague." However, the summons in the visions (and the more direct exhortations in the oracles), if heeded, will have more specific and identifiable results in the behavior of the hearers than the epideictic speech that simply "tries to affect an audience's view, opinions, or values" (1997, 601). The calls to action in Revelation are no more vague than the proposal "Let us go to war with Sparta." Deciding upon that course of action simply defines an orientation toward Sparta. It does not begin to specify the ways and means required, nor lay out a strategy by means of which the course of action will be (successfully) pursued. The call to "go to war with Sparta" remains, however, a deliberative cause, and the outcome will spawn further conversations about particular steps that must be taken. The summons "Come out of Babylon" is not more vague nor less deliberative than this.

56. Aristotle did not consider it possible for an orator to "narrate the future" and thus assigned little or no part to narration in deliberative oratory (*Rhet.* 3.16.11). This rhetorical strategy will be explored in much greater depth in chapter 11 (below).

tion upon them: "What course are *we* embarked upon or aligned with? Is this course leading to advantage or disadvantage? Is a change in course called for? Is the advantageous course compatible or incompatible with present behaviors or alternative courses being considered in our setting?" By writing indirectly and in tantalizingly allusive language, John draws the audience in to engage the deliberative import of the work for themselves, to construct for themselves the course of action that leads to advantage, and to examine how this impinges on their present actions and alliances. John does not consistently confront them with direct exhortation: rather, the audience participates alongside John in the interpretation and application of the text.

As the narrative of the visions progresses, receiving God's seal (7:1–8) proves advantageous, leading to the enjoyment of God's protection and comfort (7:13–17) as well as exemption from God's forthcoming plagues (9:4). Having God's seal, however, is incompatible with involvement in idolatry (9:20–21), the behavior that characterizes the targets of these plagues. On the other hand, receiving the beast's mark proves advantageous in regard to temporal safety and sufficiency (13:15–17), but then renders one liable to suffer the plagues that do not befall those sealed by God (16:2) and then to suffer far worse torment and disgrace for a far longer period of time in the life beyond (14:9–11; 20:15). Being marked by the beast and sealed by God correlate with worshiping the beast (13:4, 8) and worshiping God (14:6–7). The former course is pursued by those whose names are not inscribed in the Lamb's Book of Life (13:8), which in the end leads to the lake of fire (20:15). Worshiping God exclusively, living out God's commandments and faithfulness to Jesus (14:12), leads to much happier consequences to be enjoyed far longer (20:4–6; 21:1–8).

Snapshots show the hearers how saints "conquer" (12:11), directly impacting their understanding of the calls to action and the promises "to the one who conquers" in the more directly deliberative oracles. The narrative depicts a future in which continued participation in the Roman imperial economy is ultimately disadvantageous as well. "Babylon's" downfall is certain (14:8; 18:21–23a; 19:3). Rome's crimes (recited in 17:2–3, 6; 18:2–3, 7–8, 23b–24) necessitate divine action by a just God (15:2–4; 16:5–7; 19:2). Any alliance with such a system brings about alienation from God and from God's more humane and beneficent kingdom. To the extent that John can present this narration as a *plausible* depiction of the future, to that extent the hearers will examine their own situation for the ways in which they can align themselves with the advantageous courses of action and desist from the disadvantageous ones.

Revelation as Epideictic Discourse

Alongside its deployment of deliberative topics and strategies, Revelation also shows many affinities with epideictic rhetoric. Again we may take the seven oracles as a starting point. Kirby claims that the "I know" passages in these oracles (2:2–3, 9, 13, 19; 3:1, 8, 15) exhibit "a judicial aspect insofar as they deal with evaluation of the justice of past action."⁵⁷ This claim calls for some modification. These passages fall under the rubric of epideictic discourse since they set out praise and blame for each community.⁵⁸ The glorified Christ is not seeking a verdict from the audience. He is seeking to affirm and to censure, actions that are properly epideictic. In some instances, Christ's analysis of the honor and virtue of each congregation presents the grounds for taking some particular action urged in the oracle. In the oracle to Sardis, for example, Christ's censure of the congregation for failing to live up to their reputation presents the exigency to be addressed by fresh action (3:1–3b). In other instances, the praise communicated in the "I know" statement serves a purely epideictic goal, affirming those praiseworthy behaviors that ought to continue to characterize the community.

Throughout Revelation, John holds up praiseworthy models for emulation and imitation, and their opposite. The seven macarisms pronounce those who exhibit certain characteristics, behaviors, or avoidances "privileged" or "honored," nurturing the audience's inclination toward identifying themselves with those characteristics as refined and developed throughout the book (1:3; 14:13; 16:15; 19:9; 20:6; 22:7, 14). The commendatory vignettes of two witnesses (11:3–13), the holy ones who conquer the dragon (12:11), the 144,000 gathered alongside the Lamb (14:1–5), and those who maintain their loyal worship of the One God even to death (20:4–6)—these vignettes foster the audience's self-identification with these figures and the values and behaviors they have manifested. Conversely, the descriptions of those whose way of life disqualifies them from entering the Holy City (21:8; 22:15) nurture aversion toward that way of life.⁵⁹ In such passages, Revelation seeks to advance the quintessentially epideictic goal of engendering "a firm commitment to certain values in opposition to other values."⁶⁰

John incorporates more extended periods of epideictic discourse as well. He gives a prominent place to the praise of divinity—specifically, God and the Lamb—throughout the work, particularly in chapters 4–5, where laudatory acclamations give expression to the nobility and excellence of the Deity and the behaviors that have manifested such praiseworthy virtue (4:11; 5:9–10, 12; see also 15:3–4; 16:5–7; 19:2, 6–8).⁶¹ John also employs invective against rivals and enemies, harnessing the deconstructive power of vituperation to create distance between his hearers and the Nicolaitans (2:14–15), Jezebel (2:20–21), the emperors and the local promoters of their cult (13:1–18), and Roman imperial economy (17:1–18:24).⁶² The praise and blame of cities (like the description

57. Kirby 1988, 200.
58. So Royalty 1997, 611.
59. Royalty (1998, 223) observes that the vice list in Rev. 21:8 is not traditional; rather, John "has constructed here a specific, polemical message." This roster of censurable types reflects especially badly on the course of action that one could take, following Jezebel and the Nicolaitan teachers.
60. DeSilva 1998a, 79.
61. John even utilizes several of the topics for such praise outlined in Quintilian, *Inst.* 3.7.6–9; see Witherington 2003, 114–15; Schüssler Fiorenza 1991, 26.
62. See Johns 1998, 784.

of new Jerusalem and the censure of Babylon) also utilize recognizable epideictic topics and forms (like the monody), as well as the devices of amplification (ἐργασία), vivid description (ἔκφρασις), and especially, comparison (σύγκρισις), a device usually associated with encomia.[63] John provides several contrastive depictions (e.g., the worship around the throne and the adulation surrounding the beast, or the character of Babylon's domination and the character of life within new Jerusalem) without making the *synkrisis* explicit. This invites the hearers to engage constructively in the discourse, making the comparisons and evaluations themselves.

Revelation as Forensic Discourse

True forensic rhetoric, communication seeking a verdict of condemnation or acquittal from the audience, is rare in the New Testament. We find forensic speeches in Acts as missionaries defend themselves (and in one case a prosecutor accuses a missionary; see the pair of speeches in Acts 24:2–8, 10b–21). Paul occasionally engages in forensic rhetoric as he seeks, for example, a verdict of acquittal from the congregation in regard to the charge that he has acted unreliably and hurtfully (2 Cor. 1:15–2:4; 7:5–16). On the whole, however, the New Testament writings belong to the sphere of moral instruction and exhortation, thus chiefly employing epideictic and deliberative rhetoric, weaving in forensic topics where appropriate (e.g., to establish or destroy ethos), but not pursuing the goals of forensic rhetoric.

Two noteworthy rhetorical critics, however, have suggested that Revelation primarily consists of forensic rhetoric. Schüssler Fiorenza (1991, 26) writes that, while Revelation contains deliberative and ceremonial (epideictic) elements, its "indictments, warnings, and narrative symbolization of divine judgments, as well as its promises and depictions of reward and punishment, qualify it as forensic rhetoric." Warnings and promises, however, are quintessentially deliberative strategies, since they have force in regard to courses of action currently being pursued or potentially to be pursued, providing considerations in favor of some particular course of action. Even depictions of forthcoming divine judgments do not contribute to qualifying Revelation as forensic rhetoric, since these are also narrations of projected consequences, seeking to make an impact upon the decisions the hearers will make regarding their immediate and ongoing future actions.

Witherington likewise identifies forensic rhetoric as "the dominant form of rhetoric" in Revelation: "The author is not just trying to comfort his audience with the truth that God is in heaven and that all will one day be right with the world. He is calling them to repent, believe, and behave in light of the coming

---

63. Thus Aristotle (*Rhet.* 1.9.38) advises concerning how to develop the praise of one's subject: "And you must compare him with illustrious personages, for it affords ground for amplification and is noble, if he can be proved better than men of worth." See also Royalty 1997, 601–2, 615–16; Witherington 2003, 216–17.

redemptive judgment."[64] Indicting an audience, however, as John does in the seven oracles, is not a property of forensic rhetoric. Such indictments are, rather, deliberative strategies, showing the audience where it has hitherto participated in an unjust, dishonorable, or inexpedient course of action and calling them, in Witherington's own words, "to repent . . . and behave in light of the coming redemptive judgment," to adopt a particular and different course of action, desisting from their current course of action. These remain *deliberative* goals.

One cause for confusion here is the fact that forensic oratory is centrally concerned with the topics of justice and injustice, and we are accustomed to link issues of "justice" with discourse proper to the lawcourt.[65] However, topics of justice and injustice are also central to deliberative oratory. Indeed, as Witherington elaborates on the topic of justice as a rhetorical commonplace that signals, for him, John's participation in forensic oratory, he quotes a passage from the *Rhetorica ad Herennium* (3.3.4) on the various subtopics that fall under the heading of the "just" course of action. He overlooks the fact, however, that the passage he quotes actually comes from a larger discussion of *deliberative* topics (beginning at *Rhet. Her.* 3.2.3), not *forensic* topics. When he goes on, then, to identify as a major goal of Revelation that God should "be properly honored and served at the expense of other claimants, such as the Emperor,"[66] he has actually found another indication of Revelation's fundamentally deliberative orientation, and not the forensic orientation he thinks to support.[67]

The identification of Revelation as essentially forensic rhetoric leads Witherington into another uncharacteristic misstep. He states, correctly, that "in forensic rhetoric the *narratio* needed to be told in a fashion favorable to one's client," but concludes from this that John will need to tell the story he relates in a way "that does not lead his audience to despair," but that will rather "encourage them at the same time he is exhorting them."[68] The aim of the forensic *narratio*, however, is to present a narrative of the defendant's past actions that takes account of all the available evidence and puts that past action in the best, least illegal light possible (or the contrary, in the prosecutor's speech). This narration does not seek to "encourage" the client, being "favorable" in the sense of

64. Witherington 2003, 15.
65. Witherington 2003, 15.
66. Witherington 2003, 15–16.
67. Even though Loren Johns suggests that Revelation is primarily epideictic rhetoric, seeking "to reform, even revolutionize, the values and world view of the readers" (1998, 763, 767), he exhibits a similar confusion in regard to forensic rhetoric and its goal. He writes: "Instead of arguing logocentrically by means of a judicial rhetoric why such an embrace of the struggle was the only faithful response, or exhorting them directly by means of a deliberative rhetoric to engage in the struggle, he uses an epideictic rhetoric of praise to the lamb and invective against the beasts and the whore of Rome to move his readers to embrace his values" (Johns 1988, 784). The first clause is pertinent here and exhibits a strange use of the phrase "judicial rhetoric," since forensic rhetoric would not, in fact, be the genre conducive to "arguing . . . why such an embrace of the struggle was the only faithful response." Such an argument, which uses the topic of the just (defining "the only *faithful* response" [emphasis added]) with a view to affecting future action (embracing the struggle), is a deliberative argument.
68. Witherington 2003, 74.

"pleasing" the client, but rather commending the client's past actions favorably to the jury. John's narrative concerns God's future actions on behalf of God's honor and the honor of God's clients, not the *past action* of John's clients for which John is trying to provide justification, and so does not represent a forensic *narratio*.

Revelation's focus on God's judgment and the narration of the process of that judgment predisposes these scholars to see the text as forensic discourse. This is a story in which books are opened, witnesses step forward, charges are voiced, sentence passed, and justice meted out.[69] The narrative certainly utilizes forensic *topics*, but not to forensic *ends*. In regard to the familiar forensic topic of the "witness" who bears "testimony," for example, John gives voice to these witnesses and highlights their role not to gain a verdict from his hearers, but rather to arouse or solidify their commitment to give testimony. The commendation of witnesses throughout Revelation, and the depiction of the honor and good consequences that eventually befall God's witnesses, invite the hearers to ask themselves: "Should I come forward as a witness to the One God in light of the death threats and the absence of a witness-protection program, or should I not?"

Revelation, then, does not exhibit the primary goal of forensic rhetoric, namely, securing a verdict of guilt or innocence in regard to some party from the judge or jury. In the world of the visions, in every case, the verdict has already been rendered and sentence passed by God.[70] A more nuanced analysis requires that we look instead at Revelation's use of forensic *topics* and try to ascertain how they contribute to the larger argument that John constructs. For example, the indictments leveled against "Babylon" establish the necessity of Rome's demise and the certainty of God's judgment of this domination system, events that still lie in the future for the audience. This in turn puts John and his audience in a position to discern the course that holds the promise of greater "advantage" in the present, namely, to accept Revelation 18:4 as the most reasonable, expedient course of action. The ultimate rhetorical goal of the deployment of forensic topics (here, the rehearsal of charges against Babylon) is deliberative, calling for divestment from the economic and ideological systems of Roman imperialism.[71]

---

69. Johns (2003, 157) zeroes in on the "frequent resort to forensic terminology—especially that of the μάρτυς/μαρτυρία word group"—in this narrative. See also Witherington 2003, 130.

70. Witherington clearly recognizes this, though without recognizing its implications for the rhetorical genre of Revelation. He writes that the narrative of Revelation "reassures that justice will be done by this God. . . . The audience is comforted because the divine verdict is a foregone conclusion" (Witherington 2003, 16). If there is no need to persuade anyone to render a particular verdict, we have moved beyond forensic rhetoric and are instead viewing topics that may be based in courtroom imagery or functions, but that serve a goal of some other rhetorical genre. In this case, assurance of future divine verdicts and judgments functions as a topic of advantage—in particular, what course of action will lead to "security" (the other major subhead of "advantage" in deliberation besides "the honorable," according to the *Rhetorica ad Herennium*) in light of the unveiling of these future consequences.

71. See, further, deSilva 1998a, 99–101. Anaximenes speaks of "the recital of errors and offenses" as a forensic topic (*Rhet. Alex.* 1426b.25–28).

CONCLUSION

John seeks to accomplish a variety of goals by means of the communication called Revelation. An overarching goal is to foster critical distance from Roman imperial ideology and from the economic, social, and political practices of Roman imperialism, together with witness to the ways in which those practices and that ideology stand opposed to the honor and loyalty due the One God and to the realization of that God's desires for human community. John desired to see this distance and witness realized in the situations of the seven churches in a variety of ways, including (1) continued withdrawal from every setting where idolatrous rites, however minimal, would be performed, or where a person's presence might imply support for idolatrous religion; (2) caution in regard to engaging in an unjust economic system; (3) willingness to suffer marginalization and even death rather than compromise allegiance to the One God and God's Messiah.

He seeks to accomplish this, in part, by deploying topics that can be classified under each of the three principal genres of oratory, especially deliberative and epideictic topics and strategies. These rhetorical genres well suit John's goals, which involve promoting particular courses of action and instilling commitment to particular values. Which genre is "dominant" in Revelation? This might be a question best answered not so much in regard to the text itself, as in regard to the variegated audience of the text.

Aristotle had observed that the three kinds of rhetorical genre corresponded to the three kinds of audience for whom speeches would be prepared, and from whom three kinds of responses could be solicited (Aristotle, *Rhet.* 1.3.1; so also Quintilian, *Inst.* 3.4.6). Such a diverse and mixed audience as John addresses evokes a communication with multiple rhetorical goals appropriate to more than one rhetorical genre, the dominant genre shifting in practice from audience to audience, in large measure depending on where a particular audience or hearer aligns with the values, behaviors, and commitments that John promotes. The hearers who are of the mind of Antipas or of the "few" in Sardis who monitor their entanglements with pagan society closely will encounter the bulk of Revelation as a reinforcement of the values, attitudes, and commitments they already embrace. Those who are of a mind to pursue a course of action that leads to greater acceptance by and prosperity in pagan society will hear the same material as a challenge to desist and to adopt a different course of action. The narrative visions of Revelation, which invite audience engagement both in terms of making the *synkrises* or tracing out the alternative courses of action and their consequences, also allow each particular audience—even each hearer—to do so in a way that could be construed primarily in terms of epideictic rhetoric or in terms of deliberative rhetoric, depending on that hearer's orientation.

Thus epideictic and deliberative strains are interwoven and coordinated together throughout Revelation, the former portraying the ideal, the latter steering the audience more directly to choose the path that leads to the ideal.[72] The multifaceted rhetorical situations of the seven different audiences suggest that whether Revelation will be heard primarily to effect epideictic goals (continued adherence to cherished values) or deliberative goals (a call to desist from some course of action and/or embrace another course of action) may vary from locale to locale, even from hearer to hearer.

---

72. DeSilva 1998a, 108–9; L. Snyder 2000, 409.

Chapter 4

"What Is and What Will Be Hereafter"
The Cosmos according to John

Perhaps the most powerful and distinctive facet of Revelation's rhetorical strategy derives from factors alien to the forms of discourse observed by the authors of the classical rhetorical handbooks. Those theorists analyzed specimens of argumentative discourse; Revelation is largely narrative. It is a narrative, moreover, that does far more than tell a story. It creates a map of spaces and times that lie outside the realm of "lived" experience, while at the same time "remapping" and reimagining that landscape and the stories that do fall within the realm of lived experience. Before we turn to asking the questions that rhetorical criticism *does* equip us to explore, we need to devote some time to getting the "big picture" in regard to the persuasive strategy of Revelation. This means supplementing a classical rhetorical-critical analysis with models for the interpretation of religious communications or ritual acts developed by sociologists of religion.

THE RHETORIC OF REVELATION IN SOCIOLOGICAL PERSPECTIVE

John's primary strategy involves opposing "the ordinary view of reality, as anyone might experience it in Smyrna or Laodicea" with "a quite different picture of the world as seen from the standpoint of heaven."[1] Schüssler Fiorenza speaks of John seeking "to persuade and motivate by constructing a 'symbolic universe' that invites imaginative participation." John evokes and develops powerful symbols that are full of meaning for the adherents of the religion within which those symbols have force, that "engage the hearer (reader) by eliciting reactions, emotions, convictions, and identifications."[2] This different picture of the world challenges the portrayal of reality that the dominant culture wishes to nurture and robs the latter of its status as fact or commonsense reality.[3] It provides the hearers with the opportunity to enter, through their religious imagination, into an alternative cosmology that will alter their experience of normal, lived reality in such a way that promotes adherence to the values of the Christian assembly.[4]

The definition of "apocalypse" as a literary form encountered in chapter 1 highlights the fact that works of this kind are engaged, first and foremost, in the construction of a symbolic world:

> "Apocalypse" is a genre of revelatory literature with a narrative framework, in which a revelation is mediated by an otherworldly being to a human recipient, disclosing a transcendent reality which is both temporal, insofar as it envisages eschatological salvation, and spatial, insofar as it envisages another, supernatural world.[5]

An apocalypse is a literary attempt to mediate a direct, primary encounter with the cosmic underpinnings of everyday life, a radical act of world construction and world legitimation.

As an apocalypse, Revelation creates a map of the sacred cosmos. The spatial dimensions of the cosmos are mapped out as John provides descriptions of, and narrates events surrounding, places from God's throne room all the way down to the abyss. The narratives of Revelation map out the temporal dimensions of this cosmos, both in regard to how it got to be in its present state and where it is ultimately headed. In so doing, Revelation, like most specimens of the genre, places everyday realities and experiences within a broader context that provides an interpretive lens for those realities and experiences. "The religious perspective" provided by Revelation takes the hearers or participants "beyond the realities of everyday life to wider ones which correct and complete them,"[6] changing the hearers' perspective on, and engagement with, those realities. As a religious communication, Revelation, like a religious rite or religion *tout court*, "alters,

---

1. Meeks 1986, 143–44.
2. Schüssler Fiorenza 1985, 187.
3. Royalty 1997, 600.
4. Roberts (1984, 66) describes the phenomenon thus: "The role of a cosmic world view is especially evident when one studies groups that challenge the values of the dominant society. Such challenges, as in the case of counterculture movements, nearly always involve an alternative cosmology or world view to support the alternative values" (see discussion in deSilva 1993, 54; 1991, 202–6).
5. J. Collins 1979, 9.
6. Geertz 1973, 112.

often radically, the whole landscape presented to common sense, alters it in such a way that the moods and motivations induced by religious practice seem themselves supremely practical, the only sensible ones to adopt given the way things 'really' are."[7] To put this another way, Revelation does not so much seek to *be* interpreted, as to *interpret*.[8]

Clifford Geertz's choice of the word "landscape" is particularly interesting here, given that apocalypses often feature extensive descriptions of a landscape quite different from, and often much larger than, the landscape seen with the eye. It is vitally important that, within this landscape, the hearer also encounters elements of his or her "lived" landscape, even though these might now look quite different. In stretching out the canvas of the larger landscape of the group's symbolic universe, Revelation also allows the hearers to take account of competing symbolic universes in a way that neutralizes their power to threaten the Christian group's world construction. The gods of the Greeks and Romans are but faces of the dragon; the imperial ideology and its cosmic projections are the activity of beasts and a whore, all orchestrated by the dragon, the doomed enemy of God's order. All claims made on behalf of traditional Greco-Roman religion (within its own symbolic universe) or on behalf of Roman imperialism are thus swept aside—or better still, *exposed*. It enables the hearer to gain a "transcendent perspective"[9] that resolves the conflict between the group's beliefs and the values or claims promoted by adherents of the dominant culture or other groups.

Exegesis of Revelation has always tended to focus on the interpretation of its symbols, whether as "steno-symbols," by means of which a plague stands for some event in history and the beast stands for some figure in contemporary history; or as "tensive-dynamic" symbols, whose evocative power is more in focus.[10] The definition of religion and the accompanying essay offered by Clifford Geertz, which concerns itself primarily with the interpretation of systems of symbols, helps to focus the attention of the exegete of Revelation analyzing these symbols. According to Geertz

> a religion is: (1) a system of symbols which acts to (2) establish powerful, pervasive, and long-lasting moods and motivations in men [and women] by (3) formulating conceptions of a general order of existence and (4) clothing

---

7. Geertz 1973, 122.
8. So John Collins (1979, 7), who observes that an apocalypse "is intended to interpret present earthly circumstances in light of the supernatural world and of the future, and to influence both the understanding and the behavior of the audience by means of divine authority." See also deSilva 1999b, 124: "One of the primary vehicles of an apocalypse's persuasive power is its ability to set everyday realities within a broader context that provides an interpretive lens for those experiences. The disclosure of activity in other realms as well as the revelation of primordial and future history provides the context that lends meaning to present experience, making a threatened world-construction viable once more."
9. M. V. Lee 1998, 173.
10. Schüssler Fiorenza 1985, 183.

these conceptions with such an aura of factuality that (5) the moods and motivations seem uniquely realistic.[11]

John's techniques of legitimation (the means by which John clothes "these conceptions with . . . an aura of factuality" that impresses them upon the hearers as "uniquely realistic") will occupy us in the following two chapters as we examine John's appeals to (rhetorical) *ethos*. Examinations of appeals to *pathos* in Revelation will analyze more completely the moods generated by John's discourse. The present chapter concerns itself more with the first and third clauses of Geertz's definition: John's evocations of particular configurations of symbols and formulation of the "general order of existence," and the ways in which these evocations and formulations impact the congregations' experience of, evaluation of, and orientation toward their everyday situations.

Geertz's definition of a *religion* is immediately applicable to any particular instance of "religious communication," as Geertz himself shows when he uses his definition to analyze a particular religious rite in one or another tribal society, thus applicable to a particular event of religious expression within the larger religion. A religious communication (or ritual) evokes selected symbols from the religion's larger symbolic repertoire for the ongoing purposes of world construction and world legitimation, and sometimes for quite particular purposes relating to these larger group processes. This is often a strategic selection and evocation of symbols, seeking to reassert the interpretive power of a sacred order over the particular experiences of author/performer and audience, so as to reaffirm the viability of the group's distinctive worldview and ethos, or to extend the same to cover new, challenging situations.

These theoretical models invite us to explore Revelation's primary rhetorical strategy in a manner that is particularly appropriate to its self-presentation as an "apocalypse," as a symbolic religious communication that engages directly in the construction and maintenance of one worldview over against competing worldviews and the "moods and motivations" that those worldviews arouse and sustain. To what does Revelation draw attention, both within and beyond "lived" experience, as it unfolds its map of, and its metastory for, the cosmos? What mental/imaginative map of the cosmos, its inhabitants, their interrelationships, their relative authority, and so forth, does John create through the many discrete moments of "attention" he demands/invites? How does Revelation's map interact selectively and interpretively with other symbolic maps available to people, for example, in downtown Ephesus? How does John's map, and especially its reenvisioning of facets of lived experience, interpret otherwise visible, physical, and social realities? What effects does John's evocation of particular facets of this symbolic universe have upon the affections, motivations, and alignments of the hearers in the midst of their lived experience? Answering these questions will

11. Geertz 1975, 90.

allow us to see the rhetorical payoff for John of addressing an apocalypse, and not merely a sermon, to the seven congregations.

"CONCEPTIONS OF A GENERAL ORDER OF EXISTENCE"

The Cosmic Order

Leaving aside the opening vision of the glorified Christ, the major "visionary" portion of the book falls between Revelation 4:1 and 22:5. The first of these visions extends the conceptual map of the hearers outward into the realm beyond the visible heavens, figuratively accessed through a door that must crack open in the dome of the sky before mortals can observe the activity and personnel in that realm (4:2). God sits enthroned in the midst of concentric circles of heavenly beings. Four "living creatures" resembling the cherubim, seraphim, or other angelic attendants in earlier throne visions (4:6–8; cf. Isa. 6:2–3; Ezek. 1:5–11) move about the throne in the tightest orbit. Seven spirits, best understood as the seven high-ranking archangels or angels of the Presence, stand around the throne in attendance (Rev. 4:5b).[12] Twenty-four elders sit upon their thrones (4:4), arranged around and facing the throne of God. The identity of these spirit beings is elusive, but if they represent a survival of the "star gods," then "we see one manifestation of a theme that will be found throughout Revelation: the humbling of those to whom undue honor has been ascribed. The twenty-four star gods are no longer divinities in their own right, but elders in the heavenly court, totally subservient to God."[13] Around these, in ever-widening circles, move myriad hosts of angels (5:11). All of these superhuman creatures are focused on the enthroned One and the Lamb, offering continual worship and adoration. Finally, at the furthest reaches of this map, John places "every creature in heaven and on earth and under the earth and in the sea" (5:13), united in directing praise and adoration toward the center of the cosmos, God and the Lamb.

John's opening vision depicts an all-encompassing cosmic map. The most detailed attention is focused on the activity around God's throne. But John's

---

12. John speaks of "the seven angels who stand in the presence of God" in 8:2 in a manner that assumes prior acquaintance on the part of the hearers (the use of the definite article here points to them as a previously identified group). The only possible antecedent within Revelation would be the seven "spirits" of 4:5. "Angels" and "spirits" are used interchangeably in other texts (see the citation of Ps. 104:4 in Heb. 1:7, which explicitly equates the two). The tradition of seven angels/spirits standing in God's presence is attested also in Tob. 12:15 as well as several Greek manuscripts of *1 En.* 20:7; a special group of angels thus standing (though not numbered as "seven") is also referred to in Luke 1:19 and *T. Levi* 3:4–5, the latter being notably another throne vision. See Aune 1997, 34–35. This is a much more culturally proximate background for understanding the seven spirits than the alleged "sevenfold" Spirit of Isa. 11:2–3 ("seven" or "sevenfold" appears in neither the Hebrew nor the LXX texts), often adduced to provide a more Trinitarian focus in the interpretation of Rev. 1:4, and hence 4:5 as well.

13. Morton 2001, 97.

readers find themselves located in the picture as well, among the creatures "on earth" (5:13). John communicates this vision as a snapshot *of* reality, but that is not the whole story. As a coordinated collection of religious symbols, the vision is both a "model *of*" and a "model *for*" cosmic reality.[14] Religious symbols "both express the world's climate and shape it," at one time claiming to express "how reality is" and calling that very reality into being.[15] The worship scenes of Revelation 4 and 5 articulate a model *of* a well-ordered cosmos in which all created beings in every region of the map turn toward this one center—the throne of God and of the Lamb—to offer their grateful adoration. In so doing, they also articulate a model *for* the orientation of the congregations in the seven churches, whose setting presents them with several options for where to turn their attention and offer grateful adoration.

Out of Order

A tension exists within John's portrait of perfect order. On the one hand, we see "every creature in heaven and on earth and under the earth" joining in the circles of adoration around God and the Lamb, affirming the heavenly acclamations given the Lamb in 5:9–10. On the other hand, this very acclamation celebrates a work of the Lamb that involves partitioning humanity into two groups: those whom the Lamb has ransomed "out from [ἐκ] every tribe and language and people and nation" and those who have not been ransomed out from those groups.[16] That there really is an unredeemed group becomes clearer as the visions devolve.

A series of horrifying events culminates in a vision of human beings terrified at the prospect of encountering God and the Lamb, whose anger at these human beings manifests itself in dramatic disturbances of the natural cosmic order (6:12–14). The juxtaposition of a vision of the cosmos united in festal panegyrics to God and the Lamb with a vision of such a fateful and wrathful encounter between Deity and human beings forces the question: What went wrong? The tension is heightened as only a portion of humanity is sealed as God's own, falling in line with the God- and Lamb-centered focus and adoration, joining in the liturgies of the angels, elders, and celestial living creatures (7:9–12).

The answer comes swiftly. After another series of punitive judgments in chapters 8 and 9, the "problem people" are at last identified:

> The rest of humankind, who were not killed by these plagues, neither repented of the works of their hands, so as not to worship the demons and the idols of gold and silver and bronze and stone and wood, which can neither see nor hear nor walk, nor repented of their murders or their sorceries or their fornication or their thefts. (9:20–21)

---

14. Geertz 1973, 94.
15. Geertz 1973, 95.
16. The preposition ἐκ governs nouns in the, here, partitive genitive case.

John effects a coup of apocalyptic proportions. The vast majority of people living around the Mediterranean basin worshiped multiple Gods and Goddesses, almost always incorporating visible representations of their deities into their worship sites and rituals. In the city of Ephesus, for example, most residents would have oriented themselves in worship around several different cult centers in the city, joining together in major festivals of the imperial cult and traditional cults. All this cultic activity occurred within the context of a well-articulated ideology concerning the location of the center of power in the Mediterranean (Rome and her emperors) and the various means by which the region enjoyed the beneficence of the gods worshiped. Jews and Christians constituted deviant minorities, turning away from such cultic centers to perform their own rites to their tribal God in the conceptual margins of the city.

In John's vision, however, the worshipers of idols are now the deviant minority. The hosts of heaven, together with "every creature in heaven and on earth and below the earth," recognize the true center of the cosmos, and thus where to direct adoration properly. Contrary to the "public knowledge" about piety and the cosmic order, the worship of the Greco-Roman divinities does not bring one in line with the cosmic order in John's vision. These figures are identified with "demons" (cf. 1 Cor. 10:19–20), the associates of the archenemy of God and of the cosmic order (see Rev. 13:4). Idols become chaotic gravity wells, drawing human beings away from the true center and into orbit around false centers in the extreme margins of the cosmic order. Those who worship these idols, who are thus "out of order," become sources of disorder themselves, anomic forces working murder, sorcery, fornication, and theft. "Public knowledge" would attribute such chaotic acts to Christians, who were "maligned as evildoers" (1 Pet. 2:12). Pliny the Younger bears witness to this prejudice as he expresses his surprise that his "examination" of two deaconesses failed to uncover the sorts of crimes he had been led to expect from Christians (cannibalism, orgiastic gatherings, and so forth). John has enveloped and subverted the dominant culture's cosmic map and definition of "deviance," turning the tables on the majority and neutralizing the pull toward joining them in any form of idolatry.[17]

The strategy of Revelation 4–5, as this sets up and leads to 9:20–21, resembles a similar strategy employed in the much earlier apocalypse, *1 Enoch*. In *1 Enoch* 1–5, the author calls the hearers to consider a picture of cosmic order, focusing on the movements of the stars, the cycle of seasons, the life cycle of trees and plants, the movements of rivers into the sea, all exhibiting unchanging obedience to God's decree: "All his works serve him and do not change, but as God has decreed, so everything is done" (5:2). This contrasts with the behavior of most human beings,

---

17. Although we have concerned ourselves mostly with *spaces*, it is also significant that John does not divide *time* into sacred and profane seasons, such as both pagans and Jews did. The elders and the four living creatures offer worship "day and night without ceasing" (4:8). The company of redeemed humanity worship God "day and night within God's temple" (7:15). John claims all time as sacred, leaving no "profane" time in which to worship some center other than God and the Lamb, to join safely and innocently with the Greco-Roman society in offering worship to the false centers.

the vision of order highlighting what is "out of order" within God's cosmos. Both apocalypses open by presenting striking pictures of *incongruence* between the orderly worship of God (in Revelation) or obedience to the decrees of God (in *1 Enoch*), and the world of human behavior experienced by the seer and his audience (at least, the "faithful" among them). These apocalyptists point out this essential incongruence in order to move the audience to look critically upon such behaviors, distance themselves from the same, and return to or confirm themselves in that "approved way of life" that is congruent with the cosmic picture painted by the religious tradition to which they have joined themselves.

God Breaks In

The elements of a "symbolic universe" evoked in Revelation have to do not only with space, but also with time. While John establishes the cosmic center in chapters 4–5 and displays various groups around it (including the faithful disciples) or out of alignment with it (the idolaters), the dramatic movement of the narrative focuses on how this "center" breaks into and overruns—even overwrites—the realities around the seven congregations. John narrates a future in which everything that is "out of order" is set *back* in order vis-à-vis the centrality of God and the Lamb and their just requirements. The temporal dimension of Revelation expresses the conviction that, and narrates the process by which, the Christian counterculture's values and worldview will ultimately be vindicated.[18]

John locates the starting point for this action in events surrounding the throne of God, as the Lamb takes center stage as one possessing a unique dignity among all the beings in heaven, on earth, and under the earth (5:3). The Lamb alone is deemed worthy to open a certain sealed scroll in God's hand, a scroll that sets in motion the eschatological judgments that cycle down throughout the book, giving it its distinctive plot outline of series of seven seals, trumpets, and finally bowls. Since opening that scroll brings this age and all that belongs to it to an end, the Lamb holds ultimate authority over this age. One could get the impression that John sees the Lamb here having just completed his course on earth, returning as the slaughtered-but-conquering Messiah to take the scroll in hand. If this is the case, the sequence of events that mark God's breaking in upon those pockets of nonalignment with the cosmic order began some fifty years before Domitian's accession. The wheels are already in motion as John writes. The orderly, almost stately processions of the angels unleashing the series of plagues—the dignity of this "liturgy" or court protocol—amplifies the hearers' sense of God's control over the cosmos and its fate (8:1–6; 15:5–8).

---

18. The narrative dimensions of John's cosmos construction close "the gap between things as they are and as they ought to be if our conceptions of right and wrong make sense, the gap between what we deem various individuals deserve and what we see that they get" (Geertz 1973, 106). John displays how God's forthcoming visitations of plagues, judgments, and postmortem or posthistorical rewards and punishments will confirm the traditional Christian "conceptions of right and wrong," thus promoting continued commitment in the present time of cognitive dissonance.

The earth is a passive sphere, acted upon as the Lamb opens the seals (6:1–8) or as angels release the plagues prepared by God as part of God's resolution of the disorder in God's cosmos (7:1–3; 8:7–9:19; etc.). Many powerful, invisible beings stand on God's "side," assisting God's judgment, possibly acting as the congregations' intermediaries or representatives (taking the seven angels addressed in the seven oracles in the most natural, if bizarre, sense). The deviant portion of humanity steps onto the scene completely helpless, longing to be buried under landslides so they do not need to face their heavenly Antagonist (6:12–17). Even the throne of the beast (16:10–11), great Babylon itself (16:17–21; 18:21–24), and the hordes gathered against the Lamb (19:17–21; 20:7–10) cannot begin to withstand God's fury unleashed against them. These sinister figures might exercise temporary power over God's faithful ones (2:10; 11:7–8; 12:17; 13:7, 15–17), but they are helpless before the disciples' great Ally, who moves inexorably closer to vindicate the saints. The beast and his allies might act as Satan's tools, but even they are also ultimately God's puppets, executing God's judgment upon Babylon (17:17).

The picture of cosmic order and worship in chapters 4–5 stands in tension with the realities of Greco-Roman civic life, where many of God's creatures gather around false centers and direct their worship away from the One God. The narration of the course of divine judgment shows the means by which that tension will be resolved and "order" definitively and universally reasserted. In this way, John's countercosmos clearly articulates a view of what allegiances will be ultimately advantageous and in what direction "conformity" ought to proceed among the churches, namely, toward the unequivocal worship of the One God and God's Messiah, whose forces are already mobilizing to overtake the powers of this world, enforce their reign, and stamp out *all* resistance inside and outside of the congregations.

Christ as Symbol

Jesus, the focal point of early Christian faith, appears in Revelation in a variety of symbolic guises. Prominent is the symbol of the "Lamb," slaughtered-but-standing, known at the same time by the symbolic name "Lion from the tribe of Judah" (5:5–6). Key symbols perform an important function for the groups who develop and hold on to them. Clifford Geertz observes how "religious symbols, dramatized in rituals or related in myths, are felt somehow to sum up, for those for whom they are resonant, what is known about the way the world is, the quality of the emotional life it supports, and the way one ought to behave while in it. Sacred symbols thus relate an ontology and a cosmology to an aesthetics and a morality."[19]

The symbol of the Lion who conquers as a slain Lamb relates "cosmology" to "a morality" in a very important way in Revelation. The surprising "morphing" of the messianic Lion into the Passover Lamb who "purchases people for God with his blood" (5:9) creates a new symbol, "a symbol of conquest by sacrificial

---

19. Geertz 1973, 127.

death."[20] Christ is not only seen in Revelation as a Lamb, however. He appears first as a resplendent, recognizably human figure (1:12–16), described in language recalling—and combining—the Danielic "Ancient of Days" and "Son of Man," the inheritor of the kingdoms of the world (Dan. 7:9–14), as indeed Christ is destined to be (Rev. 11:18). The postmortem, postresurrection Jesus is notably more glorious, powerful, and impressive than the earthly Jesus, which is surely significant in a text promoting the sacrifice of this life in order to attain the life beyond death. He becomes a potent symbol both of life beyond death, and of the way to attain such life.

This symbol of the Lamb conquering through obedience unto death becomes a normative pattern for imitation (2:8, 10b; 3:21). The slain-but-standing Lamb acts as symbol and as historical precedent that not death but rather integrity with respect to God's commandments is of ultimate concern.[21] The story of the two witnesses—a story itself highly symbolic—further enacts Christ's pattern, making that pattern and the ethic it communicates seem more normative, "typical," and reliable. Showing Christ's witnesses enjoying the same postmortem vivification and vindication that Christ enjoyed reinforces the assurance that the faithful will indeed go where Christ has gone. The triumph of the holy ones over the dragon briefly, yet poignantly, reinscribes this symbol of conquering through faithful death (12:11).

Christ as "symbol" provides an important and powerful resource by which John can effectively address a major religious problem: suffering. Geertz defines this problem as, "paradoxically, not how to avoid suffering but how to suffer, how to make of physical pain, personal loss, worldly defeat, or the helpless contemplation of others' agony something bearable, supportable—something, as we say, sufferable."[22] Jesus' story, the story of the Lion who conquers as a Lamb, provides a lens that makes the suffering of an Antipas—or of the congregation in Smyrna, or that John envisions following upon the faithful witness to which he calls all the churches—"sufferable," even something "honorable" and "advantageous," at which point the analysis of symbols arrives squarely within the province of rhetorical criticism.

ROMAN IMPERIALISM: THE UNTOLD STORY

Although it is to some extent true that "Revelation provides the vision of an alternative world in order to motivate the audience,"[23] Revelation at the same

---

20. Bauckham 1993a, 183. I follow Bauckham's suggestion that the Lamb "suggest[s] primarily the passover lamb, for throughout the Apocalypse, and in a passage as close as 5:10, John represents the victory of the Lamb as a new Exodus, the victory which delivers the new Israel" (1993a, 184), over against the view that John presents the Lamb merely as "slaughtered," not "sacrificed" (Johns 2003).
21. A similar ethic is promoted throughout 2 Macc. 7 and 4 Macc. 5–18.
22. Geertz 1973, 104.
23. Schüssler Fiorenza 1991, 129.

time opens up an alternative vision of *the* world, the *same* world that the hearers inhabit day by day, illumining "the true character of the challenges the readers have to face" as well as the true character of the institutions and forces among which the believers live.[24] Revelation's power lies in its ability to interpret "what is" in such a way that radical witness, faithfulness to the One God, and abstinence from idolatry now constitute the course of action much to be preferred as advantageous and honorable.

A primary challenge within that "everyday world" is the availability, indeed the forceful presence, of alternative, mutually exclusive (or at least, mutually challenging) world constructions and systems of symbols existing side by side. The availability and visibility of witnesses to one world construction constitute a persistent threat to the "givenness" or simple "factuality" of any number of other world constructions. The threat is greatest to the viability of the world constructions that are least well supported socially—that is, the world constructions of minority cultures living in Asia Minor. Nevertheless, even representatives of the dominant, majority culture find it necessary from time to time to come to terms with the deviant views of minority groups living in their midst.

As a consequence, we find significant attention being given to the task of "world legitimation," shoring up the inviolability of one's own worldview, often by delegitimating competing worldviews. Many Greco-Roman authors writing about Judaism, for example, do not show a genuine interest in understanding it, but rather in neutralizing it as an inferior, aberrant understanding of the divine and the demands of piety, and thus not something that need seriously challenge the dominant culture's worldview and ethos. Similarly, Jews living outside Israel, surrounded by alternative worldviews, religious practices, and patterns of behaviors, created a significant body of literature to delegitimate Gentile religious and social practice.[25] John devotes considerable attention in Revelation to reinterpreting the central symbols of the dominant cultural worldview, notably its pantheon, emperor cult, and imperial propaganda. John finds a "place" for them within the Christian countercosmos that neutralizes their power to challenge the minority cultural worldview, even transforming them into symbols that support commitment to the Christian worldview and its ethos. He uses topics like "deception," "intoxication," or the activity of "Satan" to explain how so many people could have bought into the dominant cultural worldview and practice the behaviors it supports. As John creates "a symbolic universe which transforms and re-presents social *realia* in terms of its own order,"[26] he finds a sufficiently long lever to move the world in which he and his congregations move, relate, and think—or at least, to displace the centers of the public cosmos in favor of the Christian cosmos.

---

24. So also Frey 2006, 236; Johns 2003, 171.
25. The Letter of Jeremiah, Wis. 13–15, and 4 Maccabees are all stunning examples.
26. L. Thompson 1990, 147.

The Roman Emperor in John's Cosmos

Revelation offers a de-imperialization of the local Christians' worldview, an antidote for those still staggering under the influence of the worldview promoted and reinforced by the public discourse. He tells a story about the emperors' rise and rule, and about Rome's character and destiny, very different from the one known through public inscriptions, poetry and panegyric, coins and statuaries, and liturgies. He is also *very* thorough, taking multiple aspects of "official" Roman imperial ideology into account as he fashions his alternative story.

"Providence" was, as we saw in chapter 2, an important topic within imperial ideology, nurturing the conviction that divine destiny and beneficence were manifested in the rule of Rome and the rise of the *Augusti*. John transforms this positive etiology, giving a very different view of the supernatural forces at work behind, and manifested in, the human political sphere. Not a benign Providence, but Satan, the enemy of the divine order and the agent of chaos, stands behind the rise of the *Augusti* (Rev. 12:9; 13:2, 4). The description of the mythic conflict between the Dragon, or Satan, and the hosts of heaven in chapter 12 provides the Jewish-Christian frame for transforming the public discourse about the "divine" power at work in Roman rule.[27]

This prologue opens with a retelling of the famous myth of the birth of a divine child to a mother and the threat posed by a chaos monster.[28] Egyptian myth recounts the story of Seth's (or the monster Typhon's) assaults upon Isis and Osiris, and the eventual victory of Isis, helped by her son, Horus, who thereby establishes his rule. According to a more contemporary Greek form of this myth, the serpentine monster Python pursues Leto until she gives birth to divine twins, Apollo and Artemis. Apollo, quickly attaining maturity, turns the tables on Python, first wounding and finally slaying the monster at Delphi. The imperial house was frequently aligned with Apollo and thus would be seen represented in the "hero" of this myth.[29] In John's retelling, however, the imperial house is now aligned with the character who plays the role of Python or Typhon: Satan, the dragon-snake who is the patron and *Doppelgänger* of the Roman principate. Drawing from the domestic art of Rome and Roman cities throughout the empire, David L. Balch documents the popularity of the theme of the pregnant woman/goddess whose child would oppose a chaos monster.[30]

---

27. See also Witherington 2003, 166.
28. The classic study of these myths and their import for Revelation remains A. Collins 1976, 57–100. See also Aune 1998a, 667–76; van Henten 2006.
29. See the texts from Virgil and Dio Cassius collected by van Henten (2006, 192). John uses symbolism relevant to Apollo in other subversive ways throughout Revelation. The name of the angel of the abyss is given not only in Hebrew but also in Greek. This Greek name, *Apollyōn*, may involve "derogatory wordplay" on the Greek god Apollo (Schüssler Fiorenza 1991, 71). Moreover, the locust was associated with Apollo as a symbol for the god (Witherington 2003, 154, citing Aeschylus, *Agamemnon* 1080–1086), making the pun more deliciously subversive: John finds a place for Apollo in his cosmos as the infernal leader of these demonic locusts. Domitian's association with Apollo would, in John's portrait, link him with the leader of the demonic hordes (Schüssler Fiorenza 1991, 72).
30. Balch 2006.

As John's hearers encountered representations of this story in art, they would begin to view it quite subversively as a reminder of Christ's ascendancy and the monstrous power behind Roman rule.

As in its Greek and Egyptian counterparts, the story does not play out well for the chaos monster in Revelation. Although able to rally a third of the angels to his cause, Satan is expelled from heaven and cast down to the earth, where—unable to harm the woman or her firstborn child—he will continue to vent his spleen against the "rest of her offspring" (12:17). A hymnic interlude (12:10–12) interprets the dragon's ongoing fury, however, as a sign that the "salvation and the power and the kingdom of our God and the authority of his Messiah" have triumphed. Satan's manifestation in the rise and campaigns of the two beasts is itself a sign of defeat, a result of God's triumph over Satan in the celestial realm. The very fierceness of the campaign is a measure of his fleeting power, the death throes of the enemy of God: "for he knows that he has but a short time" (12:12).

Even here John is ringing changes on public discourse about Providence manifested in imperial rule. The Priene Inscription, in which the *Koinon Asias*, the provincial assembly of Asia Minor, instituted a new calender makes a bold affirmation about the nature of the Augustan age. The assembly resolved to begin the year with Augustus's birthday to formalize their conviction that they lived at the beginning of a new epoch. Virgil spoke of the rise of the principate as the long-awaited return of the golden age, invoking a Roman view of time and eschatology (*Eclogae* 4.1–10). According to this view, human civilization progresses through a series of deteriorating stages, symbolized by ages named after progressively inferior (and harder!) metals, until in the fullness of time the golden age returns.[31] John, however, places the rule of the *Augusti* not at the beginning of a new epoch, but at the end of the old, degenerate epoch, the epoch of Satan's rebellion against God, manifesting the "short time" left to the old dragon.

The emperors step onto the landscape of Revelation as a multiheaded beast, an unholy hybrid of the four beasts of Daniel 7.[32] The figure resembles other enemies of humanity known from extrabiblical myth (e.g., the Hydra, Typhon, and the like). Characterizing this beast as a blasphemous affront to God (Rev. 13:1, 5–6), John radically inverts the public discourse about the Roman emperor, whose chief quality was *pietas*, or proper reverence toward the gods and ancient Roman values. In John's cosmos, however, the emperors are agents of chaos and impiety. John acknowledges the titles ascribed to the emperors, like *divi filius* (son

---

31. Stephen O'Leary (1994, 46) may be mistaken when he writes that "no symbol system has yet been discovered that posits a progression from an Edenic golden age to a period of catastrophic evils while locating humanity closer to the point of origin than to the point of ending." The Priene Inscription, or Virgil's *Aeneid*, or some such piece of Augustan-era propaganda might provide the exception. The golden age had returned—but there was no sense that it would remain forever, no reason to revoke the cyclic model of decline from gold down through iron age. The audience is thus indeed closer to an Edenic age as a (new) starting point than to the period of its (next) decline.

32. References to Daniel across the NT suggest that early Christians could be presumed to be acquainted with its contents (see Matt. 11:3; 24:15, 30; 26:64; Mark 13:14, 26; 14:62; Luke 21:27; Heb. 11:34).

of the deified [predecessor]), *pontifex maximus* (chief priest [of Roman religion]), and *Augustus* (pious/revered one), but identifies them as "names of blasphemy" (13:1) since they all encode claims that locate the emperor center stage in those disorderly margins of John's cosmos where people gather around false gods.

John does not suppress the fact of widespread worship of the emperors. Far from it, he highlights and interprets this organ of imperial ideology (13:4, 8). Participation in the worship of the beast involves people in the worship of God's cosmic enemy (13:4), revealing such people to be among those whose names "are not written in the Book of Life of the Lamb slain from the founding of the cosmos" (13:8). John draws attention to this connection between beast-worship and exclusion from the Lamb's book with an emphatic formula: "If anyone has ears, let that one hear" (13:9).[33] A second beast emerges to organize religious cult for the first beast, making the worship of the beast prerequisite to continued economic and physical well-being. Here John continues to reverse public discourse concerning the imperial cult,[34] asserting that its power is essentially "manufactured charisma," not a manifestation of truly divine power at work.[35] John depicts it as an imposition upon the local populations, denying that it could be an authentic and free expression of gratitude for gifts worthy of the gods. By presenting cult as a practical necessity, he undermines the pretension that "grace" undergirds this institution.

John uses Nero as a kind of symbol to characterize the principate. While the "mortal wound" affects the beast as a whole and not merely one of its heads (13:3, 12, 14), the sword blow to one of its heads cannot help but recall Nero's suicide. The idea that a future "head" will come, in fact, from one of those that have fallen, is perhaps the clearest echo of the Nero-redux legend in the book (17:11). But Nero is not merely one aberrant head among others: he also gives the beast its character. The number of the beast, 666, is still best resolved as a Hebrew gematria concealing the name Nero Caesar; it is, serendipitously, also the sum of the Hebrew letters transliterating θηρίον, "beast."[36] John invites the hearers to see in Nero the true character of the principate, bare, exposed in all its ugliness.

Rewriting the Myth of Peace

A prominent element of Roman imperial ideology was the claim that the rise of the principate had brought "peace" to the *orbis terrarum*. "Peace" contributed

---

33. The formula normally calls hearers to pay attention to preceding, not subsequent, material, as in the Synoptic use of this formula (see Matt. 11:15; 13:9, 43; etc.) and in the use of the formula as the final or penultimate element in each of the seven oracles (Rev. 2:7, 11, 17, 29; 3:6, 13, 22).
34. See Price 1984 on the incidence and significance of the imperial cult in Asia Minor, and deSilva 1991 for a more detailed examination of the public discourse and John's reversal of that discourse in Rev. 13 and 14.
35. Glassman 1986, 118.
36. Witherington 2003, 177. Gematria refers to the numerical game of adding up the sum of the letters in a name (letters in Greek, Hebrew, and Latin also served as the numerals in those languages) and then referring to the person by that number.

functional legitimation to imperial rule and, in particular, the shift from traditional Republican government. In his portrait of the rule of Rome, however, John exposes Pax Romana and Pax Augusti to be bald-faced lies.[37] According to Schüssler Fiorenza, the first four seals are not future events but characterizations of Roman rule in the interim between Christ's ascension and John's time, highlighting Rome's military expansionist policies, the bloodshed of civil wars within Roman boundaries, the economic policies that render staples unaffordable, and the disease and death that follow "as bitter consequences of imperialistic war, civil strife, and epidemics of hunger. In sum, the first four riders function to articulate symbolically a sociopolitical critique of imperial rule."[38]

The pax Romana is, in fact, a time of "making war with the saints" (13:7) and "making war" with the witnesses of Jesus, conquering and killing them (11:7). With the opening of the fifth seal, John identifies the motivation for the judgments that are coming. The souls of Christian martyrs cry out for justice, and later two angels will praise the justice of God for bringing judgment on the earth and on "Babylon" as punishment for the shedding of the blood of saints and prophets (16:5–7; 18:24). Though it is unlikely that Revelation was written during a period of open persecution, the memory of the Christian holocaust in Rome as well as more local and individual actions against Christians such as Antipas (2:13) has not dissipated in John's mind. Roman rule is the rule of violence, spilling not only the blood of holy ones and the witnesses of Jesus (17:6), but also of "all those who had been slain upon the earth" (18:23b–24). It is a time in which those destined for slaughter by the sword and for captivity meet their destiny (13:10).

Moreover, the guardians of the "Roman peace" are the pawns of Satan, deployed as part of a last-ditch effort within a cosmic revolt that continues to play itself out as Revelation nears its climax. The acclamation of the beast in 13:4, "And who is able to make war against him?" is ironic insofar as the beast's sponsor, Satan, lost his war against Michael and God's armies. The real answer to this rhetorical question is quite different from the answer implied by the beast's followers and to be finally enacted in 19:20 as the beast is unceremoniously plucked up and deposited in the lake of fire. Rome's impressive appearance of power, which for the majority seems to assure peace through deterrence of aggression against Rome, is a sham when set against the power of God and God's Messiah.

By portraying a cosmos at war, John evokes an "attitude of resistance" to the forces that he places in the enemy's camp.[39] The *Augusti* and their minions wage war against the Christians as part of Satan's campaign against God's kingdom, and the disciples are called to "conquer," to engage this conflict victoriously, by

---

37. John was not alone questioning the integrity of the "Roman peace." Almost a half century earlier, Paul regarded the propaganda about "peace and security" (*pax et securitas*) to be delusional (see 1 Thess. 5:3).
38. Schüssler Fiorenza 1991, 63.
39. Knight 2001, 479.

not yielding to the pressures to purchase security at the cost of justice and one's very soul.[40]

Re-dressing *Roma Aeterna*

John tells a very different story about the mission and the destiny of *Roma Aeterna* from the one heard in Virgil's *Aeneid* or Plutarch's *On the Fortune of Rome*. First, John presents the goddess *Roma* in very different dress. No longer wearing the modest toga of the goddess worshiped in the temple of Rome and the *Augusti*, nor even the ascetic military garb in which she appears on the reverse of the famous *Dea Roma* coin,[41] she is dressed in her evening wear, sporting the lingerie of a self-employed courtesan and plying her trade with the utmost success. Her impact on the civilized world is entirely negative. Her curriculum vitae includes plundering the wealth of the provinces to satisfy her taste for luxury, murdering countless holy ones and witnesses to Jesus and others who have dissented against or impeded her practices, and seducing the leaders of the inhabited world into forming unholy alliances to promote their collective self-indulgent practices. As the "mother of whores," she makes the cities and cultures she encounters like herself. There is nothing here of Roma as the chosen vessel by means of which Providence renews a golden age; rather, her cup is full of abominations and the unclean things of Rome's fornication. If her mission is not what the dominant culture's mythos maintains, neither is her destiny. A dreadful irony awaits *Roma Aeterna*, "Eternal Rome," a city that will go up in flames and be laid desolate rather than live up to its name.

John has fully incorporated the public discourse about Rome into an alternative mythos about Rome seen from within the Jewish-Christian worldview. This worldview knows of a God who apportions to all kingdoms their allotted times and seasons, and history has never known a kingdom that has failed to fall from its height into obscurity and subjugation to other kingdoms. This lesson emerges explicitly and repeatedly in the court tales of the book of Daniel (see esp. 2:20–21, 36–45; 4:17, 25–27, 32; 5:18–28), a resource upon which John draws heavily throughout Revelation. God intervenes to bring low the rulers or empires that forget and affront God's sovereign oversight. Rome's claims about its divinity and destiny offer textbook affronts in this regard, such that John's story of what *must* follow becomes more than plausible within the Christian worldview. Moreover, John has drawn Rome fully into the biblical story, both the story of the Exodus and the story of God's judgment of historic Babylon and other Gentile seats of empire, a story told in the prophetic literature that is such an important resource for John (see esp. Jer. 51; Ezek. 26–27).

---

40. See Johns 2003, 182: "The promise of blessing in the Apocalypse on those who 'conquer' assumes, of course, a conflict. . . . This conflict is part of the revelation, part of the rhetorical strategy of the author, not necessarily an obvious component of the social situation of the seven churches."

41. See Aune 1998b, 920–22, and the catalog information he gives on p. 920.

John's countervision is so effective because it does not merely present an alternative worldview, but also brings major facets of the dominant cultural landscape and ideology into that worldview, subduing them with the powerful stories at the heart of Jewish subcultural discourse or with the core values of that discourse such as monolatry, which makes the cult of the emperors and of Rome appear deviant, subversive, even satanic. John's interpretation gains greater power and attractiveness because it views all of reality within a single frame of reference, resolving that nagging feeling that one can't really know which frame of reference is real or true. It is an integrated view of the world, allowing the audience to see everything in the light of God and the Lamb.

THE OVERRIDING CRISIS ON THE HORIZON

In the preceding chapter, we identified several crises facing the congregations and eliciting John's response: rival prophets eroding the distinctive identity and witness of the group; escalating tension with the synagogue; maintaining witness in the face of hostility; and sustaining the spiritual health of particular congregations. Beyond these issues, many disciples would have been concerned with more mundane challenges, such as providing for one's family, negotiating the world of business, or dealing with doubt concerning one's allegiance to this group. By writing an apocalypse, John can effectively set all of these more immediate crises against the backdrop of a greater, overarching crisis that looms on the horizon. John is thus able to motivate particular responses to the more immediate crises as the means by which to prepare for, and successfully meet, this greater crisis in which the stakes are greatly elevated. The escalation of tension with the host society that John foresees (e.g., in Rev. 6:11b; 7:14b; 13:7, 15–17) is not this crisis.[42] Rather, that escalation of tension would result as Christians kept in view the crisis that John does elevate and aligned themselves to survive *that* crisis. The critical challenge that must be given attention before all else is the forthcoming visitation of God and God's Messiah.

John foregrounds this in the opening of his discourse, the part that functions as an exordium to the whole, the aim of which was to "make clear what is the end or purpose of the speech" (Aristotle, *Rhet.* 3.14.6–7) and to "magnify or minimize the importance of the subject" (3.14.12). John describes God not only as the "one who is and was" (ὁ ὢν καὶ ὁ ἦν), but also as "the one who is coming," who is even now on the way (ὁ ἐρχόμενος, Rev 1:4, 8),[43] whose intervention in human affairs is imminent. John has significantly altered dominant cultural

---

42. Duff (2001, 72) regards John as cultivating "a crisis atmosphere most notably in the predictions and visions of persecution." Royalty (1997, 599) similarly understands John to create a crisis rather than respond to an objective crisis of "extreme oppression" at the hands of Roman authorities.

43. The use of the present participle, present aspect connoting action-in-progress, is a significant choice over against the use of a future indicative or future participle.

speech about the eternity of the gods, seen, for example, in the acclamation of Zeus: "Zeus was, Zeus is, Zeus shall be; O mighty Zeus!" (Pausanius, *Description of Greece* 10.12.10).[44] The picture is no longer of a God who exists in static eternity, but a God who will dynamically encounter God's creation.

This dynamic element of the Christian worldview is more dramatically portrayed immediately following the greeting (Rev. 1:4–6) in a startling clarion call to pay attention: "Look! He is coming with the clouds; every eye will see him, even those who pierced him; and on his account all the tribes of the earth will wail!" (1:7 NRSV). John posits an event of universal significance, amplifying this crisis by drawing attention both to the breadth and trauma of its effects (it will evoke "wailing," a response reflecting unpreparedness and failure, from "all [earth's] tribes").[45] John further amplifies the crisis by drawing attention to its imminence both in the exordium (1:3; see also 3:11) and in the peroration (22:7, 12, 20).[46] The greatest threat the hearers face is to be found unprepared to encounter God or God's Christ at his coming, thus being exposed to the threat of the "second death" (2:11) or being written out of the "Book of Life" (3:5). This challenge puts all the others in perspective, subordinates them to itself, and calls for a response to the more proximate crises that will also—and primarily—serve to position one well for encountering the returning Christ.

The visions continue to amplify the dangers of facing the "day of the wrath" of God and the Lamb and bring to the fore the importance of preparing to encounter God and the Lamb at their coming. John does this by returning frequently in his visions to Christ's visitation in judgment or to the judgment that takes place before God's throne, as well as by portraying in striking contrast the ways in which created beings will "greet" that day (cf. 6:12–17 with 11:15–18). In 6:12–17, John paints a fearsome picture of the day announced in 1:7, a picture of universal terror seizing all who have not lived each day with a view to *that* day. In 14:14–20, John weaves together Old Testament and traditional Jewish images of judgment (see Isa. 63:2–6; Dan. 7:13; Joel 3:13; *1 Enoch* 100:3–4) as a means of reminding the hearers of God's commitment to judge the world, treading down all who have acted as God's enemies. The grisly detail given to trampling the winepress impresses the danger and horror of that judgment all the more upon the hearers, and thus the paramount importance of living now so as to meet that challenge safely and be found a loyal servant of God. The same scenes are viewed from yet another angle in Revelation 19:11–21. The reference to "treading the winepress of the wrath of God" (19:15) connects the scene in 19:11–21 with 14:14–20, even as the menu for "the great supper of God" in

---

44. See the texts collected and discussed in Aune 1997, 31–32.

45. Rev. 1:7–8 does not merely stand "as a sort of heading to the narrative portion following (1.9–20)" (Kirby 1988, 198), but as an announcement of Revelation's principal stasis, or issue, toward which the speech and the hearers' attention are to be directed. This is the exigence that John asserts, the one that creates the required tension that will make the warnings and promises, exhortations and dissuasions, of chapters 2 and 3 effective.

46. Rev. 16:15 would function as a significant reminder of the imminence as suddenness of this coming.

19:17–18 repeats the categories of panic-stricken people first encountered in 6:15–17, suggesting that these scenes all depict the same focal event. In between these detailed visions of judgment, John inserts numerous announcements of the coming of "the great day of God the Almighty" (16:14), "the time for the dead to be judged and to give the reward to [God's] slaves, to the prophets and to the holy ones and to those who fear [God's] name" (11:18; see also 22:12), so that this crisis remains in focus throughout Revelation from first to last. By means of recapitulation, John keeps holding this crisis before his hearers so that they will, in turn, keep it in view.

But John also draws attention to an even more immediate "coming." Encountering Christ at his second, future coming is prefigured in the churches' encounter with the Christ who walks in the midst of his churches. The image of Christ, already invested with the glory and awesomeness of his station at God's right hand (1:12–16) and walking "among the seven golden lampstands" that represent the churches (1:20; 2:1), presents an even more immediate threat to congregations that have not kept faith with him. Unless they fall in line swiftly with his righteous demands (recovering their former love and their former commitment to avoid every semblance of idolatrous worship), Christ's immediacy threatens swift judgment:

> I will come to you and remove your lampstand from its place, unless you repent. (2:5 NRSV)
> Repent then. If not, I will come to you soon and war against them with the sword of my mouth. (2:16 NRSV)
> I am throwing her on a bed, and those who commit adultery with her I am throwing into great distress, unless they repent of her doings; and I will strike her children dead. And all the churches will know that I am the one who searches minds and hearts, and I will give to each of you as your works deserve. (2:22–23 NRSV)

At the same time, however, if one is disposed to heed Jesus' summons, his presence in the midst of the churches signifies the immediacy of help and fellowship. The oracle to Laodicea, appropriately the last of the series of seven, closes the distance between the congregations and Christ even further: the one who throughout the oracles declares that he is coming arrives, here, at the very threshold: "See! I stand at the door and knock!" (3:20). Whether for judgment or strengthening, then, Christians must come to terms at once with the glorified Christ who stands at the door. John guides the churches to see that their response to Christ's exhortations to single-hearted discipleship will determine whether they encounter him there as Judge and Executioner, or as a welcome guest.

By focusing the congregations on the visitation of God and God's Christ for judgment, John promotes accountability to this God, and therefore to the norms of God's commandments and faithfulness toward Jesus (the values and norms promoted within the Christian subculture), as the highest consideration. At this point the worldview articulated by Revelation directly reinforces the group's ethos (in the sense of its distinctive collection of alignments, attitudes, values, and practices). This establishes an interpretive interaction, in turn, between this greater crisis and all the other, more proximate decisions facing the Christians within the seven churches, who are led to examine these more immediate decisions in light of the Christian cultural values that are held out as the criteria of Christ's judgment.

This is a stunning ideological move, with John making a bid to change the focus of each disciple wrestling with the real-life issues of his or her situation. As long as the disciples remained focused on the challenge of their neighbors' pressure, or the challenge of remaining on firm economic footing, or any other of the quotidian challenges that they faced by virtue of being associated with the name of Jesus, they might move toward accommodating to the society around them, since that would generally resolve these challenges. John trumps all these rival foci by placing before the believers' eyes the ultimate crisis, the one most needing to be met successfully. The danger of the "second death" relativizes the pains of the first death (2:10); the danger of encountering God as Enemy relativizes the losses incurred as one makes an enemy of one's society. In this way, John steers each disciple to choose the course of action in regard to the proximate challenges that will best align them with "the commandments of God and faithfulness toward Jesus" (Rev. 14:12) and position them for a successful encounter with the greater challenge—the challenge that, for the moment, exists only in Christian expectation as expressed within the Christian worldview.

A POLARIZED WORLD

John's cosmos is a universe of stark alternatives. At every level of existence, there are two camps, and John has "constructed his narrative world in such a way as to emphasize the mutual exclusivity of the two realms."[47] Literary techniques such as parody, juxtaposition, and repetitive patterning help to generate this impression.

John particularly employs parody in his presentation of the beasts.[48] The beast from the sea has seven heads and a mortal wound (13:1, 3a), a monstrous reflection of the Lamb (5:6). The beast is the object of wonder and adoration, both in regard to its miraculous recovery (13:3b–4) and reign (13:7b–8), as is the Lamb in regard to the beneficial consequences of his death (5:9) and his creation of a kingdom for God (5:10). The worship offered the beast, its image, and the dragon that gave it its power parodies the proper worship centered on God's throne and the Lamb. The "mark of the beast," which ensures certain benefits and protects its bearers from the punitive measures inflicted by the beast (13:15–17), parodies the seal of God, which likewise ensures certain benefits (7:13–17) and exempts its bearers from the plagues (9:4).

---

47. Duff 2001, 76.
48. O'Leary (1993, 388) noted the importance of "the web of parody and contrast running throughout the book" as a means of forcing a dualistic interpretation upon everyday reality.

Such imitation would not be mistaken for flattery, for these imitations emerge from the context of conflict between Satan and the armies of God. They are an extension of Satan's rebellion against God's order, a rebellion in which he drew one-third of the spirit beings away from that order (12:4). They are part of Satan's plan to draw beings from the human sphere away from God, continuing the dragon's futile rebellion. Verbal repetitions underscore the dichotomy. The Lamb gave his life in order to "ransom for God" people "from every tribe and language and people and nation" (5:9). Because of the Lamb's self-giving death on their behalf, an innumerable crowd is gathered "out from every nation and tribes and peoples and languages" (7:9), with palms of victory and white garments to praise God for their deliverance. The beast, however, exercises authority "over every tribe and people and language and nation" (13:7), even as Babylon sits enthroned upon "peoples and crowds and nations and languages" (17:15).

This web of echoes fosters an environment of competition—and the competition is ongoing as John joins angels in extending the invitation to acknowledge God's accession to kingly rule to "every nation and tribe and language and people" (14:6) or to "many peoples and nations and languages and kings" (10:11). Effective witness, involving the death of the witnesses, can turn "peoples and tribes and languages and nations" (11:9) away from following the beast toward fearing God and giving God proper honor (11:13b). These repetitions reinforce a strategic picture of the human situation, according to which the Lamb and the beast are competing over these "peoples and crowds and nations and language groups," the Lamb drawing part to God, the beast and his henchthing drawing part into Satan's camp. In such a situation of competition and conflict, there can be no cooperation between followers of the Lamb and supporters of the beast.

In a monolatrous religion, any alternative focus of worship is by definition a rival one, a competitor, a counterfeit. Worship of the God "who created heaven and earth and sea and springs of water" is incompatible with worshiping the beast and its image (14:6–7, 9–11). Only the people whose names do not appear "in the Book of Life of the Lamb slain from the foundation of the cosmos" worship the beast (13:8), and only those who keep themselves from the worship of the beast and its image will stand before the throne of God, singing songs of deliverance (15:2–4) or sharing in the coming reign of God's Messiah (20:4–6). Both the kingdom of the beast and the kingdom of God are unified through worship of their respective centers, but since the kingdoms are at war, one cannot show solidarity at both the shrine of the beast and in the assembly that worships God and the Lamb. And the fate of those who worship the beast is entirely incompatible with the destiny of those who worship God and the Lamb faithfully (14:9–11; 20:4–6).

Juxtaposition also contributes significantly to this bifurcation of humanity and the cultivation of an awareness of mutual exclusivity.[49] The vision of the

---

49. Several other important instances occur in Revelation, such as the contrast created by the juxtaposition of Babylon and its practice of "empire" alongside the new Jerusalem with its very

"Lamblike beast and its followers" in 13:11–18 is strategically juxtaposed with the vision of the followers of the Lamb in 14:1–5.[50] The former join in worship around a lifeless statue, artificially enhanced by means of special effects; the latter sing hymns before the throne of God, in the company of the host of heaven, hymns that they alone are privileged to learn (13:14–15; 14:3). The former receive the mark of the beast (which seals them for disaster, as 14:9–11 makes clear); the latter have the name of God upon their foreheads (13:16; 14:1). The vision of the 144,000 stands in sharp contrast with other images as well, contributing further to the polarization of the world. They are "virgins" who "did not defile themselves with women" (14:4) in a world full of enticements to illicit alliances (globally, the whore of Babylon; locally, the prophetess Jezebel). The choice of "virgin" as an image for the redeemed is a brilliant one, fostering either/or thinking in regard to fidelity toward Jesus versus participation in local religious, economic, and social practices. These 144,000 utter nothing false (14:5) in a world full of deceptive speech (cosmically and globally, the dragon, second beast, and Babylon, all of whom "deceive" [12:9; 13:14; 18:23; 19:20; 20:3, 8, 10]; locally, false apostles and prophets and others making claims about themselves and the cosmos that are deceptive and lead others into aberrant practices [2:2, 9, 14, 20; 3:17]).[51]

This juxtaposition thus "underlines the fundamental decision that the audience faces: either to worship the anti-divine powers embodied in Rome and to become 'followers' of the beast (cf. 13:2–4) or to worship God and to become 'companions' of the Lamb on Mount Zion."[52] But more to the point, the juxtaposition *creates* the necessity for the decision. By means of these literary techniques and contrasting images, John articulates a worldview that establishes alternatives and then forces choices between them. This is highly significant in light of the rival agendas among the churches, most notably the agendas of Jezebel and of the Nicolaitans, whose position seems to envision Christians coexisting alongside and within Roman imperialism and its legitimation mechanisms. John doggedly rends asunder what Jezebel would join together. Through skillful use of parody, juxtaposition, and repetition, John creates divisions and posits incompatibility where other voices in the seven churches do not see such stark separations. John thus promotes withdrawal from imperial cult and from social networks whose gatherings involve idolatrous rites as a specific and necessary expression of the Christian's place in the camp of God and the Lamb.

By portraying a world—indeed a cosmos—at war, John eliminates cooperation with both sides as a feasible course of action. The cooperation or coexistence urged by his rivals must yield to a different reckoning of the options: capitula-

---

different practices of cultivating human society. The contrast between, and incompatibility of, the two politico-economic orders is heightened by the descriptions of the former as "prostitute" and the latter as "bride," and the like.

50. Schüssler Fiorenza 1985, 188. She underscores the importance of "the strategic position and textual relations" of particular symbols and images, setting contrasting images side by side to create textual relationships calling for creative engagement and response on the part of the audience.
51. See also Schüssler Fiorenza 1985, 190–91.
52. Schüssler Fiorenza 1985, 191.

tion or conquering. John orients the disciples toward their situation as a set of challenges to be overcome, and in light of the "larger picture," a set of forces to be overcome, not least through resistance unto the end. The identity that John asks the disciples to embrace and enact is ὁ νικῶν, the one who persists in overcoming. The ever-present possibility of lessening tension by yielding somewhat to their neighbors' expectations becomes a "test," an encounter with some outside force making an attempt on the disciple's resolution (as in 2:10). John seeks to reframe the debate in at least some of the congregations from "How much can we give our neighbors so that we can find peace, even prosperity, again?" to "Will the Enemy get the upper hand on you, or will you resist and win?"

CONCLUSION

By writing an apocalypse, John was able to draw a larger picture of the spaces of the cosmos and set this cosmos within the framework of a narrative about past events and future destiny. Both the spatial and temporal dimensions set "lived experience" firmly within an interpretive context that potentially alters the hearers' perceptions of that lived experience and thereby shapes their responses to it in ways that might seem surprising to those who look only to the realities and dynamics within that lived experience (or who look through the interpretive lenses of other worldviews).

John's picture of an ordered cosmos centered, through worship, on the One seated on the heavenly throne and the Lamb changes the hearers' perceptions of the orientation and practice of the dominant majority. The vision affirms the Christian disciples to be living in line with the cosmic majority, revealing their neighbors to be the deviants. John also presents a strikingly different picture of the major foci of the dominant culture's worldview: the pillars of the Roman imperial ideology (Rome and her emperors). He presents an interpretive depiction of the practices and pretensions of world empires as they appear sub specie aeternitatis, that is, in the light of the reign and values of the One God. Seen in this light, these focal figures engender a response of critical distance rather than partnership. John also elevates the Christian metacrisis—the coming of Christ in judgment—in his audience's consciousness, expecting this to provide the impetus to weigh their more mundane crises and decisions according to the values and practices promoted within the Christian culture, and to embrace the responses that align most closely with those values. The sharper the audience's focus on standing before Christ's judgment seat, the more the group's values will appear "not as subjective human preferences but as the imposed conditions for life implicit in a world with a particular structure."[53]

John's portrayal of the world articulates a cosmology with only one natural and self-evident response: to move in the directions John urges, rather than other

53. Geertz 1973, 131.

directions that now seem quite senseless in light of "the way things are."[54] This will be persuasive to the extent that John's portrayal of the world is accepted as a credible representation, which thus invites a more thorough investigation of John's appeals to *ethos* in the rhetorical sense of fostering his credibility, the authority of his message, and receptivity among the hearers. The advice given in the seven oracles, coupled with the summonses encountered throughout the visions (e.g., to maintain exclusive worship of the One God, to divest oneself of involvement in the unjust political and economic practices of Babylon), are "rendered intellectually reasonable by being shown to represent a way of life ideally adapted to the actual state of affairs the world view describes."[55]

Having entered this larger cosmos as John's Apocalypse was read aloud to the gathered assembly, the hearers are changed, as is "the common-sense world, for it is now seen as but the partial form of a wider reality which corrects and completes it."[56] Writing an apocalypse offers a greater rhetorical gain than, for example, a pastoral letter. The voyeuristic experience of entering into John's encounter with the unseen world—and looking back from there upon the landscape of the visible world—provides a religious "experience" (as opposed to pastoral "analysis") that disposes hearers indeed to "keep the words of this prophecy" (Rev. 22:7) as they return to the world where they will hear "Jezebel" try to defend her position, encounter further propaganda about the emperor and *Roma Aeterna*, watch goods being transported to ports for transit by ship to Rome, try to engage in their business activities again, and encounter the other quotidian realities of their cities. But these figures and activities will hardly look and feel the same, and the hearers will be raising far more critical questions as they move through their lived experience in light of the "wider reality" (and its interpretation of their immediate realities) to which John has exposed them.

---

54. "Religion supports proper conduct by picturing a world in which such conduct is only common sense . . . because between ethos and world view, between the approved style of life and the assumed structure of reality, there is conceived to be a simple and fundamental congruence such that they complete one another and lend meaning to one another" (Geertz 1973, 129).
55. Geertz 1973, 89–90.
56. Geertz 1973, 122.

Chapter 5

Why Should We Listen to John?

The Construction of Ethos in Revelation

Classical rhetorical theorists identified three fundamental kinds of appeal: the appeal to rational argument (logos), the arousal of strategic emotions in the hearers (pathos), and the construction of credibility (ethos). Aristotle regarded the last of these as the "most effective means of proof" (*Rhet.* 1.2.4), the sine qua non of persuasion. Four centuries later, Quintilian would still name "the authority of the speaker" as that which "carries greatest weight in deliberative oratory" (*Inst.* 3.8.13).

Aristotle broke down "credibility" into three main components: good sense, virtue, and goodwill (φρόνησις, ἀρετή, εὔνοια; Aristotle, *Rhet.* 2.1.5; see also 1.8.6; 2.1.3). He advised speakers to give attention to establishing credibility in the course of the speech itself, rather than relying on the audience's prior knowledge of their character and behavior (though the latter would potentially help; see 1.2.4). They needed to convey possession of the requisite knowledge to speak authoritatively and sensibly concerning the subject at hand. Speakers needed to demonstrate a personal commitment to virtue that assured hearers of their commitment to lead them only in noble directions. They also needed to communicate favorable feelings toward the audience, having the hearers' best interests at heart, wishing them well, and thinking well of them. Displaying such qualities constituted the most important step toward securing the audience's assent.

The *Rhetorica ad Herennium* takes a more audience-centered approach to thinking about the task of establishing ethos, stressing the importance of rendering the hearers "receptive, well-disposed, and attentive" (1.4.7). This is but the other side of the coin.[1] Hearers are more "receptive" toward a speaker who displays mastery of the subject and an agreeable moral character. An audience becomes well-disposed as speakers show themselves to bear the audience goodwill and to hold them in esteem (e.g., by praising their past conduct or judgment), thus establishing a sense of connection. Attentiveness is a particularly important ingredient in ethos, not just in terms of inspiring an audience to invest the energy required to hear, process, and respond to one's speech, but also to direct their attention to things that the speaker elevates as worthy of attention (and perhaps away from other concerns in their immediate situation that might draw them in a direction unfavorable to the speaker's purposes).[2]

Establishing ethos becomes especially important when multiple speakers seek to sway an audience in different directions, whether to judge a defendant guilty or innocent or to commit to one course of action over another. Because speakers often addressed an audience that may have been won over by the preceding speaker's speech, or had to yield the floor to a subsequent speaker, rhetorical theorists emphasized the importance of establishing ethos in the opening paragraphs of a speech and reaffirming credibility in the concluding moments of the speech.[3] Dispelling prejudice (against oneself) or creating the same (against opposing speakers) became a major function of the exordium and peroration.

Quite in keeping with Greco-Roman rhetorical expectations, John gives explicit attention to establishing authority and credibility both at the outset (1:1–20) and at the close (22:6–21). These sections stand apart from the main body of Revelation as a frame, in which John gives direct, explicit attention to the metalevel of communicating the content of Revelation rather than to the content itself. John speaks about being commissioned to write the contents that fall within this frame. He gives details about the means by which the content came to him, speaking *about* the "words written in this book" (1:3; 22:7) rather than communicating those words themselves. It might be inappropriate to label these sections the "exordium" and "peroration" of Revelation, since the text does not follow the form of a typical oration; yet these framing sections nevertheless achieve many of the principal goals for the exordium and peroration.

John's situation reflects the more complex situation of multiple, opposing speakers, which may help to explain the level of attention he gives to establishing credibility at the outset and the close of Revelation. Not only are there rival

---

1. Aristotle also recognized the importance of positioning the audience to "be disposed in a certain way towards" the speaker (*Rhet.* 2.1.3), as did the author of the *Rhetorica ad Alexandrum* (1436a.33–37; 1436b.8–12).
2. *Rhet. Alex.* 1436b.8–10.
3. Quintilian, *Inst.* 3.8.7; *Rhet. Alex.* 1436a.33–37; Aristotle, *Rhet.* 3.14.6–7, 12; 3.19.1.

teachers within the congregations vying for a hearing and seeking to persuade the disciples to adopt a certain stance in regard to the surrounding culture and its institutions (notably "Jezebel" and the "Nicolaitans"). There are also the strong voices of the dominant culture beyond the congregations, whether their own neighbors and fellow citizens or official representatives of Roman power. John has significant competition for the right to speak and give direction to these communities.[4] In this chapter we will give attention to the primary strategies John employs both to present himself as possessing good sense, virtue, and goodwill, and to render the hearers receptive, well-disposed, and attentive. Although many elements within the visions themselves will also contribute to ethos, our focus will remain primarily on the opening and closing frames of Revelation.

"AN *APOKALYPSIS* . . ."

If John had opened with the words of greeting found in Revelation 1:4, "John to the seven churches in Asia: Grace and peace to you," Revelation would have begun in a manner quite in keeping with other writings collected within the New Testament. His audience would have heard him addressing them as Paul and the author of 1 Peter had, and as James and Jude had addressed their readerships. But Revelation opens quite differently, with a kind of introduction otherwise found only in the classical Hebrew prophets:

> An apocalypse of Jesus Christ, which God gave him. . . . And he communicated it, sending it through his angel to his slave, John. (Rev. 1:1)
> The vision of Isaiah son of Amoz, which he saw concerning Judah and Jerusalem. . . . (Isa. 1:1 NRSV)
> The word of the LORD to Israel by the hand of my messenger [or by the hand of Malachi]. . . . (Mal. 1:1; cf. Hos. 1:1; Joel 1:1; Mic. 1:1; Zeph. 1:1)
> The word of the LORD to Israel by the hand of his angel . . . (ἐν χειρὶ ἀγγέλου αὐτοῦ, Mal. 1:1 LXX).

Revelation opens in a manner reminiscent of writings that had been received as authentic prophetic words from God. The first voice that the audience hears is not John's, but the more impersonal voice of "Scripture," introducing John's words as speech originating in the divine realm and communicated at God's bidding. The "chain of revelation" is more complicated in 1:1–3 than in most of the classical prophets, reflecting intertestamental developments such as the emphasis on the angelic mediator of divine communications (a tendency already seen in the Septuagint of Mal. 1:1), but the ultimate Origin of the revelation remains the same.

---

4. The challenge of rival *Christian* teachers is often observed and has been the focus of significant study (e.g., Duff 2001). But John's defusing of the voices of the Christians' idolatrous neighbors and fellow citizens (deSilva 1998a, 94–97) and of representatives of Roman power (Schüssler Fiorenza 1985, 192) are equally important facets of John's remedy for unhealthful ways in which his audience has potentially been won over by opposing speakers.

This impersonal voice applies the label ἀποκάλυψις (*apokalypsis*) to the communication as a whole. This Greek word gives us our label for the literary category to which Revelation is assigned: it is an "apocalypse," like *1 Enoch*, parts of Daniel, *4 Ezra*, and *2 Baruch*. But John does not name his work an "apocalypse" as an indication of genre, for which it was not yet a technical term.[5] This opening does not set Revelation apart as something distinct from prophecy (προφητεία, Rev. 1:3), but rather makes a claim that its contents represent a particular kind of "prophecy," originating in a particular mode of divine revelation.[6]

For the first hearers, the label ἀποκάλυψις would have signaled a kind of charismatic experience that generally combined visual as well as auditory impressions from the realm of the Spirit. Socialization into Christian culture would have led the hearers to accept such revelatory communications as at least worthy of testing in regard to their authenticity (and, therefore, authority).[7] The language of ἀποκάλυψις is especially prominent in Pauline Christianity. Paul himself twice uses the phrase that opens Revelation, once to refer to the end-time "manifestation of our Lord Jesus Christ" (τὴν ἀποκάλυψιν τοῦ κυρίου ἡμῶν Ἰησοῦ Χριστοῦ, 1 Cor. 1:7; cf. 1 Pet. 1:7, 13), and once to refer to his own dramatic encounter with the glorified Jesus, which he experienced as a prophetic commissioning (δι᾽ ἀποκαλύψεως Ἰησοῦ Χριστοῦ, Gal. 1:12).[8] In the second instance, Paul specifically contrasts instruction that comes through human agency against divinely revealed instruction, grounding his own apostolic authority in his experience of the latter. Paul also speaks of a "revelation" (ἀποκάλυψις) as an ecstatic experience by means of which visions or instructions are disclosed (2 Cor. 12:1, 7; Gal. 2:2), setting it alongside "prophecy" (1 Cor. 14:6). While "apocalypse" remains a useful label for a particular kind of "revelatory literature," early Christians tend to use the term to refer to an ecstatic experience (that might later be written down) in which a message is communicated from the divine realm. They perceived a continuity between prophecy and apocalypse, since a "revelation" can constitute a "prophetic word."[9]

The *titulus* summarizes the contents to follow as "whatsoever things he saw" (ὅσα εἶδεν, 1:2). The focus throughout Revelation remains on John's "seeing" and "hearing," not "creating." John's voice recedes beneath the voices of otherworldly beings, intruding chiefly to remind the hearers that he is not the inventor of this discourse by calling repeated attention to his own "seeing" and "hearing." The knowledge that John purports to convey holds great value since it is otherwise inaccessible. "Knowledge is crucial to any speaker's credibility."[10]

---

5. Schüssler Fiorenza 1985, 150.
6. See Schüssler Fiorenza 1985, 150–51.
7. Knight (2001, 487) underscores the importance of this conviction within Christian culture for the development of apocalyptic rhetoric: "Apocalyptic rhetoric is founded on the belief that authoritative information can be discerned through heavenly revelation. Apocalyptic offered the development of human knowledge by more-than-human insight."
8. Schüssler Fiorenza 1985, 150.
9. Schüssler Fiorenza 1985, 150–51.
10. Carey 1998, 753.

And there are some things John knows that he can't reveal (10:4); John reminds his audience that he is their conduit to knowledge of God's counsel, and that what he does not reveal, they do not know. His descriptions of his own physical and internal responses to what he sees and hears add vividness and authenticity to his reports of his ecstatic experience.[11] As John reports that he feels dread before the glorified Christ (1:17), experiences wonder at the sight of Babylon (17:6), or falls in awe before the feet of his angelic interlocutor (19:10; 22:8), he reinforces the impression of the "reality" of his ecstatic experience by speaking about the *effects* this experience had on him. Naming such effects reinforces the reality of the cause of these effects.

John's presentation does not automatically render his words unassailable, however, given the cultural reality of testing the prophets. But if he is received as a genuine prophet of God, the rhetorical gains of writing in this mode, rather than arguing in his own voice, are immense.[12] This has long been recognized as the foundation for the message's legitimation and hence, in rhetorical terms, for its appeal to ethos.[13]

John continues to give attention to the maintenance of ethos throughout the text, and hence throughout its oral performance as it is read to the churches. He reinforces the visionary aspect of the work, and thus its otherworldly origin, with every "I saw" (εἶδον) and "I heard" (ἤκουσα), anchoring the authority of the text in the otherworldly sources of the reported speech and vision.[14] This technique is common to apocalypses, even intrinsic to the essence of apocalypticism as revelations of realities beyond everyday experience.[15]

EXCURSUS: DID JOHN REALLY SEE THINGS?

John presents this material as the result of being able to see into and listen in on realities to which people do not ordinarily have access. However, questions naturally arise among interpreters: Is this for real? Did John *really* converse with the glorified Christ—or at least, did John really *believe* that he had such conversations? Does Revelation have its origins in an ecstatic experience, or in John's terms, being "in a spirit" (ἐν πνεύματι, Rev. 1:10), in some alternate state of

---

11. Carey 1998, 756.
12. See Hall 1996, 438: "The argument convinces to the extent that the claim to inspiration is accepted, that the comprehensive picture fits with the readers' moral and physical universe, and that it satisfactorily answers the readers' questions." As we shall see in the following chapter, John's careful and faithful alignment of himself with the voice of the tradition preserved in the Hebrew Scriptures—thus "fitting with the readers' moral . . . universe"—is an important facet of his claim to authenticity.
13. See Aune 1981, 18; A. Collins 1984, 145; deSilva 1992a, 284; 1993, 49.
14. DeSilva 1992a, 284; 1998b, 789–90. John refers to his own act of seeing no fewer than forty-five times: Rev. 1:12, 17; 4:1; 5:1, 2, 6, 11; 6:1, 2, 5, 8, 9, 12; 7:1, 2, 9; 8:2, 13; 9:1, 17; 10:1, 5; 13:1, 2, 11; 14:1, 6, 14; 15:1, 2, 5; 16:13; 17:3, 6; 18:1; 19:11, 17, 19; 20:1, 4, 11, 12; 21:1, 2, 22.
15. See, e.g., *2 Bar.* 22.1–2: "Lo! the heavens were opened, and I saw, . . . and a voice was heard from on high. . . ."

consciousness? Or does Revelation originate in John's quite conscious and self-guided processes of literary composition, crafting narratives of visions that he did not actually "see," but that he could approximate, for example, by reading other literary reports of visionary encounters such as Ezekiel 1–2 and Daniel 10? Is the seeing, hearing, conversing with otherworldly beings, and so forth, merely part of the generic trappings of apocalyptic literature (or less kindly, part of an elaborate attempt to deceive)?

Several scholars deny that any sort of ecstatic experience stands behind Revelation, preferring to view it as a purely literary creation. Schüssler Fiorenza argues that "a careful look at the inaugural vision demonstrates why one is justified in calling Revelation a 'literary vision.' It is impossible to pictorialize or draw this vision, since Revelation is full of image associations which cannot be depicted."[16] She revives an older argument against the visions' authenticity: the difficulty one would have in creating a painting of John's vision of the glorified Christ precludes John actually having "seen" or "visualized" such an image in a state of ecstasy.[17] Instead, Schüssler Fiorenza suggests that the correspondence between "the figure described in Daniel 10" and "that of Christ in Revelation 1 indicates that John worked in a literary fashion insofar as he utilizes Daniel 10 as his pattern and source text but changes this pattern in several ways (e.g., incorporating details from descriptions in Ezekiel and Exodus)." He "follows the text of Daniel 10" as he creates this description of seeing Christ, departing from the source text to introduce particular emphases of his own.[18]

Robert Royalty calls attention to the correspondences between John's description of the glorified Christ (1:12–20) and the actual words "chosen" by Christ to identify himself in each of the seven oracles. This suggests to him that John had not simply heard these oracles and transmitted the words of the glorified Christ verbatim. Rather, he argues, "Christ uses John's exact words when addressing the seven churches," borrowing, as it were, from John's description of Christ in the initial commissioning vision (1:12–20). For Royalty, this is one of several instances of "intratextuality" that "shows the literary artifice evident in John's careful rhetorical constructions throughout the Apocalypse."[19]

Other scholars forcefully maintain that genuine visionary experiences stand behind Revelation and that it is not merely the product of the writing desk. In 1971 Amos Wilder even spoke of a then-contemporary consensus—certainly now a jeopardized consensus—that "the writers not only took over earlier theophanies but that they [also] were themselves visionaries."[20] The fact that some of John's images are difficult to visualize all at once, being too strange or unnatural

16. Schüssler Fiorenza 1991, 51.
17. See Clemen 1920, 25–53.
18. Schüssler Fiorenza 1991, 29.
19. Royalty 1997, 611; 1998, 159.
20. Wilder 1971, 441; see also Böcher 1988a, 3851; Hemer 1986, 13–14; Fekkes 1994, 289–90. Aune (1986, 91) describes Revelation as "a literary replication of the original and unique revelatory experience of John the Seer which, when performed in a public, probably even a cultic setting, communicates the author's paraenetic message with divine authority."

or incoherent, seems to such interpreters *more* congruent with ecstatic experience rather than less.[21] Whether or not John's images can be pictorially represented (a factor of the imagination and skill of the artist) is hardly proof that he did not, in some sense, "see" something before formulating his written descriptions of those images. If dreams (another kind of alternate state of consciousness in which we "see" mental images) are difficult to recall, let alone paint graphically, yet are nevertheless real experiences that can even become the basis for literary works, then one should accord the same possibility to visions seen in other states of consciousness.

It does justice neither to the complexity of Revelation nor to the insights of scholars on both sides to persist in an either/or approach to the question. On the one hand, the intense degree of intertexture has to be plausibly explained. How are we to explain John's use of words snatched verbatim from Ezekiel 3:12 in his own first-person narration, "I heard a loud sound like a trumpet behind me" (Rev. 1:10),[22] or account for the stunning similarities both in detail and in lexical choices between John's vision of Christ and "Daniel's" vision of his angelic interlocutor (Rev. 1:12–15; Dan. 10:5–6)?

On the other hand, to exclude the possibility of ecstatic experience, particularly when there are so many contemporary attestations of ecstatic experience in Greco-Roman, Second Temple Jewish,[23] and early Christian sources, is to fall into the conceptual trap of discounting ecstatic experience on the basis of the antisupernaturalistic prejudices of the worldview pervasive in European and Eurocentric societies in general, and in academia in particular.[24] Such a worldview perpetuates Western prejudice against types of experiences (ecstatic, altered states of consciousness) that are *typical* among non-Western peoples. Contemporary anthropologists show a salutary reserve in this regard, avoiding "cross-cultural calculus of the relative authenticity of ecstatic experiences," paying attention rather "only where the actors themselves hold that some ecstatic states are false, whereas others are true."[25] This does not entail making faith claims

---

21. David Barr (1984, 43) finds the "element of incoherence" expected: "This is, after all, a book of ecstasy—or at least pseudoecstasy—and we ought to expect a bit of untamed disorder." Foerster (1970, 235–36) points out that while visionary experiences don't follow rational rules, the stock meaning of certain visual cues (like horns being power, heads being intelligence, and the like) could render the visual impression less difficult. The images are not, therefore, "completely plastic," but to some extent represent "visualized thought."

22. Substituting, however, the trumpet blast still resonating from Sinai in Exod. 19:16 for the loud rumbling heard by Ezekiel.

23. See the helpful survey in Levison 1999. The evidence he gathers suggests that an "emic" understanding of John's engagement with the Jewish Scriptures would not rule out the "charismatic" aspect of genuine interpretation of sacred texts. In the eyes of a Philo or Josephus, this differs from ecstasy in regard to the engagement of the interpreter's mind, but not in regard to the presence and the working of the divine to communicate through both processes (see esp. pp. 38–49). While a Ben Sira might be skeptical of dreams and visions, he nevertheless seeks the spirit's guidance—to hear the divine voice, a suprarational pursuit—through study of Scripture and other sources of wisdom (Sir. 39:6).

24. On this problem, pursued from the angle of sociology of knowledge, see deSilva 1992c.

25. Lewis 1971, 29.

that many professional academicians fear would skew, limit, or otherwise undermine the scientific nature of their inquiry. To say that God sent John this vision is a faith claim; but to say that John, in all likelihood, "saw things" is not.

Colin Hemer helpfully suggests that the seer's backgrounds and influences would naturally be drawn into an ecstatic experience.[26] John clearly possessed an encyclopedic command of the contents of the Jewish Scriptures and extracanonical apocalypses like *1 Enoch*. John's extensive knowledge of the visionary tradition supplies both his conscious and subconscious mind with the raw material for his own visionary experiences, as well as for their expression in written form. Schüssler Fiorenza's assumption that John is working in a strictly literary manner—that he "follows the text of Daniel 10"—is problematic. The similarities between the visions in Revelation 1 and Daniel 10 may not indicate that John is rewriting Daniel 10 like a scribe. He may be seeing Christ in a trance, as Daniel 10 (which he may have known by heart) and the other visionary texts alluded to therein set him up to "see." Just as dreams draw on that which has been processed by our conscious mind and seen in the light of day, so John's ecstatic experiences draw on the raw materials that John has accumulated in conscious activity.[27] Vision accounts in Daniel, Ezekiel, and *1 Enoch* do not, then, merely influence John's own vision *accounts*: they also influence the *visions* themselves. Giving weight to the role of experiences in "altered states of consciousness" in John's process of composition helps account for the often-kaleidoscopic blending of images from multiple sources across the Hebrew Bible (and beyond).[28] Thereafter, in the process of reflecting upon, shaping, and "inscribing" his visionary experiences, John again has extensive opportunity to draw quite consciously on these literary precursors.

"OF JESUS CHRIST, WHICH GOD GAVE HIM . . ."

Aristotle observed that it was sometimes strategic, in the course of a speech, to "make another speak in our place" (*Rhet.* 3.17.16). Giving voice to the victims

---

26. Hemer 1986, 14.

27. John may have utilized prophetic texts as a means of entering into an ecstatic trance (as Evan Treborn uses his own diaries in *The Butterfly Effect*). The author of *4 Ezra* may have utilized the vision of the fourth beast in Dan. 7 in such a way, leading to his reimagining/revisioning of that figure as the great eagle. Such a procedure would account for both the similarities and differences between, for example, the vision of the glorified Christ and the angelic interlocutor of Dan. 10, or between the vision of the heavenly chariot in Ezek. 1 and the throne vision of Rev. 4. If texts were the launching point for entering into alternate states of consciousness for John, his verbatim recontextualization of Ezek. 3:12 (notably, itself an incipit to a visionary experience) as an introduction to his first visionary experience becomes intelligible as an element of ecstatic experience rather than a facet of a purely literary activity.

28. Similar models are also articulated and supported in Fekkes 1994, 289–90 and Witherington 2003, 36–38. Peterson (1969, 135) makes an important observation in this regard: "Interestingly, there is not a single exact quotation from any source. It would have been impossible for anyone to copy so many things with such uniform inaccuracy." The literary-scribal model of composition is not sufficient to explain *both* the similarities *and* the differences between Revelation and its resources.

of a crime could arouse greater indignation against the perpetrator of that crime. Giving voice to how an audience's forebears might evaluate their deeds could help motivate adoption of some course of action. What was an occasional strategy in routine oratory becomes the dominant strategy in apocalyptic oratory.[29] The implied authors of *1 Enoch* and *4 Ezra* introduce the voices of angels, God, and other supramundane beings into the discourse. In the case of those pseudonymous works, even the first-person speech of the implied author represents a voice that is distant from the actual author, just as the implied audience is removed from the actual audience by many generations.

In John's Revelation, which is not pseudonymous, we nevertheless hear many voices other than John's own addressing us. We hear Christ's voice commissioning John (1:17–20) and censuring behaviors and personalities in the seven churches (2:1–3:22). We hear angelic and other heavenly voices denouncing "Babylon" (18:1–24). We hear the souls of murdered Christians crying out for vindication (6:9–11) and joining the voices of angels to praise God for enacting judgment against their enemies (16:5–7).[30] Angelic beings challenge allegiances and behaviors, while other heavenly voices, like the Spirit, pronounce felicitation upon those who walk in line with the angels' exhortations (14:6–13). Otherworldly voices, identified or not, highlight the importance of particular words (words found now within John's text) by issuing a special command to "write" them down (e.g., 14:13; 19:9),[31] affirming their otherworldly origin for the hearers who share the early Christian conviction that the gift of prophetic utterance had been renewed and accept that John genuinely exercises the prophetic gift (rather than being a "dreamer" like those denounced in Jude 8).[32] We even hear the voice of God, declaring his identity (1:8), announcing the renewal of creation (21:5a), authenticating the divine message (21:5b), and reiterating promises to those who remain faithful and pronouncing warnings against the unfaithful (21:6–8). This catalog could continue for a considerable

---

29. See Carey 1999b, 137–41.
30. An ancillary gain of John's introduction of so many otherworldly voices in this regard is that it serves to cut off objections, a goal that any good orator would keep in mind. On this point, see Carey 1999b, 128–32, who argues that this technique silences the possibility of criticizing John for being too harsh and uncompromising in his assessment of Rome and its alignment against God's righteous standards (and thus, of course, John's assessment of what Rome "deserves"). John, in fact, *never* speaks harsh, condemnatory words in his own voice. Rather, he harnesses heavenly voices to justify the severity of his visions against Rome and the beast worshipers (Rev. 15:2–4; 16:5–6; 16:7; 19:2–5). John is merely the spokesperson for "a chorus of heavenly witnesses" who, cumulatively, "protect John from objections that he is rash, violent, or exclusive" (Carey 2001, 175). Those who would object to what they hear must object against speech presented as the words of angels, martyrs, the Spirit, Christ, and God's own self. The voice of the Hebrew Scriptures and other authoritative traditions (Royalty 1997, 605; deSilva 2002b) could be added as one more voice (or chorus of voices) that John draws in as a harmonious witness to, and legitimating foundation for, his own voice.
31. Giesen 1997, 68–69.
32. Indeed, five of the macarisms in Revelation are uttered by heavenly lips (14:13; 16:15; 19:9; 22:7, 14; Bertram and Hauck, "μακάριος," 369), the first by an unknown voice that, however, does not present itself as John's own voice. Only the macarism in 20:6 is spoken in the narrator's (John's) own voice.

length. John rarely speaks in his own voice, except to narrate what he saw and heard, his responses to the experiences, and to establish the epistolary frame of the whole (1:4, 9).

A clear rhetorical gain of this tactic is that, by submerging his own voice beneath the voices of the glorified Christ, angels, the Spirit, and other supernatural beings who speak through him to the audience, for whom he merely serves as mouthpiece and scribe, John causes more authoritative figures to confront his audiences.[33] To the extent that these figures are accepted as the "source" of the content, the content is less likely to be challenged and, therefore, authoritative pronouncements may often be leveled without much supporting argumentation or evidence.[34]

This strategy also minimizes the speaker's risk of alienating the audience, since John rarely addresses even words of exhortation, let alone rebuke and correction, directly.[35] Rhetorical ethos is fostered by nurturing a receptive frame of mind in the hearers toward the speaker, which is in turn supported as the speaker communicates goodwill toward the audience. Neither is well served by berating an audience for its failures to live up to the group's standards or values. So when challenge and critique must be leveled, doing so in the voice of another—while still standing alongside the audience rather than opposite them—is a strategic tack. Apocalypses that employ pseudonymity allow an author to apply a further layer of insulation in this regard insofar as the speaker (e.g., Enoch or Baruch) does not address the actual audience directly, who rather overhear the implied author addressing a more ancient audience, leaving the actual audience to apply the words to themselves.[36]

Both facets are apparent in the seven oracles in Revelation 2 and 3. The glorified Christ confronts each congregation with its failures, censures particular teachers, and issues warnings against those who fail to respond. John steps out of the way, simply passing along—out of faithfulness both to Christ and to these congregations—what he was commanded to pass along. Each oracle's introduction leaves no doubt concerning the speaker (2:1, 8, 12, 18; 3:1, 7, 14), and therefore who is "to blame" for the harsh words. And since it is the glorified Lord to whom the congregations have pledged their loyalty and whose return to mete out rewards and punishments they anticipate, the hearers will be less likely to defend themselves against those harsh words by rejecting the speaker. The closing summons of each oracle, "Let anyone who has an ear listen to what the Spirit is saying to the churches," is not merely an attempt to claim the Spirit's authentication for each message (though it does accomplish that as well).[37] It is also "an echo of the Synoptic parables,"[38] a kind of stylistic "signature" connect-

---

33. So A. Collins 1984, 145; Kirby 1988, 199; Schüssler Fiorenza 1991, 115, 137–38; O'Leary 1993, 388; Royalty 1997, 607–10; Knight 2001, 478.
34. See chap. 9 (below).
35. See Carey 1998, 759 on this rhetorical gain in apocalyptic literature generally, particularly those that employ pseudonymity.
36. Carey 1998, 759.
37. Knight 2001, 478.
38. Royalty 1997, 610.

ing the oracles with Jesus' known speech patterns. Other echoes of Jesus traditions throughout the oracles reinforce further the impression that it is, indeed, Jesus that they are hearing (see, e.g., 3:2a, 3b, 5b).

Second, Jesus addresses his words not to the churches in the first instance, but to the *angels* of the seven churches. In this way, John and the congregations are, much of the time, each one step removed from the confrontation. The identification of these angels remains an area of significant debate. Do they represent the heavenly guardians of the churches? Such an understanding casts these angels in a role comparable to Michael, the angelic guardian of Israel (Dan 12:1), or to the angels who serve as guardians of individuals and as their representatives before God's throne, who are thus available to be addressed by God in regard to their charges (*Jub.* 35.17; Matt. 18:10; Acts 12:15), or to the angelic teachers of humankind who, in the case of *1 Enoch* 6–16, led their charges astray. They have also been seen as human representatives of the churches, possibly their bishops or messengers sent by the churches to John,[39] and even as personifications of the churches. Appreciating the rhetorical gain does not depend on solving this riddle. To a large extent, the congregation does not experience itself as being directly confronted by Jesus.

This layer of indirectness, however, is not consistently sustained, with the result that the hearers will not miss the fact that the subject matter pertains to them directly. For example, the speech shifts frequently from σύ (addressing the "angel" of the church) to ὑμεῖς (addressing the congregation as a collective) or from second-singular verbs to second-plural verbs, showing "holes" in the veil of indirect address. Revelation 2:10 affords an instructive example: "Fear nothing [singular command] that you [singular] are about to suffer. The devil is about to throw some of you [plural] into prison in order that you [plural] might be tested, and you [plural] will have tribulation during ten days. Be faithful [singular command] unto death, and I will give to you [singular] the crown of life." The angels, moreover, are not threatened with punishment themselves, though the guilty "listeners" are. Also, the refrain clearly shows that what is written "to the angel" by John at Jesus' behest is also spoken "to the churches" by the Spirit (2:1, 7; etc.).

Since Jesus is the primary speaker addressing the congregations in the opening chapters of Revelation, John also gives strategic attention to developing Jesus' ethos as well. In part, this supports John's attempt to construct, in opposition to the authoritative voices of Rome and her emperors, "an alternative locus of authority in [his] vision of the risen Christ."[40] If the emperors and their representatives are impressive and weighty figures whose voices carry authority, John wishes to show that Christ is much more so. In part, it also reflects the basic conviction that a speaker's ethos should not be assumed—even though this would be natural within the Christian assembly, since none but those who accept

---

39. Hemer 1986, 32.
40. Carey 1999b, 1.

Christ's word as authoritative would even be found among the audience—but rather created afresh within the speech.

John presents Christ in ways that will render the congregations more receptive to his "speech," first dwelling on Jesus' demonstration of favor and goodwill toward the hearers. This Jesus is "the one who loved us and released us from our sins by means of his blood," who "made us a kingdom, priests to his God and Father" (1:5–6). John reminds the hearers of Jesus' principal acts of beneficence toward them, and the personal cost of securing the same, so that they will hear his words as coming from one who has shown them the utmost goodwill, commitment, and personal investment in the past. This will, in turn, dispose them to accept his words of rebuke and correction more readily, having been reminded of the heart from which those words spring.

John's vision of the glorified Christ also contributes powerfully to Jesus' ethos (1:12–16). Using images recognizable from Daniel, and perhaps inspired overall by the transfiguration traditions that foreshadowed Jesus' postresurrection glory, John paints a truly impressive word picture of the speaker who will shortly turn his attention away from John and toward the churches and their heavenly guardians. Jesus emerges as the supreme *kyrios*, trumping the pretensions of human rulers and their manufactured aura. John also draws attention to this Christ's infallible ability to see both what we show and what we hide (2:23), even from ourselves (as is the case at least among Laodicean Christians; 3:17). This superior knowledge gives his words authority beyond the hearers' potential objections, since the latter would be based on inferior knowledge. As a claim concerning the speaker's knowledge, one that is itself grounding in an authoritative Scripture (Jer. 17:10), it would enhance the ethos of this speaker.

It is the voice of *this* Christ, *this* Lord, that speaks to the churches, confronting them and opposing the rival voices that at least some among them entertain. It is *his* strength that encourages them and shores them up in the face of hostility or deprivation, but also *his* strength that stands behind the threats and warnings against disloyalty and compromise. The self-revelation formulas that introduce each of the seven oracles recapture some facet of this overall image of power and authority, economically recalling the whole and positioning the congregations to encounter the words as John encountered the glorified Christ—with the fear and awe that cause them to prostrate themselves before his speech.[41]

The word that confronts the hearers is thus not *John's* word, but the words of the glorified Christ (1:1–2). This is reinforced in detail and enacted explicitly in Christ's appearance to and commissioning of John, and in the seven oracles themselves, in which Christ addresses the congregations (and their angels) in the first person. To the extent that the hearers accept Revelation as a genuine word of prophecy, a communication of the speech of the glorified Christ that has its source ultimately in God, it will carry great authority. Though John does not universally depend on this (e.g., his use of the authoritative Scriptures and Jesus traditions

---

41. See Kirby 1988, 202.

also contributes forcefully to both the authority and argumentation of the work), many of his arguments ultimately depend on the audience's accepting that they are spoken by Christ, who has the power, for example, to enact the consequences that he announces as "arguments" to adopt a particular course of action.

"TO SHOW ... WHAT MUST HAPPEN SHORTLY"

According to Aristotle, one goal of the exordium of a deliberative speech was to "magnify or minimize the importance of the subject" (*Rhet.* 3.14.12). Speakers needed to be able to define the precise challenge or opportunity facing the hearers, as well as capture their interest and willingness to invest themselves in meeting that challenge. Hence "amplification" was often a feature of exordia where a speaker sought to evoke a positive response to a course of action, or "minimization" when a speaker wanted to dampen enthusiasm for an opposing speaker's proposal.

John uses several topics of amplification as he opens Revelation. In the *titulus*, he employs topics of imminence. John's message will address "what will take place quickly, ... for the time is near" (ἐν τάχει, ... ὁ γὰρ καιρὸς ἐγγύς, 1:1, 3). Imminence, which also provides a foundation for the appeal to two particular emotions (fear and confidence), here advances ethos by heightening audience attention: what is presented as immediately "relevant" by virtue of being imminently forthcoming captures our attention more readily than an exercise in long-range planning.

John's announcement of Christ's "coming with the clouds" also heightens audience attentiveness. John uses the technique of vividly presenting some scene as if before the speaker's eyes, here underscored by the imperative to "look!" (ἰδού), with the result that the audience is invited to imagine the scene unfolding before them (1:7):

> Look! He comes with the clouds,
> and every eye will see him—
> Even those who pierced him,
> and all the tribes of the earth will wail on account of him.

This vivid presentation of a critical encounter that will have a sorrowful outcome for many (even "all") suggests that the author is about to treat matters of the utmost importance to the audience, since the content of his "revelation" will have some bearing on how they encounter the returning Christ. The credibility of this announcement is enhanced by the fact that it is taken directly from the authoritative texts of the community. This specific combination of Daniel 7:13, used to refer to the event of the Son of Man's coming, with Zechariah 12:10, 14, used to postulate the results or significance of the event for the majority of humankind, already appears in traditions ascribed to Jesus (Matt. 24:30 and par.). The prior combination suggests that not only the texts but also their combination and interpretation would be received as "traditional" and, therefore, authoritative here.[42] *This* event represents the primary "crisis" to which John would draw the hearers' attention, and which John will use to motivate particular responses to the situations faced by the congregations in their "here and now."

John's use of such "crisis rhetoric" serves the goals of establishing ethos. "The urgent—the unique, the precarious, and the irremediable—is a rhetorical commonplace (*topos*) sure to get attention."[43] Amplifying the significance of the challenges the author purports to address augments the audience's attentiveness. Framing the speech as an attempt to help the hearers successfully meet and survive a crisis helps the speaker to appear to offer advice out of pure rather than self-interested motives. "John is simply telling his audience what they so desperately need to know."[44] Positing a crisis—here, the well-known crisis of God's judgment—provides John with a means of addressing problems in the seven congregations from the vantage point of simply helping them overcome obstacles in their midst to successfully encountering that crisis. The focus shifts to surviving "that day" and away from criticism of the congregations, rivalry (power struggles) between prophets and teachers, and other potentially alienating facets of the discourse.

"COMMUNICATING IT . . . TO HIS SLAVE, JOHN"

Despite being the physical "author" of the text, John distances himself considerably from the "invention" of the text. In the opening lines, John is ranged alongside the recipients rather than presented as the originator of the message (1:1):

> A revelation from Jesus Christ,
> which God gave to him to show to his slaves [τοῖς δούλοις αὐτοῦ]
> what things must happen quickly,
> and he made it known,
> sending (it) through his angel to his slave, John [τῷ δούλῳ αὐτοῦ Ἰωάννῃ].

The principal links in the chain of communication are: God—Christ—slaves. John only figures in the further expansion of this chain in the second half of the verse: Christ—angel—the slave John, through whom Christ's word comes to the larger circle of God's slaves.[45]

---

42. Interesting in this connection is the recitation of Zech. 12:10 in John 19:37, applied to the crucifixion.

43. Carey 1998, 736; see also Perelman and Olbrechts-Tyteca 1969, 91–92.

44. Carey 2001, 176; 1998, 736, 760.

45. Aune (1997, 13) suggests that "slaves" may refer to a circle of prophets in Rev. 1:1; 22:6. "Slaves" clearly denotes "prophets" in 10:7, less clearly (contra Aune 1997, 13) in 11:18: "the time [came] . . . to give the reward to your slaves, to the prophets and to the holy ones and to those fearing your name." It is not apparent that "your slaves" is renamed only by "the prophets" here, rather than by all three classes of servant (prophets, holy ones, those revering God's name).

While the title "slave of God" may strike the reader as self-deprecating, it is also a traditional title of distinction, appearing frequently in early Christian literature to designate a leader (cf. Rom. 1:1; Gal. 1:10; Phil. 1:1; Titus 1:1; Jas. 1:1; 2 Pet. 1:1; Jude 1:1).[46] On the one hand, the entire body of Christian disciples is referred to collectively as "God's slaves" throughout Revelation (2:20; 7:3; 19:2, 5; 22:3, 6), as probably here in Revelation 1:1 as well, with the result that John stands alongside the hearers as one of their number. In this regard, as he diminishes his own status, he also augments the status and authority of the words that he will speak, since they are not his own. On the other hand, however, John's identity as "Christ's slave" (1:1) may also single him out from the pack as exercising a leadership role, alongside the many other Christian leaders who used that title. As that "slave" who receives this revelation and through whom it is communicated to God's *many* "slaves," John enters the scene in the role of a prophet, and it is as a prophet, by virtue of charismatic authority rather than some traditional, authority-invested office, that he exercises authority among the congregations.

Two commissioning scenes establish John's prophetic authority. In the first (1:9-20), a heavenly voice "like a trumpet" commands John to "write what you are seeing in a book and send it to the seven churches, to Ephesus and to Smyrna and to Pergamum and to Thyatira and to Sardis and to Philadelphia and to Laodicea"(1:11). John turns to discover that this voice belongs to the glorified Christ, who once again orders John to "write the things you saw, and the things that are, and the things that are about to come into being after these things" (1:19). The command to "write" will be repeated throughout the book (2:1, 8, 12, 18; 3:1, 7, 14; 14:13; 19:9; 21:5), keeping John's prophetic commission, and the otherworldly authorization of the message, ever before the hearer. This opening episode "establishes, in the customary fashion of Judaeo-Christian rhetoric, [John's] *ethos* as a prophet."[47]

The connections between John's vision of, and response to, the glorified Christ, and traditional visions of otherworldly figures experienced by prophets like Ezekiel and Daniel (cf. Ezek. 1:26-28; Dan. 10:5-6, 9) also advance ethos. John's commissioning "looks" like an authentic one, since it resembles those received in the authoritative tradition of prophetic encounters. His reaction to it confirms its authenticity, since Daniel and Ezekiel experienced similar reactions in their ecstatic encounters. The same applies to the second commissioning scene (Rev. 10:1-11), which is strongly reminiscent of Ezekiel's prophetic commission (Ezek. 2:8-3:6) without being a mere imitation or reiteration of the same.[48]

---

46. Royalty 1998, 136. Moses the "servant of God" (παῖς κυρίου in Josh. 1:13 LXX) provides the prototype for this titular usage.

47. Kirby 1988, 199.

48. Witherington finds it "improbable that the content of the scroll [in Rev. 10] is about a prophetic commission, since that was already depicted at the outset of Revelation" (2003, 157 n. 226). While the scroll *itself* is not about prophetic commission, the scene of John being commanded to *eat* the scroll clearly reinforces John's prophetic commission to speak the words that God has put in his mouth. Multiple prophetic commissions would be a contextually appropriate way for John

While John gains the authority typically ascribed to a prophet, he also establishes connections with his hearers by speaking of himself as a fellow slave (1:1) and as a "brother" and "partner" (1:9).⁴⁹ John evokes goodwill by presenting himself as a "brother," a term that carries an affective dimension likely to arouse feelings of friendship and favor supportive of ethos. Similarly, calling himself a "partner" or "fellow sharer" (συγκοινωνός) in the difficult circumstances that accompany awaiting God's kingdom (i.e., "tribulation" and "patient endurance") evokes a sense of connection with John as one who understands and experiences the same trials faced by his audiences. Indeed, his experiences of hardship become a sign of John's steadfast faithfulness to the message of Jesus, the faithful witness, and thus tokens of his sincerity and pure motives—as opposed to Jezebel and the Nicolaitans, whose accommodationist policies position them for comfort rather than tribulation, for pleasure rather than patient endurance, and hence betray the self-serving nature of their agenda. Additionally, the epistolary greeting of "grace and peace" familiar from Pauline epistles, with which John first speaks in his own voice (1:4), suggests a pastoral relationship between John and the audience, hence one marked by both caring and goodwill on his part.⁵⁰

Credibility is also advanced as the moral virtue of a speaker is demonstrated. In regard to John, this begins as early as the *titulus*, in which the "slave, John," is further described as one "who attested to the word of God and the testimony of Jesus [ἐμαρτύρησεν τὸν λόγον τοῦ θεοῦ καὶ τὴν μαρτυρίαν Ἰησοῦ Χριστοῦ]" (1:2).⁵¹ This phrase provides a snapshot of John's activity and character, presenting him (for he is not speaking about himself, but is being attested by the faceless voice of the incipit) in terms that denote praiseworthy, divinely approved behavior throughout the work (1:5, 9; 2:13; 6:9; 12:17; 19:10, 13). John immediately reinforces this picture as he claims to be present on Patmos "on account of the word of God and the witness of Jesus [διὰ τὸν λόγον τοῦ θεοῦ καὶ τὴν μαρτυρίαν Ἰησοῦ]" (1:9). John steps onto the scene already as a faithful disciple, an imitator of Jesus who is himself a "faithful witness [ὁ μάρτυς, ὁ πιστός]" (1:5). This quality will be shared by Antipas, "my [i.e., Jesus'] witness, my faithful one [ὁ μάρτυς μου, ὁ πιστός μου]" (2:13); by the many martyrs beneath the celestial altar slain "on account of the word of God and on account of the witness that they had given [διὰ τὸν λόγον τοῦ θεοῦ καὶ τὴν μαρτυρίαν ἣν εἶχον]" (6:9); by the offspring of the woman clothed with the sun who "keep the commandments of God and have the witness of Jesus [τῶν τηρούντων τὰς ἐντολὰς τοῦ θεοῦ καὶ ἐχόντων τὴν μαρτυρίαν Ἰησοῦ]" (12:17); and by those who come to life and rule with Christ for

---

to reaffirm his authority—his ethos—in the midst of the speech. If the hearer heard Ezek. 2 in the background, moreover, is it difficult to see how the hearer would have understood Rev. 10 as something other than a (renewed) prophetic commission.

49. Schüssler Fiorenza 1985, 196; Royalty 1997, 144.

50. Carey 2001, 173.

51. See Kirby 1988, 205 n.17: "The groundwork for John's *ethos* is laid as early as 1.2" (though no discussion follows).

a thousand years, who include "those who were beheaded on account of the witness of Jesus and on account of the word of God [διὰ τὴν μαρτυρίαν Ἰησοῦ καὶ διὰ τὸν λόγον τοῦ θεοῦ]" (20:4). John is part of a web of associations involving "witness," an honorable group into which the readers will also be inducted as they live in line with the testimony of Jesus in their speech, actions, and demonstrations of single-hearted allegiance.[52]

The "word of God" and "witness of Jesus" are a risky business, bringing the threat of substantial loss rather than temporal gain. It led to death for Antipas, the souls beneath the altar, and those who were (and were yet to be) beheaded. It has led to exile (*relegatio ad insulam*, deportatation to an island) for John. This fact bolsters John's ethos insofar as it shows him to be sincere in his motives rather than engaged in the religion business for the sake of material gain like the sophists and charlatans lampooned by Lucian (see his *Alexander*, *The Passing of Peregrinus*, and *Philosophies for Sale*).[53]

Finally, John's superior access to otherworldly knowledge reinforces his authority. Though he shares this knowledge with the hearers, they are continually reminded that they depend on John for this knowledge, having access to it only through him. However, John knows some things that the audience cannot,[54] for example, the meteorological message that John receives but must withhold: "And when the seven thunders had spoken, I was about to write, and I heard a voice speaking from heaven: 'Seal up the things that the seven thunders spoke, and do not write them'" (Rev. 10:4). This subtly reminds the hearers that John is more in the know than he can let on, enhancing both authority and the need for trust.[55] He surely *would* have shared it but was explicitly commanded not to do so.

John's tendency to use "as" and "like" (ὅμοιος, ὡς) may serve a similar function. The word ὅμοιος is frequent in (Greek) apocalyptic discourse, expressing the seer's struggle to find the right words to evoke precisely the visual impressions that the seer witnessed, since those visions go beyond the normal experiences for which we have words.[56] The author is thus always closer to the vision than the audience: the words do not allow them quite the same access to those scenes. John employs this word chiefly in regard to the opening Christophany

---

52. Carey 1999b, 122.
53. Paul uses hardship catalogs in 2 Corinthians similarly: a teacher's perseverance in commitment to a religion or philosophical school when such commitment has brought financial or other loss rather than gain or fame demonstrates that teacher's sincere commitment to that way of life (see Furnish 1984, 281–82).
54. So also Carey 1998, 753. Carey (1999b, 124–25, following Ruiz 1994, 201) regards the consumption of the little scroll as another "distinction in knowledge and status" separating John from the hearers, with whom he otherwise claims to share everything. This is debatable, however, since the episode of consuming the scroll can also be seen as the impetus for the revelations in chapters 12 and following, which impart the scroll's contents.
55. By attempting to recover this missing information (referring the reader to Mark 13:32 and Matt. 24:36, where no one can know the day or the hour of Christ's return, and inferring that this must be the information John hears but must suppress), Schüssler Fiorenza (1991, 75) seems to have missed the point of John's sealing up what the seven thunders revealed.
56. L. Snyder 2000, 411.

(1:13, 15), the vision of God upon the throne and his angelic court (4:3 [2x], 6, 7 [3x]), and the fifth and sixth woes (9:7 [2x], 10, 19; see also 11:1; 13:2, 11; 14:14; 21:11, 18). Positively, John's use of simile engages the hearers' imaginations as they listen, inviting them to visualize beyond the words themselves; yet it also reminds them that John's experience is larger than the words that he can find, that the words (to which they can have access) are *not* the experience (to which only John had access). This, again, subtly distances the hearers from the experience itself, reminding them that they are completely dependent upon John's mediation for access to the otherworldly insight, and thus affirming his authority by virtue of his superior knowledge.

"FAVORED ARE THOSE WHO ... KEEP WHAT IS WRITTEN HEREIN"

A number of striking assertions about the words of Revelation, and about reading and "keeping" these words, also contribute to the authority of this message. These assertions carry weight because they are not spoken in the author's own voice, but rather in the voices of entities other than John, who become "independent witnesses" to the credibility of the text—otherworldly "endorsements," as it were.

The macarisms of 1:3 and 22:7 are important examples. The first is spoken in the impersonal voice of the book's introduction, imitating the *titulus* of the scriptural prophetic books, in which John is himself spoken of in the third person. The second is spoken to John by the angelic guide who had shown John the vision of the New Jerusalem (21:9; 22:6).

> Favored is the one reading the words of the prophecy out loud, and the ones who hear the words and heed the things written therein [Μακάριος ὁ ἀναγινώσκων καὶ οἱ ἀκούοντες τοὺς λόγους τῆς προφητείας καὶ τηροῦντες τὰ ἐν αὐτῇ γεγραμμένα]. (1:3)
> Favored is the one who heeds the words of the prophecy of this book [Μακάριος ὁ τηρῶν τοὺς λόγους τῆς προφητείας τοῦ βιβλίου τούτου]. (22:7)

These two macarisms are essentially the same, framing the whole experience of reading Revelation and hearing Revelation read, except that the latter omits the felicitation of the reader and hearers. At the close of the text, these experiences are almost completed, and all that remains is to "heed" (lit., "keep") what has been read and heard. The first macarism helps to render the hearers attentive and well-disposed, since the acts of reading, hearing, and keeping the message are presented as signs of standing in a highly privileged position ("favored," "honored," "felicitated"). The second reaffirms the privilege accorded the audience, reinforcing their inclination to walk in line with what they have heard.

At the other extreme, Revelation concludes with a curse formula:

> I myself attest [μαρτυρῶ ἐγώ] to each person who hears the words of the prophecy of this book: if anyone adds to them, God will add to that person the plagues that stand written in this book, and if anyone takes away from the words of the book of this prophecy, God will take away that person's share in the tree of life and in the holy city described in this book. (22:18–19)

Context shows the "I" pronouncing this curse to be the glorified Christ. In the following verse, "the one attesting these things" (ὁ μαρτυρῶν ταῦτα, 22:20, echoing the opening of 22:18) also says, "Indeed, I am coming quickly," indicating the speaker to be the ascended Jesus, as John's response—"Indeed, come, Lord Jesus" (22:20b)—renders certain. In this curse, the glorified Christ personally attests to the importance of the whole text in all its particulars and threatens any who would dare to edit it. Given John's expectation of Christ's imminent intervention, he was probably not so concerned to preserve the integrity of the text over the course of a long history of transmission as to prevent local readers or others in the congregations from adding qualifying glosses or omitting details to make the reading of the indictments of the churches and local figures within them, or of the Roman domination system as a whole, less uncomfortable or awkward.[57]

In addition to blessings and curses, subtle transformations within the text enhance its authority as "the word of God and the testimony of Jesus" come to be closely identified with the words of this particular text. John's angelic interlocutor highlights this transformation:

> I am your fellow slave and that of your brothers and sisters holding on to the witness of Jesus [σύνδουλός σού εἰμι καὶ τῶν ἀδελφῶν σου τῶν ἐχόντων τὴν μαρτυρίαν Ἰησοῦ]. (19:10)
> I am your fellow slave and that of your brothers and sisters the prophets, and those keeping the words of this book [σύνδουλός σού εἰμι καὶ τῶν ἀδελφῶν σου τῶν προφητῶν καὶ τῶν τηρούντων τοὺς λόγους τοῦ βιβλίου τούτου]. (22:9)

Revelation relies heavily on verbal repetition to suggest meaning by creating webs of association, reinforcing boundaries and incompatibilities, and the like.[58] It may be significant, then, that the most extensive and exact verbal repetition within Revelation occurs between 19:10 and 22:8b–9.[59] "Holding on to the witness of Jesus" has become, in the second iteration, "keeping the words of this book." The second may be heard as a clarification and specification of the first. Similarly, the visions that the angel was showing John ("The Lord, the God of the spirits of the prophets, sent his angel *to show* to his slaves what must happen

---

57. Carey (1999b, 111) suggests that the blessings and curses function as topics of amplification, heightening awareness of the importance of John's message by calling attention to the high stakes of hearing and heeding the message in its entirety.
58. See deSilva 1999a, 73–81.
59. Both passages begin with John falling before the feet of the angel and the angel prohibiting this action, using many of the same words in each.

quickly," 22:6) have become "these words" (22:6; see also 22:9). The sights, for example, of the new Jerusalem, are transformed into the words John has used to record the things seen (and heard, 1:2). An especially noteworthy transformation is also evident as one moves from 1:2 to 22:20. Now, at the very conclusion, "the one testifying these things [ὁ μαρτυρῶν ταῦτα]" is not merely John, "who bore witness [ὃς ἐμαρτύρησεν] concerning . . . whatever he saw" (1:2), but also Christ himself, the same "I" of the "Indeed, I am coming quickly." The words of Revelation, therefore, are not merely John's "testimony" (1:2), but also the testimony of the glorified Christ (22:20).

There are also explicit words of authentication throughout Revelation. In two instances these affirmations concern primarily the reliability of a particular utterance. In 19:9, after commanding John to "write" the words of the fourth macarism, the angel further authorizes the words that John has just inscribed: "He says to me, 'These words are genuine words of God' [οὗτοι οἱ λόγοι ἀληθινοί τοῦ θεοῦ εἰσιν]." Similarly in 21:5, John is commanded to write—apparently by God—that "these words are reliable and authentic/genuine [οὗτοι οἱ λόγοι πιστοὶ καὶ ἀληθινοί). Here the authenticating statement refers immediately to a pronouncement made by "the one seated on the throne," "See! I am making all things new" (21:5a), but probably also includes the previous speech by the same speaker, which in turn comprises recontextualizations of familiar promises from the Jewish Scriptures (21:3–4).

In 22:6a, however, we encounter a much more sweeping authentication. Here, the angelic conversation partner repeats the affirmation made in 19:9: "These words are reliable and genuine [οὗτοι οἱ λόγοι πιστοὶ καὶ ἀληθινοί]," affirming them to originate with "the Lord, the God of the spirits of the prophets" (22:6b). But unlike the occurrences in 19:9 and 21:5, the angel uses this formula not to authenticate a discrete pronouncement, but rather, at the very least, the whole of John's description of the new Jerusalem (21:9–22:5).[60] However, 22:6b–7 may be heard to authenticate the entire body of Revelation since it explicitly recalls 1:1, 3 and forms an *inclusio* with the same:

> *God* gave to him *to show to his slaves what must happen quickly*, and he signified it, *sending it through his angel.* . . . *Favored* is the one who reads out loud and the ones who hear *the words of the prophecy* and *who keep* what is written therein. [Ἔδωκεν αὐτῷ ὁ θεὸς δεῖξαι τοῖς δούλοις αὐτοῦ ἃ δεῖ γενέσθαι ἐν τάχει, καὶ ἐσήμανεν ἀποστείλας διὰ τοῦ ἀγγέλου αὐτοῦ. . . . Μακάριος ὁ ἀναγινώσκων καὶ οἱ ἀκούοντες τοὺς λόγους τῆς προφητείας καὶ τηροῦντες τὰ ἐν αὐτῇ γεγραμμένα.] (1:1, 3)
>
> The Lord *God* . . . *sent his angel to show to his slaves what must happen quickly.* . . . *Favored is the one who keeps the words of the prophecy* of this book [Ὁ κύριος ὁ θεὸς . . . ἀπέστειλεν τὸν ἄγγελον αὐτοῦ δεῖξαι τοῖς δούλοις αὐτοῦ ἃ δεῖ γενέσθαι ἐν τάχει. . . . Μακάριος ὁ τηρῶν τοὺς λόγους τῆς προφητείας τοῦ βιβλίου τούτου.] (22:6–7)

---

60. These affirmations of reliability and genuineness appear to cluster around the visions of Christ's victory and the new Jerusalem.

Just as the macarisms themselves, together with the final curse, frame Revelation in a manner heightening audience attention and receptivity, so the angel's words of authentication, opening the epilogue to the work and recalling the opening commendation through verbal repetitions, provide a supramundane testimony to the credibility of *this* message in a situation of competing prophetic messages.

DECONSTRUCTING RIVAL VOICES

In a situation in which multiple voices vie for the audience's assent, appeals to ethos may involve undermining the credibility of rival speakers alongside positively establishing one's own. The speaker may have to give considerable attention to exciting prejudice against other speakers so as to neutralize their claims on the audience's attention and trust, as well as remove prejudice against himself or herself resulting from the rival speakers' attention to this same strategy (Aristotle, *Rhet.* 3.14.12).[61]

There are several voices competing for attention and for the right to define the boundaries of a "correct" response to the call of Jesus among the seven congregations. "False apostles" have tried to gain a hearing in Ephesus. The "Nicolaitans" have been active in Ephesus and Pergamum, although their message seems to have been rejected in the former congregation. A teacher in Thyatira claims to exercise the prophetic gift and has gathered a substantial following. Outside the churches, the local Jewish communities in Smyrna and Philadelphia have made their "voices" heard in ways that would tend to draw disciples away from the Christian assemblies ("slander," 2:9). Finally, the congregations hear the "voices" of imperial representatives and local non-Christian populations, both witnessing to Roman imperial ideology (as heard, for example, in public acclamations of the emperor or in cultic settings) and censuring individuals like Antipas (2:13) and the commitments he represented.

The fact that John submerges his own voice and allows other, supramundane voices to speak throughout Revelation is an important strategy also in regard to this "deconstructive" side of appeals to ethos. John never speaks an ill word against his rivals. At most he merely provides descriptive narration that casts them in a bad light (e.g., the emperors, their local representatives, and the general masses that involve themselves in idolatry). But it is the voice of the glorified *Christ* that denounces the Thyatiran prophetess, the Nicolaitans, the false apostles (if these are not the Nicolaitans), and the synagogue (2:1–3:22). Voices from heaven accuse and sentence Babylon, while the voices of murdered witnesses cry

---

61. See also Aristotle, *Rhet.* 3.19.1; 3.17.16; *Rhet. Her.* 1.5.8; Cicero, *De or.* 2.43.182; Quintilian, *Inst.* 4.1.14–15. These texts are cited in Carey 1998, 738. Carey has done admirable work in laying out John's techniques for casting rival speakers in the worst possible light for the sake of undermining their credibility and thus their "pull" with an audience (see Carey 1999b, 137–63; summarized in Carey 2001, 177–79). Schüssler Fiorenza (1991, 132) was an early voice calling attention to this aspect of John's rhetorical strategy.

out for vindication, arousing indignation against Roman domination. Words that might appear self-serving or hateful if John had spoken them in his own voice are placed on the lips of those whose ethos is above suspicion and beyond question. In other words, we do not hear John seeking to undermine a rival local leader (thus exposing John's potential self-interest), but rather Christ seeking to protect his congregation from the continued influence of a dangerous threat to their loyalty and therefore their eschatological destiny.

Jezebel and the Nicolaitans

One blatant strategy for undermining the more threatening rivals (i.e., those that have gained a foothold among the congregations) involves naming them not by their proper names, but by strategically chosen pseudonyms associating them with unflattering characters from the Jewish Scriptures, names that reveal their "true" character.[62] Just as John's voice is linked with praiseworthy figures like Antipas and Christ himself through the association of each of these characters with faithful witness, John's rivals are associated with notorious false prophets, associations that will adversely color the churches' perception of them—and their promotion of lower group boundaries.

As we have seen in chapter 2, the "Nicolaitans" are closely linked with Balaam (2:14–15), and their teaching with Balaam's plan to erode the identity of the people of God by luring them into participation in the cults of, and sexual intercourse with, the surrounding people groups (Num. 25:1–2; 31:16). The etymological similarity between Balaam and Nicolaus, even if not conclusive, may reinforce the connection among some of the hearers. Balaam is the prototype of the false prophet, and his teaching leads to the outbreak of a deadly plague throughout the congregation of Israel (Num. 25:8–9). Through this association, the hearers are led to view the Nicolaitans and their boundary-relaxing position as a grave threat to the integrity and safety of God's new congregation.

Jezebel was prominently associated with the prophets of Baal, for whom she acted as a patroness and protector, thus promoting the worship of false gods in ancient Israel. But she was also infamous as the "harlot queen" from the story of ancient Israel. Second Kings 9:22 LXX uses the term πορνεία (sexual immorality, fornication) to sum up Jezebel's activity, which may explain the foregrounding of sexual imagery in the oracle to Thyatira. Πορνεία also sums up the work of this prophetess, who "is not willing to repent of her fornication," with whom some members of the congregation are said to have "committed adultery," and who is ultimately to be thrown down "upon a bed" (Rev. 2:22).[63] Greg Carey speaks of this focus upon the prophetess's sexual activity as

---

62. So Johns 1998, 765: "'Naming' in the Apocalypse . . . evokes stories and images, and places value—both positive and negative—on the individuals, groups, or deities thus named."

63. The NASB's addition of the qualifier "of sickness" to describe the "bed" (κλίνη) onto which Christ will throw this adulteress may represent an attempt to avoid the sexual overtones of the scene John creates.

an example of "debasing" as a means of undermining credibility, in his view an objectionable technique.[64] While it is possible that the prophetess was involved in sexual affairs within the congregation (this is not unheard of in the history of the church), it is more likely, in keeping with the use of sexual imagery throughout Revelation, that John is labeling her activity of mentoring, teaching, and leading those who are influenced by her as "fornication" and "adultery" in order to make her activity stand out as all the more morally objectionable, arousing disgust toward her prophetic activity by painting it with the figurative overtones of uncontrolled, sexually immoral behavior. This would, in turn, place her and her teaching in a less appealing, less credible light.

Since this prophetess teaches that involvement in the local economy and in a bare minimum of the cultic activities that inevitably accompany such activity is compatible with the confession of Christ, it is perhaps not surprising that John depicts her in ways that will resemble Babylon, that domination system with which she will allow some measure of partnership for the sake of short-term security.[65] Babylon and Jezebel are linked through the repetition of the phrase "of her fornication" (τῆς πορευίας αὐτῆς, 2:21; 14:8), suggesting implicitly that the ministry of this prophetess leads believers to enter into the webs of "fornication" (that is, entangling alliances with an idolatrous domination system opposed to God's vision for human community) spun by Babylon, and thereby making a strong case against her authority and the appeal of her message.[66] According to the *Rhetorica ad Alexandrum* (1437b.18–21), a speaker can arouse prejudice against another by suggesting that the other advocates "making a discreditable peace." John uses this topic to his advantage against Jezebel, the Nicolaitans, and anyone who promotes cooperation with Roman imperialism. And, as Jezebel contributed to the northern kingdom's downfall,[67] so following the Thyatiran prophetess promises to lead to downfall for all those connected with her (2:22–23).

John links "Babylon" and "Jezebel" in many other particulars as well. Both Rome and the rival prophetess are identified with a negative name from Israel's history. Both are presented as inappropriate mothers—one, a mother of whores and abominations (17:5), the other, a mother who fornicates and commits adultery (2:20–22). Both "lead astray" (2:20; 18:23), as do Satan and the false prophet. The use of the verb πλανᾶν (to lead astray) in 2:20; 13:14; and 19:20 binds Jezebel's activity to that of the land beast (the "false prophet") as well as to the activity of the dragon (12:9) and Babylon (18:23). Since this land beast makes fire come down from heaven before a false god, he is a kind of anti-Elijah, making him an appropriate counterpart for "Jezebel," Elijah's nemesis.[68]

---

64. Carey 1999b, 157–59.
65. This is the focal point of the important study by Duff (2001).
66. DeSilva 1998b, 796.
67. Carey 1999b, 143.
68. Duff 2001, 125. The portrayal of Babylon in Rev. 17–18 would further call to mind the OT portrait of Jezebel among the more biblically literate, which would in turn further identify the

John creates such "homologies" (correspondences between images, effected through repetitions of words, phrases, and so forth) throughout Revelation, linking Jezebel, Babylon, Satan, and the second beast (notably, also called "the false prophet"). The resulting webs of contrast and correlation link acceptance of Jezebel's teaching with deception by Satan and with the crimes of the Roman order.[69] Creating homologies that link Jezebel with Satan and, more especially, with the second beast (the false prophet), leaves John in the role of true prophet—in many ways enacting the role of a new Elijah opposing Jezebel.[70] John also presents two female figures—the woman clothed with the sun and the new Jerusalem—who correlate closely with one another *and* contrast strikingly and specifically with both Jezebel and Babylon. The result is that John further censures Jezebel (and Babylon) by contrast with these positive models, a strategy recommended in Demetrius, *Style* 5.292.[71]

It is not, however, the case that John, "having little that he can use against his rival's position," simply "undertakes to malign her (as Quintilian recommends)."[72] The Thyatiran prophetess is promoting (or at least justifying) some kind of behavior that puts Christian disciples into closer contact with food offered to idols, and thus promotes lower group boundaries in an area *essential* to the group's identity and the group's witness in the midst of an idolatrous society. In other words, John has just cause for concern and calls attention both to this behavior (2:20) and to the dangers that it promotes, namely, becoming more closely linked with the "sins" of Babylon (cf. 18:4).

It is noteworthy that Balaam (with whom the Nicolaitans are identified) and Jezebel are historically the opponents of Moses and Elijah, the two faithful prophets par excellence. Indeed, Moses and Elijah are types for the true prophets and witnesses in Revelation 11, who call down fire from heaven and strike the earth with plagues. As the hearers are drawn into the role of the witnesses who resemble Moses and Elijah, they are strategically ranged against the false prophets in their midst. And John thus emerges as the "true" prophet in this contest with Jezebel and the Balaamites.

Representatives of Roman Imperialism

The Thyatiran prophetess and the "Nicolaitans" represent John's most immediate rivals for the "right" to advise and lead the congregations, but they are not

---

Thyatiran prophetess with "Babylon" (Duff 2001, 90). The "historical" Jezebel was guilty of spilling the blood of the prophets of God (1 Kgs. 18:3–4, 13; 2 Kgs. 9:7—the last text is closely recontextualized in Rev. 19:2), as was John's Babylon (Rev. 17:6; 18:24), and her flesh was ultimately devoured (1 Kgs. 21:23–24), as the flesh of Babylon would be (Rev. 17:16).

69. The indirect technique of commending or undermining by "homology" had, of course, been discussed before as "identifications" (Carey 1999b, 118–28, 141–49), under the heading of "repetitive texture" (deSilva 1998b, 796; 1999a, 73–81), or more colorfully, as "tarring with the same brush" (Royalty 1998, 163–64, 210). However, Duff's study substantially advances these incipient insights.

70. Duff 2001, 128. The parallels between Babylon and Jezebel in this paragraph are found in Duff 2001, 91.

71. Duff 2001, 75.

72. Duff 2001, 75.

the only opposing voices to which the congregations are listening. Voices in the cities shout out, "Who is like the beast, and who is able to fight against him?" (13:4). Of course, they do not use exactly those words, stolen away here from the praise of God (cf. Exod. 15:11). But the seven cities are each, in varying degrees, home to discourse about Rome and her emperors, and about the allegiance and honor due these pillars of the Roman imperial system. While John is concerned that teachers within the churches not draw the disciples back into partnership with the larger society, especially in matters involving idolatry, he devotes far more space to undermining the credibility of, the authority of, and any positive emotions felt toward Rome and her emperors. Though we will explore this more fully through the appeals to emotions John will orchestrate throughout the visions, it may be appropriate to give some attention to this aspect of his rhetorical strategy under the heading of "ethos."

John uses the technique of "debasing" once again in regard to Rome. He gives no attention to her positive achievements, no credit to the ideals that the principate sought to embody at its best. Rather, he presents Rome as a depraved and self-indulgent prostitute, such that the "normal" practice of everyday business is overlaid with the negative connotations of playing with a whore.[73] Representing the goddess Roma as a drunken, bloodthirsty prostitute allows John also to create a new mythology (and destiny) for Roman rule, radically different from the publicly articulated one, and thus promote distance between his audiences and Rome.[74]

A technique closely related to debasing is dehumanizing. John presents the emperors, who are flesh-and-blood human beings, as a collective, monstrous animal: the "beast" (Rev. 13:1–10). This "beast," moreover, is painted with the brush strokes of the mythic chaos monster, casting the head of the Roman Empire as a force of disorder and subversion in the cosmos. John obscures the emperor's humanness and any legitimate claim that the emperor might have on the audience's loyalty and gratitude, which is particularly significant in cities that celebrate the emperor's patronage so enthusiastically.[75] The local voices charged with promoting the imperial cult receive similar attention: their humanity is also suppressed, as they constitute merely another beast, "leading people astray" (13:14) and employing coercive measures to enforce adulation of the emperors where deception and chicanery fail (13:15–17). John knows that Rome, her emperors, and their local promoters have previously attracted many members of the churches, and so he portrays them here as unsympathetically as possible so

---

73. Carey 2001, 179; see also Royalty 1998, 191. I disagree, however, that John employs "taunting" as a means of further debasing Babylon. If Rev. 18 represents a taunt, its restraint when compared to the taunts represented, for example, in the reported speech of the psalmist's enemies is extraordinary. Whether or not one hears "John's glee over the catastrophe" (Carey 1999b, 156–57), moreover, is a function of the emotional tone supplied by the reader/interpreter. One could with perhaps more justification hear sincere regret over the tragic waste that accompanies Babylon's inevitable judgment, and over the personal tragedies that it entails. See the section "Such a Pity?" in chap. 8 (below).

74. Carey 2001, 178.

75. See deSilva 1998b, 799; 1999a, 109.

as to undermine any appeal they might have and arouse revulsion rather than attraction.⁷⁶

Finally, John attacks the credibility of the voices of those non-Christian neighbors who would be closest to the members of the congregations in a variety of ways, insulating the disciples from the persuasive power of their non-Christian peers' practice and pressure. The credibility of the non-Christian Jewish neighbors voicing their critique of the disciples' convictions is assaulted with the label "synagogue of Satan" (2:9; 3:9), and their speech dismissed as "slander" (βλασφημία, 2:9).⁷⁷ John neutralizes the persuasiveness of the voices (and social pressures) of the believers' non-Christian Gentile neighbors by displaying their lack of virtue and knowledge. The idolaters behave unjustly insofar as they take the worship due the One God who gave them life and give it to the demons that lurk behind their idols (9:20). These idolaters are, moreover, the deviant source of every social ill (9:20–21), laboring under demonic deception and unable to perceive the truth of their situation (12:9; 13:14; 18:23), and therefore unable to formulate a reliable assessment of the Christians or their commitments. These neighbors, moreover, will maintain their folly to the end (16:9, 11).⁷⁸ Whatever social sanctions they impose upon the believers, however much they display their contempt for the Christians, the disciples must bear in mind that it all stems from a deadly error and a commitment to vice on the part of the outsiders, and so they must not allow any such trials to turn them away from God's truth.

DOES JOHN GO TOO FAR?

Scholars studying John's construction of his own authority and deconstruction of other voices often express concern or discomfort in regard to John's aims and methods. This is justified to some extent. In recent times we have had sufficient reminders of the dangers of authoritarian prophets who claim to be the sole spokespersons for the divine will, and who will not engage—nor allow their followers to engage—in open dialogue with other, potentially critical viewpoints. On the other hand, many modern people are simply challenged by John's conviction that God's perspective can be truly known and brought to bear on a particular situation, to the exclusion of other positions. These critics write from a modern cultural preference, placing a higher value on inclusiveness, recovering all imaginable voices, and bringing everyone to the table rather than on commitment to a particular tradition and on discerning its correct interpretation

---

76. So rightly Carey 1999b, 159.
77. Royalty (1998, 163–64) observes that "Rome, the Jews, and other Christian teachers [especially Jezebel] . . . are united by John's rhetoric under Satan's name" (see Rev. 2:9, 13, 24; 3:9). However different these parties are from one another, John groups them all together as tools being used by God's archenemy as part of his rebellion against the cosmic order.
78. DeSilva 1998a, 94–97.

or application. To put it another way, we tend, particularly in postmodern discourse, to value "perspective" over "Truth."

In their critique of John, however, recent scholars have unduly exaggerated John's authoritarian stance and distorted his claims to unique and exclusive authority—and then criticized John on the basis of those distortions. Robert Royalty reads the curse of 22:18–19 (regarding adding to, or taking away from, the message of Revelation) as a proscription of "text criticism, editing, translation, or allegorization," as well as borrowing John's words, for example, to keep them alive in the liturgy of the worshiping community (where Revelation has had its broadest and most lasting impact).[79] He works in a rabbinic manner to erect a considerable fence around this proscription, but then criticizes *John* for that fence and the ways that fence limits engagement with the text.

From another angle, Paul Duff claims that "John's followers [must] accept his leadership to the exclusion of any other person."[80] Similarly, Greg Carey cites 1:1 as evidence that John presents his work as the "only revelation of Jesus Christ."[81] But this reading of 1:1 says more about Carey's aversion to John's claims to authority than about those claims. In point of fact, John does not even use the definite article to preface his claim: it is simply "*a* revelation of Jesus Christ," presented as one more among any number of valid revelations. It is not John, but the prejudice of the interpreter, that turns this into an *exclusive* claim.

In making such statements about John's exclusivity, Duff and Carey (and all the more, Royalty) do not give adequate attention to the role of the other prophets whose voices and activity are affirmed. The angel who shows John the new Jerusalem, to whom he twice bows down and must be corrected, describes himself as "your fellow slave, and that of your brothers and sisters, the prophets [σύνδουλός σού εἰμι καὶ τῶν ἀδελφῶν σου τῶν προφητῶν]" (22:9). While many of the references to "prophets" throughout Revelation could refer to the classical prophets of the Hebrew Bible or the larger, transtemporal company of prophets, this particular reference suggests prophets who are John's contemporaries. David Aune sees this same group of prophets behind the "you" (plural) in 22:16: "I, Jesus, sent my angel to attest these things to you [ὑμῖν] for the churches.[82]

Although some have suggested that these prophets are all part of one "school" or "guild" of which John himself is the head, evidence for this position is difficult to come by.[83] Rather, such a claim functions subtly to support the image

---

79. Royalty 2004, 291.
80. Duff 2001, 49.
81. Carey 1999b, 133.
82. Aune 1998b, 1225–26; so also Schüssler Fiorenza 1985, 106. In an earlier study, Aune (1989, 110) blended together the hypothesis that the "you" (plural) refers to a circle of prophets with the possibility that they were the envoys who bore John's message to the seven churches. This position explains, in part, the addition of the strange preface (1:1–3), which locates these prophetic envoys in the chain of revelation and dissemination ("his slaves," 1:1).
83. Schüssler Fiorenza (1985, 106–7, 112 n. 76) deduces the existence of a school on the basis of the author's knowledge of prophetic-apocalyptic traditions and forms, access to the traditions of other schools (e.g., Pauline and Johannine), and use of "'coded' language and imagery." The first of these, however, requires not a school context for the exercise of prophecy in Asia Minor, but merely

of John as authoritarian and concerned primarily about power and influence rather than the spiritual health of the congregations. The mention of the "other prophets" who exercise a discerning role in 1 Corinthians 14:29–33, a primary witness for proponents of the hypothesis of prophetic "schools" or "guilds" in the first Christian century, need refer to nothing more than those who have an established record of exercising the prophetic gift, without any claims concerning their organization, functioning as a unit, or internal leadership.[84] Moreover, Paul's very democratic view of the gifts of the Spirit—"for you are all, each one of you, capable of prophesying" (1 Cor. 14:31)—militates against any notion of a closed circle of prophets in Corinth (even if it is offered as a corrective of such a practice, though glossolalia seems to have been the preferred and more prized gift there). In other words, claiming that John only acknowledges the prophets under his authority or in his school is another example of reading too much into the text in a way that is prejudiced against John.

While John clearly believes that not all prophets adequately represent Christ's intentions for the churches (and this might be the crux of the problem for some modern interpreters), he does acknowledge other prophets who stand alongside him under the authority and guiding norms of the Hebrew Scriptures and the Jesus tradition, who are deeply concerned that the commandments of God, the warnings of the prophets, and the witness of the Psalms (e.g., to God's kingship, to the necessity of acknowledging this kingship above all others, and to the future, in which all nations will come and do the same) be preserved and lived out in the churches of Asia Minor (and elsewhere).

John's self-representation fits the expectations of the early Christian culture that God would communicate to God's people through those who experienced alternate states of consciousness, and moreover, that these words would be "tested" or weighed in order to discern their authenticity and therefore credibility. In Pauline circles (which overlap considerably with the churches addressed by Revelation; certainly Ephesus and Laodicea were influenced by Paul and his legacy), the expectation both of allowing ecstatic utterances *and* testing them is well attested (see 1 Cor. 14; 1 Thess. 5:19–22). The guidelines for such testing are not fully developed, but alignment with the received tradition is underscored at two points. In the exordium to Galatians, Paul asserts that a new proclamation, even if delivered by an angel (perhaps through a prophet or charismatist), must not be accepted if it conflicts with the apostolic proclamation of the gospel (Gal. 1:6–9). In Johannine circles, such testing clearly involved doctrinal litmus tests at one point in the community's history (1 John 4:1–4). Notably, 1 John

---

the author's access to hearing and reading formative texts throughout the course of his life. The second requires only attention to the emerging patterns of Christian discourse, such as would be expected of someone so involved in the life and leadership of the churches. The third is, frankly, a myth whose expiration date is long overdue. Revelation is not written in "code" for an esoteric conventicle, unless by "code" we simply mean "OT language" and by "esoteric conventicle" we mean the Christian assemblies themselves. See further chap. 2, n. 8 (above).

84. Although citing 1 Cor. 14:29–33 as evidence for prophetic "schools," Aune (1989, 111) recognizes that the text conduces to other readings.

itself begins by calling attention to the received tradition of the community as the larger context for testing new proclamations. In perhaps the most important extracanonical witness to the phenomenon of early Christian prophecy, the *Didache*, communities are directed to discern whether or not the prophet is acting out of self-interest, using (the appearance of) prophetic speech as a cloak for gain (11–13).

John communicates his prophetic word within this Christian culture of "testing" prophecy, especially by other prophets (1 Cor. 14:29). John knows this culture to exist in these churches and even encourages the practice, for after all, the Ephesian community "tested" some teachers claiming to be apostles and found them lacking by some criterion or criteria (Rev. 2:2). This larger context, and the established tradition of weighing prophecy, allows for the possibility that John is himself quite antiauthoritarian, submitting his word to the other prophets in the community for testing and verification. This culture creates the reasonable expectation for John that he will be held accountable to standards external to his own speech, thus mitigating what modern critics regard as his authoritarian strains and keeping him honest in regard to a larger stream of received tradition. Prophecies would surely not be weighed simply on the basis of who was "louder" or more extravagant in one's claims concerning divine inspiration. Christians were well accustomed to charlatans claiming inspiration, but who were in reality merely "dreaming" (Jude 8). Prophets would be tested, rather, at least in part on the basis of their consonance with the foundational beliefs, ethos, and traditions of the group. John's thoroughgoing alignment of his own voice with the voice of the Hebrew Scriptures may, in fact, reflect John's awareness of this need to conform himself to, and to discover and "invent" his argument in line with, the greater norm under which he, other prophets, and his audiences stand. It is to John's use of the Jewish Scriptures and other early Christian traditions, and the contribution of the same to John's message being "approved," that we turn in the following chapter.

Chapter 6

Stealing Authority?
John's Use of the Hebrew Bible

John's use of the authoritative Scriptures shared by synagogue and church is an area of perennial interest and vexation. The latter stems from two concurrent observations that (virtually) no one would deny: On the one hand, John incorporates hundreds of phrases and even essentially complete verses from the Jewish Scriptures;[1] on the other hand, John never once actually *quotes* material from those Scriptures. Why does John incorporate so much material from the Old Testament without ever explicitly citing it? What are the rhetorical gains of doing so, as opposed to drawing explicit attention to the origin of this material? With what motives, techniques, and degree of exegetical responsibility is John reading and interpreting the Old Testament and re-presenting it to his audience? What are his expectations for his hearers' engagement with the Old Testament and with his use of its contents?

---

1. Swete (1908, cxl–cliii) finds 278 verses in Revelation with allusions to particular texts from the Jewish Scriptures.

THE RHETORICAL GAINS OF EXTENSIVE INTERTEXTURE

Many New Testament authors use the recitation of Old Testament texts in much the same way as Greco-Roman authors cite some authoritative text from within their own tradition (e.g., a line from Homer or Hesiod).[2] Paul, for example, writes: "Are we [Judeans] any better off? No, not at all; for we have already charged that all, both Jews and Gentiles, are under the power of sin, as it is written: 'There is no one who is righteous, not even one'" (Rom. 3:9–10 NRSV). Here, Paul recites Psalm 14:1 as evidence—proof from a written authority—for the argumentative claim he has just advanced and upon which he will go on to build. The use of the Old Testament in Paul, Hebrews, 1 Peter, and other argumentative texts often has this, or a closely related, character. For example, the recitations of Old Testament texts in Galatians and Hebrews often have the flavor of arguments from close readings of the wording of legal documents. John, however, avoids explicitly appealing to the authority of the Old Testament by using this specific, self-conscious practice.[3] Nevertheless, intertexture remains a primary resource for him in establishing the credibility of this future he narrates. John never explicitly points to Scripture as an external norm that authorizes and undergirds his moral assessments of particular elements of the hearers' situation, his diagnosis of the particular challenges that merit attention, and his identification of the salutary way forward. Yet he still harnesses the power of these authoritative texts to render his message credible and persuasive.

By recontextualizing the content of authoritative prophecy, John subtly invites these Scriptures to lend their authority to his own visions. If the words of the prophets and psalms were inspired in their original contexts, they remain recognizable as inspired material in the new context. For example, John recontextualizes—that is, he weaves into his new composition significantly long strings of words from—portions of Daniel 7:13 and Zechariah 12:10 as he announces the imminently coming One (Rev. 1:7):

> *Look! He is coming with the clouds,*
> *and every eye will see him,*
> and whoever *pierced* him,
> *and all the tribes of the land will wail on his acount.*

Many hearers would recognize such recontextualizations, all the more since these texts in this particular combination had already circulated within early Christian culture in a saying of Jesus (Matt. 24:30 par.).[4] The hearers would recognize that

---

2. The NT authors very occasionally cite Greco-Roman authorities: see the quotation of Aratus in Acts 17:28 and Menander in 1 Cor. 15:33.
3. See Paulien 1988, 38.
4. This is not to say that audiences would catch every scriptural *allusion*, a matter about which even scholars focusing their work on John's allusions disagree. Paulien (1988, 37–38), for example, carefully tabulated the allusions discovered by ten commentators in Rev. 8:1–9:21; 11:15–19 and found a surprising lack of overlap. Commentators might agree on a few allusions, but then each offer

these texts had a life long before John's utterance of the words, and that these texts were authoritative oracles of God. Nevertheless, they would also hear them afresh within John's text, used here in particular to create a mental image of the coming of Christ. The audience would recognize, in other words, that they were hearing "Scripture," even as they were hearing John's proclamation.[5] The biblical word becomes John's word. The voice of the Hebrew Scriptures and other authoritative traditions is one more voice (or chorus of voices) that John draws in as a harmonious witness to his own voice.

The infusion of texts already accepted as divine revelations helps John's vision come across as an authentic revelation. John gives the texts new shape, referents, and direction, but the older texts lend their power to that new shape. His frequent weaving in of small phrases and descriptions known from Daniel or other prophetic and apocalyptic literature, for example in the opening vision of the glorified Christ, enhances the hearers' impression that they are hearing another authoritative vision, another species of the same genre, as it were.[6] Even the Semitic flavor of John's Greek, which might make "an audience composed of modern philologians . . . respond with a mixture of perplexity and scorn," enhances this effect, reinforcing "the impact of the subject-matter by echoing the pungent cadences of the OT. As a result, style bolsters invention, most of all in the area of *ethos*."[7]

John does not explicitly *cite* his Old Testament sources, however, because for John to say "as it is written in the prophet Isaiah" would detract from the immediacy of the hearers' experience of John's vision, just as footnotes would detract from the experience of reading a novel, interrupting the readers' immersion in the narrative world. Indeed, it would threaten to make the visions appear derivative or secondary, rather than genuine charismatic experiences. Although such citations lend authority to other New Testament arguments, here they would actually diminish the authority that John claims for the apocalypse, which he has consistently presented as a firsthand revelation from God.

ANTHOLOGICAL OR EXEGETICAL?

The pervasiveness of Old Testament recontextualizations and allusions in Revelation leads naturally to questions about *how* and *how well* or *how faithfully*

---

many other suggested allusions not observed by the rest. The question of whether John intended such allusions is equally elusive, although John's level of consciousness about referring to some OT passage may be presumed to increase with the length and obviousness of references and to diminish with the brevity and obscurity of allusions. That is to say, John *himself* probably would not "catch" every scriptural allusion in his text since the language and thought of the Scriptures had become so much his own.

5. Royalty (1998, 143) affirms that the older texts used in Rev. 1:7 were "meant to be recognized by the audience and to provide legitimation for John as a trustworthy prophet." John's use of "a legitimate prophetic oracle at this point in the proem" contributes to establishing his ethos.

6. So, also, Royalty 1997, 605.

7. Kirby 1988, 203.

John is interpreting these Scriptures. The conversation has tended to center on the question of John's sensitivity to the original literary context of the scriptural verses upon which he draws. Does John simply use the language of the Jewish Scriptures with "little interest in the significance or meaning that a verse or an image or an idea originally had,"[8] or does he honor the original meaning and intent of those texts that he borrows in the way that he brings them to bear on his audience's situation? A much deeper ethical question fuels this ongoing conversation: with what integrity and intent does John harness the voices of Scripture to the chariot of his own rhetorical agenda? Does Scripture become servant to John's ideological interests and political agenda, or does John strive to remain the servant and spokesperson of the scriptural tradition, to which he considers himself—and holds others—accountable?

One pole in this conversation regards John's use of the Old Testament to be "anthological," a term first applied by Elisabeth Schüssler Fiorenza: "John . . . does not interpret the OT but uses its words, images, phrases, and patterns as a language arsenal in order to make his own theological statement or express his own prophetic vision."[9] John simply takes up "traditional symbols and mythological images," putting them into his new vision "like mosaic stones," to give his work rhetorical power.[10] The image of the mosaic is informative. The artist looks for appropriately shaped and colored shards of material amid the heaps of discarded, broken pottery, stone, and tile for the raw materials out of which to construct his or her new decorative pictures. The "original context" of these shards is of no importance, and has no bearing upon, their use in the mosaic. According to this model, we uncover the meaning of this language and these symbols not through analysis of their original occurrences in the Hebrew Bible, but "from their present position within the overall symbolic framework and rhetorical narrative of the book."[11]

The opposite pole in this conversation insists, to the contrary, that John remains highly attuned to the original meaning and purpose of the texts that he weaves into his new text, and that this original meaning and purpose informs his use of the Scriptures throughout Revelation. Jan Fekkes, a recent champion of this view, argues that John does not "simply use the OT as a religious thesaurus to pad his visions with conventional symbolism and rhetoric."[12] Rather, John's use of a passage "extends also to the setting and purpose of the original biblical passage."[13] This model does not envision John undergoing a process of exegesis

---

8. Witherington 2003, 11 (though Witherington himself argues in favor of the second position, that John honors the original meaning).
9. Schüssler Fiorenza 1985, 135.
10. Schüssler Fiorenza 1991, 31; see also Ruiz 1989 and Royalty 2004. The latter writes, rather sensationally, that the Scriptures "have become pieces in John's vision of destruction with no reference to their prior life. The Apocalypse is the death of scripture" (Royalty 2004, 294).
11. Schüssler Fiorenza 1991, 31.
12. Fekkes 1994, 288. The "exegetical" view is also supported by Beale (1999, 98), Witherington (2003, 13), and Bauckham (1993a, 38–91).
13. Fekkes 1994, 102.

in regard to every allusion he makes while writing Revelation, although a strong case can be made that he read and reflected deeply on a *few* key texts in the process of composing some of his visions. It does affirm that John's reading of the Hebrew Bible and his attempts to hear *its* prophetic word throughout his lifetime deeply inform his own prophetic word in a manner that gives integrity to his use of those scriptural resources. As one weighs John's exegetical work, it is also vitally important that John's fidelity to the meaning and intent of the texts he incorporates not be judged on the basis of modern historical-critical methods, but by the standards and methods of first-century exegesis and application.

A revealing case in point here concerns the reference to "the Song of Moses" in Revelation 15:3, John's most explicit reference to a text from the Jewish Scriptures. Schüssler Fiorenza did not find the actual song in 15:3–4 to be "connected in any literary way with the song of Moses in Exodus 15 or Deuteronomy 32."[14] In a tour de force article, however, Richard Bauckham showed otherwise. While Revelation 15:3–4 contains no recontextualizations from Exodus 15:1–18, Bauckham argues that there is nevertheless a close literary connection.[15] John follows an established tradition of reinventing a biblical song of deliverance, such as one finds in Pseudo-Philo (comparing the Song of Deborah in *LAB* 32 with Judg. 5:2–31) and Isaiah 12:1–6 (a reinvention of the song of deliverance by the sea using motifs found in Exod. 15:1–18). The Song of the Redeemed shares several points of interest with the Song of Moses: God's mighty act of judgment on God's enemies (Exod. 15:1–10, 12), which also revealed God's superiority to the pagan gods (15:11); God's judgments resulting in awakening "fear" among the nations (15:14–15); and the manifestation of God's reign (15:18).[16]

John has created this new song, moreover, using phrases from biblical texts (e.g., Ps. 86:8–10; Jer. 10:6–7a) that themselves relate to Exodus 15 by *gezera shawa*, in particular to the declaration of God's incomparable superiority over the gods of the nations (Exod. 15:11), a verse of particular significance for the question of whom to worship, so central in John's setting.[17] "Thus John's version of the song takes as its starting point the key verse Exodus 15:11, which is taken for granted, without being quoted, because it is the common denominator which links the passages to which allusion is made (Jer 10:6–7; Ps 86:8–10; Ps 98:1–2)."[18] On the basis of such careful—and contextual, in regard to first-century Jewish hermeneutical practice—exegetical work, Bauckham (1993a, 238) successfully maintained his claim that "one of the principal ways in which Revelation conveys meaning is by very precise reference to the Old Testament." Discovering such connections, however, requires that we examine John's "exegesis" more in terms of first-century Jewish practice than modern practice.

14. Schüssler Fiorenza 1985, 135.
15. Bauckham 1993a, 298–300.
16. Bauckham 1993a, 301.
17. Bauckham 1993a, 302.
18. Bauckham 1993a, 305.

Proponents of the "anthological" view of John's use of Scripture find the "exegetical" view difficult to accept. Against Fekkes's arguments, Royalty comments: "It is difficult to imagine that the free recombination and rewriting of scriptural texts in the Apocalypse has any correspondence with the purposes of the original passages (were such purposes even discernible)."[19] Unfortunately, he offers only this dismissive remark, rather than serious, critical engagement of Fekkes's work. Within the parenthetical remark above, moreover, Royalty also conveniently dismisses the possibility of speaking about authorial meaning and intent in regard to the texts of the Hebrew Bible and, in so doing, eliminates the only control for assessing John's use of the Old Testament, that is, for adjudicating between Fekkes's and his own position.

Both positions contribute valid observations concerning John's mode of interaction with the Old Testament. Royalty's description of John's engagement with the Jewish Scriptures as a "free recombination and rewriting" is more appropriate in regard to the blending of allusions in Revelation 17:1–6,[20] and perhaps also in the vision of the glorified Christ in 1:12–16.[21] In these passages, the "anthological" model may explain the data better. But Nelson Kraybill, for example, observes a far more exegetical engagement with the Jewish Scriptures in Revelation 18:1–24, where he finds "a veritable midrash" on specific sections of Isaiah, Jeremiah, and Ezekiel.[22] In the speeches uttered over Rome, John has focused closely on the oracles against Tyre in Ezekiel 26–27 and against historic Babylon in Isaiah 47 and Jeremiah 51, rather than blending together many disparate texts in short compass. Indeed, the specific criticisms of seats of economic and political empires in these oracles inform—even enable—John's critique of Roman imperialism. The anthological model does not do justice to such extended and close interaction.[23] In chapter 11 (below) we will also see how John utilizes particular scriptural texts as premises or historical precedents in developing appeals to rational argumentation, suggesting a much more "exegetical" approach in those places (though he will also simply use details from scriptural episodes more loosely to make his projected future more credible by depicting it as resembling the past).

In this debate, a both/and approach to John's overall use of the Old Testament better suits all the evidence. The claim that "Scripture is only a language"[24] may apply to certain passages in Revelation, but it will not apply to other pas-

---

19. Royalty 2004, 289.
20. Royalty 1998, 191.
21. See Paulien 1988, 37–38. This anthological use of Scripture in Rev. 1:12–16 or 17:1–6 remains consonant with the model of inspiration articulated in chap. 5 (see "Did John Really See Things?"). Details and images from scriptural visions, present to John either through conscious meditation or subconsciously, provide the raw material both for ecstatic experiences and for the description of the same.
22. Kraybill 1996, 148–49.
23. Bauckham's analysis of Rev. 15:3–4 (1993a, 296–307) provides another such example where the anthological model falls far short of the evidence.
24. Patte 1975, 172.

sages where Scripture is not just a thesaurus of imagery, but a collection whose interpretation has enlightened John's understanding of the challenges around him and his congregations and provided the basis for his expectations of God's forthcoming interventions.

READING OR REPLACING SCRIPTURE?

John's pervasive practice of weaving in the content of Scriptures without drawing explicit attention to his sources has aroused deep suspicion concerning his intent. Perhaps the most extreme and sensationalist expression of this suspicion finds a voice in Robert Royalty's article "Don't Touch *This* Book!" Royalty tries to advance the thesis that, by incorporating so much material from the Hebrew Bible, John is trying to replace these Scriptures with his own revelation. When John urges his hearers to keep the words of "*this* book" (Rev. 1:3; 22:7, 9), he tries to exclude "what God has written before through other slaves and prophets."[25] By incorporating the words of Daniel and Zechariah into his own speech in 1:7, John "announced with divine voice that other books of prophecy [beside his own] are no more."[26] In this way, Revelation becomes "the death of Scripture," devouring the latter in the process of creating the new text.[27] Less extreme is Greg Carey's observation that, while *4 Ezra* urges the keeping of the Torah, Revelation "is the first apocalypse to claim that salvation depends upon response to its own message."[28] Again from another angle, such statements raise the question of John's relationship to the Hebrew Bible and other traditions received within the Christian community. If he does, indeed, seek to replace the received Scriptures with his own message and call for absolute obedience to his *own* word, John becomes an eerie precedent for many cult leaders who have done the same on the basis of Revelation itself.

It is hardly likely, however, that John expected his hearers to cease reading and engaging the Hebrew Bible and authoritative Christian texts alongside his own work. Indeed, John refers to the Hebrew Bible in some direct ways that tell against any desire to eliminate awareness of, and ongoing reference to, the same in his audience's practice. John refers explicitly to the Song of Moses in 15:3,[29] and Bauckham has shown this to be a genuine invitation to conversation between texts.[30]

Second, in 10:7 an angel announces the imminent fulfillment of the mystery of God, "as he announced to his own slaves, the prophets." While John would consider himself and faithful prophets contemporary to him to be "God's

---

25. Royalty 2004, 293.
26. Royalty 2004, 293.
27. Royalty 2004, 294.
28. Carey 1999b, 178.
29. Schüssler Fiorenza 1985, 135.
30. Bauckham 1993a, 298–305.

slaves" (1:1; 22:9), his usage of this term allows for a broader body of referents to include, for example, "Moses the slave of God" (15:3) and all who have borne faithful testimony to, and prophetic witness on behalf of, God throughout the long history of God's people (see 11:18). John's own narration of the fulfillment of this mystery of God, pervasively using the words of the Hebrew prophets, moreover, demonstrates his own understanding that "the angel" is pointing to those prophetic texts as the locus of God's pre-announcements of this mystery, thus making it appropriate for John to describe its fulfillment in *their* words.

Third, John assumes the hearers' familiarity with Zechariah 4:1–14, referring to the two witnesses in a way that forces intertextual conversation: "These are the two olive trees and the two lampstands standing before the Lord of the earth" (Rev. 11:4). The definite articles indicate John's awareness that the hearers will have encountered these olive trees and lampstands before—in Zechariah—inviting them to bring information from that text back into their understanding of these witnesses, and to bring these witnesses and their activity back into their reading of Zechariah.

Fourth, John refers the hearer to "the commandments of God," that body of divine legislation and oracles revealing God's requirements for God's people, in order to flesh out the picture of "the saints" (Rev. 14:12). The readers must now refer back to those commandments in order to know how they themselves can be assured of being found among "the saints" rather than among those who experience God's wrath. The major issue in Revelation 13–16 is idolatry versus the worship of the One God, an issue prominently announced in the opening of the Decalogue. The call to "keep the words of the prophetic utterance of this book" (1:3; 22:7) is ultimately a call to "keep the commandments of God [as revealed in the Law and the Prophets] and faith with Jesus" (14:12), resolving the dichotomy Carey perceived between urging the keeping of Torah and urging the keeping of the prophet's own word as salutary.[31]

Royalty does not actually support the charges he levels against John. The statements quoted at the outset of this section remain mere assertions. In each case, Royalty pairs an unobjectionable observation with an unsupported assertion, which he slips in to ride on the coattails of the first part of the statement. Thus, for example, while it is true that "the words of Daniel and Zechariah become John's words (Rev 1:7)," Royalty never explains how speaking the words of Zechariah and Daniel necessarily constitutes an attempt to eliminate those books as ongoing communal resources. He provides no argument concerning the move from the observation that John recontextualizes words from Daniel and Zechariah to the conclusion that "John announced with divine voice that other books of prophecy are no more."[32] Similarly, he offers no evidence for his claim that John's desire for his hearers to obey *his* prophetic message entails *also* that they no longer heed "what God has written before through other slaves and other prophets." Royalty

---

31. Carey 1999b, 178.
32. Royalty 2004, 293.

simply asserts that they are mutually exclusive rather than complementary, even though the latter would be the far more natural understanding in a traditional culture where one's innovations add to the cultural heritage without eliminating the earlier tradition.[33] Moreover, the references to *"the* two olive trees" (11:4) and to "the commandments of God" (14:12), as we have shown, demand that the audience continue to look to the traditional Scriptures in order fully to understand John's new text and its summons.[34]

A subsidiary question within this conversation concerns whether the audience could have been expected to catch John's many scriptural allusions, exploring possible implications of their recognition or nonrecognition of the same. Even Royalty (ironically) expects hearers to recognize the source texts behind 1:7 and sees such recognition to contribute to the authority of John's word.[35] On the other hand, he rightly questions to what extent, if at all, hearers would recognize allusions in other passages. For example, the pastiche of allusions in 1:12–16 "begins a tangled web of intertextual confusion difficult for even the hardiest exegete to unravel."[36]

Royalty reads this "intertextual confusion" as a sign that John tries to hide the derivative nature of his "visions"—to cover his tracks, as it were.[37] But John's visions *must* be derivative in some sense, and must be understood to be derivative, to constitute a valid utterance within the Christian community. If his message is to be accepted, John must be heard to stand within and upon, and thus derive his message from, the received tradition of God's revelations in the Hebrew Bible, the sayings of Jesus, and the apostolic tradition. Moreover, there is widespread agreement, including agreement by Royalty himself, that at least some of his allusions will be recognized, and that it is this recognition, not *non*-recognition, that will contribute to the credibility of the work.

The question of whether or not the audience will recognize John's allusions cannot be answered monolithically. Several variables are at play. One set of variables concerns the nature of the allusions themselves: Are they brief or more extensive? Are they periphrastic or more exact replications of strings of words from traditional texts? Are they derived from more-or-less familiar texts (the Psalms,

---

33. As expressed, e.g., in Sir. 21:15: "When an intelligent person hears a wise saying, he praises it [thus *preserving* it] and adds to it."
34. Comparing *4 Ezra* 11–12 with Rev. 13, Royalty (2004, 297) rightly observes that, in the former, the use of Daniel is "acknowledged and updated rather than subsumed as in Revelation." An often-overlooked dynamic in this regard, however, concerns the different expectations regarding the prophetic voice in Christian circles, where the "Spirit" flowed freely, giving visions, utterances, and the like; and on the other hand in non-Christian Jewish circles, with their more reserved sense of prophetic utterance and firmer basis in texts and their (inspired) interpretation as the ultimate source of authority.
35. Royalty 1998, 143.
36. Royalty 1998, 147. Paulien's comparison of lists of allusions perceived within this passage among representative commentators established this point a decade earlier (1988, 38–39). Royalty (1998, 191) makes a similar point again in connection with the multiple allusions to Isa. 23:17; Jer. 25:15; 51:7, 13; and Nah. 3:4 in Rev. 17:1–6.
37. Royalty 1998, 147.

e.g., appear to have been prominently used in Christian worship and preaching)? Another set of variables concerns differences among the hearers in regard to their level of familiarity with the Hebrew Bible. One need not assume that John would expect most hearers to recall *all* the prophetic texts and their contexts, though most might recognize and recall a few key ones, especially those to which John draws repeated attention. Royalty, however, speaks as though the hearers would *need* to recognize each allusion for John's work to have integrity as a creative interpretation and application of that text, though this is certainly not the case.[38]

Different levels of recognition would yield different levels of rhetorical payoff. We can, perhaps, identify some of these thresholds. If the language simply sounds familiar, there is a slight rhetorical payoff: the familiarity itself contributes to acceptance since the new communication sounds consonant, at least superficially, with traditions already accepted within the community. If the language sounds *biblical*, this yields an additional rhetorical payoff insofar as the new message is invested with the authority of the scriptural voice. If the allusions are recognized to communicate something as specific as recognizable historical precedents for the allegations John brings or the consequences John forecasts, the rhetorical gain is even greater and more precise (here, contributing to the text's rational argumentation, and that with the voice of authority). In many scenes, however, we might also agree with Schüssler Fiorenza that the power of John's vision, for example, of the throne and the activity around it, comes not as a result of tracking down the sources of each component, but from the "overall impression of the whole composition of the vision."[39] That is to say, there can be a substantial rhetorical impact even where allusions are minimal, or minimally recognized.

Those familiar with literary theory have much to contribute to this conversation. First, they helpfully distinguish between "outright allusion," whereby an author clearly intends to "point the reader to a previous work as a means of expanding the reader's horizons," and "echoes," which may enter a text with or without an author's conscious intent.[40] There are many "echoes" in Revelation, particularly where John describes visual impressions that may, indeed, have come to him while in an altered state of consciousness ("ecstasy"). Reading intentionality—and especially, intention to deceive, as Royalty does—into such passages becomes, by definition, problematic.

Second, literary theorists emphasize the fact that allusion, recitation, and other forms of intertextuality "force . . . readers into a 'dialogue with the text and with the texts within the text.'"[41] Allusion and intertextuality nurture an environment in which the Old Testament continues to be read alongside Rev-

---

38. From another point of view, the allusions show us more about John's process of invention and his understanding of the thing he describes than about how the audience would experience the text. Whether or not one can presume audience recognition of these allusions, one may still investigate, as Bauckham, Fekkes, and others have, the consonance of John's new expression with the meaning and effects of the traditional texts upon which he draws.
39. Schüssler Fiorenza 1991, 58–59.
40. Paulien 1988, 39–40.
41. Moyise 1995, 137, quoting Ruiz 1989, 520.

elation, creating conversation between the older and the new text, rather than allowing the new to subsume or replace the old. "The reader of John's book will look at the Old Testament in quite a different light from one who has not read it (and vice versa)."[42] Significantly, "the reader of John's book" is indeed expected to continue to "look at the Old Testament," and this intertextual reading will affect how both texts are understood.

John's failure to draw explicit attention to the sources of his allusions is a failure common to *all* poets. John does what all poets do, refusing to rend the poetry he weaves for the sake of footnotes and references. If John Milton did not intend to supplant Genesis when he spoke of "the fruit of that forbidden tree whose mortal taste brought death into the world" without explicitly citing Genesis, and if John Donne did not erase the words of Revelation 21:4 when he wrote "One short sleep past, we wake eternally, / And Death shall be no more," then it is impossible to substantiate the claim that, through allusions to traditional texts, John seeks to supplant them. On the contrary, by alluding to those texts, John actually helps to preserve their voices and increases the attention given to them in the seven churches, when the voice of those texts was being marginalized in favor of rational(izing) arguments promoting accommodation, participation in idolatry, and the like.

John's manner of interaction with the Hebrew Bible also reminds us again that John is primarily interested in the acts of seeing and hearing—not just seeing the divine visions, but also seeing the world around him and his audiences. He is not focused on the interpretation of other texts and drawing attention to the process and hermeneutical keys involved in their interpretation. Recitation is less appropriate in Revelation than Matthew, which is vitally concerned with how one reads the prophets in order to find Jesus' life therein foretold. John is more concerned with the act of "reading" and interpreting the world of first-century Roman Asia for his congregations in light of the tradition of the Jewish Scriptures and the witness of Jesus, and allowing them to see *their world* in the light of this tradition. The techniques of recontextualization and allusion allow the horizons of the biblical world and the congregation's world to blend and interact more directly, whereas recitation reinforces the boundaries and the distance between those worlds.

Nevertheless, John *has* read and expects the congregations to *continue* to read the Scriptures. He expects them to continue to deepen their engagement with their world and to thicken their understanding of a faithful response to that world, doing so through ongoing engagement with his own text, the older oracles of God, and the traditions of Jesus. The contents of Revelation, moreover, bear out the claim that John regards himself as standing *under* the authority of the Hebrew Bible, discerning its guidance as he identifies and interprets the challenges facing the congregations on whose behalf he exercises his prophetic ministry, rather than regarding himself as having power *over* the Hebrew Bible, to use its words at will for his own agenda. By blending together so many texts

---

42. Moyise 1995, 135–36.

from the Hebrew Bible, John unites the voices of the received tradition, allowing them to speak anew in what Eugene Peterson has called "a fusion of voices and images."[43] Allusion and reference to the content of these books manifests John's conviction that all prophets, himself and Jezebel equally, stand accountable before this greater tradition, in light of which their utterances are to be tested.

JOHN'S FAITHFULNESS TO THE GREATER TRADITION

As John writes to these seven congregations, he is mindful of the well-established practice of testing prophetic utterances. He has himself commended the Ephesian Christians for their examination and rejection of "those claiming themselves to be apostles and they are not, and you have found them to be liars" (Rev. 2:2). One important test for evaluating a new revelation was establishing its consonance with the "canonical" revelation, whether the apostolic tradition (as in Gal. 1:6–9 and 1 John 1:1–4; 4:1–3) or the Scriptures that the apostles themselves used to legitimate their own message, demonstrating its consonance with the same. It is to this larger tradition that John and other prophets remain accountable, by which their words are to be tested and either approved or rejected.

John's extensive use of the Old Testament will invite the hearers to test his words in regard to their faithful representation of those Scriptures. At this point, we need to push beyond the "anthological versus exegetical use" debate. Both models adequately describe particular uses of the Old Testament in certain passages within Revelation. But there is another level at which to examine John's presentation of the voice of the Scriptures within his composition. Does John's message provide a faithful representation and application of the received tradition? Whether John is reading the Scriptures closely and inviting his hearers to "read along" (as in Rev. 15:3–4; 18:1–24), or whether he blends multiple Old Testament images together rather more loosely (as in 1:12–16; 17:1–6), does the resulting speech nevertheless align with the received, authoritative tradition, or does John use the Old Testament "against its will," as it were, to support innovations that could not be considered consonant with the received tradition?

Writing in the early fifth century CE, Augustine provides an interesting perspective on the "true" interpretation of religious texts (*De doctrina christiana* 1.36.40–41). He discerns that such texts seek to achieve particular effects in their readers, principal among which are the cultivation of love of God and love of neighbor, and the diminishment of concupiscence. Interpretations that miss the particular intention of an author in a particular passage, but that nevertheless tend to the accomplishment of the larger purposes of the text in the formation of the interpreter's audience and are in keeping with the *regula fidei*, the "rule of faith," are not "unfaithful" interpretations. A person whose

---

43. Peterson 1969, 135.

> mistaken interpretation contributes to building up love, which is the commandment's goal, . . . goes astray as does a man who mistakenly leaves the high road, but still reaches through the fields the same place to which the road leads. He should be corrected and shown how much better it is not to leave the straight road, lest, if he become accustomed to straying, he may sometimes take cross roads, or even go in an entirely wrong direction. (Augustine, *De doctrina christiana* 1.36.41)

Such a person is to be "wholly acquitted of the charge of deception" (1.36.40). The question concerning John's use of the Old Testament might better be pursued by inquiring whether it is in harmony with the *regula fidei*, as it were, of the Old Testament. What would a reader of the whole of the canon of the Jewish Scriptures take away as the essential message? What view of God and God's actions emerges from that canon? What is the "biblical theology" that would constitute the "rule of faith" nurtured by the Hebrew Bible? To the extent that elements of such a *regula fidei* can be discerned, is John's message, and his use of material from the Old Testament to communicate that message, consonant with that rule? Scholars of the Hebrew Bible may indeed find places where they need to take John aside and correct him, as Augustine recommended. But the overall judgment on John must be that his own revelation of God's character, actions, and purposes is overwhelmingly consonant with the "rule of faith" he learned from his exposure to the breadth of the Jewish Scriptures.[44] And if this is the case, he, like Augustine's preacher, should be acquitted of these charges of deception leveled against him by recent critics.

The following themes show John's continuity with the Hebrew Bible.

The God Who Is *Alone* Worthy of Worship

As other prophets and the gathered communities weighed Revelation, they would be confronted, first and foremost, with a prophetic word that forcefully proclaimed the One God who is *alone* worthy of worship and that targets idolatry as a behavior supremely to be avoided. The Shema is the appropriate starting point for the *regula fidei* of the Jewish Scriptures: "Hear, O Israel: The LORD is our God, the LORD alone" (Deut. 6:4 NRSV). And the Shema is, indeed, a *faith* claim, followed by behavioral prescriptions growing out from this claim: "You shall love the LORD your God with all your heart, and with all your soul, and with all your might. Keep these words that I am commanding you today" (6:5–6 NRSV). The faith claim concerns the uniqueness of the God of Abraham, Isaac, and Jacob, and the unique right this God has to the loyal obedience of the people who hear this sentence pronounced.

---

44. This discussion is largely limited to John's faithfulness to the worldview and ethos nurtured by the Hebrew Bible but could be fruitfully extended to include the literature written during the Second Temple Period that found no lasting place in that canon (particularly Jewish apocalyptic texts), as well as Jesus traditions, which were collected as part of a different canon.

Foremost among those behavioral prescriptions are the opening commandments of the Decalogue, the first of the "words" to which the Shema refers: "I am the LORD your God. . . . You shall have no other gods before me. You shall not make for yourself an idol, whether in the form of anything that is in heaven above, or that is on the earth beneath, or that is in the water under the earth. You shall not bow down to them or worship them" (Deut. 5:6–9 NRSV). The Hebrew Bible is replete with commentary upon, and application of, this central summons. It is a theme that pervades historical books (e.g., 2 Kgs. 17:9–18), sapiential and liturgical texts (Pss. 96:1–9; 97:6–7; 115:3–11; 135:13–21; Wis. 13:1–15:17), and prophetic literature (e.g., Isa. 44:6–24; Jer. 10:1–11). John's heart beats with this same pulse as he manifests his intense concern with "keeping the commandments of God" (Rev. 12:17; 14:12), and the first and second commandments are foremost in his mind as he calls the churches away from "food sacrificed to idols [εἰδωλόθυτα]" (2:14, 20) and from *any* compromise with idolatry (9:20–21), especially imperial cult (13:1–18).[45] John gives voice to the eternal call to "fear God and give him glory," to offer God worship as "the one who made heaven and earth and sea and springs of water" (14:6–7), rather than offer worship to "the gods that did not make the heavens and the earth" (Jer. 10:11; see also Ps. 96:5).[46]

The God Who Indicts Domination Systems

John's indictment of Rome (Rev. 17–18) is entirely in keeping with the strain within the prophetic tradition that critiques any ordering of society setting the pursuit of wealth or power as the highest consideration, which inevitably leads to the disregard for the fair distribution of this world's goods and for the socially, politically, and economically vulnerable and is often accompanied by an ideology of self-aggrandizement, if not self-worship. This strain emerges throughout

---

45. Talbert (1994, 87) rightly calls Revelation a summons to "First-commandment faithfulness."
46. On the Hebrew scriptural and early Christian resonances with this summons, see deSilva 1999a, 85–90; on the theme of calling humanity to worship the One God and to abandon the worship of idols that pervades Revelation, see deSilva 1998a, 87–99.
   Richard Bauckham (1993a, 287–88) has shown the deep consonance between Ps. 96 and Rev. 14:6–7. Psalm 96 calls the hearers to "Announce the good news of his act of deliverance from day to day" (96:2; cf. the "eternal good news" that the angel proclaims in Rev. 14:6). "Nations," "peoples," and "tribes" are the audience for this declaration of God's "glory" and "marvelous works" (Ps. 96:3, 7) and the "families/tribes of the peoples" are summoned to "ascribe to the LORD glory and strength," to "give the LORD the glory due his name," and to "worship the LORD" and "tremble before him" (the last being addressed to "all the earth"; 96:7–9; cf. Rev. 14:7). Psalm 96:5 calls attention to the distinction between God and the idols worshiped by other nations, particularly in reference to the act of creation: "For the gods of the peoples are idols, but the LORD made the heavens" (NRSV). This also provides part of the rationale in Rev. 14:6–13 for worshiping God and avoiding the worship of manufactured substitutes. Finally, Ps. 96:10, 13 speaks of God's acts of judgment, especially in God's forthcoming visitation, a topic that is also introduced as a rationale to honor and worship this God (Rev. 14:7). "The eternal gospel [of Rev. 14:6–7] is therefore the call which Psalm 96 itself contains, the call to all nations to worship the one true God who is coming to judge the world and to establish his universal rule" (Bauckham 1993a, 288).

the major prophets, particularly in the texts upon which John draws (e.g., Isa. 23; 47; Jer. 51; Ezek. 26–27). It is rooted in the exodus event itself, when God took the side of an oppressed and enslaved people, at the cost of whose dehumanization the great treasure cities of Egypt were being constructed (the treasures themselves often coming from violent conquest, enforced tribute, and economic rapine). The classical prophets did not only turn this critical eye to foreign powers, but also indicted Israel as well when it put the enjoyment of luxury by the few ahead of the survival of the many, or when it forgot the covenant loyalty due God, reveling instead in its alliances with other powers that allowed the elites to achieve greater economic growth or political influence.

As Nelson Kraybill aptly observes, "These passages of the great prophets deal with the interplay of Empire, commerce and idolatry; they help explain John's attitude toward Rome and his reasons for rejecting economic involvement with her."[47] In other words, from his close reading of the prophets, John has discerned what the response of the God of the prophets would be to a new, grander, more overtly self-deifying, and more violently expansive domination system. Indeed, where Matthew, Romans, and Hebrews show a markedly greater interest in the Pentateuch, with fewer allusions to the Psalms and major prophets, John shows a greater interest in the prophetic corpus (and the liturgical corpus) of ancient Israel,[48] bringing those traditions to bear on the situation facing his congregations to help them see their context in light of those paradigms of violent oppression, luxurious overconsumption, and self-legitimating ideology.

John was not alone in presenting such a close correspondence between Roman domination and the prophetic critique of empire. The authors of *4 Ezra* and *2 Baruch* come to the same conclusion regarding Rome's status in the sight of the One God on the basis of their reading of the Hebrew scriptural tradition as well:

> You, the fourth [beast] that has come, have conquered all the beasts that have gone before; and you have held sway over the world with great terror, and over all the earth with grievous oppression; and for so long you have lived on the earth with deceit. You have judged the earth, but not with truth, for you have oppressed the meek and injured the peaceable; you have hated those who tell the truth, and have loved liars; you have destroyed the homes of those who brought forth fruit, and have laid low the walls of those who did you no harm. Your insolence has come up before the Most High, and your pride to the Mighty One. . . . Therefore you, eagle, will surely disappear, . . . so that the whole earth, freed from your violence, may be refreshed and relieved. (*4 Ezra* [= 2 Esd.] 11:40–46 NRSV)

Fourth Ezra is more directly (and explicitly) dependent upon Daniel (cf. *4 Ezra* 12:11–12), whereas John draws upon the greater prophets in his denunciation of Rome. Yet the charges of violence, oppression, deception, and pride are essentially

47. Kraybill 1996, 148–49.
48. Moyise 1995, 15–16.

the same (John will dwell more upon luxurious consumption, in addition) and suggest that deep immersion in the Hebrew scriptural tradition led two apocalypticists independently to one inescapable conclusion concerning the domination system of Roman imperialism.[49]

The God of the Exodus

The importance of the exodus story for shaping the Jewish people's knowledge of God cannot be overestimated. Its centrality is evident from the opening words of the Decalogue: "I am the LORD your God, who brought you out of the land of Egypt, out of the house of slavery; you shall have no other gods before me" (Exod. 20:2-3 NRSV; see also Deut. 5:6-7). The exodus story as a revelation of the character of God and God's interventions was held continually before the worshiping community in its Psalms (see, e.g., Pss. 78, 105, 106) and canticles (e.g., the Song of Moses in Exod. 15:1-18).[50] It provided the material for sustained theological reflection on the workings of Wisdom and the ways of God in the sapiential traditions (most notably, Wis. 10:15-11:20; 12:23-27; 15:18-19:22). Prophets invoked the exodus as the beneficent act on the basis of which the obligations of the covenant were grounded (e.g., Ezek. 20:3-26), and as the paradigm and precedent for the hope of a new exodus from the Babylonian captivity (as in Isa. 40:3-5; 43:16-19; 52:1-6).

John stands in line with this tradition, proclaiming the One seated upon the throne as the God of the exodus, who now effects the final deliverance of God's people in a new exodus that is the eschatological exodus.[51] This exodus typology has been amply explored.[52] John draws his description of the Christian communities as "a kingdom and priests to our God" (Rev. 5:10; cf. 1:5-6) from God's address to the exodus generation, calling them to be "for me a priestly kingdom"

---

49. David Aune (2006, 6) has also shown the correspondences between the vision of humanity's terror before the throne of judgment in Rev. 6:15-16 and *1 En.* 62:3-5. The *1 Enoch* passage especially targets "the kings and mighty and the exalted and those who *possess* the earth," i.e., the empowered groups (62:3, 6, 9; 63:1, 12)—whose response of terror and fear/prostration receives threefold notice (62:3, 6, 9)—rather than the more general body of "those who dwell on the earth" (62:1; 67:8), even though this more universal group is called to account at the beginning of the passage (62:1). Similarly, even though John does include "every slave and free person" in the scene of terror before the "face of the One seated upon the throne," John first singles out "the kings of the earth and the potentates and the generals and the rich and the powerful," who are thus more prominently foregrounded in this scene of terror. Similarly, it is the kings, powerful merchants, and sea captains who lament the fall of Babylon (i.e., those who most profited from Babylon's domination) in Rev. 18.

50. Evidence for use of this canticle in synagogue worship is admittedly slight. The fact that John can confidently refer to Exod. 15 by title (Rev. 15:3) suggests a familiarity gained through liturgical usage. Its inclusion at the head of the book of *Odes* in several Septuagint codices (Alexandrinus, Veronensis, and Turicensis) attests to its established use in post-Nicene churches, a practice that, along with the use of Psalms in the Christian church, may have been taken over from the synagogue.

51. Benjamin Wold brought to my attention the importance of the reconfiguring of the exodus as a deliverance from exile in Babylon during the prophetic period.

52. See, e.g., Casey 1987.

(Exod. 19:6 NRSV).⁵³ The plagues that God visits upon the inhabitants of the earth in the seven trumpets and seven bowls recall, in many of their particulars, the plagues visited upon Egypt in Exodus 7:14–11:10.⁵⁴

John shows an awareness of the kind of commentary on the exodus plagues that one finds in Wisdom of Solomon, in regard both to the principle of making the punishment fit the crime (Rev. 16:2, 4–5; see Wis. 11:15–16), and to the view that the plagues were not just God's strategy for changing Pharaoh's mind about releasing the Israelites, nor only for gaining international repute, but rather also a means of *punishment* for the Egyptians' refusal to recognize and worship the One True God rather than their idols and sacred animals: "To escape from your hand is impossible; for the ungodly, refusing to know you, were flogged by the strength of your arm, pursued by unusual rains and hail and relentless storms, and utterly consumed by fire" (Wis. 16:15–16 NRSV). John explicitly underscores the punitive nature of the plagues: "You are just . . . because they shed the blood of the holy ones and prophets, and you have given them blood to drink" (Rev. 16:5–6). The idea that the plagues, as in Exodus, were meant to induce repentance, however, is not abandoned: they are simply unsuccessful in this regard, as they were also in Exodus (Exod. 8:15, 19, 32, etc.; Rev. 9:20–21; 16:9, 11, 21).⁵⁵

As in Exodus, the people of God are sealed for protection from the plagues (Rev. 7:1–8; 9:4; 16:2). The marking of the doorposts and lintels of the Hebrews' houses with the blood of the (Passover) lamb is the most striking image associated therewith, but God's protection was evident also when the plagues did not affect the land, livestock, and human inhabitants of Goshen, where the Hebrews resided (Exod. 8:22–23; 9:6–7, 25–26; 10:22–23). Perhaps it is significant that Moses' pretext for the exodus was the need for his people to worship God beyond the borders of Egypt, since the Hebrews and Egyptians cherished mutually offensive religious practices (5:3; 7:16; 8:1, 20, 25–27; 9:13; 10:3, 7–11). In Revelation's new exodus, worship remains a primary concern, one that again involves separation from the rites cherished by the oppressor (e.g., 13:11–18; 14:9–11). The redeemed finally sing of God's deliverance by the side of a new sea (15:2–4): "The linking of the song of Moses and the song of the Lamb also demonstrates unmistakably John's appreciation of the Exodus as a paradigm of the redemption now come in Christ."⁵⁶ The exodus—combined with the new exodus paradigm in which the faithful are brought out of Babylon (cf. Rev. 18:4–8) and into a new land of promise (Rev. 21:1–22:5)—becomes the conceptual framework within which to speak of a much grander deliverance. In this respect, once again, John's visions of the future would be received as fully

---

53. Casey 1987, 34–36. Notably, John shares in the Christian conviction that this priestly kingdom transcends ethnic identity, being constituted not merely by Jacob's descendants, but also by people drawn from "every tribe, nation, people, and language" (see also Bauckham 1993a, 306).

54. Casey 1987, 36–37; Schüssler Fiorenza 1991, 27. John blends together the common apocalyptic tradition of end-time disturbances (now explicitly acts initiated by God) with the exodus tradition to make a statement concerning end-time catastrophes.

55. Contra Casey 1987, 37.

56. Casey 1987, 39.

grounded in the scriptural tradition (the exodus), and even in the scriptural tradition's ongoing use of the exodus tradition (e.g., the prophetic "new exodus").

The God Who Vindicates God's Faithful Ones

The psalmists expressed confidence in God's commitment not only to deliver God's people collectively when they fell into distress or oppression, but also to deliver each faithful person from his or her distress: "Many are the afflictions of the righteous, but the LORD rescues them from them all" (Ps. 34:19 NRSV). The underlying rationale for such bold confidence derives ultimately from Deuteronomy, which promised that covenant loyalty would result in the safe enjoyment of the land and, when that was threatened, God's aid. The covenant promises were passed along through the wisdom tradition (e.g., Prov. 3:1–11) and in the liturgical tradition as well (as in the "wisdom psalms"; see esp. Ps. 1).

In seasons of distress, whether from natural calamity or hostile aggression, the faithful would wait expectantly for God's intervention. Their knowledge that they had walked in line with God's commandments (often coupled with the suspicion that their enemies did *not*) gave them the grounds for expecting deliverance. Since God was just, God would necessarily intervene to bring the promised blessings to the righteous and just punishment to the wicked. If the ungodly gained ascendancy over the righteous person, the cry went up for vindication (Ps. 13:1–2 NRSV):

> How long, O LORD? Will you forget me forever?
>   How long will you hide your face from me?
> How long must I bear pain in my soul,
>   and have sorrow in my heart all day long?
> How long shall my enemy be exalted over me?

The just God could not allow the wicked to put the righteous person to shame and to gain honor or profit at the expense of the godly or the weak (see Pss. 35:24–26; 94:1–6). This same conviction found expression in regard to the fortunes of the nation as well. This was announced in the Song of Moses in Deuteronomy: "The LORD will vindicate his people, have compassion on his servants" (32:36 NRSV), an assurance that also appears in the liturgical traditions of the psalms (Ps. 135:14). Therefore, the cry for vindication can go up on behalf of the slain and oppressed of the entire nation (as in Ps. 79).

In the events prior to the Maccabean Revolt, the fact that the righteous were being killed by the ungodly, often in a degrading and painful manner, led to the expectation of postmortem vindication of the righteous person's commitment to God in two forms: the reward of the righteous one, who would enjoy the covenant blessings in the life beyond death, and the punishment of their lawless persecutors, who would be made to acknowledge the nobility and wisdom of the righteous ones whom they made sport of and killed (see 2 Macc. 7:9, 11, 14, 17, 19, 23, 31, 35–36; 4 Macc. 9:8–9, 32; 10:11, 15; 12:11–12; 17:4–6; Wis. 1:16–5:23).

When John depicts the souls of the righteous, slain for the sake of God's word, crying out for vindication (Rev. 6:9–11), he stands in line with this tradition, confessing the justice of God and therefore the expectation of God's intervention to uphold the cause of the righteous. He stands firmly in the tradition that claims that even death is insufficient to thwart God's commitment to give justice to those who had walked faithfully in line with God's commandments: "How long, holy and true Sovereign, will you not give judgment and require our blood from the inhabitants of the earth?!" (6:10).[57] As the narrative unfolds, John affirms the truthfulness of the tradition's foundational premises: God is indeed just in all God's ways (15:2–4), as will be seen when God dramatically avenges the blood of God's holy ones: "You are just, you who are and were, the Holy One, because you have rendered these judgments, because they poured out the blood of holy ones and prophets, and you have given them blood to drink, for they deserve it" (16:5–6). The martyrs themselves give voice to their confirmation of this foundational premise, adding their "Amen" from beneath the altar to the angel's declaration (16:7). The scenes of God's judgment throughout Revelation are anchored in this traditional expectation that God vindicates God's servants, an expectation relevant to the past and forthcoming violence against the Christian community and the people of God more broadly (2:10, 13; 6:9–11; 11:18; 13:15–17; 17:6; 18:24).

The God Who Exercises Sovereign Rule over the Cosmos

John proclaims God as the *Pantokratōr* (παντοκράτωρ, Rev. 15:3), the One who holds all things within his grasp. This God consistently appears as One sitting enthroned (4:2, 9, 10; 5:1, 7, 13; 6:16; etc.), a posture declaring that God reigns over the cosmos. Once again, Revelation's depiction of God, and the precise manner in which God's reign is actualized, is entirely consonant with the witness of the scriptural and derivative traditions.

God's sovereign rule is especially foregrounded in liturgical texts, keeping God's rule in the forefront of the worshipers' consciousness, as in the following samples (NRSV):

> The LORD is king. . . .
> Your throne is established from of old.
> (Ps. 93:1–2)

> The LORD is king!
> (97:1; 99:1)

---

57. Revelation 6:9–11 bears a stunning resemblance to the scene of the just calling for their promised reward in *4 Ezra* 4:35–37 (see also *2 Bar.* 23:4–5a). The earlier *1 Enoch* also attests to the expectation that God will hear the prayers of the righteous for vindication, and require their blood at the hands of their enemies, specifically when the full "number of the righteous had been reached" (47:4). Revelation, *4 Ezra*, and *1 Enoch* all solve the problem of God's delaying the vindication of the unjust deaths of God's saints by appealing to God's measured ordering of the cosmos: there is a particular number of such souls that must first die.

God sits in session, presiding over a heavenly court populated by supernatural beings who stand and wait to do God's bidding and pay God homage as sovereign (NRSV):[58]

> Bless the LORD, O you his angels,
>   you mighty ones who do his bidding,
>   obedient to his spoken word.
> Bless the LORD, all his hosts,
>   his ministers that do his will.
>   (103:20–21)

> Praise him, all his angels;
>   praise him, all his host!
>   (148:2)

> Blessed are you in the temple of your holy glory, ...
>   who look into the depths from your throne on the cherubim.
>   (Sg. Three 31–32)

Songs such as the last one were inspired by the physical representations of God in the temple (or at least, memories of the same), where God sits enthroned invisibly above the ark of the covenant, the top of which is decorated with the two cherubim that uphold God's throne, God's "seat." Visionaries like Isaiah elaborate upon this, providing visions of God upon this throne, surrounded by multiple angelic beings offering ceaseless worship (6:1–6). Ezekiel gives a rather different, more daringly detailed, and more colorful depiction of the same (1:4–28). The author of *Testament of Levi* 2–5 elaborates still more upon this foundation, providing a vision of God enthroned in the highest heaven, surrounded by several distinct orders of angels performing different functions within the heavenly court, all visually expressive of God's rule over the cosmos.

John's vision of the enthroned One, and of the activity of the orders of heavenly beings around the throne, stands firmly in line with this tradition of imaging God as enthroned and surrounded by a heavenly court occupied preeminently with worship, though the other activities of angels throughout the text also align well with established roles for the same as God's messengers and as those who do God's bidding (as in the Psalms), particularly in regard to attending to the prayers of God's holy ones and executing God's judgments upon the earth (as in *T. Levi* 2–5). Details drawn from Ezekiel's vision, enhanced by the liturgical acclamation from Isaiah's vision, cause John's vision to be heard as all the more traditional and therefore legitimate.

---

58. The heavenly court appears in other streams of the tradition as well, as in the Deuteronomic historian's account of Micaiah ben Imlah: "I saw the LORD sitting on his throne, with all the host of heaven standing beside him to the right and to the left of him. And the LORD said, 'Who will entice Ahab, so that he may go up and fall at Ramoth-gilead?' Then one said one thing, and another said another ..." (1 Kgs. 22:19–20 NRSV).

Alongside the depiction of God as the enthroned Pantokrator, John gives significant attention to the enthronement of God's Anointed (e.g., Rev. 5:1–14). This, too, is deeply rooted in the tradition of the Hebrew Scriptures, and the particular form that it takes in Revelation—the enthronement of this *Jesus*—represents the unanimous interpretation of this tradition within early Christian culture (a sine qua non of belonging to the group). The enthronement psalms celebrate the accession of the Davidic king to the throne of David, which also represents a kind of share in the divine rule: "The LORD says to my lord, / 'Sit at my right hand / until I make your enemies your footstool" (Ps. 110:1 NRSV). In the period after the dissolution of the monarchy, these psalms (together with passages such as 2 Sam. 7:12–16) became the foundation for hopes that God would once again raise up a king for Israel, a descendent of David, under whose reign prosperity and political independence, even ascendency, would return to Israel. The early Christian movement claims Jesus of Nazareth to be this "righteous Branch" from the house of David (Jer. 23:5–6; cf. Luke 1:32; Rom. 1:3–4), envisioning a much greater reign than a kingdom over a particular ethnic group. When John speaks of the "Lamb" as the "Root of David" (Rev. 5:5), he expresses the conviction that the kingdoms of this world would cede themselves to "the kingdom of our Lord *and* of his Anointed" (11:15), or depicts Jesus as somehow sharing in the throne of God or appearing "in its midst" (3:21; 5:6; 7:17); he thus faithfully represents the Christian culture's interpretation of the Hebrew scriptural tradition of the enthronement of God's anointed. His application of the enthronement traditions to Jesus will be received as consonant with the apostolic traditions according to which prophets would be tested.

The Hebrew Scriptures are particularly interested in the realization of God's sovereign rule as God brings justice to human affairs. The liturgical traditions of Israel particularly emphasize God's reign in judgment, judging the earth, the nations, and their peoples (NRSV):

> He will judge the peoples with equity. . . .
> He will judge the world with righteousness,
>   and the peoples with his truth.
>   (Ps. 96:10, 13)

> Righteousness and justice are the foundation of his throne.
>   (97:2)

> He will to judge the world with righteousness,
>   and the peoples with equity.
>   (98:9)

> The LORD is king. . . .
>   He sits enthroned upon the cherubim. . . .
> Mighty King, lover of justice,
>   you have established equity;
>   you have executed justice.
>   (99:1, 4).

John also foregrounds this particular aspect of God's rule. The "good news" about God's accession to the reins of the kingdoms of this world is the manifestation of God's justice in this human sphere:[59]

> We give thanks to you, Lord God Pantocrator,
>   who is and who was,
> because you have taken up your great power and exercised sovereign rule.
> And the nations were enraged, and your wrath came,
>   and the right time to judge the dead,
> and to give the reward to your slaves,
>   to the prophets and the holy ones and those fearing your name,
>   the small and the great,
> and to ravage the ravagers of the earth.
>
> (Rev. 11:16–18)

> Alleluia!
> The deliverance and the glory and the power of our God! . . .
> Because he judged the great prostitute, who ravaged the earth in her fornication,
> and he required the blood of his slaves from her hand. . . .
> Alleluia!
> Because the Lord God, the Pantocrator, exercised sovereign rule.
>
> (19:1–2, 6)

God's exercise of punitive judgment makes way for a new order of human community, as the latter hymn goes on to celebrate the coming marriage feast of the Lamb, which leads, in turn, to the vision of the new Jerusalem, a multinational human community "done right." Nevertheless, the hearers will recognize in John the spokesperson for the same God whose rule-through-executing-justice was already well established in the Psalms (among other traditional texts).

A fourth and final aspect of the reign of God in Revelation vis-à-vis the tradition concerns God's sharing of kingly rule with God's holy ones as an extension of the enthronement of God's Anointed. The author of Daniel 7, a text of great importance for John (cf. Rev. 13:1–10 with the four beasts of Dan. 7:2–8), speaks of "one like a Son of Man coming with the clouds of heaven" (Dan. 7:13; cf. Rev. 1:7) and receiving the kingdom from the Ancient One seated upon the throne. In the interpretation that follows, this act signals the day when "the kingship and dominion and the greatness of the kingdoms under the whole heaven shall be given to the people of the holy ones of the Most High" (Dan. 7:27 NRSV). John, like other early Christian leaders, reads these two texts as complementary, the latter adding to the former rather than replacing it (demythologizing the "one like a Son of Man," as it were). The Messiah receives a share in the kingdom of God and shares the exercise of rule with the loyal people gathered around him:

---

59. "An eternal gospel" (Rev. 14:6) probably reflects not eschatological evangelism so much as a call to acknowledge the imperator of the cosmos whose reign, whose "empire," is now bursting in upon the provinces of the earthly rulers.

And the one who conquers and keeps my works to the end, I will give to that one authority over the nations, to shepherd them with a rod of iron. (Rev. 2:26–27)
The one who conquers, I will give to that one to sit with me in my throne, as I also conquered and sat with my Father in his throne. (3:21)

Revelation 20:4–6 provides the most famous depiction of this, as the "souls of those beheaded on account of the testimony of Jesus and on account of the word of God, and whoever did not worship the beast nor its image nor received the mark upon their forehead or right forearm, . . . came to life and exercised sovereign rule with Christ for a thousand years." John may have described Daniel's "people of the holy ones of the Most High" in a way that reveals his own rhetorical agenda (though this, too, can hardly be considered a departure from the tradition), but the promises he extends in the name of Christ are themselves thoroughly grounded in the tradition on whose behalf he speaks.

The God Who Promises Shalom in God's Presence

God's reign moves toward establishing the order in the natural and human spheres that reflects God's just character and God's designs for human community in relationship with the divine. In Revelation, this finds its full expression in the vision of the new Jerusalem, where God's promises to God's people and indeed to the nations are consummated. John remains thoroughly aligned with Hebrew scriptural traditions, giving voice to these promises and to the shape of this hope, modulating the pitch in two important ways that remain, however, harmonious with early Christian reinterpretation of the tradition.

The image of this consummation as the wedding of God and God's people was poignantly expressed by the prophet Hosea (see 2:14–20), whose own actions toward Gomer became a living parable of God's intentions toward Israel. Isaiah applies this image more particularly to Jerusalem as the bride of God (an extension of his tendency to refer to Jerusalem as "daughter Zion") in the context of God's vindication of the fortunes of God's people:

> The nations shall see your vindication,
>   and all the kings your glory;
> and you shall be called by a new name. . . .
> You shall no more be termed Forsaken,
>   and your land shall no more be termed Desolate;
> but you shall be called My Delight Is in Her,
>   and your land Married;
> for the LORD delights in you,
>   and your land shall be married.
> For as a young man marries a young woman,
>   so shall your builder marry you,
> and as the bridegroom rejoices over the bride,
>   so shall your God rejoice over you.
>   (Isa. 62:2, 4–5 NRSV)

The tradition of the covenant as a wedding or marriage comes to expression in early Christian discourse as the wedding of Christ (the "Son") to the people of God, with the eschatological age being depicted as a wedding banquet. This has strong roots in the Jesus tradition (Matt. 22:1–14 and pars.) and in Pauline traditions (2 Cor. 11:2–3; Eph. 5:22–32) and blends with the tradition of Zion/Jerusalem as God's bride in John's visions of "the holy city, new Jerusalem . . . descending out of heaven from God, prepared as a bride adorned for her husband" (Rev. 21:2; see also 19:6b–9; 21:9; 22:17).[60]

The very idea of the "new heavens and new earth," together with the passing away of the "former things" and the re-creation of Jerusalem, reprises the hope expressed by Isaiah (65:17–18). When John represents the speech of "a great voice from the throne" announcing this great consummation, he speaks entirely in the idiom of the prophets who had previously communicated this hope:

> Look—the tent of God is with humankind,
> and he will make his home with them,
> and they will be his people,
> and God himself will be with them,
> and he will wipe away every tear from their eyes,
> and death will no longer be, nor grief, nor crying,
> neither will there be suffering, because the former things passed away.
> (Rev. 21:3–4)

Several promises previously articulated in God's name would be recognizable (NRSV): "I will dwell in your midst" (Zech. 2:11). "I will walk among you, and will be your God, and you shall be my people" (Lev. 26:12). "Then they shall be my people, and I will be their God" (Ezek. 11:20). "My dwelling place shall be with them; and I will be their God, and they shall be my people" (Ezek. 37:27). "Then the Lord GOD will wipe away the tears from all faces" (Isa. 25:8). "No more shall the sound of weeping be heard in it [Jerusalem], or the cry of distress" (Isa. 65:19). In the promise that immediately follows in Revelation 21:7, that "I will be to the one who overcomes a God, and that person will be to me a son or a daughter," the hearers encounter the familiar promise from 2 Samuel 7:14, applied first to the Davidic dynasty, then to the Messiah, and here extended to the whole of the Christian community in keeping with the theme of the "people of the holy ones" sharing in the rule of God's Anointed. Paul had previously joined a number of these promises, applying them to the Christian community (2 Cor. 6:16–18).

When John gives expression to the consummation and especially when he represents the speech of God, he is very careful to do so on the basis of traditional material already associated with the same hope and the same lips. He

---

60. *Fourth Ezra* 10 illustrates the fluidity with which the image of a woman can be transformed into the image of a city, though the representation of cities personified as women is also a commonplace in the Greco-Roman world.

stands under, and for, that traditional vision of intimate communion with God, and the vision for a healing community that such shared intimacy generates.

John differs from his sources in two significant particulars. The first of these concerns the scope of God's promises. Ezekiel was concerned with the vindication of Israel, while the nations looked on to witness God's acts on Israel's behalf. Though John can interweave strands of Ezekiel 37:27 into his vision, he stops short of 37:28: "Then the nations shall know that I the LORD sanctify Israel, when my sanctuary is among them forevermore" (NRSV). In keeping with major streams of the early Christian movement, John rejects an ethnocentric focus in favor of a more inclusive, universalizing scope for the redemptive work of God. The same light that illumines new Jerusalem will enlighten the nations: "The nations will walk by her light, and the kings of the earth will bring their glory into her" (Rev. 21:24). This is not, however, to arrogate the authority of Ezekiel for an innovative interpretation on John's part; it is to interpret Ezekiel's vision in light of the broader vision of Isaiah and Zechariah (see Isa. 60:3–5; Zech. 2:11–12), the latter of which had already applied the promise that "they shall be my people" to the nations that join themselves to God.[61] John's estimation of the broader scope of Christ's interests in building a kingdom of priests for God "from every tribe and language and people and nation" (Rev. 5:9–10; 7:9; 14:6–7) and his preference for the more universalizing stream would be readily received as consonant with the sacred tradition, since that view stands in line with major streams of early Christian interpretation of the Hebrew scriptural hope (e.g., Luke 3:1–6; Acts 10–11, 15; Rom. 15:7–13; Gal. 3:1–4:7; Eph. 3:1–6; 1 Pet. 2:4–10).

The second point of divergence is more pronounced: the emphatic *absence* of a temple in the new Jerusalem.[62] This contrasts starkly with Ezekiel, who reserves substantial textual space for the construction of the new temple (40–48).[63] This divergence is all the more striking given the formal similarities between John's vision and Ezekiel's vision, both involving an angelic being with a measuring rod ushering the seer around the complex and exploring every gate, wall, and structure.[64] John, however, gives careful attention to expressing the rationale for this difference (21:22): the full presence of God and the Lamb in this city eliminate the need for a temple, since the graded access to God and the limitations placed on the presence of God implied by the temple structure have been completely transcended in God's consummation.

---

61. See also Bauckham 1993a, 310–11.
62. Including the names of the twelve apostles on the foundations alongside the names of the twelve patriarchs is also a notable difference (Rev. 21:12–14; cf. Ezek. 48:30–35), but one that would readily be accepted by the hearers who have themselves embraced the apostolic tradition with their conversion.
63. See further Aune 2006, 16–28. Aune also discusses the development of visions of eschatological temple and city in the *Temple Scroll* and *Description of the New Jerusalem* found in the caves near Qumran, though he concludes that "common dependence on Ezek 40–48" explains most similarities between these documents and Revelation (Aune 2006, 28).
64. Aune 2006, 22.

The God Whose Patience Has an End

It is not John's visions of cosmic renewal and healing that elicit criticism, but rather his claims about the exclusion of certain groups of people and the more dire destiny he forecasts for them. Royalty considers the warnings in the seven oracles to be "eschatological threats" used "to bully the churches into accepting his views (see Rev. 2:22–23; 3:5; 3:9; and 3:16)."[65] The visions of people being cast into the lake of fire or barred from entering the new Jerusalem because they chose a different path would surely also belong to this class of "bullying" words. These were the visions that set D. H. Lawrence on edge: he condemned John for betraying the New Testament vision of love with his "lake of burning brimstone in which devils, demons, beasts, and bad men should frizzle and suffer for ever and ever and ever, Amen!"[66]

And yet we must admit that even in the most objectionable parts, the words that rub most gratingly against our cultural predilection for inclusivity, tolerance, and pluralism—even here John does no more than speak in line with the tradition of which he has become the curator and spokesperson. When he proclaims a God who, having created a just kingdom, excludes, punishes, or extirpates what is unjust, rebellious, and not aligned with God (but aligned, rather, with "lawlessness," ἀνομία), he faithfully portrays that "other side" of God that shows through the Torah, the former and later prophets, and ultimately Jesus himself.

In Isaiah's celebration of the new Exodus that God would make for God's people, the prophet includes a note of exclusivity concerning God's new highway through the desert: "The unclean shall not walk on it" (35:8). When the same prophet comes to his vision of the renewed Jerusalem, he calls Zion to rejoice in part because "the uncircumcised and the unclean shall enter you no more" (52:1 NRSV).[67] In Ezekiel, immediately following the promise that "they shall be my people, and I will be their God" (11:20 NRSV), so prominent in early Christian discourse (including Rev. 21:3–4), the prophet shows God turning his attention to those who will not heed the call to obedience so as to experience these benefits: "But as for those whose heart goes after their detestable things and their abominations. . ." (Ezek. 11:21 NRSV).

In keeping with the presentation of God's city and, in Ezekiel and *11QTemple*, restored temple precincts as holy, these texts all focus as well on excluded classes of the polluted.[68] John's vision of the Holy City in which God dwells in all God's fullness, therefore, quite naturally invites similar discussion of classes of pollution that disqualify one from approaching the Holy One in the holy places of God's dwelling. John's lists (Rev. 21:8, 27; 22:15) are notable insofar

---

65. Royalty 1998, 33.
66. Lawrence 1931, 117.
67. By "same prophet," I identify the stream of tradition associated with the name of Isaiah by John and his contemporaries, the book of Isaiah as it would have been read. This is not a claim about the actual authorship of the various parts of the book.
68. See discussion in Aune 2006, 26.

as they involve not ritual pollution, but moral failure, particularly the failure to take a courageous and loyal stand by God and God's Christ. In this manner they align with broadening the scope of God's salvation to members of every nation ("the uncircumcised," e.g., do not appear on John's list of excluded groups, as in Isaiah's list).

Above all, John's presentation of a God who holds rebellious humanity accountable for their affronts against God's honor and rightful claim to obedience resonates with the sayings of Jesus. Matthew 13:41–43 is a case in point: "The Son of Man will send his angels, and they will gather together out of his kingdom all the stumbling blocks and those practicing unlawfulness and 'will throw them into the fiery furnace': weeping and gnashing of teeth shall be there. Then the righteous will shine like the sun in the kingdom of their Father. Let the one having ears listen." Jesus' exclusion of "the stumbling blocks and those practicing unlawfulness [τὰ σκάνδαλα καὶ τοὺς ποιοῦντας τὴν ἀνομίαν]" from the kingdom of the Son of Man corresponds quite closely with Revelation 21:8, 27; 22:15. John simply defines more precisely what constitutes a σκάνδαλον or ἀνομία in his pastoral situation.

Furthermore, the place of exclusion is described in terms suggesting severe pain and torment: "They 'will throw them into the furnace of fire'" (Matt. 13:42, recontextualizing Dan. 3:6), where there will be "weeping and gnashing of teeth," a detail not suggestive of quick incineration (Matt. 13:42). Revelation 14:9–11 elaborates this image of judgment by the Messiah, again with specific ἀνομίαι identified, here very much in line with the first commandments of the Decalogue. The prohibitions against worshiping other gods and making cult images for worship have been disregarded by the offenders in this vision. Interesting is the reconfiguration of Daniel 3 (a story about enforced idolatry and its consequences) implicit in both Matt. 13:41–42 and Revelation 14:6–13, particularly when Daniel 3 is *not* about eschatological judgment.[69]

Matthew 25:41–45, the close of Jesus' Apocalyptic Discourse in Matthew and perhaps the most vivid description of the Last Judgment, is also a noteworthy act of exclusion. Here, the Son of Man sends away those who have failed to return gratitude to him in the persons of the hungry, naked, homeless, and imprisoned, to a place of endless torment—the "eternal fire prepared for the devil and his angels," which closely resembles the "lake of fire" in Revelation, also populated by Satan, his minions, and those human beings deceived by him (14:9–11; 19:20; 20:10, 14–15). In these regards, John is not more exclusive or

---

69. Recalling Royalty's allegation that John seeks to replace the Hebrew Scriptures with his own work by recontextualizing without citing (2004, 293), it is informative to observe that the Jesus saying (Matt. 13:41–43) recontextualizes Dan. 3:6; 12:3 without citation. Is Matthew's Jesus guilty, then, of the same crimes against Scripture of which John stands accused? Or is Mark guilty of trying to obliterate Ps. 22 by recontextualizing and reconfiguring the same in the passion narrative without notice? On the contrary, the fact of recontextualization functions rather to keep the conversation between texts alive, nurturing an environment in which the older texts will be revisited by the hearers of the new text in a mutually informing conversation.

vindictive than Jesus (at least as the latter is represented in the traditions attributed to him).

The question here is not whether John's vision is therefore "right" or "good" or "ethically (in)offensive," but whether John is fairly representing and applying the tradition of the Jewish Scriptures, other intertestamental Jewish literature, Jesus, and the early church—or giving expression to violence, hatred, or venom beyond the tradition (e.g., "bullying his audience into accepting his views," as asserted by Royalty). And in light of John's alignment with the *regula fidei* of the Hebrew Scriptures, the Jesus tradition, and the apostolic tradition in so many points, it is also hardly the case that John is merely trying to get the hearers to accept "his" views.

CONCLUSION

When the canonical authority of Revelation has been questioned—from Luther's preface to his translation of Revelation to Eduard Lohse's article[70] asking "Just how Christian is the Revelation of John?"—it has not been on the basis of its discontinuity from the message of the Hebrew Scriptures. Rather, it has been on the basis of its extreme *continuity* with those texts, indeed, Revelation's greater continuity with the Jewish Scriptures than other texts from the apostolic period. In the early Christian context of testing prophets, however, the continuity of John's portrayal of God's character, activity, and interventions with the portrayal of the same throughout the Jewish scriptural tradition, either as carried over in or modified by the emerging traditions of the early Christian movement, would have recommended "the words of the prophecy of this book" as a genuine prophetic utterance. And if John's authority was grounded in the recognition of this consonance among the congregations, he can hardly be dismissed as a power-hungry authoritarian leader. Rather, he emerges as one whose claim to authority rests ultimately not in hearing voices and seeing visions, but in giving new life and new voice to the sacred traditions to which John, other prophets, and the congregations themselves stood accountable, at least as long as they wished to continue claiming to be followers of Jesus.

70. Lohse 1988b.

Chapter 7

The Strategic Arousal of Emotions in the Oracles to the Seven Churches

Revelation regularly provokes strong emotional responses in its readers, whether those readers resist John's rhetoric[1] or yield themselves fully to John's rhetoric and reinscribe John's strategies in current contexts.[2] And yet, despite the self-evident nature of Revelation's emotionally evocative power, rhetorical critics have given little attention to the appeals to emotion in John's Apocalypse, focusing most energetically instead on appeals to ethos, and then, to a lesser extent, on appeals to logos and other facets of its rhetorical composition.[3] To be sure, rhetorical critics affirm the importance and prominence of appeals to the emotions in Revelation and the evocative power of John's imagery.[4] However,

---

1. See, e.g., Lawrence 1931, 87–88; Jung 1954, 125. Both authors seek to be alert to the emotions expressed within/behind the text as well as evoked by the text.
2. Contemporary sectarian literature is instructive in this regard. Herbert W. Armstrong (1959, 44–45), for example, correctly identifies John's appeal to fear in Rev. 6:5–17 and uses this, with the help of Gruenewaldesque illustrations by Basil Wolverton, to terrorize his readers into accepting the seal of God, meaning the yoke of Armstrong's own instruction concerning keeping God's commandments.
3. See the survey of research in deSilva 2008b. A rare exception is A. Collins 1984, 151–53, though she does not use rhetorical theory as a resource.
4. For example, Schüssler Fiorenza 1985, 187; Johns 2003, 157–58; Witherington 2003, 90. The importance of appeals to the emotions as an integrated part of an orator's rhetorical strategy is, of course, well evidenced by the space devoted to the subject in classical rhetorical handbooks, as well

many studies remain imprecise in their analysis of particular appeals to pathos. Critics frequently observe that a particular feature of Revelation "evokes pathos" without taking the step of specifying *which* emotion is likely to be aroused,[5] let alone the further step of analyzing the particular literary means by which this emotion might be evoked (and on the basis of what criteria the analyst discerns such an appeal to that particular emotion).

In this chapter we begin to remedy this lack of attention, first in regard to the seven oracles of Revelation 2–3.[6] For this exploration to be fully rhetorical, we need to attend to three questions in regard to the analysis of pathos. The first question concerns "Which emotions, and where?" Where do we suspect John of trying to arouse particular emotions among his hearers, and what particular emotions would these be? The second is the question "How can we tell?" What features of the text can we identify as likely to arouse these particular feelings, and on what basis can we make these claims? Here the near-contemporary discussions of evoking emotions in the rhetorical handbooks will provide us with a reliable guide. The third and final question concerns "Why." To what end is John potentially evoking this emotion at this place in the text?[7]

METHODOLOGICAL CONSIDERATIONS: IDENTIFYING APPEALS TO THE EMOTIONS

To pursue the analysis of appeals to emotion on a less subjective foundation than "knowing them when we feel them," this study relies heavily on the near-contemporary discussions of how to evoke emotions in Greek and Latin rhetorical handbooks. Aristotle's *Art of Rhetoric* (2.2–11) provides a lengthy elaboration of topics that an orator might use to build a case, as it were, for the provocation of a particular emotional response, covering a wide range of human feeling (anger, calm, friendship, enmity, fear, confidence, shame, shamelessness, favor/gratitude[8] and its negation, pity, indignation, envy, and emula-

---

as more recent analyses of the difference between "convincing" someone (i.e., of the validity of some logical theorem) and "persuading" someone (i.e., to commit his or her personal resources to taking some action). See P. Smith 1998, 4; Thuren 2001, 109.

5. E.g., Schüssler Fiorenza 1991, 31, 129; Royalty 1997, 609; 1998, 138, 190; Johns 1998, 763; 2003, 162, 163 n. 46.

6. The seven oracles recommend themselves for study as a discrete textual unit on the basis of the unity of (highly stylized) form that sets them apart from the remainder of Revelation, the unity of implied speaker (the glorified Christ), reinforced by references in the opening of each oracle to the vision of this speaker (1:12–20), and the unity of addressees (individual churches, though also to be heard by the whole circle of congregations).

7. Although developed independently, these three questions align with, and thereby confirm, those posed in Keck 2001, 87–88: "What emotion does Paul seek to elicit? How does he attempt to do so? And, what is its role in the whole undertaking?"

8. The designation of the emotion treated by Aristotle in *Rhet.* 2.7 merely as "favor" or "benevolence" is too one-sided both for the range of meanings covered by the term χάρις itself as well as for the situations that Aristotle includes, some of which clearly would arouse gratitude in response to favor.

tion).⁹ His discussion pertains thus to material that the analyst can discover in a text (topics) rather than to techniques that could only be observed in the performance (emotional tone, demeanor, or gesture of the speaker, a prominent feature of Roman rhetoricians' discussion of the subject).¹⁰

Aristotle's treatment is supplemented in important ways by Latin orators. Because of a greater focus on forensic rhetoric, texts in the Ciceronian corpus (including the misattributed *Rhetorica ad Herennium*) provide detailed discussions only of indignation and pity (*Inv.* 1.53.101–1.56.109; *Rhet. Her.* 2.30.48–2.31.50), with only some passing attention given to love (*amor*), compassion (*misericordia*), and jealousy (*invidia*; *De oratore* 2.51.205–2.52.211). Cicero (*De or.* 2.53.215–216) and Quintilian (*Inst.* 6.1.18, 20, 46) call attention to the orator's obligation to sweep aside the feelings evoked by an opposing speaker by means of arousing the contrary emotion, just as surely as the opponent's proofs must be deconstructed. They also highlight the speaker's own genuine experience of particular emotions as an effective catalyst for kindling the hearers' emotions (Quintilian, *Inst.* 6.2.26; Cicero, *De or.* 2.45.189–2.47.197). Quintilian recommends the technique of vividly imagining the scenes about which one speaks as a means of conjuring one's own emotions (*Inst.* 6.2.29–30; cf. also *Rhet. Her.* 4.55.68), to the point that one will "not so much narrate as exhibit the actual scene" (*Inst.* 6.2.32), even calling attention to the imagined "sights" as if pointing with his finger, inviting the audience to "see" what he wishes them to "see" in those spaces, augmenting the immediacy of the scenes and their emotionally evocative content for the audience (Longinus, *On the Sublime* 15.1–2). John achieves this and more as he displays the scenes themselves before his audience, both as one who witnessed the scenes himself and as one who enables them to see the same vividly before their own minds' eyes.

The material in these classical handbooks has already been extensively employed in detailed analyses of appeals to pathos in other early Christian texts, particularly the epistolary literature.¹¹ No presumption need be made that John

---

9. According to Steven J. Kraftchick (2001, 56), Aristotle believed that "*ethos* and *pathos* arguments are indeed arguments.... The πάθη are emotions that can be caused in the audience by demonstrating to the listeners that the conditions for those emotions are present," focusing those emotions, showing "that they are justifiable," and finally suggesting "actions that are consonant with the emotions." See also T. Martin 2001, 188.

Aristotle does not provide comprehensive coverage of the full range of human emotions that can be strategically evoked to serve rhetorical ends, limiting his treatment to emotions appropriate for arenas of human debate or celebration, the forum, council chamber, and hall of justice (Cooper 1996, 251). He does not treat the emotion of "awe" or "wonder," which would be evoked in the religious contexts of the temple of Artemis, the altar of Zeus, the temple of *Roma et Augustus*, or the Christian ἐκκλησία—religious contexts of great interest and concern to John.

10. Kraftchick (2001, 47–57) provides an excellent, succinct analysis of the differences between Greek and Latin rhetorical theory concerning appeals to the emotions.

11. This method is employed in Johanson 1987; Watson 1988a; deSilva 2000b, 103–7, 151–52, 183, 210–14, 239–40, 343–54, 380; and several of the studies collected in Olbricht and Sumney 2001, which have substantially helped confirm and refine the methodological approach of the present study.

learned or consciously imitated these conventions.[12] As a distillation of their authors' observation of rhetorical practice and its effects, the handbooks provide near-contemporary evidence concerning how first-century audiences responded to particular rhetorical prompts (e.g., "topics"). Where an analyst discovers the presence of these prompts in a New Testament text, even one so far removed from the Greek oration as Revelation, the analyst has a solid textual basis for presuming an emotional response on the part of the hearers, and an invitation to explore how this emotional reaction would help guide the hearers' response to the author's discourse in a manner favorable to the author's rhetorical goals.[13]

GENRE AND RHETORICAL ORIENTATION

Readers are generally disposed to encounter, and therefore analyze, these chapters as a collection of seven "letters," a generic label that has almost come to be assumed.[14] Such a generic frame leads, in turn, to the application of epistolographic theory and conventions in interpretation, even against the evidence of the text itself. John Kirby[15] gives an example of this as he writes: "Each begins, after what may be termed the salutation ('to the church at X write:'), with the phrase τάδε λέγει. . . ." The formula, "To the church at X, write," is not, however, a "salutation." It is explicitly an instruction to John, not a greeting as in Revelation 1:4: "John to the seven churches that are in Asia, grace and peace."

There is a growing awareness, however, that the "seven letters" are not "letters" at all. In an important article, David E. Aune[16] correctly observes that the formula "To the church at *X,* write" is part of the literary setting, since the actual messages begin with the "thus says" formula. This formula, in turn, signals an immediate correspondence with the prophetic oracles of the Hebrew Scriptures as well as pagan oracles,[17] and secondarily with Persian royal diplomatic letters and edicts and later edicts issued by Roman magistrates and emperors.[18] The instruc-

---

12. See Kraftchick 2001, 42–43; Sumney 2001, 149.
13. The point is often made that rhetorical criticism needs, in general, to take into account more recent theory (see Olbricht 2001a, 2; Classen 1992, 321–22). In terms of their attention to appeals to the emotions, however, recent rhetorical and speech theorists actually fall short of Aristotle. Perelman and Olbrichts-Tyteca (1969) give only passing attention to the subject. See Olbricht's survey of, and conclusions concerning, the contributions of contemporary theory (2001a, 2–3). Moreover, in regard to the analysis of appeals to emotion (particularly in Revelation), we have not begun even to employ the insights of classical rhetorical theory to their fullest.
14. As in Barr 1984, 45: "The risen Christ dictates seven letters." The use of the label "letters" in landmark works such as Ramsay 1994 (1904) and Hemer 1986 strongly reinforces this disposition.
15. Kirby 1988, 200.
16. Aune 1990, 185.
17. Aune 1990, 187–88; so also Schüssler Fiorenza 1991, 46; deSilva 1992a, 286–87; Duff 2001, 32.
18. Aune 1990, 188; Schüssler Fiorenza 1991, 46. Aune (1990, 201–3) argues that, within the identification of these communications as prophetic oracles, the particular pattern of the imperial edict gives further definition to the form of each pronouncement. He especially notes the similarities in form, with both edicts and the pronouncements including a *"praescriptio* ('introduction'), which gives the title(s) and name(s) of the issuing magistrate, followed by a verb of declaration" (1990,

tion to John to "write" signals not dictation of a "letter," but of an "oracle." It is an instruction quite at home in the Greco-Roman milieu, where "gods command various individuals, usually through the medium of a dream, to write books."[19] Aune's conclusion that "the seven proclamations . . . exhibit few features derived from the Hellenistic epistolary tradition" has been increasingly accepted.[20]

This clarification of genre carries significant implications for our appreciation of how the first hearers would have encountered these proclamations, and thus for the analysis of the rhetorical effects of the proclamations on these hearers. As oracles (and all the more if they are heard as oracles proclaiming edicts) these communications arouse fewer expectations for involved attempts at persuasion, but rather more forthright diagnosis and command.[21] The form raises the issue of the superior and unquestionable authority of the speaker. John intends for his audience to hear Christ speaking to them,[22] and Christ's position in the worldview shared by John and the congregations allows him indeed to command, whereas John, even if a respected leader, could only come alongside to persuade. The letter form nurtures the expectation of a more "friendly" communication that might "enjoin," where the oracles can "command" and are thus to be sharply distinguished from epistolary paraenesis.[23] In light of this, the features that the seven oracles do share with paraenesis stand out more starkly and carry, potentially, a greater rhetorical impact since they are the less expected.[24] Oracular form also gives greater room for the use of threat and promise (rather

---

201); a *narratio*, functioning similarly to the οἶδα clauses in the seven proclamations (what does the magistrate know, on which knowledge the present communication is based? 1990, 202); a *dispositio* giving the magistrate's commands or instructions or decree (1990, 203); and *sanctiones*, the threats and promises inducing obedience (1990, 201). This introduces a useful secondary generic frame for these oracular communications, a means by which John voices his conviction that "Christ is the true king in contrast to the Roman emperor who is both a clone and tool of Satan" (1990, 204).

19. Aune 1990, 187.

20. Aune 1990, 194; Royalty 1997, 609; Witherington 2003, 41, 90.

21. Argumentation is not absent, as Kirby (1988, 202–3) has rightly observed. We will explore rational argumentation in the seven oracles in chap. 9 (below).

22. Royalty 1997, 610. Royalty rightly observes that the closing summons of each oracle, "Let anyone who has an ear listen," is "an echo of the Synoptic parables" (1997, 610). This constitutes a kind of stylistic "signature," marking the style of the oracles in a way that connects them with Jesus' known speech patterns, increasingly the likelihood of acceptance on the part of the hearers that this represents Jesus' "true" speech.

23. In this regard, the seven oracles more closely resemble "the Mosaic law, which prohibits or commands, but hardly engages in paraenesis" (Starr and Engberg-Pedersen 2004, 2). Those features of the seven oracles that command, prohibit, and moreover, threaten and promise would not be seen here to nurture a paraenetic environment, which relies rather on "benevolent injunction" (see Popkes 2004, 28; Engberg-Pedersen 2004, 52).

24. Following Starr and Engberg-Pedersen 2004 and Perdue and Gammie 1990, this study tends toward the narrower definition of "paraenesis" that rejects the practice of using "paraenetic" interchangeably with "hortatory" (as, e.g., in Aune 1997, lxxxvii–lxxxviii, cxxv, where precisely the same list of textual features, chiefly in the seven oracles, is first described as "hortatory" and later as an example of "parenesis"). Starr and Engberg-Pedersen 2004 sought to establish that "what may be called 'hortatory,' need not be 'paraenetical'" (Popkes 2004, 38). The specific commands given in the seven oracles stand at some distance from the "clear, concrete guidance" concerning behavior within established domestic or social roles that characterizes speech or texts properly called "paraenetic" (Popkes 2004, 42; Engberg-Pedersen 2004, 53, 62).

than moral exhortation) as effective motivators, which is exactly what we find in the seven proclamations. At the same time, these oracles are couched within a larger epistolary framework (1:4; 22:21), the genre that John has chosen for the delivery of his own voice. God gives a "revelation" (1:1); Christ commands in oracles (2:1–3:22). John himself, however, can write a "letter" (1:4), coming alongside the hearers in a way that creates strong feelings of association (e.g., presenting himself as a "brother" and "fellow sharer" in both the hope and the costs of discipleship, in 1:9) and signals pastoral intent,[25] while including oracles (2:1–3:22) and other more authoritative and authoritarian communications speaking with the power of divine command. He can thus "have it both ways" in terms of constructing authority for his message.

APPEALS TO THE EMOTIONS IN THE ORACLES TO THE SEVEN CHURCHES

The congregations' experience of hearing the seven oracles is necessarily colored by the opening chapter of the book, which provides the narrative frame for the whole. Two features of this introductory chapter are of special importance here: the establishment of "imminence" as the overall temporal frame of reference and the evocations of "awe" in connection with the narrated vision of the glorified Christ.[26]

The opening sentences of Revelation twice evoke the topic of "imminence" (ἃ δεῖ γενέσθαι ἐν τάχει, 1:1; ὁ γὰρ καιρὸς ἐγγύς, 1:3), establishing "imminence" as a frame for all the material that John is about to describe. Precisely "what" is imminent comes into sharper focus as the decisive visitation of God/Christ is held vividly before the audiences' eyes: "Look! He comes (ἔρχεται) with the clouds!" (1:7).[27] The description of God, moreover, as "the one who is and who was and the one who comes" (1:4, 8), modifies a widespread, traditional formula concerning the "eternity" of God (e.g., "Zeus is, Zeus was, Zeus will be"), and thus, in a sense, the timelessness of God, in favor of crafting an image of the "imminently intervening" God (not ὁ ἐλευσόμενος, "the

---

25. Carey 2001, 173.
26. The verbal repetitions of phrases from Rev. 1:12–20 in the self-introduction of the speaker in each of the seven oracles shows intentional connection between these passages, as does the verbal repetition of Christ "coming" or "coming quickly" in 1:7–8; 2:5, 16; 3:11.
27. Where the MT of Dan. 7:13 employs a perfect-tense verb, LXX/Old Greek an imperfect indicative, and Theodotion a periphrastic imperfect construction to speak of this "coming," John has used the present tense of vivid narration. John seems to see this very sight happening before his eyes. Although Quintilian was talking about the benefits of a vivid imagination rather than ecstatic visionary experiences, it is still noteworthy that such "internal imaginings" (φαντασία, *visiones*) were recommended as a means by which a speaker could effectively evoke emotional responses in himself or herself, so as to provide the spark to ignite the flames of emotion in the audience as well (*Inst.* 6.2.29–32). Since John is narrating what he claims to be a visionary experience, however, his vivid and immediate descriptions may present the scenes not only to himself, but also to his hearers' internal sight, evoking their emotional responses more directly.

The Strategic Arousal of Emotions in the Oracles   181

one who will come [at some point]," but ὁ ἐρχόμενος, "the one who is [in the process of] coming").²⁸

As we have seen, these opening evocations of the topic of imminence effectively heighten the hearers' attention (hence, contributing to ethos). Imminence, however, is also the foundation for appeals to the emotions of fear and confidence.²⁹ Aristotle defines fear (φόβος) as "a painful or troubled feeling caused by the impression of an imminent evil (κακοῦ) that causes destruction or pain" (*Rhet.* 2.5.1). He stresses the proximity of harm: people will be afraid "only if [harmful things] appear to be not far off but near at hand and threatening" (2.5.2). Similarly, confidence (θαρρεῖν), as "the contrary of fear," is evoked by "the hope of what is salutary, . . . accompanied by an impression that it is quite near at hand" (2.5.16). This topic of imminence will be significantly reinforced as Revelation proceeds.³⁰ Imminence, and the evocations specifically of fear and confidence in the face of imminent events posing threat or promise, heighten the urgency that helps create a situation in which the hearers are disposed to deliberate,³¹ to consider possible changes in their courses of action (a rhetorical function highlighted by Aristotle specifically in regard to fear; 2.5.14), and to adopt the actions commanded in the seven oracles.

In Revelation 1:12–20, John brings the glorified Christ before the eyes of his congregations by using language drawn from scriptural theophanies and angelophanies (notably recontextualizing details from Daniel and Ezekiel). Kirby³² had helpfully suggested that Christ is pictured in a way evocative of the feeling of awe. While Aristotle did not provide a detailed list of topics or situations to which an audience could be expected to respond with "awe," we can readily understand how this emotional response would be generated by means of religious ritual in the context of, for example, impressive temples with grandiose representations of deities.

Revelation 1:12–16; 4:1–5:14 can be understood largely as representations of God, Christ, heavenly "personnel," and heavenly court ceremonial designed

---

28. The translation of Rev. 1:4, 8 comes from Aune 1997, 57. That God "was, is, and will be" is a widely attested tripartite formula for Deity in the classical and Roman periods (many examples are helpfully collected in Aune 1997, 30–32).

29. Royalty (1997, 609) had observed that Rev. 1:1–3 "heightens the emotional impact, or *pathos*, of the text on the audience," first by creating a sense of "eschatological urgency" and second by pronouncing a blessing, though he did not specify which emotions would be evoked by these two features, nor how. Similarly, Schüssler Fiorenza (1991, 115) sensed that "the urgency of Revelation's imminent expectation clearly serves rhetorical functions" without probing more fully what those functions would be.

30. See ἔρχομαί σοι ταχύ (2:16); ἔρχομαι ταχύ (3:11); χρόνος οὐκέτι ἔσται (10:6); ἃ δεῖ γενέσθαι ἐν τάχει (22:6); καὶ ἰδοὺ ἔρχομαι ταχύ (22:7); ὁ καιρὸς γὰρ ἐγγύς ἐστιν (22:10); ἰδοὺ ἔρχομαι ταχύ (22:12); ναί, ἔρχομαι ταχύ (22:20). The concentration of the last five of these statements in the functional peroration of the book suggests that John is giving special attention to closing appeals to pathos, especially in regard to reinforcing fear and confidence (*which* emotion a hearer feels will correspond with where one sees oneself reflected in the contents of the seven oracles and the visions).

31. See Kraftchick 2001, 45–46 on the role that "emotions play . . . in initiating thought and creative thinking."

32. Kirby 1988, 199.

to arouse genuine awe—and all this is most strategic. The extensive scholarly literature on Revelation's interaction with, and opposition to, Roman imperial cult and court ceremonial leaves little room for doubt that John attempted to evoke such a response, in part, in order to draw members of the audience away from being impressed by the emperor, especially through all the pomp and circumstance of the manifestations of imperial cult in their cities, toward being *more* impressed—feeling more *awe*—in response to Jesus. John's own response reflects the emotional response he seeks to kindle among his audience—being so overcome by the vision of Christ as he exists now in his postresurrection, postascension state that physical strength fails (Rev. 1:17).[33]

This is not to say, however, that John's presentation should not also evoke "fear" in the more normal sense, especially in the context of the topics of imminence (temporal, in regard to Christ's second coming, but also now spatial, in regard to Christ standing in the midst of the seven lampstands; 1:12–13, 20). John acknowledges such fear to be naturally generated by such a vision, which certainly colors the "awe" that Kirby discerned here, for it is *this* emotional response that Christ himself allays as he places his hand upon John to reassure him and utters the words Μὴ φοβοῦ, "Do not fear" (1:17). The same dual rhetorical potential that inheres in the topic of "imminence" inheres in the presentation of the glorified Christ: both topics can be nurtured now in a direction that evokes fear or in a direction that evokes confidence. It is this "awesome," divine figure who confronts the churches in Revelation 2–3. His power and strength stands ready to enforce the warnings (fear), but also to encourage the believers, setting before them open doors that no one can close (confidence).

Fear and Confidence

Rather than proceed through the seven oracles seriatim, this study will focus on the arousal of particular emotions throughout the seven oracles, following Aristotle's own pairing of contrary (but often complementary) emotions.

The oracle to Ephesus begins with a topic of proximity: the glorified Christ is not far off in the world beyond, but stands in the midst of the seven congregations (Rev. 2:1).[34] He is thus close at hand to carry out the threat made at the close of the oracle: "I will . . . remove your lampstand from its place unless you repent" (2:5). Spatial proximity functions in much the same way as temporal

---

33. We recall here Cicero's advice (*De or.* 2.45.189–2.47.197) that speakers must themselves feel the emotions they would wish to arouse in their hearers. This principle needs to be applied with caution, of course, since not every such expression signals an appeal to pathos, or at least to that particular emotion. This is abundantly clear from Rev. 5:3–4, where John weeps when no one is found who is worthy to open the scroll. John surely does not intend to arouse sorrow among the hearers at this juncture; rather, his weeping serves as part of a narrativization of a topic of encomium, namely, the unique achievement of the subject of the encomium, who here is the Lamb.

34. In the discussion that follows, I will speak of John orchestrating topics in the seven oracles, but also of "the glorified Christ" speaking to the congregations. Neither constitutes a claim in regard to the vexed question of the genuineness or artifice of these oracular pronouncements.

proximity ("imminence," which is nevertheless also present as a foundation for the entire experience of hearing Revelation): the threatened loss or harm is close at hand. John plays a similar change on the topic of "imminence" within the oracle to Sardis: "If, then, you will not be watchful, I will come as a thief, and you will certainly not know in what hour I will come upon you" (3:3).[35] Here it is not that Christ will come "quickly" against them, but that he will come suddenly, without warning. The vision of Christ in 1:12–20 reinforces the impression that he has the power to carry out his threats if he continues to be provoked by the congregation's lack of responsiveness.[36] The topics productive of fear, if successful, help to move the congregations toward discovering the "works" that manifest the recovery of their "first love," or genuine "life" so as to avoid encountering this powerful figure to their harm.[37]

Appeals to fear are more fully developed in the oracles to Pergamum and Thyatira. In 2:12, Christ confronts the congregation as the one "having the sharp, double-edged sword."[38] This sword is pointed specifically at the Nicolaitans, who have provoked God (thus aroused the "anger" of one who is "able to injure"; see Aristotle, *Rhet.* 2.5.3, 5) with their promotion of "eating foods sacrificed to idols and fornication" (Rev. 2:14–15), and not at the congregation as a whole (2:16).[39] The topic of imminence ("I will come to you quickly," 2:16) is also explicitly introduced in connection with the fate of the Nicolaitan party in Pergamum, completing the recipe for eliciting fear. Since the threat clings specifically to being associated with the Nicolaitans, fear contributes to motivating the members of the congregation sympathetic to the Nicolaitans' message and practice to distance themselves from the same.

Similarly, in the oracle to Thyatira, the glorified Christ announces the threat of imminent harm to Jezebel and those who are connected with her (2:22–23).

---

35. That the speaker (Christ) anticipates disagreement or resistance, to the point even of announcing plans for dealing with such a response ("but if not, . . ."; see Rev. 2:5b, 16b; 3:3b), distinguishes these oracles from paraenesis as defined by, e.g., Pseudo-Libanius ("paraenesis is a word of advice not expecting opposition, as if someone would say that it is necessary to honour the divine; for nobody objects to that advice, unless he were crazy beforehand"; quoted in Popkes 2004, 45) and by the working group that shaped the Oslo definition of the phenomenon (Starr and Engberg-Pedersen 2004, 4).

36. The identification of a powerful figure who has been or is being provoked, especially a figure of principle, is an important constituent of an effective appeal to fear. Signals of fear include "the enmity and anger [ὀργή] of those able to injure us in any way . . . and outraged virtue [ἀρετὴ ὑβριζομένη] when it has power, for it is evident that it always desires satisfaction, whenever it is outraged, and now it has the power" (Aristotle, *Rhet.* 2.5.3, 5).

37. Some hope of escape must be left, or else people will not be afraid (Aristotle, *Rhet.* 2.5.14), and this is indeed the case in regard to constellations of topics of fear in Revelation. There is a way out for anyone on the wrong side of the glorified Christ (except, perhaps, for "Jezebel," who "refuses to repent"; Rev. 2:21).

38. The presentation of the speaker (Christ) as one who stands equipped and ready violently to enforce his commands (2:5b, 12, 16b, 21–23; 3:3b) is another prominent feature that significantly distances these oracles from paraenesis.

39. Appropriately in regard to the historical precedent invoked, Christ makes war with these contemporary Balaamites "with the sword of [his] mouth," even as the Israelites killed the historical Balaam "with the sword" (Num. 31:8).

John employs the present tense as a means of making the threatened consequences more vivid, more imminent (ἰδοὺ βάλλω, 2:22), despite the fact that they are still *future* consequences, occurring only if the way of escape is not taken first (ἐὰν μὴ μετανοήσωσιν).[40] The amplitude of this threatened harm is magnified in 2:23b: It will be so stunning that "all the churches" will feel its repercussions, giving rise to a new and profound reverence for the "one who searches minds and hearts." The overtones here of God's gaining glory by means of the plagues God will visit upon Pharaoh, striking fear into the hearts of other nations, are unmistakable and contribute to the dread of what this judgment will look like for anyone caught in bed with Jezebel.[41] By contrast, 2:24–25 evokes confidence among "the rest" in Thyatira by equating "not holding to her teaching" with being found in need of no major adjustment in their walk in order for it "to be well with them in regard to the gods" (Aristotle, *Rhet.* 2.5.21), specifically, God and God's Christ. The juxtaposition of arousing fear in connection with following Jezebel's teaching and offering confidence in connection with distance from the same clearly serves the rhetorical goal of distancing the Christians in Thyatira from this prophetess, even potentially motivating them to put an end to her teaching within the congregation.

The oracle to Smyrna contains a description of a situation of imminent harm that could be expected naturally to arouse a response of fear (Rev. 2:10). The glorified Christ, however, explicitly seeks to allay that emotional response, cutting it off ahead of time: "Fear nothing that you are about to suffer" [μηδὲν φοβοῦ ἃ μέλλεις πάσχειν]" (2:10a). Instead, his speech nurtures a different kind of emotional response to the situation of fearsome opposition, namely, confidence, as he recalls his own conquest of death, the most fearsome evil (2:8b), minimizes the danger by specifying its short duration (ἡμερῶν δέκα, 2:10), and promises safety from a far more fearsome evil for the disciples who successfully meet the challenges set before them (2:11b).

The oracle to Philadelphia is especially rich in topics that were recognized to evoke confidence. Christ presents himself as a powerful Ally who will open the way forward to the congregation, with no one to hinder: "These things says . . . the one who opens and no one will close, who closes and no one opens: . . . I set in front of you an open door that no one is able to shut" (3:7–8). This opening combines the topics of having "means of help" (Aristotle, *Rhet.* 2.5.17), allies whose "interests are the same as ours" and who are "stronger" than the opposition (2.5.18), and the assurance of divine favor delivered through an oracle (2.5.21)

---

40. A few scribes "correct" John on this point, writing βαλῶ for βάλλω, missing the rhetorical contribution of the present-tense verb here.

41. In Num. 25:1–9, eating food sacrificed to idols and committing fornication resulted in death by plague for many among the Hebrews. Here, it is noteworthy that Jezebel's punishment is to be cast upon a bed (κλίνη), which many commentators read as a "sickbed" (Duff 2001, 92; Witherington 2003, 104; though its multiple valences are also aptly noted by Harrington 1993, 64; Krodel 1989, 125; Roloff 1984, 55), and that her children will be killed "with death," a redundancy that almost certainly indicates that θάνατος should be heard here to denote a certain manner of death, namely "plague" (as in BDAG).

in regard to a present conflict. Whatever the precise nature of this conflict,[42] this same, powerful Ally will bring it about that the synagogue will come to acknowledge the congregation's beloved place in the eyes of the Son of God (3:9). Similarly, the congregation receives assurance of safety in regard to "the hour of testing that is about to come upon the whole inhabited world to test those dwelling on the earth" (3:10), which will be developed at length in the course of the visions to follow. The exact sense of this assurance is rendered problematic by the unusual expression "τηρήσω ἐκ" insofar as it is not clear whether the congregation will be "kept from" this trial or "preserved through and out of the midst of" the same.[43] If the former sense, this topic corresponds with Aristotle's suggestion that making fearful things seem far-off or nonexistent will arouse confidence; if the latter sense, the emotional response is still the same, though grounded in different affirmations (the presence of help, strong and capable Allies, and other such resources as assure a successful outcome). In this oracle the topic of imminence invoked by Christ's declaration, "I am coming quickly" (3:11), would serve to further nurture confidence, "the hope of what is salutary" being "accompanied by an impression that it is quite near at hand" (Aristotle, *Rhet.* 2.5.16). Feelings of confidence are aroused to compensate, in part, for the congregation's awareness of its own relative powerlessness (3:8b), and to embolden it to continue in the course of "not denying [Christ's] name," not bending before any pressure that might be applied by the local synagogue there (3:9).

Friendship and Enmity

Words that show "good feelings," that manifest admiration or appreciation, and that praise the hearers' good qualities all potentially arouse feelings of friendship (Aristotle, *Rhet.* 2.4.14, 19). The words of commendation in five of the seven oracles (2:2a, 3, 9, 13, 19; 3.8), then, are very likely to have this effect.[44] Aristotle especially finds that speakers "who praise our good qualities, especially those which we ourselves are afraid we do not possess" (2.4.14), evoke friendly feelings, something that may apply in the case of Smyrna, whose material poverty may have hidden from their own eyes—but not from Christ's—the fact

---

42. The conflict with the synagogue is not developed here in the same degree of detail as it is in the oracle to the church in Smyrna.

43. See discussions, e.g., in Aune 1997, 239–40; Beale 1999, 290–92. In the context of visions that show disciples consistently emerging as "victors" on the other side of trial (see esp. Rev. 7:13–17; 15:2–4), the latter option (preferred by both Aune and Beale) seems by far the most likely.

44. This is also a point at which the seven oracles resemble paraenesis: "Paraenesis typically compliments present behavior, indicating a degree of personal acquaintance between the speaker and the audience. Thus paraenesis was aptly suited to the letter genre, since a chief characteristic of the letter was that it should be a friendly, personal communication" (Starr 2004, 79, referring to Malherbe 1986, 125). The speaker's complimenting of the congregations introduces an element of affirmation that is less characteristic of the oracle genre to which these proclamations belong, and may therefore have fostered a greater sense of friendly feeling/disposition, a positive emotion that would help to encourage the church to face the criticism and have greater confidence concerning their recovery. That such complimentary language was strategic may be inferred from the fact that it is least developed in the oracle to Smyrna, where there is also no rebuke or criticism.

that they are rich in those things that have value before God (Rev. 2:9). Words of commendation are especially well developed in the oracles to Pergamum and Thyatira (2:13, 19).

The connection of praise and friendly feelings is self-evident enough; the words of censure embedded in the majority of the seven oracles are a little more difficult in terms of the potential evocations of emotions. Frank naming of faults can be employed as a further evocation of feelings of friendship (Aristotle, *Rhet.* 2.4.27). However, the exposure of faults could also arouse anger if the motives are not perceived to be friendly, for example, intended to humiliate another for one's own advantage (2.2.22; 2.4.16). A number of factors suggest that even the moments of censure will not jeopardize the feelings of friendship that John hopes will shape the hearers' response to these oracles and to the Christ who confronts them.

First, John has previously reminded the addressees how Jesus has acted on their behalf in such a way as to arouse their deep gratitude (Rev. 1:5–6); his love for them and acts on their behalf establish an overarching framework of "friendship" as a dominant pathos (Aristotle, *Rhet.* 2.4.2, 5, 29). Second, Jesus acts out a well-established script appropriate for a divinity in the mode of prophetic confrontation. This is, further, consistently presented as a confrontation that has the best interests of the audience at heart (Cicero, *De or.* 2.51.206), for example, to move them back to a place of experiencing covenant blessings rather than judgment. Third, where virtues are identified as being lacking, the glorified Christ may express the conviction that the congregation *formerly* exhibited those virtuous behaviors (as in Rev. 2:4–5). To be upbraided for falling short of one's own former example interweaves a topic of praise and admiration, hence, a topic evocative of friendship (Aristotle, *Rhet.* 2.4.14, 19), into the rebuke.[45] Fourth, Christ shows every expectation that, if the congregations are willing, they are able to overcome these faults. The rebukes express no lack of esteem. Fifth, Christ enthusiastically offers promises of reward for those who heed his correction of their faults (Rev. 2:7, 11, 17, 26–28; 3:5, 12, 21). Aristotle suggested that people are disposed in a friendly way toward "those who bear no malice and do not cherish the memory of their wrongs, but are easily appeased" (*Rhet.* 2.4.17), and Christ's overtures and promises to the defective congregations communicate such an attitude toward the hearers. Finally, in some oracles, such as those addressed to the church in Pergamum and Thyatira, the words of censure do not focus on the congregation as a whole, but on some narrow segment or third party.

---

45. The speaker twice enjoins the hearers to "remember" (Rev. 2:5; 3:3). The topic of "reminding" addressees about their training with a view to calling them to live up to what they already know is closely identified with paraenesis (Aune 1997, 147; Malherbe 1987, 7). The speaker, in the midst of rebuke and command, reaffirms "the listener's dignity" (Starr 2004, 84) by presenting the necessary action as an outworking of what is already within their intellectual grasp (esp. emphasized in Rev. 3:3) and even a characteristic of their own past behavior (more to the fore in 2:5). The command to "hold fast" (2:25; 3:11), signaling again that what is needful is within the addressees' grasp and practice, would have a similar effect.

The interrelatedness of feelings of friendship and enmity is especially clear from the fact that the topic of having common enemies was also seen to support the feeling of friendship. Friends "love and hate the same persons" (Aristotle, *Rhet.* 2.4.4). "Those whose enemies are ours, [and] those who hate those whom we ourselves hate," tend to be regarded as friends, being united by a common enemy (2.4.6–7). We might well expect this topic to function in this way in the seven oracles as well, as, for example, when Christ commends the disciples in Ephesus because they "hate the works of the Nicolaitans, which I also hate" (Rev. 2:6).

Alignment with Satan, the common enemy of both the glorified Christ and the Christian community, provides a topic that both unites the latter in friendship and reinforces feelings of enmity in regard to the "locals" outside the Christian community. The local Jewish communities in Smyrna and Philadelphia are labeled "synagogues of Satan" (2.9; 3.9), a label that both explains any hostile actions the Christian community is experiencing from the parent body *and* mitigates any tendency toward capitulation to any pressures being applied to the Christians. The glorified Christ also names Pergamum the place "where Satan's throne is" and "where Satan lives" (2:13), reinforcing enmity by recalling the locals' act of hostility in making off with one of "their own." If friendship is created by an act of beneficence (Aristotle, *Rhet.* 2.4.2), and if "we like those who have done good either to us or those whom we hold dear" (2.4.5), the opposite feeling would be evoked by opposite actions, and a reminder of overt acts of hostility (such as this oracle presents) would serve to rekindle both the awareness and feeling of enmity. In a situation in which some voices (the Nicolaitans) are advocating lowering boundaries between the community and the society and moving toward a more accommodationist position, arousing feelings of enmity strategically positions the audience *against* such a course of action.

John gives more extended attention to evoking the emotion of enmity, along with emotions supportive of creating distance and antagonism (e.g., anger and indignation), toward the Nicolaitans and Jezebel. These feelings are strategically aroused to dispose the congregations to distance themselves from these figures, and thus address the main criticism—that they tolerate these voices in their midst (Rev. 2:14–15, 20, 24–25). If he is to achieve his goal, he must replace any feelings of friendliness toward these figures since at least *some* in the congregations have been open to the influence of these voices.

Describing people within or among the congregation as persons who "hold the teaching of Balaam" taps into the story of the prototypical false prophet in the Jewish epic as a means of creating distance. Balaam plotted against the common good of the people of God for gain. Unable to call a curse upon them at the request of his patron, Balak, he nevertheless found a way to earn his commission, resulting in a plague falling upon the assembly of Israel and causing many deaths (Num. 25:1–9; 31:16). Identifying the Nicolaitans as a modern resurgence of Balaam's destructive teaching (Rev. 2:15) is apt to arouse several negative emotions against them.[46] If "love is won" when a person is "thought to be upholding the interests of your audience," and the contrary topics excite hatred (Cicero, *De or.* 2.51.206, 208), the audiences will feel enmity against the Nicolaitans to the extent that they perceive the latter to be indeed acting out of self-interest and leading their fellow disciples on a path that will provoke God's anger and hence lead them to come to harm as a result of the Nicolaitans' activity.[47] The identification may crystallize feelings of indignation against them, since they are gaining a hearing in the congregation that they do not deserve, given the destructiveness of their message for those who follow them (as Balaam's plot led to plague, the Nicolaitans' practice will lead to Christ's intervention "with the sword of his mouth"; Rev. 2:16).[48]

In the oracle to the church in Thyatira, censure is directed primarily toward "Jezebel," and only at the church as a whole insofar as they "permit" Jezebel to exercise a prophetic ministry there. The repetition of the (alleged) summary of her influence as "leading my slaves astray to commit fornication and eat foods sacrificed to idols" (2:20; cf. 2:14) connects her to the historic figure of Balaam and the contemporary figures of the Nicolaitans; the feelings of enmity and indignation roused against them will provide a boost to appeals to enmity and indignation within this oracle as well. The glorified Christ's denial of Jezebel's claim to the status of "prophet" potentially directs indignation against her (again, for enjoying an undeserved status and authority, gained by deception; 2:20). Jezebel's contumacy is emphasized (2:21), which would tend to provoke anger.[49] Her behavior is also made to appear as deplorable as possible, with the images of fornication and adultery employed to amplify Jezebel's "crimes," thus stoking the fires of indignation further (2:20–22).[50]

---

46. "Balaam" plays a different role in Revelation than "Jezebel." The former functions as a historical example of leading God's people toward assimilation (with an eye to gain) and is evoked as a means of (negatively) interpreting the activity of teachers contemporary with John. Balaam, however, is not a name applied to a particular teacher in Pergamum (contra Witherington 2003, 102), since no contemporary of John could consult Balak in the way Balaam is remembered to have done (Rev. 2:14). "Jezebel," while of course recalling the infamous queen of Israel, *is* applied as a label directly to a prophet contemporary with John.

47. *Rhetorica ad Alexandrum* names ill-treatment of one's friends by some third party as a prod to feeling enmity against that third party (1440a.30–39). The Nicolaitans' threat to the safety of the disciples in Pergamum, leading them into paths that bring them into conflict with the Deity, would surely qualify as a form of ill use.

48. The essence of indignation is pain at undeserved good fortune, that is, seeing bad or unworthy people enjoy what ought, in all justice, be the reward reserved for the virtuous and worthy (Aristotle, *Rhet.* 2.9.1). The corollary involves seeing good people *not* receive what is due them (2.9.11). Aristotle himself asserts that "indignation" is an emotional response of virtuous people and the product of good character: "We ought to be indignant with those who prosper undeservedly; for that which happens beyond a man's deserts is unjust, wherefore we attribute this feeling even to gods" (2.9.1).

49. Aristotle (*Rhet.* 2.3.5) observes that people grow mild (the opposite of angry) toward those who admit their faults. The opposite stimulus (lack of repentance when confronted) must, then, promote the opposite emotional response, as Quintilian (*Inst.* 6.1.14) observed in judicial cases (anger can be aroused by drawing attention to a defendant's "disrespectful attitude toward the court, if, for instance, he be contumacious, arrogant or studiously indifferent").

50. Quintilian, *Inst.* 6.1.15: "The best way, however, for the accuser to excite the feelings of the judge is to make the charges which he brings against the accused seem as atrocious or, if feasible, as deplorable as possible."

Feelings of friendship and enmity (and supporting emotions, such as gratitude on the one hand, and indignation on the other) are thus rather extensively nurtured throughout the seven oracles, and in the oracles to Pergamum and Thyatira in particular, with a view to creating distance between the disciples and influences John perceives to pose a threat to Christian identity and witness.

Shame and Emulation

Shame and emulation constitute a third pair of emotions prominently at work in the seven oracles. First, the actual social dynamics of reading Revelation in the seven congregations, and realizing what is being said in the hearing of one's sister churches, contribute substantially to the evocation of shame. The public nature of these oracular pronouncements is seven times emphasized by the refrain concluding each "individual" message: "Let the one who has ears hear what the Spirit is saying *to the churches*" (2:7, 11, 17, 29; 3:6, 13, 22).[51] The seven churches become a public audience of "significant others" whose opinion would probably be valued by the individual Christians within the circle.[52] This circle of churches is made witness to what each congregation has attained, and in what regards each had not lived up to the mark (2:23 explicitly speaks of "all the churches" witnessing and learning from Christ's forthcoming interventions to punish Jezebel and her followers);[53] each congregation individually is thus positioned to imagine its sister congregations looking on to witness their responses now that their shortcomings have been brought to light—whether they will prove shameless in light of Christ's correction, or act to repair their reputation.

It will arouse shame, therefore, among one congregation as its defects are exposed before the other congregations, as when, for example, the Ephesians' decline from their "former love" and its accompanying works is heard in the context of the ability of the church in Thyatira to attain Christ's praise for their ever-increasing works and fruitfulness, or when the Pergamenes' inability to

---

51. Noted by Aune 1990, 184. Witherington (2003, 109) also draws attention to the rhetorical pressure applied by John by having the congregations "read[ing] each other's mail, even if it is embarrassing."

52. Aristotle had observed that "people feel shame before those whom they esteem, . . . whose opinion they do not despise [μὴ καταφρονεῖ τῆς δόξης]" (*Rhet.* 2.6.14–15). Early Christians had been widely and consistently directed by their leaders to be attentive to their honor and reputation in the eyes of their fellow Christians, both locally and translocally (see deSilva 2000a, 58–61).

53. A textbook example of this technique of conjuring a specific audience to one's decision as a means of arousing the feeling of shame (with a view to motivating a particular response) appears in Aristotle, *Rhet.* 2.6.24: "Cydias, when haranguing the people about the allotment of the territory to Samos, begged the Athenians to picture to themselves that the Greeks were standing round them and would not only hear, but also see what they were going to decree." John may also harness here something of the broader civic competition in which these cities regularly found themselves, competing, e.g., for the honor of being recognized for their promotion of imperial cult and the honorific title νεωκόρος. On the latter phenomenon, see Price 1984, 248.

exercise appropriate discernment is heard in contrast to the Ephesian congregation's successful deflection of the Nicolaitan threat.[54]

The exposure of such defects is especially blatant in regard to the congregations in Sardis and Laodicea, which are publicly shown not to merit the reputation they enjoy or would wish to enjoy. The glorified Christ publicly and explicitly rejects their claims to honor, and his opinion is of such a quality as not to be overturned by any riposte on the congregations' part.[55] He tersely strips Sardis of its reputation, based as it is, in his eyes, on fiction: "You have a name that you are alive, and you are dead" (3:1). Laodicea fares even worse. This congregation is also not what it should be, and Christ publicly exposes their failure to live up to expectations (3:15b–16). The claims to honor that they might make on their own behalf are publicly rejected as empty and as the result of self-deception: "You say, 'I am rich and I have been enriched and I have need of nothing,' and do not know that you are wretched and pitiable and poor and blind and naked" (3:17). They are publicly stripped of the public image they think to project, exposing their "naked" state (ἡ αἰσχύνη τῆς γυμνότητός σου, 3:18b) to broad view. Moreover, there is no word of commendation, not even about "a few," to help them save face.

The Sardian Christians, however, have what it takes to rebuild a more secure reputation (3:3a). They even have in their midst a "few names" of note, a few models of what constitutes an honorable walk in the eyes of Christ (3:4).[56] Calling them "a few names" is surely significant, since the "name" of the Sardian church as a whole has been found to be empty. These "few" alone retain a secure reputation ("name"). The commendation of the few may serve to rouse emulation among the many. Emulation (ζῆλος) involves pain at another's enjoyment of honor or other goods but, unlike envy, remains a noble emotion. The envious person seeks to deprive another of deserved enjoyment of these goods; the emulous person seeks to fit himself or herself to attain the same goods (Aristotle, *Rhet.* 2.11.1). People tend to be emulous of those who are close to them and like them (2.11.3), as well as "those who are praised or eulogized either by poets

---

54. One of the causes of shame (αἰσχύνη) is for someone to be seen to lack the praiseworthy things that those like him or her have been able to attain (Aristotle, *Rhet.* 2.6.12). Again, it is a basic response to not "measuring up" to an expected—and in this case, elsewhere attained and exemplified—norm. At the same time, the Ephesians will not feel unduly put to shame, since they also exhibit virtues or behaviors that other churches lack and that they must now strive to achieve to "measure up" to Ephesus on that particular point.

55. Aristotle did not name this as a topic in his own discussion of evoking shame, although examples of discussing endangered or falsified reputation do exist in the repertory of actual orations. In his oration *To the People of Rhodes* (*Or.* 31), for example, Dio Chrysostom avers that the Rhodian assembly's reputation, which is otherwise secure, is in one particularly serious regard endangered by practices that have crept in during more recent times involving renaming old statues after new benefactors. Notably, Dio considers himself to be doing the assembly a friendly service by exposing the shamefulness of the practice, so that the assembly can properly repair the reputation of the city.

56. We might presume that the Sardian Christians would be able to discern who, specifically, was meant: these "few names" would be the ones who currently look the most like those who "keep the commandments of God," "keep faith with Jesus" (14:12), and thus "keep the words of the prophecy of this book" as well (22:7).

or prose writers" (2.11.7). Jesus promises, moreover, to confess the "name" of any who rise now to the challenges he sets before the churches (i.e., any who "overcome," 3:5), which is the explicit remedy for their defective "name," their false reputation, having as a whole *not* having risen to the challenges posed by following Christ (3:1). This, too, can serve to flame "emulation." What is in the grasp of the "few" in Sardis can be in the grasp of all if they apply themselves.

In regard to Laodicea, Christ could not show himself more easily reconciled with the congregation (a topic evocative of friendly feelings). Christ has what they need to restore their honor, indeed, to build a more secure honor, and shows himself more than willing to provide it to cover the nakedness that is now exposed and otherwise to reverse their shortcomings (3:18). He further interprets the rebuke itself as an expression of love for the congregation, connecting with the topic of frank speech offered for friends' edification as evocative of friendly feelings ("love").[57] This is done, moreover, in language that evokes the "philophronetic tone" of a parent tending to the moral edification of a child (and thus a strategy of paraenesis).[58] Finally, 3:20 shows Christ poised at the threshold, not standing aloof from a congregation that has failed to meet his expectations. The open offer of rapprochement and intimate fellowship, again, evokes friendly feelings through negating any sense of Christ bearing malice, being hard to appease, or cherishing any memory of their failure and his disappointment (see, again, Aristotle, *Rhet.* 2.4.17).[59]

In one of the rare instances where a word with an emotional component is used as an imperative, Christ calls the Laodicean church to "be emulous" (ζήλευε, 3:19b). In part, this provides a corrective to being "tepid" (3:16), but in part it also directs the attention of the Laodiceans to the positive models around them, and directs the energies of the Laodiceans to acquiring what those praiseworthy models already possess, as the means by which their lukewarmness will be resolved. The Laodicean Christians, having been put to shame for claiming to be rich while, in Christ's eyes, being in fact impoverished (3:17), cannot fail to take notice of Smyrna, praised among the circle of churches for having what makes one "rich" in Christ's sight, despite their poverty (2:9). But indeed, several traits of several congregations have been held up as admirable in the seven oracles, and emulation is naturally aroused where we see people like us in possession of praised and highly valued goods.[60]

---

57. This interpretation of rebuke, moreover, is anchored in an authoritative text (Prov. 3:12) that connects Christ's rebuke with God's traditional role as the One who offers loving παιδεία for God's children, something that the author of Hebrews will offer as a token of God's esteem and the honor of the Christians (Heb. 12:4–11, esp. 12:7a). See deSilva 2000b, 446–54, esp. 454.

58. Malherbe 2004, 299.

59. In light of such attention to encouragement and overtures to rapprochement on the part of the glorified Christ, it is difficult to agree with Duff (2001, 35–36) that John believed he had little hope of "winning over" Laodicea.

60. Similarly, the Christians in Ephesus may become emulous of the Thyatiran congregation, hearing the latter praised for their consistent increase in "works" praiseworthy before Christ (Rev. 2:4–5, 19), or Pergamum emulous of Ephesus, since the latter's deflection of Nicolaitan influence won them praise while the former's toleration brought them the one blot on their report (2:6, 14–15).

Shame and emulation, then, are employed throughout the seven oracles to turn the hearers' ambitions toward achieving the mark Christ holds out before them, so that they will be highly esteemed before his "court" and the court of opinion formed by the circle of congregations. In several instances, this might provide an antidote to the Christians' aspirations and ambitions being drawn overly much toward goals achieved only through collusion with Babylon's economy, through winking at Roman imperial ideology or participating in idolatry in some form.[61]

CONCLUSION

The seven oracles, together with the introduction to the whole of Revelation, have the capacity especially to arouse three related pairs of emotional responses: fear and confidence, friendship and enmity, and shame and emulation. While some of these emotional responses are evoked in multiple oracles, certain ones tend to be more fully nurtured in particular oracles (e.g., confidence in the oracle to the Christians in Philadelphia, shame and emulation in the oracles to Sardis and Laodicea, enmity in the oracles to Pergamum and Thyatira), being more strategic to achieving the speaker's goals in those settings. In most of these cases, John gives attention to multiple dimensions of appeals to a particular emotion (i.e., nurturing the frame of mind that is disposed to that particular emotion, identifying particular "others" toward whom that emotion is rightly directed, and inscribing situations that naturally give rise to that emotion; see Aristotle, *Rhet.* 2.1.9.)

Yet these remain only rhetorical potentialities. Not every hearer responds to every prompt, and among those who respond to a particular prompt, not every one does so to the same degree—especially in regard to appeals to pathos. But even where the response is slight, it creates an opportunity for the hearers to reexamine their assessment, alignment, and inclinations in regard to particular features of their situation, and thus an opportunity for John to draw the disciples forward in the direction that, he is convinced, the glorified Christ would have them go.

---

61. The promises to the "one who overcomes" (2:7, 11, 17, 26–28; 3:5, 12, 21) also contribute to this realignment of aspirations.

Chapter 8

"I Saw a Monster Rising Up!"
Appeals to Pathos in the Visions of Revelation

In the previous chapter we saw that the seven oracles of Revelation 2–3 were composed with a view to eliciting particular, strategically selected emotions among the hearers, particularly three related pairs of emotion: friendship and enmity, confidence and fear, shame and emulation. We should, then, not expect the more fully visionary parts of Revelation to be less evocative of emotional response, as indeed the history of interpretation—with the frequently emotional reactions to Revelation on the part of many interpreters—amply attests. In this chapter we will focus first on the potential arousal of certain key emotions surrounding Rome and Roman imperialism among Revelation's first audiences. John seeks to redirect the positive emotions of awe and gratitude toward God and the Messiah, combating the dominant cultural impulses to direct these feelings toward Rome and the emperor. Instead, by calling attention to the ways in which Rome, the emperors, and local promoters of imperial cult violate God's just requirements and draw (or pressure) others to violate the same, John nurtures responses of enmity and indignation toward these pillars of Roman imperialism and their local manifestations.[1]

---

1. It is not claimed here that the idea *that* John arouses indignation and feelings of enmity is a new discovery, although this study may advance a more precise understanding of the emotional

Such emotional responses create the affective distance between the hearers and their politico-economic environment that facilitates their acceptance of John's counsel to make that distance visible in their behavior and give testimony about the value of that distance.[2] In particular, appeals to pathos support the summons of the glorified Christ to avoid food sacrificed to idols (and idolatry generally) and to avoid "fornication" (that is, entanglement with the Roman economy and other facets of Roman domination), not buying into the pursuit of tainted wealth that other voices among the churches (e.g., "Jezebel," the Nicolaitans, and the compromised believers in Laodicea and Sardis) promote. In a situation in which some voices are advocating lowering boundaries between the community and the society and moving toward a more accommodating position, arousing feelings of enmity strategically positions the audience *against* such a course of action. Further, we will explore the ways in which the visions continue the evocation of fear, confidence, and emulation begun in the oracles, and the rhetorical goals that these somewhat ancillary appeals to pathos are likely to advance.

THE GENUINE EXPOSES THE COUNTERFEIT: REVELATION 4–5 AND THE EVOCATION OF AWE AND GRATITUDE

John's opening vision of the scenes of worship around the throne of God, while evoking important emotional responses in its own right, also lays a strategic foundation for the emotional responses that John will seek to evoke in regard to the emperors and the cultic expressions of loyalty and gratitude that formed so prominent a feature of the cultural and architectural landscape of the seven cities. Classical rhetoricians were keenly aware that, just as an opponent's arguments had to be swept aside and attempts to establish superior credibility undone, so also the emotions that an opposing speaker tried to evoke in regard to a particular prospect or person would need to be replaced with emotions more conducive to one's own agenda (Cicero, *De or.* 2.53.215–16; Quintilian, *Inst.* 6.1.18, 20, 46). As scholars investigating the imperial cult and propaganda in the cities addressed by Revelation have amply demonstrated, Christians in Asia Minor were exposed to many influences that sought to arouse feelings of awe and gratitude toward Rome and its emperors.[3] John seeks to displace such feelings. Directing awe and gratitude back toward the Creator God and the Redeemer Lamb, the genuine Savior/*divi filius*, provides the groundwork for evoking indignation against

---

response John seeks to evoke, whether truly "envy" (as suggested forcefully in Lawrence 1931, 87–88), "resentment" (A. Collins 1984, previously the only substantial investigation of John's arousal of particular emotions), or "indignation." The exploration of the mechanics of *how* adversative emotions are aroused, however, contributes new insights to the analysis of Revelation.

2. On the contributions of appeals to the emotions to deliberative goals, see *Rhet. Alex.* 1439b.15–18; Quintilian, *Inst.* 3.8.12.

3. See esp. Price 1984; Friesen 1993. A summary of research on this subject appears in deSilva 1991, 187–97.

the pretensions of those promoting the cult of Rome and the *Augusti* in the later visions.[4]

Neither Aristotle nor the other rhetorical theorists treat the entire range of human emotions, and "awe" appears not to have been deemed relevant or strategic for oratory in the forum, council chamber, and hall of justice.[5] Awe constitutes, however, a primary emotional response generated by religious rituals and impressive edifices, with their grandiose representations of deities, like the temple of Artemis, the altar of Zeus, the temple of *Roma et Augustus*, or the temple of Domitian—religious contexts of great interest and concern to John. It is an emotional response evoked by the ceremonial representation of earthly rulers. Esther's response of being overwhelmed at the sight of Xerxes attests to the "aura" generated by earthly monarchs' self-representation: "'I saw you, my lord, like an angel of God, and my heart was shaken with fear at your glory. For you are wonderful, my lord, and your countenance is full of grace.' And while she was speaking, she fainted and fell" (Add. Esth. 15:13–15 NRSV).

Roman imperial court ceremonial and, more especially, the imperial cult with its representations of the emperor and its rites of adoration, sought to achieve no less an impact upon the provincials in Asia Minor. The colossal statue of Domitian (Titus?) in Ephesus, the presence of cult statues and temples throughout Asia, the impressive processions and other rites involving these cult sites and simulacra, replete with choral associations singing hymns to the emperors as to gods, all sought to excite awe among the residents of the seven cities (and beyond), contributing thus to the popular legitimation of imperial rule.[6]

John's vision of the glory of God displayed in the activity and arrangement of God's court offers an antidote to feelings evoked in settings of imperial cult, a counterexperience of awe that will expose the other as counterfeit.[7] The medium of apocalypse allows John to invite his audience into the scene, to "see" the

---

4. The Letter of Jeremiah shows another spokesperson for the monolatry at the heart of the Jewish tradition seeking to defuse the power of the neighboring peoples' religious practices to lead the Jews in Diaspora into feeling "awe" before their gods (see deSilva 2002a, 217–21).

5. Aristotle, and to an even more limited extent Cicero and Quintilian, discuss only "the range of emotions that the orator needs to know about in order to compose his public address with full effectiveness" (Cooper 1996, 251), and not necessarily the range of emotional responses appropriate to Christian (religious) discourse (Olbricht 2001b, 16). While Aristotle discusses "fear" (φόβος) at length (*Rhet.* 2.5.1–15), the topics therein listed do not cross into the more positive experience of "wonder" or "amazement" mingled with caution that constitutes "awe."

6. See Price 1984. On the role of hymn singers in imperial cult (e.g., the organization of a choral society in Pergamum to "sing hymns to the god Augustus in the temple precinct dedicated by Asia"), see Kraybill 1996, 61–62 (citing *I. Eph.* 18d.11–14); Witherington 2003, 193; Brent 1999, 194–95. Tacitus (*Annals* 14.15) recalls how, under Nero, "Roman knights were enrolled under the title of *Augustiani*, men in their prime and remarkable for their strength.... Day and night they kept up the thunder of applause, and applied to the emperor's person the voice and epithet of deities." John's vision of the endless praise offered to God by celestial beings that "do not rest by day and by night" offers a striking counterpoint.

7. Schüssler Fiorenza (1991, 123) similarly understands the scenes of heavenly cult to provide "a symbolic alternative to the splendor of the imperial cult," while Russell Morton (2001, 105) correctly perceives the resulting contrast to critique imperial cult as an encroachment on the prerogatives of the One God.

scenes and "hear" the choral adulation along with him.[8] To the extent that our imaginations are engaged by John's descriptions, our emotions will be the more directly aroused by the impressions made upon our imaginations.

John invites the audiences to see God seated upon God's throne, projecting an aura resembling nothing on earth except its most precious gems and frightening natural phenomena (4:3, 5). God is surrounded by magnificent, supernatural orders of beings, including fiery attendants and cosmic priests,[9] together with the Lamb receiving the praise and adoration of increasingly wider circles of beings until, finally, "every created being which is in heaven and upon the earth and under the earth and in the sea and all things in them" (5:13) join in adoration. Such a vision, if imaginatively engaged, cannot fail to arouse genuine awe in response. The vision of God and the Lamb, and of their adoration, trumps all the pretensions of human rulers and their pomp, their "aura."[10]

The experience of awe is layered with evocations of gratitude toward God and the Lamb. This, too, is strategic in regard to calling into question the cultic activities surrounding the emperors. The cult of *Roma et Augusti* was first and foremost an expression of gratitude toward Augustus and his successors. In the words of Nicolaus of Damascus, a contemporary of Herod the Great, people address Octavian as *Sebastos* "in accordance with their estimation of his honor" and "revere him with temples and sacrifices over islands and continents, organized in cities and provinces, matching the greatness of his virtue and repaying his benefactions toward them."[11] John claims, on the contrary, that the gratitude merited by God and the Lamb preclude the offering of cultic honors to human "benefactors" (and indeed, potently challenges the claims of Rome and its emperors to be "benefactors" of the populations outside Rome's walls).

8. The frequent use of the verbs "I saw" and "I heard," which contribute to the impression that John has indeed had an authentic visionary and auditory experience (hence, to the ethos of the work as a divine revelation), also contribute to the power of his words to engage the imaginations of his hearers. John's frequent use of ἰδού (Rev. 1:7, 18; 4:1, 2; 5:5; 6:2, 5, 8; 7:9; 9:12; 11:14; 12:3; 14:1, 14; 16:15; 19:11; 21:3, 5; 22:7, 12) constitutes an ongoing invitation to the audience to "look" and "see" with their mind's eye, so that the impressions made upon their emotions will also be deeper and more immediate. Even the use here of ὅμοιος (Rev 4:3 [2x]; 4:7 [3x]) and ὡς (4:6, 7; 5:6) may function to invite the audience into that space between the weakness of verbal description and the realities John describes, asking them to "see" better than John can find words to describe.

9. On the twenty-four elders as a heavenly archetype for the twenty-four orders of priests and Levites in the earthly temple (1 Chr. 24:4–6), see Witherington (2003, 117). The elders' accoutrements (harps, suggestive of Levitical duties in the temple, and bowls of incense, suggestive of priestly duties in the temple) strengthen this suggestion. I also prefer the identification of the "seven spirits" as seven archangels (as in Witherington 2003, 75), both on the basis of widespread parallels in Jewish representations of the heavenly court (Tob. 12:15; *T. Levi* 2; though without enumeration of the archangels; Greek *1 En.* 20:1–8) and internal parallels (cf. Rev. 1:4 and 8:2).

10. John does not merely transpose imperial cult ceremonial into the heavenly worship (as in Brent 1999, 204). Rather, John builds on a long-standing tradition of throne visions and depictions of heavenly worship (Isa. 6; Ezek. 1; *T. Levi* 2–5; *2 Bar.* 21:6–7). John crafts an alternative to the imperial cult, but not purely by way of "reaction formation," though elements of this are present, e.g., in the forms of the acclamations, which do not appear in the Hebrew Bible but are familiar from Roman imperial court ceremonial. See Aune 1983, 16, though Jörns (1971, 36) suggests that the Greek "Worthy are you" derives from the Hebrew "Blessed are you" (Morton 2001, 100 n. 36).

11. As quoted in Price 1984, 16. See further deSilva 1991, 187–93.

Gratitude (χάρις) is the response to expressions of favor or kindness (also χάρις). Aristotle provides an extended discussion of topics productive of χάρις, freely moving back and forth between the uses of that term to capture the benefactor's favorable disposition and the beneficiaries' reciprocal feelings of gratitude.[12] Topics that amplify the importance of a favor or the magnitude of the favorable disposition behind it could be expected, within this reciprocal arrangement, to amplify feelings of gratitude in response. The topics that would prompt this response of gratitude are found chiefly in the hymns, which have an enthymematic quality in these chapters.[13]

The first hymn (Rev. 4:11) asserts that God deserves public acknowledgment (glory), honor, and power *because* (ὅτι) God has created all that is. The unstated premise that completes the logic comes from the universally held conviction that benefactors (among whom God is supreme as the Giver of life, habitable and fruitful environment, and the like) merit a grateful response, typically including honor and service (the latter contributing to the benefactor's power base). Greco-Roman ethicists would concur that God (or the gods) merit worship for their benefactions (cf. *Rhet. Alex.* 1421b.37–1422a.2; *Rhet. Her.* 3.3.4), the difference being that John makes this claim in the context of the Jewish affirmation of one Creator God, who alone is worthy of worship, and whose beneficence in the gift of life requires a response of obedience to live that life in accordance with God's commandments, including the prohibition of worshiping any other would-be divinity (cf. *4 Ezra* 7:21–24; 8:59–61).

The second hymn (Rev. 5:9–10) proclaims the Lamb worthy to take the book and open its seals (that is, to exercise judgment over the earthly kingdoms and usher in God's kingdom) *because* (ὅτι) the Lamb redeemed a people for God to constitute that kingdom by giving up his own life on their behalf, dramatically depicted in terms of being slain and giving his blood as the ransom, fulfilling at last the promise of the creation of a priestly kingdom. As such, the Lamb has acted clearly in the interest of the recipients rather than out of self-interest (Aristotle, *Rhet.* 2.7.2; Cicero, *De or.* 2.51.206), rendering an important service to people in significant need ("redeeming" or "ransoming" suggests a situation of significant distress), and thus fulfilling the basic conditions for the evocation of "gratitude" (χάρις, although Cicero calls this *amor*).[14] Moreover, the Lamb alone has attained such a significant benefit on behalf of humankind (Aristotle, *Rhet.* 1.9.38; 2.7.2). The uniqueness of this benefactor's achievement is dramatically, rather than discursively, demonstrated in Rev. 5:1–6. The episode of looking for one who is "worthy" to initiate divine judgment, the disappointment with the reported failure to find *anyone* who is worthy, and the dramatic

---

12. DeSilva 2000a, 104–6.
13. See Schüssler Fiorenza 1991, 61–62 on Rev. 5:9–10.
14. The Lamb's actions would also be seen as supremely noble in light of the criteria offered in Aristotle's *Rhetoric* and the anonymous *Rhetorica ad Alexandrum*. The Lamb's actions produced significantly good results (*Rhet. Alex.* 1426a.22–23), were undertaken "not for his own sake, but . . . for the sake of others" while in fact "neglecting his own interests" (Aristotle, *Rhet.* 1.9.16–17, 19).

resolution as the Lamb is revealed—these constitute a narrative development of the encomiastic topic of being the first or only person to succeed in a particular venture or achieve a particular end.

Passing over other prominent "savior" figures available in the Mediterranean here, especially the emperor, is salient. Augustus's power over the fate of the known circle of inhabited lands was grounded in the rhetoric of beneficence and beneficial achievement,[15] as well as the rhetoric of enacting the will of the gods. The slaughtered Lamb now steps forward as an alternative and superior picture of what it means to serve God's design for humanity and to act as a perfect benefactor. The repetitive texture of Revelation reinforces this contrast, especially in regard to the Lamb and the beast or Babylon competing for people "from every tribe and language and people and nation" (5:9; 13:7; 17:15). Where unique or outstanding achievement constitutes a claim to precedence, John's claim on behalf of the Lamb is especially relevant to establishing Jesus' claim to worship (as a human-become-God), above and beyond the claims of the emperors and members of their families (lauded as *divi*, humans-become-gods), who are not qualified to step into the silence of 5:3–4 to fill the void.

The circles of praise, predicated upon God's creation of all things (ὅτι σὺ ἔκτισας τὰ πάντα, 4:11) extend at last to "every creature" (πᾶν κτίσμα, 5:13). Since all have benefited from God's creative and life-sustaining activity, all properly stand before God in awe and gratitude. This is the norm, the proper order, that is violated wherever people gather around their idols or around the image of the "beast."

EVOCATIONS OF ENMITY AND INDIGNATION: THE MONSTER, THE WHORE, AND THEIR FOLLOWERS

The Unholy Scam: Revelation 12–13

Awe and gratitude are two emotional responses that local representations of imperial cult ceremony, presence, and propaganda sought to arouse toward Rome and its emperors among the local populace. John's vision of the glorified Christ (1:12–20) and the worship around the throne of God extending throughout the cosmos (4:1–5:14) provide an antidote to the impressions potentially made by those local phenomena. John also presents Rome and her emperors in such a way as to nullify responses of awe and gratitude, replacing these with enmity and indignation.[16] Beginning with the cosmic backdrop, the war pitting the dragon (Satan) against God and God's people sets the stage perfectly in this regard.

15. The *Res gestae divi Augusti*, prominently inscribed in public spaces, served such a dominion-legitimating function.
16. Schüssler Fiorenza (1985, 192) correctly claims that John seeks to "alienate [the audience's] allegiances and affects from the present symbols of Roman power by ascribing to it images of degradation, ugliness, ultimate failure, and defeat." The present analysis seeks to supplement and refine her seminal insights.

"Friendship" is demonstrated by procuring goods for our friends insofar as lies within our power (Aristotle, *Rhet.* 2.4.2). "We also like those who have done good either to us or to those whom we hold dear" (2.4.5). If acts of beneficence done "to us or those whom we hold dear" generate feelings of friendship (2.4.5, 29), the opposite feeling—enmity—would be evoked by opposite actions, and a reminder of overt acts of hostility would serve to rekindle both the awareness and feeling of enmity. The author of the *Rhetorica ad Alexandrum* also names illtreatment of oneself or one's friends by some third party to be a prod to feeling enmity (ἔχθρα) against that party (1440a.30–35). Finally, enmity is predictably aroused against those who are shown to be enemies of our friends or benefactors (Aristotle, *Rhet.* 2.4.4, 6–7).

John does not need to work hard to demonstrate the enmity of the dragon, who is *de facto* the enemy of God and God's people and would readily be accepted as such within both Jewish and Christian culture. Nevertheless, John describes the dragon's activity in such a way as to remind the audience of this basic fact. The dragon's activity against the male child (Rev. 12:4), clearly identified as Christ by the use of Ps. 2:7, 9 (Rev. 12:5–6); his warring against the hosts of God (12:7–8); his identification as the historic enemy of humankind (the "serpent," 12:9), the deceiver and accuser (the "Satan") of the whole world; and his hostile activity against the woman and the rest of her offspring among whom the audience will locate themselves ("the ones keeping the commandments of God and holding the testimony of Jesus," 12:17)—all nurture feelings of enmity against this diabolical figure.

Feelings of enmity against a well-established enemy are transferred to a potentially more ambiguous figure, one regarded favorably by the majority of people outside the churches—and perhaps some within these churches (even if only in the guarded, "demythologized" ways reflected in Rom. 13:1–7; 1 Pet. 2:13–17). Along with the dragon's gifts of "power and throne and great authority" (Rev. 13:2), John ensures the transfer of the enmity and hostility felt toward the dragon to the Roman emperor as beast from the sea, the friend of the enemy of the audience and of their great Ally (cf. Aristotle, *Rhet.* 2.4.4, 6–7). Enmity is enhanced as this beast advances the dragon's agenda of making war against the saints and overcoming them (Rev. 13:7; cf. 12:17), employing the topic that one feels enmity against those who attack one's own (Aristotle, *Rhet.* 2.4.5; *Rhet. Alex.* 1440a.30–35).[17] This portrait of "a world at war"—an ironic one, given public discourse about the Pax Romana—steers the audience away from "cooperation and compromise."[18]

---

17. Another trait borrowed from Daniel, esp. Dan. 7:21 (Aune 1998a, 746).

18. Barr 1984, 40. John gives a preview of the beast's hostility against God's witnesses in Rev. 11:9–10, evoking feelings of enmity in a preliminary way as the "beast" (whose identity has not yet been developed) injures figures who would be seen as "friends" of the audience (11:9), adding insult to injury by denying them burial. The beast's subjects' celebration of what is clearly not in the audience's interest (the deaths of two of its own, in some sense) further reinforces feelings of enmity between the audience and the beast's followers (11:10).

The presentation of Rome's emperors and the local organizers of imperial cult as "beasts" helps augment feelings of aversion and enmity. The imagery is derived from Daniel,[19] an important precedent for such a presentation of human rulers and kingdoms. The *Augusti* appear as a monstrous aberration, prodigious in the worst sense, as when Philostratus's Apollonius speaks of Nero as a beast (θηρίον): "I know not how many heads it has," but it is nevertheless "more savage than the beasts of mountain and forest."[20] John invites his audience to regard their character and rule as something out of all harmony with the divine and natural orders. Hiding the humanity of these figures also helps to subvert any feeling of social obligation toward them as rulers and benefactors, and thus counter feelings of (positive) awe and gratitude.[21]

Alongside enmity, John generously employs topics evocative of indignation in his depiction of the emperors and the promoters of their local cults.[22] The essence of indignation is pain at undeserved good fortune, seeing bad or unworthy people enjoy what ought, in all justice, be the reward reserved for the virtuous and worthy (Aristotle, *Rhet.* 2.9.1). The corollary involves seeing the virtuous *not* receive what is due them (2.9.11). Aristotle regards "indignation" as an emotional response of virtuous people and the product of good character, since it stems from a sense of justice, "wherefore we attribute this feeling even to gods" (2.9.1). Aristotle carefully distinguishes between envy and indignation, the former being a vicious characteristic (since it is indifferent to matters of justice, and potentially inimical to them) and the latter a virtuous one (since it is rooted in justice).[23] Envy includes pain at the *deserved* good fortune or joy at the *undeserved* bad fortune of another person, while indignation is pain at another's *undeserved* good or *undeserved* bad fortune (2.9.5).

---

19. The beast from the sea is, however, not Daniel's fourth beast (Witherington 2003, 181), although this is the case in *4 Ezra* 12 and Josephus. Rather, it is a hideous hybrid of all four (deSilva 1991, 191, 203; Schüssler Fiorenza 1991, 83; Aune 1998a, 779; Royalty 1998, 184). That in itself is quite a statement about Rome on John's part, one that finds a parallel development in John's blending together of elements of God's prophets' denunciations of multiple precedent cities and seats of empire like Tyre, Babylon, and even Jerusalem, in his denunciation of Babylon the Great.
20. Philostratus, *Vita Apollonii* 4.38, cited in Bauckham 1993a, 410. Philostratus invokes the image of the Hydra, the many-headed (and thereby grossly unnatural) monster here. The myth of the monster who grows more heads than one can cut off seems to underlie the image of the beast who sustains and recovers from a "death wound" to one of its heads (Rev. 13:3).
21. DeSilva 1998b, 799; Carey 1999b, 159.
22. DeSilva 1998b, 797.
23. Anaximenes (*Rhet. ad Alex.* 1440a.34–39), however, uses the term φθόνος to designate the emotion aroused against "those whom we have shown to have been or to be or to be going to be undeservedly prosperous." Despite the terminological confusion, it is clear that Anaximenes is describing something other than the base "envy" described by Aristotle, of which Lawrence (1931, 87–88), e.g., accuses John: "How the late apocalyptists love mouthing out all about the gold and silver and cinnamon of evil Babylon! How they *want* them all! How they *envy* Babylon her splendour, envy, envy! . . . . How the apocalyptists would have loved to drink out of her cup! And since they couldn't: how they loved smashing it." "Indignation" in Aristotle's sense is also not precisely the same as "resentment" (the term chosen by A. Collins [1984, 153] alongside "fear" to name the two principal emotions evoked by John), the usage of which can cover some aspects of indignation, but also envy.

At this point the significance of Revelation 4–5 as a strategic foundation becomes evident. The temporary power of the dragon and the beast (Rev. 12:12c; 13:2b, 5b) and the adulation they receive from "the inhabitants of the earth" (13:3b–4) parody the cosmic enthronement of God and the Lamb and the adoration they receive from "every creature" (5:13). The parody is extended in the depiction of the beast having one head with a mortal wound, but restored to life, seeking to bring together people from "every tribe and people and language and nation" under its dominion (13:7), recalling the Lamb's redemptive activity both in terms of being slaughtered, yet standing, and ransoming people "from every tribe and language and people and nation" (5:9).[24] Whatever the mark of the beast is determined to represent (13:16), it is first and foremost a parody of the seal of God (7:2–3).[25] As Greg Carey has perceptively observed, "John uses parody to unmask imperial *hybris*. . . . Parody is especially appropriate where appearances are deceptive; it is the perfect tool for revealing imperial pretensions."[26] Parody raises awareness of counterfeit.

Within this parody, John invokes topics of indignation in connection with the acclamations and adoration of the beast and his sponsor. The beast and Satan—God's enemies and rivals of the Lamb for humankind—enjoy what they do not deserve: worship. Especially provocative is the speech placed on the lips of the beast worshipers: "Who is like the beast?" (Τίς ὅμοιος τῷ θηρίῳ; 13:4), a rhetorical question implying that there is no one equal to this great and powerful being.[27] This phrase, however, is stolen from the worship of God, even as worship offered to the beast and the dragon is worship stolen from the God to whom it is uniquely due as Creator of all that is, sharpening the impropriety and injustice of this beast-worship:[28]

> Who is like you among the gods, Lord?
> Who is like you, glorified among the holy ones?
> τίς ὅμοιός σοι ἐν θεοῖς, κύριε;
> τίς ὅμοιός σοι, δεδοξασμένος ἐν ἁγίοις;
> (Exod. 15:11 LXX)
>
> Lord, who is like you?
> κύριε, τίς ὅμοιός σοι;
> (Ps. 34:10 LXX [35:10E])

---

24. As observed in Schüssler Fiorenza 1991, 83. The obvious competition that the beast and its activities pose to the Lamb's program of bringing people together into God's priestly kingdom (the mention of the Lamb and the Lamb's slaughter [13:8] in close proximity with the phrase "every tribe and people and tongue and nation" establishes a clear connection between the two passages) also potentially evokes indignation, as the audience finds here an "inferior contending with the superior," and that "in the same pursuit" (Aristotle, *Rhet.* 2.9.11). Since the Lamb has acted to purchase this people *for God* (Rev. 5:9), the beast is shown to be trying to detract from God's enjoyment of the fruits of this purchase.
25. Aune 1998a, 768.
26. Carey 1999b, 154.
27. Bauckham 1993a, 235.
28. Showing that an act adversely affects the perpetrator's superiors gave ground for indignation (Cicero, *De inventione rhetorica* 1.53.101; *Rhet. Her.* 2.30.48).

O God, who is like you?
ὁ θεός, τίς ὅμοιός σοι;
(Ps. 70:19 LXX [71:18E])[29]

Notably, the Hebrew prophets remembered the king of Babylon as a figure who harbored the arrogant ambition to rival God: "I will ascend above the clouds, I will be like unto the Most High [ἔσομαι ὅμοιος τῷ ὑψίστῳ]" (Isa. 14:14 LXX). Now "the whole earth" (Rev. 13:3b–4) uses the language of acclaiming the unique dignity and power of the Most High to flatter the beast who carries "Babylon" on its back.

John further nurtures indignation through several other strategies. The "blasphemous names," by which are intended "the titles and epithets used by Roman emperors, including κύριος, 'lord', σωτήρ, 'savior', and *divi filius*, 'son of god,'"[30] present additional evidence that the emperors enjoy more than is their due, and this at the cost of God and God's Messiah receiving their due.[31] Similarly, the beast himself speaks ill of God and God's hosts (Rev. 13:1, 5–6), refusing to give God due honor, and instead slandering.[32] Quintilian suggested that the impropriety of an act "may be enhanced by considerations of the nature of the act, the position [status, relationship] of its author or the victim, the purpose, time, place, and manner of the act" (*Inst.* 6.1.15). Here the beast slanders its superiors, and the violation is further amplified by the author's multiplication of objects of this slander: not just God, but also "God's name" and "God's dwelling" (13:6).[33] John makes the beast's activity seem as deplorable as possible (Quintilian, *Inst.* 6.1.15), speaking here not in terms of misdirected acclamations of other gods, but of "profaning" God, God's name, God's dwelling.

As for the beast from the land, feelings of enmity are immediately transferred by the identification of this figure as a supporter of the enemies of God and of the Christian community (one feels enmity toward the friends of one's enemies). As "another" beast, that also speaks "like a dragon" (i.e., words appropriate to Satan),[34] it is presented from the outset as standing squarely in the enemy camp (13:11).

---

29. In the LXX see also Pss. 85 (86E):8; 88:9 (89:8E), together with the more extensive lists taking the Qumran literature into account provided by Bauckham 1993a, 235; Aune 1998a, 741. Isaiah 46:6–7a (clearly reflected in Rev. 1:17; 22:13) is also relevant, using the phrase "Who is like?" in the context of an affirmation that there are no comparable divinities, thus negating competing objects of worship: "I am the first and I am the last; *besides me there is no god. Who is like me?*" This makes the application of the phrase ("Who is like?") to the beast (1) clearly a claim about its divinity and (2) clearly incompatible with the worship of the One God.

30. Aune 1998a, 734. See also Cuss 1974, 53–74.

31. John presents imperial cult as a relatively recent innovation. Certainly John and his audience would have been familiar with the phenomenon of new *divi* emerging with the passing (or accession) of another emperor or member of the imperial family. Aristotle (*Rhet.* 2.9.9–10) discusses indignation as a response to the newly rich or powerful, especially if they rival those who have long been wealthy or powerful. The innovation of giving cultic honors to new would-be gods in competition with the cult of the "Ancient of Days" might subtly serve as a goad to indignation at the phenomenon.

32. An allusion to Dan. 7:25a (cf. also 8:9–14; 11:36; Aune 1998a, 743).

33. So also Cicero, *Inv.* 1.53.101; *Rhet. Her.* 2.30.48.

34. Aune 1998a, 757.

"I Saw a Monster Rising Up!" 203

It actively diverts worship away from the One God toward the beast from the sea (now involving idolatry, as the "image of the beast" comes prominently into focus; 13:14–15), using deception (13:13–14; Satan's long-standing strategy, 12:9; 20:3, 8, 10) and coercion (13:15, 17).[35] The threat to those who do not worship the beast (murder, economic disenfranchisement) arouses feelings of enmity as the second beast, like the first beast and the dragon before it, injures the Christian communities. At the same time, these sanctions also potentially arouse indignation, since a particular misdeed (here the promotion of idolatrous cult, contrary to God's prime directive) has been perpetrated by violent force (13:15) and the influence of wealth (13:16–17).[36] The beast's use of deceptive measures to make the cult of the image of the beast more impressive, and thus make the counterfeit seem more real, also nurtures indignation against the whole complex of ruler cult, since the "special effects" manufacture the impression of "merit" where none exists.[37]

The local manifestations of imperial cult seek to foster ongoing awe and gratitude toward the emperor and Rome. John replaces these feelings with indignation, enmity, and anger in order to support his agenda for Christian presence in Roman Asia: fostering critical witness, with no room for idols, no room for assimilation to, and support of, the mechanisms of imperial legitimation.

The Harlotry and Violence around Us: Revelation 17–18

John creates one of the most memorable—and negative—pictures of Rome in extant literature. Like the picture of the emperor and provincial organization in Revelation 12–13, the picture of Rome in chapters 17–18 is crafted to foreground the multiple levels of injustice that inhere in Roman imperialism, so carefully muted in public discourse, with a view to arousing feelings of enmity against the Roman domination system and indignation at its practices, propaganda, and successes.[38]

John uses the techniques of personification and character delineation (*Rhet. Her.* 4.50.63; 4.53.66) in his portrait of Rome, presenting the seat of empire in

---

35. Suggestions regarding the identification of the "beast from the land" have included the emperor himself, the provincial governor, the *Koinon Asias* (which figured prominently in the promotion of imperial cult), and the imperial priesthood in Asia (Aune 1998a, 736). The latter is preferred by Aune, following Cuss (1974, 96) and Beasley-Murray (1978, 216). Titles of these priests, including "high priest of the goddess Roma and the emperor Caesar Augustus, son of a god," would have been particularly offensive to Christians like John (Friesen 1993, 77–81).
36. Cicero, *Inv.* 1.53.102.
37. On the use of special effects in pagan cults, see especially Scherrer 1984; Aune 1998a, 762–64. The use of special effects (13:13–14) in this cult is akin to those employed in the story of Bel and the Dragon, as the priests of idolatrous cults attempt to defeat the accusation that the gods they serve are not "living" because they cannot eat or speak (cf. Rev. 9:20–21; on Bel, see deSilva 2002a, 240–42). The fact that calling down fire from heaven was used to demonstrate the genuineness of the God of Israel in a contest against Baal (1 Kgs. 18:38–40) makes its use here fall somewhere between the ironic and the studiously subversive (see Duff 2001, 122).
38. The negative side of Roman imperialism in Asia Minor has been amply documented in Kraybill 1996; Howard-Brook and Gwyther 1999.

the guise of a (successful, upscale) prostitute.[39] This choice has subjected John to trenchant criticism in recent decades, but it must be remembered that he is also looking at another feminine portrait of Rome—as a stately goddess, as in the temples to *Roma et Augusti* in Ephesus and Pergamum, the temple to *Dea Roma* in Smyrna, or on the reverse of many first-century Roman coins.[40] It is specifically this public image of Rome that he wishes to address (or perhaps better, *re*dress). John had also inherited the prophetic tradition of speaking critically of cities and nations as "prostitutes," which provided an effective overlay for the image of Roma as goddess.[41] Moreover, John presents Babylon and the new Jerusalem as foils for one another, much as the portraits of the worship around the heavenly throne (Rev. 4–5) and the worship surrounding the beast (chap. 13) formed a telling diptych, revealing John to be drawing on the "two women *topos*" in his portrayal of Rome, using its traditional resources and inherent logic to arouse aversion to partnership with Rome.[42] This technique again allows John to portray Rome as a counterfeit society, a distorted image, a parody of the divine vision for a community that nurtures justice and wholeness, creating critical distance and the potential for arousing indignation at the power and position that Rome occupies, hindering God's ideal as it does.[43]

Quintilian's advice concerning the arousal of feelings of revulsion, aversion, and indignation certainly applies to John's portrait of Rome: "The best way

---

39. Some critics of John import modern structures of prostitution, in which the women are indeed victimized by their purveyors and clients, and thus accuse John of blaming the victim in this vision. Hylen (2003, 209), for example, questions the "problematic assumption that prostitutes really benefit from their activities or undertake them because of economic benefits," and tries to establish that the actions of the kings of the earth (among others) are in fact responsible for the city's downfall, that "the whore deserves punishment because of the actions of others" (2003, 215–16). Such a move unhelpfully obscures the fact that "Babylon" is very much in business for herself and drinks in the full share of the profits. Babylon actively and uncoercedly solicits her own clientele (14:8; 18:2); she is drunk with her own acts of violence (18:6), and not merely scapegoated because others "nations" have gotten drunk because of her; she bears responsibility for spreading deception and befuddlement (18:2 and 14:8). See further 18:7, 23–24; 19:2. The fact that the kings and merchants remain alive to lament Babylon's punishment may seem to support Hylen's claims about the logic of scapegoating the innocent prostitute while the male partners get away free, but what is indeed their end in the narrative world John creates? Does John not expect us to see them caught up in the final rebellions against God and ushered into the lake of fire? It is true that the image of harlot implicates the hearers in the crimes of the harlot, but there is no ground in these texts to exonerate Babylon (all the more as we remember that it is not a prostitute but the center of a worldwide web of imperial exploitation and oppression that is in John's crosshairs).

40. Aune 1998a, 922. Magie (1950, 2.1613–14) provides a list of cult sites of Roma and *Roma et Augustus*. Aune's discussion of the *Dea Roma* coin provides a helpful background to John's impressionistic redrawing of the same (1998b, 920–22). Hylen (2003, 215) asserts that "in the image of the coin, the 'goddess' is depicted as a *male* warrior," with the result that "its image reminds us that the goddess Rome does not necessarily have to be imaged as a woman." The extra fold in the garment falling over the girdle around the breasts, however, reveals this to be a woman's dress, in keeping with the customary iconography of Roma as a female warrior.

41. Jerusalem: Isa. 1:21; Tyre: Isa. 23:16–17; Israel: Jer. 3:6–10; Ezek. 16:15–22; 23:1–49; Hos. 4:12–13; 5:3; Nineveh: Nah. 3:4; see Aune 1998a, 929.

42. See the excellent study by Rossing (1999). The gendered guise will be largely dropped in chap. 18, where we see the city itself rather than its personification.

43. See Duff 2001, 88–89.

for the accuser to excite the feelings of the judge is to make the charges which he brings against the accused seem as atrocious or . . . deplorable as possible" (*Inst.* 6.1.15). Presenting Rome as a prostitute and her international influence and dealings as "fornication," as "trafficking" with a harlot (Rev. 17:1, 2, 5; 18:3) certainly puts the facts of Roman imperialism in "as deplorable" a light "as possible,"[44] while at the same time arousing revulsion at the idea of (continued) entanglement with Rome. This was a major point of contention among certain of the seven churches (notably Pergamum and Thyatira, but also rich Laodicea), where such "fornication" also appears as a (metaphorical) practice promoted or tolerated by other Christian teachers.

John dedicates much of chapters 17–18 to naming the crimes perpetrated by Babylon and depicting the consequences that should properly follow such crimes (but have not as yet!), with the result that these chapters will arouse indignation against the position and success Rome currently and undeservedly enjoys. This serves further to dissuade the Christians addressed by John from adopting practices that lead to partnership with this ugly system of domination and economic exploitation, promoting instead a vocal, critical distance in the form of witness and nonparticipation in key activities. Adela Yarbro Collins finds John to present the following charges against Babylon, which will mitigate any evocations of pity in the portrayal of her judgment: "(1) the idolatrous and blasphemous worship offered and encouraged by Rome, especially the emperor cult; (2) the violence perpetrated by Rome, especially against Jews and Christians; (3) Rome's blasphemous self-glorification; and (4) Roman wealth."[45] John develops each of these in such a way as to arouse indignation or alleviate the positive feelings of awe and gratitude that public discourse sought to maintain in regard to Rome.

The first and third charges emerge from a number of details in the text. Rome stands in close connection with "the beast" that is "full of blasphemous names" (17:3), an alliance that reinforces enmity against Babylon as a participant in the promotion of unmerited cultic honors. The cry of the seafarers, "Who is like the great city? [τίς ὁμοία τῇ πόλει τῇ μεγάλῃ;]" (18:18), also recalls the rhetorical question used in acclamation of the beast (Rev. 13:4), an acclamation "taken" from the acclamation of the One God non pareil. The linking of Rome with the emperors in cultic worship throughout Asia Minor is here subtly (and in context, ironically) recalled to remind the hearers that Rome claims for itself—and receives—what is due the Creator God alone.[46] Related to this charge is the presumption inherent in the public discourse about Rome as the

---

44. See Aune 1998a, 930–31 on commercial trade and political alliances here as prostitution (with important precedents in Isa. 23:17 in regard to Tyre and Nah. 3:4 in regard to Nineveh): "Such alliances inevitably had significant economic, social, and religious implications and usually worked to the detriment of the kingdoms involved." John may have been thinking of the effects of Roman "alliances" with Judea, and the former's manipulation of domestic affairs, since 63 BCE.

45. A. Collins 1980, 203.

46. Aune (1998a, 936) marshals substantial evidence to suggest that the "abominations" with which Babylon has filled her cup represent idolatrous practices.

"Eternal City," *Roma Aeterna*,⁴⁷ claiming for Rome what has never belonged to any kingdom or empire before her (Rev. 18:7–8), signaling Rome's refusal to apply the lessons of history to a more humble and humane rule. John's principal resource for such a philosophy of history would have been the visions of Daniel 2 and 4, where Daniel is seen trying to teach the king of Babylon these very lessons (2:21; 4:32). The "attitude" inherent in such public discourse, then, is presented here as a cause for indignation.

John exposes these pretensions in his vision of Rome's demise, which will reveal the emptiness of Rome's claims in favor of the persistent truth that all human domination systems run their course. Every seat of empire, no matter how prosperous at its peak, will one day sit as a ruin, and Rome will be no different (Rev. 18:2). In the course of this display, John sweeps aside feelings of awe toward Rome, such as the public discourse and iconography sought to maintain. John presents himself as a model of recovery in this regard. At first, he "marvels" at the sight of the figure of Roma: "And, seeing her, I was awestruck with a deep awe" (17:6b).⁴⁸ The angel questions him as to "why" he marvels (17:7a), promising to show him the revelation of the mystery and fate of "the woman" as a remedy for such "awe."⁴⁹ "Marveling" is the response of the inhabitants of the earth to the beast (17:8; cf. 13:3b, 8); it is the emotional response of people "whose names are not written in the book of life." The scene of *Roma Aeterna* stripped, naked, devoured by her allies, and burned up (17:16–17) provides the final antidote to any such feelings.⁵⁰

---

47. See deSilva 1998a, 99; Witherington 2003, 221.

48. Without any argument or justification, Tina Pippin (1992, 57) gives John's "amazement" an erotic cast: "The desire of the male who views her erotic power is brought quickly under control by the angel. . . . The desire is controlled by the angel's explanation." This is, however, a point to be argued rather than assumed and used as the starting point for further argument. The reader has already encountered the response of "amazement" in the inhabitants of the world who follow the beast (13:3), and who will have the same response to Babylon (17:8); the word group is also used to speak of the awesome sight of the conquerors hymning God by the crystal sea (15:1, 3). These other cues in the text (aside from John's avoidance of any words from the ἐπιθυμία/ἐπιθυμέω group in this context) suggest that "amazement" here falls within the larger contrast of appropriate versus inappropriate objects of "awe," not "sexual excitement" or "desire."

49. Aune (1998a, 927) suggests that John's reaction here is a standard feature of the literary form of *ekphrasis*, in which the narrator is left to puzzle over the significance of the image being viewed until an interlocutor relieves the narrator's confusion by explaining the work. It is noteworthy that one of these narrators is left θαυμάζων, "wondering," about a depiction of Hercules (Lucian, *Herc.* 4) and another describes a statue of Lysippus as a θαῦμα, "a marvel" (Callistratus, *Imagines* 6), giving Aune strong lexical support for his reading of 17:6. However, the inhabitants of the earth also experience "amazement" as they witness the woman riding the beast (17:8; cf. 13:3), amazement (surely not, in this case, puzzlement) that found expression in the worship of the beast and the dragon (13:4), something that does not escape Aune's notice (1998a, 940). While Aune's observations about literary form, then, argue strongly for "puzzlement," the immediate and broader literary context necessarily color any "puzzlement" with a more sinister "amazement" that can draw one's focus away from true objects of worship. See also Bartsch 1989, 25–27.

50. The substantial debate concerning this scene (see the conversation begun in Pippin 1992 and carried forward in Hylen 2003) appears to turn on the degree to which the interpreter/analyst reads it through the lens of the political critique and forecast for which the figure of the prostitute serves as a vehicle (which is surely the lens that John would have the readers continue to hold before themselves) as opposed to allowing the figure (a woman) to displace the reality for which it stands.

Throughout Revelation, John gives attention to Rome's violence, the second charge noted by Adela Yarbro Collins: "I saw the woman drunk with the blood of the saints and with the blood of the witnesses of Jesus" (17:6; see also 18:23b–24).[51] This is, first, a topic of enmity. John reminds the Christians that Rome has savagely hurt "our own," amplified by the image of drinking blood to the point of intoxication, recalling the Levitical prescriptions against drinking blood as an abomination and evoking general taboos against cannibalism (after all, this is human blood). The strange blending of "blood" with the effects of wine suggests that Babylon engaged in this slaughter for her own wanton amusement (getting a "rush," as it were, out of doing injury to God's friends). By depicting the suppression of Christian witness in such provocative terms, and presenting the victims as virtuous witnesses of Jesus who did not merit such ill treatment, John has also woven in two topics evocative of indignation (cf. Quintilian, *Inst.* 6.1.15).

John has previously raised awareness of Rome's violence. The vision of the martyrs crying out under the altar in Rev. 6:9–11 calls attention to righteous people not getting what they deserved in life, having been killed by the powers that be for their faithful testimony concerning the One God and God's requirements. Their evident pain at the lingering delay of divine judgment against the empire signals, moreover, that the perpetrators still enjoy a reprieve that they do not deserve. The violence and injustice, moreover, must continue against God's righteous ones for a time (6:11b), heightening feelings of enmity and indignation against the powers of this world. By giving voice to these victims, John has incidentally employed the strategy of placing "fictitious speeches in the mouths of our characters" and calling "the dead to life" to testify against the ills they have suffered or to rail their own indignation against the accused, thereby contributing to the arousal of indignation among the audience (Quintilian, *Inst.* 4.1.28).[52]

These same victims express relief when justice is finally given (16:5–7). But if such plagues are indeed, as angel and martyrs affirm, what earth's inhabitants deserve, they have not yet received their due and hence still enjoy undeserved good fortune. The distance between the "justice" envisioned in 16:15–17 (and 17:1–18:24) and the hearers' present experience of Rome's ascendency continues to nurture indignation. It is perhaps in this light that we should hear 18:20: "Rejoice over her, heaven and holy ones and apostles and prophets, because God judged your case against her."[53] "Rejoicing" here is not the gloating or taunting

---

The image is not itself without precedent, appearing in Ezek. 23:25–29, where Jerusalem is personified as a woman stripped naked, with the survivors of Jerusalem being burned to death (Aune 1998a, 956–57).

51. Robert Royalty (1998, 190) speaks of the details of this verse "increasing the *pathos* of this vision," but not specifying *which* emotion is being augmented, how, or to what end.

52. That which arouses pity at the fate of the victim (Quintilian, *Inst.* 6.1.18) could be expected, reciprocally, to arouse indignation against the perpetrator.

53. On what factors would lead hearers to "hear" this injunction as the conclusion of the hypothetical lament placed on the lips of the sailors or as the "voice from heaven" speaking in his own voice, see deSilva 2007a, 363–65.

of the vicious, but the experience of relief at last enjoyed by the victims who first suffered the brutality of a repressive regime, and suffered again to witness that regime prospering and successfully promoting its lies about its crimes for so long. Moreover, since this relief belongs still to an unrealized future for John and his audiences, John is not actually seeking to provoke "rejoicing" as a response to Rome's (unrealized) fall,[54] so much as indignation against the crimes perpetrated by this domination system that as yet go unpunished. In other words, the invitation to the narrative victims to "rejoice" at as-yet-unrealized events works upon the flesh-and-blood hearers rather differently, calling attention to what is still wrong in the present (hence, arousing indignation: the plaintiffs have not yet been given justice; the defendant still enjoys privilege and power to which she is not entitled).

The final charge pertains to the Roman imperial economy, which John portrays as structured chiefly to benefit Rome. This first emerges in the portrayal of Rome as a prostitute as John calls attention to her luxurious clothing ("purple and scarlet"), adornment ("gold and precious stones and pearls"), and luxury goods (not just a cup, but a "golden cup"; 17:4), and is reinforced by the denunciation of Rome for "indulging in her excesses" (18:5) and her "luxuriating" (18:3). It emerges also from the focus on the extensive cargoes flowing from the ports throughout the known world, taking both staples (like grain and oil) and luxury items away from the provinces to satiate a single city's cravings (18:12–13).[55] It is further evidenced as merchants rise to positions of power and influence through the increase of trade with the city (cf. Jer. 51:49).

This "view" of the Roman economy counters the feelings of gratitude toward Rome by drawing attention to the pervasive self-interest that underlies Roman rule.[56] Roma is an antibenefactor, whose influence and interventions ultimately seek to secure self-serving ends. John includes no notice of anything Rome has done purely on behalf of her subjects.[57] The emphasis on luxury, intemperance,

---

54. As suggested in A. Collins 1980, 203.

55. Aelius Aristides (*To Rome* 11–13) provides a strikingly similar portrait of the provinces being literally stripped bare, given the volume of goods brought to the capital city. Aune (1998b, 981) observes that John uses polysyndeton here to "produce the effect of 'extensiveness and abundance by means of an exhaustive summary' (BDF § 460); i.e., it rhetorically emphasizes the conspicuous consumption of Rome," her "profound materialism." Adela Yarbro Collins (1984, 153) correctly observes that John's manifest "is purposely selective and perspectival," emphasizing luxury items. However, John does in fact list "fine flour and grain" in 18:13, drawing attention to the fact that even the more mundane cargoes in the shipping lanes manifest the injustice of the system, supplying some 200,000 families in Rome with their "regular 'dole' of free grain," also a (parasitic) luxury when "provincials paid high prices for grain and sometimes had none" (Kraybill 1996, 107–8).

56. According to Aristotle (*Rhet.* 2.7.5), an orator could negate feelings of gratitude by showing an act to have been motivated not by benevolence, but in the self-interest of the doer. See also Cicero, *De or.* 2.51.206, 208.

57. A defender of Rome might ask whether or not this a "fair" critique, pointing, e.g., to Rome's marshaling of resources to relieve famines and rebuild cities after earthquakes in Asia Minor, or to its effective elimination of piracy and brigandage from the Mediterranean basin. John might respond, however, that all such "beneficence" was undertaken ultimately to serve Rome's interests, safeguarding her supply in the lands of production and in transit to her lap.

and conspicuous consumption also nurtures indignation, as Rome is seen to consume more of the world's goods than is the share of any one city, enjoying more than is due—and this often to the detriment of the provinces under her far-from-beneficent rule.[58]

The angel closes this episode with a summary of Babylon's crimes (18:23b–24). Rome is guilty of "the blood of prophets and saints . . . and all the slain upon the earth," naming not only the violence targeting Christian dissenters but also the violence of conquest and suppression of revolt upon which empire is ultimately founded.[59] Rome is guilty of spinning a web of propaganda and supplying enough of a share in the rewards to deceive the majority into viewing empire as a good thing, even as a divinely ordained state of affairs. John provides ample reason, then, for his hearers to allow their passions against Rome to be excited by such calls to (imaginative) action as 18:5–6, with their explicit arousal of desire for "payback,"[60] which is essentially the goal of indignation.

God's Anger and the Arousal of Indignation

Several rhetorical theorists mark the importance of the audience witnessing the speaker's own genuine experience of emotions as a catalyst for the stirring of their own.[61] John reveals fairly little of his own emotional responses throughout Revelation,[62] but he does foreground the emotional responses of other characters, especially God's experience of anger (ὀργή, 6:16, 17; 11:18; 14:10; 16:19; 19:15; θυμός, 14:19; 15:1, 7; 16:1, 19; 19:15). John elaborates the reasons for

---

58. The economic situation in 6:6 might also contribute to the arousal of indignation, since production and markets have been so mismanaged on account of the demands of the imperial economy (and the ruling consideration of the profitability of certain crops for export over others for internal consumption) that hardworking people are unable to purchase the food they need simply to feed their families. See Schüssler Fiorenza 1991, 63.

59. "Christians were only a small minority among countless victims of the great imperial beast," and John is able to step back to "take a panoramic view of the carnage" in 18:24 (Kraybill 1996, 200).

60. Aune (1998a, 994) rightly rejects readings of 18:6 that suggest that angels or some characters other than the obvious ("my people") are the ones invited to "pay her back double" as examples of theological-ethical convictions trumping the meaning of the text. However, it is noteworthy that Christians are not actually given any role in the punishment of beasts or Babylon other than to keep their necessary (ideological and behavioral) distance until God intervenes. Adela Yarbro Collins's insight that Revelation stirs up these feelings so as to resolve them and allow for their release as the disciples await God's future intervention is helpful in this regard (1984, 152–53). However, many in the audience simply need to be made to *feel* this desire for vindication and acknowledge its basis in Rome's unjust practices, so that they will cease to entertain notions of coexistence or even collusion. Many among John's audience appear willing to forget that Rome ever spilled so much Christian blood (and so creatively at times!) in order to get on with a comfortable life. Rather than reflecting a commendable pursuit of Christian forgiveness, however, John avers that this course of action amounts to abandoning the witness to the unjust and impious practices that, in part, it is the survivors' duty to remember and protest.

61. Quintilian, *Inst.* 6.2.26; Cicero, *De or.* 2.45.189–2.47.197.

62. Notable exceptions include his narration of his experiences of fear (1:17), sorrow (5:4), and awe or wonder (17:6b), none of which, however, are offered as a catalyst for imitation (he is told explicitly *not* to fear in 1:17; the angel seeks to dispel any awe or amazement he feels in 17:7; and John's disappointment in 5:4 merely serves to amplify the uniqueness of the Lamb's achievement).

God's anger more implicitly and narratologically than one finds in *1 Enoch* 1:9 or in Pauline texts (e.g., Rom. 1:18–23; Eph. 5:3–6), but his analysis of how God must "feel" about what God witnesses on earth is essentially the same: God is fed up with human disregard of God's commands and beneficence and with the mistreatment of God's faithful clients.

Ingratitude prompts anger (Aristotle, *Rhet.* 2.2.3; 2.2.17). John has established gratitude and worship as the proper responses to God and the Lamb, both through example and enthymeme (esp. in 4:1–5:14). The first of three message-bearing angels reinforces the fact that worship and honor from God's creatures is God's due (14:7). In an environment, then, where large pockets of humanity resolutely refuse to give God due honor and instead worship their idols, the beast, and the dragon, God's anger would be readily understood as a response to ingratitude (exacerbated by occasions of slandering—not just failing to honor, but actively speaking ill of God; 13:1, 5–6; 16:9, 11, 21).

Anger abates when people admit their wrongdoings but grows more severe when people deny their offenses (Aristotle, *Rhet.* 2.3.5; Quintilian, *Inst.* 6.1.14). John repeatedly displays the recalcitrance of the disobedient and ungrateful in spite of God's warnings. These displays occur at prominent junctures, including the effective climax of the trumpets (Rev. 9:20–21)[63] and interspersed among the bowl plagues (16:9, 11, 21). The objects of God's (just) anger further provoke God with abusive speech (ἐβλασφήμησαν, 16:9, 11, 21) or affronting behaviors (the continued worship of idols and violation of other commandments; 9:20–21) at the very points where they ought to be admitting their wrongdoing. The height of this, of course, is speaking ill of God for their experiences of plague as if God is to blame (and is therefore acting unjustly, being a "bad God") rather than themselves.

People "are also angry with those who slight such persons as it would be disgraceful for them not to defend, for instance, parents, children, wives, and dependents" (Aristotle, *Rhet.* 2.2.23). Throughout Revelation, John spotlights God's "dependents" as the targeted victims of these same recalcitrant, disobedient, ungrateful pockets of humanity and the spiritual forces of evil behind them (1:9; 2:13; 6:9–11; 11:7; 12:17; 13:7; 16:5–6; 17:6; 18:24). Moreover, John explicitly connects avenging these righteous victims with the pouring out of "the seven gold vials full of the wrath of the God who lives for ever and ever" (15:7), both as they begin to be poured out (16:5–7) and in the climactic liturgy in heaven praising God for God's judgment of Babylon (19:2).[64]

Thus the relevant question for an investigation of appeals to pathos is What does the *audience* feel when they envision God being thus provoked by earth's inhabitants? The audience sees God's anger as the response to not receiving God's due (cf. Aristotle, *Rhet.* 2.9.11), with the result that these images are likely

---

63. "Effective," because a long parenthesis separates the sixth from the seventh and largely breaks the forward drive of the rhythm, such that 9:20–21 falls at the peak of that movement.

64. This connection is also made explicit in *4 Ezra* 7:79, 81, 83, 87.

to further fuel the audience's indignation against those who behave so unjustly toward God. They see a population confronted with God's warnings and judgment, and yet refusing to admit wrongdoing on their part, the emotional response to which would be, in modern colloquial parlance, "I don't believe the *nerve* of these people!" Similarly, God's anger at seeing God's faithful clients receiving ill treatment that they do not deserve is likely to nurture indignation among the audience against the perpetrators. The topos of God's anger, then, supports the arousal of indignation among the hearers against those who have affronted God, who have not yet met with their deserved punishment. This again contributes to creating distance between the audience and those who participate in such affronts, making it less likely that they themselves will, for example, "eat foods sacrificed to idols" or condone such behavior as appropriate.

Such a Pity?

John's indictment of Rome and narration of her doom have led some critics to surmise that John has no sense of the tragedy, the human loss, connected with the events he describes: "There is nothing in Revelation 18 to conceal John's glee over the catastrophe."[65] But there are cues in the text that suggest that we ought not to hear *unmitigated* glee in John's narrative voice.[66] Indeed, several noteworthy critics have suggested that Revelation 18 is more expressive of pity and regret over Babylon's fall.[67] A rhetorical analysis of John's potential evocation of topics of pity can help us discern whether John evokes the overtones of regret in the upper harmonics of his arousal of indignation, or rather a more ethically questionable delight in human suffering.

Robert Royalty[68] has suggested that Revelation 18 resembles the monody, a Greek lament expressing pity, suggesting that the form of the chapter itself might have disposed the hearers to temper their responses of indignation, anger, and enmity with pity. Beyond form, the content of Revelation 18 aligns with topics evocative of pity at several points. John takes a rhetorical risk when he describes the calamities that will befall Babylon as thoroughly and as sensitively as he does, for it creates the necessity on the part of John and his audience to remain mindful that the piteous calamity they are witnessing is in fact deserved.

Contrasting "the prosperity . . . once enjoyed" with "what evils they now suffer" (Cicero, *De inventione rhetorica* 1.55.107; see also Quintilian, *Inst.* 6.1.23) was productive of pity, although John has so carefully positioned the audience

---

65. Carey 1999b, 156–57.
66. Even Rev. 18:20, the verse that comes closest to supporting Carey's claim, could be read not as an expression of glee, but as an acknowledgment of vindication, the "rejoicing" that comes from *relief* after living with the lingering pains of injustice (martyrs) and with the official "spins" that deny any wrongdoing and thus fail even to acknowledge the injury.
67. E.g., Caird 1966, 227; Beckwith 1919, 285; Lilje 1957, 237; Glasson 1965, 105; Kiddle and Ross 1946, 365, 370–73. See A. Collins 1980, 186 n. 4 for a complete list, though she herself concludes that John neither seeks to arouse true sympathy nor bitter joy.
68. Royalty 1997, 615.

to regard the fall of Babylon as *deserved*, even necessary, that pity would not be automatically excited (Aristotle, *Rhet.* 2.8.2). Babylon is "in distress contrary to all expectation," another topic potentially evocative of pity (Cicero, *Inv.* 1.55.108). The political and military might of Rome gave no hint of such forthcoming collapse. Moreover, the repetition of the phrases "in a single day" and "in one hour" (Rev. 18:8, 10, 17, 19), together with the image of the millstone sinking into the sea (18:21), all stress the suddenness, and hence unexpectedness, of this dramatic reversal. Babylon's speech (18:7–8), preceding the first instance of the topic of suddenness, shows her obliviousness to God's standards and power to enforce them through judgment, and hence drives home the fact that the catastrophes come "contrary to all expectation." John again mitigates the arousal of pity, however, by showing that Babylon's lack of awareness is culpable insofar as she has violently silenced those who bore witness to the truth about her practices in the light of God's commandments (17:6; 18:24).

Amplifying the misfortune by viewing it from various angles provided another means of evoking pity. A bereaved father's grief could be amplified by talking about the different pleasures he had from his child's life, which would no longer be enjoyed, as well as the joys that he would now never have (Cicero, *Inv.* 1.55.107). Alternatively, a catastrophe could be broken down into discrete, lamentable experiences, each one of which could then be presented "to view one by one, so that the auditor may seem to see them, and may be moved to pity by the actual occurrence, as if he were present, and not by words alone" (Cicero, *Inv.* 1.55.107).

John's extended monody engages this topic in a number of ways. First, he allows the audience to see Babylon's fall from the perspective of various parties affected by the loss (kings, merchants, seafarers, 18:9–20) and voicing their lament, as well as the stark silence resulting from the sudden and permanent cessation of music, crafts, and new beginnings in Babylon (18:22–23).[69] John mitigates the power of these laments to evoke pity by presenting the kings unsympathetically as those "who fornicated with her and indulged in excess with her" (18:9),[70] as well as by underscoring the obvious self-interest on the part of other "mourners" (18:11, 15, 19),[71] which distances them from the displays of wife and children being brought out in tears and wretched attire to evoke pity for the defendant (Quintilian, *Inst.* 4.1.28).

John dwells significantly on the topic of separation from relationships and the pleasures they bring.[72] This emerges first in Revelation 18:14, although somewhat ironically insofar as the focus is solely on deprivation of material goods rather than social relationships. It is more sensitively evoked in John's

---

69. In this regard, I find Carey's observation that "the mourners are silenced" (1999b, 157) to be problematic. It is rather remarkable, on the contrary, that John gives them such room to speak at all, potentially to arouse pity and regret that things must be so.
70. A. Collins 1980, 195.
71. So rightly Aune 1998a, 998.
72. See Cicero, *Inv.* 1.55.109.

narration of the joys that would no longer be experienced in Babylon (18:22–23a): the "sound of harpists and musicians and flutists and trumpeters," "craftsmen of every art," "the sound of the mill," "the light of a lamp," and especially "the sound of bridegroom and bride," which are all unobjectionable facets of Babylon's civic life.[73] This elaboration of the deserted-city topos first invoked in 18:2[74] calls attention to these wholesome facets of society that will be lost, the needless "waste" that Babylon will have brought about in her reckless collision course with the God of justice.[75] John thus adds a more fully tragic dimension to the scene, a more "human" dimension to what is otherwise a caricature of Roman society. In anticipating the relief that will come with the collapse of a global domination system, John does not fail to acknowledge the personal tragedies in the stories of weddings that would never happen, songs of joy that would never be sung, and productive crafts that would cease to be practiced. It is this segment of the lament that would most potentially arouse pity for the *people* in Babylon, who are caught up in her fall, and John does nothing to mitigate pity at this juncture. Such an emotional response would balance indignation against the "system," as it were, with a concern for witness to call the individuals out from that system before it is too late. In this way, indignation is allowed to have its full force, reinforcing a sense of incompatibility and separation (and the return to the topic of Rome's crimes in 18:23b–24 reinforces this, assuring that pity will not be misdirected toward the "system"), while the topics evocative of compassion help the audience remain sensitive toward the ordinary people who exist within and under that system, perhaps spurring on the witness and evangelism that some noteworthy scholars understand to be critical to John's larger agenda (i.e., to bring about the conversion of the nations).[76]

Ethical Evaluation of John's Evocation of Emotions Related to Enmity

Quintilian speaks of the practice of *deinōsis* (δείνωσις), by means of which "the force of eloquence . . . awakens emotions that either do not naturally arise from the case or are stronger than the case would suggest." Such a practice amplifies "things unjust, cruel or hateful" beyond what the offenses would actually merit, falling into the ethically questionable realm of manipulating emotions for the sake of achieving one's rhetorical goals (*Inst.* 6.2.24), even if it requires moving "the minds of the judges . . . away from the contemplation of the truth"

---

73. Howard-Brook and Gwyther (1999, 172) suggest that the cessation of music in Babylon in Rev. 18:22 signifies that "the imperial cults and local cults will be silenced." While musical instruments might have accompanied cult hymns and the silencing of *all* music necessarily includes the silencing of cultic music, neither the scriptural precedents (Isa. 24:8; Ezek. 26:13) nor the specific content of Rev. 18:21–24 support their suggestion that John particularly targets pagan cultic music here.

74. Aune 1998a, 1012.

75. See also Kraybill 1996, 24 n. 2.

76. E.g., Schüssler Fiorenza 1991, 79; Bauckham 1993b, 103.

(6.2.5).[77] Does John overstate his case? Does he excite the emotions of enmity and indignation beyond what Rome's practices merit? Or does he make a sufficient case to justify the emotional responses he seeks to arouse? In evaluating these questions, it is significant that several voices bear witness against Roman domination by using similar language and to a very similar degree.

The authors of the near-contemporary apocalypses, *4 Ezra* and *2 Baruch*, use language and amplitude very similar to John's as they set forth their own experience of Roman imperialism, corroborating his witness. The author of *2 Baruch* denounces the "nations" in general for their exploitation and violence, their misuse of creation, and their failure to honor the God who provided creation and its fruits: "But now, ye peoples and nations, ye are guilty because ye have always trodden down the earth, and used the creation unrighteously. For I have always benefitted you, and ye have always been ungrateful for the beneficence" (*2 Bar.* 13:11–12). He further indicts "Babylon" (Rome) for its imperialistic expansion and the sufferings this policy brought upon the subject peoples. Conquest, in turn, facilitated the widespread dissemination of Rome's "wickedness" (36:8). The end of the cedar is to be burned (37:1). In the interpretation of the vision of the cedar tree, Rome's pride and insolence come to the fore, as well as its suppression of "the truth" (39:5–7).

In *4 Ezra*, the Messiah indicts Rome for establishing dominion through violence and terror, and for its widespread destruction of fruitful communities for the sake of expansion. Rome is upbraided for its oppressive exercise of that rule, for the perversion of justice and the use of deceit, for its enmity against "those who tell the truth," and for its insolence and pride (11:39–12:1). The author anticipates the day when the world will be "freed from your violence" and "refreshed and relieved" by the removal of the terrible burden of Roman imperialism. Moreover, the author of *4 Ezra* regards the Flavian emperors as the empire's most oppressive rulers, who "sum up [the eagle's] wickedness" (12:23–25). The foregrounding of the Messiah's judicial role in both *2 Baruch* and *4 Ezra* suggests that multiple communities experienced Roman rule as an intolerable situation of injustice for which there was simply no appeal save to God's court. The authors of the third and fourth books of *Sibylline Oracles* also attest to Rome's economic exploitation of the province of Asia.[78] Even Tacitus, a privileged member of the dominant culture, knows how Roman domination looks from the margins: "Robbery, savagery, and rape they call 'government'; they make a desert and call it 'peace'" (*Agricola* 30).

---

77. Quintilian (*Inst.* 6.2.5, 24) takes a neutral stand in regard to this practice, while Aristotle expresses disapproval for the use of emotions to create unjustified bias (*Rhet.* 3.1.5).

78. See, e.g., *Sib. Or.* 3.350–52: "However much wealth Rome received from tribute-bearing Asia, Asia will receive three times that much again from Rome and will repay her deadly arrogance to her"; 4.145–148 (late first century CE), in connection with return of Nero (4.137–39): "Great wealth will come to Asia, which Rome itself once plundered and deposited in her house of many possessions. She will then pay back twice as much and more to Asia, and then there will be a surfeit of war." These are helpfully cited in Bauckham 1993a, 379, 382.

"I Saw a Monster Rising Up!" 215

Therefore, John does not appear to engage in *deinōsis*. He forcefully gives voice to the cost of imperialism, adding his voice to a veritable chorus of voices that the dominant cultural rhetoric seeks to drown out, whether by volume or violence. The multiplicity of witnesses (including non-Jewish, non-Christian witnesses) suggests that John appropriately (if colorfully) draws attention to the underside of Roman imperialism. He has identified features of Roman imperialism that he can justifiably criticize or even demonize on the basis of the Jewish scriptural tradition on which he takes his stand. This is not to say that John "fairly" represents the sum total of Roman imperial interventions in Asia Minor. John's presentation is certainly one-sided, giving no voice to Rome's positive contributions to life in that province (although John might well question whether Rome's motives for "helping" the provincials in terms of famine relief, development, and provision for safety for trade on land and sea were altruistic or self-interested). All elements of imperial ideology that promote gratitude toward the *Augusti* or legitimate their rule (e.g., as the vessels chosen by the gods to bring peace and rule of law) are suppressed or subverted. But in what John *does* say, he resonates with a significant number of contemporary witnesses that would corroborate his case.

EVOCATIONS OF FEAR AND CONFIDENCE IN THE VISIONS

The topics of imminence in the opening chapters lay the foundation for appeals to both fear and confidence throughout the entire book. The opening announcements of the imminent "coming" of Christ and of God give way to descriptions of that coming, thrusting the hearers into the midst of those forthcoming events, making the imminent more fully present through the imagination.[79]

John seeks to evoke fear at several points throughout the visions, particularly in connection with the experience of God's wrath through plagues and judgments. Such arousal of fear in regard to encountering God as Judge (rather than as Ally) should distance the hearers from pursuing any course of action upon which God would be known (e.g., from the information in the Hebrew Scriptures) to look with disfavor. Furthermore, though John is forthright about the fearsomeness of the faithful witnesses' temporal opponents, he demonstrates the fearsomeness of the consequences of opposing God to be far greater both

---

79. Periodic reminders of imminence still appear, such as the oath sworn by the "strong angel" that "no time remains" (Rev. 10:6). An oath is itself a form of rhetorical proof, normally employed in judicial cases by witnesses to past events (see, e.g., *Rhet. Alex.* 1432a.33–37), here applied to testimony in regard to the "present" circumstances in which John finds himself. Similarly, Christ's interjection of first-person speech in 16:15 ("See! I am coming as thief") evokes the topic of unexpectedness or suddenness in connection with the dangers of the final bowl plagues (16:12–16). "Suddenness" here acts as a functional equivalent of the topic of imminence (both call forth the response of immediate attention, watchfulness, and wise deliberation in light of the eventualities) in supporting an appeal to fear.

in terms of amplitude and duration. The opening of the seven seals, the blowing of the seven trumpets, the pouring out of the seven bowls, the visions of the decisive acts of judgment, and the pictures of postmortem punishment—all contribute to the arousal of feelings of fear in connection with finding oneself opposed to God, feelings that should provide strong disincentives to the same. We will here examine only a sample.

The grisly gallop of the four horsemen, with the grim and all-too-well-known consequences of their ride, begins the process of arousing fear. Unlike the judgments that follow, there is no indication that the faithful are spared the experience. The sequence of imperialist expansion, civil war, famine, and disease was not unknown to the hearers, particularly those who had lived through the reigns of Claudius and Nero (a period of some expansion) and then the disastrous "year of the four emperors." It is with the opening of the sixth seal, however, that terror breaks forth most explicitly. In the face of the cosmic disruptions that accompany the appearance of God and the Lamb in judgment—the landscape and skyscape themselves, as it were, fleeing in terror (6:14)—all the inhabitants of the earth express their fear by hiding themselves, even crying out to the mountains to cover them and shield them in death from the fearsomeness of this encounter with the Living God (6:15–16), whose face they cannot endure. Portraying these characters displaying such fear is the narrative equivalent of an orator feeling and making visible the very emotion the orator hopes to arouse at a certain point in the speech (Quintilian, *Inst.* 6.2.26–30; Cicero, *De or.* 2.45.189–2.47.197). The cries of terror in the scene become the spark to kindle fear in the hearts of the audience.

That the "kings of the earth and the magnates and the chiliarchs and the rich and the strong" express utter terror at this encounter draws upon another topic of fear. According to Aristotle, an audience will fear "those who are feared by those who are stronger than we are, for they would be better able to injure us, if they could injure those stronger than ourselves" (*Rhet.* 2.5.10). The first five categories of people named in Revelation 6:15 would certainly qualify as stronger than most members of the seven congregations, and hence this scene might be expected to arouse fear as the hearers see "those who are stronger" quaking before the appearing of God and the Lamb. Moreover, the hearers are themselves implicitly included in this response, for it is not only the kings and potentates, but also "*every* slave and free person" who trembles before God and the Lamb (6:15). This intones a strange counterpoint to 5:13, where "every creature" shouts in worship rather than in fear, but John's diptych of universal, contradictory visions accentuates the alternatives he sets before his congregations. The hearers are driven to "see" themselves in both scenes, to experience the concomitant feelings, and thus to resolve themselves to remain consistently centered on God and the Lamb in all their doings.

The scene of panic ends most poignantly with the rhetorical question borrowed from an older prophetic text contemplating the fearsomeness of encountering God at his appearing (Mal. 3:2): "The great day of their wrath has come, and who is able to stand?!" (Rev. 6:17). After a brief and dramatically effective pause, the answer is given in the vision of the 144,000, and of the uncountable number standing (indeed ἑστῶτες, 7:9) before God's throne. Before the terror of the coming of God and the Lamb on the day of their wrath, a terror that is so severe that it simply cannot be *faced* (6:16–17), there is only one remedy, one path to relief and safety: to be of such a sort (in one's alignment, behaviors, and so forth) that one receives the seal of God, which exempts one from the plagues that God is prepared to unleash upon the world (7:1–17).[80]

The images of the redeemed gathered before God and the Lamb in 7:13–17 (appropriately read in many Christian communions on All Saints' Day and at funerals) evoke feelings of confidence in regard to the outcome of the "great ordeal" that lies ahead. That which is harmful is seen, from this vantage point, now to be "far away or nonexistent" (Aristotle, *Rhet.* 2.5.16), a topic made explicit by a recontextualization of Isaiah 49:10 (Rev. 7:16). Danger stands only behind the disciple, who has moved beyond the reach of harm forever. Further, strong help (another topic productive of confidence, as in Aristotle, *Rhet.* 2.5.17) could not be nearer: "The one seated upon the throne will spread his tent over them" (Rev. 7:15b), sheltering them, even as the Lamb shepherds them, ushering them into life in its abundance (7:17a). There *is* restoration, healing, and blessedness after the storms of life; therefore, disciples can brave those storms faithfully. The possibility of standing before God with confidence, experiencing the favor and help of God and the Lamb, draws the audience to identify themselves with this group in 7:9–17 and thus to avoid the fearful encounter with "the one seated upon the throne" anticipated for those who have not lived as God's own (6:15–17).

The rhetorical power *and* strategy of this diptych portraying two starkly different encounters with God at the end of history (6:15–17; 7:9–10, 13–17) is not lost on contemporary religious leaders, particularly leaders of apocalyptic cults who otherwise would not agree with the contemporary-historical orientation of the present study. Herbert W. Armstrong, late Pastor General of the Worldwide Church of God, for example, participates in an interpretation of Revelation shared by several other Christian groups that retain Saturday (the Sabbath) as their distinctive day of worship, which becomes now the primary mark distinguishing true followers of Jesus Christ (those "who keep the commandments of God" [14:12], and this one commandment in particular) from those who have compromised with the empire-church and gone the way of the Nicolaitans and Jezebel. Armstrong showed a keen awareness of the power of the images of Revelation and sought to harness this power with the help of cartoonist Basil Wolverton.[81]

---

80. "Just as the Israelites were spared from the Egyptian plagues, so the cosmic plagues will not touch those who have the protection of God's seal" (Schüssler Fiorenza 1991, 71). A similar recurrence of this motif from Exodus appears in *2 Bar.* 29:2–3; 71:1, although there one finds divine protection of the *land* of Israel and those therein dwelling (rather than of the *people* of God wherever they might happen to be).

81. Armstrong 1959, 44–45.

Wolverton created a dark cartoon depiction of 6:12 (and its parallels: 11:13; 16:18) to help readers visualize and thereby feel the terror of that scene. Armstrong provides a lengthy caption (about 40 percent of the facing page) that twice instructs readers to "STUDY this picture" (emphasis orig.). The caption begins and ends with invitations to the readers to place themselves in that scene and to experience the terror, even as John had implied the readers' potential presence in that scene. This is used, in turn, to impel them toward the alternative, namely "turn[ing] to God in REAL EARNEST . . . and being supernaturally PROTECTED from the real event soon to strike." This protection is the much-to-be-desired seal of God. John sought to evoke this series of mental images and corollary emotional responses with precisely the same goal in mind, though without the benefit of illustrators.

The value of the seal, and therefore the importance of living as one who receives it, is further underscored in chapters 8 and 9, which depict the first six of the seven trumpets and continue to employ topics evocative of fear. The first four trumpet blasts, with their disruptions of nature and disastrous results for sea and land, rather straightforwardly evoke fear. The threefold cry of "woe" (8:13) amplifies the fearsomeness of the threat of harm yet to come in response to the last three trumpets, notably also incorporating the topic of imminence ("the three angels *who are about to* sound," τῶν μελλόντων σαλπίζειν). The two woes narrated in chapter 9 contain perhaps the most fantastic images of Revelation. What God *could* have done in the exodus/conquest (Wis. 11:17–19), God now does, sending "newly created unknown beasts full of rage, or such as breathe out fiery breath, or belch forth a thick pall of smoke, or flash terrible sparks from their eyes" (11:18 NRSV) upon the inhabitants of the earth lacking God's seal (Rev. 9:4, 7–10, 17–19). Identifying the instruments of God's punishment as Parthians or Goths is, in effect, a misguided attempt at demythologization. John's point is, rather, that God will punish those who have opposed him with fearsome instruments beyond our imagination, capable of inflicting such pain as makes death a wished-for escape. These fear-evoking images serve chiefly to underscore the value of the seal of God as the one path to exemption from these imminent experiences of harm (9:4).

Yet God is not the only fearsome force in John's vision. The seer frankly acknowledges the fearsomeness of the "enemies" of the faithful and the dangers of opposing them. He is realistic about the path of resistance and its psychological and material costs. The spiritual and corporeal forces arrayed against those who remain committed to the worship of One God and to walking in God's ways are powerful indeed. Empowered by Satan himself, depicted as monstrous beasts, dealing death and disenfranchisement to all who refuse to acknowledge their power through cultic venues—the political potentates of Rome and proconsular Asia are displayed in ways productive of fear. They possess the combination of injustice and power that Aristotle described as inherently fearsome (*Rhet.* 2.5.4); they freely exercise their power to injure, or to withhold this world's goods from, their subjects (2.5.8). They orchestrate harm, directing it intentionally toward the "saints" (Rev. 12:17; 13:7, 15–17).

John acknowledges the feelings that accompany resisting Roman authority, even augmenting them for the faithful and *evoking* them afresh for those who do not presently experience Roman power as hostile.[82] However, he puts these feelings in perspective in regard both to God's help (which nurtures confidence that the opposition, though fearsome, will be overcome) and God's judgment (which entails far more fearsome experiences and consequences). Chapters 6–9 have provided one side of the frame to assure that the threat of Roman power was properly weighed vis-à-vis the threat of God's power; the later visions of God's wrath and the punishment of those who yield to the pressures toward idolatry around them complete the interpretive framework.

The scenes of judgment in 14:9–11, 19–20, for example, are so depicted as to arouse fear in regard to the terrible consequences of beast-worship. The vivid details (e.g., the action of fire and molten sulfur upon the bodies of the disobedient, or the expressing of blood from the victims as if in a winepress) heighten the emotional effect by playing more strongly upon the audience's imaginations.[83] Such ongoing appeals to fear continue to implant absolute aversion to the course of assimilation or continued cooperation with the cultic mechanisms of Roman imperialism, no matter how fearsome its representatives. That those bearing the mark of the beast (who have consented to participate in behaviors that legitimate and cooperate with imperialism) are the specific target of the bowl judgments (e.g., 16:2, 10) continues to arouse fear in connection with this alignment. Finally, the depiction of the fate of Babylon at God's hands (18:1–24) and of the monstrous representatives of Roman imperialism at the hands of Christ (19:20) potentially heighten the audience's fear of the God who is able to defeat such powerful temporal forces (see Aristotle, *Rhet.* 2.5.15). These visions help the audience to master the fear they would feel before Roman authorities and other representatives of the dominant culture: first, by raising the fear of God to a position of first prominence; second, by displaying the effective help

---

82. Uncompromising Christians had significant cause to fear the reactions of the powers that be. First, they were no doubt afflicted with "a feeling of powerlessness . . . evoked by the exclusion of Christians from Jewish and Gentile institutions." Morover, "fear was elicited by the denunciation of Christians before Roman authorities and by the impressions left by the traumas of Nero's persecution, the destruction of Jerusalem, the execution of Antipas, and John's banishment" (A. Collins 1984, 142–43). John does nothing to allay the fear. Instead, "fear of Roman power is evoked or intensified" (A. Collins 1984, 152–53), though not ultimately with the goal of allowing *this* fear to guide the hearers in their deliberations.

83. See Perelman and Olbrichts-Tyteca 1969, 147: "General notions and abstract schemes have hardly any effect on the imagination. . . . An audience that had remained unmoved by a general description of carnage . . . was moved to tears by a little detail concerning the death of two young men. . . . The more specific the terms, the sharper the image they conjure up, and, conversely, the more general the terms, the weaker the image." Thus Shakespeare has Marc Antony refer to the conspirators "not as those who 'killed Caesar' but as those 'whose daggers have stabbed Caesar.' The concrete term increased the sense of actuality."

that God would bring to God's allies (i.e., the audience, if they remain among "those who keep God's commandments," Rev. 14:12) against those fearsome but still-weaker enemies.

John gives equal attention to arousing confidence in connection with the behaviors and commitments he promotes. Feelings of confidence are likely to be engendered by the visions of the myriads of angels and heavenly beings, joined eventually by "every creature" in heaven, on earth, and under the earth, giving worship to God. The hearers (particularly those who are already exclusively oriented in this direction) are allowed to see that "those whose interests are the same as ours are more numerous, or stronger, or both" (Aristotle, *Rhet.* 2.5.18) than the networks of those who participate in the worship of idols. The Christians in Asia Minor whose worship practices mirror those of the angels (i.e., who worship God and the Lamb day and night, without stopping to pay homage to other gods) will encounter these heavenly beings as allies throughout the remainder of Revelation, regarding their actions as ultimately undertaken on behalf of their own deliverance and vindication. Thus as strong angels appear, making proclamations or bringing plagues and disasters upon the enemies of God and God's people, the hearers who share John's perspective (or adapt themselves quickly to it) will be awakened to the power and resources of their allies who will fight on their behalf. Such feelings of confidence (on the basis of enjoying powerful allies) will be most powerfully aroused where Christ himself acts against the hearers' enemies (see Rev. 19:11–21; 20:7–10, in the latter passage specifically defending the faithful gathered around him), as well as in the multiple assurances that God will intervene to vindicate God's own honor and that of God's witnesses, with which God's honor is inextricably linked (11:11–13; 16:5–7).[84]

Topics of confidence are especially prominent and concentrated in the description of the new Jerusalem. Aristotle had defined confidence (θαρρεῖν) as "the contrary of fear and that which gives confidence [as the contrary] of that which causes fear, so that the hope of what is salutary is accompanied by an impression that it is quite near at hand, while the things to be feared are either nonexistent or far off" (*Rhet.* 2.5.16). The last component of this definition—the removal of all that is threatening—expresses a topic prominently invoked throughout the description of the new Jerusalem.

> Death will no longer be, nor mourning nor crying nor sorrow,
>   because the former things passed away.
>
>   (Rev. 21:4)
>
> Its gates will surely never be shut during the day, for night will no longer exist. (21:25)
>   Anything unclean will by no means enter it, nor a person committing an abomination nor a liar, but only those who are written in the Lamb's book of life. (21:27)
>   Every curse[d thing] will no longer exist. (22:3)

---

84. See deSilva 1998a, 98.

"I Saw a Monster Rising Up!" 221

City gates are closed at night as a safeguard against invasion or attack in more turbulent places or periods. The bold declaration that the gates will never be shut asserts the nonexistence of any such threat, even the nonexistence of the darkness of night under the cover of which any assault might occur. The exclusion of certain groups from the city (21:27) recalls the establishment of the *pomerium* around Rome and Roman cities at a mile from the city walls, past which "no strange cults or other detestable practices" could pass so as to enter the city and introduce discordant customs (Livy, *History of Rome* 1.44).[85] New Jerusalem is a place that exists beyond threat, beyond harm, and therefore beyond fear.

Confidence is engendered not only by the remoteness of that which harms, but also by the nearness of that which supports, protects, and helps. People feel confident "if there are means of help, either great or numerous, or both" (Aristotle, *Rhet.* 2.5.17). The Deity was an especially important source of help (2.5.21). The sheltering closeness of God stands out as perhaps the most prominent feature of the new Jerusalem:

> See! The tent of God is with humanity, and God will pitch his tent with them, and they will be God's people, and God will be with them and will wipe away every tear from their eyes. (Rev. 21:3–4)
> The ones who overcome will inherit these things, and I will be God to each, and each will be a son or daughter to me. (21:7)
> And I did not see a temple in it, for the Lord God Almighty and the Lamb are its temple. . . . The glory of God illumines it, and the Lamb is its light. (21:22–23)
> The throne of God and of the Lamb will be in it, and his slaves will worship him, and they will see God's face. (22:3–4)

Through the language of association (pitching God's tent with these blessed ones), adoption (naming them God's own sons and daughters), and intimate care (restoring and comforting the blessed after their trials—indeed, the trials of the entire cosmos—are over), John paints a picture of divine presence and nurture that assures the hearers that God is "for them," as they continue now to walk for God. The immediate presence of their great Ally, so near that, at last, God's followers will see God's face, is thus established as a source of strength and support for eternity.

Confidence is further evoked as John describes the availability of other resources that promote wholeness and security (Aristotle, *Rhet.* 2.5.16). The inhabitants of new Jerusalem have access to the "water of life" (21:6; 22:1) and to the "tree of life" and its fruits (22:2), both powerful symbols of enjoying a quality of life that cannot (again) be interrupted or threatened by death. The leaves of the tree of life are specifically indicated "for the healing of the nations" (22:2). The assurance of a never-failing structure or shelter (21:7–21; 22:14–15) and food supply (22:2) also nurtures confidence in regard to this future, particularly in a setting in which many families lived from day to day or season to

---

85. Discussed in Kraybill 1996, 212.

season and lacked such assurance about their long-term enjoyment even of life's most basic necessities.

As a corollary to confidence, the vision of the new Jerusalem also appears to be designed to awaken "awe," particularly through the extensive descriptions of the city's grandeur and opulence. In contrast to Babylon as a city and seat of empire for which John felt a misplaced wonder (17:6–8), new Jerusalem is a sight worth "marveling" at. The vision of a place of security and blessedness functions to provide incentive to the hearers to maintain a "faithful" response to God in the midst of their particular challenges. The threat of exclusion from such a place, moreover, is offered as a disincentive to actions that compromise the group's witness and ethos (21:8; 22:15).[86] The arousal of confidence (and to a lesser extent, awe) supports these incentives, inviting the hearers to feel the positive emotions of being "at home" in such a place, and in such community, as the vision opens up before them.

EVOCATIONS OF EMULATION IN THE VISIONS

The glorified Christ himself specifically enjoins the Christians in Laodicea to experience the emotion of emulation ("be emulous," ζήλευε, 3:19b), directing their attention to the positive models around them (e.g., the Christians in Smyrna whose "poverty" results from behaviors and commitments that actually make them "rich" in Christ's sight), but also orienting them toward the praiseworthy models yet to be developed throughout the visions.

Emulation (ζῆλος) was an ethically positive emotional response to seeing others enjoying the fruits of their character and actions, whereby the viewer fits himself or herself to attain the same (Aristotle, *Rhet.* 2.11.1). Emulation makes people make themselves better, more virtuous, more fruitful. "Honours obtained by ancestors, kinsfolk, intimates, nation, or city make people emulous" (2.11.3), motivating them to embody more fully the virtuous commitments and behaviors that led to those honors. John will describe several privileged and honored groups throughout Revelation, each of which holds the potential to arouse emulation, drawing the hearers in turn toward embodying the same behaviors and attitudes seen in these groups. The subjects of the seven macarisms—indefinite, open classes of people lauded as μακάριος (blessed, favored, honored)[87]—arouse emulation in the hearers, moving them to hear and heed John's word (Rev. 1:3), to stay the course of faithfulness to God and Christ that leads to dying "in the Lord" and enjoying the wholesome consequences of the same (14:13), to remain alert to the coming of Christ and the need to make decisions day-by-day in view of *that* Day (16:15), and so forth.[88] The privileged 144,000 standing beside the

---

86. Kraybill 1996, 199.
87. See Hanson 1996.
88. See deSilva 1998a, 103–7.

"I Saw a Monster Rising Up!" 223

Lamb on Mount Zion (14:1–5) and the redeemed standing before the throne of God (15:2–4) will surely arouse emulation. The latter are described with the praiseworthy attribute of "overcoming" or "conquering," having risen to the challenges ranged against their faithful commitment (whether the deceit of the dragon or the coercion of the beast from the earth) and thus having proved themselves to be neither dupes nor cowards. But the most focused appeal to emulation may be the story of the Two Witnesses of Revelation 11. Looking at this episode from the vantage point of the story's effects on the audience's emotions helps to illumine its rhetorical effect and function within the whole of Revelation.

Conversation concerning the two witnesses has tended to focus on solving the problem of their identity, whether they represent Elijah and Moses redivivus, or the First and Second Testaments,[89] or some other possibility. But what if the anonymity of these witnesses is not a mystery to be solved, but a rhetorical potentiality? Adela Yarbro Collins suggests that the anonymity of the witnesses allowed them to become "a point of orientation for the hearers," who "aspired to being God's witnesses, to giving testimony about God's cause in the world. At least it is clear that John wished them so to aspire."[90] That is, the story of the witnesses, far from being a prediction of events involving two specific people (or less likely, the Scriptures), constitutes an appeal to emulation. Their namelessness invites the hearers more easily to supply their own faces to the picture.

These rhetorical effects of the story of the Two Witnesses reinforce other appeals to emulation throughout Revelation. Jesus, who is held up as a model for imitation throughout early Christian literature,[91] is characterized at the outset as

---

89. See, e.g., Mueller 2002, who defends the position taken by E. G. White 1950 (1911), 267. Like most analysts, Mueller (2002, 34) locates the significance of the number "two" in the Deuteronomic prescription that one must have two or three witnesses to build a case (Deut. 19:15). He acknowledges that "they are two prophets and prophesy" (2002, 36), which alone, in the context of the appearance of "prophets" throughout Revelation, should militate against equating them with bodies of texts rather than embodied voices. Mueller finds the alternation between singular and plural in regard to the witnesses' body/bodies (11:9), their singular "prophecy" (11:6) and "testimony" (11:7), and their singular "mouth" (11:5) to fit "the interpretation of the two witnesses as Scriptures" best (2002, 40), though in light of the general tendency in biblical Greek to use a singular noun distributively among a plural population and to move freely between singular and plural in this regard (e.g., "This people honors me with their *lips*, but their *heart* is far from me," Mark 7:6; Isa. 29:13 LXX; "They shake the head," Ps 21:8 LXX [22:7E]; "Their *throat* is an open grave, they deceive with their *tongues*; the poison of asps is under their *lips*, whose *mouth* is filled with curse and bitterness," Ps. 13:3 LXX) mitigates the significance of this observation. Moreover, even among human witnesses there must be only one message (cf. Rev. 11:6–7) in order for their witness to some event to be valid (e.g., in Susanna, where the two witnesses are found not to speak the same thing on one detail, as well as in Mark 14:57–59 in regard to Jesus' trial). Mueller's evidence consistently does not necessitate, or even render probable, the conclusion that he promotes as the "better" one.

90. A. Collins 1984, 151. Bauckham (1993a, 285) understands this story to nurture a sense of "the church's role in the final period of world history," which is "portrayed primarily by means of the image of prophetic witness." Appeals to emulation (and supporting appeals to confidence) encourage the hearers to take up this role.

91. Swartley (1996), e.g., argues that "the model of the Lamb is paradigmatic and normative for believers." The theme of *imitatio Christi* appears explicitly in numerous streams of early Christian tradition. See, perhaps most directly, Phil. 2:5–11; 1 Pet. 2:21–25; 1 John 2:6. Numerous texts on this topic are discussed in deSilva 1999c, 51–63.

"the witness, the faithful one" (ὁ μάρτυς, ὁ πιστός; 1:5), who triumphs by giving his life for God's purposes (5:9–10), with the result that he enjoys the praise and tribute of the court of heaven. Only one individual is praised by name in the seven oracles, and that is Antipas, described by the glorified Christ as "my witness, my faithful one" (ὁ μάρτυς μου ὁ πιστός μου; 2:13)—thus, as one who has followed Christ's example and achieved, like Christ, a praiseworthy remembrance.[92] John presents himself, a person privileged with supernatural encounters, as a spokesperson for "the word of God and the witness [μαρτυρία] of Jesus" (1:2, 9). John also sees the souls of those slain "on account of the word of God and the witness which they bore" first given a place of shelter under the altar of the heavenly temple (6:9), and finally a share in the reign of Christ, enthroned alongside the One whom they imitated (20:4). The seven oracles orient the audiences to look for the path to "victory," for it is "to the one who conquers" that the stunning promises throughout the seven oracles are made (τῷ νικῶντι, 2:7, 17; ὁ νικῶν, 2:11, 26; 3:5, 12, 21). Throughout Revelation, it is the power of Christlike witness that "conquers," achieving a share in that victory that brings access to eschatological, eternal honor and prestige (1:5; 5:5; 12:11; 20:4).[93]

The vision of the two witnesses provides a detailed close-up of this activity of witness as the path to overcoming, and thus as the means by which to enter into Christ's story of witnessing (to the point of death) and into the rewards of reigning in eternal life with Christ.[94] The praiseworthy model of Elijah, the prototypical prophet and witness, provides the stitch for this tapestry of witness. His story is reflected in the supernatural availability of fire to consume hostile opponents (Rev. 11:5; 2 Kgs. 1:10), the witnesses' ability to prevent rainfall (Rev. 11:6; 1 Kgs. 17:1), the witnesses' ascension upon a cloud (Rev. 11:12; 2 Kings 2:11), and the number 7,000 (Rev. 11:13; 1 Kgs. 19:18), though used here to speak of a relatively small number of people killed in the earthquake that accompanies the witnesses' ascension, resulting in the conversion of the many (whereas in the Elijah story the number was the total of the faithful remnant).[95] Echoes of the story of another celebrated prophet, Moses (most notably in the witnesses' authority to summon plagues upon the land, particularly turning water into

---

92. Aristotle observed that a speaker could arouse emulation by dwelling upon "those whom many or ourselves admire," or "those who are praised or eulogized either by poets or prose writers" (*Rhet.* 2.11.7).

93. The essence of the mimetic pattern that the audience is invited to embody, as David Barr (1984, 42) correctly discerns, is that "faithful witness brings both salvation and judgment." In this regard Rev. 12:11 is a very important text, as that hymn of triumph claims that the disciples' faithful witness (rather than simply the military might of the hosts of Michael) brings victory over Satan himself (1984, 42), paralleling the transformation of the image of the Messiah as "lion" into the "slaughtered Lamb" standing before God (1984, 41). Barr goes on to observe that "this conviction is not argued, or even stated; it is portrayed. It is enacted in story" (1984, 42), thus hitting on a very important insight into how apocalyptic rhetoric approaches logos. It creates a plausible story by means of which fundamental convictions about "the way things work (out) in God's world" are displayed and rendered credible.

94. Johns (2003, 174) rightly surmises that "the paradigms of witness and death in Rev 11 and 12 reinforce the pattern of the Lamb" as witness.

95. This last point comes from Koester 2001, 111.

blood), enhance the stature of the Christian witnesses. Moving in the power of God and ultimately effective in their witness (11:13), their career follows Christ's pattern—martyrdom on account of their testimony, the experience of disgrace before human eyes, vindication by God through resurrection and ascension in the sight of their enemies—that is consistently lauded as the path to honor in Christian culture. Their story therefore has great potential to excite emulation, emboldening the congregations in Asia Minor to faithful witness.[96]

Feelings of emulation toward these witnesses (and indeed, commitment to *emulate* them) is further supported throughout this episode by details that invoke topics of confidence, primarily the topic of divine help being available to meet the challenges confronting the witness. Christian witness is presented as something that God empowers. John describes the witnesses' activity in terms recalling the witness of Moses and Elijah, who function implicitly as a kind of "historical precedent," reinforcing the plausibility of divine empowerment supporting new witnesses. There are spiritual resources available, then, to help the witnesses carry out their commission in the face of the challenges. Moreover, even though witness is here (as elsewhere) projected as being a costly course of action entailing martyrdom and public humiliation, God's help is again evident where it counts most, in overturning both death and disgrace through resurrection and *public* vindication.[97] God provides effective help to overturn the worst that could befall the witness.

Witness is also portrayed as effective, even if its effects are not realized until after the witnesses' deaths. Revelation 11 provides the only picture of people turning toward the Living God in reverent fear, responding as the angel would call humanity to respond in 14:6–7. Such an impact is made *not* through divine judgments (9:20–21), but through obedient and empowered witness. The audience can feel confident about this course of action, then, on the basis of several topics: assured success in the endeavor, and the availability of God's help to overcome obstacles to witness on *both* sides of death.

Arousing feelings of emulation toward these two witnesses serves an additional goal. The two witnesses exercise powers reminiscent of Moses and Elijah, who in turn are the positive counterparts of Balaam and Jezebel, respectively. As the hearers are drawn into the role of these witnesses, they are strategically ranged against the "false prophets" in their midst, who seek to lead the church in a different direction from John. If the Nicolaitans are seen as successors to Balaam and the female prophet in Thyatira as "Jezebel," those who oppose them and their accommodationist message are encouraged to stand up against them in the roles and with the power of Moses and Elijah.

Because the passage has so often caused difficulties in the history of interpretation, it seems appropriate also to give some attention to Revelation 14:1–5

---

96. The importance of the theme of witness in Revelation, and the vision's assurance that witness is ultimately an effective form of resistance (not to mention a means of turning helpless victims into active contestants), is widely recognized. See Blount 2000, 399; Witherington 2003, 161; Barr 1984, 50.

97. DeSilva 1998a, 98.

here. John describes the 144,000 as a privileged group standing beside the Lamb as a foil for the group that gathers in the worship of the beast (13:4, 8, 12). The element of "privilege" is communicated in their participation in special rites in which no one else can join (perhaps akin to initiation into the mysteries in Greek culture; 14:3). They are also distinctively marked with the names of Christ and of God upon their foreheads, a seal that protects the bearers from God's punishments (14:1; cf. 7:2–8). That this seal is a desirable commodity was well established in chapters 6–9.

If emulation toward the 144,000 is roused, 14:4–5 fleshes out some qualities to embody if the hearers wish to fit themselves to attain to such privileges. The first trait has occasioned the most difficulty: "these are the ones who have not defiled themselves with women, for they are virgins" (14:4a). Does John literally recommend virginity, or at least abstinence? If so, does he do so in a misogynist way that labels women as defilements and limits the company of the 144,000 to male disciples?[98] Schüssler Fiorenza has convincingly argued that, since sexual imagery is abundant in Revelation and can generally be taken metaphorically (as in the Hebrew prophets) to denote inappropriate levels of accommodation to, or interaction with, the non-Christian society (or its religious practices), so it should be taken here as well.[99] The avoidance of defiling entanglements with "women" in the particular context of Revelation orients the emulous hearers to distance themselves from both "Jezebel," a prophet whose message legitimates accommodation, and from "Babylon," the economic, political, and religious system that has otherwise ensnared the known world.[100]

This is not a case of special pleading to avoid the misogynistic implications of the text, for even "following the Lamb wherever he goes" (14:4b) must be taken in a similarly symbolic manner, as an expression of walking after the example of Christ, maintaining his witness and obedience to God in the face of the world's hostility and rejection. The further detail that "no lie was found in their mouth" (14:5) again calls the audience's attention to the importance of speech, particularly not uttering any speech that might reinforce the deceptions perpetrated

---

98. Tina Pippin (1992, 70) reads Rev. 14:1–5 as a sign that females are excluded from the new Jerusalem, which she takes to be the "logical conclusion" of the identity of the 144,000. While the cues in the text, if taken literally, do lead to this conclusion, Pippin reads against the tendency to regard Revelation as, in fact, largely symbolic in its figurations. And John poses equal-opportunity challenges in this regard. If the image of the 144,000 ostensibly male virgins in 14:1–5 is one that tends to exclude women from picturing themselves there, the image of a bride for the very male Lamb is just as potentially exclusive for male readers (leaving aside the problem of cross-species intermarriage). The imagery of Revelation, far from simply reinscribing patriarchal values and gender roles, consistently pushes us past gender and gender roles into the symbolic meaning of its images, where women find a place among the army of (male) virgins and men find a place identified with the bride of the Lamb.

99. Schüssler Fiorenza 1985, 190–91.

100. Bauckham understands "faithful witness to the point of death" (1993a, 233) to provide the means by which disciples participate in the holy war waged by the Lamb, who has already won the decisive battle through his own "faithful witness and sacrificial death" (1993a, 234). Witness is, for John, "as active as any physical warfare and his use of holy war imagery conveys this need for active engagement in the Lamb's war" (1993a, 234).

"I Saw a Monster Rising Up!"   227

by false apostles, "false Jews," or the false prophet (second beast). Rather, those who will be privileged speak only the truth about God and about idolatrous cult, rather than the "lie" of joining in, even to pay mere lip service.

In her groundbreaking treatment of this passage, Schüssler Fiorenza advises that interpreters of Revelation need to "look first for the strategic position and textual relations of the symbols and images within the overall dramatic movement of the book. Second, we must pay attention to the explicit rhetorical 'markers' that seek to 'channel' the audience's understandings, emotions, and identifications in such a way that it is persuaded and moved to the desired action."[101] The literary context of the vision of the 144,000 is indeed key to its rhetorical function and effects. It is preceded by scenes that inspire indignation against the emperors and their supporters, as well as fear in regard to the temporal power that these figures can wield against those who refuse to participate in the religious legitimation of Roman rule (13:1–18). The audience comes to realize, however, that the same figures who are the victims of violent repression in chapter 13 also stand alongside the victorious Lamb in 14:1–5. The latter vision provides an interpretive perspective on witness and its temporal costs: what leads to marginalization in Roman Asia also confers high privilege in the court of God.

Emulation of the 144,000 is further encouraged by the depiction of the consequences of failing to withstand the beasts' coercive measures, and thus failing to stand alongside the Lamb that was slain. The fear-inspiring vision of the pain and humiliation that awaits those who bend the knee to the beast and its image, or receive its mark in place of the name of God (14:9–11), casts a positive, retrospective spotlight on the company of the 144,000 and the desirability of being "in that number." Revelation 14:1–5 thus functions in tandem with 14:12–13, another description of the characteristics of the redeemed, and the positive consequences of "keeping God's commandments and faith with Jesus" (14:12), drawing hearers toward emulation of those figures who enjoy honor and rest beyond life's contest.

CONCLUSION

Classical rhetorical theorists help us pinpoint the topics and strategies by means of which a first-century text produced within the Greco-Roman world, even a text as far removed from the worlds of Aristotle and Cicero as Revelation, potentially prompts emotional responses. These theorists help us discern what those responses would be and enable further theorizing about the ways in which those responses advance an author's rhetorical goals. John dampens any feelings of awe or gratitude toward Rome and its emperors, redirecting these responses to God and the Lamb. In their place, he evokes feelings of enmity and indignation toward Roman imperialism at its center and in its local manifestations, which in

---

101. Schüssler Fiorenza 1985, 188.

turn position his audiences to accept his summons to maintain critical distance and witness, and to avoid any behaviors that suggest support for, or toleration of, a domination system whose ideology and practices stand condemned before the Creator God. John further evokes fear in connection with being found to be in league with the enemies of God, but confidence in connection with being found to be a loyal ally of God and the Lamb, despite the heavy cost such loyalty will carry in this life. Models of powerful prophets and victorious martyrs arouse emulation in regard to a course of action that entails obloquy and marginalization in this life. In these and other ways, engaging the emotions of the hearers plays an essential role in the rhetorical strategy—and the success—of Revelation as a call to live faithful lives of dangerous witness.

Chapter 9

Appeals to Rational Argument (Logos) in Revelation
The Seven Oracles

INTRODUCTION

In 1969 Eugene Peterson offered a perceptive critique of those who approached Revelation strictly as a written text composed of a pastiche of written texts. He called attention to the "nonliterary" origins of the Revelation in John's experiences of seeing and hearing, and to the multisensory evocations throughout the text: seeing, hearing, smelling, touching (chiefly through the sensory impressions evoked by number),[1] and tasting. He sought thus to revive "the place of the imagination and the effect of sensory media" in encountering Revelation, opposing attempts to distill static theological propositions or, worse, an end-time playbook. In other words, he suggested that more attention be given to *experiencing* the book rather than seeking to derive its message as something communicable apart from the experience.

---

1. "The mass numbers provide a sensory response of victory. The effect of the numbers in the vision of chapter seven on a sensorily alive person is to extend [the] *feeling* of God's protection and victory in the face of pressing evil" (Peterson 1969, 138).

This study has sought to honor this call, beginning, as it did, by exploring the hearers' experience of entering and living for a span within the countercosmos that John's visions open up and the impact this would have on their experience of the everyday realities that surrounded them, and advancing through detailed exploration of the potential evocations of emotional responses to the experience. Interpreting so complex a work as Revelation, however, is not reducible to an either/or engagement, but always invites a broader both/and. Peterson himself offered his hermeneutical critique without intent "to minimize the place of the rational, understanding mind in reading the Apocalypse," which is also explicitly invited to engage the experience (13:18; 17:9).

Revelation stands apart from other early Christian writings collected in the New Testament in many ways, not least in the apparent lack of sustained argumentation. This impression is heightened by its position in the canon, following many instances of careful, extensive development of argumentation in the epistolary literature. Appeals to logos in Revelation tend to be overlooked in favor of its other strategies of effecting persuasion. Greg Carey, for example, writes that John's program "depends not so much on his arguments against his opponents as upon his own ability to represent them effectively. Rather than prove his case against them, he appeals to his audience's sensibilities by constructing stories and images that align his audience against the Empire and those who support it."[2] Ben Witherington similarly observes that "there is not a syllogistic logic to Revelation, but there is a narrative logic."[3]

Although these critics rightly emphasize the contributions of the narrative art (characterization, plot, and the like) to the persuasive force of Revelation, neither is it the case that Revelation completely *lacks* argumentation. John T. Kirby made a keen observation in regard to the presence of "inferential particles" in the seven oracles:

> The argument from *logos* consists basically of logical reasoning, known in the sciences as syllogism and in rhetoric as enthymeme. Enthymemes advance conclusions on the strength of premises which may or may not be explicitly formulated. Premises are often expressed in Greek by ὅτι or γάρ, conclusions by οὖν. The use of *logos* here is important because the pronouncements, though absolute, are seen not to be irrationally despotic: there is *logos*, a rationale, underlying them all.[4]

Kirby cites the use of ὅτι in 2:14; 3:8, 10, 16; γάρ in 3:2; and οὖν in 2:5, 16; and 3:19 as a sign of enthymematic-argumentative elaboration within the seven oracles.[5] Although Kirby does not enter into an analysis of the argumentation to which he draws attention, he underscores the presence of "argumentative

---

2. Carey 1999b, 163.
3. Witherington 2003, 83.
4. Kirby 1988, 202–3.
5. Kirby 1988, 206 n. 33. He suggests further within this note that ἰδού "is also sometimes tantamount to οὖν (2.22; 3.8, 9; but probably not 2.10 and 3.20, where it seems merely expletive)."

texture" within the seven oracles, the lexical invitations to the hearer to consider the rational argumentation that supports the claims, exhortations, and warnings made within these messages, and indeed throughout the visions.[6]

Though they may not carry the day in terms of this text's ability to engage and persuade an audience, John's appeals to rational argumentation merit close attention at least as a supportive element in the attainment of the same. In this study we will investigate the presence of enthymematic-argumentative reasoning, analyze how the argument works in terms of employing common topics and deductive patterns, and examine what ends such reasoning seeks to serve. An important facet of this investigation involves the assessment of the cultural premises and ideological convictions that John presumes his hearers will share and be willing to supply in order for John's logic to be persuasive.[7] In particular, we will examine appeals to logos in the seven oracles, in the visions as a whole (focusing on the three propositions in the messages of the three angels of 14:6–13), and in the seven macarisms. It is not our goal to promote Revelation as a noteworthy specimen of sustained reasoning, but to examine the presence and contributions of appeals to logos within the text, particularly enthymematic-argumentative forms of elaboration, in order that this dimension not be lost to view within the larger task of analyzing a visionary, affective text.

PRIMARY ARGUMENTATIVE STRATEGIES IN REVELATION

Revelation both gives advice and presents models of behavior. That is, it pursues both deliberative goals (seeking to shape the ongoing behavior of the hearers in specific ways in regard to specific circumstances or settings) and epideictic goals (seeking to praise and censure particular figures with the aim of reinforcing or shaping the values of the Christian groups John addresses). John presents directives (exhortations, commands, advice) in high concentration in the seven oracles, but also scattered throughout the visions (e.g., 14:7; 18:4). He also holds up models of behavior for praise (and therefore imitation) or censure (and therefore nonimitation) in the seven oracles, in the seven celebrated macarisms ("Blessed is/are the one/s who . . ."; 1:3; 14:13; 16:15; 19:9; 20:6; 22:7, 14), and throughout the visions (e.g., the 144,000 and the two witnesses). But how does

---

6. V. K. Robbins (1996a, 21–29; 1996b, 58–64, 77–89) directs attention to "argumentative texture" as an important feature of analyzing the "inner texture" of a text. The use of inferential particles does not always guarantee the presence of logical argumentation: fallacious arguments, e.g., using the word "therefore" to give the appearance of having reached a conclusion when no logical process of inference has truly been followed, were common enough to merit significant attention in Aristotle's *Art of Rhetoric* (2.24.1–10).

7. "One of the most characteristic aspects of logical argumentation is the function of unstated premises in the discourse. Identifying and articulating these premises reveals aspects of the argumentative texture in its social and cultural environment that the narrator may never state" (Robbins 1996b, 59).

John support these calls to action or declarations of praise (or censure), if at all? What is required of the hearers if they are to accept these summons to actions or ascriptions of value as "reasonable" advice and evaluations? How does the author help the hearers accept the content by providing some form of rationale or reasoned argumentation to facilitate persuasion?

In some instances John makes no appeal to logos. Persuasion would depend upon the sheer authority of the speaker. In these cases, John exemplified what George Kennedy called "radical Christian rhetoric," which exercises its power through "authoritative proclamation, not rational persuasion."[8] Such speech "does not arise out of a process of inference, but authoritatively proclaims the truth," unlike rational speech, which is "based on formally valid inference from accepted premises."[9] Thus an angel declares, "Blessed are they who have been called to the marriage feast of the Lamb" (19:9), offering no explanation concerning why such people should be considered favored. Rather, it is followed by the solemn declaration: "These are genuine words of God." It is an authoritative pronouncement, to be accepted on the weight and at the word of the speaker, not on the basis of argumentation promoting the reasonableness of the claim. The presentation of the "words of this prophecy" as a credible ecstatic-prophetic experience (one that resembles traditional and therefore accepted accounts of ecstatic experiences) facilitates the acceptance of such "radical rhetoric."

More often, however, John softens the "radical rhetoric" of his message, facilitating the hearers' acceptance by means of enthymemes and other discrete pieces of argumentation. Aristotle described an enthymeme as a statement supported by a rationale, the adding of the "why and wherefore" (*Rhet.* 2.21.2). Thus the statement "No one is truly free" becomes an enthymeme when it is joined with an explanation: "No person is truly free, for one is the slave of either wealth or fortune" (2.21.2). Enthymemes are preferred in oratory since they are less pedantic than syllogisms (and thus more appealing to the listener). A syllogism articulates all the necessary steps in deduction; an enthymeme does not state what the speaker can expect the hearer to supply (see *Rhet. Alex.* 1434a.35–37), thus subtly enlisting the hearer's partnership, in effect, in constructing and completing the argumentation.[10] Thus a syllogism might run like this:

Major (general) premise: All benefactors deserve honor;

Minor (particular) premise: Demosthenes has benefited the city;

Conclusion: Therefore, we ought to confer the honor of the wreath upon Demosthenes.

---

8. Kennedy 1984, 6–7.
9. Kennedy 1984, 6, referring to Grassi 1980, 103–4.
10. Lloyd Bitzer (1974, 149–51) calls attention to the need for "audience participation" in supplying premises from "its stock of opinion and knowledge" as the audience negotiates enthymemes. See also Conley 1984, 168–69.

The logic has force as long as speaker and hearers agree upon both the general premise learned from the experience of the social systems of beneficence and patronage and the particular premise that Demosthenes has actually done some good for the city. An enthymeme encapsulates the deductive process more economically:

Thesis/proposal: We ought to confer the honor of the wreath upon Demosthenes,

Rationale: for he has benefited our city.

Or,

We ought to confer the honor of the wreath upon Demosthenes,

for all benefactors deserve honor.

In either case, the orator assumes that the hearers can and will supply the missing link that makes the logical transference viable.

While New Testament rhetorical critics focus on Aristotle's definition of the enthymeme, David Aune has helpfully reminded them that it is not the only one. Quintilian (*Inst.* 5.10.1–3) lists five categories of enthymeme: "(1) a thought, (2) a maxim supported by a reason, (3) an inference from consequents or contraries, (4) a rhetorical syllogism, and (5) an incomplete syllogism."[11] Rhetoricians and rhetorical critics alike tend to privilege the second and fifth of these categories,[12] but the addition of "inferences from consequences" and arguments from the contrary is significant.[13] These were listed by Aristotle among the "common topics" that would provide the basic logic of an enthymeme, and that possessed their own "plausibility which they shared with the enthymemes derived from them."[14]

A second corrective introduced by Aune concerns the goal of the enthymeme, which is to convince an audience, not achieve logical certainty.[15] A formally valid syllogism built upon scientific premises need not undergird every enthymeme. All that is needed is that the logic be *probable*, not *certain*.[16] New Testament scholars seeking to reconstruct the fuller syllogisms behind an enthymeme often create syllogisms that are not formally valid and that do not belong to one of the principle formal types (categorical, hypothetical, and disjunctive).[17] This further reflects the principle that the writer merely sought to establish likelihood, since people respond to what they believe is *likely* to happen, and not only

---

11. Aune 2003, 300.
12. E.g., Corbett 1990, 60; Hurley 1988, 256; Kennedy 1984, 7.
13. Indeed, Cicero (*Topica* 55–56) and the *Rhetorica ad Herennium* (4.17.25–4.18.26) focus on the enthymeme specifically as an argument from contraries.
14. Aune 2003, 305; Ryan 1984, 48.
15. Aune 2003, 305.
16. Thus Bitzer 1974, 151; Conley 1984, 168; Ryan 1984, 55, 69–77.
17. Aune 2003, 320.

to what will *certainly* happen (if such certainty were even possible). In light of these criticisms, we will cast our net more widely than the "maxim with a rationale" or "incomplete syllogism" in our analysis of enthymemic-argumentative elaboration in Revelation, and speak of "deductions" rather than "syllogisms" undergirding this elaboration.[18]

Explicit inferential markers—"for" (γάρ), "therefore" (οὖν), "on account of this" (διότι), and the like—can point to the presence of enthymemes. However, the reader must also be attentive to the presence of enthymemes even where such inferential particles are absent. When John falls at the feet of the angel who proclaims God's "genuine words," the angel responds, "Don't do that. I am your fellow slave, and that of your brothers and sisters keeping the witness of Jesus. Worship God" (19:10; see also 22:9). Even without an explicit γάρ, the angel's statement that he is John's "fellow slave" clearly serves as a rationale for why John should heed his command not to prostrate himself. Similarly, Jesus' affirmation, "See! I am coming quickly!" precedes the sixth macarism, which claims "the person who keeps the words of the prophecy of this book" to be "blessed" or "divinely favored" (22:7). These again are not simply two unrelated assertions standing side by side. Jesus' imminent return provides the grounds for the "blessedness," the favored or privileged status, of the person who walks in line with Revelation's message. It is simply a more vivid way of saying, "Blessed is the person who keeps the words of the prophecy of this book, *for* I am coming quickly."[19]

Once such argumentative steps have been identified, the analyst needs to determine what makes the argument work, or perhaps better, what the audience would be expected to know and to supply for the argument to work. In regard to Revelation, the premises needing to be supplied and the knowledge that is presupposed often belong to the special knowledge transmitted within Jewish and Christian culture. These faith communities would accept many things as valid foundational premises for argumentation that would be hotly disputed (or even ridiculed) outside these groups. It remains "insider" logic, not likely to persuade outsiders who would not, for example, share in the foundational conviction that Christ will return with authority to judge, punish, and reward. As a result, our aim is not to analyze the argumentation in Revelation in terms of "valid" or "invalid" syllogisms. Rather, our interest is to uncover the argumentation as fully as possible, and to inquire into what the hearers must accept as true in order to engage this argumentation as "rational" discourse within the worldview and ethos into which the Christian audiences were socialized.

---

18. Aune 2003, 309, 313.

19. Rev. 1:3, the opening macarism of the book, does present just such an enthymeme, including the inferential particle γάρ: "*Blessed* is the one reading aloud and *the ones* hearing the words of the prophecy *and keeping the things written therein*, for [γάρ] the time is near"). Aristotle provided several examples of enthymemes in which the rationale is given subtly or implicitly, e.g., as an adverbial phrase, rather than more pedantically with explicit attention being called to the logical connections through the use of inferential particles (*Rhet.* 2.21.6).

Besides radical rhetoric and basic argumentation, John also develops what Witherington calls "narrative logic."[20] The visions as a whole provide a vivid, narrative depiction of what proves to be advantageous or productive of honor in the future.[21] This depiction is supported, in turn, by extensive interweaving of texts and paradigms from the Jewish Scriptures, evoking historical precedents that render John's projection of the future and its consequences more credible, and by evocations of Old Testament promises and expectations, accepted as reliable because they are part of the received tradition (that is, divinely authorized), the fulfillment of which is now being depicted. Because this is such an important and extensive facet of John's appeal to logos, it will be treated in its own chapter.

ARGUMENTATION IN THE SEVEN ORACLES

The Oracle to Ephesus

Each oracle begins with the speaker's self-identification, chiefly using phrases drawn from the initial, awe-inspiring vision of the glorified Lord (1:12–20), strategically selected to undergird some feature of the oracle itself. The briefer echoes of that initial vision serve as economical reminders of the power and stature of the explicated speaker, establishing his ethos: his authority to speak and the importance of giving him an attentive hearing. This element is followed here by a substantial catalog of the church's commendable achievements. That Christ recognizes and gives voice to these achievements nurtures, as we have seen, feelings of friendship and openness toward the speaker, which further serves the goals of ethos, fostering receptivity and attentiveness from an audience convinced of the speaker's goodwill. Up to this point, rational argumentation is not necessary or even appropriate in each miniature oracular "oration."

This changes, however, as the speaker comes to the point at issue, the circumstances or conditions that need to be addressed. Classical rhetoricians used the term *stasis*, particularly in regard to forensic rhetoric, to label the principal "sticking point" of a speech, the relevant question to be decided. There were four kinds of forensic stases: Did an action actually occur? If it did, was it truly illegal? If it was illegal, was it truly *wrong* under the circumstances? Does this court really have the jurisdiction to decide? (*Rhet. Her.* 1.10.18–1.15.25). I use the term here as a helpful designation for the sticking point of a deliberative speech: the identification of the challenges or problem in the present situation requiring adoption of a course of action by the assembly.

---

20. Witherington 2003, 83.
21. "Thus, the visions also give deeper reasons for the admonitions of the seven letters. Only from the visionary part does it become clear why the readers should 'leave Babylon' (Rev 18:4)," namely, because of the pervasiveness of "idolatrous veneration" of empire and the eternal consequences of the same (Frey 2006, 246).

In the oracle to the Ephesian Christians, the stasis is succinctly identified: "I have against you that you have forsaken your first love" (Rev. 2:4). This is followed by statements that employ inferential conjunctions inviting the hearers to engage this section as rational discourse:

Premise (identification of stasis): "You have forsaken your first love." (2:4)

Conclusion (in the form of an exhortation): "Remember, therefore (οὖν), whence you have fallen and repent and do the first works." (2:5a)

Argument from the contrary, using topic of the consequences: "But if not (εἰ δὲ μή), I am coming to you, and I will remove your lampstand from its place, unless you repent." (2:5b)

The speaker offers no evidence for the premise in the way of a list of specific acts or behaviors that reveal this alleged failure of love.[22] The audience is expected to accept the diagnosis on the basis of the speaker's authority (accepting that the glorified Christ indeed addresses them) together with, perhaps, that "intuitive response to the message" that acknowledges the truth of the accusation in their own experience.[23] This is more radical than one often finds in the Hebrew prophets, who facilitate such perception and acknowledgment by naming specific examples of abuse observable in the hearers' context.

The statement "I have this against you" is a major component of the persuasive force of this oracle, as indeed in the oracles to Pergamum, Thyatira, Sardis, and Laodicea. The foundational premise is this: "Whatever Christ does not like about you is disadvantageous or dangerous for you." Or in more Pauline terms: "Pleasing Christ is of paramount importance" (see 2 Cor. 5:9). John's rationale is ultimately the same as Paul's in this matter: "We must all appear before Christ's judgment seat," to receive due recompense for the works performed while in the body, whether good or evil (2 Cor. 5:10). John brought this rationale into focus with his announcement of Christ's coming in glory and power to the detriment of many (Rev. 1:7), as well as through the impressive portrait

---

22. Because of this lack of examples or further explication, scholars have not been able to come to agreement concerning the precise import of this falling off of love. Some suggest that love for God or for Christ is at issue. Prigent (1988, 42), for example, points to Jer. 2:2 as a precedent for a prophetic word lamenting the cooling of the people's love for their God. Beale (1999, 230), who also prefers love for Christ here, further specifies this failure of love as a flagging zeal for witness to outsiders as an expression of their love for Christ. Loisy (1923, 89) and Lohse (1988a, 25) emphasize the horizontal dimension of love summed up in the "second greatest commandment" of love toward neighbor or the "new commandment" promoting "Bruderliebe," love among the Christian community. Lohse cites the prediction in Matt. 24:12 that "the love of many will grow cold" as a parallel, though there the direction of this love is also unspecified. Murphy (1998, 115–16) specifies this love toward the neighbor even further, suggesting that the Ephesians have, in their zeal to detect and guard against heresy, failed to maintain "a loving attitude toward the wayward." Hemer (1986, 41) prefers not to separate love for God and neighbor here, and Aune (1997) perhaps shows the most wisdom in not attempting to further specify what the Seer left unspecified.

23. The phrase is borrowed from Kennedy's description of "sacred language," which he calls, in the Christian context, "radical Christian rhetoric" (1984, 6–7).

drawn of the power and stature of this figure (1:12–20). The portrayals of judgment at Christ's coming (14:14–20; 19:11–20:15) and the pervasive connection between one's eternal fate and Christ's pleasure or displeasure in one's deeds (e.g., Rev. 14:9–11) all reinforce this shared Christian cultural knowledge about Christ's return and Christ's activity as judge. This still belongs more to the realm of "radical rhetoric" (the authoritative pronouncement) than rational argumentation, though it is notably well rooted in shared early Christian premises about the nature of the world.

Further, if they are to accept the conclusion as a logical inference from the premise, the hearers would have to agree that the diminution of expressions of love is indeed a bad thing in need of remedy. Hence, they would need to supply the premise "Love must be maintained" or "A diminution of expressions of love among Christians is disgraceful or disadvantageous." John can reasonably expect them to supply this premise, however, since love is commended as an essential virtue, the sine qua non of discipleship, within *many* streams of Christian culture.[24] The statement would have the same rhetorical effect as saying to an assembly of rich elites, "You have forgotten how to be generous." It questions their embodiment of a cardinal virtue universally and consistently upheld as valuable within that culture. John facilitates the supplying of this premise, moreover, by strategic word choices: "forsaken" and "whence you have fallen" color the lack of love in a particularly negative way, presenting it as a current lack that needs to be filled before the church will again enjoy the stature it once had in Christ's eyes and now, since they have overheard this diagnosis, in the other communities' estimation.

The importance of the authority and power of Christ, and the gravity of displeasing this figure, emerge again in the argument from the contrary course of action that supports the conclusion and completes this cycle of argument.

Argument from the contrary: Failure to resuscitate the virtue of love in your engagements will lead to disadvantage. (Rev. 2:5c)

Conclusion: "Remember, therefore, whence you have fallen and . . . do the former works." (2:5a)

The specific disadvantage is supplied by a personal threat: Christ, already depicted as walking in the midst of the churches, will visit them in judgment to remove their presence from their locale.[25] The seriousness of these consequences functions as a topic of amplification, showing that the matter is indeed sufficiently grave to merit the hearers' immediate attention and positive response.

24. See, e.g., Mark 12:28–34; John 13:31–35; 15:12–14; Rom. 13:8–10; 1 Cor. 13; Gal. 5:13–14; Eph. 5:1–2; Heb. 13:1; Jas. 2:8; 1 Pet. 1:22; 2:17; 3:8; 1 John 3:11–18.

25. Commentators from English, French, and German scholarly traditions (Aune 1997, 147; Murphy 1998, 116; Loisy 1923, 90; Prigent 1988, 42; Lohse 1988a, 25) agree that "removal" here denotes the dissolution of the church as a viable presence in Ephesus, and not some milder consequence.

The "reasonableness" of these arguments and their persuasive force depend on the hearers' willingness to accept that Christ will indeed intervene in their community's story at some future coming, potentially to punish them for failing to heed his injunctions to make themselves fully pleasing in his sight. Similarly, the promise concluding the oracle adds incentive to the Christians in Ephesus to heed the exhortation, but not on the basis of rational argumentation concerning how "doing the former works" would lead to "eating from the tree of life" (2:7). Rather, the latter is offered as a future gift (δώσω) by the One who is presumed to possess the power and authority to supply access to this gift, simply because it pleases this One to do so for those who respond positively to his exhortation.

For both the disincentive (presented in the argument from the contrary) and incentive to be effective, the hearers must accept that the glorified Christ is indeed the originator of this message, and that he has the ability to follow through with both threat and promise. John facilitates this acceptance by conforming the oracles to the diction of otherwise known Jesus sayings. Most obvious in this regard is the signature saying that appears toward the end of all seven oracles, offering internal, "stylistic" corroboration for the attentive hearer, as Jesus was remembered to have closed parables with similar words:

> Let the one who has an ear listen! [ὁ ἔχων οὖς ἀκουσάτω] (Rev. 2:7, 11, 17, 29; 3:6, 13, 22)
> Let the one who has ears keep listening! [ὁ ἔχων ὦτα ἀκούειν ἀκουέτω] (Matt. 11:15; 13:9, 43).[26]

Similarly, the oracle to Ephesus, together with the remaining oracles, echoes Jesus traditions at several key points: "Repent!" (μετανόησον, Rev. 2:5, 16; 3:3, 19; μετανοεῖτε, Matt. 4:17); "unless you/they repent" (ἐὰν μὴ μετανοήσῃς, Rev. 2:5; ἐὰν μὴ μετανοήσωσιν, 2:22; ἐὰν μὴ μετανοῆτε, Luke 13:3, 5); "you kept my word" (Rev. 3:8, 10; cf. John 8:51, "if you keep my word"); "I will confess his name before my Father and before his angels" (Rev. 3:5; Matt. 10:32); "be watchful" (γίνου γρηγορῶν, Rev. 3:2; γρηγορεῖτε, Matt. 24:42; 25:13; Mark 13:35, 37). The "idiom" of the glorified Christ strategically resembles the idiom of the sayings Jesus was remembered to have spoken while present in the flesh.[27]

---

26. Aune (1997, 150) compiles this impressive list of parallel expressions in the Jesus tradition: Mark 4:9, 23; Matt. 11:15; 13:9, 43; Luke 8:8; 14:35; *Gos. Thom.* 8, 21, 24, 63, 65, 96; and also as variant readings in Mark 7:16; Matt. 25:29; Luke 12:21; 13:9; 21:4.

27. See also the conclusions in Aune 1997, 264–65 and Vos 1965, 224. The latter argues that the words spoken by early Christian prophets in the name of Jesus did not become part of the body of known sayings attributed to the earthly ministry of Jesus; rather, a prophet like John used the language of Jesus sayings, whether known through oral tradition or in written form, as a means of giving expression to his prophecy in the name of the risen Lord, authenticating "the written presentation of his own revelatory encounter with the exalted Jesus" (Aune 1997, 265), though Aune would caution against drawing the conclusion that "these allusions were primarily the result of a fully conscious literary artifice."

The Oracle to Smyrna

No inferential particles or conjunctions occur within the oracle to Smyrna. Nevertheless, there is a clear deliberative stasis. The glorified Christ wants the Christians to choose a particular course of action in regard to imminently forthcoming circumstances.

Exhortation: "Do not fear what you are about to suffer." (Rev. 2:10a)

Case: "The devil is about to throw some of you into prison in order that you may be tested, and you will have tribulation during ten days." (2:10b)

Restatement of exhortation: "Be faithful to the point of death." (2:10c)

Argument from the consequences: "And I will give you the crown of life." (2:10d)

While the explicit argumentation is slight, the author has woven in material that provides substantial support for both the picture of future circumstances and the reasonableness of the course of action promoted (as opposed to the course of "making peace with one's adversary quickly" by finding a mode of behavior that would diminish tension between the Christian congregation and outside parties).

First, Christ's commendation of the congregation (2:9) details several sources of trouble for the congregation, as well as previous and present experiences of marginalization, providing a reasonable basis for the prediction (2:10) that functions as the focal "case." The Christians experience material poverty (πτωχεία), other (?) unspecified hardship (θλίψις), as well as verbal abuse (βλασφημία) by members of the closely related synagogue. The present experience, then, of marginalization makes the prediction of heightened marginalization more credible since, "as a rule, the future resembles the past" (Aristotle, *Rhet.* 2.20.8). Examination of the past (or the present) makes it possible credibly to "divine the future" (1.9.40) since similar causes and conditions could be expected to spawn similar effects. The glorified Christ is simply suggesting that matters will go from bad to worse, not that the congregation will experience a reversal from prosperity to penury, a claim that might require substantially more evidence.

Second, the speaker offers an interpretation of the forthcoming adverse conditions that helps enable steadfast endurance. The time of imprisonment is a time of "testing," an opportunity to demonstrate endurance in virtue. The speaker introduces a readily recognizable topic of "courage" (enduring what is fearsome for the sake of reward, or because is it ignoble not to endure), which in turn is a standard topic in deliberation (representing "the right," a subtopic of "advantage" in the *Rhetorica ad Herennium*; cf. *Rhet. Her.* 3.3.5). It therefore embeds a rationale for the exhortation not to fear, but rather to endure these trials:

Exhortation: "Do not fear what you are about to suffer." (Rev. 2:10a)

Embedded rationale: "For it is an opportunity to prove your virtuous character and commitment, and to reap the rewards of loyalty toward me." (2:10b)

The explicit argumentation is drawn primarily from the consequences: if the Christians endure the coming trials, even to the point of death, the consequences will still be advantageous to them: they will receive "the crown of life" (2:10b).[28] What potentially inclines the hearer to accept this argument from the consequences as sound? The author had earlier invoked Jesus' own example ("he who was dead and came to life," 2:8) as a kind of historical precedent that provides evidence for the reasonableness of the course urged and the credibility of the incentive offered. Just as Christ bore witness in the face of opposition, remained faithful unto death, and was rewarded with an unquenchable life beyond death, so the disciple who bears witness in the face of opposition, even unto death, can be assured of the same reward. The *imitatio Christi* was a quintessential presupposition within early Christian discourse.

The concluding promise posits a second consequence motivating compliance with the exhortation: the assurance of not being "harmed by the second death" (2:11). The one who overcomes, who successfully endures the "test" of forthcoming anti-Christian actions, will escape an even greater danger by means of heeding Christ's advice. This additional argument from the consequences employs the topic of relative expediency: it is better to endure a temporary hardship than one of longer duration and greater severity.

The effectiveness of these arguments depends upon the hearers' prior conviction that disciples are called to participate, by imitation, in Christ's example of attaining the resurrected life through obedience to the point of death, and further, that divine justice is far more to be feared than human hostility. The first conviction is so basic to early Christian discourse that one could hardly join and remain in the community without embracing it (Mark 8:34–35; Rom. 6:1–11; Phil. 3:10–11; 2 Tim. 2:11–12; Heb. 12:2; 1 Pet. 1:11; 2:21), and the second is common to (and prominent within) both Jewish and Christian discourse (see 2 Macc. 6–7; 4 Macc. 5–13; Matt. 10:28 par.; Acts 5:29).

---

28. The speaker foresees the hardships of imprisonment leading to death, not merely indicating the discomfort of being incarcerated for a short while and then released. Imprisonment was not a judicial punishment, but was used to detain someone before a trial, "as a means of coercion to compel obedience to an order issued by a magistrate," or a place of detention until execution could be carried out (Aune 1997, 166). Aune suggests that detention before execution is in view, given the precedent of Antipas and John's anticipation of further martyrdoms (1997, 176). This also clarifies how enduring the test of brief imprisonment (until execution!) entails remaining "faithful until death" and leads to receiving the wreath or crown of life. The wreath is a frequent image for postmortem reward in contemporary Jewish and Christian literature. See 4 Macc. 17:15; 1 Cor. 9:25; 2 Tim. 4:8; Jas. 1:12; 1 Pet. 5:4.

The Oracle to Pergamum

The point of deliberation in Pergamum concerns the presence of "some holding to the teaching of the Nicolaitans." The claim that their presence is disadvantageous to the congregation, and therefore requires action in the form of "repenting" of the tolerant attitude that allows this group to operate there, is supported by the introduction of a historical precedent. This precedent is advanced as an argument from a comparable situation (οὕτως, ὁμοίως, Rev. 2:15) from which conclusions about the present situation can be reliably derived:

> Historical precedent: "Balaam . . . tried to teach Balak to throw a stumbling block before the sons of Israel, to eat food offered to idols and to fornicate." (2:14)
>
> Case: "In this way you also have some who hold the teaching of the Nicolaitans [who are teaching] likewise." (2:15)
>
> Result: "Repent, therefore." (2:16a)
>
> Consequences of contrary course: "But if not, I am coming to you quickly, and I will make war against them by means of the sword of my mouth." (2:16b)

The comparison with Balaam suggests that the Nicolaitans' teaching is misleading (as a σκάνδαλον, it "trips up" those who receive it) and exposes the congregation to danger (Balaam's success resulted in a plague striking the congregation of Israel, in which "many died"; Num. 25:1–9). The topic at work is that similar causes have similar effects. If Balaam's teaching (involving the seduction of the Israelites, with the result that the latter joined in the worship of the gods of the Midianites) resulted in disaster for the congregation of Israel, the continuing presence of the Nicolaitans will also lead to inexpedient consequences.

The underlying argumentation could be expressed more deductively, transforming the single historical precedent (which builds a case for *probability*) into a universal premise that would likely be accepted within the world construction nurtured in both synagogue and church:

> Rule: All who teach God's people to compromise their allegiance to God and God's commandments lead their followers into danger. (Rev. 2:13–14)
>
> Case: The Nicolaitans teach God's people to compromise in regard to the principal prohibitions of idolatry and worshiping other gods. (2:14)
>
> Result: The Nicolaitans lead their followers into danger (and thus the congregation acts reasonably in distancing themselves from this group). (2:14–15)

For the argument to be effective, the hearers need to be able to perceive and validate the connection between the Nicolaitans' practice and the teaching of Balaam. If, for example, the Nicolaitans are *not* in fact advocating making room for occasional participation in an idolatrous ritual or ingestion of food sacrificed to idols, it is difficult to see how linking the Nicolaitans with Balaam would have any persuasive force. The visions of Revelation will amply illustrate the "rule" given above, as idolaters in general, and those involved in the worship of the image of the beast in particular, are seen to come to a pass far more dire than the plague that swept through the congregation of Israel.

The argument from the contrary course (the option of *not* repenting, 2:16b) utilizes the topic of the consequences to dissuade the hearers from that option. This argument again builds on the fundamental conviction within Christian culture that Christ will indeed intervene in the community's story at some future "coming," potentially to punish them for their failure to heed his injunctions to make themselves fully pleasing in his sight. John utilizes traditional language that recalls the power of God's own speech (the "word" that leaps forward like a warrior brandishing a sharp sword; Wis. 18:14–16) and traditions that attribute effective speech to the Messiah (such that his speech consumes the enemies of his people like fire; see *4 Ezra* 13:9–11, 27–28, 37–38) to render the image more plausible.

As is typical in these oracles, the speaker makes no explicit argumentative connection between the opening commendation of the church and the argumentation supporting the proposed course of action. The qualities that receive praise here (withstanding hostility from the surrounding, demonic society rather than seeking means of accommodation; 2:13), however, are contrary to those exhibited and promoted by the Nicolaitans (accommodating on the point of participation in social settings involving food sacrificed to idols). The speaker raises a contradiction in behavior: costly resistance on the one hand and toleration of accommodation on the other. The former is praised while the latter is censured, further underscoring the contradiction and supporting the rejection of the Nicolaitans' influence.[29] Aristotle's catalog of common topics for framing enthymemes includes two topics involving the consideration of the contrary (*Rhet.* 2.23.1, 19), the second of which underscores contradictions in behavior. John provides the material needed for the hearer to perceive the contradiction, and to formulate implicitly an enthymeme that could be stated explicitly thus: "If it seemed good to you to endure hardship for the sake of your commitment to discipleship, with Antipas even enduring to the point of death, how can you now after such investment and single-mindedness make room for teachers of compromise?"

---

29. Antipas is cited as an example of the praiseworthy courage of the whole community, "the model Christian, the one who has already done what all other Christians must be prepared to do" (Murphy 1998, 130; see also Loisy 1923, 96).

The Oracle to Thyatira

The point at issue in Thyatira, as in Pergamum, concerns the presence of a teacher whose influence and practices do not align with the seer's vision of unbroken monolatry: "You tolerate the woman Jezebel, who calls herself a prophetess and is teaching and misleading my slaves to commit fornication and eat foods sacrificed to idols" (2:20). This statement of the issue includes a subtle use of a rhetorical species called "investigation." The *Rhetorica ad Alexandrum* lists this alongside the three major genres of oratory as one that can be used independently or as an ancillary tool in other species of oratory. Investigation is "the exhibition of certain intentions or actions or words as inconsistent with one another or with the rest of someone's conduct" (1427b.12–15). Here the speaker calls Jezebel's claim to the status of "prophet" into question on the basis of an inconsistency between her work and the traditional understanding of the prophet's vocation. How can she be a prophet, as she claims, when she leads people to do what the true prophets (e.g., Elijah, who stood up for the uncompromising worship of the One God against the Baal-worship led by the historical Jezebel and her priests) opposed? In leading her followers to "eat foods sacrificed to idols," she moves more closely in line with the false prophets, who are to be expunged from the congregation (Deut. 13:1–5).[30]

Rather than introduce direct exhortation and supporting argumentation concerning how the congregation should respond, the speaker provides a brief narrative explaining why Christ has "tolerated" her (the very thing the Thyatiran Christians are *not* to do) up to this point, using a familiar topic of both Jewish-Christian and Greco-Roman discourse: Divine vengeance delays to make room for repentance and emendation of life.[31] "Jezebel," however, has not made good use of the delay, which now nears its end. The exhortation that follows in regard to this issue is indirect: Christ announces the consequences that will follow "unless they repent of [their association with] her works" (2:22). Those who have associated themselves with Jezebel and who hear this oracle would readily construct the following:

---

30. Aune (1995, 204) cites a close parallel from the writings of Philo, suggesting that the phenomenon of contemporary prophets counseling accommodation was not an exclusively Christian problem: "If anyone cloaking himself under the name and guise of a prophet and claiming to be possessed by inspiration lead us on to the worship of the gods *recognized in the different cities*, we ought not to listen to him and be deceived by the name of 'prophet.' For such a one is no prophet, but an imposter, since his oracles and pronouncements are falsehoods invented by himself" (Philo, *Spec. Laws.* 1.315–317, emphasis added). The italicized phrase underscores Philo's own recontextualization of the situation envisioned in Deut. 13:1–5, as he now addresses Jewish communities trying to thrive in cities whose citizens find the Jews' refusal to worship the cities' gods to present a stumbling block to the Judeans' enfranchisement there. This in turn provides the motivation for contemporary Jewish "prophets" to teach their fellow Jews to make some room for the worship of the same for the sake of acceptance.

31. See Wis. 12:8–10, 18; Rom. 2:4; 2 Pet. 3:8–9; Plutarch, "On the Delays of Divine Vengeance" (*Mor.* 548–68), 5–6, 9.

Exhortation: Repent of her works, therefore. (2:21)

Consequences of contrary course: If you will not repent, I will throw you, who have committed adultery with her, into great tribulation. (2:22)

These consequences, when they eventuate, will increase Christ's prestige among the churches (2:23), even as the plagues upon Egypt increased the prestige of the God of the Hebrews ("And all the Egyptians will know that I am the LORD"; Exod. 7:4–5; 14:4, 18). This statement functions as a topic of amplification in regard to the implicit call to dissociation from Jezebel: the spread of the report of their fate, implicitly calling to mind the fearsome precedent of God's visitations upon Egypt as an analogous situation, signals its severity.

Revelation 2:23 also affirms, appropriately at the midpoint of these oracles, a foundational conviction undergirding all seven: Christ has an infallible ability to see both what we show and what we hide, even from ourselves (as is explicitly said to be the case among Laodicean Christians; 3:17). This superior insight gives his words authority beyond the hearers' potential objections, since the latter are based on inferior self-knowledge. The hearers are further reminded that Christ "will give to each according to each one's own works" on the basis of this knowledge, which he is graciously sharing with each congregation before his intervention, thus reintroducing the foundational premise: "Pleasing Christ is of utmost importance," or "Everything that displeases Christ jeopardizes safety and honor." John's use here of traditional language clearly reminiscent of Jeremiah 17:10 supports the claim made on behalf of Christ's abilities, assuming that the hearers will consent that what was predicated of God in the Hebrew Scriptures can also be predicated of God's Anointed.[32]

For the first time in one of these oracles, there is a shift away from the problematic back to the positive elements in the situation (Rev. 2:24–25).

Counterstasis: You, the remainder of the congregation, do not hold to this teaching. (2:24ab)

Consequences: On you I lay no further burden, (2:24c)

Exhortation: except to hold on to what you have until I come. (2:25)

The threat and implicit exhortation of 2:22–23 do not apply to this "remainder," the disciples in Thyatira who have not followed the teaching of Jezebel (colorfully labeled the "deep things of Satan"), and who have only to persevere in their course. These disciples stand approved before him who "searches minds and hearts," lacking nothing that would make them fall short of the reward that

---

32. Aune 1997, 206–207. Only in Jer. 17:10 are the ideas of God "trying the heart and mind" and "giving to each according to each one's works" joined, though the ideas appear individually in many other texts from the Hebrew Scriptures.

Christ promises for approved deeds. Although overtly affirming those who have not become Jezebel's partisans, this shift of focus has a strategic impact on those from Jezebel's circle who "overhear" this oracle. Christ's positive evaluation of these others, and his suggestion that they enjoy a secure position in regard to Christ's forthcoming inspection and judgment, potentially arouses feelings of emulation, disposing Jezebel's partisans more strongly toward a change of course (as we saw in chapter 7). Christ's "coming" remains a fundamental premise for the argumentation as a whole, both as the threat that looms over Jezebel's partners and children (2:22–23) and as the promise of reward (2:23b) to be conferred to those who hold fast till Christ comes (2:25).

The concluding promise to the one who overcomes the challenges to faithful discipleship strikingly applies *messianic* texts (chiefly Ps. 2:8–9) to the destiny of the victorious believers (Rev. 2:26–27). The speaker offers a historical precedent in support: the disciple will receive authority over the nations "as [ὡς] I also received from my Father" (2:28a). The unexpressed premise that the audience would be expected to supply is, once again, that Jesus' career (faithful obedience, even involving suffering and death, leading to vindication and elevation in God's presence) is the template for the disciples' career (as Jesus' followers). The assumption of this foundational premise was already evident in the oracle to Smyrna and will appear again in the oracle to Laodicea.

The Oracle to Sardis

Argumentative texture is most fully developed in the oracle to the congregation in Sardis, even though the identification of the challenge to be addressed (the stasis) remains the most opaque to those outside the situation.

Stasis: "You have a name [= a reputation] that you live, and you are dead." (3:1cd)

Conclusion (in the form of an exhortation): "Be vigilant and strengthen the things that remain and are about to die," (3:2a)

Rationale: "for [γάρ] I have not found your works complete before my God." (3:2b)

Restatement of conclusion (in the form of an exhortation): "Remember, therefore [οὖν], how you received and heard, and keep [it] and repent." (3:3a)

Consequences of contrary course: "If then [ἐὰν οὖν] you are not vigilant, I will come as a thief, and you will certainly not know in what hour I come upon you." (3:3b)

The basic pattern (stasis, conclusion in the form of exhortation, argument from the consequences of the contrary course) closely resembles the argumentation in the oracle to Ephesus (2:4–5). Here, however, the speaker does not use the familiar phrase "I have this against you" to signal that the disparity between reputation and reality is a deficit requiring attention; instead, he expects the audience immediately to recognize and accept it as such. Furthermore, the speaker offers no evidence for this startling claim, no particulars in the congregation's behavior or attitude that betray a lack of "life." Such particulars might have helped the congregation acknowledge the accuracy of the point at issue, directing it to facets of their own experience that they might recognize as problematic. As it is, the speaker expects the congregation to accept the diagnosis and to sift through their own experience to discover what is lifeless about their witness and work as well as to determine where to begin to revivify their congregation and validate their endangered reputation. In other words, this oracle begins strongly in the realm of "radical Christian rhetoric," relying on the authority of the speaker and intuitive confirmation of the message.[33]

The exhortation is supported formally by a rationale, but the force of the rationale depends not on a logical commonplace so much as the speaker's opinion that the "works" of the congregation are deficient. John continues to presume that the hearers will share the conviction that Christ has superior insight into the churches' condition than the members do themselves (cf. 2:23), that Christ's is indeed the voice that addresses them, and that Christ's opinion of a congregation or individual, whether approving or disapproving, is in itself sufficiently weighty to require corrective action because of the long-lasting consequences Christ's opinion carries.

The argument from the consequences of the contrary course of action repeats the verb "be vigilant" (γίνου γρηγορῶν, 3:2; γρηγορήσῃς, 3:3), suggesting that the second exhortation is an elaboration of the first one, explicating (though still not precisely enough for outsiders) what "vigilance" and "strengthening what remains" means in their situation—a return to a more faithful, well-aligned response to the message they received in the beginning. As in the oracles to Ephesus, Pergamum, and Thyatira, the argument from the contrary course names consequences that will follow as the direct result of Christ's intervention in the affairs of the congregation, coming upon them unexpectedly "as a thief" (3:3). The speaker does not use argumentative topics common to deliberation both outside and within Christian culture, such as the topic of "honor": "If you will not be vigilant, the emptiness of your reputation will become known to others and you will be put to shame." Rather, the discourse remains firmly grounded upon distinctively Christian premises (Christ exists in the realm beyond death and can intervene in the stories of his churches, whether for encouragement or judgment).[34] As in the oracle to Ephesus, the glorified Christ speaks in the dis-

---

33. Kennedy 1984, 7.

34. Prigent (1988, 63) suggests that the command to "be vigilant" would evoke the larger matrix of Christian apocalyptic expectation, an observation that is immediately confirmed in 3:3b.

tinctive idiom of the historical Jesus, facilitating the hearers' acceptance of the words as those of their Lord.[35]

As in the oracle to Thyatira, the speaker gives attention to another, positive aspect of the situation:

Counterstasis: "You have a few names in Sardis which did not soil their garments." (3:4a)

Consequences: "They will walk with me in white," (3:4b)

Rationale: "because [ὅτι] they are worthy." (3:4c)

Like "the rest" in Thyatira (2:24), this group provides a positive model within the situation that may rouse the others to emulation (see chapter 7). The repetition of "name" (ὄνομα, 3:1; ὀνόματα, 3:4) communicates implicitly that the fundamental problem articulated in the stasis (the false reputation, the lack of a genuine name) does not apply to this select group and can be reversed for any who heed the exhortation and follow their example.

The promise attached to this oracle (3:5) aligns closely with the stasis, functioning as an argument from the consequences of heeding the exhortation to "be vigilant" and thus to return to walking solidly in line with the foundations laid earlier in the church's history: "Whoever overcomes will *in this manner* be clad in white garments," making explicit now the function of 3:4 as a positive example to be imitated: "I will certainly not scratch out that person's name from the book of life, and I will confess that one's name before my Father and before his angels." Once again, the repetition of "name" (ὄνομα, 3:1, 5) suggests that what is undesirable in the situation (the stasis, the challenge to be addressed by deliberation and action) will be adequately resolved by following the counsel given in the oracle. It employs a topic of advantage, here the securing of lasting honor and a repaired reputation when Christ bears positive witness to their "name," owning them as his own before the throne of God, as a means of promoting the recommended course of action.

The Oracle to Philadelphia

Analysis of the opening steps of argumentation in this oracle is complicated by lack of clarity concerning the relationship of the first four components (3:8–9):

---

35. Rev. 3:2–3 particularly recalls Jesus' command to his disciples to "watch" or "be vigilant" (γρηγορεῖτε, Matt. 24:42; Mark 13:35, 37), the affirmation that "you do not know on what day" Christ will come (Matt. 24:42; Rev. 3:3, "what hour"), and the analogy of the thief breaking in upon a householder (Matt. 24:43; cf. 1 Thess. 5:2). Aune (1997, 227) points out that "only in Rev 3:3 and 16:15 is the thief identified with Christ." Resonances with sayings attributed to Jesus continue in Rev. 3:5 (cf. Matt. 10:28; Luke 12:8).

Component 1: "I know your works." (3:8a)

Component 2: "See! I have put in front of you an opened door, which no one is able to close," (3:8b)

Component 3: "because/that [ὅτι] you have little power and you kept my word and you did not deny my name." (3:8c–e)

Component 4: "See! I will grant that some from the synagogue of Satan—the ones claiming themselves to be Jews, and they are not but they are lying—I will make them so that they come and prostrate themselves before your feet and know that I have loved you. (3:9)

Commentators have proposed several different readings. In the first reading scenario, the second component is a parenthetical interjection, with the result that the third component provides the elaboration of the congregation's "works" (with ὅτι being read as "that").[36] In this reading, there is little argumentation, but rather a series of three affirmations (what Christ knows about the church, and what Christ has done and will do on behalf of the church). A second reading scenario understands the third component to provide the rationale for the action taken in the second component. Christ has set this "opened door" before the congregation *because* they have heeded Jesus' teaching and acted loyally toward him, despite their lack of social influence and support.[37] A third possibility would be to construe component 3 as the rationale for component 4. The second reading enjoys the widest support, though the third merits consideration, since the pattern of presenting a rationale using a ὅτι clause *preceding* the main clause appears (again?) in the following verse (3:10).

Jesus' declaration concerning "an opened door that no one can shut" evokes the topic of the "feasible," one of the topics commonly associated with deliberative rhetoric (*Rhet. Alex.* 1421b.21–1422b.12). One of the strategies that an orator could employ to promote a course of action was to argue that it was possible, that the hearers had the necessary resources to follow it through to its end, and so forth. Here the glorified Christ affirms that the way forward is clear and open, with no hurdles or dead ends, assuring the hearers that they can successfully continue in their confession and commitments, progressing ever forward to their reward.[38]

---

36. Beale 1999, 286. This has the benefit of parallel expressions in the neighboring oracles to Sardis (Rev. 3:1b) and Laodicea (3:15), where οἶδα governs a ὅτι clause. Interrupting sentences with parenthetical ejaculations, however, has not been a feature of the prose up to this point, and so is a less natural construal of the flow of the text. Even Rev. 16:15, a clear interruption of the flow of the narration of the consequences of pouring out the sixth bowl, does not break an otherwise complete sentence in two.

37. Aune 1997, 236.

38. The two principal options for the significance of this open door are "opportunity for witness," argued on the basis of the use of this imagery in Acts 14:27; 1 Cor. 16:9; 2 Cor. 2:12; Col. 4:3, and entrance into the place of deliverance and salvation, e.g., new Jerusalem. The latter option is favored by Loisy (1923, 112), Lohse (1988a, 33), Aune (1997, 236), and Murphy (1998, 152).

Whether the third component is taken as the rationale for the preceding or following actions of the glorified Christ, the logic remains the same: faithful and obedient action on the part of the disciples meets with deliverance or vindication by the faithful and gracious action of Christ. The socially observed and learned ethics of reciprocity in the unequal relationships of patrons/benefactors and clients/beneficiaries undergirds this logic. The junior party shows gratitude through loyalty and faithful action which, in turn, prompts further acts of beneficence. The specific content of these actions is rendered more plausible through the use of intertexture. As the Davidic Messiah (a facet of Christian cultural knowledge), Jesus appropriately presents himself as having the key of David (3:7), and hence the power of opening a door that no one else has the ability (the "key") to lock again (3:8). Similarly, the declaration of future action on behalf of Christ's disciples recontextualizes the promise given to God's historic people in Judah regarding their vindication before their Gentile oppressors (notably, Isa. 60:14).[39] The audience is expected to accept that (1) Christ has the power and authority to fulfill God's promises (a premise affirmed elsewhere in earlier Christian literature, e.g., 2 Cor. 1:20; Gal. 3:14)[40] and (2) that the people of God gathered in the name of Jesus are the heirs of these promises to historic Israel (again, a commonplace in Christian discourse).

The next argumentative step in this oracle is much clearer:

Rationale (topic of the cause): "because [ὅτι] you kept (ἐτήρησας) the word of my patient endurance," (Rev. 3:10a)

Consequence: "I also will keep [τηρήσω] you out from the hour of testing that is about to come upon the whole inhabited world to test those dwelling on the earth." (3:10b)

The logic is derived again from social knowledge of reciprocity within patron-client relationships, a reciprocity here highlighted by the repetition of forms of τηρέω to express both the past action of the clients and the forthcoming action of the patron: You have kept, so I will keep. The loyal stance embodied

---

While Beale (1999, 286) tries to promote the former reading, he must also admit that "the 'open door' primarily means the church's 'own assured entry into the New Jerusalem'" (1999, 287, quoting Wilcock 1975, 56). The promise that closes this oracle, assuring the one who overcomes a firm place within the new Jerusalem (3:12), also favors hearing this "opened door" as the promise of entrance into the goal of the Christian journey.

39. The application of this promise is quite ironic, with Judeans (the descendants of the original recipients of the promise) bowing down before a probably mixed body of Gentile and Jewish Christians (Murphy 1998, 153).

40. I do not presume that John was familiar with these texts, though these Pauline letters could well have circulated through the churches by 90 CE. My point is simply that John presupposes the kind of conviction or premise that was already being nurtured and evidenced in Christian discourse, and thus something reasonably presupposed when communicating with these congregations.

by these disciples will meet with continued loyal action—here, protection—on their behalf by Christ.[41]

Up to this point the congregation has not been challenged to do anything, or to respond to their situation in any particular way (although the affirmations of their past stance will confirm them in that stance for the future). Moreover, the first three consequences all announce what Christ has done or will do on behalf of this congregation because of its past behavior. Only in 3:11 do we find anything like an identification of a situation to be addressed and advice concerning the same.

> Stasis: "I am coming quickly." (3:11a)
>
> Exhortation: "Hold on to what you have," (3:11b)
>
> Argument from the consequences (topic of the inexpedient): "so that no one takes your crown." (3:11c)

There is, however, no deficiency observed and challenged in Philadelphia; they are merely exhorted to prepare for the general crisis for which all churches need to prepare themselves, primarily through continuing in the stance of loyalty and obedience that they have already manifested quite well. An incentive is offered in the form of an argument from the consequences asserting that failure to persevere would prove inexpedient (another major deliberative topic), endangering existing goods (their claim on the "crown," their entrance into the place that Christ holds open before them). The affirmation of the imminence of Christ's return provides further incentive, invoking the topic of the "feasible." The implication is that the believers will not need to "hold on" for too long. Activity to be pursued or deprivations to be endured for a short time are more feasible than those to be pursued or endured for a long or an indeterminate period.

The Oracle to Laodicea

The oracle begins with an elaboration of Christ's disapproval of the congregation, presenting the circumstances requiring corrective action at the outset:

---

41. Prigent (1988, 71) and Murphy (1998, 155) rightly understand this promise of protection to refer not to the persecution of Christians, but to the experience of God's plagues and judgments ("the inhabitants of the earth" is a phrase that, throughout Revelation, tends to be used negatively for those who live in rebellion against God, are in league with the beast and with Babylon, and act with hostility against Christian witnesses: 6:10; 8:13 [here, clearly those who do not have God's seal, 9:4]; 11:10; 13:8, 12, 14; 17:2, 8). Such a reading falls well in line with the remaining content of the visions, according to which Christians are subjected to marginalization and execution at the hands of the beasts and their party, but divinely protected from the plagues that God sends upon the unrepentant. That Christ says he will keep the Philadelpian Christians from this tribulation does *not* mean that Christ will not do the same for the other faithful Christians throughout the seven churches, any more than the promise to Smyrna that those who are faithful to the point of death will receive the crown of life (2:10) is limited to them, and not rather a particular application of a general promise (contra Aune [1997, 240], who asserts that "the promise made here pertains to Philadelphian Christians *only* and cannot be generalized to include Christians in the other churches of Asia").

Stasis: "You are neither cold nor hot. Would that you were cold or hot!" (3:15)

Consequences: "I am about to spew you out of my mouth" (3:16b)

Rationale: "Because [ὅτι] you are in this way lukewarm, and neither hot nor cold." (3:16a)

The exclamation ("Would that you were!") communicates the negative assessment of their present deficiency.[42] An implicit argument from analogy both elaborates the undesirability of their condition and contributes to the persuasiveness of the connection between the Laodiceans' condition and the response that the glorified Christ will have if it persists: "Just as tepid water makes the drinker feel nausea and wish to vomit, in this way your 'lukewarmness' makes me nauseous and about to vomit."[43]

The stasis is restated in a way that becomes more clearly the rationale for the course of action proposed (the language of deliberation—"symbouleutic" oratory—is explicitly used here):

Rationale: "Because [ὅτι] you say 'I am rich and I have prospered and I have need of nothing' and you do not realize that you are wretched and pitiable and poor and blind and naked," (3:17)

Exhortation: "I advise you [συμβουλεύω] to buy from me gold smelted in fire in order that you may be rich, and white garments in order that you may clothe yourself and the shame of your nakedness not be seen, and ointment to anoint your eyes in order that you may see." (3:18)

---

42. The images of "hot," "cold," and "lukewarm" have invited much speculation concerning the more precise nature of the speaker's censure of the Laodiceans' performance and attitudes. Those who understand both "hot" and "cold" to label positive qualities (rather than fervor on the one hand and complete indifference on the other, following Loisy 1923, 117; Murphy 1998, 161), are more firmly grounded in observations of the uses of cold and hot water in the first-century social context in general and the local setting of Laodicea in particular (i.e., hot water is healing and salutary, cold water is refreshing, but lukewarm water is nauseating and even used as an emetic—which can be salutary, but Christ's reaction does not suggest that any positive, medicinal use of lukewarm water is in view here). Prigent (1988, 76) rightly complains of the subjectivism involved in interpreting "lukewarmness," although his solution (asserting some Christian gnostic heresy's success in Laodicea, supposedly also evidenced in the other six oracles) is no better. Reading the more specific critique of Laodicea in Rev. 3:16–18 as an elaboration of "lukewarmness" seems a sufficient safeguard against subjectivity and avoids the worse error of introducing heresy as a cause when John himself does not use any language suggestive of its presence (a topic he is not reticent to name explicitly where relevant).

43. The audience had ready access to the experiences that would make this analogy credible, whether one follows Colin Hemer's discussion of Laodicea's tepid and nauseating water supply in contrast to neighboring Colossae's cold water or Hierapolis's hot springs (1986, 186–91), or Craig Keener's less localized and more socially widespread suggestion of the practice of serving both hot and cold water at banquets (2000, 159), with tepid water being offered as an emetic.

The rationale provides a more detailed explanation of what is amiss in this congregation.[44] The principal assertion is that their own self-assessment of the happiness of their state (wealth and security being major components of "happiness" in Aristotle's definition of this elusive subject; see *Rhet.* 1.5.4) is the result of utter self-deception.[45] There is no support offered for this claim, however, beyond its presentation as an authoritative word from the Christ whose knowledge surpasses our knowledge even of ourselves (Rev. 2:23). It is couched as an antithesis, a rhetorically effective form (*Rhet. Her.* 4.15.21) that might create the illusion of syllogistic force (Aristotle, *Rhet.* 3.9.8), and carries at least the potential to raise doubt in the hearers' minds about their degree of need, motivating self-examination and opening them up to the possibility of exploring remedies such as Christ offers.

The proposed course of action, admittedly left far from concrete, is supported by arguments from the consequences, embedded as purpose clauses, that use familiar topics of advantage to provide incentives to accept the exhortation: embracing this course will allow the hearers to secure a more genuinely enriching wealth ("expediency"), avoid disgrace ("honor"), and attain more reliable knowledge and perception (again, the topic of "expediency"). It thus promises the complete and positive reversal of the deficiencies in their present condition.

The remaining verses of the body of this oracle (3:19–20) make the message to Laodicea stand out from the preceding ones insofar as it adds two additional motivations for those whose behavior stands disapproved to respond positively to the speaker's rebuke and advice.

> Premise (claim about the speaker's motivation): "As many as I love, I convict and discipline." (3:19a)
>
> Conclusion (exhortation): "Be zealous, therefore [οὖν], and repent." (3:19b)

The audience would be disposed to accept the premise both on the basis of its clear evocation of a sacred text (Prov. 3:12) speaking of the reasons to accept God's discipline in a good and pliant spirit and on the basis of their own experi-

---

44. Duff (2001, 35) claims that there is "no significant elaboration of problems" and "little, if any, encouragement" in the oracle to the Laodicean community, so that he can relegate it to the same category of Sardis rather than read it alongside the oracles to Ephesus, Pergamum, and Thyatira, the oracles that notably provide him with the picture of factionalism that he promotes as *the* crisis behind Revelation. However, Rev. 3:17–18 represents a significant elaboration of the problem of being "lukewarm," with significant resonances with material in the visions (cf. 3:17 with 18:7–8). Furthermore, this oracle offers proportionately extensive encouragement, often considered the most intimate of the seven in this regard (3:19–20), suggesting that John did not, in fact, write off Laodicea as a congregation that he had little hope of winning over. Duff's analysis of this oracle and its presenting situation suffers insofar as it does not elaborate the problem that Duff otherwise seeks to foreground.

45. A close parallel to this "hubris soliloquy" appears in Epictetus, *Discourses* 3.7.29: "But I am rich and need nothing" (Aune 1997, 258; see also Hos. 12:8; *1 En.* 97:8–9). The proud or prosperous misperceiving their situation is something of a topos in prophetic and philosophical literature.

ence of parenting and education, where concern for the full and sound formation of the child/student undergirded correction and discipline, even though these experiences are unpleasant (see also Heb. 12:4–11).[46] Because the rebuke is motivated by love and concern for the successful formation of the Laodicean disciples (lodged by one with superior insight into their situation than they themselves possess, and hence salutary), it would be reasonable that they should respond favorably (that is, "be zealous, and repent").

To this is added a second additional incentive, similarly affirming Christ's goodwill toward the congregation and desire for renewed connection with them: "See! I stand at the door and knock. If anyone hears my voice and opens the door, I will come in to that one and sup with that one, and that one with me" (Rev. 3:20). If the hearers accept the opening premise (the proximity of Christ's potential intervention, here portrayed quite positively), which has been a premise undergirding, and explicitly invoked within, most of the seven oracles, the plausibility of the second half of the verse follows from the routine script of opening up one's home to an invited guest or friend.

The concluding promise (3:21) incorporates a historical precedent as an implicit argument supporting the plausibility of the promise:

Historical precedent: Christ conquered and, as a result, sat enthroned with the Father. (3:21b)

Conclusion: Those who conquer after the manner of Jesus may plausibly expect to enjoy similar honors. (3:21a)

This historical precedent is an established part of Jesus' story, based on the widespread application of Psalm 110:1 to the career of Jesus in early Christian discourse.[47] The particular logic of the promise, which rests in the foundational

---

46. Rev. 3:19a paraphrases Prov. 3:12. The doubling of "discipline" and "rebuke" (ἐλέγχω καὶ παιδεύω) suggests the influence also of Prov. 3:11: "Child, do not despise the discipline (παιδείας) of the Lord, nor grow weary when rebuked (ἐλεγχόμενος) by him." The tendency to link these two verbs appears also in Prov. 3:12 LXX Codex B, where "rebukes" replaces "chastises" (Prigent 1988, 78).

Murphy (1998, 164–65) suggests that this verse did not apply to the Laodicean Christians, to whom it is addressed, but to the Christians who were currently suffering for their faith in a way that the Laodicean Christians are not. "When Christ is speaking about those whom he loves, he does not mean the Laodiceans. If he really loved them, they would be suffering like the church at Smyrna." He claims that this reading "fits more securely into the book as a whole," especially the theme that God's favor is upon those who suffer. However, Rev. 3:19b–20 suggests, on the contrary, that this reading is the least to be preferred. The recontextualized proverb is offered as motivation for zeal and response: "Be emulous, therefore, and repent." The Laodiceans would have experienced hearing 3:15–18 as a rebuke and act of chastening; 3:19a in this context would be most naturally heard as an explanation of the motivation behind the rebuke that has just been leveled. Moreover, language of rebuke and discipline is *never* used in Revelation to interpret suffering for the sake of Christ (in fact, the word groups never appear elsewhere in Revelation, which prefers probative, athletic, and military images to interpret the experiences of suffering—as indeed, in 2:10), unlike Heb. 12:4–11 (which Murphy may be reading into Rev. 3:19 to arrive at, and sustain, his preferred interpretation).

47. See Matt. 22:44; 26:64; Mark 12:36; 14:62; 16:19; Luke 20:42–43; 22:69; Acts 2:34–35; Rom. 8:34; 1 Cor. 15:25; Heb. 1:3, 13; 8:1; 10:12.

principle that like causes have like effects, once again reflects the equally widespread conviction that Jesus' story of arriving at glory through suffering and death establishes a pattern that will apply to Jesus' followers as well, a conviction already seen at work to undergird argumentation in the oracles to Smyrna and Thyatira.

CONCLUSION

The seven oracles contain significant appeals to rational argumentation (logos). This argumentation largely involves the most basic strategies known from classical rhetorical handbooks, even from the most rudimentary level of progymnasmic (preparatory) exercises. There are instances of radical rhetoric, to be sure, most notably in declarations of the stasis in which no supporting evidence is provided (2:4; 3:1), with the speaker depending on the hearers' intuitive response to the authoritative pronouncement concerning what is amiss. The speaker offers supporting argumentation throughout, however, in several different forms, with multiple forms often being combined in a single oracle. The speaker articulates premises, provides rationales, and draws conclusions (often in the form of exhortations, appropriate to the deliberative or advisory environment). The stasis and related advice are supported by arguments from analogy (3:15–16), from the consequences (2:10; 3:18), from the contrary (normally also involving the topic of the consequences; 2:5b, 16b, 22–23; 3:3b), from historical example (2:14–15), and from the revelation of contradictions (2:13, 15; 2:20). Enthymemes are based on the topics of courage (2:10), the just (particularly in terms of reciprocity; 3:8–10), the feasible (3:8, 11), the (in)expedient (2:5, 16, 22–23; 3:11), and relative expediency (2:11). Positive examples for imitation also appear within specific oracles, elaborating upon the course of action that leads to advantage (2:13, 24–25; 3:4).

The argumentation of Revelation requires, however, that the hearers have previously accepted certain premises derived from the distinctive cultural knowledge of the Christian group (sometimes shared with the larger Jewish ethnic subculture). For example, the arguments from the contrary course of action (i.e., the projected consequences of *not* following the speaker's preferred course of action) chiefly depend on the audience's willingness to accept the premises that (1) Jesus is available to intervene personally in the congregation's future and (2) the words spoken reflect the glorified Christ's intentions in this regard. In other words, the arguments work within a framework of belief that, to borrow from the Apostles' Creed, Christ "will come again to judge the living and the dead," both finally and in interim interventions, and that Christ makes his intentions known through prophetic speech. The use of diction associated with the historical Jesus (particularly in the oracles to Ephesus and Sardis) helps to reinforce the second premise. The argumentation within the oracles presupposes the audience's willingness to assent also to other distinctive elements of Christian "knowledge," for example, Christ's story as a paradigm for believers and the elevation of "love" as a primary virtue. The oracles indeed temper the authoritarian dimension with appeals to rational argumentation, as Kirby had asserted—but these appeals to reason will only work within Christian culture and would be likely to be dismissed, even ridiculed, outside of early Christian congregations.

Chapter 10

Argumentation in John's Visions
Revelation 14:6–13 as Focal Summary of Main Points

Argumentation proceeds on two different levels in John's Apocalypse. At the basic level, listeners can discern the presence of argumentative texture on the surface of the text, whether in the form of unsupported assertions or in the form of more fully developed argument employing either implicit or explicit enthymemes and drawing on such topics as cause, consequence, honor, or security. At a deeper level, argumentation is implicitly evoked through the author's invocation of traditions and precedents known to the audience through their shared body of Scripture (the Hebrew Bible) and other cultural knowledge (e.g., extracanonical apocalypses, or stories about, and sayings of, Jesus). Premises and supporting arguments are *narrated* rather than *stated*. In this chapter, we will continue the previous chapter's exploration of the more basic level of appeals to logos, or rational argumentation, now in the more visionary portions of Revelation.[1]

While argumentative texture is relatively dense in the seven oracles, it is less concentrated in the main body of the work, since the visions are, by their nature,

---

1. Some observations concerning the argumentation present "under the surface" will naturally emerge in the course of this chapter, though this will be the focus of chapter 11.

largely descriptive of *scenes* rather than the recounting of *speech* (as were the seven oracles). The emphasis on "scenes" distinguishes Revelation from *4 Ezra*, where dialogue between the seer and an angelic intermediary dominates the first three episodes, with the result that argumentative texture is far more prominent and argumentation far more developed. Even so, argumentative texture is present in Revelation's visions in the hymns embedded within the scenes of worship (e.g., 4:11; 5:9–10; 7:15–17; 11:15–18; 15:2–4; 19:1–8), in the speech of angelic figures who call for action or make pronouncements in the course of the scenes (e.g., 14:6–11; 18:2–8, 21–24), and in assertions that punctuate the visions, often with some accompanying rationales (e.g., the seven macarisms: 1:3; 14:13; 16:15; 19:9; 20:6; 22:7, 14). In this chapter, we will focus on the messages of the three angels and other heavenly voices in 14:6–13. These messages provide a concentrated sample of the exhortations and pronouncements made indirectly to the audience, representing a summary statement of the argumentative appeals throughout the whole of Revelation's vision.[2]

These messages primarily raise the issue of who is worthy of worship—God or the beast?—and secondarily the issue of alliance, whether to align oneself with the One God or with Babylon, the beast, and its image.[3] In chapter 8, we saw how John underscores the question of worship in the scenes of worship of God and God's Messiah in Revelation 4–5 and the parody in the worship of the dragon and his beast in Revelation 13, as people from "every nation, tribe, language, and people" are drawn to one or the other epicenter of worship. Throughout Revelation, but more clearly in these three messages than anywhere else, John forces a choice between the worship of God and the worship of the beast. The focus on the question of whom to worship, and why, locates Revelation's rhetoric within the context of discussions of "justice" (δικαιοσύνη) in the Greco-Roman world.[4] Revelation's readers are invited into a deliberative arena as they view the relative advantages and disadvantages of the exclusive worship of the One God over against participation in the cult of the beast. Either choice carries a cost, but it is John's aim to demonstrate (not merely illustrate) that the exclusive worship of the living and true God is the far more advantageous course. To this end, John marshals a wide array of deliberative topics in the enthymemes he constructs for this demonstration (including the "just," the "honorable," the "expedient," the "safe/secure," and arguments from the consequences).[5]

---

2. See deSilva 1998a. Aune (1998a, 848) says of Rev. 14: "The many parallels with other passages in Revelation suggest that Rev 14 is a pastiche of the author's favorite themes and formulas."

3. DeSilva 1998a, 87–89; so also Frey (2006, 239–41), who emphasizes "who is the true God," and "whom are we to worship" as main questions in Revelation: "We can even say that the topic of true and false worship dominates the whole main section of the book" (2006, 241).

4. DeSilva 1998a, 88. Worship of the gods is a prominent subject in discussions of "justice" in (Pseudo-) Aristotle, *Virt. vit.* 5.2; *Rhet. Her.* 3.3.4; *Rhet. Alex.* 1421b.36–40.

5. As Frey (2006, 246) observes, "The visions also give deeper reasons for the admonitions of the seven letters. Only from the visionary part does it become clear why the readers should 'leave Babylon' (Rev 18:4)" and should respond to local concerns as John outlines in the oracles.

HONOR GOD! (REVELATION 14:6–7)

The first angel's announcement is a call to a particular course of action: "Revere God and give God honor," restated as a call to "worship God" (14:7). Residents in the cities of Asia Minor are exposed to many invitations to worship different gods and indeed find it advantageous to do so. John's audience, in particular, must weigh the respective "cases" to be made for the exclusive worship of the One God non pareil of the Jewish and Christian tradition or for the inclusive worship of the indigenous gods and the imperial divinities alongside the God of the Christian movement. The first angel's message therefore articulates the main point at issue in a deliberative environment.

The course of honoring the One God and showing reverence ("fear") through observing God's commandments[6] is recommended here on the basis of two rationales. The first is explicated in the ὅτι clause of 14:7: "Revere God and give God honor, *because* the hour of God's judgment came." The rationale invokes a topic of "safety" or "security," one of the two major categories of deliberative topics according to the *Rhetorica ad Herennium* (3.2.3). This topic involves adopting "some plan or other for ensuring the avoidance of a present or imminent danger." God's commitment to hold human beings accountable in judgment and to mete out rewards and punishments creates a crisis that poses potentially grave danger to all. Acting in a way that shows reverence for God is a path to survival through that crisis.[7]

The second rationale is presented indirectly in an elaboration of the identity of this God who is to be feared: "Worship the One who made heaven and earth and sea and springs of water" (Rev. 14:7b). Aristotle had observed that the most effective maxim was one with a rationale embedded in it, as in "Do not harbor immortal wrath, being mortal," rather than appended, as, for example, in "Do not harbor immortal wrath, *because/for* mortal beings ought to moderate their feelings" (*Rhet.* 2.21.6). John thus introduces his second rationale more subtly into the discourse, embedding it in the description of the proposed object of veneration ("the God who made . . ."). This rationale utilizes the topic of the "just," a subtopic of "the right," the other major category of special deliberative topics (*Rhet. Her.* 3.2.3). As the Creator of the cosmos, God—and God *alone*—merits the honor and obedience of all who have received the gift of life and enjoy the bounty of creation.[8]

---

6. The "fear" of God is consistently linked with, and explicated as, obedience to the commandments of this God throughout the Hebrew Scriptures (see Lev. 19:14, 32; 25:17, 36, 43; Deut. 6:2, 24; 10:12; 13:4; 17:19; 31:12–13; 2 Kgs. 17:35–38; Ps. 112:1; Prov. 16:6; Eccl. 12:13; Tob. 4:21; Sir. 10:19; 19:20; 23:27).

7. The first, explicit rationale of 14:7 is further supported throughout the work by statements about the necessity and consequences of God's judgment (e.g., 11:15–18; 15:3–4; 19:1–8) and by the display of the negative consequences of failing to reserve worship exclusively for the One God (most relevant here, in Rev. 14:9–11).

8. See deSilva 1998a, 90; 1998b, 791–93. Showing gratitude to the One God is a proper enactment of the "just," and therefore "right" and "advantageous," course of action (cf. *Rhet. Alex.*

The first angel's summons, however, follows much more extensive treatments of the issue of the worship of God (and God's Messiah) and the rationales for doing so—and doing so exclusively—in a pluralistic religious environment. Especially important in this regard is the extended scene of worship in Revelation 4–5. In particular, the angel's second rationale is grounded in the enthymemic-argumentative contributions of the hymns and other liturgical acts articulated during that earlier vision.

The hymn sung to God by the twenty-four elders (4:11) is overtly enthymemic in form:

> You are worthy, our Lord and God,
>   to receive the glory and the honor and the power,
> *because* [ὅτι] you created all things,
>   and by your will they were and were created.

The first part of the hymn lays out an assertion: God deserves public acknowledgment (glory), honor, and power. The second part marshals evidence in support of that assertion: *because* (ὅτι) God has created all that is.[9] The unstated premise that completes the deduction comes from the universally held conviction that benefactors (among whom God is supreme, having given to all the ultimate benefactions of life, habitable and fruitful environment, and the like) merit a response of gratitude.[10] Greco-Roman ethicists would concur that God (or the gods) merit worship for their benefactions,[11] the difference being that John makes this claim exclusively on behalf of One God who alone is worthy of worship, and whose beneficence in the gift of life merits the reciprocal commitment to live that life in accordance with God's commandments, including the prohibition of worshiping any other would-be divinity.

The next hymn (5:9–10) follows precisely the same pattern of assertion followed by rationale:

1421b.37–1422a.2; *Rhet. Her.* 3.3.4). The identification of God as "the one who made heaven and earth," etc., which is common in the Jewish Scriptures, is particularly used in contexts to distinguish this God from all the counterfeit gods worshiped among the peoples surrounding the faithful Israelites and Judeans (see Exod. 20:11, in the context of Exod. 20:2–5; 2 Kgs. 19:15; Neh. 9:6; Isa. 37:16). Especially poignant is the parody of this description of the One God in Jer. 10:11, applied to the idols, "the gods who did *not* make heaven and earth." For those with ears to hear, these intertextual resonances will further support the deliberative edge to the call to worship the God of Israel *rather than* the gods venerated in the local contexts of the seven churches.

9. The two steps in this and the following hymn resemble Quintilian's prescription for "praising the gods": "our first step will be to express our veneration of the majesty of their nature in general terms: next we shall proceed to praise the special power of the individual god and the discoveries whereby he has benefitted the human race" (*Inst.* 3.7.7; thus Harris 1988, 276; Morton 2001, 102). Revelation's examples of such praise make explicit what is implicit in Quintilian: the deity's achievements and benefits merit recognition (specifically in the form of veneration and worship).

10. On the social practices of patronage and beneficence, and the ethos that governed it, see Moxnes 1991; Elliott 1987; deSilva 1996b; 2000a, 95–156.

11. See *Rhet. Alex.* 1421b.37–1422a.2; *Rhet. Her.* 3.3.4; Aristotle, *Eth. Nic.* 8.14.4.

You are worthy to take the scroll and to open its seals,
because [ὅτι] you were slain and you bought back for God with your blood
[people] out of every tribe and language group and people and nation
and made them a kingdom and priests for our God,
and they will reign over the earth.

The hymn proclaims the Lamb worthy to take the book and open its seals (initiating judgment over the kingdoms of the world and ushering in God's kingdom) *because* (ὅτι) the Lamb redeemed a people for God to constitute that kingdom by giving up his own life on their behalf. The Lamb has acted clearly in the interest of the recipients and of God rather than out of self-interest,[12] and has rendered an important service to people in significant need ("redeeming" or "ransoming" suggests a situation of significant distress), thus enacting a recognizable benefactor script and evoking the logic associated with the social arena of benefaction and reciprocity.[13] The unstated premise might run: only the person who has truly selflessly given himself in service to God/the gods to benefit others merits dominion. Augustus's dominion was built upon the rhetoric of beneficence and beneficial achievement. The *Res gestae divi Augusti*, prominently inscribed in public spaces, fulfilled such a dominion-legitimating function by listing the many political and military achievements of Augustus, but also the many public benefactions bestowed by the same. The Lamb now steps forward, having been slaughtered for the sake of bringing benefit to many (showing a greater, indeed ultimate, commitment to the virtue of generosity), as an alternative and superior picture of serving God's design for humanity and acting as a perfect benefactor.[14]

At this point, John's narration provides additional argumentative topics. First, John claims that the Lamb has attained a unique dignity through his beneficence, displaying this uniqueness dramatically, rather than discursively, in 5:1–6. The episode of the universal search for one who was "worthy" to initiate the breaking in of God's kingdom, the reported failure of finding *anyone* who is

---

12. A prominent topic for praise and for arguing in favor of the appropriateness of praise involved the deeds performed or successes gained not for one's own sake, but for the benefit of others (Aristotle, *Rhet.* 1.9.16–17, 19; Quintilian, *Inst.* 3.7.16). This would tend to evoke, in turn, responses of "gratitude" (Aristotle, *Rhet.* 2.7.2; Cicero, *De or.* 2.51.206).

13. The Lamb's actions would also be seen as supremely noble in light of the criteria offered in Aristotle's *Rhetoric* and the anonymous *Rhetorica ad Alexandrum*. The Lamb's actions produced significantly good results (*Rhet. Alex.* 1426a.22–23), were undertaken "not for his own sake, but . . . for the sake of others" while in fact "neglecting his own interests" (Aristotle, *Rhet.* 1.9.16–17, 19). Schüssler Fiorenza (1991, 61–62) had already observed that this hymn "underlines three reasons why the Lamb is worthy to assume the eschatological reign over the world," although she does not go on to analyze the fuller argumentation undergirding each rationale: (1) The Lamb suffered the violent death that signaled the eschatological Passover. (2) The Lamb ransomed people back for God from every nation, tribe, people, and language group. (3) The Lamb creates thus an alternative kingdom of priests, whose allegiance will be to God.

14. Repetitions reinforce this contrast, especially in regard to the Lamb and the beast (or Babylon) competing for people "from every tribe and language and people and nation" (5:9; 13:7; 17:15). See deSilva 1999a, 75–76.

worthy, and the dramatic resolution as the Lamb is revealed—all this constitutes a narrative development of a standard encomiastic topic: being the first or only person to succeed in a particular venture or achieve a particular end.[15] This was one of several means by which to amplify (to augment the significance of) a person's achievement. Here the amplification heightens appreciation of Jesus' status and of the value of his death, thus supporting the argument that he is worthy of worship (5:9–10). It is particularly relevant to establishing that Jesus' claim to worship (as a human-become-God) is superior to the claims made on behalf of the imperial household (lauded as *divi*, humans-become-gods), whose members are not worthy to step into the silence of 5:3–4 to fill the void.

The heavenly scenes of worship contribute a second argument in narrative form, the highly relevant "argument from universal consensus" (*argumentum e consensu omnium*):

> And I heard every creature in heaven and upon the earth and under the earth and upon the sea, and all things in them saying, "Blessing and honor and glory and power forever and ever to the One seated upon the throne and to the Lamb!" (5:13)

Shaye Cohen succinctly describes the "logic" of the argument: "If all people believe something to be true, it must be true; that which is accepted by a larger number of people is better than that which is accepted by a smaller number. This argument presumes that the people as a whole is an arbiter of that which is good and true, and that agreement proves truth."[16] The *argumentum e consensu omnium* was an important prop for the legitimacy of the principate.[17] As early as the *Res gestae divi Augusti*, we find Augustus reflecting on "having obtained all things *by universal consent*," before boasting of being given the title "'Augustus' *by universal decree*," thereby legitimating his ongoing primacy over the affairs of empire (*Res gestae* 34). In this environment, John boldly narrates a scene whereby "universal consent" upholds the reign of the God of Israel and this God's Messiah.[18] As Revelation devolves, those who worship other gods bring a minority report that deviates from the truth perceived by "all." John will also challenge public discourse that the emperors' beneficence evoked the "universal consent" awarded their rule: "and all the earth marveled at the beast and worshiped the dragon because it gave the authority to the beast and worshiped the beast, saying, 'Who is like the beast, and who can make war against it?'" (13:3–4). Although the Lamb receives rule by universal consent on the more

---

15. On uniqueness as a topic of amplification (frequently used in encomium), see Aristotle, *Rhet.* 1.9.38; 2.7.2; Quintilian, *Inst.* 3.7.16. Aristotle lists amplification as a "common topic" for enthymematic elaboration alongside arguments from the consequences, from incentives and disincentives, from precedents, and the like: amplification involves "enthymemes which serve to show that a thing is great or small, just as other [enythmeme]s serve to show that it is good or bad, just or unjust" (*Rhet.* 2.26.1).

16. Cohen 1988, 6–7. See also Oehler 1961.

17. See Aune 1983, 18–19.

18. So also Barnett 1989, 115.

Argumentation in John's Visions   263

noble and praiseworthy basis of his other-centered sacrifice, the beast receives it on the basis of his military might and his use of violence as the mechanism of unification of multiple peoples, languages, nations, and tribes into "empire."

Substantial "rational" argumentation, then, supports the first angel's summons. Two rationales are offered within the summons itself in support of the course of action promoted. The second rationale recalls and summarizes argumentation presented in an earlier visionary sequence (Rev. 4–5) through enthymematic reasoning *and* the narrative elaboration of argumentative topics. The first rationale is elaborated through graphic depictions of future judgment (e.g., 14:14–20; 20:11–15), as well as evidence marshaled to demonstrate the necessity of this judgment (e.g., 11:15–18; 15:3–4). The summons will be further developed through both enthymematic and narrativized arguments from the consequences of this and the alternative course of action, both in the immediate context (14:9–11) and more broadly throughout Revelation (e.g., 16:1–21; 20:11–22:5).

COOPERATION WITH BABYLON DEFILES! (REVELATION 14:8)

The second angel issues not an explicit call to action, but an assertion concerning the fate of the seat of a world empire:

> She fell, she fell, Babylon the Great, who gave all the nations a drink from the wine of the passion of her fornication. (14:8)

Argumentation is implicitly present here, however, in the same manner that we observed in the second component of the first angel's summons: the description of the central character embeds the rationale for the principal statement. Fornication represents a moral failure recognizable as such by the standards both of Augustan morality and of the Jewish-Christian tradition, within which John speaks. Babylon emerges here as a contaminant, defiling and unraveling the moral order by her activity. In a moral universe, such contaminants must be purged, such sources of disorder expunged.[19] Thus the second angel's message implies the following enthymeme in a manner that Aristotle would commend as artfully indirect:

> Great Babylon fell,
> *because* she gave all the nations to drink from the wine of the passion
>   of her fornication.

19. Aristotle, *Rhet.* 1.2.18 on necessary signs: "If one were to say that it is a sign that a man is ill, because he has a fever, or that a woman has had a child because she has milk, this is a necessary sign. This alone among signs is a τεκμήριον (evidence); for only in this case, if the fact is true, is the argument irrefutable." Babylon's crimes are a "necessary sign" of her downfall in a cosmos ruled by a God of justice.

This reconstruction of the implicit enthymeme in 14:8 is corroborated by the explicit and formal articulation of the same in 18:2–3:

> Thesis (effect): "She fell, she fell, Great Babylon, and became a dwelling place of demons and a keep of every unclean spirit and a keep of every unclean and hateful bird." (18:2)
>
> Rationale (cause): "*Because* [ὅτι] she gave all nations to drink from the wine of the passion of her fornication, and the kings of the earth committed fornication with her, and the merchants of the earth grew rich from the power of her luxuriating." (18:3)

The first angel's message *recalls* and *recapitulates* previous argumentation concerning the justice of worshiping the One God and the expediency of doing so in light of God's forthcoming judgments; the second angel's message *anticipates* the much fuller argumentation concerning Babylon and the inexpediency of partnership with her in Revelation 17–18.[20]

Because John is giving voice to these statements within a situation marked by particular challenges and options, and because John has a clear agenda for positioning his hearers to respond to those challenges and options, we should not miss the deliberative *force* even of an epideictic statement (indeed, a statement of "fact"). A primary issue among the churches concerns the question of partnership with Roman imperialism in its local manifestations. Persuasive Christian prophets and teachers have defended some level of partnership as consistent with the beliefs and practice of the Christian community, with the result that the Christian group could experience considerably less tension with its environment and enjoy readier access to the material and social benefits offered within that environment.

John opposes any such "compromise," seeking, if anything, to augment the Christian group's withdrawal from activities suggesting any level of support for, or participation in, Roman imperialism and its religious forms of legitimation. He has proleptically painted the prophetess "Jezebel" in Babylon's scarlet hues, particularly in regard to "fornication": Jezebel teaches other Christians to "fornicate" (πορνεῦσαι, 2:20) and has not herself repented "of her fornication" (τῆς πορνείας αὐτῆς, 2:21); Babylon disseminates her defilement through "the wine of the passion of her fornication" (τῆς πορνείας αὐτῆς, 14:8). These verbal associations suggest that Jezebel's ministry leads believers into the webs of fornication spun by Babylon (that is, into partnership with Rome), who thus incur a share of responsibility for the injustices of Roman imperialism, for the sake of the temporal benefits that partnership brings.[21] John raises serious questions about the expediency of such a partnership.

---

20. In this particular instance, Rev. 14:8 stands in relation to 18:2 in precisely the same way as 14:7 stood in relation to the enthymematic hymn of 4:11.

21. See deSilva 1998b, 796; 1999a, 79. Duff (2001) masterfully traces out the correspondences created between Jezebel and Babylon, the contrasts of these figures with the "desirable" woman clothed with the sun and the bride of the Lamb, and the rhetorical effects of the same. See also Carey 1999b, 141–49.

The second angel's message takes a strategic first step toward this end, introducing Babylon from the outset as a censurable entity, association with whom entails dishonor insofar as it embroils the associate in her vices. It thus applies the topic of "the honorable" negatively to association with Babylon. The second angel's message also implicitly invokes the topic of "security," specifically the subtopic of "allies." If Babylon "fell," alliance with Babylon does not improve one's security and so proves ultimately inexpedient (and potentially quite disastrous).[22]

The deliberative aim of the second angel's message is not fully expressed, however, until Revelation 18. Argumentative texture is particularly dense in this chapter, especially in 18:2–8 and 18:21–24, the segments that frame the heavenly voice's projection of the lament that Babylon's partners will take up over the fallen city (18:9–20). In 18:2–3, as displayed above, Babylon's desolation (18:2) is forecast as a direct result of her practice of imperialism, negatively depicted using the language of fornication, conspicuous consumption, and self-indulgence (18:3). Then, a second heavenly voice introduces a thesis in the form of an exhortation, supported by thick argumentative texture:

> Come out from her, my people
> *in order that* [ἵνα] you may not share in her sins,
> and *in order that* [ἵνα] you may not receive (a share) of her punishments.
> *Because* [ὅτι] her sins have piled up as far as heaven
> and God remembered her crimes.
>
> (18:4–5)

The exhortation to "come out" from Babylon is supported by two arguments from the consequences (the two ἵνα clauses), the second consequence following upon the first. Remaining "in" Babylon, continuing in partnership with Roman imperialism, means participating in the injustices of that system (both against other human beings who are exploited, excluded, or victimized by that system, and against God, whose unique claim on human allegiance is belied by that system).[23] The first consequence—sharing in Rome's crimes—leads, in the moral cosmos of Revelation, to the second, sharing in the punishment that those crimes merit and that will inevitably follow. The final ὅτι clause provides a confirmation of the argument from consequences, providing the grounds for believing that these punishments are certain and imminent. Empirical evidence for these grounds is unavailable, but the framework of a heavenly revelation with otherworldly voices speaking on behalf of God to make God's perspective known renders the claim plausible. Moreover, the piling up of crimes in 18:3 and 18:23–24 (each contains a triple statement of Babylon's ethical failures as a

---

22. Although not explicitly developed, the description of Babylon as a female figure who lures the nations into fornication also makes her a clear and present danger to those who might wish to be included among the 144,000 holy ones "who have not defiled themselves with women, for they are chaste persons" (14:4), an exemplary group introduced just prior to the passage containing the announcements of the three angels.

23. See Aune 1998b, 991, on the symbolic nature of the summons to "come out" here: John is not calling Christians to leave their cities in a physical sense.

world power) further supports the impression that her crimes are indeed stacked up as high as heaven and cannot escape God's notice. These argumentative steps provide a disincentive against remaining in league with the Roman imperial economy and idolatrous religion.

The remainder of this heavenly voice's speech continues to unfold by argumentative elaboration:

> Give back to her as she gave back
> and double the double measure according to her deeds;
> In the cup she mixed, mix up for her a double portion;
> As much as she glorified herself and luxuriated, give her that much torment and mourning.
> *Because* [ὅτι] in her heart she says, "I sit a queen and I am not a widow, and I will surely never see mourning."
> *On account of this* [διὰ τοῦτο], her punishments will come in a single day—plague and mourning and famine—
> and she will be burned with fire,
> *Because* [ὅτι] the Lord God who judged her is powerful.
> (18:6–8)

The voice issues a second exhortation (18:6), addressed to those who constitute "my people" (18:4). Many have found this summons, apparently calling human beings to take vengeance—and that by violence and out of proportion ("double")[24]—ethically problematic. But there is no corroboration elsewhere in Revelation for hearing this as a genuine call to violent retaliation. The only place that we see Christians "tormenting" those who are in league with Rome is in the tale of the two witnesses (11:10), and there it is specifically effected *by means of* their witness. Throughout Revelation it is consistently God and God's heavenly forces who execute judgment *on behalf of* the faithful disciples, rather than those disciples themselves. The purpose of this solitary exhortation must, then, not be to call Christians to act in a sub-Christian manner.

The ὅτι clause of 18:7 presents a rationale supporting the summons to "give her that much torment and mourning" to the extent that "she glorified herself." The speaker claims that Babylon has taken an attitude unmindful of all accountability to God—the God who establishes kingdoms and plucks them up again—and so merits what she has coming. The speaker expects the audience to share the assumption that hubris is indeed a moral flaw, one that merits the visitation

---

24. Rev. 18:6–7b forms a chiasm, with the outer elements speaking of simple retribution and the middle elements intensifying this to double retribution.

> Give back to her *as* she gave back
> and *double* the double measure according to her deeds;
> In the cup she mixed, mix up for her a *double* portion;
> As much as she glorified herself and luxuriated, give her that much torment and mourning.

If this is correct, the internal lines speaking of doubling the revenge may be seen more as devices intended to heighten indignation against Rome, while the outer lines propose repayment in kind, replicating the logic of the previous verses, where punishment is the fitting, expected, even divine response to crime.

of divine nemesis. The consequences, the "effects" that follow this "cause," are explicated in 18:8 (where, notably, it now is God, not the believers, who inflicts "mourning" upon Babylon; compare 18:8 with 18:6b). The speech concludes with a rationale (the ὅτι clause of 18:8) supporting the plausibility of these consequences, while at the same time revealing the self-deception behind Babylon's lack of awareness of accountability to the God served by the Christian communities.

The speech of the angel who drops the millstone into the sea (18:21–24) is not nearly so developed in its argumentation, but it is enthymematic in form, consisting of an assertion of future consequences (the "thesis") supported by a triple rationale:

> In such a violent rush, Great Babylon will be thrown down and will surely no longer be found. . . .
>
> *because* [ὅτι] her merchants were the magnates of the earth,
> *because* [ὅτι] all the nations were deceived by means of her sorceries
> and the prophets' and saints' blood was found in her,
> and (the blood) of all the slain upon the earth.
>
> (18:23c–24)

Babylon's future downfall is assured, this angel claims, on the basis of three charges leveled against her imperium. The first concerns the power attained by Babylon's merchants, suggesting that John perceived unjust redistributions of power and wealth as a result of Babylon's economic practices. The second concerns Babylon's practice of "luring" other nations into partnership and subjugation through various wiles—luxury goods, entertainment, and special privileges for local elites being among the most prominent "spells" cast by Babylon over other people groups. Tacitus bears witness to such "seduction" or "enchantment" in the voice of Civilis in Batavia, who calls out to his people: "Away with those pleasures which give the Romans more power over their subjects than their arms bestow!"[25] Where there was resistance to Roman expansion, the introduction of luxury, to which local elites would slowly become addicted, and the establishment of the "privilege" of Greek and Roman education for the children of the elite, could often prevail where violence failed. The third names the violence by means of which Babylon silenced dissent (the prophets and the saints witnessing to the greater empire of God and more authentic community promised by Jesus), stamped out opposition, and sustained its military-based system and slave-based economic structure.

No further evidence (e.g., the naming of specific incidences of offense) is offered to support these charges; rather, John expects them to be accepted on the basis of the authority of the speaker (an angel) or of the text (a divine revelation). The fact that other voices name the same crimes in their critique of Rome, however, suggests that John could also rely on the hearers' own memories and perceptions providing sufficient confirmation of the charges to allow the argumentation

---

25. Tacitus, *Hist.* 4.64.3, cited in Howard-Brook and Gwyther 1999, 96. See also Plutarch, *Sertorius* 13–14.

to promote critical distance between them and local manifestations of Roman imperial rule. The logic "works" on the basis of a shared conviction that, in a just cosmos, such institutionalized inequity and such perpetration of violence must lead to an accounting.

The angel's announcement receives further elaboration from "heaven," as celestial choirs sing another hymn in response to the judgment of Babylon:

> Hallelujah! The deliverance and glory and power of our God!
> *because* [ὅτι] his judicial decrees are true and just:
> *because* [ὅτι] he judged the great whore who ravaged the earth by means of her fornication,
> and required restitution for the blood of his slaves from her hand.
> (19:1–2)

The opening line presents a thesis about God and God's achievements (such as "God and God's accomplishments are worthy of acclamation") in an ejaculatory form. This thesis is supported by a rationale citing the virtue that God's actions have manifested, virtuous activity being a universally acknowledged basis for acclamation. The hymn adds a confirmation of the rationale, citing the particular deed manifesting justice and truth (in the sense of "faithfulness," אֱמֶת). The argumentation of 19:1–2, then, makes explicit the cultural premise about the governance of the cosmos assumed in 18:4–8, 21–24.

How, then, does this argumentation support John's agenda? John seeks to dissuade the hearers from fostering partnership with Rome and her local representatives, even though such partnership promises the greater and more secure enjoyment of temporal benefits. Rather, he wants the congregations to seek out ways to "come out" from participation in Roman domination systems. His aim aligns well with a major topic of classical rhetorical theory: the topic of "allies." Alliances were a regular topic of debate in Greek civic deliberation and continued to a limited extent in the Roman period. If one proposed an alliance, one would try to prove that the proposed ally "is reliable in character, and has done the state some service previously, and is very powerful" (*Rhet. Alex.* 1424b.36–40). A speaker opposing such an alliance would "show first that it is not necessary to make it now, secondly that the proposed allies are not really reliable, thirdly that they have treated us badly before" (1425a.2–4).

Using several of these standard topics, John urges against pursuing any alliance. He suggests that Rome has acted dishonorably in the spread of its imperium, painting the divinized personification of the senate and people of Rome (*Roma Aeterna*) as a wanton, lascivious prostitute, spreading moral pollution across the nations. The "proposed ally" is thus not "reliable in character," but depraved, self-indulgent, and self-serving.[26] Second, he reminds the hearers that the proposed ally has indeed "treated us badly before," certainly in the person

---

26. John's accumulations of the negative results of Roman rule (e.g., 18:3, 21–24), together with the agglomeration of the system's moral failures, serves to amplify the censure of Babylon (*Rhet. Alex.* 1426a.22–23), which in turn supports his arguments against partnership with Rome.

of the Christian apostles and martyrs (Rev. 18:23–24), not to mention Jesus himself. The depiction of intense enmity between the beast and his forces, with whom Babylon is herself in league (chap. 17), and those who refuse to participate in the cult of the beast intensifies the force of the application of this topic. Finally, to the extent that John has successfully established his forecast of Rome's destiny, he has also shown that such an alliance would not be advantageous, but would in fact be ultimately inexpedient: the hearers would find themselves ranged against God in partnership with a system doomed to fall by decree of divine justice. Partnership with Rome offers not security but rather the danger of incurring the wrath of God as Rome's clients are led to participate in Rome's sins against God.

We have spoken about the charges brought against Rome in Revelation (14:8; 18:2–8, 20–24). The prominence of these accusations has led several rhetorical critics to suggest that Revelation is largely "forensic rhetoric." While John indeed employs a plethora of forensic topics, neither Revelation 18 in particular, nor Revelation as a whole, constitutes forensic rhetoric. The goal of forensic oratory is to win a particular verdict of guilt or innocence from the judge or jury. Here, in the world of the visions, the verdict has already been rendered—and that by a heavenly judge, not the audience, who do not function as "jury" in any sense—and the sentence passed. Rather, forensic topics establish the necessity of Rome's (forthcoming) demise, which in turn positions John and his audience properly to discern "advantage" in the present, here to accept the summons of 18:4 as the most reasonable, advantageous course of action in their setting, given the forecast for the future. The ultimate rhetorical goal of the deployment of the forensic topics is thus deliberative.[27]

The second angel's declaration introduces another significant argumentative contribution. In an important sense, the second angel's assertion is historically true at the time John relays it: Babylon, the eastern empire that flourished under Nebuchadnezzar, did indeed fall and lay in ruins. The angel's message itself recontextualizes (that is, incorporates without citing) elements of phrases from Isaiah 21:9 and Jeremiah 51:7–8 (LXX 28:7–8), prophetic oracles spoken against that historic seat of empire, thus inviting the knowledgeable reader to blend the two horizons of Babylon's exercise of imperialism and its fate and Rome's imperialism and its prospects. In the fuller denunciation of Babylon/Rome in Revelation 17–18, John recontextualizes significant verbiage from Isaiah, Jeremiah, and Ezekiel, establishing a typological relationship with Rome as the antitype of Babylon (a typology shared by *4 Ezra* and *2 Baruch*), and applying Isaiah's and Jeremiah's prophecies about the type to the antitype. Having committed many of the same crimes as Babylon, Rome will most assuredly fall under the judgment of the same God.

This is an unusual but strikingly effective way of considering a historical precedent to predict the outcome of a new venture. Historical precedents were a

27. See further deSilva 1998a, 99–101.

"common topic" for enthymematic elaboration.[28] In this instance, the underlying deduction might run as follows:

> The Babylonian empire fell as the inevitable result of its injustice, violence, and arrogance.
> Roman imperialism exhibits the same systemic behaviors.
> Therefore, the Roman empire will also fall.

All of this, however, is communicated implicitly through John's artful use of label and allusion, intertexture, and narration.

WORSHIPING THE BEAST IS ULTIMATELY INEXPEDIENT! (REVELATION 14:9–12)

The third angel's message, like that of the first angel, moves more fully in a deliberative mode. Where the first angel summoned the inhabitants of the earth to pursue one course of action, the third angel seeks to dissuade hearers from an alternative, competing course of action.[29] The argumentation employs the topic of the consequences, a primary topic in exhortation and dissuasion.[30] John employs the technique of vivid description—a "clear, lucid, and impressive exposition of the consequences of an act" (*Rhet. Her.* 4.39.51)[31]—in order to impress the undesirability of these consequences more firmly upon the minds of the congregations:

> Course of action: "If anyone worships the beast and his image and receives a stamp upon one's forehead or upon one's hand,"
>
> Consequences: "that same person will drink from the wine of the violent fury of God, spiked and undiluted, in the cup of God's anger, and will be tortured with fire and sulfur in the presence of the holy angels and in the presence of the Lamb." (14:9–10)

These consequences are then further elaborated, and the course of action leading to such consequences restated:[32]

---

28. Aristotle, *Rhet.* 2.23.12. On the use of historical example as a premise on the basis of which to draw conclusions about future circumstances, see Aristotle, *Rhet.* 1.2.8; 1.4.9; 1.9.40; 2.20.8; *Rhet. Alex.* 1428b.12–17; 1429a.25–28.
29. Thus rightly Bauckham 1993a, 286.
30. Aristotle, *Rhet.* 2.23.14; 3.17.4.
31. Notably, the example given in the *Rhetorica ad Herennium* also uses vivid description of the consequences in the context of a dissuasive summons.
32. The third message thus also utilizes the figure of diction known as "reduplication," the "repetition of one or more words for the purpose of amplification" or appeal to emotion (*Rhet. Her.* 4.28.38), here using repetition to emphasize both the dire consequences and the actions that lead to the same.

Consequences: "And the smoke of their torture goes up forever and ever, and they do not have rest by day and by night,"

Course of action: "those people who worship the beast and his image, and if anyone receives the stamp of his name." (14:11)[33]

The third angel invokes topics related to both honor and security. Participation in imperial cult, he asserts, would mean exposure to everlasting torment at God's judgment, thus putting one's safety in the greatest possible jeopardy. Moreover, it would lead to public degradation and loss of honor as the angels and Lamb bear witness to one's punishment.[34]

The angel offers no explicit argumentation in support of this stark assertion. How, then, can John expect his hearers to accept it as a sufficiently reliable projection of the consequences upon which to base potentially costly decision making in the present? An important contribution in this regard is the evocation of the topic of God's anger (14:10) and the implicit argumentation it would nurture. Participation in the imperial cult will lead to such dire consequences, the angel implies, because it represents a course of action that provokes God to anger.

John and his congregations shared cultural knowledge that would readily provide what was needed to complete this deductive process. Participation in idolatry shows complete and utter disregard for perhaps the most prominently communicated commandments of God: Do not worship other gods, and do not engage in the worship of idols. These are the first two commandments in both listings of the Decalogue (Exod. 20:2–6; Deut. 5:6–9), and apart from the commandment to keep the Sabbath, the most fully elaborated of those commandments. The prohibition, rejection, and denunciation of idolatry recurs throughout the scriptural tradition (Exod. 23:33; 34:13; Lev. 26:1; Deut. 8:19; 11:16; 30:17; Josh. 23:16; etc.), extrabiblical Jewish literature (Letter of Jeremiah; Wis. 13:1–14:31; etc.), and early Christian instruction (Rom. 1:18–32; 1 Cor. 10:14–22; Gal. 5:19–21; 1 Thess. 1:9; 1 Pet. 4:3; 1 John 5:21). As the heavenly hymns and the first angel's message have already intimated, however, participation in idolatry also enacts ingratitude toward the Creator God, taking away the honors due God and giving them to "the gods that did not make heaven and earth." Paul provides an explicit statement of this logic in Romans 1:18–23, where the ingratitude and the dishonor shown God in the practice of idolatry—when creation itself revealed the goodness of the divine Benefactor and invited people into a grateful and obedient response—provokes God to "wrath" (ὀργή) and leads to the experience of punishment both now and

---

33. The angel's message is thus an instance of chiasmus at the level of ornamentation as discussed in ancient literary theorists. On the abuse of "macrochiasm" in attempts to outline large segments or the whole of Revelation, see deSilva 2007a.

34. Reading these messages as attempts at persuasion in the context of an honor culture (where public dishonor is a greatly feared evil) helps us to understand why this punishment should take place in the sight of the angels and the Lamb, a detail that several commentators have found "difficult" (Ford 1975, 249) or "strange" in light of modern sensibilities (Roloff 1993, 176).

hereafter (1:24–32; 2:6–11).[35] Since John has already described the beast as the ally and pawn of God's archenemy, the dragon (Rev. 13:1–8), the affront to God is amplified, and the worshiper of the beast who thus challenges God's honor should expect all the more to suffer God's punishment.[36]

Aristotle (*Rhet.* 2.2.1, 8) regarded anger as an expected response to an affront to one's honor, particularly when the affront comes from those whom one has benefited (as God has benefited all; 14:6–7). God's anger is the anger of a slighted benefactor, whose favor meets not with gratitude (such as the first angel calls for) but with disobedience of his commands—the refusal to render the Patron the service he requires of the client.[37] In the perpetual punishment of the idolater, God reasserts God's honor.[38] The third angel's assertion, therefore, is completely reasonable within the context of Jewish and Christian cultural knowledge about God and the worship of idols, and the broader context of the responses of benefactors to displays of ingratitude and even insult.

Heard within the larger literary context of Revelation 13:11–14:13, the third angel's announcement contributes another argumentative topic, an argument concerning "relative expediency." Aristotle gave considerable attention to arguments of this sort in his *Art of Rhetoric*, since, as he observed, people often agree that two courses of action might both bring benefit, or might both bring unwanted consequences, and so must dispute which brings the greater good or the lesser evil (1.7.1–2). That which causes greater loss is more to be avoided (1.7.16). Unpleasant situations of shorter duration and lesser dangers are to be preferred over long-lasting evils and more serious dangers (1.7.26). Avoiding a greater evil, pain, or loss by embracing a lesser one is expedient (1.10.18). "Those things are greater evils," and therefore more to be avoided, "the punishment for which is greater" (1.7.30).

John has already acknowledged that nonparticipation in the imperial cult can carry an increasingly heavy cost, both in terms of economic disenfranchisement and even loss of life (Rev. 13:15–17). The Christians in Smyrna and Pergamum appear already to have experienced and witnessed such consequences firsthand.

---

35. See also *4 Ezra* 7:20–24, 78–87, where the everlasting fate of the ungodly is also the result of their provocation of God, slighting God and God's law by their disobedience and denial of the One God's existence and claim on their devotion.

36. Appropriately, those who wish to be seen as grateful clients of the beast, and who are thus seen by God as ungrateful enemies, share the fate that will also befall Satan, the beast, and the false prophet. Repetitions of "torment" (14:10; 20:10), "fire and sulfur" (14:10; 19:20; 20:10), and "day and night" (14:11; 20:10) associate their fates.

37. On the obligations of clients, see Danker 1982; deSilva 1996b.

38. According to Aulus Gellius (*Attic Nights* 7.14.2–4), punishment allows for the restoration of the dignity of the affronted or assaulted party, "lest the omission of punishment bring him into contempt and diminish the esteem in which he is held." The expectation of everlasting rewards and punishments following upon obedience or disobedience to God in this life was a foundational aspect of converts' resocialization within the Christian worldview (see, e.g., Heb. 6:1–2, a text stemming from the mission fields of the Pauline circle and bearing significant affinities with the social situation presumed in 1 Peter—thus quite possibly reflecting the practice of Christianity in Asia Minor or its neighboring provinces. The Nicolaitans were swimming against the strong current of the tradition both in regard to the dangers of idolatry and the certainty of eternal condemnation as a result of the practice.

However, the third angel's message provides a counterpoint that makes such disadvantages pale in comparison with the disadvantages that attend participating in idolatrous worship for the sake of lessening tension and hostility between sect and society (see also 14:14–20; 16:1–21; 20:11–15). Weighing temporary advantages and disadvantages against "eternal" ones is a rhetorical technique common to subcultures and countercultures, found in Greco-Roman ethical philosophy, Hellenistic Jewish texts, as well as Christian literature, since members of these groups must frequently accept some degree of disadvantage as the price of maintaining their alternative culture and practicing its distinctive commitments.[39]

Whether 14:12 is heard as part of the angel's pronouncement or as John's comment on the angel's message, this statement offers a conclusion that makes the topic of relative expediency more explicit: *"Here* is the patient endurance of the holy ones, the ones keeping the commandments of God and the faith of Jesus."[40] The statement suggests that the consequences of dishonoring God through disobedience (in particular, giving to idols and other "gods" the honor due the One God) provide the holy ones with incentive to "endure." But what do the saints "endure"? The hearer immediately recalls 13:15–17, a proximate picture of the negative consequences imposed upon those who refuse to participate in this same idolatrous cult. The "holy ones" know that the consequences of betraying God and God's commandments are far more inexpedient than the consequences of running afoul of the expectations of human society where walking in line with God's law requires it.

John is still drawing on logic pervasively inculcated within Jewish and Christian culture. The author of 4 Maccabees provides a striking parallel when he opens a window into the reasoning of the brothers as they face the choice of disloyalty to God's covenant or death by torture:

> Let us with all our hearts consecrate ourselves to God, who gave us our lives, and let us use our bodies as a bulwark for the law. Let us not fear him who thinks he is killing us, for great is the struggle of the soul and the danger of eternal torment lying before those who transgress the commandment of God. (13:13b–15 NRSV)

Here one finds the same awareness of the debt of gratitude (and hence obligation of loyalty) owed God as the giver of life (cf. Rev. 14:7), and rejection of unjustly seeking to preserve one's life or improve one's circumstance at the cost of disloyalty to the divine Patron. These brothers face brutal execution by torture if they refuse the king's command to act against their native law, but they weigh

39. See, e.g., Plato, *Gorgias* 526D–527A; 4 Macc. 15:2–3, 8; 2 Cor. 4:16–18.
40. Or, perhaps better, "keeping ... faith *with* Jesus," understanding πίστις more in the sense of faithfulness displayed rather than belief held (or even faithfulness imitated), and construing the genitive Ἰησοῦ as an objective genitive. Prigent (1988, 57) observed that πίστις appears three out of four times in parallel with ὑπομονή (2:19; 13:10; 14:12) and that the adjectival form appears eight times in the sense of fidelity, and not belief. Frederick J. Murphy (1998, 135) concurs: "'Faith' in Revelation always means absolute loyalty to Christ, especially when engagement with surrounding culture might mitigate such loyalty."

this against the "danger of eternal torment lying before" them if they show more regard for the king than for God. Therefore, they deduce that patient endurance of temporary pain and loss is, indeed, the more expedient course of action. This logic pervades early Christian culture as well (see, e.g., Matt. 10:28; Acts 5:29). John thus invokes a well-established argument from relative expediency to make living and dying as a faithful witness to God and God's Messiah through conspicuous nonparticipation in the imperial cult (and, hence, nonparticipation in the rituals legitimating Roman rule) emerge as the model to be embraced.[41]

Revelation 14:12, by effectively summarizing the posture of those who escape the horrific consequences announced in 14:9–11, also recapitulates the course of action that the whole discourse promotes: the course that shows commitment to walk in line with God's commandments (among which avoidance of idolatry remains prominent) in such a way as shows loyalty to Jesus (e.g., through not making alliances with the beast or other enemies of God and God's Christ). Distancing those who practice such behaviors from the consequences announced in 14:9–11 disposes the hearers to identify themselves with, and conform themselves to, this model.

DYING IN THE LORD BRINGS REAL ADVANTAGE! (REVELATION 14:13)

The series of three angelic messages closes with a coda in the form of a "macarism," a statement declaring a certain class of people to be μακάριος, "happy," "favored," "honored," or otherwise "privileged" to enjoy a highly valued good. The term is classically connected with the "gods" (οἱ μάκαρες) and "the happy state of the gods above earthly sufferings and labours."[42] Classical authors frequently ascribe the enjoyment of this state to certain persons who fulfill particu-

---

41. Ian Smith (2002), an economist, has provided an excellent discussion of John's treatment of relative expediency, providing a helpful supplement to classical rhetorical analysis. Smith identifies John's primary rhetorical problem to be the human tendency to place higher value on the benefits to be gained or costs to be avoided that are near at hand, and to "discount" (value less) those that are far off (2002, 99), a tendency observed as early as Aristotle as a rhetorical "problem" (*Rhet.* 2.5.1). He pays particular attention to the ways in which John "discounts" the value of the benefits of participation (or costs of nonparticipation) in the imperial cult by stressing the shortness of the time in which one is likely to enjoy/suffer such benefits/costs (2002, 110), while heightening the import of eschatological benefits and costs by affirming their certainty and by using vivid description of consequences (good and bad) so that the hearers will "imagine the future and future experiences" more fully, with the result that they will weigh more heavily on present choices (2002, 112–13, citing Becker and Mulligan 1997 on the relationship between discounting future costs and the individual's ability and tendency to imagine those future experiences). "Imaginative capacity itself can be accumulated by investing time and effort in running mental simulations of future scenarios and in training the imagination to anticipate distant experiences more readily" (Smith 2002, 113). Revelation provides its audiences with just such an exercise. Smith (2002, 113) rightly stresses that Revelation achieves its effect not by imparting necessarily new *information* about the future, but by stimulating the *imagination* of that future so that it weighs more heavily as a factor in present decision making.

42. Bertram and Hauck 1967, 362.

lar characteristics (e.g., achievements, virtues, and the like). Dissatisfaction with the adequacy of "blessed" as a translation has led to several alternative suggestions that better capture the force of a macarism, such as "How honored!" "How privileged!" (or "favored").[43]

Rhetorical theory helps unpack the persuasive force of a "macarism." Aristotle, indeed, comments specifically on this kind of pronouncement: "Blessing and felicitation [μακαρισμὸς καὶ εὐδαιμονισμός] are identical with each other, but are not the same as praise and encomium, which, as virtue is contained in happiness, are contained in felicitation" (*Rhet.* 1.9.34 [1367b.33]). "Praise" or "encomium" are thus considered to be included within the macarism or congratulatory affirmation, the added feature being the notice of the "happy," "privileged," or "favored" condition of those who are also praised.

A macarism is thus an epideictic statement that can contribute to deliberative rhetoric in the same way that praiseworthy examples support adoption of a particular course of action. In the paragraph directly following his treatment of the macarism, Aristotle compares praise and advice, encomium and deliberation, thus:

> Praise and counsels have a common aspect; for what you might suggest in counseling becomes encomium by a change in the phrase. Accordingly, when we know what we ought to do and the qualities we ought to possess, we ought to make a change in the phrase and turn it, employing this knowledge as a suggestion. For instance, the statement that "one ought not to pride oneself on goods which are due to fortune, but on those which are due to oneself alone," when expressed in this way, has the force of a suggestion; but expressed thus, "he was proud, not of goods which were due to fortune, but of those which were due to himself alone," it becomes praise. Accordingly, if you desire to praise, look what you would suggest; if you desire to suggest, look what you would praise. (*Rhet.* 1.9.35–36; see also Quintilian, *Inst.* 3.7.28)

The macarism, as a form that includes praise, directs attention to what is valuable and thereby advantageous to acquire for oneself. It carries the implicit potential for exhortation. This has been consistently recognized by scholars studying macarisms in a variety of contexts. By declaring a certain class of people to be μακάριοι, a macarism exerts subtle pressure upon the hearers. The hearers will engage in self-examination, to discern whether or not they fit in with the category of people who are thus beatified.[44] If they do "fit," they may tacitly recommit themselves to maintain the required behaviors, attitudes, and

---

43. Hanson (1996, 90) makes a strong case in favor of the former: Macarisms "represent the public validation of an individual's or group's experience, behavior, or attitude as honorable." Yet deSilva (1998a, 104) suggests the latter as modest expansions of the scope of μακάριος, since in many instances macarisms are predicated upon *receiving* a special favor, not (solely) upon the attributes or achievements of the subjects. "Enviable," proposed by W. Janzen (1965, 224–26), is a less viable option (see Lipinski 1968, 322 n. 7), in part because of the negative connotations of "envy" in both classical and modern ethical conversations.
44. Sweet 1979, 280.

commitments identified in the macarism, even if costly.⁴⁵ If they do not, they may be pushed "to range themselves alongside the category of the 'beatified,'" and thus to change their behaviors or dispositions.⁴⁶ The macarism proposes a "condition" that leads to a highly desirable state, and thus exercises a "paraenetic function" by fostering the hearers' desire to meet that condition.⁴⁷

Moreover, while macarisms were originally simple pronouncements (often made in cultic settings), they were quickly adapted to more didactic settings, in part by the addition of supportive argumentation,⁴⁸ demonstrating the recognition of the macarism's paraenetic potential within Israelite, Hellenistic- and Roman-era Jewish, and early Christian contexts. Macarisms are frequently supported by ὅτι or γάρ clauses,⁴⁹ explicitly signaling the presence of argumentation, as well as by supporting rationales introduced more subtly.⁵⁰ The additions of these rationales create a variety of enthymemes employing the argument from consequences, from the contrary, or from the cause, often using familiar topics traditionally linked with deliberation (honor, expediency, security, and so forth).⁵¹ In a few cases, the argumentation combines several "common topics" of enthymemes.⁵²

The first of Revelation's seven macarisms exhibits both a "hortatory tone" as well as supportive argumentation fostering assent to the macarism's fundamental claim:

> How honorable [Μακάριος] is the one who reads aloud, and the ones who hear the words of this prophecy and continue to keep what is written therein, for [γάρ] the time is near. (Rev. 1:3)

The macarism, an endorsement spoken in the impersonal voice of the book's incipit, renders the reader and hearers well disposed toward the process of communicating the contents of the book as it occupies them for the next hour and encourages them to align their behaviors with those contents. The macarism thus evokes particular behaviors from the audience in the present (attentive and receptive hearing) and near future (walking in line with what will be heard). The macarism is supported by explicit argumentation, the rationale (γάρ) that "the time is near."⁵³ The proximity of the realities described in the book explains why the one who

---

45. Giesen 1997, 64–72, esp. 66.
46. Lipinski 1968, 322.
47. Strecker 1991, 376–77; Windisch 1937, 45.
48. Lipinski 1968, 322–25, 359.
49. Lipinksi (1968, 359 n. 14) cites Gen. 30:13; Tob. 13:16; Bar. 4:4; Matt. 5:3–10; 13:16; 16:17; Luke 1:45; 6:20–21; 14:14; Jas. 1:12; 1 Pet. 4:14 as examples of macarisms with ὅτι in the LXX and NT, and Isa. 31:9–10; Prov. 3:13–14; 8:34–35; Sir. 28:19–20; 48:11; 50:28–29; 4 Macc. 18:9; Luke 14:14; Rev. 1:3; 14:13 as examples of macarisms with γάρ in the LXX and NT.
50. See, e.g., Pss. 41:1–3; 89:15; 112:1–3; Sir. 28:19–20; Bar. 4:4; *Pss. Sol.* 4:23; 5:16; 6:1–2.
51. Consequences: see, e.g., Pss. 41:1–3; 89:15; 112:1–3; 127:5; 128:1–2; Tob. 13:16; Sir. 26:1; 50:28–29; *Pss. Sol.* 4:23; 6:1–2; 10:1; Jas. 1:12; contrary: Ps. 32:1–4; *Pss. Sol.* 5:16; cause: Bar. 4:4.
52. For example, arguments from the consequences and the contrary are combined in Prov. 8:34–36; 28:14; while Ps. 1:1–5 weaves in enthymemes based on consequences, arguments from analogy, and the contrary.
53. Royalty 1997, 609.

reads it aloud (to the gathered congregation), those who hear it (the assembled congregations), and those who keep it (as they would also keep the commandments of God; 12:17; 14:12) are "privileged" or "favored": they are put in a better position to overcome the challenges of the forthcoming future successfully.[54]

Revelation 14:13, the second of the seven macarisms, provides the "clincher" to the argument of the relative expediency of participating in the worship of the beast (and the constellation of accommodating practices of which this is the central representative for John) versus visibly and uncompromisingly withdrawing from settings where anyone or anything other than the God of Israel and God's Messiah is the focal point of worship. It does this by pronouncing those who have been faithful unto death "privileged," "honorable," "enjoying the divine life beyond the temporal realm":

> And I heard a voice from heaven, saying, "Write:
> "How privileged are the dead, the ones dying in the Lord from henceforth!"
> "Yes, indeed," says the Spirit,
> "in order that [ἵνα] they may rest from their labors,
> for [γάρ] their works follow with them."

The macarism elevates all who "die in the Lord," who have lived out the core values of keeping the commandments of God and keeping faith with Jesus (14:12), whether or not this has led to a violent end.[55] The use of the more general ἀποθνῄσκειν (to die) rather than a passive form of ἀποκτείνειν (to kill) supports this observation. Nevertheless, John has been leading the audiences to expect violent responses from the non-Christian world to their faithful witness to the One God (as in 2:10), since their deaths contribute to completing the number of the martyrs (6:9–11) as they find themselves among the targets of the beast and his ally (13:8, 15–17). The related macarism of 20:6 also especially highlights the positive value of being executed for the sake of one's loyalty to God and the Lamb. Thus, with the irony characteristic of several early Christian macarisms that is, in part, a source of their rhetorical power, John elevates as honored and privileged those whom society will have most devalued and marginalized.[56]

---

54. The content is very similar to other macarisms found in the NT. Compare Luke 11:27–28: "Blessed, rather, are the ones hearing and keeping [guarding] the word of God [μακάριοι οἱ ἀκούοντες τὸν λόγον τοῦ θεοῦ καὶ φυλάσσοντες]"; and Jas. 1:25: "Blessed is this person in his doing [of the law]." To the extent that such macarisms are "commonplace" in early Christian culture, John's assertion of what constitutes "a blessed state" will be the more readily accepted.

55. Thus Harrington 1993, 152; Giesen 1997, 68; Prigent 1988, 230; Cruz 1991, 275; against Beckwith 1919, 659; Bousset 1906, 386–87; Kraft 1974, 195; and Mounce 1977, 277, who relate the macarism exclusively to the martyrs.

56. Bertram and Hauck (1967, 368) have observed that NT macarisms are often paradoxical, citing Matt. 5:3–11; Luke 6:20–22; 1 Pet. 3:14; 4:14; and Rev. 14:13 as prominent examples. "The power of the statements lies in their reversal of all human values" (Bertram and Hauck 1967, 368). Jesus' own elevation of faithfulness in the face of persecution as a condition of "blessedness" (Matt. 5:10–11) may provide something of a precedent available to the audiences through their shared tradition, and possibly thus a kind of authority or foundation that renders the macarisms in Revelation more readily credible.

The central assertion of "blessedness" is supported by an argument from the consequences (or perhaps more properly, the *incentives* connected with the course of faithfulness unto death, taking the ἵνα clause as fully expressing purpose, and not merely result).[57] Dying "in the Lord" conveys privilege because it results in enjoying a state of rest from the exertions of faithful discipleship. This enthymeme would persuade hearers who share the cultural knowledge that, despite the circumstances of their deaths, the "righteous" who die "rest in their chambers" (Isa. 57:1–2) and are "at peace" (Wis. 3:1–3). John has already depicted a voice telling the souls of those previously killed for God's word and their witness to "continue to rest" (ἵνα ἀναπαύσονται) until their number is completed (Rev. 6:9–11). This "rest" significantly entails freedom from the consequences of yielding to the pressures and enticements of imperial cult and related cultic practices. John's skillful repetition of words reinforces the contrast between consequences of competing courses of action:

They do not have rest by day and by night [οὐκ ἔχουσιν ἀνάπαυσιν]. (14:11)

That they may rest from their labors [ἵνα ἀναπαήσονται]. (14:13)

The grim picture of public torment without rest or reprieve for those who worship the beast or receive its mark is juxtaposed with the rest enjoyed by those who have died "favored" or "blessed" by God. The repetition of "rest" reinforces the message that those who maintain their exclusive, faithful obedience to the One God—even if the cost is grim (13:15–17)—rather than submit to participation in the emperor cult have chosen wisely, since they will enjoy what is eternally denied the beast-worshipers. The contrasting postmortem fates seal John's case regarding relative expediency for those who sufficiently value the traditional affirmations that he brings to bear on their present situation.

A confirmation of this rationale provides the "evidence" that the faithful disciples' expectation of entering into rest is a firmly grounded one: the record of these souls' "works" crosses the threshold of death together with them, ostensibly to "speak" on their behalf and assure their enjoyment of blessedness in God's realm beyond this mortal life. It also evokes a topic identified by Aristotle as tending to identify something as a greater good than other things. Those things "which follow us after death" and "are accompanied by honor" are "greater goods" (Aristotle, *Rhet.* 1.9.25). The macarism identifies works of loyal obedience to be among those things that "follow us after death" (as Rev. 14:9–11 painted a picture of how works showing ingratitude and disobedience toward God follow one after death). The essential deduction might be stated as follows:

---

57. Incentives and disincentives were another "common topic" for enthymematic elaboration (Aristotle, *Rhet.* 2.23.21).

God assigns people postmortem rewards and punishments according to their works.

God will view the works of faithful people favorably.

The faithful dead will find reward (as rest).

The first, general premise is assumed here, being amply attested throughout Jewish and Christian literature[58] as well as throughout Revelation itself.

The idea that (faithful, righteous, obedient) works stored with God can give the faithful confidence in the face of death is prominent in Jewish apocalypses contemporary with Revelation. *Second Baruch* affirms that "the righteous justly hope for the end, and without fear depart from this habitation, because they have with Thee a store of works preserved in treasuries. On this account also these without fear leave this world, and trusting with joy they hope to receive the world which Thou hast promised them" (14:12–13). Both *2 Baruch* 24:1–2 and *4 Ezra* 7:77; 8:32, 36 speak of treasuries of good works. John speaks from within this cultural background as he frames this confirmation of the rationale.

The value of "possessing" such works is also supported throughout Revelation. In the oracle to Ephesus, Jesus asserts that "works" and "labors" (ἔργα, κόποι) are already known to him (Rev. 2:2), even preceding rather than following the disciple (see also 2:19; 3:1 [ironically]; 3:8, 15 [ironically again]). Jesus affirms that he renders to each according to their works (2:23), a premise affirmed again in the visions of the final judgment and the epilogue (20:12–13; 22:12; cf. also 18:6). The gains to be had by works of "compromise" with the local society and its cultic expressions of loyalty, solidarity, and plain sociability pale in comparison with the gains to be enjoyed through works displaying loyalty to God's commandments and to Jesus (14:12–13), making the pursuit of the latter the path of greater expedience. The macarism in 14:13 thus supports Christians in their resistance to the cult of the emperors and its compulsions, holding before their eyes a paradigm of the "saints" who are "blessed," characterized by obedience to God's commands and lifelong loyalty to God and to Jesus, as honorable models for imitation and self-identification.

Macarisms continue to punctuate Revelation, holding up certain responses as advantageous or commendable, contributing thus to the overall paradigm of faithful response that John wishes to foster, as well as to the argumentative support for the same. A third appears in 16:15 as a parenthetical remark in the midst of John's description of the results of pouring out the sixth bowl:

> See! I am coming like a thief! How fortunate are those who keep a sharp eye out, and keep hold of their garments in order that they not walk about naked and people see their shame.

---

58. Within the NT, see Rom. 2:6–11; 2 Cor. 5:9–10; Heb. 11:6.

The opening sentence, "I am coming like a thief," establishes a context in which people can be caught off guard by an event to their own disadvantage.[59] The principal assertion of the macarism, then, elevates the value of living as one who expects Christ's coming, who would not be caught in tangled alliances and compromising positions at Christ's return. This assertion is supported by an enthymeme based on the consequences: the ἵνα clause affirms that those who maintain the posture of watchfulness and readiness (keeping their "garments") will avoid the negative consequences of being exposed and disgraced.[60] This avoidable eventuality carries strong overtones of Genesis 3, where awareness of "nakedness" reflected humanity's awareness of their shame, sin, and betrayal being exposed as God came to visit them in the evening (2:25; 3:7–11). This macarism essentially keeps the audience focused on Christ's return and readiness for that event, drawing their attention away from, and diminishing the importance of, other challenges in their immediate situations that could draw them into courses of action that compromise their adherence to the dispositions and behaviors fostered by the Jewish and Christian traditions they had accepted.

An angelic being pronounces a fourth macarism (Rev. 19:9) without offering explicit or implicit argumentation: "How privileged are those who are invited to the marriage feast of the Lamb!" Instead, the angel makes an extraordinary assertion of the reliability of the macarism as "genuine words of God [καὶ λέγει μοι· Οὗτοι οἱ λόγοι ἀληθινοὶ τοῦ θεοῦ εἰσιν]."[61] This approaches George Kennedy's "radical rhetoric,"[62] the rhetoric of authoritative pronouncement, whereas previous macarisms have shown the tendency to support "radical rhetoric" (i.e., divine pronouncements) with some "secular" argumentation (causes, consequences, rationales). For hearers inclined to grant such authority to these words, the macarism would naturally invite self-examination.[63] The description of the bride as adorned with "the righteous deeds of the saints" might give particular direction to this self-examination: Am I living in such a way as to be

---

59. The macarism, spoken by Christ (the "I" in "See! I am coming quickly!"; cf. 2:16; 3:11), incorporates words and phrases from the tradition of Jesus sayings. The macarism resembles Luke 12:37: "Blessed are those slaves, whom the Lord, upon coming, will find watching." Although Jesus does not speak of *himself* coming as a thief in the sayings traditions, he does use the figure of the thief breaking in at an unknown time as an image of his coming (Matt. 24:43; Luke 12:39). Connections with Jesus' speech may assist the acceptance of the prophetic word as authentically representing the ongoing speech of Jesus to his followers.

60. This macarism explicitly recalls the language of several of the seven oracles. The Laodicean Christians had been described as "naked" (γυμνός), requiring from Christ "white garments, in order ... that the shame of your nakedness not be seen [ἱμάτια λευκὰ ἵνα ... μὴ φανερωθῇ ἡ αἰσχύνη τῆς γυμνότητός σου]"; Rev. 3:18). The Sardian Christians were warned to "become watchful [γίνου γρηγορῶν]"; 3:2), and to "keep [τήρει]" not garments, but what instruction in the way of discipleship they had hitherto received (3:3). Failure to be watchful (ἐὰν μὴ γρηγορήσῃς) would result in this very situation announced in 16:15: "I will come as a thief [ἥξω ὡς κλέπτης]"; 3:3). Finally, some in Sardis are commended for not defiling their garments (τὰ ἱμάτια αὐτῶν), who will walk around with Christ clothed in white robes (3:4–5).

61. Like the macarism in 14:13, the significance of 19:9 is highlighted by a preceding command from a heavenly voice to "write down" the macarism (Giesen 1997, 68–69).

62. Kennedy 1984, 6–7.

63. Sweet 1979, 280.

invited to this marriage feast, contributing to the adornment of the bride by deeds of justice performed in the midst of an unjust system that both lures and pressures me to participate in injustice? Given that the "marriage supper" is an image of the messianic banquet, and that this union between the Lamb and the bride represents the life of the saints in God's kingdom (see 19:7–8; 21:1–4), the macarism would likely be accepted as a truism and, therefore, effective in redirecting the hearers' ambitions toward attaining this privilege by living in line with God's commandments and just decrees.

The fifth macarism (20:6) is the only one spoken in John's own narrative voice. After describing "the first resurrection" (20:5), the raising of the souls of those beheaded "on account of the testimony of Jesus and on account of the word of God" and "whoever did not worship the beast nor its image and did not receive the mark,"[64] and the elevation of the same to coregency with Christ (ἐβασίλευσαν μετὰ τοῦ Χριστοῦ, 20:4), John pronounces them favored:

> How favored and holy is the one having a share in the first resurrection: over them, the second death has no claim, but they will be priests of God and of Christ and they will reign with him [βασιλεύσουσιν μετ' αὐτοῦ] for a thousand years. (20:6)

Two reasons are offered for the "favored" status of those who take part in the first resurrection, who came to enjoy this privilege at an otherwise substantial cost. Both are arguments from the consequences: a negative consequence avoided ("Over these the second death has no authority"), and a positive one enjoyed ("but they will be priests of God and of Christ, and they will reign with him for a thousand years"). Previous argumentation supports the first of these rationales: the faithful have the "works" that demonstrate that they belong to Christ (and thus are written in the Lamb's Book of Life) and hence will enjoy rest and honor in the presence of the Lamb rather than be sentenced to have a part in the second death (2:11; 14:12–13; 20:14–15). The second rationale is rendered more plausible (if not confirmed) by the continued use of language drawn from Exodus 19:6, God's promise concerning the formation of God's people, which becomes the necessary precedent for asserting the final and complete fulfillment of the promise in Revelation 20:6 (seen also in 1:5–6; 5:9–10, which nurture the conviction that the promise of Exodus is in the process of being fulfilled in the gathering together of the Christian assemblies). The fifth macarism, then, further promotes the withdrawal from local manifestations of imperial cult as urged in previous argumentation (including the second macarism). Bearing testimony by word and deed, though admittedly costly in terms of the safe enjoyment of life in this world, remains the more expedient path since it leads to significantly greater and longer-lasting privileges in the world to come.

64. This macarism pronounces salvation not only over martyrs, but also over all Christians who "prove themselves in the present oppression" (Giesen 1997; 70; with Schüssler Fiorenza 1972, 305–6; Prigent 1988, 310–11; Roloff 1984, 193; Bieder 1954, 25; Cruz 1991, 277–78; against Mounce 1977, 355–56; Böcher 1988b, 105).

The sixth macarism (22:7) opens the "epilogue" that follows the visionary portions, essentially repeating the first macarism, though with the appropriate omission of "reading" and "hearing," since those acts are, by this point, nearly completed. All that remains is the "keeping," the comprehensive observance of John's prophetic word.[65] It also repeats the rationale ("for the time is near," 1:3), though now in the form of an affirmation ("See! I am coming quickly!") rather than a dependent clause with an explicit inferential particle. The argumentation remains the same: the imminence of Christ's coming (to judge the opponents and to reward the faithful witnesses) provides the grounds or reason that those who "keep the words of the prophecy of this book," who walk in line with what is revealed in Revelation, are "privileged" or "favored," since they will encounter Christ advantageously and favorably.

The final macarism (22:14–15) returns to the image of "washing one's robes" to describe the privileged group with whom John wants his hearers to identify themselves:

> How fortunate are the ones washing their robes [οἱ πλύνοντες τὰς στολάς], in order that authority over the tree of life might be theirs and that they might enter by the gates into the city. Outside are the dogs and the sorcerers and the sexually immoral and the murderers and the idolaters and everyone who loves and lives a lie.

The macarism promotes "washing one's robes" as a behavior to be emulated, offering supporting arguments from the incentives to such action (see the purposive ἵνα) and from the contrary. The consequences have been described within the vision (see 21:25–27; 22:2) and rely on the persuasiveness of that vision for their own argumentative strength here. The beauty, peace, and security of life in new Jerusalem (particularly in contrast to the conditions of life under the beast and Babylon) heighten the desirability of entering that city, and hence the expediency of "washing one's robes."

The assertion that such "washing" of robes is prerequisite to entering the holy city where God's presence dwells in its fullness (21:3–4, 22–23; 22:3–5) draws on Jewish cultural premises concerning the divinely appointed preparation for a theophany or for entering God's presence. Prior to the Sinai theophany, God instructed Moses to have the people wash their garments (πλυνάτωσαν τὰ ἱμάτια) in preparation for the encounter (Exod. 19:10, 14). The full deduction might be spelled out thus:

> Rule (deduced from historical precedent in Exod. 19:10, 14): It is necessary to wash one's clothes before coming before the presence of the Holy God.

---

65. Giesen 1997, 70–71.

Case: These Christ-followers washed their clothes by means of the blood of the Lamb.
Result: They are eligible to enter God's presence in the Holy City.

Throughout Revelation, the prominence of God's promise that the people would be a "priestly kingdom" (Exod. 19:5–6; see Rev. 1:5–6; 5:9–10; 20:4–6) renders more plausible the assertion that John draws upon the nearby regulations for God's people coming before God as God's priestly kingdom.

This ideal is clarified in part by the statement of the contrary (22:15), describing the traits of the disprivileged group that will not enjoy these consequences. The list of dispositions and behaviors in 22:15, like that of 21:8, is not merely a general vice list, but one that has been pointedly crafted toward John's hearers' challenges (and the courses of action that would denote, for John, failure to meet those challenges). Each represents some form of compromising one's Christian loyalties and witness, as well as relevant facets of the behavior of non-Christians.[66] Hearers would have encountered the image of washing robes in the vision of those who had successfully emerged on the other side of the "great tribulation" (7:14), where identification with the blood of the Lamb in faithful witness resulted in the washing of their garments.[67]

Revelation's seven macarisms thus contribute to John's prioritizing of the hearers' ambitions or goals (attaining the rest of the holy ones [14:13], being prepared at Christ's return [16:15], being invited to the marriage feast of the Lamb [19:9], and so forth), and to John's depiction of an "ideal" Christian response, identifying the traits and behaviors of those who are held to be most honorable before God's court of reputation (and thus within the Christian group to the extent that John's values and visions are embraced). They provide "a kind of summary" of Revelation's summons by

> spell[ing] out the adequate response to John's prophecy (reading/hearing and keeping: 1.3; 22.7; faithfulness as far as death: 14.13; 22.14; readiness for the Lord's coming: 16.15) and the fulness of divine blessing that attends that response (rest from labours: 14.13; invitation to the Lamb's marriage supper: 19.9; participation in the first resurrection: 20.6; the tree of life and entry into the new Jerusalem: 22.14; but these are only *representative* of the complete blessing indicated by the number seven).[68]

Alongside other, more developed paradigms of praiseworthy commitments and actions (e.g., 7:13–17; 11:3–12; 12:10–12; 14:1–5), they lay out the path

---

66. Kraybill 1996, 199. Informers who denounce Christians would be, according to Kraybill, the "murderers."
67. "Washing" one's robes refers not to a single act, like baptism, but to how one has conducted oneself after baptism, signaling the living out of one's Christian conviction (Giesen 1997, 67, 71), whether that has eventuated in martyrdom or not (Giesen 1997, 67, with Prigent 1988, 355; against Lohmeyer 1970, 180; Caird 1966, 285).
68. Bauckham 1993a, 30.

to honor and the enjoyment of a secure "happiness" for the members of the seven churches.

CONCLUSION

Despite its visionary nature, its appeals to the emotions of the hearers, and its imaginative power, Revelation contains significant rational argumentation. John employs enthymematic strategies and topics familiar from Greco-Roman rhetoric as part of his larger program of persuasion. Such argumentation is only "rational" within the context of a particular worldview, in this case the worldview nurtured by the Scriptures and other Jewish and emerging Christian traditions. While rational argumentation is by no means the most prominent facet of John's rhetorical program, its contributions ought not to be overlooked.

Throughout Revelation's argumentation, epideictic and deliberative strains work together, the one portraying the ideal, the other assisting the audience to choose the path that leads to the ideal, as well as the contrary (looking at censurable models and the courses of action from which the audience is dissuaded).[69] As one would expect from a mixture of epideictic and deliberative rhetoric, the exhortations throughout Revelation both seek to inculcate *general* values, dispositions, and behaviors to be lived out in day-to-day situations (an effect of classical funeral orations), as well as *particular* responses to particular situations that John has in view, whether peculiar to each congregation (as in the seven oracles) or encountered by all disciples in their local settings (as in the visions, particularly in regard to participation in the imperial cult or other facets of Roman imperial domination).

---

69. DeSilva 1998a, 108–9; 2002b, 219.

Chapter 11

Literary Logic in Revelation
Rational Argument through Narrative and Intertexture

Thus far in our study of appeals to logos, we have focused on the more deductive, discursive elements within Revelation. This focus has served to counteract the tendency to regard Revelation as essentially *irrational*, rather than to look for the ways in which Revelation does engage in rational appeal alongside and within its more imaginative and emotive modes of communication. But this focus has also left large blocks of Revelation untouched—the lengthy sections of vivid description (in rhetorical-critical terms, ἔκφρασις) that sets this work apart from the epistolary literature of the New Testament.[1] What are we to say, for example, about the lengthy descriptions of the plagues that befall humankind, which occupy the bulk of chapters 6, 8–9, and 15–16?

At the outset of the previous chapter, we observed that explicit argumentation was expected to be less dense in such sections, and indeed throughout the visionary portions of Revelation, since these sections describe scenes and narrate action. We would expect narrative to affect the emotions of the audience (see chapter 8). But do these narratives make no appeal to the minds of the hearers? Or is it

---

1. John's mastery of the technique of "vivid description" has been often noted by rhetorical critics (Royalty 1997, 601; Aune 1998b, 919–28; Rossing 1999, 24–25; Witherington 2003, 216–17).

possible to read these as "narrative demonstrations" of theses or premises that John wishes to impress upon their minds and build upon in the course of guiding their deliberations, or as "narrative projections" of theses or premises that John expects his hearers to hold firmly in mind as a result of their socialization into Christian culture? In the first two sections of this chapter, we will explore how the stories John crafts communicate important cultural premises or invite evaluative judgments and responses that undergird John's broader argument.

A second mode in which John lodges more subtle appeals to the mind emerges through his use of intertexture, the evocation of passages and episodes from the Scriptures and other received traditions (e.g., extrabiblical apocalypses and sayings of Jesus). Allusion to the Old Testament is pervasive. Indeed, the most "creative" text in the New Testament is also, quantitatively speaking, the most "derivative," since many of the images, phrases, and actions in Revelation have identifiable antecedents in the Jewish Scriptures. Weaving in such quantities of traditional material bolsters the authority and fosters the reception of the work; in several distinct ways it also contributes to the rational argumentation of the book.

As he seeks to shape his hearers' responses to the challenges in their situations, John does what deliberative orators ordinarily could not do: "narrate" the future (Aristotle, *Rhet.* 3.16.11). A deliberative orator must often forecast consequences and lay them out so convincingly that the hearers will make a decision about action in the present on the basis of the same, but those consequences are not available for "narration" in the same way as the facts of a criminal case (as in judicial rhetoric). The medium of Christian prophecy, in the vivid mode of apocalypse, opens up the possibility of narrating future events (see Rev. 1:1, 19; 4:1; 22:6).[2] Intertexture contributes to this strategy's success in several ways: (1) It provides the language by means of which to make the future "crisis" of Christ's judgment more vivid and convincing, since it is resonant with the oracles of God. (2) It reinforces central premises about God's actions in God's cosmos that John will narrativize throughout Revelation, particularly in regard to God's commitment to intervene on behalf of God's faithful ones. (3) It evokes historical precedents, examples, and previous verdicts (i.e., of the divine court) that render more plausible John's description of events yet to occur, "since, as a rule, the future resembles the past" (Aristotle, *Rhet.* 2.20.8).

COMMUNICATING PREMISES THROUGH NARRATIVE: REVELATION 7–9

Narrative is widely used to communicate knowledge about the way things work in the cosmos and the way to live advantageously in such a cosmos. The fables of Aesop, for example, are purely fictive creations valued throughout the classical and Hellenistic-Roman periods for their engaging communication of cul-

---

2. DeSilva 1998a, 785; 2002b, 220.

turally valued information or guidance. Fables become an element in the art of argumentation, one of two forms of example (παράδειγμα), a main category of inductive proof (Aristotle, *Rhet.* 2.20). Aristotle prefers the second form, the historical precedent, as a stronger form of inductive argument, since it is not fictive and since "the future, as a rule, resembles the past" (2.20.8). Nevertheless, a relevant fable may be more readily available since clever speakers may invent them as needed. The narratives of Revelation differ from fables in that there is no element of analogy. Fables usually look to the realm of animals and their (fictive) interactions in order to illustrate a principle that can then be applied to the realm of human activity, whether generally (as in Aesop's collection) or specifically (as when Aesop invents a fable in the midst of a forensic speech; see Aristotle, *Rhet.* 2.20.6). John does not speak of the behavior of fleas and foxes in order to bring some induction to bear on the situations calling for decision in the seven congregations. Rather, he looks to the behavior of God, angels, and monsters, revoicing the mythos of Jewish apocalypticism, as a means of accomplishing the same. Like the fable, however, John's episodes frequently have a "moral," articulating strategically selected premises that have direct bearing on the deliberations at hand.

After the first six seals are opened—accompanied by horrific devastation that will surely evoke the question "Is there any way out from this?"—John tells a story about angels being restrained from releasing further winds of devastation "until we seal the slaves of our God upon their foreheads" (Rev. 7:1–3). The scene is extended through a census of those who are sealed (7:4–8) and through a triumphant scene of an innumerable multitude worshiping God for God's deliverance and enjoying the shelter of God's protection from hunger, thirst, and every scorching heat (7:9–17). The contrast with the sequences of chapter 6 and chapters 8–9, where great multitudes do *not* enjoy such divine protection (pointedly linked with the worship of God) could not be more poignant. As the disasters resume with the seven trumpets, John narrates what befalls those "who do not have the seal of God upon their foreheads" (9:4), including, among other things, subjection to scorching heat and thirst (8:6–11). And as the sealed ones who enjoyed protection gather around God's throne in worship (7:9–12), so those who experience God's judgments gather around "the works of their hands," worshiping "demons and idols of gold, silver, bronze, stone, and wood, which can neither see nor hear nor walk about" (9:20).

Explicit argumentative texture in these scenes is limited to two enthymemes (7:14–15 and 7:16–17).[3] The story itself, however, invites several relevant inductions on the part of the hearers. First, God's sending down widespread plagues

---

3. The first enthymeme, utilizing the common topic of cause and effect, is signaled by the presence of an explicitly inferential prepositional phrase:

> These are the ones coming out from great tribulation, and they washed their robes and made them white by the blood of the Lamb.
>
> *On account of this* [διὰ τοῦτο], they are in the presence of the throne of God, and they worship God by day and night in God's temple, and the One sitting upon the throne will pitch his shelter over them. (7:14–15)

upon some human beings, but sparing others who have been specifically set apart for God, communicates the premise that God makes a distinction between God's people and the other peoples of the earth.[4] This is not new information: it was a prominent and explicit "moral" of the Exodus story, as God sent plagues upon the Egyptians but kept the Israelites out of harm's way. Before the fourth plague, God announces: "I will make a distinction between my people and your people" (Exod. 8:23 NRSV). Similarly, prior to the devastating plague against the firstborn, Moses announces that no harm will befall firstborn Israelites, "so that you [Pharaoh] may know that the LORD makes a distinction between Egypt and Israel" (11:7 NRSV). This principle is extended in Leviticus: God's distinguishing the Israelites from other nations to be God's own people places ethical and other behavioral burdens upon the Israelites after the exodus (20:25–26). The Israelites cannot simply behave like the Canaanites or the Egyptians; they must "live out" the distinction God has made.

The second induction to be made is that "worship" is central to the distinction between those who suffer God's judgments and those who are protected.

The necessity of washing one's clothes before coming into God's presence at the Sinai theophany (Exod. 19:10, 14) provides the cultural information that supplies the causal connection between "washing one's robes" and the privilege of coming into God's presence, establishing the former as a prerequisite for the latter:

Rule (deduced from historical precedent in Exod. 19:10, 14): It is necessary to wash one's clothes before coming before the presence of the Holy God.

Case: These Christ-followers washed their clothes by means of the blood of the Lamb.

Result: They are eligible to stand before God's throne.

The second enthymeme presents an assertion about the ongoing life of these redeemed, a picture of security (here, specifically, freedom from injury) supported by a rationale introduced once again by an explicit inferential marker:

They will not hunger anymore nor thirst anymore nor will the sun or any scorching heat fall upon them,

because [ὅτι] the Lamb in the midst of the throne will shepherd them and will lead them beside springs of waters of life, and God will wipe away every tear from their eyes. (7:16–17)

Lengthy recontextualizations of God's promises from Isa. 25:8 and 49:10 provide the substance of Rev. 7:16, 17b. The Lamb (Christ) is presented as the promised good shepherd, acting on behalf of God and in God's interests, who will effectively and faithfully tend to the needs of the sheep rather than of himself (Ezek. 34; Ps. 23). This larger Jewish-Christian cultural knowledge about God as Shepherd provides the "rule" that undergirds the deduction:

Rule: Where God (or God's select and true representative) leads the people, the people will be well cared for.

Case: The Lamb shepherds the throng of disciples who have passed through the tribulation.

Result: The throng will enjoy safety from all harm and shall have their needs met abundantly.

This analysis anticipates the discussion in the second half of this chapter, in which the rhetorical contributions of intertexture, primarily from the Hebrew Scriptures, are the focal point of investigation.

4. See also 2 Pet. 2:9, where the author adduces several stories from the Jewish tradition (2:4–8) to affirm that God knows how to preserve the righteous and keep the ungodly under judgment.

John coordinates worshiping God and the Lamb with deliverance and safety in regard to God's future acts of judgment, and refusing to disassociate from idols with being deprived of God's seal and thus suffering the horrors of divine punishment. The narratives of Revelation 7–9, then, support the explicit summons to exclusive worship of God and the Lamb issued in more discursive passages (e.g., 4:11; 5:9–10; 14:6–13), while also working against any impetus toward accommodating to the idolatrous practices of the audience's neighbors—an impetus fostered by the interpretations of the gospel promoted by Jezebel and the Nicolaitans. The line between Goshen and Egypt was salutary: security depended upon drawing it as sharply as possible.

While a fable is usually a simple story illustrating one and only one point, the narratives of Revelation are far more complex. The opening of the seventh seal inaugurates an exquisite scene of liturgical action in the heavenly temple often treated as an interlude because, at some level, it is recognized to communicate a different "moral" or invite a different (though complementary) "induction." After the seal is opened, there is only "silence," dramatic in its very stillness after the calamitous chaos of the first six seals. Into this silence step seven angels with the next sequence of punitive judgments and another angel who burns incense before the altar, explicitly "for the prayers of all the saints" (8:3). The smoke of the incense ascends, carrying these prayers before God (8:4), after which the angel takes fire from the altar and throws it down to earth in the very censer used to offer the prayers (8:5).

This liturgical "drama" expresses in narrative form the conviction that the cries of God's righteous ones (the martyrs located under the altar of incense, 6:9) rise before God, resulting in judgment upon the perpetrators of injustice and all their allies. Hence the prayers of the saints provide the prelude to the judgments announced by the trumpets, and the martyrs will return in 16:5–7, alongside an angel, making the connection between the judgments and God's vindication of his martyred righteous ones explicit.[5] What we see pictorially reinforces convictions about God responding to prayer as known from other Jewish and Christian texts (e.g., Luke 18:7–8), communicated within the mythos and liturgical practice of the Jewish tradition, where angels bring people's prayers before God and the burning of incense is a constant visual and olfactory experience symbolizing the sending of gathered worshipers' prayers up to God.[6]

The episode's focus on prayer and its efficacy, an obvious induction in this case, also offers support for John's case that the path of covenant loyalty and

---

5. A. Collins (1980, 190) rightly observes that "the trumpets are presented as the answer to the prayer of the saints for vengeance," though perhaps the word "vengeance" is not as appropriate here as "vindication," as when an unjust sentence from a lower court is overturned by a higher court and "justice" is restored. Witherington (2003, 139) also holds that 8:1–5 communicates the efficacy of the prayers of the saints in bringing about justice.

6. On the role of angels, see Tob. 12:12, 15; *1 En.* 47:1–2; 99:3 (Bauckham 1993a, 81). Luke poignantly captures the liturgical significance of burning incense at the hour of prayer in the opening scene of his Gospel (1:8–10), which also weaves in the role of angels as bearers of prayers *and* their responses (1:11–20).

visible witness will ultimately prove more advantageous. Access to divine help is a major subtopic of security throughout Jewish and early Christian literature, particularly in situations of deprivation or marginalization.[7] Prayer is the principal practice by means of which this help is secured. Revelation 8:2–5 affirms the efficacy of the practice, "displaying" the unseen mechanisms of the practice that also link prayer and real consequences as cause and effect, whether or not those effects are experienced during one's lifetime or after one's transition from this world to the places of rest (e.g., with the martyrs in 6:9–11; 14:13). As John affirms the reliability and efficacy of prayer, he thus also promotes the feasibility of the path of resistance (since help is available and effective).

A third example will conclude this brief exploration of how story nurtures argument. As John narrates the grander story of God's judgment, readers are brought to the "end" several times. The sixth seal (6:12–17) already speaks in the idiom of the "Day of the Lord," the "great Day of the wrath" of God and the Lamb, portraying the celestial disruptions commonly associated with that day.[8] The seventh trumpet leads to a celebration of the arrival of God's kingdom (11:15–18). The plagues initiated by the pouring out of the seventh bowl are accompanied by the finality of the divine pronouncement: "It has come to pass" (16:17). Such observations gave rise to the theory of recapitulation within Revelation's structure. In its simpler form, this means that John leaps at various points to the "end," after which he returns to fill in some more details about the plagues preceding the end. In its more rigorous form, an interpreter might suggest that the seven bowls (with their emphasis on the complete devastation of the targets of each plague) describe the very same actions as the seven trumpets (with their emphasis on the partial devastation of their targets, limited to "one third"), only from the vantage point of being in the midst of the devastation caused by these plagues, with the resulting perception of "totality."

In recent narrative-critical analysis, J. L. Resseguie has affirmed important cautions against theories of wholesale recapitulation.[9] John explicitly distinguishes the series of seven bowls as the *last* series of plagues (15:1), thus affirming a serial rather than a recapitulative view of these septets (leaving open the likelihood of the milder version of the recapitulation theory articulated above). We are left, then, with John devoting a substantial part of Revelation—at least chapters 6–9, 15–16—to the detailed narration of variegated and incremental punishment. The rhetorical contributions of such narration are manifold. Such a display is more horrific than instantaneous global annihilation. Judgment is seen in all its particulars, and thus amplified; it also engulfs the world in ever greater degrees, prolonging the experience.

Perhaps counterintuitively, John stresses the failure of these plagues to evoke repentance. This is most explicit in 9:20–21, which serves as a kind of con-

---

7. Heb. 4:14–16 is an outstanding example.
8. Compare Rev. 6:12–14 with Joel 2:10, 30–31 and the use of the latter in Matt. 24:29–30; Acts 2:20.
9. Resseguie 1998.

clusion to the series of six trumpets (the seventh being deferred until after a lengthy interlude, appropriately concerning prophetic commission and prophetic witness):

> The rest of humanity, those who had not been killed in these plagues, neither repented from the works of their hands, in order not to worship demons and idols made of gold and silver and bronze and stone and wood, nor did they repent from their murders or their sorceries or their sexual infidelities or their acts of theft.

This failure to respond with repentance is also underscored in the course of the final series of plagues:

> The fourth poured out his bowl, ... and the people were burned with a great scorching, and they slandered the name of the God who had authority over these plagues, and they did not repent, so as to give God glory. (16:8–9)
> The fifth poured out his bowl, ... and they [the people] slandered the God of heaven on account of their burdens and their sores, and they did not repent from their works. (16:11)

"Speaking ill of God" follows the final bowl plague as well (16:21).

As John narrates the story of the trumpets and the bowls, he introduces the implicit expectation—by dwelling on the noneventuation of this result—that these judgments should produce a change of heart among the people who are not giving their allegiance and obedience to the God of heaven. Reading from this perspective, the relationship of the trumpets to the bowls becomes especially significant. The attentive hearer recognizes that the bowls repeat the punishments of the trumpets. The first four trumpets and bowls are virtually identical except that the trumpets are partial, affecting only one-third of their targets, whereas the bowls effect complete devastation. John thus narrativizes the conviction voiced elsewhere in Jewish literature that God judges or punishes by increments rather than all at once in order to allow room for repentance:[10]

> You were not unable to give the ungodly into the hands of the righteous in battle, or to destroy them at one blow by dread wild animals or your stern word. But judging them little by little you gave them an opportunity to repent. (Wis. 12:9–10 NRSV)

This represents a substantial theological development of the exodus tradition, which originally presented God's motivation for driving the Canaanites out "little by little" as a concern to keep the land from becoming overrun and overpopulated by wild animals (Exod. 23:29–30). This tradition regarding the conquest is blended with the tradition of the (new) exodus plagues in Revelation (with "those inhabiting the land" recalling descriptions of the Canaanites in

---

10. Schüssler Fiorenza 1991, 72; Witherington 2003, 147. On Wisdom of Solomon, see deSilva 2002a, 147–48, 151–52.

Num. 32:17; 33:52–53, 55). As in Wisdom's interpretation of the destruction of the Canaanites, so also in Revelation: John does not expect "those inhabiting the land" to respond with repentance, except in response to the active witness of Christ-followers working in conjunction with God's hand (Rev. 11:3–13).

Thus John's narration suggests that repentance stands as a goal behind God's punitive actions, even though the recalcitrance of the general population will prevent the realization of this goal. In so doing, these narrations potentially motivate the audiences to walk in line with their own repentance (distancing themselves from the "targets" of these judgments), as well as to live out the "testimony of Jesus" in a way that will support God's general call to repentance, since the narratives emphasize the ineffectiveness of God's forthcoming judgments to bring about a change of heart on their own.[11]

A TOPOS OF TWO WOMEN

The act of "showing" is prominent in this text, as is appropriate for a book that presents itself as a "revelation" of ordinarily unseen mysteries. In two parallel statements, an angel invites John to see particular sights, drawing special attention thus to their importance:

> And one of the seven angels having the seven bowls came and spoke with me, saying, "Come, I will show you the judgment of the great prostitute seated over many waters." (17:1)
> And one of the seven angels having the seven bowls full of the seven last plagues came and spoke with me, saying, "Come, I will show you the bride, the wife of the Lamb." (21:9)

Each of these invitations is followed by an extended and vivid description of the spectacle (a compositional technique called *ekphrasis*). The graphic nature of the first—the great prostitute, described as an actual female figure who first exudes sensuality and later suffers a brutal death—continues to excite strong reactions among readers.[12] Nevertheless, both Babylon (as a female image) and new Jerusalem (as an architectural image) are described in significant detail, inviting the hearers truly to imagine the scene as it unfolds before John's gaze (17:3–18; 21:10–22:5). But is such "showing" in any sense "argumentative"?

Barbara Rossing has convincingly demonstrated that it is.[13] John is not simply presenting two "sights": he is presenting two *alternative* sights, two alternative women whom the hearers will perceive as mutually exclusive, potential partners. The underlying structure is already present within the personifications of Wisdom and Folly in Jewish wisdom texts (Prov. 1–9). Both are portrayed

---

11. These narratives contribute to other rhetorical effects as well, e.g., arousing indignation against the members of the non-Christian society who do not respond to witness (see chapter 8).
12. Most notable in this regard is Pippin 1992.
13. Rossing 1999.

as women; both offer something to those who pass by. One must, however, choose between them: one cannot enjoy Wisdom's feast *and* Folly's couch. This essential structure is not limited to Jewish literature. An extremely well-attested and thus presumably influential Greek fable tells of the choice of Heracles. In this coming-of-age story, Heracles sits in a quiet place to ponder what path his life should take. Two women appear to him, the first beautiful but simple and modest, the second artificially adorned and immodest. Both speak to Heracles, offering their promises and trying to win his devotion. Finally, Heracles chooses the first woman, Virtue, leading to his trials but also to his divinization.[14] This story is told repeatedly, often developed more explicitly as an exhortation to virtue, to choose a particular career, even to choose to go to war or to maintain civic concord.[15] Christian writers like Justin and Clement of Alexandria know and use the story in its original form.[16]

When John introduces and describes first a prostitute and later a bride, he invokes what Rossing calls the "two women *topos*," a rhetorical commonplace with a recognizable pattern and structure calling for a particular response.[17] The essential components of this topos include (1) the personification of both elements of some either/or choice as two female figures, (2) an elaboration of the physical appearance and bearing of these women designed to guide the audience to respond positively to one and negatively toward the other, and (3) an ethical appeal to make a decisive choice for one over the other.[18] The first component draws on the rhetorical technique of *prosōpopoiia*, the second on *ekphrasis* (vivid description) and *synkrisis* (comparison), though the comparison is often communicated simply through contrasting description. Whether or not the exhortation is made explicitly, the topos itself evokes a framework of decision, and the elaborated description of the women guides the hearers to align themselves with the preferred figure.[19]

Playing on the tendency in the ancient world to personify cities as women or goddesses, John transforms the public image of Rome into a lascivious, gratuitously indulgent prostitute.[20] Even though in some ways a compelling and enticing figure, as is typical for the negative figure in this topos, John warps the

---

14. The story is first told in Xenophon, *Mem.* 2.1.21–22.
15. Philostratus (*Vit. Apoll.* 6.10), Dio Chrysostom (*Or.* 1.66–84), Lucian (*Somn.* 6; *Bis acc.* 21; *Merc. cond.* 42; *Rhet. praec.* 6–7; *Hermot.* 22–28), Julian (*Or.* 2.57), Philo (*Sacr.* 20–35), Cicero (*Off.* 1.32.118), Quintilian (*Inst.* 9.2.36), Athenaeus (*Deipnosophistae* 12.510), Maximus of Tyre (*Or.* 14.1), and Silius Italicus (*Punica* 15.1–132). Rossing (1999, 18–37) very helpfully collects and surveys this material.
16. Justin, *2 Apol.* 11; Clement of Alexandria, *Paed.* 2.10.110.
17. Rossing 1999, 18.
18. Rossing 1999, 18, 37–40.
19. Rossing 1999, 39.
20. Among the Dead Sea Scrolls, 4Q184 and 4Q185 contain a more elaborate physical description of the seductress with very little elaboration of the physical features of the positive female figure (see 4Q185 11–12; Rossing 1999, 50–51). This is very similar to what we find in John's descriptions of the prostitute and the bride: or rather, while there *is* extensive description of the bride's physical appearance, it is in her existence as a city, not her hypostatization as a female.

portrait sufficiently to turn any stirrings of attraction quickly to revulsion. If one is intrigued by the golden cup, one would push it aside after learning that it is full of "abominations and the unclean things of her fornication" (Rev. 17:4); if Babylon's devil-may-care attitude holds appeal, the fact that violence against fellow Christians is her intoxicant of choice would surely turn John's hearers off. And she is not nearly so attractive at the end of the vision: Her allies will come to "hate the whore and leave her desolate and naked and eat up her flesh and burn her with fire" (17:16). On the other hand, the bride is presented as pure, virtuous, and radiantly clad in the garments of righteous deeds (19:7–8). When John turns to physical description, he creates an image of the most beautiful city imaginable, where the adornments formerly enjoyed only by the elite few are now the daily pleasure of all (21:9–22:5).[21]

John's extensive narrativization of the two-women topos, then, directly supports his deliberative agenda, calling his congregations to (continue to) "come out" of Babylon (18:4) and live so as to be granted admittance into the new Jerusalem.[22] The topos invokes a structure that reinforces the mutually exclusive nature of participation in the economic and political system of Babylon, with its promised goods, and participation in the economic and political system of new Jerusalem, with its (substantially longer-lasting) promised goods.[23] As such, it counters the opposing position of Jezebel and the Nicolaitans that one can move from Babylon's table to the wedding feast of the Lamb as part of one progressive dinner. Presented with the two female figures, the audience understands from the deep logic of the topos that it must make a choice between them, allowing John to guide their attachments to the bride.

NARRATIVE DEMONSTRATION AND THE RHETORICAL CONTRIBUTIONS OF INTERTEXTURE

John's use of the Jewish Scriptures consistently commands the attention of interpreters.[24] In vision after vision, hymn after hymn, John weaves in multiple phrases from those texts, creating complex conversations between the original

---

21. Rossing (1999, 14–15) does not find losing sight of both figures as "females" and moving to direct speech about cities (Rev. 18; 21:9–22:5) remotely problematic since the women in the topos regularly represent some other area of interest (ethical choices, career choice, and so forth). This becomes a principal reason for rejecting Pippin's reading of Revelation, since the latter "reifies" the female dramatis personae of the fable into flesh-and-blood women, about whom it is appropriate to have human and humane concern (1999, 12–14).

22. Rossing 1999, 162.

23. Royalty (1998, 216–18) argues that original readers would have understood the new Jerusalem as an actual city where they would one day live, not merely a symbol for Christian community, on the following grounds: (1) Revelation addresses people in real cities. (2) New Jerusalem is set against Babylon, a real city, and is repeatedly called a city (12 times in 21:1–22:19). (3) Babylon and Jerusalem (i.e., the fundamental sources for the Rome/heavenly city contrast) were real cities. (4) The moral aspects of Rev. 21–22 are appropriate to praise of cities, not just a community.

24. See Cambier 1955; Lohse 1961; Beale 1984; 1998; Ruiz 1989; Fekkes 1994; Moyise 1995.

Scripture and the new utterance wherever hearers discern the resonance. This pervasive (and ever indirect) use of intertexture, invoking the very language of Scripture throughout, is one important way in which John departs from traditional rhetoric, forcing analysts also to move beyond the stricter modes of classical rhetorical criticism in order to treat John's rhetoric adequately.[25] At this level, rational persuasion is more allusive and associative than overtly argumentative, more experiential than explicated.[26] Many scholars have attempted to classify the ways in which John refers to older traditions.[27] Vernon Robbins's discussion of intertexture makes a very important contribution to this conversation.[28] Robbins provides a sophisticated taxonomy commensurate with the complexities of John's use of Jewish Scriptures and extrabiblical literature, raising the level of precision possible in this discussion, and his terminological distinctions will be observed here.

Although we have been able to discern significant "argumentative texture" in the visionary portions of Revelation, explicit argumentation is clearly not John's primary mode of persuasion. The primary mode of Revelation is, rather, "narrative demonstration."[29] John traces out various possible courses

---

25. Revelation pursues intertextual conversations not only with Jewish literature but also with local phenomena in the seven cities (Hemer 1986; Ramsay 1994 [1904]; Scobie 1993) and with the Roman imperial ideology articulated in coins, inscriptions, and most prominently, the architectural representations and performance of ruler cult (Cuss 1974; Stauffer 1952 [1955]; L. Thompson 1990; deSilva 1991; Friesen 1993). John certainly plays on "the 'evocative power' of shared experiences" in addition to "the 'evocative power' of texts" (Moyise 1995, 125), though we here restrict our inquiry to oral-scribal intertexture particularly involving the sacred traditions shared by John and his hearers.

26. Socio-rhetorical interpretation is very promising in this regard, opening up the model of "rhetorical" analysis to include repetitive patterns, intertextual associations, social and cultural topics, and ideological analysis. For a preliminary attempt to probe how this mode of analysis can display John's persuasive techniques more fully than classical rhetorical criticism, see deSilva 1999a.

27. The critical editions of the Greek NT, for example, have identified "allusions and citations" or "allusions and verbal parallels." Several scholars have attempted to refine these categories, making meaningful distinctions within the broad category of "allusions." See Vanhoye 1962, 473–76; Fekkes 1994; Beale 1986; Paulien 1988, 39–43. Paulien distinguishes between "direct allusions" and "echoes," the former indicating intertexture that John intended for the attentive hearer to catch, the latter indicating a connection between Revelation and some other text the hearer could have made, but without being consciously employed by John as such. Direct allusions would include verbal parallels (shared strings of words), thematic parallels (shared concepts using different words), and structural parallels (modeling a passage on an OT antecedent without using the same words). This last category is very much in keeping with the breadth of what literary critics would consider under the heading of intertexture. John Hollander, for example, is willing to contemplate intertextual echo in "pieces of voices as small as single words, and as elusive as particular cadences" (1981, 88), by which he means poetical rhythms sharing no actual lexical terms in common, but a mere "tuneful correspondence" (Moyise 1995, 109) rather than shared words. "Structural" allusions are thus as potentially informing and evocative as lexical correspondence.

28. Robbins 1996a, 40–68; 1996b, 96–143. Robbins's model also calls us to be more attentive to conversations between the NT and Greco-Roman texts, as well as to expand the definition of "text" to include oral and written texts, texts on paper, metal, and stone, as well as "scripts" of a nonverbal but nonetheless commonly shared sort.

29. The author of 4 Maccabees uses this term to name the strategy that he himself follows for the bulk of his work (3:19). There, the stories of the nine martyrs provide proof in narrative form of the proposition he has previously demonstrated by more deductive means. In his narration, the author

of action—compliance with the demands of ruler cult and partnership with Roman imperialism, as opposed to nonparticipation in idolatry and in the polluted prosperity of the imperial system—and graphically depicts incentives, disincentives, and consequences related to either course of action. The hearers can "see" what will be the end of the course they have chosen or are contemplating choosing. As they engage the vision, they are positioned to examine their current situation and possible courses of action in light of the standard deliberative topics explored in the previous chapters. The explicit argumentation and appeals to emotion are all embedded within this narrative demonstration.

The cultural environment of Christian prophecy (according to which divine revelations are both possible and expected) and the specific mode of apocalypse (which nurtures narration of visions of events yet to come) allow John to harness a persuasive strategy that was, for Aristotle, an impossibility: "In deliberative oratory narrative is very rare, because no one can narrate things to come" (*Rhet.* 3.16.11). Narration was an important element of judicial oratory since it pertained to past events that were known (although it could still be "colored" to prejudice a jury for or against a defendant). Narration was crucial to some forms of epideictic oratory: through narration of a person's deeds, that person's virtues could be exhibited and "demonstrated." But who can "narrate" what has not yet happened?

John claims to be able to narrate what will happen in the future—"what must shortly take place" (Rev. 1:1, 19; 4:1; 22:6)—from God's judgments being poured out upon all who refuse to "fear God" and "give God glory" (as in 8:1–9:21; 16:1–21) to God's promises being delivered to those who have maintained God's commandments and kept faith with Jesus (as in 7:13–17; 15:1–4; 21:1–22:5). He almost never "intrudes" in the visionary chapters to give instructions or exhortations to the hearers. He instead relies on the plausibility and even inevitability of the future he presents in order to engage the hearers and foster commitment to respond faithfully against innovation within the group, intimidation outside the group, and potential partnership with those outside the group. This rhetorical strategy is sufficiently flexible to address every element within John's diverse audience, both those who are wholly committed to preserving the distinctive contours of the Christian witness at any cost as well as those who seek innovative ways in which to negotiate commitment to this group and peaceful (even profitable) coexistence with the larger society.

Revelation's success as an instrument of persuasion, then, largely depends on the persuasiveness of the future John narrates. What strategies does he use to impress upon the hearers that his description of what will happen "shortly"

---

includes deliberative speeches, both protreptic and apotreptic, but these are placed on the lips of the characters spoken in the ears of other characters (e.g., Antiochus to Eleazar). They are not spoken directly to the audience, but the audience nevertheless hears the speeches and will ponder its own situation and life choices in light of those speeches. This is a very similar strategy to the embedding of arguments and speeches in the visions of Revelation.

is actually reliable information upon which to make choices in the present?[30] Intertexture—the pervasive interweaving of texts from the sacred tradition shared by John and his audiences—is a primary resource for John as he seeks to establish the credibility of this future. In chapter 6 we have already explored how intertexture serves in general to establish the ethos of John and the authority (persuasiveness) of his message, as John unites the biblical word to his own and, in effect, enables the sacred tradition itself to speak to the situation of John's hearers. Here we instead focus on the contributions of intertexture to the underlying appeals to logos throughout Revelation, especially as this is at work in 14:14–16:21. In particular, intertexture (1) contributes to defining the real crisis to which the hearers must give their attention and in light of which make decisions in the midst of their immediate settings, (2) reinforces major cultural premises that undergird John's deductive processes, and (3) introduces indirect arguments from example and historical precedent to render the projected future more plausible.

Defining the Main Point of Deliberation

Revelation 14:14–20 reinforces the "hour of judgment" as the principal challenge facing the hearers requiring judicious action and preparation in the present. This and nothing else, John would aver, should dominate the minds of the hearers. John recontextualizes Daniel 7:13 to present the first character in this episode:

Upon the cloud one like *a son of man* (Rev. 14:14)

*Upon the cloud*s as it were *a son of man* (Dan. 7:13)[31]

In Daniel the "one like a son of man" comes to receive the kingdom and represents the "holy ones" of God. For those who hear the Danielic overtones—and John uses Daniel so pervasively that he either could safely presume his audience to know Daniel or failed miserably in terms of writing for his audience—John continues to connect God's coming to claim the kingdom with the execution of judgment (as in Rev. 11:17–18).

---

30. John's challenge aligns with the primary challenge facing the deliberative orator, who must "prove . . . that the facts are what the supporter of a measure maintains they are" (Aristotle, *Rhet.* 1.1.10). See also *Rhet. Alex.* 1428b.12–17: "In exhortations and dissuasions it has to be proved about the matter under consideration that the line of action which we are urging or opposing itself has the effect that we assert it has; or if not, that actions resembling this line of action generally or invariably turn out in the way we assert."
31. For the sake of non-Greek readers, throughout this section I will attempt to convey verbal parallels in the Greek through the use of italics in the English translation.

ἐπὶ τὴν νεφέλην ὅμοιον υἱὸν ἀνθρώπου (Rev. 14:14)
ἐπὶ τῶν νεφελῶν ὡς υἱὸς ἀνθρώπου (Dan. 7:13)

The description of this judgment consists of three scenes: the harvesting of the earth, the gathering in of the vineyard, and the trampling of the winepress. The whole is a narrative amplification of Joel 3:13 (4:13–14 MT/LXX): "Put in the sickle, for the harvest is ripe. Come, tread, for the winepress is full. . . . Multitudes, multitudes in the valley of decision! For the Day of the Lord is near in the valley of decision."[32] John heightens the drama of Joel's scene by first drawing attention to the "sharp sickle" in the hand of the "one like a son of man" (14:14). He then recontextualizes the first part of Joel 3:13 in the angel's invitation to that figure: "*Send out your sickle* and reap, because the hour to reap came, *because the harvest* of the earth *ripened*" (Rev. 14:15). John then adds a brief narration of the harvest being carried out (14:16).[33] Next he creates a logically intervening scene between grain harvest and treading of the winepress: the harvesting of the vineyard.[34] This scene closely parallels the first: an angelic figure appears already holding a "sharp sickle" (14:17); another angel gives a similar command with a similar rationale ("Send out your sharp sickle and harvest the clusters of the vineyard of the earth, for its grapes are ripe"; 14:18–19); the action is then carried out (14:19a).

Finally, John elaborates the treading of the winepress. First the "grapes" are "thrown into the great winepress of the wrath of God" (14:19). John's description of this action comes from another prominent text using the treading of a winepress as an image for judgment:

---

32. The Hebrew word translated "decision" חָרוּץ makes a clever pun since it can also signify a sharp threshing instrument.

33. This first harvest could be heard as a positive ingathering of the elect in contrast to the harvest of the vineyard (which is indisputably negative; see Bauckham 1993a, 290), or as a doublet for the punitive judgment expressed by the winepress scene. Hearers aware of Jesus' sayings featuring the image of harvesting to describe both the ingathering of the righteous and the burning of the wicked (see Matt. 13:24–30, 37–43) might be inclined to hear Rev. 14:14–20 in terms of such contrasting images. Bauckham suggests that the presentation of the 144,000 as the firstfruits of a much larger harvest creates the expectation of the depiction of that larger, positive harvest, which 14:14–16 would provide (1993a, 291–92), all the more as it uses the more positive image of "reaping" (see Mark 4:29; John 4:35–36) as opposed to threshing (Jer. 51:33; Mic. 4:12–13; Hab. 3:12; Matt. 3:12; Luke 3:17) or the chaff being blown away or burned up (Pss. 1:4; 35:5; Isa. 17:13; 29:5; Dan. 2:35; Hos. 13:3; Matt. 3:12; Luke 3:17), the images commonly denoting destruction or loss of the wicked.

On the other hand, there are some indications that John intended both harvests to be heard as two expressions of a single, punitive judgment. First, there is an obvious parallelism between 14:7, "because the hour of his judgment came [ὅτι ἦλθεν ἡ ὥρα τῆς κρίσεως αὐτοῦ]," and 14:15, "because the hour to harvest came [ὅτι ἦλθεν ἡ ὥρα θερίσαι]." Second, Jer. 28 (51E):33 LXX, a text that John clearly knew, had already used the image of a grain harvest to speak of the (destructive) judgment of Babylon (thus strengthening the link between 14:7 and 14:15): "yet a short while and the time of her harvest will come." It would be impossible, however, to demonstrate that the *hearers* would all take the vision this way, especially since there are contemporary references to a dual harvest (Jesus' parable being a prominent example) and counterindications within the text itself. See Aune 1998b, 800–803 and Beale 1999, 773–79 for a detailed review of arguments.

34. The LXX translators had already taken this step in Joel 4 (3E):13, translating the more neutral Hebrew word for harvest (קָצִיר) with a word distinctly associated with fruit harvesting: τρύγητος.

"Why are your garments as of one coming from *trampling the winepress* (ἀπὸ πατητοῦ ληνοῦ)?" . . . "*I have trampled* (κατεπάτησα) them in *wrath* (ἐν θυμῷ), . . . and I have poured out their *blood* (τὸ αἷμα) *upon the ground* (εἰς γῆν). For the day of payback came for them, . . . and my *wrath* (ὁ θυμός) arose, and *I trampled* (κατεπάτησα) them in my *wrath* and poured out their *blood* (τὸ αἷμα) *upon the ground* (εἰς γῆν)." (Isa. 63:2–6)

The angel cast his sickle *into the earth* (εἰς τὴν γῆν) and harvested the vineyard of the earth and threw it into the great *winepress* (ληνόν) of the *wrath* (τοῦ θυμοῦ) of God. And the harvest was *trampled* (επατήθη) outside the city and *blood* (αἷμα) went out *from the winepress* (ἐκ τῆς ληνοῦ). . . . (Rev. 14:19–20)

The detail that the winepress was trampled "outside the city" (ἔξωθεν τῆς πόλεως) recontextualizes the Pentateuchal phrase "outside the camp" or, in references to laws holding after the Israelites take possession of Canaan, "outside the city." While this sometimes refers to a "clean place" (Lev. 6:11; Num. 19:3, 9), or even a holy place where God's tabernacle is pitched (Exod. 33:7), it is most often an unclean place where sin offerings are burned (Exod. 29:14; Lev. 4:12, 21; 8:17; 9:11; 10:4; 16:27), all things leprous and polluted are cast (whether people or building materials, Lev. 13:46; 14:40–41, 45; Num. 5:3–4), and most poignantly here, sinners are executed (blasphemers, Lev. 24:14, 23; Sabbath violators, Num. 15:35–36).

As treading this winepress signifies bloodshed in Isaiah, John elaborates upon the spilling of blood as well. In describing the quantity of blood exuding from the trodden winepress ("blood went out . . . as high as the horses' bridles"; Rev. 14:20), John alludes to another description of God's execution of judgment:

> And the horse shall walk up to the breast in the blood of sinners, and the chariot shall be submerged to its height. . . . In those days the angels shall descend into the secret places and gather together into one place all those who brought down sin, and the Most High will arise on that day of judgment to execute great judgment among sinners. (*1 En.* 100:3–4)

John's extensive use of oral-scribal intertexture in Revelation 14:14–20 weaves together Old Testament images of judgment, reminding the hearers of God's thoroughgoing commitment to tread down the ungodly. John recalls for his audience the witness born by multiple prophetic voices (Joel, Daniel, Isaiah, and Enoch) to God's intervention to judge particular people groups as well as all humanity, adding his voice to the chorus of witnesses that *God's judgment* is indeed the crisis that must ultimately command attention. He expands those images in order to impress upon the hearers the danger and horror of that judgment and thus the paramount importance of settling upon a strategy for meeting that challenge in safety, such as the strategy that John commends to each congregation (in the oracles) as well as to the churches as a whole (in the visions). This impending crisis thus rises to the fore, trumping the less dire crises of temporal hardship or deprivation, regarding which other speakers like Jezebel and the Nicolaitans are advancing their own strategies.[35]

Reinforcing Major Cultural Premises

Recontextualization—importing strings of words from an older text into a new context without explicitly drawing attention to the fact—is prominent in two hymns celebrating God's justice: 15:2–4 and 16:5–7. These poetic passages, declarations from the mouths of the redeemed and their angelic advocates, serve the rhetorical purpose of reinforcing major Jewish cultural premises concerning God's justice. Here the premises, in turn, reinforce the necessity of the consequences John posits and thus the plausibility of the future he narrates. Rome, guilty of the same crimes as Babylon in the eyes of John (as also in the eyes of the authors of *4 Ezra* and *2 Baruch*), will most assuredly fall under the judgment of the same God whose commitment to justice and bringing forth justice never ceases, and whose opposition to injustice, greed, and self-glorification never changes.

Chapters 15 and 16 interact extensively with Exodus 1–15.[36] "Conquerors" singing the "song of Moses (and of the Lamb)" while standing "beside the sea" (Rev. 15:1–2) recalls the Exodus setting in a rather obvious way.[37] While the content of the "Song of Moses" in Deuteronomy 32 is more evident on the surface of this hymn (esp. in Rev. 15:3c, 4b), Bauckham has shown that the Song of Moses in Exodus 15 lies at the heart of John's reflection and John's choice of intertexture throughout this reinvented "song of Moses and of the Lamb."[38] Those who "overcome" the beast and its image by virtue of enduring the cost of nonparticipation in the cult now celebrate the Lord's deliverance of the faithful ones as a second and grander exodus.

> Great and wonderful are your works, Lord God Almighty! (Rev. 15:3b)
>
> Just and true are your ways, O King of the nations: (15:3c)
>
> Who will not fear, Lord, and glorify your name? (15:4a)
>
> For you alone are holy, (15:4b)

---

35. John reinforces this effect in 16:15 through intertextural references to the sayings of Jesus, particularly his warnings concerning the importance of "watching" for the day of his coming (Matt. 24:42; 25:13; Mark 13:35, 37) and his use of the image of the thief suddenly and unexpectedly breaking in upon the unwary householder (Matt. 24:42–44), exhortations and images prominent throughout early Christian discourse about the Day of the Lord (see Acts 20:31; 1 Thess. 5:2–4, 6; 1 Pet. 5:8; 2 Pet. 3:10).

36. Beale (1999, 787) aptly notes the tendency to view God's eschatological deliverance in terms of God's prototypical deliverance in Exodus. The *Apocalypse of Abraham* also speaks of God preparing ten plagues (as in Egypt) against the heathen (29.15; 30.1–8).

37. Rabbinic texts speak of the Red Sea becoming "a crystallized . . . kind of glass" (*Midr. Pss.* 136.7; see also *Mekilta de Rabbi Ishmael*, Beshallah 5.15), a tradition drawn out from the detail in Exod. 15:8, "the deeps were congealed" (Beale 1999, 791–92).

38. Bauckham 1993a, 297–306.

for all the nations will come and worship before you, (15:4c)

for your just decrees have been made manifest. (15:4d)[39]

Almost every line of this song recontextualizes some earlier declaration about God and God's dealings with humanity. Perhaps the single most important subtext is Ps. 85 (86E):9–10 LXX. This psalm praises God as *"great"* and as one who "does *wonders*" (μέγας . . . καὶ ποιῶν θαυμάσια; cf. Rev. 15:3b), and as "God *alone*" (θεὸς μόνος; cf. Rev. 15:4c). It also affirms that *"all the nations* that you made *will come and worship before you* and *glorify your name*" (πάντα τὰ ἔθνη . . . ἥξουσιν καὶ προσκυνήσουσιν ἐνώπιόν σου, . . . καὶ δοξάσουσιν τὸ ὄνομά σου). John recontextualizes the first part of this affirmation in Revelation 15:4d in a slightly abbreviated but otherwise verbatim manner, and the latter part of the affirmation in 15:4a, though in the form of a rhetorical question anticipating an affirmative answer.

Alongside the striking and concentrated correspondences with Psalm 85 (86E) LXX, several other passages have also contributed to the invention of this hymn. Revelation 15:3b resonates with a number of texts confessing the "great and wonderful works of the Lord":

They acknowledged the *great* and *wonderful works* of God. (Tob. 12:22)

Great are the *works* of the Lord! (Ps. 110 [111E]:2 LXX)

Wonderful are your *works*! (Ps. 138 [139E]:14 LXX)[40]

While it is difficult (and perhaps superfluous) to decide with certainty, Revelation 15:3b may represent a combined recontextualization of Psalm 110 (111E):2 and Psalm 138 (139E):14. Since the hymn responds to the emergence of the seven angels with the seven last *"plagues"* (πληγάς), a sight that John describes as a *"great and wondrous"* (μέγα καὶ θαυμαστόν) sign (15:1), it is likely that he understood these "works" to be enactments of judgment, akin to the *"great and wondrous plagues"* (πληγὰς μεγάλας καὶ θαυμαστάς, Deut. 28:59) that God promised to bring upon disobedient Israel. The divine title "Lord God Almighty" (κύριε ὁ θεὸς ὁ παντοκράτωρ) recontextualizes verbatim (but in the vocative case) the title of God from Amos 3:13 and 4:13 LXX.

---

39. Μεγάλα καὶ θαυμαστὰ τὰ ἔργα σου, κύριε ὁ θεὸς ὁ παντοκράτωρ·
δίκαιαι καὶ ἀληθιναὶ αἱ ὁδοί σου, ὁ βασιλεὺς τῶν ἐθνῶν·
τίς οὐ μὴ φοβηθῇ, κύριε, καὶ δοξάσει τὸ ὄνομά σου;
ὅτι μόνος ὅσιος,
ὅτι πάντα τὰ ἔθνη ἥξουσιν καὶ προσκυνήσουσιν ἐνώπιόν σου,
ὅτι τὰ δικαιώματά σου ἐφανερώθησαν.
40. ἐξωμολογοῦντο τὰ ἔργα τὰ μεγάλα καὶ θαυμαστὰ τοῦ θεοῦ. (Tob. 12:22)
μεγάλα τὰ ἔργα κυρίου. (Ps. 110 [111E]:2 LXX)
θαυμάσια τὰ ἔργα σου. (Ps. 138 [139E]:14 LXX)

Similarly, Revelation 15:3c resonates with several Jewish scriptural texts celebrating the "truth" and "justice" of God's ways and works:

His works are *true* and all his *ways* are judgments. (Deut 32:4 LXX)

You are *just*, . . . all your works are *true* and *your ways* straight, and all your judgments are *true*. (Dan. 3:27 LXX [Pr. Azar. 4E])

The Lord is *just* in all his *ways* (Ps. 144 [145E]:17 LXX)[41]

The divine title in Revelation 15:3c is a translated recontextualization of Jeremiah 10:7 (MT): *"King of the nations"* (מֶלֶךְ הַגּוֹיִם). Revelation 15:4a continues to recontextualize Jeremiah 10:7 (MT), which also asks the rhetorical question "Who would not fear you?"[42] This is an especially poignant intertext since Jeremiah 10:1–10 offers an elaborate contrast between the gods of the nations and the God of Israel, underscoring the folly of worshiping the former and the self-evident correctness of worshiping the latter.

The second half of Revelation 15:4a, as seen above, is derived from LXX Psalm 85 (86E):9. Revelation 15:4b, which declares that God is "alone holy" (μόνος ὅσιος), alludes to two epithets of God celebrated frequently in Jewish hymns, but never together (see, e.g., Deut. 32:4 LXX: "Just and *holy* is the Lord," δίκαιος καὶ ὅσιος κύριος; Neh. 9:6 LXX: "You yourself are Lord *alone*," Σὺ εἶ αὐτὸς κύριος μόνος; Isa. 37:16 LXX: "You are God *alone*," σὺ θεὸς μόνος). While Rev 15:4c most clearly recontextualizes LXX Psalm 85 (86E):9, it also resonates with other texts articulating the same hope (e.g., Isa. 66:23: "All flesh will come before me to worship"; Zech. 14:16: "the nations coming . . . to worship the LORD, the King"). The final element of Revelation 15:4 does not recontextualize any clearly identifiable passage. Rather, it refers with new words to the conviction, also expressed in Ezekiel and the *Psalms of Solomon*, that God's righteous judgments will be made known to the earth (*Pss. Sol.* 2:10: "And the earth will know all your righteous judgments," καὶ γνώσεται ἡ γῆ τὰ κρίματά σου πάντα τὰ δίκαια; cf. 8.8; Ps. 97 [98E]:2 LXX), with the result that the nations will at last acknowledge the One God (see Ezek. 38:22–23, which includes blood, fire, and hail among the punishments, as does John).

By weaving together phrases from Psalms, the Song of Moses, a hymnic passage of Jeremiah, and the like into a new, eschatological song of deliverance, John affirms that the old songs about God—God's power, justice, and truth manifesting themselves in God's judicial actions on behalf of God's people and

---

41. ἀληθινὰ τὰ ἔργα αὐτοῦ καὶ πᾶσαι αἱ ὁδοὶ αὐτοῦ κρίσεις. (Deut 32:4)
δίκαιος εἶ . . . πάντα τὰ ἔργα σου ἀληθινά, καὶ αἱ ὁδοί σου εὐθεῖαι, καὶ πᾶσαι αἱ κρίσεις σου ἀληθιναί. (Dan. 3:27 LXX)
δίκαιος κύριος ἐν πάσαις ταῖς ὁδοῖς αὐτοῦ. (Ps. 144 [145E]:17 LXX)

42. The LXX lacks Jer. 10:5–8, as do several mss. of Jeremiah found at Qumran, which has suggested to text critics that these verses are a later interpolation into Jeremiah's denunciation of the folly of idolatry.

against God's adversaries—will be renewed in the future. John's narration of the celebrations of those who overcome the present contest asserts that the unfolding future will demonstrate the ongoing validity and reliability of the premises articulated in those ancient songs. God's justice and power will continue to manifest themselves in divine action against the unjust and on behalf of those who do justice (that is, "keep God's commandments and faith with Jesus," 14:12). John also affirms the conviction articulated by the ancient witnesses (e.g., Ps. 85 [86E]:9–10 LXX; Isa. 66:23) that outsiders to God's people, acting now according to their different values and even pressuring the disciples to conform, will recognize their folly. All nations will yet recognize the truth that they currently suppress in their idolatries, violence, economic rapine, and false ideologies. These are foundational premises that John hopes will guide the hearers' present deliberations.

Revelation 16:5–7, the second hymnlike passage, also affirms God's commitment to bring justice to human affairs as a core premise illumining the hearers' times and choices. After the waters are turned into blood, the "angel of the waters"[43] exclaims:

> Just are you, the One who is and who was, the Holy One, because you judged these things, (16:5b)
>
> because they poured out the blood of the holy ones and prophets, (16:6a)
>
> and you have given to them blood to drink, for they deserve it. (16:6b)[44]

The voices from below the altar,[45] those "slaughtered on account of the word of God and the testimony they bore" (6:9), speak a second time, this time to affirm

---

43. This is probably not one of the two angels involved in turning the waters into blood, but rather an angel whose sphere of authority is "water," similar to the "angel having authority over fire" introduced in 14:18.

44. δίκαιος εἶ, ὁ ὢν καὶ ὁ ἦν, ὁ ὅσιος, ὅτι ταῦτα ἔκρινας,
ὅτι αἷμα ἁγίων καὶ προφητῶν ἐξέχεαν
καὶ αἷμα αὐτοῖς [δ]έδωκας πιεῖν, ἄξιοί εἰσιν.

45. The opening of Revelation 16:7, ἤκουσα τοῦ θυσιαστηρίου λέγοντες, could be translated as "I heard the altar saying" or "I heard [a voice] from the altar saying," depending on whether one understands the genitive case of θυσιαστηρίου, "altar," to denote merely that it is the direct object of the verb ἤκουσα (ἀκούω can take its direct object in either the accusative or genitive case) or to denote the source of what John heard (a "genitive of source"). The scribes of two Greek minuscules clearly read this as the latter, emending the text to ἤκουσα ἐκ τοῦ θυσιαστηρίου λέγοντες in order to resolve the ambiguity for their readers. The altar first appears in Revelation in connection with the martyrs who are gathered beneath it (6:9–11). In the next scene, the altar is intimately connected with the prayers of the saints that result in divine judgments being hurled upon the earth, resonating quite closely with 6:9–11 and taking the martyrs' cries for vengeance one step forward toward fulfillment (8:3–5). The angel's declaration in 16:5–6 directly recalls these same martyrs' cry for the vindication of their blood and for God to manifest God's justice, leading me to conclude that the voice pronouncing the "Amen" to the angel's declaration is none other than the voice of the martyrs beneath the altar. In effect, either resolution of the grammatical ambiguity noted above could support this interpretation: if the θυσιαστήριον is the direct object, the "altar" could stand for those gathered under the altar by metonymy; if it is a genitive of source, it points again to those whose voices have been heard before from the altar on the topic of blood and justice (6:9–11).

that God has brought the vindication for which they had cried out in 6:10: "Yes, Lord God Almighty, true and just are your judgments" (16:7b).[46]

The angel's declaration reaffirms the familiar words of Psalm 118 (119E):137 LXX and Daniel 3:27 LXX (Pr. Azar. 4E): "*Just are you*" (Δίκαιος εἶ). Significantly, both of these older texts continued, in context, to declare the reliability or constancy of God's judgments. The *Psalms of Solomon*, moreover, make frequent declarations concerning God's justice being demonstrated in the judgments God brings upon both Gentiles and Jerusalem:

> In your judgments is your justice. (2:15)
>
> God is justified in his judgments among the nations. (8:23; see also 17:10)

The angel thus reaffirms Jewish cultural knowledge about God's character and commitment to bring justice to the earth.

The angel's description of the crime of the inhabitants of the earth recontextualizes the complaint of Psalm 78:3 LXX against the Babylonians who had besieged and subdued Jerusalem:

> *They poured out* the *blood* of holy ones and prophets. (Rev. 16:6a)
>
> *They poured out* their *blood* like water around Jerusalem. (Ps. 78 [79E]:3 LXX)

The psalm goes on to ask God to "make known among the nations . . . the vindication of the outpoured blood of your slaves" (Ps. 78 [79E]:10), essentially the prayer uttered by the martyrs (Rev. 6:9–11), which is affirmed to have been answered at this point in the narrative. The Song of Moses in Deuteronomy had also affirmed that God "will avenge the blood of his children" [τὸ αἷμα τῶν υἱῶν αὐτοῦ ἐκδικᾶται, Deut. 32:43 LXX).

Most appropriately, then, the very souls of the martyrs sing the antiphon to this verse. Those who had cried out for justice (Rev. 6:9–11) now affirm firsthand the reliability of the premise articulated earlier in 15:3 (a premise that their deaths had called into question), with the significant specification of "ways" now as "judgments":

> Lord God Almighty, true and just are your judgments. (16:7)
>
> Lord God Almighty: just and true are your ways. (15:3)[47]

---

46. Ναί, κύριε ὁ θεὸς ὁ παντοκράτωρ, ἀληθιναὶ καὶ δίκαιαι αἱ κρίσεις σου.
47. Κύριε ὁ θεὸς ὁ παντοκράτωρ, ἀληθιναὶ καὶ δίκαιαι αἱ κρίσεις σου. (16:7)
Κύριε ὁ θεὸς ὁ παντοκράτωρ, δίκαιαι καὶ ἀληθιναὶ αἱ ὁδοί σου. (15:3).

While this antiphon (16:7) is a variant of the earlier hymn of the conquerors, it also exhibits a closer recontextualization of Daniel 3:27 LXX (Pr. Azar. 4E) than its predecessor ("True are your judgments," αἱ κρίσεις σου ἀληθιναί), specifying acts of judgment as the "works" or "ways" evoking such acclamation.

John's narration of God's judgment of Babylon, the pouring out of the plagues upon the beast and his kingdom, and the heavenly celebration of the conquerors—all provide a narrative confirmation of the truth of these basic Jewish-Christian convictions about God's power, God's justice, and God's manifestation of these attributes to the unbelievers. The faithful will be vindicated in the sight of those who now live heedless of God's decrees. In John's vision of the future, the victims of human injustice themselves speak as witnesses (almost in a forensic sense here) to God's unfailing commitment to bring justice. The many texts within the Jewish tradition that speak of God's justice, woven extensively and transparently into John's narrative, focus the hearers on the major enthymeme implicitly at work in John's narration of future events: since God is just, God intervenes to punish the unjust and oppressor and to deliver God's faithful clients.

This enthymeme, furthermore, combines with John's bridging of the horizons between historic Babylon and Rome to provide further support for the future he posits for the Roman imperial system. Aristotle had advised studying one's own city's past wars and other cities' wars when advising about war, since "similar causes are likely to have similar results" (*Rhet.* 1.4.9). John has conducted a similar investigation as he pondered the fall of pagan empires in the past, as interpreted by Israel's prophets, and then considered what must be the outcome of Rome's excesses and sins.[48] Oral-scribal intertexture, then, elevates God's justice almost as a necessary sign of Rome's demise.[49] Rome's arrogance, violence, idolatries, and economic rapine cry out for the inevitable intervention and judgment of a just God (for which Babylon and her fate serve as a remarkable precedent).

Revelation 16: Historical Precedents and the Plausible Future

Revelation 16 narrates the pouring out[50] of the bowls of God's wrath upon the kingdom of the beast, culminating in the destruction of Babylon, "the great

---

48. Aristotle lists this among the commonplaces for enthymemes (*Rhet.* 2.23.25): When the cause exists, the effect exists.

49. On necessary signs, see Aristotle, *Rhet.* 1.2.18 (and chap. 10, n. 19). In a cosmos governed by a just God, Rome's idolatry, violence, and the like, can be offered as necessary signs that it will come under God's judgment. The historical precedents appealed to (always indirectly) by John will support this argument.

50. The command to "pour out the seven vials of the wrath of God upon the earth [ἐκχέετε τὰς ἑπτὰ φιάλας τοῦ θυμοῦ τοῦ θεοῦ εἰς τὴν γῆν]" (16.1) refers to Jewish cultural intertexture about God's interaction with the ungodly, in which God is frequently said to "pour out wrath" upon the nations. Noteworthy among these texts is Jer. 10:25 (ἔκχεον τὸν θυμόν σου ἐπὶ ἔθνη τὰ μὴ εἰδότα σε ... ὅτι κατέφαγον τὸν Ιακωβ), which cites the nations' ravaging of God's people as the motivation for God's pouring out God's wrath. John preserves this as the motivation behind the plagues, explicating this connection in Rev. 16:5–7. In the LXX see also Ps. 68:25 (69:24E); Zeph. 3:8.

city," and the cities of the nations.[51] As in the *Apocalypse of Abraham* (29–30) and several rabbinic texts,[52] John looks to the exodus, the narration of God's first great deliverance of God's holy people, for language by which to describe God's final deliverance of God's people. Where John describes the plagues that God will unleash upon the godless Roman world, intertexture with Exodus is at its thickest, as the following comparisons show:

And there came a boil . . . upon the people. (Rev. 16:2)

And there came boils . . . among the people. (Exod. 9:10)

And [the sea] became *blood* . . . and every living soul that was in the sea *died.* (Rev. 16:3)

And all the water in the river turned into *blood* and the fish in the river *died.* (Exod. 7:20–21)

The third poured his bowl into *the rivers,* . . . and it became *blood.* (Rev. 16:4)

He struck the water in *the river,* . . . and all the water in the river turned into *blood.* (Exod. 7:20–21)[53]

And his kingdom *became darkened.* (Rev. 16:10)

And *let darkness be* upon the land of Egypt. (Exod. 10:21)

three unclean spirits like *frogs* (Rev. 16:13)

He drew out the *frogs,* and the *frog* came up and covered the land of Egypt. (Exod. 8:2–3 LXX [8:6E])[54]

And great *hailstones* . . . came down from heaven upon people, . . . *exceedingly great.* (Rev. 16:21)[55]

many *exceedingly great hailstones* (Exod. 9:24)

---

51. Buchanan (1993, 428–31) argues that "the great city" refers to Jerusalem, which was divided between three parties during the civil strife of 68–70 CE (*J.W.* 5.1.1–5); the reference to Babylon would thus not be resumptive but would add "Rome" to the list of casualties after Jerusalem and the other cities. John himself, however, clearly identifies "the great city" with "Babylon" immediately following (Rev. 17:18, where the "woman" named "Babylon" in 17:3–6 is interpreted by the angel as "the great city that has dominion over the kings of the earth"). Additionally, those who lament over Babylon lament her as "the great city" (18:10; see also 18:16, 19).

52. Rabbinic texts (e.g., *Lev. Rab.* 6.6; *Exod. Rab.* 14.3; *Midr. Pss.* 22.3; 27.1) anticipate the Egyptian plagues falling upon Rome in the end time (Beale 1999, 825).

53. See also Ps. 77 (78E):44 LXX: "And he turned their *rivers* into *blood.*"

54. The Egyptian priest, like the false prophet, was also able to command the frogs (Exod. 8:3, 7). The identification of the frogs and "unclean" spirits may allude to the frog's uncleanness (Lev. 11:9–12, 41–47; Beale 1999, 832).

55. The fourth plague (the sun being made to burn the beast and his people "with fire [ἐν πυρί]"; Rev. 16:8) may recall Exod. 9:23 as well, where the hail was accompanied by fire, which "ran down to the earth."

At three other points, John's seven last plagues intersect with the exodus plagues. First, by means of a structural parallel, John preserves the sense of purposeful action behind these plagues. That Moses (or Aaron) must first stretch out his hand or that an angel first pours out a bowl to initiate a plague conveys the same impression: they happen not merely "on their own" but expressly by God's direction. Second, John chooses to express the amplitude of an earthquake that forms part of the seventh plague by recontextualizing an expression found in Exodus 9:18:

such as *did not happen since* human beings were upon the earth
(Rev. 16:18)

of *such a kind* as *has not happened since* the day [Egypt] was established
(Exod. 9:18; cf. 10:6; 11:6)

This expression had already been taken into the Jewish apocalyptic tradition,[56] another sign of the influence of exodus traditions on Jewish speculation about God's future acts of deliverance. Finally, the response of the beast and his subjects to these plagues, slandering God's name rather than repenting (16:9, 11, 21), recalls the response of Pharaoh and his subjects, who were similarly hardened rather than won over by these visitations of judgment (Exod. 7:22; 8:15, 19, 32; 9:7, 12, 34–35; etc.). The recalcitrance of God's enemies thus also binds the episodes together.

Oral-scribal intertexture serves two principal rhetorical purposes here. First, it contributes directly to the plausibility of John's narration of the future by invoking a historical precedent. Speakers seeking to move an audience to take one course of action rather than another usually do so, in part at least, by demonstrating certain consequences that will serve as incentives or disincentives.[57] Aristotle and Anaximenes both observe that historical examples, invoking historical precedents rather than inventing fables, assist deliberative orators in their primary task: demonstrating that matters will turn out as they allege:[58]

> Examples are most suitable for deliberative speakers, for *it is by examination of the past that we divine and judge the future.* (Aristotle, *Rhet.* 1.9.40)
> While the lessons conveyed by fables are easier to provide, those derived from facts are more useful for deliberative oratory, because *as a rule the future resembles the past.* (Aristotle, *Rhet.* 2.20.8)

---

56. Notably, Dan. 12:1: "There will be . . . tribulation *such as has not happened since* a nation came into being on the earth"; Mark 13:19: "There will be . . . *such* tribulation of *such a kind* as *has not happened since* the beginning of creation."

57. Thus Aristotle, *Rhet.* 3.17.4: "In deliberative oratory, it may be maintained either that certain consequences will not happen, or that what the adversary recommends will happen, but that it will be unjust, inexpedient, or not so important as supposed." See also Anaximenes, *Rhet. Alex.* 1428b.12–17.

58. Anaximenes refers to judicial situations here. Well-documented previous cases can render a jurist's reconstruction of the present case under scrutiny more plausible. Mutatis mutandis, the same should still hold true for deliberative causes.

[Examples should be used] in order that your audience may be more ready to believe your statements when they realize that another action resembling the one you allege has been committed in the way in which you say that it occurred. (Anaximenes, *Rhet. Alex.* 1429a.25–28)

Calling to mind historical examples is a form of induction (Aristotle, *Rhet.* 1.4.9; 2.20.2). Since similar results follow upon similar causes, speakers and audiences expect to be able to predict outcomes of incomplete or future scenarios on the basis of analogy with completed, past scenarios. The fact, then, that God was indeed able to work great and wondrous plagues upon Egypt (and chose to act in this colorful manner, punishing by degrees and by diverse phenomena) so as to bring justice and deliverance to God's people—this fact lends plausibility to John's narration of a future in which God does this again. The scale may be grander, but the action is consistent. John also capitalizes on the tendency within Scripture and within Jewish culture to portray God's future interventions in terms of God's prior ones, itself perhaps another sign that people were willing to embrace a vision of the future more readily when it resembles the past.

Second, oral-scribal intertexture nurtures an evaluative framework for guiding the hearers in their assessment of their condition and their possible responses in a direction that is favorable to John's agenda. Immersing the hearers' situation (local life in Asia Minor under Roman imperial rule) in the scriptural situation of God's visitations upon Egypt guides them to see their present situation in light of the exodus. While it is true that "the Exodus pattern gives shape to Revelation's depiction of oppression and redemption in these judgment visions,"[59] this pattern also sheds interpretive light on the Christians' present experience as a state of bondage and oppression from which redemption, not more complete assimilation into this situation, is required. Given God's historically proven ability and commitment to pour out God's wrath upon injustice, identifying with God's holy ones will always be more secure and advantageous than identifying with God's enemies. Although temporarily afflicted, when the "hour of God's judgment came" (14:7), it was far more advantageous to be found among the Hebrews than the Egyptians.

The details John includes in his description of the sixth bowl plague (Rev. 16:12–16) point to a second arena of intertexture in which historical references contribute to the plausibility of John's future by shaping that future to resemble the past and supporting it with historical precedents. Prophetic texts frequently name the "great river Euphrates"[60] in announcements of the disasters that would befall Judah. The powers east of the Euphrates ("north" of Israel) threatened to

---

59. Schüssler Fiorenza 1991, 27.
60. The Euphrates figures prominently in both Jewish and Roman conceptual maps of geographic space. It sets the eastern boundary of Israel's inheritance in the promises given to Abraham and to the exodus generation (Gen. 15:18; Exod. 23:31; Deut. 11:24; Josh. 1:4) and figures in the descriptions of Solomon's kingdom (1 Kgs. 4:21, 24; 2 Chr. 9:26), when Israel's boundaries were at their most expansive. Although the boundary of the Roman Empire was sometimes east and sometimes west of the Euphrates, that river still served as an approximate boundary of the Roman map until Trajan's victory over the Parthians in 114–116 CE (Caird 1966, 122).

sweep not only over Israel (Isa. 8:7–8; Jer. 1:14–16; 6:22–26; 25:9–11; 47:2) but also over all the Gentile nations in the region (Jer. 46:6–10). The association of the forces beyond "the great river" with bloody destruction is quite strong.

Drying up the Euphrates ("Its water was dried up," Rev. 16:12), while possibly evoking images of God's parting of the Red Sea ("He made the sea dry," Exod. 14:21), provides a notable reference to military history. Cyrus, coming from Persia in the East, captured Babylon when the flow of the Euphrates stopped (whether Cyrus's armies diverted the river from its bed, as in Herodotus, *Histories* 1.189–191, or whether it was the naturally low time for the river). Deutero-Isaiah also speaks of this event: "I will dry up your rivers" (Isa. 44:27; see 44:24–45:6).[61] The drying up of the river to allow the "kings from the east" to cross over and enter into a battle continues to reconfigure this historical precedent, particularly as scripted in Isaiah. Deutero-Isaiah had spoken of God arousing "one from the east," meaning Cyrus, to crush Babylon and liberate Israel (Isa. 41:2, 25). John evokes and reconfigures this scene, as many kings "from the east" are roused against "Babylon."[62]

The site chosen for the battle is also rich with historical reminiscences preserved in the Jewish Scriptures. Ἀρμαγεδών is the Greek transliteration of the Hebrew "Mount of Megiddo."[63] The expression refers to the mountain nearest to the city of Megiddo, much like the expression "waters of Megiddo" (Judg. 5:19) refers to the Wadi Kishon, the torrent close by Megiddo. Mount Carmel would fit this description.[64] Megiddo was a strategically critical stronghold between West and East, and the plain stretching before it is rich in military history, particularly in international battles for domination. Here Sisera was defeated (Judg. 4:15), Gideon repulsed the Midianites (Judg. 7:1), Saul and Jonathan died in battle against the invading Philistines (1 Sam. 31:1–6), King Ahaziah died after being shot by Jehu's forces (2 Kgs. 9:27–28), and King Josiah perished in his attempt to stop Pharoah Necco from crossing through Palestine to wage war on the king of Babylon (2 Kgs. 23:29). If there was a single spot in Israel's geography where one should sit upon the ground and tell sad stories of the death of kings, it was Megiddo. Shea suggests that the historic "battle" between Ahab and Elijah, between Baal and Yahweh on Carmel, should also be heard as a resonance here.[65] This would be particularly appropriate since John's plot also concerns the final demonstration of who is, indeed, God.

61. Shea 1980, 157–58.
62. Buchanan reads this as a reference to the Jewish hope that the Parthians would join forces with them and overthrow Rome (1993, 417, 419), something for which their assistance to Judea against Roman-imposed rule in the late Hasmonean/early Herodian period (see Josephus, *J.W.* 1.248–270) provided precedent. These eastern kings would not, in his view, be the beast's allies but his adversaries (Buchanan 1993, 425, 427). The fact that *1 En.* 56:5–7 speaks of Parthian kings laying siege to Jerusalem should not preclude, however, the possibility that they are hostile not only to Rome.
63. Possibly "city of Megiddo" if the first syllable represents Hebrew ʿîr (עִיר) rather than *har*.
64. Shea 1980, 159–160.
65. Shea 1980, 160–61. Shea isolates this as "the" resonance, but there is neither need nor warrant for choosing a single referent.

By patterning the final battle in which God defeats "Babylon" and brings relief to God's people after the model of a prominent precedent in which God did the same to end the historic Babylonian exile, John nurtures the plausibility of the future he narrates, since it continues to resemble known historical facts. John adds to the plausibility by laying out at some length God's "strategy" for accomplishing this end, the ways and means by which God will position God's enemies for defeat. Rather than speaking vaguely about God's victory, John uses specificity and detail to make that victory appear more feasible and real. God has chosen a location known for its strategic importance,[66] one where large hostile forces could be routed (as was Sisera's army), and now by defeating "the kings of the earth," God will add to the historic wailing of the armies assembling in that space.

Chapter 16 closes with the announcement of the fall of Babylon, to whom God remembered "to give to her the cup of the wine of the violent passion of his anger" (Rev. 16:19; cf. 14:10). Identifying Rome with "Babylon" allows John to bring together many pieces of authoritative texts denouncing historic Babylon and other pagan seats of empire in Isaiah, Jeremiah, and Ezekiel into a deconstruction of Roman imperial ideology in chapters 17 and 18.[67] The label "Babylon" affords an unusual but strikingly effective way of considering a historical precedent to predict the outcome of a new venture. Despite the fact that there were few indicators of "decline" in terms of Roman power and stability during the reign of Domitian,[68] John is able to use historical reference and intertexture to build a plausible case for the forthcoming judgment of Rome, chiefly by establishing that the same causes for judgment are present in Rome as were present in Babylon (as well as other cities similarly judged by God).[69] The example also thus becomes a "previous verdict" (Aristotle, *Rhet.* 2.23.12) that can be counted upon to guide the divine court in pronouncing its sentence upon Babylon's new manifestation.

The essential deduction undergirding the "appeal to logos" in 16:17–19:8 could be outlined as follows:

---

66. Buchanan (1993, 422) suggests that "if Parthians had come to rescue Palestine from the Romans during the war between Vitellius and Vespasian, there would have been Jewish volunteers to meet them at Mount Carmel, just as there were at the beginning of Herod's rule, because Megiddo was one of the most strategic fortresses in Palestine, and it was the first one the Parthians would have reached as they came to Palestine from the north ([Josephus,] *War* 1.13.2 §250)."

67. As Kraybill (1996, 150) observed, "Equating Rome with Babylon gave John and his readers a familiar paradigm of oppressive power."

68. Kraybill 1996, 24. There were, no doubt, memories of 68–69 CE, when provincials watched to see if the empire would collapse under the weight of the civil wars. If the earlier date for Revelation is to be preferred, of course, then the observable political conditions themselves would be far more favorable to supporting John's forecast.

69. Most noteworthy among these would be Tyre, indicted for its economic "prostitution" (Isa. 23:15–18), the power amassed by its merchants (Isa. 23:2–3, 8), and the overweening pride of its king born of economic success (Ezek. 28:2, 5). Tyre's cargo list overlaps significantly with Rome's (cf. Ezek. 27:12–24 with Rev. 18:11–13); its fate is to be burned up and exposed (cf. Ezek. 28:17–18 with Rev. 17:12–13); and over its fall pilots and mariners lament (cf. Ezek. 27:28–36 with Rev. 18:9–20). See the detailed discussion in Kraybill 1996, 152–61.

Step 1: Rome has embraced the following practices:
  a. It uses violence against dissenting groups and rebellious nations or people groups (that is, against people who miss their former political independence).
  b. It orchestrates a global economy that makes traders, merchants, producers of exports rich and happy while making it harder for the local nonelites to obtain bread.
  c. It spreads an ideology legitimating these practices, while claiming to be answerable to none (not even to the God who appoints times and seasons for earthly kingdoms).

Step 2: From the written record of the sacred oracles of the Hebrew Scriptures, we know that God opposed such practices where they have emerged in past empires.

Step 3: Therefore, we can confidently project how this same God assesses Rome's practices and how God will respond to them in the course of events, having ended the rule of past regimes that embraced similar practices, including ancient Israel.

Step 4: On the basis of these projections, we can further discern the course of action that will result in advantage, in honor and safety, when God does intervene to judge.

John's actual presentation, with its extensive use of intertexture from the major prophets, deftly conflates the first two steps in this progression, so that we only see Rome and Roman imperial practice from "inside" the scriptural prophetic tradition—from God's own viewpoint, as it were.

John's mode of presentation has the potential to be far more effective than a more discursive argument from example. Aristotle knew that deliberative proofs worked on probabilities. Analogies and examples were used to establish the *probability* that the consequences would be as the orator predicted, but could never establish their *certainty*. John is able to suppress the element of analogy, never saying that the fate of Rome will be "like" that of Babylon. Rather, he completely closes the distance between the historical precedent that informs his language and the present case under consideration by identifying the two, thus also closing the distance between probability and certainty. The element of "certainty" is reinforced as John continues to narrate the reasons for Rome's downfall and the execution of the same by using recontextualized material from the very oracles of God from Isaiah, Jeremiah, and Ezekiel denouncing historic Babylon (and other such seats of empire) in Revelation 17 and 18.

By embroidering portions of the Old Testament prophets into his denunciation of Rome, John again causes the hearers to set their present situation and their present world in the interpretive context of authoritative Scriptures. This is a central mode of persuasion in John's visionary rhetoric. In effect, he causes them to inhabit the world of everyday experience and the world of the Scriptures simultaneously, knowing that this will lead them both to see and respond to the world in ways that John considers faithful to the Christian tradition. Without John ever having to exhort the hearer directly on this point (18:4 will come very close to this), John's addressees will nevertheless discern that any course favoring partnership with Rome, an enemy of God certain to be judged and toppled, will be less expedient than a course favoring exclusive allegiance to the One God.

CONCLUSION

Alongside explicit argumentative texture and enthymematic elaboration, John employs narration as a means of appealing to the hearers' minds. Indeed, this is his *primary* means of lodging appeals to logos, within which hearers occasionally encounter more explicit forms of argumentation. Both subcategories of induction Aristotle labeled "example"—the fable (the invented story with a "point") and the historical precedent—have counterparts within John's rhetorical strategy.

As the "fable" creates a scenario in order to narrativize some element of argumentation that will contribute to the speaker's case, many episodes in Revelation narrativize some premise or provide an invented, illustrative "demonstration" of the expediency of some course John recommends. In one of the more detailed examples, John utilizes a rhetorical commonplace, the "two women topos," itself a rhetorical structure derived from Greek fable, in order to guide perceptions and elicit particular decisions.

John employs older texts and cultural traditions (oral-scribal and cultural intertexture) as, among other things, a means of invoking the historical precedents that contribute to rendering his narration of the future plausible. John's visions will not have the appearance of flights of fancy but will present a future that very much resembles the past and in which the same relationships of cause and consequence are observable that have been at work throughout God's dealings with humanity. At critical junctures in this narrative demonstration, the older texts about God's character and commitment to do justice upon the earth are affirmed and reinvigorated, reminding the hearers of the principal, unchanging premises that guide the unfolding of history and thus provide a reliable basis for divining the future. Perhaps most central to the success of John's cause, intertexture promotes the prioritization of that forthcoming crisis concerning which John wants the congregations to deliberate wisely. The "Day of the Lord" is prominently featured and dramatically depicted so that securing safety on that Day will displace any contrary agenda that threatens total commitment to the Christian group and its distinctive values.

Chapter 12

John's Vision beyond the Roman World

What Might the Spirit Continue to Say to the Churches?

Revelation exhibits an uncanny appeal among many twenty-first-century Christians, just as it had throughout the last quarter of the twentieth century. Granted, the constituencies of some denominations still proceed as though the biblical canon ended with Jude (better make that 3 John). The immense popularity enjoyed by the books of Hal Lindsey or the Left Behind series by Jerry Jenkins and Tim LaHaye, however, attest to the ongoing appeal of the Apocalypse. The question is not *whether* to apply Revelation but *how* to apply it, since it already exerts a strong influence on many Christians, some of whom exert, in turn, a strong influence upon American politics—and not consistently in a manner that challenges modern domination systems.[1]

Many Christians who are drawn to Revelation do not share its author's social location. They are often well connected within the politics, economics, and social networks of the dominant culture. The way they live out their faith does not bring them into conflict with the representatives of the dominant culture. Quite the opposite: many of our most eschatologically-minded Christian

---

1. C. D. White (1998) provides a helpful primer on the identification and working of several domination systems. See also Wink 1983; 1986; 1992; Howard-Brook and Gwyther 1999, 236–77.

leaders are welcome guests on Capitol Hill. Any rhetoric of persecution among such Christian groups is just that: rhetoric. In the words of Stephen O'Leary, "If the largely middle-class group of fundamentalist Christians in the United States who today form the core of Hal Lindsey's readership believes itself to be similarly persecuted, this is surely a rhetorically induced perception; for there is an obvious difference between being torn apart by lions in front of cheering crowds and being forced to endure media onslaughts of sex, violence, and secular humanism."[2]

There is one sense in which the fundamentalist Christian would be eased by the lion scenario more than the scenario of sex, violence, and secular humanism. The former confirms the importance of one's religious commitments and allows one to conform to well-established paradigms within the Christian tradition. Martyrdom can be—certainly at a significant cost to oneself—immensely reinforcing of one's commitment to one's world construction. The trouble with the "media onslaught of sex, violence, and secular humanism" is that it makes one's religious commitments seem rather unimportant and easily ignored. When religion does come up, it is often relativized, sometimes trivialized, and all too often uncomfortably "taken into account" and explained away by the competing world construction of secular humanism. Sociologists or psychologists of religion have an annoying habit of being able to explain why evangelical Christians should be so deeply committed to, and certain of, their religious convictions without giving any indication that those convictions are any more "true" or even "interesting" or "praiseworthy" than those held by Javanese who gather around the dance of Barong and Rangda.

This, in turn, makes apocalypticism highly appealing to such an audience. It can turn the tables on those who speak of religious commitment as but one facet of life, and not all that important a facet at that, making it once again the most important determining factor, since eternal destiny—and often, end-time safety (e.g., being "raptured")—depends entirely on this factor. Revelation (the apocalypse of choice for such an audience) presents a multimedia picture of reality that has the ideological and rhetorical power to answer the "media onslaught" and everything else that conspires to erode their commitment to the worldview and ethos of conservative Christianity.

Apocalyptic theology and texts are applied not only to reassert the centrality of a particular Christian worldview. Revelation continues to be utilized to promote a perception of marginalization within, and hostile tensions with, the larger society as a strategy for developing group identity and strengthening the ideological boundaries that protect the group against assimilation, as John used it in his context. The rhetoric of persecution found in publications such as A. Jan Marcussen, *The National Sunday Law*, provides a case in point.[3] This book seeks to confirm Christians whose distinguishing feature is worshiping on

2. O'Leary 1994, 11.
3. Marcussen 1983.

Saturday (the book was given to me by my Seventh-day Adventist grandaunt) in their practice and in their commitment to their particular religious bodies, and does so by imagining national (and spiritual) conspiracies to close down stores on Sunday (the horror!), which are, in turn, interpreted as attempts to enforce worship on Sunday.[4]

Such forms of application of Revelation and its rhetoric in the contemporary scene—from supporting right-wing political agendas to legitimating strongly sectarian positions, not to mention the pervasive trivialization of John's message by reducing it to an end-times playbook—have tended to marginalize Revelation in mainstream Christian discourse, save for the book's contributions to the liturgy and hymnody of these churches.[5] What has Revelation to contribute to the reflection and practice of Christians who, fully cognizant of the changes in the rhetorical situation, are allergic to using its rhetoric either to foster the interests of contemporary imperial pursuits (which, as they correctly intuit, run counter to John's intentions for his text) or to promote divisions within the Christian church by looking across the street or across the theological spectrum for the "whore of Babylon" or the "Nicolaitans"?

Before we can explore this question, we need to return to several significant challenges and cautions posed regarding the applicability of Revelation *tout court*. These challenges must be heard and considered in order to ensure that the ongoing application of Revelation will be done in such a way as to nurture health within the Christian culture and just interaction with the world outside the church. In regard to the study of the *rhetoric* of Revelation, two challenges emerge in particular. The first concerns John's allegedly authoritarian posture vis-à-vis his communities, coupled with his lack of toleration for divergent viewpoints within the church. The second concerns Revelation's deployment of feminine imagery and the ways in which this deployment contributes to the alienation of women readers and the perpetuation of ideological and physical violence against women. These will be explored in turn before formulating any statement about how our study of the rhetoric of Revelation might open up venues for the application of John's word and strategies.

JOHN: AN AUTHORITARIAN AND INTOLERANT RELIC?

Rhetorical critics who have focused on John's construction of ethos (including John's deconstruction of the ethos of rival speakers) have sharply criticized

---

4. This is manifestly not the case since the lack of availability of shopping does not exactly compel people to go to worship, as if that were the only alternative to unbearable boredom, though the legislation would not *help* people who have jobs in retail *and* want to worship on Saturday.

5. In my experience in Episcopal, Lutheran, and United Methodist churches, I have encountered Revelation's voice in hymns like "Holy, Holy, Holy," "O Holy City, Seen of John," "O What Their Joy and Their Glory Must Be," canticles like "This Is the Feast," the liturgical reading of several of the acclamations found in Revelation, and readings from Rev. 7 and 21 on All Saints' Day.

John's authoritarian stance and the power dynamics of John's speech. These criticisms challenge any facile application of John's text and certainly of John's model, particularly in a postmodern environment that highly values pluralism and toleration, and that locates "authority" increasingly less in external norms and more in the perspectives and experience of the individual. The principal points of concern are the following:

1. John seeks to limit, or even prevent, other people's creative engagement with the tradition. Only his "dream" will do.
2. John forbids reading, critically engaging, and excerpting his work.
3. John seeks to silence other voices, establishing his own hegemony within the Christian community.
4. The replication of John's rhetoric demonizing opponents is highly problematic in a modern context where dialogue is an increasingly essential value.

We have already performed some "checks" on John's construction of his authority vis-à-vis the activity of other prophets, the community and its role in discernment, and the Hebrew Scriptures. In regard to all three foci, we found evidence that would substantially mitigate claims about John's authoritarianism and quest for prophetic hegemony. Nevertheless, it remains to consider these related criticisms, particularly from the perspective of what to "do" with Revelation in a modern context.

In his thoughtful study of John's appeals to ethos, Greg Carey writes that, while "John seeks to provide his audience with the resources to endure" in their resistance to colonial domination, he nevertheless "denies them the freedom to do their own imagining. Resistance must be on John's terms, and his terms only."[6] But is John really so exclusive? We have already seen that John affirms the activity of a number of prophets alongside himself, finding no substantial evidence for the claim that these prophets were in some sense under John's control or tutelage. John affirms the legitimacy of multiple prophetic voices, as long as they also speak in line with the higher norm that John believes (and surely not John alone) must guide the community—the witness of the Hebrew Scriptures and the "testimony of Jesus" that inspires prophecy (Rev. 19:10). John leaves a great deal of room for ongoing imagining, insofar as John encourages all disciples to hold on to the "witness of Jesus" that is the "spirit of prophecy." *Fifth Ezra* (2 Esd. 2:38–48) provides a striking example of such ongoing imagining. The author has read and internalized Revelation as part of the tradition and now gives voice to a vision very similar to the vision of Revelation 7 in terms of content, imagery, and even form. But it is a new vision, giving new voice to the image of "conquering" and promoting, in a new context, the value of witness.

6. Carey 1999b, 117.

John was not understood to have squelched such imagining, but to have modeled and enabled it.[7]

Carey's fundamental critique of John's rhetoric is that "it cannot sustain its own vision—that of a priestly dominion in which John is a partner under God's rule (1:9)," because John raises his voice authoritatively and in an authoritarian manner above other voices, commanding assent to his vision if anyone wishes to experience the blessedness that God prepares for the faithful.[8] In Carey's understanding, the egalitarian impulses of Revelation's vision conflict with John's authoritarian rhetoric. But Carey's claims that John thinks himself "alone" possessing "the authority to bless and to curse," and that he thinks "his message the only revelation of Jesus Christ (1:1)," are simply not *John's* claims.[9] As we have seen, John does not make claims about exclusive power to bless and to curse, nor does he present his apocalypse as "the only" authentic message in opposition to all other messages. The words "only" and "alone" are imposed by the critic, not asserted by John, who presents his work simply as "*a* revelation of Jesus Christ" (1:1), refusing to use so much as a definite article. Moreover, we have shown that, in calling the hearers to "keep what is written" in Revelation (1:3; 22:7), John is calling the hearers to continue to live aligned with the greater tradition of the Hebrew Scriptures and the sayings and deeds of Jesus (see, e.g., 14:12). This tradition, and not his own peculiar message, is at the heart of John's concern.

The real problem with John is not a bifurcation between egalitarian vision and authoritarian rhetoric. It is that John affirms the existence of boundaries at the edges of Christian identity, practice, and witness. A "priestly dominion"—*especially* a priestly dominion—retains its codes of holiness and defilement, purity and pollution, its awareness of boundaries. Carey is really faulting John for not making room at the table for Jezebel, for declaring her vision for Christian practice "out of bounds" in regard to the tradition under which, in John's view, both he and she stood. And as we shall see below, Jezebel's reformulation of Christian practice might have been far more problematic than our pluralistic ideological commitments would admit.

John acknowledges the prophets who stand alongside him in the same tradition of interpreting the authoritative texts of the Hebrew Scriptures and the Jesus tradition, who are deeply concerned that the commandments of God, the warnings of the prophets, and the witness of the Psalms (e.g., to God's kingship, to the necessity of acknowledging this kingship above all others, and to the future in which all nations will come and do the same) be preserved and lived out in the

---

7. One would be reading too much into Rev. 22:18–19, perhaps subconsciously influenced by its placement at the end of the canon, to think that John allows no more room for Christian prophetic activity. He simply seeks to protect the integrity of his own message in an environment in which it could easily be blunted in the course of transmission on the authority of some local leader or through the sensitivity of some copyist within the church circles.
8. Carey 1999b, 173.
9. Carey 1999b, 133.

churches. This is the common ground that provides unity and toleration amid diversity. But, then, there are boundaries as well, beyond which one moves from the possibility of unity to a different gospel that rends common practice, witness, and unity. Here John confronts *our* cultural location's fear of boundaries and of claims about some center of authority beyond our own consent.

Robert Royalty raises the second criticism, that John forbids reading, critically engaging, and excerpting his work. The focal text here is 22:18–19, in which Jesus threatens eschatological harm to those who tamper with the text:

> I myself bear witness to everyone hearing the words of the prophecy of this book: If anyone adds to them, God will add to that person the plagues written in this book, and if anyone takes away from the words of the book of this prophecy, God will take away that person's portion of the tree of life and of the holy city, [that person's portion] of the things written in this book.

Royalty asserts that "adding or subtracting (ἐπιτίθημι, ἀφαιρέω) would involve textual criticism, editing, translation, or allegorization—interpretive moves in any act of reading. John is afraid that someone will *read* what he has *written*. Reading, the construction of alternative interpretations and meanings, has been circumscribed by the text."[10] His last sentence reflects a postmodern prejudice and predilection for "alternative interpretations and meanings": Royalty excludes the form of reading as the disciplined effort to hear and understand the meaning of the author.

In his interpretation of John's warning, Royalty significantly expands it. He builds his own fence around John's sentence and then proceeds to blame John for that fence. He claims that 22:18–19 proscribes interpretation, borrowing, excerpting, or keeping John's words alive in the liturgy of the worshiping community, even though Revelation has had its broadest and most enduring impact in Christian liturgy (something Revelation's harsher critics have overlooked in their castigation of John for his violence and envy). This fact shows, moreover, that early Christian readers of 22:18–19 did not understand the curse to prevent excerpting for the purpose of crafting liturgy, regarding themselves rather as faithful readers of a text that was itself full of liturgical expressions, incorporating John's language into liturgy as a means of "keeping the words written in this book." The use of the imagery, language, and form of Revelation 7 by the author of *5 Ezra* similarly demonstrates that early Christians did not understand Revelation 22:18–19 in the way that Royalty wants to promote.

If John is safeguarding *interpretation* with this curse, one might better say that John insists that the act of reading take the whole work into account rather than reading selectively (taking away) or in a supplementary fashion (adding to

---

10. Royalty 2004, 291. This becomes a refrain in Royalty's article: "Any act of interpretation brings with it the inscribed curses of the Apocalypse" (2004, 295). "Revelation threatens plagues and taking away salvation from anyone who attempts to act as a strong reader and dares to allegorize, interpret, connect—in short, to read" (2004, 299).

the work that which might blunt it). But John may indeed simply be concerned with the faithful copying and reading of the text as it passed from church to church, fearing perhaps that copyists or readers would allow their pastoral sensitivity (or fear of confrontation) to blunt John's message to the church. This proved to be a reasonable-enough fear, given the history of emotionally charged reactions against John's text—hence how much more reasonable when "Jezebel" or "Nicolaitans" would be sitting in the congregation? In this regard, this curse offered a kindness to the local reader, who is thereby excused before the audience for not being more diplomatic in confronting local teachers and members of the congregations.

Royalty recognizes that John has (yet again) used a technique bequeathed to him by the tradition of the Hebrew Scriptures. The legal material of Deuteronomy is sandwiched between two similar commandments regarding adding and deleting:

> You must neither add anything to what I command you nor take away anything from it, but keep the commandments of the LORD your God with which I am charging you. (4:2 NRSV)
> All the curses written in this book will descend on them [who think they can follow "their own stubborn ways" rather than the Law of God], and the LORD will blot out their names from under heaven. (29:20 NRSV)

Royalty argues that, while Deuteronomy was concerned with deeds, Revelation is only concerned with words, with "reading the text."[11] However, this overlooks the fact that reading, hearing, and keeping are intimately bound together in the opening blessing of Revelation 1:3, reiterated in the macarism of 22:7, "Blessed is the one keeping the words of this prophecy." John's concern with the integrity of the text (the words) arises from his understanding that deeds are affected by words. Specifically, the audience's response of obedience to God's commandments (12:17; 14:12) in their local setting, notably the obligation of exclusive worship of the aniconic God, may be jeopardized by the editing of John's prophetic message. He seeks to safeguard the words in order to safeguard the response. John's inclusion of a curse that recalls the prohibition of additions or deletions from the body of God's commandments in Deuteronomy is also a potent reminder that, ultimately, John is calling disciples to "keep the commandments of God," now in tandem with, and interpreted by, "the testimony of Jesus" (12:17).

The third focal point of criticism is John's obvious lack of tolerance for opposing viewpoints, particularly the vision for Christian practice supported by "Jezebel" and the "Nicolaitans." "The Apocalypse . . . excises alternative Christian voices within the ἐκκλησίαι of Asia Minor. . . . Revelation envisions a New Jerusalem from which alternative voices have been cast into fire and perdition (20:15)—the ultimate marginalization of the other."[12] It may be well not to

---

11. Royalty 2004, 292.
12. Royalty 2004, 285.

generalize. We cannot demonstrate that John is intolerant of any other viewpoint, but only that he is intolerant of the suggestion that Christian practice can accommodate participation in idolatry for the sake of increasing the disciple's access to the prosperity and security offered by the Roman imperial system, and we have already explored *why* John would have regarded this practice as jeopardizing Christian witness.

As a counterpoint, it may be useful to examine the voices that John still allows to speak and perhaps even enables to speak. This, in turn, sheds light on what is at stake for John if certain other voices are not actually excised from the Christian churches. John gives renewed voice to the many voices that the domination systems of the world would prefer to drown out beneath the accolades of their accomplishments and benefits. Prominent among these are the voices of the victims. The martyrs under the altar twice cry out (6:9–11; 16:7); those whom the domination systems of the first century had violently silenced are allowed to find a voice again and are not allowed to be forgotten or conveniently swept aside by those who now preach "peace" with those domination systems.

John preserves the voice of the prophetic witness of the Hebrew Scriptures. We have already closely examined and refuted the criticism that John wants to eliminate the Hebrew Scriptures from the ongoing engagement and reading of the Christian communities, replacing them with his own text. John's use of the Old Testament represents, on the contrary, an attempt to keep the voices of the prophets and other witnesses to God, God's commandments, and God's standards of justice alive in a context where Roman imperialism and the lure of material success and a secure "peace" (preserved by Roman power and violence against dissent and resistance) threatens to stifle those voices. Isaiah and Jeremiah's tirades against empire are not welcome voices when there is such promise of enjoying the fruits of imperialism. Arguably, these voices have been excised in the preaching of Jezebel and the Nicolaitans, and in the witness of the congregation in Laodicea. In this regard, John does the very opposite of what Royalty charges him with doing: "eliminat[ing] the prophets as authoritative texts."[13] Rather, he gives fresh voice to those traditions with their alternative visions, practices, and values (notably derived from a subaltern people within the empire).

Further, John enables the Christians in the seven churches to find their voice as they join in "witness." He gives individuals the power to stand before the governor Pliny the Younger fifteen years later and to say "I am a Christian," just as the Maccabean martyrs celebrated in Jewish literature were able to stand up before Antiochus IV, holding fast to the dictates of their moral conscience. He enables Christians to speak the truth under the principate: "You are *men*! Climbing to the top of the social pyramid does not make you *gods*!" And this is an appropriate reminder to those who still think to live out the strategy of Babel, that prototypical domination system whereby another kind of pyramid was built to allow a few people to think to touch heaven. John empowers Christians to live

---

13. Royalty 2004, 299.

out the witness, rather, that the way to become like God is to become like Christ: to give oneself to others in love, to lay down one's own agenda for God's and be part of a community that will do so, to proclaim the poor and the marginalized to be the recipients of God's favor, and to confront domination systems and be crushed, knowing that God will have the last word.

If postcolonial interpretation "is a counter-hegemonic discourse which pays special attention to the hidden and neglected voices in the Bible,"[14] Revelation is a first-century specimen of (post)colonial resistance literature insofar as it, too, represents a "counterhegemonic discourse" that seeks to elevate and give utterance to the "hidden and neglected voices," even the violently *silenced* voices, at the margins of Roman imperial discourse. Jezebel, by contrast, seeks to elevate within the church the voices at the *center* of Roman imperial discourse, the voices calling for conformity to the mechanisms of the religious legitimation of imperial society.

Royalty asserts that "a just society includes tolerance for dissent and alternative points of view and the means of expression for all voices."[15] This may indeed be true of a just society, but is it possible in the midst of resistance to an oppressive, overwhelming imperialist domination system and the loud clamor of its legitimating ideologies? At least one ancient author of resistance literature articulated a paradigm of resistance demonstrating that members of a dissenting, minority culture needed to exhibit solidarity and unified witness under such circumstances, rather than tolerate a diversity that would undermine commitment.[16] John also recognized that a "just society" would not emerge until certain points of view— for example, the points of view that affirmed the securing of the prosperity of the few at the expense of the many, or that countenanced winking at the use of brutal force to secure one's party's assets—ceased to be embraced. For John, the voices that called for Christianity to become a private, individualistic, hidden faith that outwardly participates in the legitimating machines of self-glorifying empire— and in the lies these machines spin about the violence of empire and the like— prevented the emergence of this just society and indeed threatened the existence of God's very means of bringing it about (i.e., through witness).

We also need to recognize that Jezebel *does enjoy* the means of expression and has exercised those means to express her alternative point of view. John does not *silence* Jezebel. He makes his best case against her influence. Her voice has been heard before Revelation is read aloud, and she can still rebut after Revelation is read. If the community is persuaded by John that her influence does corrode Christian identity and witness by altering its practice, it has no moral obligation to keep listening to her; her word will have been tested and found wanting when set alongside the tradition to which the community looks for its ongoing formation. Carey accuses John of reinscribing the practice of empire: John's "message is in a profound sense no different from that of the Empire: Neither

---

14. Schüssler Fiorenza 2007, 123.
15. Royalty 2004, 286.
16. See deSilva 2007b, 123–25 on 4 Maccabees.

allows dissent."[17] Yet it is clear that John's strategy for "excising" alternative or dissenting points of view is fundamentally different from empire's style. The latter can exercise the physical means by which to disallow dissent; John can only exercise persuasion, the common strategies of civil discourse that we have explored in chapters 5 through 11 of this volume. In the end, John and Jezebel must both submit their prophetic word to the congregations, with whom rests the authority to follow one or the other.

Toleration is clearly a core value in a multicultural and pluralistic environment, and it is particularly important for those who are a part of the privileged and empowered class (e.g., professors of New Testament studies) to keep this value in view lest the society that they continue to shape move away from the ideal of the "just society." For such persons, however, to criticize John for his intolerance in regard to one (radically) opposing view is problematic for a number of reasons. First, as we have already mentioned, John does not write as a member of the privileged, empowered class. Second, tolerance of a diversity of voices is *our* value. It is, to a great extent, a *Roman* value, which was intolerant only of atheism and such exclusive expressions of piety that threatened to come across as insulting to the majority of gods—or the gods of the majority of the people. But for John to embody and model toleration of a multiplicity of divergent voices (i.e., Jezebel's opinion regarding how to follow Christ), he would have had to betray his own tradition.

The tradition of the Hebrew Scriptures (and of Jesus) is not a tolerant tradition, and the Jewish God is not a tolerant one. "I am the LORD your God. . . . You shall have no other gods before me" (Exod. 20:2–3 NRSV; Deut. 5:6–7). There would be no Asherah poles or enclaves of Baal worship, no vestiges of pluralism in the cleansed "Holy Land" of Deuteronomy or the prophets. There would be no accommodation to the idolatrous practices of the Gentile majority and dominant culture in the lands of exile, for the Gentiles' gods were not gods at all. There would (ultimately) be no concession to the worship needs of Greco-Syrian residents in Jerusalem under Hellenistic monarchs, no innovations of the temple service to be more inclusive. God had commanded that the prophet who urged the people of God to go after (make room for) other gods be put to death (Deut. 13:1–5); John does not presume to stand in judgment upon the tradition, but calls for the community to cease entertaining such prophets in their midst.

In the end, what qualifies John to speak as a prophet to his communities (his deep faithfulness to the Jewish and early Christian tradition) *dis*qualifies him as a role model in the eyes of many modern interpreters. This is not to say that we all need to act like John. When those who have not adequately submitted themselves to the process of understanding and interpreting the tradition jump to the stance of proclaiming its exclusive demands too quickly, the results are disastrous. But we should not blame John for trying to silence or undermine

17. Carey 1999b, 117.

those whom he believed to be the contemporary false prophets leading God's new Israel into idolatry. We should not blame John for trying to be faithful to the very tradition whose words he interweaves into his own as a signal of his "ideological location" as a prophet of that tradition. If John were to speak in the idiom of the Jewish Scriptures to argue for tolerance of multiple positions regarding how to interact with idols and other issues of "religious pluralism" in his setting, he might be applauded by his modern critics—but then (and *only* then) would he be acting disingenuously in regard to his use of those Scriptures. In light of this, when modern critics pronounce judgment on John from their positions of power and privilege, they replicate the dominant Roman culture's inability to stomach the exclusive claims made by a particular subaltern people (the Jews and their religious offspring, the church) and become one more example of how we, in our culture of toleration, can tolerate anything except exclusive claims about Truth.

It is this changed rhetorical situation, however, that makes these critics' fourth concern entirely apt. The replication of John's rhetoric demonizing opponents is indeed highly problematic in a modern context, all the more as this rhetoric is too often employed by those who are actually among the empowered and privileged in American society (and in the service of American imperialism!), and not by members of a minority culture resisting, for example, American imperialism. Carey draws attention to the work of Chinua Achebe, the author of *Things Fall Apart*, the first in a series of novels detailing the decline of the Ibo culture through the process of colonization, as an informative example.[18] Achebe's treatment of the (unwitting) contributions of the work of missionary Mr. Brown among the Ibo to the decline of the same as the vanguard of the colonialism to follow "demonstrates that one may criticize the imperial power without resorting to demonization." Carey uses this observation to criticize John's language, having lost sight of the very different rhetorical situations behind the works he compares. If Achebe had written *during* the period of Mr. Brown's missionary work among the Ibo and had perceived then the dangers to the Ibo way of life presented by the foreign power beyond the sea, of which Mr. Brown was a representative and forerunner, would he then have refrained from painting the missionary and the imperial power as beasts from land and sea? However, Carey's observation remains an important caveat for us in *our* very different rhetorical setting and social location, if we were to pursue such a critique of our own or other political settings. As people embedded in a web of overlapping and mutually reinforcing domination systems, our approach should rather be one of inquiry than labeling.

Revelation's meaning and certainly its rhetoric are limited by its rhetorical situation; its message is easily perverted where that situation no longer persists. "The book is written 'with a jail-house' perspective, asking for the realization of God's justice and power. It therefore can only be understood by those 'who

---

18. Carey 1999b, 182, citing Chinua Achebe, *Things Fall Apart* (London: Heinemann, 1958).

hunger and thirst for justice.'"[19] Schüssler Fiorenza suggests that Revelation "cannot be understood when its 'rhetorical situation' no longer 'persists,'" even though it will powerfully evoke an appropriate response in parallel rhetorical situations (Allen Boesak's reading of Revelation from the setting of apartheid South Africa remains a monument in this regard).[20] It is not the case, however, that Revelation fails to be understood in a changed rhetorical situation, as long as its readers think critically about the significance of the distance between their own and John's situation before reinscribing its rhetoric. The application of John's labeling of the church's adversaries in changed situations, such that papal Rome or Hussein's Babylon are made to wear the dress of beast and harlot, does not represent a faithful reading of Revelation in a changed rhetorical situation; but the inquiry into the degree to which *we* are imitating Babylon or muting (or even failing to notice) the witness of the Christian tradition because of our commitment to prosperity would be a faithful application.

REVELATION AND WOMEN

Standing in the tradition of D. H. Lawrence, Tina Pippin offers a radical critique of Revelation's vision—now from the standpoint of what John has to say about women—and holds out little or no prospect for the text's ongoing application to Christian thought and practice. Pippin approaches the work quite self-consciously *not* from the perspective of its historical situation, and *not* with a view to recovering John's challenge to his contemporaries. Rather, she approaches Revelation from a reader-response perspective, particularly highlighting her response to the text as a woman reader (as opposed to, for example, a "first-world" reader, a "Caucasian" reader, a reader from a privileged class, and so forth). Pippin engages Revelation as a specimen of "fantasy literature" rather than as an "apocalypse,"[21] and discovers, as she enters into this fantasy, that "the Apocalypse is not a safe space for women."[22] As a result, she approaches the text with this goal: "I want to show that all the females in the Apocalypse are victims;

---

19. Schüssler Fiorenza 1985, 198.
20. Schüssler Fiorenza 1985, 199. See Boesak 1987.
21. Pippin 1992, 89. Pippin's decision to exclude the historical-contextual reading facilitates her application of the label "fantasy literature" to Revelation, leaving her puzzled by the "slowness" with which biblical scholars adopt such a generic title for apocalyptic literature. However, the move from "apocalypse" to "fantasy literature" is not as simple a generic transition as Pippin seems to think. When reading a work of fantasy, one does not tend to see particular political figures and systems not only reflected in, but actually represented and interpreted by characters in the text. While many aspects of Revelation would qualify as "fantastic"—such as the actions of angels and divine and infernal beings, the descent of swarms of unearthly insects and herds of infernal horses—it is precisely those elements that are regarded as interpretive symbols of real-world political entities that prevent interpreters from regarding it as "fantasy." The label "apocalypse," in other words, encodes something of the historical-contextual orientation of the interpreters who use that generic label, whereas "fantasy literature" is more in keeping with an ahistorical, reader-response orientation.
22. Pippin 1992, 80.

they are objects of desire and violence because they are all stereotyped, archetypal images of the female rather than the embodiment of power and control over their own lives in the real or fantastic worlds."[23]

Pippin refers to the four explicitly female characters one encounters in Revelation: "Jezebel," the only flesh-and-blood woman, the woman clothed with the sun, Babylon, and the bride of the Lamb. Pippin is not content to read the latter three merely as figurations, however. "Having studied the evils of Roman imperial policy in the colonies, I find the violent destruction of Babylon very cathartic. But when I looked into the face of Babylon, I saw a woman."[24] Revelation 17 becomes, thereby, a story of sexual exploitation of a prostitute, and ultimately a voyeuristic episode of the torture and murder of a woman. The fate of the woman clothed with the sun is to be "exiled,"[25] though this is perhaps a harsh way to view the woman's removal into the desert as an attempt to preserve her life from the violence not of a male, but of a dragon. Even the bride seems to Pippin to have been swept aside in the narrative: "The role of the female is subordinate in the text; once women are used or abused they are either denied a place in the future world or their future function is left undefined."[26] She concludes: "The Apocalypse is not liberating for women readers. . . . I find in the Apocalypse only negative and male-dominated images of women. The biblical text of the end of time is so misogynist that I continue to be shocked by its blatant voice."[27]

Pippin's provocative monograph proclaimed a thesis that, in Hegelian fashion, called for a counterthesis and eventually (although this is still being forged) a synthesis. On the one hand, if one were to read Revelation 17 as the story of a *woman*, one must be appalled by the denouement. A woman who uses her sexuality to become rich from her elite male "guests," who plies them with promises, who promotes all manner of crimes and debasement for her infatuated lovers so that they can continue to afford her bed—I cannot help but think of (the Babylonian!) Nefer-nefer-nefer in Mika Waltari's *Egyptian* when I try to join Pippin seeing "a woman" in Babylon the Great—is a responsible agent and therefore vicious. Yet she is also acting out a stereotype that she has not invented for herself but merely selected as a means of remaining independent and prospering in the male-crafted world. It is not justice if, at the end of the story, her lovers drag her out of her house, strip her naked, and torture her with burning and flesh-rending violence.

But the problem with Pippin's reading remains precisely here: Babylon is not a woman. "She" is a city. "She" is not an individual with a face who has been shaped by male fantasies and uses these, in turn, to her profit. "She" is the powerful center of a political and economic system of domination, enforced by

23. Pippin 1992, 72.
24. Pippin 1992, 80.
25. Pippin 1992, 107.
26. Pippin 1992, 69–70.
27. Pippin 1992, 80.

generally irresistible military might and legitimated by such heady propaganda as makes self-critique impossible. When we look into the face of *that* "woman," we see a politico-economic complex established on a slave economy, on military and "legal" violence when the complex is threatened (or even questioned), on the redirection of local populations' goods, services, and even longings from the interests of their native lands to the interests of the seat of empire.

Elisabeth Schüssler Fiorenza, another feminist theologian, thus contends that "although Babylon is figured as a queen and a whore, an elite wo/man of great power, the rhetorical-symbolical discourse of Revelation clearly wants us to understand it as an imperial city and not as representing an historical wo/man."[28] John himself makes this identification explicit in 17:18, establishing "Babylon" as a steno-symbol for the capital of the Roman Empire.[29] "Just as the figure of 'beast' or the 'lamb' does not constitute 'animal,'" with the result, perhaps, that we should also accuse John of acts of cruelty toward animals, particularly of the seven-headed variety, "so 'harlot' does not connote 'woman' nor does it mean actual 'prostitutes' in the rhetoric of Revelation . . . but rather signifies seductive imperial power."[30] As a result, the stories of Babylon, the woman clothed with the sun, and the bride do not reveal the author's understanding of flesh-and-blood women.[31] Schüssler Fiorenza does not find the figure of Babylon to have been activated "for misogynist ends," but rather "against the imperial domination of Rome."[32]

Moreover, because the woman, Babylon, and the bride are truly *figures* and not *women*, it is expected that they should disappear from the scene once the author has made the point that needs to be made. These are not, then, further instances of women being tossed aside after they have served their purpose,[33] but further instances of what happens in symbolic discourse. Barbara Rossing observes that the transformation of the female figures into cities "once they have served the purpose of introducing the basic either/or ethical contrast" is "typical of ancient authors' use of the two-women *topos*, since their primary subject of argument is not real women but some unrelated topic such as politics, morality, careers, or even entertainment."[34] If we were to read Revelation 17 in the context of the following chapter, we would not see a woman naked and burning (17:16), but a city desolate and burning (18:2, 9, 18). Habeas corpus? No, for this is not about a woman. The "reality" replaces the "figure"; the "figure" is not to be reified (i.e., read as the story of an actual woman).

---

28. Schüssler Fiorenza 2007, 133. Susan Hylen (2003, 207) agrees with Schüssler Fiorenza's critique at this point: "By establishing a one-to-one relationship between female/feminine language and symbol on the one hand and actual wo/men on the other, Pippin's reading does not destabilize but rather literalizes the gender inscriptions of the Apocalypse."
29. Schüssler Fiorenza 2007, 134.
30. Schüssler Fiorenza 2007, 133.
31. Schüssler Fiorenza 1991, 96.
32. Schüssler Fiorenza 2007, 135.
33. Pippin 1992, 69–70.
34. Rossing 1999, 14–15.

Pippin has made a categorical shift in her reading and critique of John that is somewhat unfair to John. Pippin's critique of John's story about the woman clothed with the sun, about the great prostitute, and about the bride would be apt if John were indeed writing a "story" about women (a piece of "fantasy literature"). But he is instead writing an apocalypse, a symbolic discourse. Pippin faults John insofar as "the female figures in the Apocalypse are given symbolic names and symbolic tasks; they are not allowed to speak their own identity. This technique distances the reader from the female images, leaving only women stereotypes of good and evil and no real flesh-and-blood women."[35] But in so doing, she faults John for writing an apocalypse rather than a fantasy novel.

One important aspect of Pippin's thesis must survive in any synthesis. John's figurations involving female symbols are inherited by him in two essential ways. The first line of inheritance derives from the figuration of the people Israel in their relationship with God, or the figuration of international seats of empire, using images of modest woman and prostitutes.[36] The second line of inheritance derives from the dominant culture's figuration of the seat of empire as *Dea Roma* or *Roma Aeterna*, using the image of the goddess to represent Rome to the world and to serve as part of the legitimating structures of imperial power. This image would have been thrust before the eyes of John and John's audience time and again in statues, coins, and the like, and John responds by refiguring *Roma* by using the resources inherited from the Hebrew prophets. Pippin's critique presses upon us the inescapable fact that the objectification and stereotyping of women over the millennia preceding John certainly facilitates and even provides the imagery we find in Revelation (the unfaithful people or the seat of empire as "harlot"), and to some extent constrains John since he is also responding to prior figurations (*Roma*) based upon such stereotyping. John does not take the important metastep of critiquing either the figuration or the stereotyping process that facilitated this figuration.[37]

Though John's figuration was extremely strategic and effective in his historical context, he did not *have* to use female images at all. He could have stepped back from his tradition at this point, asking what effects imaging the people of God as "bride" would have on the ongoing promotion of marital relationships as relationships between two unequal parties, whose socially inscribed roles and role-formed identities would continue, then, to be informed by the relationship of God to human beings. Although this tradition no doubt brought humanizing elements to Christian marriage (as, for example, in the expectations placed upon husbands in Ephesians 5:25–33 to replicate in their marriages the self-giving love that Christ showed to all disciples), it also reinforced the inequality of status between the partners. John certainly could have stepped back and inquired into the impact of using a female figure to depict a vice-ridden and debauched imperial system upon

35. Pippin 1992, 103.
36. See, e.g., Schüssler Fiorenza 2007, 135.
37. "They are all stereotyped, archetypal images of the female" (Pippin 1992, 72); the figurations perpetuate female "stereotypes of good and evil" (1992, 103).

how his audiences would view actual women. Neither was it unavoidable that, when speaking of the one flesh-and-blood woman "Jezebel," he should use sexual stereotypes of the "bad woman" to talk about a rival teacher (however odious he found her teaching). John does not critique the figuration, but we must.

We are left, then, with a picture of John caught in contradiction: while fervently challenging the domination systems that he saw to be ravaging God's creation, including human community, John also reinscribes facets of those domination systems. Although he cared passionately about liberation, his vision for what was in need of redemption and liberation was not as broad as it could have been. Part of the variegated ideology of domination into which he had been socialized—but much of which he had also come to recognize and challenge—kept its hooks in his flesh.

The formulation of the antithesis, then, would not only involve an insistence on reading symbolic discourse as *symbolic*, thus maintaining a focus on John's critique of particular facets of domination and John's call to disengage from practices that would tend to support and prolong domination.[38] It would also insist that concerns about the oppression of women and dismantling the ideologies that facilitate and enact such oppression be held together and pursued in tandem with the full range of concerns about the complex web of domination systems and the ways in which they interweave to maintain power and exploitation across a great many lines of differentiation, and not just across the male-female line.

Schüssler Fiorenza brings this forcefully to the fore when she questions the claim made by Jean K. Kim that female readers must identify with the female character Babylon or else "betray our sexual identity in order to share the perspective of the author/God."[39] Rather, Schüssler Fiorenza asks,

> Why should a conquered, exploited, enslaved, and prostituted Jewish wo/man not rejoice in the downfall of the imperial power Rome that has destroyed her home and crucified her son, even though Rome is figured in feminine terms? Why should we assume that such a wo/man has to deny her own sexual identity if she looks hopefully at the visionary destruction of the imperial power of Rome? Since the imperial power of Rome is figured as an "elite woman" (*kyria*), why shouldn't a wo/man at the bottom of the kyriarchal pyramid experience and resent this power as a violent force which enslaves and exploits her?[40]

Gender is only *one* category at work and is not automatically the category to privilege in interpretation: there is also the matter of class distinction (the

---

38. As maintained forcefully by Schüssler Fiorenza (2007, 140) in reading the contrast between Babylon and new Jerusalem as "the *political contrast* between the capital of the world of oppression and the capital of the world of G*d in which tears, hunger, and death—the characteristics of the world of injustice—have passed away," that is a contrast "not between two types of wo/men but between two types of world."

39. Kim 1999, 61.

40. Schüssler Fiorenza 2007, 145.

elites and the poor) and national distinction (the foreign imperial power and the indigenous person) to consider. In this reading, Revelation does not preach "sexual violence against wo/men," but rather underscores "the exploitation and violence of empire against wo/men,"[41] which remains a relevant proclamation in light of "globalizing capitalism's exploitations . . . seen in the international sex trade and in violence against wo/men and children in war, poverty, migration, and global exploitation."[42]

Viewing John as a misogynistic enemy of liberation means privileging only one facet of the struggle for liberation and electing to give this lens totalizing power over John's discourse, marginalizing the latter for this particular failure. One might well ask whose interests would be served by silencing John's witness or succeeding in getting modern churches not to read Revelation or to seek its word of challenge for application in a modern context. It would not be the interests of oppressed women, but the interests of the domination systems that John would challenge as forcefully today if he were present, and that John equips us to continue to challenge by means of his text. John is a champion of liberation in regard to certain aspects of domination, and his boldness in challenging certain facets of domination facilitates the ongoing work of challenging others, including those that John himself reinscribes. He is an ally of liberation who, like many of us to some extent, has come to see—and oppose in God's name— certain facets of how domination systems operate and the violence they have done to human community, and still retains certain blind spots to other facets, from which his own discourse yearns to be liberated for the sake of continuing to advance the entire program of liberation in all its facets.

Part of the "call of the Apocalypse for women readers" is "to face the divisions of women by the patriarchy [e.g., into the roles and spaces for virgins and whores] and to face our own roles in the violence,"[43] but this is not the sum total of its call for women readers, nor is the "call" of responding to Revelation completely reactive and negative. That call also involves continuing to name, challenge, and withdraw support from other facets of domination that are all part of a mutually sustaining and supporting web.

One possible effect of Revelation's imagery remains to be addressed, an effect that is named also by the spokespersons for the antithesis and, to some extent, the synthesis. This is the particular issue of violence against women (which, however, we need to hold together with all other forms of violence that delay the emergence of a truly humane and just society—such as violence against the poor, violence against particular ethnic groups, violence against the environment, and with it, all future human beings). John himself never calls upon the audience to enact violence against any human subject, male or female. He forecasts the destruction of the city of Rome and the collapse of its economic web as its partnership with

---

41. Schüssler Fiorenza 2007, 146.
42. Schüssler Fiorenza 2007, 146.
43. Pippin 1992, 107.

other rulers goes bad, perhaps specifically referring to Roman rulers (hence, self-destruction). It is not a judgment in which Christians are called to participate through acts of violence, except insofar as they *suffer* acts of violence intended to silence their witness. There is no suggestion that the violence done to Rome by her partners should be imitated by Christians in regard to any real-life women, including Jezebel, whose judgment lies in Christ's hands alone.[44] John issues no call to the Thyatirans to act against Jezebel in any way except for rejecting her teaching and falling in line again with John's vision for Christian exclusivity.

Nevertheless, the figuration itself does introduce danger to women into the history of appropriation of Revelation,[45] and of this we certainly need to be aware, critical, and cautious. John's figuration "must be problematized as engendering an ideological tradition that has been and is activated against wo/men in the interest of a misogynist politics,"[46] including specific acts of violence against flesh-and-blood women. If Christ is seen casting Jezebel onto a bed for punishment, perhaps that is a sanction for me to do the same to some woman that I can "type" as Jezebel. If heaven rejoices over Babylon, the mother of all whores, being stripped, ripped apart, and burned, perhaps that is a sanction for me to do the same to some woman that I can typecast as Babylon. John never intended any such effects, and it is difficult to imagine a reader of Revelation who could so thoroughly miss the point. Nevertheless, the imagery itself, particularly divorced from the context of its historical setting, and John's struggle for liberation within that setting, could tend to support such acts *insofar* as it supports and continues to perpetuate the *types*.[47]

If we are inclined, then, to continue to stand in line with the prophet John and to proclaim his challenge to the domination systems that persist in our setting, we should do so after benefiting both from John's clear-sightedness in regard to the complex of economic, political, and ideological domination *and* from the clear-sightedness of feminist theologians critiquing John's blind spots. Perhaps it is possible to imagine an apocalypse taking a different tack with "Babylon," showing her the respect that she did not give her victims. Rather than reinscribing the image of a woman being stripped and mauled, we could turn to other images from the Hebrew prophets, for example, of a defendant—even a war criminal!—standing trial in a court of law and being duly but impassionately executed. If John's imagery too easily mirrors acts of violence against

---

44. Jezebel is not singled out for punishment because she is a woman but because she proclaims a message that endangers the integrity of the Christian community's identity and witness (in John's eyes). Christ threatens similar punitive intervention in regard to the Nicolaitans in Pergamum (cf. Rev. 2:16 and 2:22). In John's understanding, this is not a gender issue but an issue of prophetic accountability.
45. Schüssler Fiorenza 2007, 135.
46. Schüssler Fiorenza 2007, 136; see also Hylen 2003, 209.
47. "Rev. engages the imagination of the contemporary reader to perceive women in terms of good or evil, pure or impure, heavenly or destructive, helpless or powerful, bride or temptress, wife or whore. Rather than instill 'hunger and thirst for justice,' the symbolic action of Rev. therefore can perpetuate prejudice and injustice if it is not 'translated' into a contemporary 'rhetorical situation' to which it can be a 'fitting' rhetorical response" (Schüssler Fiorenza 1985, 199).

actual women, contributing in turn to the perpetration of the same under the domination system of patriarchy, we need to find alternative imagery in our own work of speaking out against modern manifestations of imperialism that both faithfully captures John's critique *and* goes the extra step of freeing that critique from its own perpetuation of domination. And indeed, we need to think long and hard about any feminine figurations we might use.

Although I certainly cannot prescribe such a reading for women readers, I would hope that, once the limitations of John's vision for liberation are named and understood and once John's passion for liberation again qualifies him as an ally even in those struggles to which he seems oblivious or worse, women can indeed find a "safe place" in Revelation in precisely the same place that male readers must—in the bride of the Lamb. And if the image of the 144,000 ostensibly male virgins in 14:1–5 tends to exclude women from picturing themselves there, the image of a bride for the very male Lamb is just as potentially exclusive for male readers. But precisely such imagery pushes us past gender and gender roles into the symbolic meaning of the images, where women find a place among the army of (male) virgins and men find a place identified with the bride of the Lamb. In this new Jerusalem, it is not the case that "the natural order of patriarchy will at last be manifested in unchallenged perfection."[48] Rather, the leveling of gender roles and differences as redeemed humanity takes on its new identity as "bride" in relationship to Christ might indeed suggest the *opposite*. If the text is silent about "what happens to female believers other than being subsumed under this image of the Bride,"[49] it is also silent about what happens to male believers after they, too, are subsumed under the same image. What new Jerusalem offers, it offers to all who have washed their robes in the blood of the Lamb, without comments differentiating what is offered to women from what is offered to men. "The future function [of the women] is left undefined,"[50] but this lack of definition is salutary. If John had defined the function of the female in the new Jerusalem, that would represent just another act of limiting or oppressing women, forcing them into male-determined roles. But, "left undefined," the woman just like the man has the opportunity to discover a new mode of life in the new Jerusalem beyond patriarchal roles and beyond reactions against patriarchy.

THE CHALLENGE OF APOCALYPSE

The Boundaries That Preserve Witness

The maintenance of Christian witness—and the identification of the boundaries of confession and practice that maintain this witness—was of central concern to John. A perpetual tension exists between the need for creative reformulation of

---

48. Pippin 1992, 97.
49. Pippin 1992, 103.
50. Pippin 1992, 69–70.

Christian identity and practice and for the discovery of those boundaries beyond which Christian discourse ceases to be *Christian* discourse, where practice ceases to be witness. John raises the question of the distortion of both as he identifies apostles who are "liars" and a prophetess who does not speak for God, even as he questions the witness and practice of a sister community—the synagogue—in regard to the modus vivendi it has embraced in the wake of the First Jewish Revolt.

What is so bad about "eating food from idol sacrifices" and getting in bed with existing social, political, and economic structures and their mechanisms of self-legitimation that Jezebel's position must be declared out of bounds for Christian discourse and authentically *Christian* practice? When Christians sit alongside their neighbors and join in eating food sacrificed to idols or making other required compromises to enjoy prosperity and safety within Roman Asia, they cease to raise the problematic issues regarding Roman imperialism in their neighbors' consciousness by moving away from prophetic practice. As Christians participate, even if only in halfhearted and marginal ways, in the religious legitimation that upholds the Roman order; as they orient their practice (and hearts) toward increasing their access to the peaceful enjoyment of the goods offered to the loyal subjects of that order; as they seek to live out a more private allegiance to the One God—in all these compromises they silence the witness of the prophets and apostles and martyrs. They withhold from themselves and from their society the gift of preserving the voice that could call into question the "world-taken-for-granted"[51] as presented and lived out under Roman imperialism, a voice that could create a space for critical distance and the discovery of alternative ways of being human together.

Barry Harvey identifies the failure to discover the boundaries where Christian discourse ceases to be *Christian* discourse, where practice ceases to be witness, as a major problem facing American Christianity:

> Christians, particularly in North America, constitute for the most part a rather indistinguishable lot in the modern world, assuming along with virtually everyone else that their purpose in life is to pursue their own interests in every sphere allotted to them by the institutions of our commercial republic. A majority of those who continue to call themselves Christian "retain a vague notion of religious identity but their lives are distinctively secular, with the experience of God in worship and prayer not figuring very prominently in all that they do. Increasingly these nominal Christian . . . Americans embrace the heady hedonism and narcissism of popular culture and do not see that this contradicts biblical faith." . . .[52] Firmly ensconced in the well-worn tracks of the City, they regard religion almost exclusively as a private and inward matter, quite often as a form of therapy designed to

---

51. Alfred Schütz (1967; Schütz and Luckmann 1973) coined this phrase to describe the aggregate of values, roles, scripts, logic, and contours of "reality" embraced by a society and imprinted upon its members. Berger (1963, 117) describes the "world-taken-for-granted" as "the system of apparently self-evident and self-validating assumptions about the world that each society engenders in the course of its history."

52. Guroian 1994, 89.

make their lives more fulfilling. They see little or nothing wrong in regarding the church as simply another vendor of goods and services.⁵³

According to Harvey and Guroian, many American Christians live (and even think) in a way that bears witness to the propriety of relegating religion to the private, internal sphere, of turning religion into a commodity of self-help and self-actualization, and of elevating the "values" of consumerism and gratification as the uniting principles that join them in solidarity with their non-Christian, fellow Americans.

Here is one manifestation of the triumph of Jezebel's gospel over John's Gospel. Moreover, this privatization and internalization of Christian faith, something clearly not manifested in the practice of the communities reflected in the New Testament, itself serves the interests of the dominant culture. A major threat to the "world-taken-for-granted" is neutralized by being affirmed as an appropriate component of a respectable life, while having its jurisdiction so severely circumscribed that it is likely never to challenge that world. Indeed, it would not occur to one in a hundred such "North American Christians," if this description is accurate, that the New Testament *should* challenge that world.

Individuals cannot break through the socially imprinted "world-taken-for-granted" on their own. This requires "the social practices of a certain type of community, or . . . a parallel *polis*."⁵⁴ Herein lies the heinousness of the threat posed by Jezebel, the Nicolaitans, and even the self-satisfied Laodicean congregation. If personal deliverance from the lie requires a community of practice and witness, then blunting that community's practice and witness, merging that practice and witness toward the lifestyle of the lie, destroys the medium of salvation (or if that term is too evangelical, then the de-alienation) of all.

John does not merely challenge the lowering of religious boundaries in Pergamum and Thyatira. He also challenges the lack of that personal and spiritual vigilance required to keep disciples from being swept up by the dominant culture's definition of "the good life" and its recruitment of members who will seek their own fulfillment in the pursuit of that ideal, thus serving the domination systems sustained by mass involvement in that pursuit. What is so bad about seeking wealth or reputation, and taking pride in the same? The voice of Christ confronts the Christians in Laodicea (and possibly Sardis) with questions: Does seeking the "good life" mask spiritual hollowness? Does it mask a lack of awareness about oneself, one's group, or the system in connection with which one gains the wealth and status used to reassure oneself of one's value and "success"?

Here, too, John's probing is eerily relevant for America's culture of unabashed consumerism and consumption. The legacy of modernity is "a self without substance, frantically searching for something, anything, to fill it up."⁵⁵ The self has become empty

53. Harvey 1999, 3.
54. Harvey 1999, 137.
55. Harvey 1999, 8.

in part because of the loss of family, community, and tradition. It is a self that seeks the experience of being continually filled up by consuming goods, calories, experiences, politicians, romantic partners, and empathic therapists in an attempt to combat the growing alienation and fragmentation of its era.[56]

Laodicea's coping mechanisms, trying to fill up the self and numb the lingering emptiness by acquiring wealth and amassing goods, are familiar indeed, making Christ's promise all the more relevant.

The insidiousness of the domination systems sustained by consumerism, however, shows itself in the fact that facets of the system work energetically to *perpetuate* the empty condition of the human being and the illusion, most notably through the advertising empire, that a full self is possible through consumerism. "This is a powerful illusion. And what fuels the illusion, what impels the individual into this illusion, is the desperation to fill up the empty self."[57] It is in the system's interests to perpetuate the emptiness and promote consumerism as the cure, since the "post-World War II economy ... is dependent on the continual consumption of nonessential and quickly obsolete items and experiences."[58] Powerful subsystems thus cooperate in the production and maintenance of emptiness in the self, distracting attention and energy away from pursuits that might lead to fullness (and to correcting the sociohistorical factors that have led to the widespread experience of emptiness) for the sake of amassing the wealth that will not fill their members' own emptiness. In this way, consumerist America becomes another example of the sociological dictum "Each society produces the men [*sic*] it needs."[59] It also becomes another example of enslavement—of the advertising mogul as much as the shopaholic—to the "powers and principalities," to suprasocial forces whose human origins are now hidden and whose mandates go unquestioned.

John calls his own congregations to remain within the boundaries of Christian practice—or better, to recover the *center* of Christian practice—as a counterwitness to the dominant culture and a challenge to the values and practices it instills in order to maintain its "essential" systems. To talk about boundaries represents a minimalist attempt to talk about the center, where a greater deal of energy and focus ought to be invested. The boundaries appear where the community discerns that the "center" is being violated or, in John's picture, where behavior reflects an orientation toward and orbit around a "center" different from God and the Lamb. Recovering this center might mean simply taking the prophets' and Jesus' prescriptions concerning the acquisition and use of wealth and property at face value and living them out. A community whose practice reflected the prioritization of the quest for spiritual, social, and relational progress ("seeking first the kingdom of God and his justice") over the

---

56. Cushman 1990, 600.
57. Cushman 1990, 606.
58. Cushman 1990, 600.
59. Berger 1963, 110.

quest for capital and consumer goods, the prioritization of sharing with those in genuine need rather than hoarding or indulging in "impulse buying" or luxury upgrades, the adoption of a lifestyle of simplicity, the mobilization of resources to support Christians in prison and distress in restricted nations—all practices specifically promoted in the New Testament—would confront the "world-taken-for-granted" with a striking alternative and raise the possibility of critical examination, questioning, and ultimately rejection in favor of a more hopeful (since not futile) alternative.

Witness that Invites De-alienation

Alienation, in Peter Berger's terminology, describes the state of a person who has lost sight of the ongoing dialectic between who one "really" is in one's totality and the "self" constructed for the person by the social order (along with the roles assigned to this "self"). It entails losing sight of the possibilities that exist outside of one's socially defined self and roles. Though in many ways we as individual members of a society can be compared to puppets, we have the possibility denied them of "looking up and perceiving the machinery by which we have been moved. In this act lies the first step toward freedom."[60] The alienated person, however, has become unaware of the strings and machinery. Religion often heightens alienation, bolstering those socially prescribed roles with the power of divine fiat. Religious perspectives, however, can also nurture de-alienation by allowing one to view one's society *sub specie aeternitatis*, that is, from a perspective that stands outside of, and relativizes, the society's projected image of itself.[61] "Before the face of God, the institutions are revealed as nothing but *human* works, devoid of inherent sanctity or immortality," and the possibility of action beyond—even outside—the socially prescribed roles dawns.[62]

John offers his congregations such a perspective. He confronts them with a well-developed picture of how their society's practices, policies, and ideologies "look" sub specie aeternitatis, in the light of eternity, from the perspective of that "longer view" that reaches before and after the story of Roman imperialism. The inclusion of Revelation in the Christian canon provides a model and a mandate for continuing to examine the social, political, economic, and ideological contexts of the Christian assembly in every locale, in every age. As we work at seeing our society, its practices, and its values from the perspective of "heaven," we create a starting point for gaining critical distance from the roles, scripts, values, and knowledge that our society seeks continually to imprint upon us. We engage the critical and self-reflective practices that can deliver us from "alienation," from accepting the "given" or "self-evident" nature of our society and the social self and roles it aggressively promotes within us for its own interests.

60. Berger 1963, 176.
61. Berger 1967, 96–97.
62. Berger 1967, 98–99.

Such activity benefits not only the Christian, but the Christian's neighbors as well, calling others by word and example to question those practices and propaganda, initiating conversations about the possibility of a better way of being human together than the ways inscribed by the domination systems, which continually seek to keep people thinking and running within the grooves most congenial to the interests of those in power within the system.[63] "Few see any realistic alternative to what the modern world offers them."[64] This is precisely what the Apocalypse, and the ongoing work within Christian community seeking "apocalyptic adjustments" to our perceptions, invites us to discover and to offer.

Revelation itself surely risks provoking alienation in regard to the Christian subculture's ideology and the religiously constructed self and roles it promotes. A critical perspective requires that we examine this tendency as well, and choose what stance we will take and what practices we will adopt on the basis of what promotes the integrity of our lives rather than the perpetuation of social constructions. The willing martyrs of Daniel 3:17–18 are paradigmatic in their resistance to the roles and scripts the domination systems of Babylon would force upon them. This resistance is based not only on some promise of deliverance offered via the ideological repertoire of the Jewish world construction, but also on their own integrity as people who will not violate their own conscience for the sake of peace with the colonial power: "If our God whom we serve is able to deliver us from the furnace of blazing fire and out of your hand, O king, let him deliver us. But if not, be it known to you, O king, that we will not serve your gods and we will not worship the golden statue that you have set up" (NRSV).

Working toward an "Apocalyptic Adjustment"

John's principal rhetorical strategy involved getting a glimpse of, and communicating effectively, the bigger picture that reaffirmed the Judeo-Christian world-

---

63. In the postmodern setting, the relativizing of all religious worldviews and perspectives, even of all political ideologies, by the publicity and the availability of the "other" has not resulted in emancipation. Rather, it has given rise to another system of central, core values that routinely go unquestioned and unexamined. Two friends might engage, with self-pleasing sophistication, in a vigorous examination of the effects of a particular religious worldview on limiting a person's willingness to grapple with certain issues over a latte macchiato and oversized slice of cheesecake before blowing off three hours and $340 at the mall, grabbing a slice of pizza at 3:00 p.m. before going to aerobics at 4:00 p.m. to work off the calories, meeting with other friends for dinner and the latest movie, and hooking up with someone over drinks afterward.

If these new core values of consumerism and self-gratification are examined, the examination does not proceed on terms that ultimately challenge the new "system," but merely shift practice from one area of behavior within that system to another. If we examine indulgent eating habits, it is for the purpose of looking better for some event where we want the satisfaction of being "seen" in a particular way, not because we question *why* we are slaves to overconsumption. If we check our impulse spending, it is for the purpose of buying something bigger at the end of the month or giving more attention to cushioning ourselves against financial risk, not because we are struck with the global inequities of access even to subsistence goods and determined to alter our lives and reorient our use of wealth toward meeting the needs of others.

64. Harvey 1999, 3–4.

view and the values and practices that worldview sustained, interpreting the dominant culture and its legitimation structures from within that worldview. John discovered this bigger picture as he looked beyond the facades of Roman imperialism and its ideology. He was well positioned to do so, being himself a provincial and a member of one of a subaltern people group subsumed into empire. His native traditions provided him with an interpretive lens "from outside" the situation of Roman imperialism by means of which to examine, name, and evaluate its practices, policies, and propaganda. "The perception of the reality behind the facades . . . demands a considerable intellectual effort,"[65] an effort readily apparent in John's intense study and meditation both on the tradition *and* on the nature of life under Roman imperialism.

To us who continue to live under the power of the domination systems of this world, the challenge of Revelation is "to do a better job of seeing ourselves as others see us,"[66] so that we can move from a state of alienation to a state of seeing and living out available alternatives that are more reflective of God's justice and *shalom*. "The sins hardest to see are those where our culture shares the same blind spots we have,"[67] and so we need the aid of those who can speak to us from beyond that culture and our particular social location.

Although John's own presentation of his challenge might lead us to expect this to come by means of an apocalypse, there certainly are many other strategies by means of which to pursue this larger perspective. The first derives from John's location looking "in" toward Babylon as a member of a subaltern *ethnos* and from his vision of the people of God drawn out "from every tribe and language and people and nation" (5:9), a vision that ever reminds us of the distance between any one national "perspective" and the perspective of the kingdom of God and God's Messiah.

What is the view of our nation from other nations? Does this view help us "see" a more complete picture of our practices and policies, and our impact beyond our borders, than we can see from our own location? Does our experience of the practices and policies of our own country conflict with our commitment to the people of God in every place (the church catholic), when those practices and policies are seen from the outside? Conversations with international students have helped me see America's global economic practices and international affairs—and my participation in and support for the same—in challenging ways. I recall how I inquired one evening into how Revelation was read among Christians in India, and in particular, how disciples there read the vision of Babylon. My guests looked at me like I was an idiot. Follow the goods. Follow the money. Follow the local impetus to collude with foreign powers for a piece of the action. How would *anyone* with an ounce of sense think about Babylon's presence in today's world? While I did respond that the United States was

---

65. Berger 1963, 32.
66. Witherington 2003, 235.
67. Keener 2000, 435.

not the Babylon that John had in mind, I did have to admit that our consumer-driven economy, into which the goods of the world flow, did have something Babylonish about it in a world in which many developing countries struggle in the face of plague and starvation. What is our responsibility to such people? Is it worth giving up the present order to have a world where all are fed and free to pursue the joy of family, friends, and work? Is there something Babylonish in the current distribution and consumption of this world's resources and wealth? As long as the hungry die for want of food while millions of others amass superfluous commodities, God's priorities are certainly not being honored.

And what is the view of our nation—or our churches or our own social or educational sector—from other social locations *within* our own nation? What is the experience of America from the inner city? From the poorer sections of one's own town? How do these other views, insofar as they provide a larger or fuller picture, challenge the nation's rhetoric, practices, and policies—and *our* participation in that rhetoric, those practices, and those policies?

An indispensable facet of seeing ourselves as others see us, from John's point of view, is to see ourselves as God sees us, as the religious tradition and heritage that we claim as our own diagnoses and interprets us. John's immersion in the classical prophets gave him eyes to see beyond the veneer of imperial propaganda and past the immediate displays of prosperity. It allowed him to see Rome sub specie aeternitatis, in the light of God and of the Lamb. It gave him the vantage point from which to raise questions from outside the imperial system and to expose its underside. He challenges us to immerse ourselves fully in the "scriptural world" as well, which now includes his own analysis of Roman imperialism in light of the outside voices of the prophets and Jesus, in order that we might also see ourselves from yet another angle from outside the world construction (and propaganda) of our own society.

Nor should we neglect the perspective that religious experience brings to these questions. To do so would be to play to the rules of an epistemology promoted within a particular domination system—the academy that seeks to advance the epistemological hegemony of the scientific method, limiting inquiry to factors that can be observed and largely controlled. This epistemology conveniently brackets out what has been, historically, a *major* source of critique of the "world-taken-for-granted."

> The confrontation between God's messianic regime and those rulers and authorities who currently exercise their dominion over the world no longer seems like the husk of a primitive apocalyptic mythology that can be stripped away without damaging the kernel of true religion within. Under the tutelage of such myths diasporic politics prepares the pilgrim people of God to be the bearer of habits and relations that locate all of life within the context of a promised but as yet unfulfilled future, thereby defying the darkness of the secular void.[68]

---

68. Harvey 1999, 159.

Sociologists, to be true to the discipline, must also question the rules of that discipline at least far enough to recognize that reality may exceed the bounds of those rules, or else risk alienation themselves. John's example challenges us also to explore the view of our practices and policies when considered from the experience of worshiping and adoring the divine Other, who confronts and convicts every human pretension, starting with our own, and our involvement in the pretensions of other persons, of powers, and of principalities.

John's vision takes him to visions of human community beyond what is possible within Babylon, whether it be to the community of the sealed and redeemed in Revelation 7:13–17 or the community of the new Jerusalem in 21:1–22:5. He thus models the importance of making room for the vision that transcends our present reality, interprets and critiques it, and calls our community forward into a better reality. "Better" entails a value judgment, to be sure, and the basis for those value judgments must always be held up to scrutiny. I think, for example, of that most celebrated speech of Martin Luther King Jr., "I Have a Dream," in which the vision for a future reconciliation between people of different races gave expression to a state of interpersonal relationships and national *shalom* that was better than the state experienced by those who listened that day. And those hearers who were elevated to glimpse that vision and whose inner light bore witness within that it was, indeed, "better" would be drawn closer by the experience toward committing to its realization.

John reminds us of the power of vision to expand our capacity to see past our present and to learn to desire a better future, a more just future, a future more reflective of the prophets' vision, Jesus' vision, the apostles' vision—if I might be permitted—God's vision for human community. That power lies in awakening desires that would never stir in imaginations shaped only by the values, logic, and stories of this world's domination systems. These desires internalize that vision, moving people, in prophetic witness amid the present, to speak and act in line with that future, pressing toward the possibility and preferability of that future rather than the future toward which domination systems drive us.

Authority, Passion, and Logic in the New Community

In chapters 5 and 6 we inquired into John's construction of the credibility of his own message and deconstruction of the credibility of particular opposing voices. Since this has been a major focal point of criticism, we have already looked closely at several issues relevant to the ongoing application of John's "model" for constructing authority in Christian discourse. Ultimately, John grounds his own authority—and challenges the authority of "Jezebel" and the "Nicolaitans"—on the basis of alignment with the religious and ethical traditions of the church and of the Jewish *ethnos* that provided the formative matrix for early Christianity. In John's practice and model, legitimate authority derives from speaking with and for those traditions, preserving their voice and enabling it to continue to speak to our social location and its challenges and concerns *over* the voices perpetuating the interests of domination systems.

John's delimitations of boundaries for Christian practice and his deconstruction of other voices advocating what *he* believes to lie outside those boundaries are problematic, particularly where toleration of a diversity of views is a core value. Is this a viable part of a model for discovering, communicating, and living out new "apocalyptic adjustments"? The answer depends, in part, on the decisions made by the discerning community regarding its own core values. Where faithfulness to the tradition is a core value, John's model remains viable. There will always be positions and practices that vary in their degree of alignment with the Judeo-Christian tradition, the adjudication of which will be the task of prophets advocating one or the other and of communities discerning together in which direction God leads. Remembering that this tradition is itself variegated, with the result that divergent practices may be equally "faithful" to the tradition, will help prevent premature excision of particular voices and facilitate accepting that one may honor God by observing a certain calendar and another may honor God by not observing any particular liturgical calendar, all within the same faith community. However, some positions or practices will be advanced that so strongly and directly contrast with core positions or practices within the tradition—and different positions and practices may be more important than others for the sake of Christian witness in different situations—that the argument can be made, and the community can confirm, that they lie outside of Christian witness and practice.

John does not exclude Jezebel. This is ultimately a matter for community discernment. Moreover, it is also ultimately a matter of Jezebel's own choosing, if the community discerns that a more accommodating stance toward the imperial religion and economy violates the values of keeping God's commandments and keeping faith with Christ. Where speakers can assume a culture of "testing the prophets," speaking like John is not ultimately authoritarian or exclusive. It is a word submitted to the community for testing. In the modern ecclesiastical context, several denominations have developed rigorous structures to ensure this process. In the United Methodist Church, for example, positions can be presented and argued as vehemently as desired at Annual and General Conferences, but ultimately it is the assembly gathered that will discern and decide.

John's construction of *ethos* alerts us to the importance of cultivating a culture of "testing" (combining critical thinking and spiritual discernment) in congregations, with the result that individuals' words are submitted to the collective discernment of the "body." Following John's model as it was enacted in first-century congregational practice would require us to foster a dialectic whereby we seek to keep one another honest in regard to our tradition, our witness, our practice, while at the same time replacing authoritarian proclamation (the pervasive model in our churches where "the Word" is preached but the proclamation is not critically examined, sifted, extended) with community inquiry and discernment (which was, in fact, in place in the seven churches that heard Revelation, mitigating John's perceived authoritarianism).

Intentionally evoking particular emotions is the facet of rhetoric most often described as manipulation, but neither John nor the modern Christian prophet calling a congregation toward a more faithful alignment with God's commandments is the one who *introduces* appeals to pathos into the rhetorical situation. It is not a question of whether or not emotions are to be directed, engaged, "manipulated." Appeals to the emotions are already at work in social, cultural, economic, and political communications at all times. It is rather a question of raising the possibility and making the opportunity for affects and ambitions to be engaged by the countervision of the Christian traditions in ways that promote our integrity and preserve the countervoice of Christian witness, rather than *continue* to allow these emotions to be engaged in ways that conduce to assimilation and alienation or, at best, cowardice.

John's example challenges us to become more conscious of the emotions that particular sectors of our society arouse in us, seeking our support for their ends and participation in the processes that lead to those ends. In political addresses, news reports, and advertisements, speakers target our emotions. John understood how Roman imperial propaganda in its various forms sought to arouse awe and gratitude toward Rome and her emperors and emulation for the Roman life. John further understood how these affective experiences oriented people toward participation in practices that continued to support Roman imperialism at all levels. Redirecting these emotions toward other objects, and thus fostering other goals that would conduce to preserving the witness of the group and the group's quest for God's justice, was a necessary part of the rebuttal to society's rhetoric.

Some of John's focal appeals to pathos—redirecting our awe and nurturing experiences of awe through worship of the One God, and redirecting our emulation toward those virtues and practices that promote critical distance rather than alienation—remain timely antidotes in the midst of the domination systems that continually hold up models of power and wealth (the ability to coerce and consume) for our awe and emulation. But in the present context we may also need to look critically at ways in which fear and enmity are nurtured to promote the exercise and maintenance of the domination system of militarism. And it is important to look critically at the ways in which consumer confidence is aroused in order to increase spending and the assumption of greater debt. Perhaps the view from the new Jerusalem would call us, rather, to make contact with fellow Christians from the lands of the "enemy," approaching them with friendly feeling and with confidence that, in the power of God, cooperation between the people of God can effect a nonviolent solution. Perhaps the view from the new Jerusalem would call us to look with indignation and revulsion upon attempts to increase the glut of consumerism and bolster a Babylonish economy, motivating Christians more fully to seek out alternative economic practices that would disentangle us from the luxury and seduction. In the process, we need to discern and avoid *deinōsis*—the arousal of emotions of inappropriate amplitude in relation to the actual object of those emotions—both in society's attempts to work upon our feelings and in our prophetic responses.

Our study of appeals to rational discourse in Revelation suggests that John would have us take account of the Christian confession and the premises of our faith in our deliberations, so that our actions will conform to and reflect the "logic" of the alternative values and story, bringing them to life in embodied actions in this world. Following John's own model of immersion in the Scriptures and the tradition that confronts our "world-taken-for-granted" from outside, we would seek to discover through Bible study and "Christian conferencing" (in local gatherings of the Christian assembly, but also in dialogue with disciples from other social locations, national and international) the decisions and practices that proceed from the logic of the gospel. Executing these decisions and practices, in turn, becomes a witness to the countertruths with which our neighbors need to be confronted, if they are to have opportunity to step into that space of critical distance and the liberation that distance brings from the constraints imposed by the "givenness" of our society's worldview, values, and foundational "logic." Peter Berger observed that "in the Durkheimian perspective, to live in society means to exist under the domination of society's logic. Very often men [*sic*] act by this logic without knowing it."[69] The availability of an alternative logic that can engage one persuasively—for example, the logic of the gospel, the persuasiveness of which is bolstered by social and religious experience—makes examination of society's logic a genuine possibility, even a necessity.

Concerning the "logic" of society, Berger further observes that "violence is the ultimate foundation of any political order. . . . Even in the politely operated societies of modern democracies, the ultimate argument is violence."[70] Berger has in mind the power of the state to compel its members when persuasion has failed and to protect its interests against external threats by means of violence. But the logic of violence pervades society at many other levels in varying degrees, for example, in the antagonism and competition that stand at the root of economics and politics.

Is violence also "the ultimate argument" in Revelation? John has been charged with reinscribing the dominant culture's logic and practices of violence in the devastating plagues and the violent elimination of the dragon, beasts, Babylon, and their followers.[71] But there is also a strain within Revelation that pushes the violence and the logic of violence to a secondary position, almost as a cleanup operation. The ultimate argument in Revelation is the argument of self-giving love and self-sacrificing witness—the arguments embodied in the actions by which the Lamb conquered and attained a unique authority, by which the martyrs are crowned as victors, by which the two witnesses share in Christ's resurrection and ascension. These arguments are made in the face of violence

---

69. Berger 1963, 40.
70. Berger 1963, 69.
71. Howard-Brook and Gwyther regard both the violence of God and the opulence of the new Jerusalem as rhetorical foils to Rome's strategies of compulsion and seduction: "These are metaphors, not literal descriptions. They are John's visionary means of reminding people that God's ways are more powerful and more joyous than those of empire" (1999, 267).

(cross, execution) and violent exploitation—thus in the face of society's ultimate argument—and are made on behalf of the victims of the same. And those who live in line with *these* arguments *prevail.* It is an argument that has been made too infrequently in the history of the world "AD." Nevertheless it is an argument that entered the world most powerfully in the example of the Church's Lord.

Of great importance to the logic of Revelation is the historical precedent given in Jesus, whose self-giving love, as the perfect expression of obedience to God, resulted in vindication and exaltation, and this in stark contrast to the world's logic. Also important is the foundational conviction that this Jesus will come again in judgment, that God will hold the world accountable to standards revealed not in its own operating principles, but in the Judeo-Christian tradition of the Torah and the prophets, of Jesus and the apostles. These premises, among others peculiar to Jewish and Christian culture, contribute to the deductive reasoning within Revelation; they ultimately "take on flesh" in the practices and witness of the Christians convinced by Revelation. In contrast to the logic of the world, "the mission of the church is thus to reveal to the world its *archē* and *telos* by offering to it the means and media for living in love and therefore in the truth."[72]

Coming out of Babylon

John's vision forces us to look at Western political arrangements and economies differently. John looks long and hard at the Roman imperial economy and concludes that the resources and labor of a world are being siphoned off to cater to the excessive luxury and conspicuous consumption of an imperial power. He looks at the use of force and violence across the empire and concludes that they are deployed in the service of maintaining that economy and the political arrangements that make that economy possible. He looks at the official propaganda and sees it as nothing more than a cover-up for greed, which is idolatry. His critique of his world provides us with a set of questions by which to uncover the injustices and self-legitimating mechanisms of our own society.[73] By seeking out analogous dangers to faithful response in the modern congregation's world, speaking prophetically against these dangers, and discovering the stance among the realities that reflects faithfulness to the church's tradition and to the God to which it witnesses, John's prophecy can still be kept (and this in sharp contrast to the more popular method of trying to identify John's images with events in the modern or premodern world).

Whose interests does our country's excessive consumerism serve? And what are we masking, both as individuals and as a population, with all this spending

---

72. Harvey 1999, 161.
73. Nelson Kraybill (1996, 10) suggests asking, "What should Christians do when governments seek our personal or financial support for acts of violence or nationalistic self-interest? What ideology or pseudo-religion do political powers use to justify their deeds? How are Christians tempted to take part or benefit?"

and stockpiling and displaying? To what extent have we really done an inventory of our spiritual and relational and moral poverty, wretchedness, blindness, and nakedness? Although I do not consider us to be living in the "age of Laodicea"—for the oracle to Smyrna equally well characterizes so many of our sister congregations in restricted nations, and the oracles to Thyatira or Sardis characterize many of our churches alongside the oracle to Laodicea—nevertheless, on the matter of wealth and consumerism, there is a lot to be gained by asking to what extent we share Laodicea's misapprehension of the gospel, distorted view of their own health, and therefore their reproach.

Revelation poses questions about the use of power and use of force or, in other words, about violence as an ultimate argument. Where these are employed for domination by one part of society over another, or by one nation over another, or for securing endless resources for a privileged few, the great harlot is back in business, and all her partners stand under God's impending judgment. But Revelation also sets clear limits on the use of force to protest such practices. In a world where a Lamb conquers by dying and the dragon is defeated by believers who lay down their lives rather than collude with an idolatrous system, the path for resistance is clear. Disciples are called to protest, to bear witness to what society *could* be if God were allowed to break in and reign, but not to defile ourselves with blood as God's enemies have done.

An important facet of Christian witness involves coming out from Babylon, disentangling oneself from violence and exploitative economics and from seeking and sharing in the benefits of unjust practices. There is a mystical connection between the person who fires an automated weapon, those who have applied themselves to its design and construction, and those who paid the taxes that supported the research, development, and deployment of the same.[74] God's commitment to justice—to vindicate the deaths of the innocent and the faithful ones, and to visit destruction upon those who have inflicted, or collaborated with those who inflict, destructive practices upon the earth and its inhabitants—impels us to learn how to "come out from Babylon," both to witness to God's justice *and* to avoid falling afoul of God's justice.

We can easily be overwhelmed both by the power of the systems against which we are called to witness and by the intricacies of our entanglement therein. As a result, because we cannot see our way to "come out from Babylon" entirely, we might wish to throw up our hands and not attempt to come out at all. Aware of these dynamics, William Stringfellow recalls the importance of taking the small steps, performing the symbolic acts of resistance, under the Nazi regime. The Resistance

> consisted, day after day, of small efforts. Each one of these, if regarded in itself, seems far too weak, too temporary, too symbolic, too haphazard, too meek, too trivial to be efficacious against the oppressive, monolithic, pervasive presence which Nazism was. . . . To calculate their actions . . .

---

74. Stringfellow 1973, 72–73.

in terms of odds against the Nazi efficiency and power and violence and vindictiveness would seem to render their witness ridiculous.[75]

Nevertheless, people took those steps and made those efforts at tremendous risks to themselves—risks that far outdistanced the possible results—because

> *resistance became the only human way to live.* To exist, under Nazism, in silence, conformity, fear, acquiescence, obeisance, collaboration—to covet "safety" or "security" on the conditions prescribed by the State—caused moral insanity, meant suicide, was fatally dehumanizing, constituted a form of death. Resistance was the only stance worthy of a human being, as much in responsibility to oneself as to all other humans, as the famous Commandment mentions.[76]

Not all choose the path of being fully human, however. Václav Havel indicts those who consent to "live the lie" because of the "general unwillingness of consumption-oriented people to sacrifice some material certainties for the sake of their own spiritual and moral integrity."[77] The seductiveness of a more-or-less secure enjoyment of some goods led—and leads—many not to inquire too closely into the systems that could, if provoked, harm them, even though it means self-willed alienation to the realities of that system, the selling of one's birthright for a pot of stew.

Hearing the scriptural witness to an alternate way under Nazism provided the possibility, and fostered the boldness, to live out that alternative. "*Recourse to the Bible was in itself a primary, practical, and essential tactic of resistance.* Bible study furnished the precedent for the free, mature, ecumenical, humanizing style of life which became characteristic of those of the confessing movement"[78]—as, indeed, it did for John and his communities! This seemingly simple and pietistic step also lay at the foundations of numerous projects that inject new life into persons and communities, and do so quite apart from, and following a strategy different from, the political and economic processes of domination systems. The work of the Tacoma Catholic Workers and the "Guadelupe Gardens" in the most derelict area of Tacoma, Washington, "happened out of the base of prayer, worship, and study.... The Tacoma Catholic Worker folks simply trusted that if they started the project, God would provide what they would need."[79]

In the study of Scripture, prayer, and Christian conversation, disciples learn afresh what is due God, what it means to "fear God . . . and worship the One who made heaven and earth and sea and springs of water" (Rev. 14:7), and what practices align with this fear and worship. It is to build a house on a new foundation, a foundation that faith regards as unshakable rock, and the process of building becomes the essence of Christian witness. "The greatest threat to the

75. Stringfellow 1973, 118.
76. Stringfellow 1973, 119.
77. Havel 1987a, 54.
78. Stringfellow 1973, 120.
79. Howard-Brook and Gwyther 1999, 266–267.

system" remains to "dare to suggest in deed as well as word that there might be an alternative."[80] John continues to challenge disciples to discover this alternative and to bear witness to it as they reorganize their lives around practices that incarnate the logic of Christ's self-giving and the logic of commitment to the global *shalom* of the kingdom of God.

New Jerusalem

John challenges definitions of "happiness," "the good life," and being "blessed." The disciples in Laodicea adopted a definition involving the secure enjoyment of wealth: "I am rich and I have become wealthy and I have need of nothing" (3:17). Perhaps the desire for more of *this* kind of happiness led some in Thyatira and Pergamum to push their own practice further off into (and beyond) the boundaries of Christian witness, making some room for participation in idolatrous settings, rather than pushing their practice further toward the center of Christian witness. Continuing to embrace a vision of "fulfillment" nurtured by the propaganda of the imperial culture (where *Ploutos*, *Fecunditas*, and *Securitas* were promoted as divine ideals) would continue to draw people into practices and pursuits that sustained the Roman domination systems.

John's prophecy continues to challenge disciples not to define happiness in terms of access to the enjoyment of commodities and the containment of risks threatening such enjoyment, but rather in terms of a soul-filling moral vision, divine encounter, and principled walk. "Privileged," "favored," "*happy* are those who keep the words of the prophecy of this book" (22:7), whose fidelity to God's commandments and to Jesus crafts a life with integrity now that will be recognized as such beyond death, whose vigilance provides protection from going about naked and thus wearing the emperor's new clothes, the wardrobe of self-deceived Laodicea and of Babylon itself (3:17; 18:7–8).

John develops his alternative vision of happiness most fully as he sketches the life of the new Jerusalem. Cultivating new definitions of "the good life" rooted in God's vision of human community liberates one to live for its realization in the new Jerusalem. John shows us that our task involves far more than simply critiquing our society, pushing us to form a vision for human community reflective of God's desires for people. For John, this vision differs from the world in which he lives as a pure bride differs from a depraved harlot. The contrast between the two cities, depicted as women from such different walks of life and of such different character, could not be more striking. John has not given up on human society. "The pagan vision of the future is Eden or Arcadia—a primitivistic return to uncomplicated individualism. . . . But the biblical vision is a perfection of the city. This artifice of society for living consciously together is culminated, not eliminated."[81] "City" is not the problem. The agendas and

---

80. Harvey 1999, 135.
81. Peterson 1969, 139.

ideologies driving the life of the city and of the webs of cities and lands caught in the orbit of the "great city" are the problem. John's final vision is of human community, human urbanized society, organized with God—God's reign, God's light, God's justice—at the center of all things. John has never seen anything like this in life, not in Rome, not in Ephesus, not even in Jerusalem. This point is important. John does not suggest that a theocracy is the answer to the problems of godlessness in the world. Wherever he has looked at a human society that organized itself as a theocracy, he has seen God's name and God-talk simply used to legitimate human domination. The vision of William Blake for his native land is not John's:

> I will not cease from endless strife,
> Nor shall the sword sleep in my hand
> Till we have built Jerusalem
> In England's green and pleasant land.[82]

New Jerusalem is not "brought about by famine and war and pestilence and natural disaster," nor does Revelation's place in the canon legitimate the desert-making systems that John indicts.[83] This society emerges as a bride from her wedding chamber, longing for her husband. It is prepared as the people of God engage the acts of justice and righteousness that spin the fine linen in which the bride is robed. Disaster and war and pestilence and famine (Rev. 6:1–8) are the tools of this world's domination systems. They run their course (e.g., in the seals) and reap their harvest (in the trumpets and bowls). Living with Babylon, not bringing in the new Jerusalem, necessitates the judgments of the Apocalypse. Only God and God's Anointed can usher in the consummate reign of God. All we can do is *witness* to that reign through speech and practice aligned with God's reign. Blake's approach has been far too common throughout Christian history.

The new Jerusalem is inclusive, joining people from every ethnic group, every nation, every tribe, and every language into one humanity, divided no longer by the barriers erected and defended by the fallen mind. In this new kingdom the dignity of priesthood, of access to God, is bestowed upon all. The distinction between priest and layperson was fundamental to the hierarchy in Israel and Judea, and an important marker of status in the Greco-Roman world as well. In God's kingdom, there is the absence of hierarchy, of haves and have-nots, of castes and divisions (1:5–6; 5:9–10). All are elevated to privileged status.

The new Jerusalem is clothed with the righteous acts of God's holy ones (19:8), quite a different wardrobe from Babylon's. Justice, mercy, keeping God's commandments, keeping the testimony of Jesus—these adorn the alternative society. It is built on the foundations of the apostles (21:14), not on the foundations of violence or greed, but on the gospel of the truth of God. The distance between humanity and God is closed proportionately as righteousness and

---

82. William Blake in prefatory poem for *Milton* (ca. 1809).
83. Contra Pippin 1992, 102–3.

peacemaking flourish. The city exists to bring peace and healing to the nations (22:2), rather than to establish "peace" by controlling, dominating, and subduing. The city faces no threat (the gates are never shut; 21:25). Military conquest, international strife, struggles for maintaining a balance of power—all are done away with in this vision. Resources are no longer expended in futile wars and power struggles but rather for the well-being of all.

New Jerusalem is a costly alternative. One cannot profit from Babylon's partnership and violence and then expect a welcome in the new Jerusalem (21:8, 27). Refusing to participate in those activities and pursuits that legitimate Babylon's rule will bring hardship. Throngs of faithful ones pass through great tribulation to arrive at the new Jerusalem. Their need for God's consolation after a hard struggle with the powers of this world that resist such a vision is great, but solace is assured (7:13–17; 21:4). The vision of new Jerusalem is *not* a "pie in the sky in the sweet by-and-by" compensator. It is a proclamation of God's purpose for creation, in light of which all human purposes and societies are judged, critiqued, weighed in the balance and found wanting. Christians are challenged not only to *wait* but also to *witness*, hence to proclaim and protest, to encourage and direct, in light of God's vision. Our society's failure to enact God's righteousness, however this failure manifests itself, cannot be legitimated either by our participation or our silence.

John's vision of the new Jerusalem suggests some particulars for this witness. First, where an ideology stands in the way of perfecting God's vision of a world at peace, whose inhabitants would all have access to the gifts that God intended for all and would accord one another the full respect due to children of God, John calls disciples to unveil that ideology for what it is: another facet of the dragon's activity in leading people astray from God's truth. Second, the naming of the city's foundations calls disciples to build their lives individually, as families, and as local and global communities of faith fully and squarely on the foundations of the apostolic witness. The visions for discipleship and community in the New Testament provide the blueprints.[84] As we see these blueprints more clearly, with the lenses of our own culture and location stripped away one by one, and as we build more closely on the foundation, our lives together will more surely reflect a way of being "community" that resembles the new Jerusalem and stands out more distinctly and provocatively from our own society. Third, the multiethnic and nonhierarchical population of new Jerusalem challenges us to discover ways of living beyond economic caste and ethnic or national boundaries in our life together and our cooperative ventures as a global church, challenging the lines of differentiation within and around our society. Finally, the provisions within new Jerusalem call us to pursue policies and practices that extend healing, restoration, and dignity to the "other," offering leaves from the tree of life

---

84. The image of "blueprint" does not suggest facile replication, as anyone who has tried to build a house from blueprints on an actual site with all the challenges of a new terrain and environment knows.

to people in our own most at-risk areas and to people suffering dehumanization at the hands of domination systems.

Revelation issues a summons to a particular way of being "in the world." John urges disciples to learn how to live as aliens in a land that is not our own, looking away to our native land, the city that none of us has yet seen but that is the consummation of the Judeo-Christian witness. He challenges disciples to yearn with a countercultural yearning, to remember who they are, to whom they belong, to what "laws" they remain committed and bound during the time of their sojourn. In calling Christians into this posture, John's voice speaks in harmony with those of Paul (Phil. 3:21), the author of Hebrews (11:13–16; 13:13–14), and the author of the *Epistle to Diognetus* (5.1–5). It is a posture insisting that religious discourse and practice nurture de-alienating processes rather than accommodate and further reify the "world-taken-for-granted" that seeks our cooperative participation.

> Now, in the meanwhile, with hearts raised on high,
> We for that country must yearn and must sigh;
> Seeking Jerusalem, dear native land,
> Through our long exile on Babylon's strand.[85]

---

85. From "O quanta qualia," "O What Their Joy and Their Glory Must Be," text by Peter Abelard, translated by John Mason Neale (1851).

Bibliography

Anderson, R. Dean. 1998. *Ancient Rhetorical Theory and Paul.* Rev. ed. Leuven: Peeters.
Applebaum, S. 1976. "Economic Life in Palestine." In *The Jewish People in the First Century,* edited by S. Safrai and M. Stern, 2:631–700. Philadelphia: Fortress Press.
Armstrong, Herbert W. 1959. *The Book of Revelation Unveiled at Last!* Pasadena, CA: Ambassador College.
Aune, David E. 1981. "The Social Matrix of the Apocalypse of John." *BR* 26:16–32.
———. 1983. "The Influence of Roman Imperial Court Ceremonial on the Apocalypse of John," *BR* 28:5–26.
———. 1986. "The Apocalypse of John and the Problem of Genre." *Semeia* 36:65–96.
———. 1989. "The Prophetic Circle of John of Patmos and the Exegesis of Revelation 22.16." *JSNT* 37:103–16.
———. 1990. "The Form and Function of the Proclamations to the Seven Churches (Revelation 2–3)." *NTS* 36:182–204.
———. 1997. *Revelation 1–5.* WBC 52A. Dallas: Word Books.
———. 1998a. *Revelation 6–16.* WBC 52B. Nashville: Thomas Nelson.
———. 1998b. *Revelation 17–22.* WBC 52C. Nashville: Thomas Nelson.
———. 2003. "The Use and Abuse of the Enthymeme in New Testament Scholarship." *NTS* 49:299–320.
———. 2006. "The Apocalypse of John and Palestinian Jewish Apocalyptic." *Neotestamentica* 40:1–33.
Bainbridge, W. S., and R. Stark. 1980. "Sectarian Tension." *Review of Religious Research* 22, no. 2:105–24.
Baird, A. Craig. 1965. *Rhetoric: A Philosophical Study.* New York: Ronald.
Bal, Mieke. 1988. *Murder and Difference: Gender, Genre, and Scholarship on Sisera's Death.* Chicago: University of Chicago Press.
Balch, David L. 2006. "'A Woman Clothed with the Sun' and the 'Great Red Dragon' Seeking to 'Devour Her Child' (Rev 12:1, 4) in Roman Domestic Art." In *The New Testament and Early Christian Literature in Greco-Roman Context: Studies in Honor of David E. Aune,* edited by John Fotopoulos, 287–314. Supplements to Novum Testamentum 122. Leiden: E. J. Brill.
Barnett, Paul. 1989. "Polemical Parallelism: Some Further Reflections on the Apocalypse." *JSNT* 35:111–20.

Barr, David L. 1984. "The Apocalypse as a Symbolic Transformation of the World: A Literary Analysis." *Interpretation* 38:39–50.
———. 2003. "Introduction." In *Reading the Book of Revelation*, edited by D. L. Barr, 1–9. Resources for Biblical Study 44. Atlanta: SBL.
Bartsch, S. 1989. *Decoding the Ancient Novel: The Reader and the Role of Description in Heliodorus and Achilles Tatius.* Princeton, NJ: Princeton University Press.
Bauckham, Richard. 1993a. *The Climax of Prophecy: Studies in the Book of Revelation.* Edinburgh: T&T Clark.
———. 1993b. *Theology of the Book of Revelation.* New York: Cambridge University Press.
Beale, G. K. 1984. *The Use of Daniel in Jewish Apocalyptic Literature and in the Revelation of St. John.* Lanham, MD: University Press of America.
———. 1986. "A Reconsideration of the Text of Daniel in the Apocalypse." *Biblica* 67: 536–43.
———. 1988. *John's Use of the Old Testament in Revelation.* JSNTSup 166. Sheffield: Sheffield Academic Press.
———. 1999. *The Book of Revelation.* New International Greek Testament Commentary. Grand Rapids: Wm. B. Eerdmans Publishing Co.
Beasley-Murray, G. R. 1978. *Revelation.* Rev. ed. New Century Bible. London: Marshall, Morgan & Scott.
Becker, G. S., and C. B. Mulligan. 1997. "The Endogenous Determination of Time Preference." *Quarterly Journal of Economics* 112:729–58.
Beckwith, I. T. 1919. *The Apocalypse of John.* New York: Macmillan.
Bell, A. A., Jr. 1978. "The Date of John's Apocalypse: The Evidence of Some Roman Historians Reconsidered." *NTS* 25:93–102.
Berger, P. L. 1963. *Invitation to Sociology: A Humanistic Perspective.* Garden City, NY: Doubleday.
———. 1967. *The Sacred Canopy.* New York: Doubleday.
———. 1970. *A Rumor of Angels.* New York: Doubleday.
Berger, P. L., and Thomas Luckmann. 1967. *The Social Construction of Reality.* New York: Doubleday.
Bertram, G., and F. Hauck. 1967. "μακάριος, etc.," *TDNT* 4:362–70.
Betz, Hans Dieter. 1979. *Galatians.* Hermeneia. Philadelphia: Fortress Press.
Bieder, W. 1954. "Die sieben Seligpreisungen in der Offenbarung des Johannes." *Theologische Zeitung* 10:13–30.
Biguzzi, G. 1998. "Ephesus, Its Artemision, Its Temple to the Flavian Emperors, and Idolatry in Revelation." *NovT* 40:276–90.
Bitzer, Lloyd F. 1968. "The Rhetorical Situation." *Philosophy and Rhetoric* 1:1–14.
———. 1974. "Aristotle's Enthymeme Revisited." In *Aristotle: The Classical Heritage of Rhetoric*, edited by K. Erickson, 141–55. Metuchen, NJ: Scarecrow Press.
Bloomquist, L. Gregory. 1993. *The Function of Suffering in Philippians.* JSNTSup 78. Sheffield: Sheffield Academic Press.
———. 1999. "Methodological Criteria for Apocalyptic Rhetoric: A Suggestion for the Expanded Use of Sociorhetorical Analysis." In *Vision and Persuasion*, edited by G. Carey and L. G. Bloomquist, 181–203. St. Louis: Chalice Press.
Blount, Brian. 2000. "Reading Revelation Today: Witness as Active Resistance." *Interpretation* 54:398–415.
———. 2005. *Can I Get a Witness? Reading Revelation through African American Culture.* Louisville: Westminster John Knox Press.
Böcher, Otto. 1988a. "Die Johannes-Apokalypse in der neueren Forschung." In *Aufstieg und Niedergang der römischen Welt*, edited by Wolfgang Haase, 2.25.5:3850–93. Berlin: Walter de Gruyter.

———. 1988b. *Die Johannesapokalypse.* 4th ed. Erträge der Forschung 41. Darmstadt: Wissenschaftliche Buchgesellschaft.
Boesak, Allen. 1987. *Comfort and Protest: The Apocalypse from a South African Perspective.* Philadelphia: Westminster Press.
Booth, Wayne. 1983 [1961]. *The Rhetoric of Fiction.* 2nd ed. Chicago: University of Chicago Press.
———. 1961. "Distance and Point-of-View: An Essay in Classification." *Essays in Criticism* 11:60–79.
Bousset, Wilhelm. 1906. *Die Offenbarung Johannis.* 6th ed. Göttingen: Vandenhoeck & Ruprecht.
Bowersock, G. W. 1982. "The Imperial Cult: Perceptions and Persistence." In *Jewish and Christian Self-Definition,* edited by B. F. Meyer and E. P. Sanders, 3:171–83. Philadelphia: Fortress Press.
Brent, Allen. 1999. *The Imperial Cult and the Development of Church Order.* Leiden: E. J. Brill.
Brinton, Alan. 1988. "Pathos and the 'Appeal to Emotion': An Aristotelian Analysis." *History of Philosophy Quarterly* 5:207–19.
Buchanan, G. W. 1993. *The Book of Revelation: Its Introduction and Prophecy.* Lewiston, NY: Edwin Mellen.
Caird, G. B. 1966. *A Commentary on the Revelation of Saint John the Divine.* New York: Harper & Row.
Cambier, J. 1955. "Les images de l'Ancien Testament dans l'Apocalypse de Saint Jean." *Nouvelle revue théologique* 77:113–22.
Carey, Greg. 1998. "Apocalyptic Ethos." In *SBL Seminar Papers 1998,* 2:731–61. SBLSP 37. Atlanta: Scholars Press.
———. 1999a. "Introduction: Apocalyptic Discourse, Apocalyptic Rhetoric." In *Vision and Persuasion: Rhetorical Dimensions of Apocalyptic Discourse,* edited by G. Carey and L. G. Bloomquist, 1–17. St. Louis: Chalice Press.
———. 1999b. *Elusive Apocalypse: Reading Authority in the Revelation to John.* Studies in American Biblical Hermeneutics 15. Macon, GA: Mercer University Press.
———. 2001. "The Apocalypse and Its Ambiguous Ethos." In *Studies in the Book of Revelation,* edited by Stephen Moyise, 163–80. Edinburgh: T&T Clark.
Carey, Greg, and L. G. Bloomquist, eds. 1999. *Vision and Persuasion: Rhetorical Dimensions of Apocalyptic Discourse.* St. Louis: Chalice Press.
Casey, Jay. 1987. "The Exodus Theme in the Book of Revelation against the Background of the New Testament." In *Exodus, a Lasting Paradigm,* edited by Bas van Iersel and Anton Weiler, 34–43. Edinburgh: T&T Clark.
Charles, R. H. 1920. *A Critical and Exegetical Commentary on the Revelation of St. John.* 2 vols. Edinburgh: T&T Clark.
Classen, C. Joachim. 1992. "St. Paul's Epistles and Ancient Greek and Roman Rhetoric." *Rhetorica* 10:325–32.
Clemen, C. 1920. "Die Bildlichkeit der Offenbarung Johannis." In *Festgabe für Julius Kaftan,* 25–43. Tübingen: Mohr Siebeck.
Cohen, Shaye. 1988. "History and Historiography in the *Against Apion* of Josephus." *History and Theology* 27:1–11.
Collins, Adela Yarbro. 1976. *The Combat Myth in the Book of Revelation.* Harvard Dissertations in Religion 9. Missoula, MT: Scholars Press.
———. 1980. "Revelation 18: Taunt-Song or Dirge." In *L'Apocalypse johannique et l'apocalyptique dans le Nouveau Testament,* edited by J. Lambrecht, 185–204. Bibliotheca ephemeridum theologicarum lovaniensium 53. Leuven: Leuven University Press.

———. 1983. "Persecution and Vengeance in the Book of Revelation." In *Apocalypticism in the Mediterranean World and the Near East*, edited by David Hellholm, 729–49. Tübingen: J. C. B. Mohr (Paul Siebeck).
———. 1984. *Crisis and Catharsis: The Power of the Apocalypse*. Philadelphia: Westminster Press.
Collins, J. J. 1979. *Apocalypse: The Morphology of a Genre*. Semeia Studies 14. Missoula, MT: Scholars Press.
Conley, Thomas M. 1982. "Aristotle *Rhet*. II 2–11." *Hermes* 110:300–315.
———. 1984. "The Enthymeme in Perspective." *QJS* 70:168–87.
Cooper, John M. 1996. "An Aristotelian Theory of the Emotions." In *Essays on Aristotle's Rhetoric*, edited by Amelie O. Rorty, 238–57. Berkeley: University of California Press.
Corbett, E. 1990. *Classical Rhetoric for the Modern Student*. 3rd ed. New York: Oxford University Press.
Cruz, V. P. 1991. "The Beatitudes of the Apocalypse: Eschatology and Ethics." In *Perspectives on Christology: Essays in Honor of Paul K. Jewett*, edited by M. Shuster and R. A. Muller, 269–83. Grand Rapids: Zondervan.
Cushman, Philip. 1990. "Why the Self Is Empty: Toward a Historically Situated Psychology." *American Psychologist* 45:599–611.
Cuss, Dominique. 1974. *Imperial Cult and Honorary Terms in the New Testament*. Fribourg: University Press.
Danker, F. W. 1982. *Benefactor: An Epigraphic Study of a Graeco-Roman and New Testament Semantic Field*. St. Louis: Clayton House Publishing.
deSilva, David A. 1991. "The Image of the Beast and the Christians in Asia Minor." *Trinity Journal* 12, n.s.: 185–206.
———. 1992a. "The Social Setting of the Apocalypse of John: Conflicts Within, Fears Without." *Westminster Theological Journal* 54:273–302.
———. 1992b. "The Revelation to John: A Case Study in Apocalyptic Propaganda and the Maintenance of Sectarian Identity." *Sociological Analysis* [now *Sociology of Religion*] 53:375–95.
———. 1992c. "The Meaning of the New Testament and the *Skandalon* of World Constructions." *Evangelical Quarterly* 64:3–21.
———. 1993. "The Construction and Social Function of a Counter-Cosmos in the Revelation of John." *Forum* 9:47–61.
———. 1995. *Despising Shame: Honor Discourse and Community Maintenance in the Epistle to the Hebrews*. SBLDS 152. Atlanta: Scholars Press.
———. 1996a. "Meeting the Exigency of a Complex Rhetorical Situation: Paul's Strategy in 2 Corinthians 1 through 7," *AUSS* 34:5–22.
———. 1996b. "Exchanging Favor for Wrath: Apostasy in Hebrews and Patron-Client Relations." *JBL* 115:91–116.
———. 1998a. "Honor Discourse and the Rhetorical Strategy of the Apocalypse of John." *JSNT* 71:79–110.
———. 1998b. "The Persuasive Strategy of the Apocalypse: A Socio-Rhetorical Investigation of Revelation 14:6–13." In *SBL Seminar Papers 1998*, 2:785–806. SBLSP 37. Atlanta: Scholars Press.
———. 1999a. "A Socio-Rhetorical Investigation of Revelation 14:6–13: A Call to Act Justly toward the Just and Judging God." *Bulletin for Biblical Research* 9:65–117.
———. 1999b. "Fourth Ezra: Maintaining Jewish Cultural Values through Apocalyptic Rhetoric." In *Vision and Persuasion: Rhetorical Dimensions of Apocalyptic Discourse*, edited by G. Carey and L. G. Bloomquist, 123–39. St. Louis: Chalice Press.
———. 1999c. *New Testament Themes*. St. Louis: Chalice Press.

———. 2000a. *Honor, Patronage, Kinship and Purity: Unlocking New Testament Culture.* Downers Grove, IL: InterVarsity Press.
———. 2000b. *Perseverance in Gratitude: A Socio-rhetorical Commentary on the Epistle "to the Hebrews."* Grand Rapids: Wm. B. Eerdmans Publishing Co.
———. 2002a. *Introducing the Apocrypha: Message, Context, and Significance.* Grand Rapids: Baker Academic.
———. 2002b. "Final Topics: The Rhetorical Functions of Intertexture in Revelation 14:14–16:21." In *The Intertexture of Apocalyptic Discourse in the New Testament*, edited by D. F. Watson, 215–41. SBL Symposium Series 14. Atlanta: Scholars Press.
———. 2003. "Toward a Socio-Rhetorical Taxonomy of Divine Intervention: Miracle Discourse in the Revelation to John." In *Fabrics of Discourse: Essays in Honor of Vernon K. Robbins*, edited by D. B. Gowler, L. G. Bloomquist, and D. F. Watson, 303–16. Harrisburg, PA: Trinity Press International.
———. 2004. *An Introduction to the New Testament: Contexts, Methods and Ministry Formation.* Downers Grove, IL: InterVarsity Press.
———. 2007a. "*X* Marks the Spot? A Critique of the Use of Chiasm in Macro-Structrual Analyses of Revelation." *JSNT* 30:343–71.
———. 2007b. "Using the Master's Tools to Shore Up Another's House: A Postcolonial Analysis of 4 Maccabees." *JBL* 126:99–127.
———. 2008a. "The Strategic Arousal of Emotions in the Apocalypse of John: A Rhetorical-Critical Investigation of the Oracles to the Seven Churches." *NTS* 54:90–114.
———. 2008b. "What Has Athens to Do with Patmos? Rhetorical Criticism of the Revelation of John (1980–2005)." *Currents in Biblical Research* 6:256–89.
Diefenbach, Manfred. 1994. "Die 'Offenbarung des Johannes' offenbart, dass der Seher Johannes die antike Rhetorklehre kennt." *Biblische Notizen* 73:50–57.
Downing, F. G. 1988. "Pliny's Prosecutions of Christians: Revelation and 1 Peter." *JSNT* 34:105–23.
Duff, Paul B. 2001. *Who Rides the Beast? Prophetic Rivalry and the Rhetoric of Crisis in the Churches of the Apocalypse.* New York: Oxford University Press.
Elliott, John H. 1987. "Patronage and Clientism in Early Christianity." *Forum* 3:39–48.
———. 1990 [1981]. *A Home for the Homeless: A Sociological Exegesis of 1 Peter and Its Situation and Strategy, with a New Introduction.* Minneapolis: Fortress Press.
———. 1993. *What Is Social-Scientific Criticism?* Minneapolis: Fortress Press.
Engberg-Pedersen, Troels. 2004. "The Concept of Paraenesis." In *Early Christian Paraenesis in Context*, edited by J. Starr and T. Engberg-Pedersen, 47–72. Berlin: Walter de Gruyter.
Engelmann, H., and D. Knibbe. 1989. "Das Zollgesetz der Provinz Asia: Eine neue Inschrift aus Ephesos," *Epigraphica Anatolica* 14.
Engels, F. 1964 [1894]. "On the History of Early Christianity." In *On Religion*, edited by K. Marx and F. Engels. Atlanta: Scholars Press.
Eriksson, Anders. 2001. "Fear of Eternal Damnation: *Pathos* Appeal in 1 Corinthians 15 and 16." In *Paul and Pathos*, edited by T. H. Olbricht and J. L. Sumney, 115–26. SBL Symposium Series 16. Atlanta: SBL.
Fee, Gordon D. 1997. *Philippians.* NICNT. Grand Rapids, MI: Wm. B. Eerdmans Publishing Co.
Fekkes, Jan. 1994. *Isaiah and the Prophetic Traditions in the Book of Revelation: Visionary Antecedents and Their Development.* JSNTSup 93. Sheffield: Sheffield Academic Press.
Finley, Moses I. 1985. *The Ancient Economy.* Berkeley: University of California Press.
Foerster, W. 1970. "Bemerkungen zur Bildsprache der Offenbarung Johannis." In *Verborum veritas: Festschrift für Gustav Stählin*, edited by O. Böcher, 225–36. Wuppertal: Theologischer Verlag Brockhaus.

Ford, Josephine M. 1975. *Revelation*. AB 38. Garden City, NY: Doubleday.
Fortenbaugh, William. 1970. "Aristotle's *Rhetoric* on Emotions." *Archiv für Geschichte der Philosophie* 52:40–70. Reprinted in *Aristotle: The Classical Heritage of Rhetoric*, edited by K. V. Erickson, 205–34. Metuchen, NJ: Scarecrow Press, 1974.
———. 1975. *Aristotle on Emotion: A Contribution to Philosophical Psychology, Rhetoric, Poetics, Politics, and Ethics*. New York: Harper & Row.
———. 1985. "Theophrastus on Emotion." In *Theophrastus of Eresus: On His Life and Work*, edited by W. W. Fortenbaugh, P. M. Huby, and A. A. Long, 209–29. Rutgers University Studies in Classical Humanities 2. New Brunswick, NJ: Transaction Books.
Frede, Dorothea. 1996. "Mixed Feelings in Aristotle's *Rhetoric*." In *Essays on Aristotle's Rhetoric*, edited by Amelie O. Rorty, 258–85. Berkeley: University of California Press.
Frey, Jörg. 2006. "The Relevance of the Roman Imperial Cult for the Book of Revelation: Exegetical and Hermeneutical Reflections on the Relation between the Seven Letters and the Visionary Main Part of the Book." In *The New Testament and Early Christian Literature in Greco-Roman Context: Studies in Honor of David E. Aune*, edited by John Fotopoulos, 231–55. Leiden: E. J. Brill.
Friesen, Steven. 1993. *Twice Neokoros: Ephesus, Asia and the Cult of the Flavian Imperial Family*. Leiden: E. J. Brill.
———. 2001 *Imperial Cults and the Apocalypse of John: Reading Revelation in the Ruins*. Oxford: Oxford University Press.
Furnish, V. P. 1984. *II Corinthians*. AB 32A. New York: Doubleday.
Gager, J. G. 1975. *Kingdom and Community*. Englewood Cliffs, NJ: Prentice Hall.
Garrow, A. J. P. 1997. *Revelation*. New Testament Readings. London: Routledge.
Geertz, Clifford. 1973. *The Interpretation of Cultures*. New York: Basic Books.
Gelin, A. 1951. "L'Apocalypse." In *Le Sainte Bible*, edited by L. Pirot and A. Clamer, 12:581–667. Paris: Letouzy et Ané.
Giesen, Heinz. 1986. *Die Johannes-Apokalypse*. Stuttgarter kleiner Kommentar, Neues Testament 18. Stuttgart: Verlag Katholisches Bibelwerk.
———. 1997. *Die Offenbarung des Johannes*. Regensburg: Verlag Friedrich Pustet.
Glancy, Jennifer A. 2002. *Slavery in Early Christianity*. New York: Oxford University Press.
Glassman, R. M. 1986. "Manufactured Charisma and Legitimacy." In *Charisma, History, and Social Structure*, edited by R. M. Glassman and W. H. Swatos Jr., 115–28. New York: Greenwood Press.
Glasson, T. F. 1965. *The Revelation of John*. Cambridge: Cambridge University Press.
Grassi, Ernesto. 1980. *Rhetoric as Philosophy: The Humanist Tradition*. University Park: Pennsylvania State University Press.
Gregg, Steve. 1997. *Revelation, Four Views: A Parallel Commentary*. Nashville: Thomas Nelson.
Griffin, Miriam. 2000. "The Flavians." In *Cambridge Ancient History*, vol. 11, *The High Empire, AD 70–192*, edited by A. K. Bowman, P. Garnsey, and D. Rathbone. 2nd ed. Cambridge: Cambridge University Press.
Guroian, Vigen. 1994. *Ethics after Christendom: Toward an Ecclesial Christian Ethic*. Grand Rapids: Wm. B. Eerdmans Publishing Co.
Hall, Robert G. 1996. "Arguing Like an Apocalypse: Galatians and an Ancient *Topos* outside the Greco-Roman Rhetorical Tradition." *NTS* 42:434–53.
Hansen, G. 1967. "Herrscherkult und Friedensidee." In *Umwelt des Urchristentums*, edited by J. Leipoldt, 127–42. Berlin: Evangelische Verlagsanstalt.
Hanson, K. C. 1996. "How Honorable! How Shameful! A Cultural Analysis of Matthew's Makarisms and Reproaches." *Semeia* 68:81–111.

Hanson, P. D. 1976. "Apocalypticism." In *Interpreter's Dictionary of the Bible: Supplement*, 28–34. Nashville: Abingdon.
Harrington, Wilfrid. 1969. *The Apocalypse of Saint John: A Commentary.* London: Geoffrey Chapman.
———. 1993. *Revelation.* Sacra Pagina 16. Collegeville: Liturgical Press.
Harris, Michael A. 1988. "The Literary Function of Hymns in the Apocalypse of John." Ph.D. diss. Southern Baptist Theological Seminary, Louisville, KY.
Hartlib, Samuel, and John Drury. 1651. *Clavis apocalyptica, or, the revelation revealed in which the great mysteries in the Revelation of St. John and the prophet Daniel are opened: it being made apparent that the prophetical numbers come to an end with the year of our Lord 1655.* London: Printed by William Du-Gard for Thomas Matthewes.
Harvey, Barry A. 1999. *Another City: An Ecclesiological Primer for a Post-Christian World.* Harrisburg, PA: Trinity Press International.
Havel, Václav. 1987a. "The Power of the Powerless." In Havel, *Living in Truth*, edited by J. Vladislav, 36–122. London: Faber & Faber.
———. 1987b. *Living in Truth.* Edited by Jan Vladislav. London: Faber & Faber.
Hayes, John H. and Sara R. Mandell. 1998. *The Jewish People in Classical Antiquity: From Alexander to Bar Kochba.* Louisville: Westminster John Knox Press.
Hemer, Colin J. 1986. *The Letters to the Seven Churches of Asia in Their Local Setting.* England: JSOT Press.
Hengel, Martin. 1989. *The Zealots: Investigations into the Jewish Freedom Movement in the Period from Herod I until 70 AD.* Translated D. Smith. Edinburgh: T&T Clark.
Hermansen, G. 1981. *Ostia: Aspects of Roman City Life.* Edmonton: University of Alberta Press.
Himmelfarb, Martha. 1993. *Ascent to Heaven in Jewish and Christian Apocalypses.* Oxford: Oxford University Press.
Hollander, John. 1981. *The Figure of Echo: A Mode of Allusion in Milton and After.* Berkeley: University of California Press.
Horsley, G. H. R., and S. R. Llewelyn, eds. 1981–92. *New Documents Illustrating Early Christianity.* 6 vols. North Ryde: Macquarrie University.
Howard-Brook, Wes, and Anthony Gwyther. 1999. *Unveiling Empire: Reading Revelation Then and Now.* New York: Orbis Books.
Humphrey, Edith M. 1999. "In Search of a Voice: Rhetoric through Sight and Sound in Revelation 11:15–12:17." In *Vision and Persuasion: Rhetorical Dimensions of Apocalyptic Discourse*, edited by G. Carey and L. G. Bloomquist, 141–60. St. Louis: Chalice Press.
Hurley, P. J. 1988. *A Concise Introduction to Logic.* 3rd ed. Belmont: Wadsworth Press.
Hylen, Susan E. 2003. "The Power and Problem of Revelation 18: The Rhetorical Function of Gender." In *Pregnant Passion: Gender, Sex, and Violence in the Bible*, edited by C. A. Kirk-Duggan, 205–19. Semeia Studies 44. Atlanta: SBL.
Janzen, E. P. 1994. "The Jesus of the Apocalypse Wears the Emperor's Clothes." In *SBL 1994 Seminar Papers*, edited by E. H. Lovering Jr., 637–61. SBLSP 33. Atlanta: Scholars Press.
Janzen, Waldemar. 1965. "*Ašrê* in the Old Testament." *HTR* 58:215–26.
Johanson, Bruce C. 1987. *To All the Brethren: A Text-Linguistic and Rhetorical Approach to 1 Thessalonians.* Stockholm: Almqvist & Wiksell.
Johns, Loren L. 1998. "The Lamb in the Rhetorical Program of the Apocalypse of John." In *SBL Seminar Papers 1998*, 2:762–84. SBLSP 37. Atlanta: Scholars Press.
———. 2003. *The Lamb Christology of the Apocalypse of John: An Investigation into Its Origins and Rhetorical Force.* WUNT 167. Tübingen: Mohr Siebeck.

Jörns, Klaus-Peter. 1971. *Das hymnische Evangelium: Untersuchungen zu Aufbau, Funktion und Herkunft der hymnische Stücke in der Johannesoffenbarung.* Gütersloh: Gerd Mohn.
Jung, C. G. 1954. *Answer to Job.* London: Routledge & Kegan Paul.
Keck, Leander E. 2001. "*Pathos* in Romans? Mostly Preliminary Remarks." In *Paul and Pathos*, edited by T. H. Olbricht and J. L. Sumney, 71–96. SBL Symposium Series 16. Atlanta: SBL.
Kee, Howard C. 1989. *Knowing the Truth: A Sociological Approach to New Testament Interpretation.* Philadelphia: Fortress Press.
Keener, Craig. 2000. *Revelation.* New International Version Application Commentary. Grand Rapids: Zondervan.
Kennedy, George A. 1984. *New Testament Interpretation through Rhetorical Criticism.* Chapel Hill: University of North Carolina Press.
Keresztes, P. 1989 *Imperial Rome and the Christians.* Lanham, MD: University Press of America.
Kiddle, M., and M. K. Ross. 1946. *The Revelation of St. John.* London: Hodder & Stoughton.
Kim, Jean K. 1999. "Uncovering Her Wickedness: An Inter(con)textual Reading of Revelation 17 from a Postcolonial Feminist Perspective." *JSNT* 73:61–81.
Kirby, John T. 1988. "The Rhetorical Situations of Revelation 1–3." *NTS* 34: 197–207.
Kirk-Duggan, C. A., ed. 2003. *Pregnant Passion: Gender, Sex, and Violence in the Bible.* Semeia Studies 44. Atlanta: SBL.
Klauck, H.-J. 2001. "Do They Never Come Back? *Nero Redivivus* and the Apocalypse of John." *Catholic Biblical Quarterly* 63:683–98.
Knight, J. M. 2001. "Apocalyptic and Prophetic Literature." In *Handbook of Classical Rhetoric in the Hellenistic Period: 330 B.C.–A.D. 400,* edited by S. E. Porter, 467–88. Boston: E. J. Brill.
Koester, Craig. 2001. *Revelation and the End of All Things.* Grand Rapids: Wm. B. Eerdmans Publishing Co.
Kraft, H. 1974. *Die Offenbarung des Johannes.* HNT 16A. Tübingen: Mohr Siebeck.
Kraftchick, Steven J. 1985. "Ethos and Pathos Appeals in Galatians Five and Six: A Rhetorical Analysis." PhD diss., Emory University.
———. 2001. "Πάθη in Paul: The Emotional Logic of 'Original Argument.'" In *Paul and Pathos*, edited by T. H. Olbricht and J. L. Sumney, 39–68. SBL Symposium Series 16. Atlanta: SBL.
Kraybill, Nelson. 1996. *Imperial Cult and Commerce in John's Apocalypse.* JSNTSup 132. Sheffield: Sheffield Academic Press.
Krodel, Gerhard A. 1989. *Revelation.* Minneapolis: Augsburg.
Lawrence, D. H. 1931. *Apocalypse.* New York: A. A. Knopf.
Lee, Irving J. 1939. "Some Conceptions of Emotional Appeal in Rhetorical Theory." *Speech Monographs* 6:66–86.
Lee, Michelle V. 1998. "A Call to Martyrdom: Function as Method and Message in Revelation." *NovT* 40:164–96.
LeGrys, A. 1992. "Conflict and Vengeance in the Book of Revelation." *Expository Times* 104:76–80.
Leon, Harry J. 1995. *The Jews of Ancient Rome.* Updated ed. Peabody, MA: Hendrickson.
Levison, John R. 1999. *Of Two Minds: Ecstasy and Inspired Interpretation in the New Testament World.* Dead Sea Scrolls and Christian Origins Library 1. North Richland Hills, TX: BIBAL Press.
Lewis, I. M. 1971. *Ecstatic Religion: An Anthropological Study of Spirit Possession and Shamanism.* Harmondsworth: Penguin.

Lilje, Hans. 1957. *The Last Book of the Bible.* Philadelphia: Muhlenberg Press.
Lipinski, Eugene. 1968. "Macarismes et Psaumes de Congratulation." *RB* 75:321–67.
———. 1969. "L'Apocalypse et le martyre de Jean à Jerusalem." *NovT* 11:225–32.
Lohmeyer, E. 1970. *Die Offenbarung des Johannes.* HNT 16. Tübingen: Mohr Siebeck.
Lohse, Eduard. 1961. "Die alttestamentliche Sprache des Sehers Johannes." *Zeitschrift für die neutestamentliche Wissenschaft* 52:122–26.
———. 1981. *The Formation of the New Testament.* Nashville: Abingdon.
———. 1988a. *Die Offenbarung des Johannes.* Das Neue Testament Deutsch 11. Göttingen: Vandenhoeck & Ruprecht.
———. 1988b. "Wie christliche ist die Offenbarung des Johannes?" *NTS* 34:312–38.
Loisy, Alfred. 1923. *L'Apocalypse de Jean.* Paris: Nourry.
Longenecker, Bruce W. 1995. *2 Esdras.* Sheffield: Sheffield Academic Press.
———. 2001. "'Linked Like a Chain': Rev 22.6–9 in Light of an Ancient Transition Technique." *NTS* 47:105–17.
Mack, Burton L. 1990. *Rhetoric and the New Testament.* Minneapolis: Fortress Press.
Magie, David. 1950. *Roman Rule in Asia Minor to the End of the Third Century after Christ.* 2 vols. Princeton, NJ: Princeton University Press.
Malherbe, A. J. 1977. "Ancient Epistolary Theorists." *Ohio Journal of Religious Studies* 5:3–77.
———. 1986. *Moral Exhortation: A Greco-Roman Sourcebook.* Library of Early Christianity. Philadelphia: Westminster Press.
———. 1987. *Paul and the Thessalonians: The Philosophic Tradition of Pastoral Care.* Philadelphia: Fortress Press.
———. 2004. "Paraenesis in the Epistle to Titus." In *Early Christian Paraenesis in Context,* edited by J. Starr and T. Engberg-Pedersen, 297–317. Berlin: Walter de Gruyter.
Marcussen, A. Jan. 1983. *National Sunday Law.* Thompsonville, IL: Amazing Truth Publications.
Martin, Clarice. 2005. "Polishing the Unclouded Mirror: A Womanist Reading of Revelation 18:13." In *From Every People and Nation: The Book of Revelation in Intercultural Perspective,* edited by David Rhoads, 82–109. Minneapolis: Fortress Press.
Martin, Troy W. 2001. "The Voice of Emotion: Paul's Pathetic Persuasion (Gal 4:12–20)." In *Paul and Pathos,* edited by T. H. Olbricht and J. L. Sumney, 181–202. SBL Symposium Series 16. Atlanta: SBL.
Mede, Joseph. 1627. *Clavis apocalyptica.* Cambridge: printed by T. and J. Buck.
Meeks, W. A. 1983. *The First Urban Christians.* New Haven, CT: Yale University Press.
———. 1986. *The Moral World of the First Christians.* Philadelphia: Westminster Press.
Mellor, R. 1975. ΘΕΑ ΡΩΜΗ: *The Worship of the Goddess Roma in the Greek World.* Hypomnemata 42. Göttingen: Vandenhoeck & Ruprecht.
Michaels, J. Ramsey. 1997. *Revelation.* IVP New Testament Commentary. Downers Grove, IL: InterVarsity Press.
Moore, B. R. 1983. "Rhetorical Questions in Second Corinthians and in Ephesians through Revelation." *Notes on Translation* 97:3–33.
Morton, Russell. 2001. "Glory to God and to the Lamb: John's Use of Jewish and Hellenistic/Roman Themes in Formatting His Theology in Revelation 4–5." *JSNT* 24:89–109.
Mounce, Robert H. 1997 [1977]. *The Book of Revelation.* NICNT. Grand Rapids: Wm. B. Eerdmans Publishing Co.
Moxnes, Halvor. 1991. "Patron-Client Relations and the New Community in Luke-Acts." In *The Social World of Luke-Acts: Models for Interpretation,* edited by J. H. Neyrey, 241–68. Peabody, MA: Hendrickson.
Moyise, Steven. 1995. *The Old Testament in the Book of Revelation.* JSNTSup 115. Sheffield: Sheffield Academic Press.

Mueller, Ekkehardt. 2002. "The Two Witnesses of Revelation 11." *Journal of the Adventist Theological Society* 13:30–45.
Müller, Ulrich B. 1984. *Die Offenbarung des Johannes*. Gütersloh: Gerd Mohn.
Murphy, Frederick J. 1998. *Fallen Is Babylon: The Revelation to John*. New Testament in Context. Valley Forge, PA: Trinity Press International.
Newport, Kenneth G. C. 2000. *Apocalypse and Millennium: Studies in Biblical Exegesis*. Cambridge: Cambridge University Press.
Nikolakopoulos, C. 2001. "Rhetorische Auslegungsaspekte der Theologie in der Johannesoffenbarung." In *". . . Was ihr auf dem Weg verhandelt haten": Beiträge zur Exegese und Theologie des Neuen Testaments; Festschrift für Ferdinand Hahn zum 75. Geburtstag*, edited by C. Gerber, T. Knöppler, and P. Müller, 166–80. Neukirchen-Vluyn: Neukirchener Verlag.
Nussbaum, Martha C. 1996. "Aristotle on Emotions and Rational Persuasion." In *Essays on Aristotle's Rhetoric*, edited by Amelie O. Rorty, 303–23. Berkeley: University of California Press.
O'Leary, S. D. 1993. "A Dramatistic Theory of Apocalyptic Rhetoric." *QJS* 79:385–426.
———. 1994. *Arguing the Apocalypse: A Theory of Millennial Rhetoric*. New York: Oxford University Press.
Oehler, Klaus. 1961. "Der consensus omnium als Kriterion der Wahrheit in der antiken Philosophie und der Patristik." *Antike und Abendland* 10:103–29.
Oepke, Albrecht. 1957. *Der Brief von Paulus an die Galater*. 2nd ed. Theologischer Kommentar zum Neuen Testament 9. Berlin: Evangelische Verlagsanstalt.
Olbricht, Thomas H. 2001a. "Introduction." In *Paul and Pathos*, edited by T. H. Olbricht and J. L. Sumney, 1–4. SBL Symposium Series 16. Atlanta: SBL.
———. 2001b. "*Pathos* as Proof in Greco-Roman Rhetoric." In *Paul and Pathos*, edited by T. H. Olbricht and J. L. Sumney, 7–22. SBL Symposium Series 16. Atlanta: SBL.
Olbricht, Thomas H., and Jerry L. Sumney, eds. 2001. *Paul and Pathos*. SBL Symposium Series 16. Atlanta: SBL.
Patte, Daniel. 1975. *Early Jewish Hermeneutics in Palestine*. SBLDS 22. Missoula, MT: Scholars Press.
Paulien, Jon. 1988. "Elusive Allusions: The Problematic Use of the Old Testament in Revelation." *BR* 33:37–53.
Perdue, Leo G., and John G. Gammie. 1990. *Paraenesis: Act and Form*. Semeia Studies 50. Atlanta: SBL.
Perelman, Chaim, and L. Olbrechts-Tyteca. 1969. *The New Rhetoric: A Treatise on Argumentation*. Notre Dame, IN: University of Notre Dame Press.
Peterson, Eugene H. 1969. "Apocalypse: The Medium Is the Message." *Theology Today* 26:133–41.
Pieters, Albertus. 1937. *The Lamb, the Woman and the Dragon*. Grand Rapids: Zondervan.
Pippin, Tina. 1992. *Death and Desire: The Rhetoric of Gender in the Apocalypse of John*. Louisville, KY: Westminster John Knox Press.
Popkes, Wiard. 2004. "Paraenesis in the New Testament." In *Early Christian Paraenesis in Context*, edited by J. Starr and T. Engberg-Pedersen, 13–46. Berlin: Walter de Gruyter.
Porter, Stanley E., ed. 2001. *Handbook of Classical Rhetoric in the Hellenistic Period: 330 B.C.–A.D. 400*. Boston: E. J. Brill.
Poster, Carol. 2001. "The Affections of the Soul: *Pathos*, Protreptic, and Preaching in Hellenistic Thought." In *Paul and Pathos*, ed. T. H. Olbricht and J. L. Sumney, 23–38. SBL Symposium Series 16; Atlanta: SBL.
Price, S. R. F. 1984. *Rituals and Power: The Roman Imperial Cult in Asia Minor*. Cambridge: Cambridge University Press.

Prigent, Pierre. 1988. *L'Apocalypse de Saint Jean*. Commentaire du Nouveau Testament 14. Geneva: Labor et Fides.
Ramsay, William Mitchell. 1909. *The Letters to the Seven Churches of Asia*. New York: Hodder & Stoughton.
———. 1994. *The Letters to the Seven Churches*. Updated edition. Edited by Mark W. Wilson. Peabody, MA: Hendrickson.
Redditt, Paul L. 2001. "The Rhetoric of Jewish Apocalyptic Eschatology." *Perspectives in Religious Studies* 28:361–71.
Reid, Ronald F. 1983. "Apocalypticism and Typology: Rhetorical Dimensions of a Symbolic Reality." *QJS* 69:229–48.
Resseguie, James L. 1998. *Revelation Unsealed: A Narrative-Critical Approach to John's Apocalypse*. Leiden: E. J. Brill.
Robbins, Vernon K. 1996a. *Exploring the Texture of Texts*. Valley Forge, PA: Trinity Press International.
———. 1996b. *Tapestry of Early Christian Discourse*. London: Routledge.
Roberts, Keith A. 1984. *Religion in Sociological Perspective*. Chicago: Dorsey Press.
Robinson, J. A. T. 1976. *Redating the New Testament*. Philadelphia: Westminster Press.
Roloff, Jürgen. 1993. *The Revelation of John*. Translated by John E. Alsup. Continental Commentaries. Minneapolis: Fortress Press.
———. 1984. *Die Offenbarung des Johannes*. Zürcher Bibelkommentar, Neues Testament 18. Zurich: Theologischer Verlag.
Rossing, Barbara R. 1999. *The Choice between Two Cities: Whore, Bride, and Empire in the Apocalypse*. Harvard Theological Studies 48. Harrisburg, PA: Trinity Press International.
Rowland, Christopher. 1982. *The Open Heaven: A Study of Apocalyptic in Judaism and Early Christianity*. New York: Crossroad.
Royalty, Robert. 1997. "The Rhetoric of Revelation." In *SBL Seminar Papers 1997*, 596–617. SBLSP 36. Atlanta: Scholars Press.
———. 1998. *The Streets of Heaven: The Ideology of Wealth in the Apocalypse of John*. Macon, GA: Mercer University Press.
———. 2004. "Don't Touch *This* Book! Revelation 22:18–19 and the Rhetoric of Reading (in) the Apocalypse of John." *Biblical Interpretation* 12:282–99.
Ruiz, Jean Pierre. 1989. *Ezekiel in the Apocalypse: The Transformation of Prophetic Language in Revelation 16,17–19,10*. Frankfurt am Main: Peter Lang.
———. 1994. "Hearing and Seeing but Not Saying: A Look at Revelation 10:4 and 2 Corinthians 12:4." In *SBL Seminar Papers 1994*, edited by E. H. Lovering Jr., 182–202. SBLSP 33. Atlanta: Scholars Press.
———. 2001. "Praise and Politics in Revelation 19:1–10." In *Studies in the Book of Revelation*, edited by Steve Moyise, 69–84. Edinburgh: T&T Clark.
Ryan, E. 1984. *Aristotle's Theory of Rhetorical Argumentation*. Montreal: Les Éditions Bellarmin.
Saffrey, H. D. 1975. "Relire L'Apocalypse à Patmos." *RB* 82:385–417.
Sanders, E. P. 1983. "The Genre of Palestinian Jewish Apocalypses." In *Apocalypticism in the Mediterranean World and the Near East*, edited by D. Hellholm, 447–59. Tübingen: J. C. B. Mohr.
Scherrer, Steven J. 1981. "Revelation 13 as an Historical Source for the Imperial Cult under Domitian." *HTR* 74:406.
———. 1984. "Signs and Wonders in the Imperial Cult: A New Look at a Roman Religious Institution in the Light of Rev 13:13–15." *JBL* 103:599–610.
Schüssler Fiorenza, Elisabeth. 1972. *Priester für Gott: Studien zum Herrschafts- und Priestermotiv in der Apokalypse*. Münster: Aschendorff.

———. 1985. *The Book of Revelation: Justice and Judgment*. Philadelphia: Fortress Press.
———. 1991. *Revelation: Vision of a Just World*. Proclamation Commentaries. Minneapolis: Fortress Press.
———. 2007. *The Power of the Word: Scripture and the Rhetoric of Empire*. Minneapolis: Fortress Press.
Schütz, Alfred. 1967. *The Phenomenology of the Social World*. Evanston, IL: Northwestern University Press.
Schütz, Alfred, and Thomas Luckmann. 1973. *The Structures of the Life-World*. Translated by R. M. Zaner and H. T. Engelhardt Jr. Evanston, IL: Northwestern University Press.
Scobie, C. H. H. 1993. "Local References in the Letters to the Seven Churches." *NTS* 39:606–24.
Scott, K. 1936. *The Imperial Cult under the Flavians*. Stuttgart: W. Kohlhammer.
Shea, William H. 1980. "The Location and Significance of Armageddon in Rev. 16.16." *AUSS* 18:157–62.
———. 1982. "Chiasm in Theme and by Form in Revelation 18." *AUSS* 20:249–56.
———. 1984. "Revelation 5 and 19 as Literary Reciprocals." *AUSS* 22:248–57.
———. 1985. "The Parallel Literary Structure of Revelation 12 and 20." *AUSS* 23:37–54.
Slater, T. B. 1998. "On the Social Setting of the Revelation." *NTS* 44:232–56.
Smalley, Stephen S. 2005. *The Revelation to John: A Commentary on the Greek Text of the Apocalypse*. Downers Grove, IL: InterVarsity Press.
Smallwood, E. M. 1976. *The Jews under Roman Rule: From Pompey to Diocletian*. Leiden: E. J. Brill.
Smith, Ian. 2002. "A Rational Choice Model of the Book of Revelation." *JSNT* 85:97–116.
Smith, P. Christopher. 1998. *The Hermeneutics of Original Argument: Demonstration, Dialectic, Rhetoric*. Evanston, IL: Northwestern University Press.
Snaider Lanser, Susan. 1981. *Narrative Act: Point of View in Prose Fiction*. Princeton, NJ: Princeton University Press.
Snyder, Barbara W. 1991. "Combat Myth in the Apocalypse: The Liturgy of the Day of the Lord and the Dedication of the Heavenly Temple." PhD diss., Graduate Theological Union and University of California, Berkeley.
Snyder, L. 2000. "Invitation to Transcendence: The *Book of Revelation*." *QJS* 86:402–16.
———. 2004. "The Rhetoric of Transcendence in the Book of Revelation." In *Rhetorics and Hermeneutics: Wilhelm Wuellner and His Influence*, edited by J. D. Hester and J. D. Hester (Amador), 193–217. Emory Studies in Early Christianity 9. New York: T&T Clark International.
Solmsen, F. 1938. "Aristotle and Cicero on the Orator's Playing to the Emotions." *Classical Philology* 33:390–404.
Stamps, Dennis L. 2001. "The Johannine Writings." In *Handbook of Classical Rhetoric in the Hellenistic Period: 330 B.C.–A.D. 400*, edited by S. E. Porter, 609–32. Boston: E. J. Brill.
Starr, James. 2004. "Was Paraenesis for Beginners?" In *Early Christian Paraenesis in Context*, edited by J. Starr and T. Engberg-Pedersen, 73–111. Berlin: Walter de Gruyter.
Starr, James, and Troels Engberg-Pedersen, eds. 2004. *Early Christian Paraenesis in Context*. Beihefte zur Zeitschrift für die neutestamentliche Wissenschaft 125. Berlin: Walter de Gruyter.
Stauffer, Ethelbert. 1952. *Christus und die Caesaren*. Hamburg: Friedrich Wittig.
———. 1955. *Christ and the Caesars*. Philadelphia: Westminster Press.
Strand, Kenneth A. 1976. *Interpreting the Book of Revelation*. Worthington, OH: Ann Arbor Publishers.

———. 1978. "Chiastic Structure and Some Motifs in the Book of Revelation." *AUSS* 16:401–8.

———. 1982. "Two Aspects of Babylon's Judgment as Portrayed in Revelation 18." *AUSS* 20:53–59.

Strecker, Georg. 1991. "Μακάριος." In *Exegetical Dictionary of the New Testament,* edited by H. R. Balz and Gerhard Schneider, 2:376–79. Grand Rapids: Wm. B. Eerdmans Publishing Co.

Strecker, Georg, and Udo Schnelle, eds. 1996. *Neuer Wettstein: Texte zum Neuen Testament aus Griechentum und Hellenismus.* Vol. 2/2, *Texte zur Briefliteratur und zur Johannes-apokalpyse.* Berlin: Walter de Gruyter.

Striker, Gisela. 1996. "Emotions in Context: Aristotle's Treatment of the Passions in the *Rhetoric* and His Moral Psychology." In *Essays on Aristotle's Rhetoric,* edited by Amelie O. Rorty, 286–300. Berkeley: University of California Press.

Stringfellow, William. 1973. *An Ethic for Christians and Other Aliens in a Strange Land.* Waco: Word.

Sumney, Jerry L. 2001. "Paul's Use of Πάθος in His Argument against the Opponents of 2 Corinthians." In *Paul and Pathos,* edited by T. H. Olbricht and J. L. Sumney, 147–60. SBL Symposium Series 16. Atlanta: SBL.

Swartley, Willard. 1996. "War and Peace in the New Testament." In *Aufstieg und Niedergang der römischen Welt,* edited by Wolfgang Haase, 2.26.3:2297–2408. Berlin: Walter de Gruyter.

Sweet, J. P. M. 1979. *Revelation.* London: SCM Press; Philadelphia: Westminster Press.

Swete, H. B. 1908. *The Apocalypse of John.* 3rd ed. London: Macmillan.

Talbert, C. H. 1994. *The Apocalypse: A Reading of the Revelation of John.* Louisville: Westminster John Knox Press.

Thompson, James W. 2001. "Paul's Argument from *Pathos* in 2 Corinthians." In *Paul and Pathos,* edited by T. H. Olbricht and J. L. Sumney, 127–46. SBL Symposium Series 16. Atlanta: SBL.

Thompson, Leonard L. 1986. "A Sociological Analysis of Tribulation in the Apocalypse of John." *Semeia* 36:147–74.

———. 1990. *The Book of Revelation: Apocalypse and Empire.* Oxford: Oxford University Press.

Thomson, Ian H. 1995. *Chiasmus in the Pauline Letters.* JSNTSup 111. Sheffield: Sheffield Academic Press.

Thuren, Lauri. 2001. "'By Means of Hyperbole' (1 Cor 12:31b)." In *Paul and Pathos,* edited by T. H. Olbricht and J. L. Sumney, 97–114. SBL Symposium Series 16. Atlanta: SBL.

Ulrichsen, J. H. 1985. "Die sieben Häupter und die zehn Hörner zur Datierung der Offenbarung des Johannes." *Studia Theologica* 39:1–20.

van Henten, Jan Willem. 2006. "Dragon Myth and Imperial Ideology in Revelation 12–13." In *The Reality of Apocalypse: Rhetoric and Politics in the Book of Revelation,* edited by David L. Barr, 181–203. SBL Symposium Series 39. Atlanta: SBL.

Vanhoye, A. 1962. "L'utilisation du livre d'Ezékiel dans l'Apocalypse." *Biblica* 43: 436–76.

van Kooten, George H. 2005. "'Wrath Will Drip in the Plains of Macedonia': Expectations of Nero's Return in the Egyptian *Sibylline Oracles* (Book 5), 2 Thessalonians, and Ancient Historical Writings." In *The Wisdom of Egypt: Jewish, Early Christian, and Gnostic; Essays in Honour of Gerard P. Luttikhuizen,* edited by A. Hilhorst and G. H. van Kooten, 177–215. Ancient Judaism and Early Christianity 59. Leiden: E. J. Brill.

———. 2007. "The Year of the Four Emperors and the Revelation of John: The 'Pro-Neronian' Emperors Otho and Vitellius, and the Images and Colossus of Nero in Rome." *JSNT* 30:205–48.

Vos, L. A. 1965. *The Synoptic Traditions in the Apocalypse.* Kampen: Kok.
Wainwright, Arthur W. 1993. *Mysterious Apocalypse: Interpreting the Book of Revelation.* Nashville: Abingdon.
Walvoord, John F. 1966. *The Revelation of Jesus Christ: A Commentary.* Chicago: Moody Press.
———. 1991. *Armageddon, Oil and the Middle East Crisis: What the Bible Says about the Future of the Middle East and the End of Western Civilization.* Grand Rapids: Zondervan.
Watson, Duane F. 1988a. *Invention, Arrangement, and Style: Rhetorical Criticism of Jude and 2 Peter.* SBLDS 104. Atlanta: Scholars Press.
———. 1988b. "A Rhetorical Analysis of Philippians and Its Implications for the Unity Question." *NovT* 30:57–88.
———, ed. 2002. *The Intertexture of Apocalyptic Discourse in the New Testament.* SBL Symposium Series 14. Atlanta: Scholars Press.
———, ed. 2006. *The Rhetoric of the New Testament: A Bibliographic Survey.* Blandford Forum, UK: Deo Publishing.
Weber, M. 1963 [1922]. *The Sociology of Religion.* Boston: Beacon Press.
Wengst, K. 1987. *Pax Romana and the Peace of Jesus Christ.* Translated by J. Bowden. Philadelphia: Fortress Press.
Wettstein, Joannes Jacobus. 1752. *Novum Testamentum Graecum.* 2 vols. Amsterdam: Officina Dommeriana.
White, C. Dale. 1998. *Making a Just Peace: Human Rights and Domination Systems.* Nashville: Abingdon.
White, Ellen G. 1950 [1911]. *The Great Controversy between Christ and Satan during the Christian Dispensation.* Mountain View, CA: Pacific Press.
Wilcock, Michael. 1975. *I Saw Heaven Opened.* Downers Grove, IL: InterVarsity Press.
Wilder, Amos N. 1971. "The Rhetoric of Ancient and Modern Apocalyptic." *Interpretation* 25:436–53.
Wilson, B. R. 1967. "An Analysis of Sect Development." In *Patterns of Sectarianism*, edited by B. R. Wilson, 22–45. London: Heinemann.
Wilson, J. Christian. 1993. "The Problem of the Domitianic Date of Revelation." *NTS* 39:587–605.
Wilson, R. R. 1981. "From Prophecy to Apocalyptic." *Semeia* 21:79–95.
Windisch, H. 1937. *Der Sinn der Bergpredigt.* 2nd ed. Leipzig: J. C. Hinrichs Verlag.
Wink, Walter. 1983. *Naming the Powers.* Minneapolis: Fortress Press.
———. 1986. *Unmasking the Powers.* Minneapolis: Fortress Press.
———. 1992. *Engaging the Powers.* Minneapolis: Augsburg Fortress.
Wisse, Jakob. 1989. *Ethos and Pathos: From Aristotle to Cicero.* Amsterdam: Hackkert.
Witherington, Ben, III. 1995. *Conflict and Community in Corinth: A Socio-Rhetorical Commentary on 1 and 2 Corinthians.* Grand Rapids: Wm. B. Eerdmans Publishing Co.
———. 2003. *Revelation.* New Cambridge Bible Commentary. Cambridge: Cambridge University Press.

Index of Ancient Texts

JEWISH SCRIPTURES

Genesis
2:25	280
3	280
3:7–11	280
15:18	308n50
30:13	275n49

Exodus
1:15	299
5:3	163
7:4–5	244
7:14–11:10	163
7:16	163
7:20–21	306
7:22	307
8:1	163
8:2–3	306
8:3	306n54
8:7	306n54
8:15	163, 307
8:19	163, 307
8:20	163
8:22–23	163
8:23	288
8:25–27	163
8:32	163, 307
9:6–7	163
9:7	307
9:10	306
9:12	307
9:13	163
9:18	307
9:23	306n55
9:24	306
9:25–26	163
9:34–35	307
10:3	163
10:6	307
10:7–11	163
10:21	306
10:22–23	163
11:6	307
11:7	288
14:4	244
14:18	244
14:21	309
15	151, 162n50
15:1–2	299
15:1–10	151
15:1–18	151, 162
15:8	300n37
15:11	141, 151, 201
15:12	151
15:14–15	151
15:18	151
19:5–6	283
19:6	163, 281
19:10	282, 288n3
19:14	282, 288n3
19:16	123n22
20:2–3	162, 322
20:2–5	260n8
20:2–6	271
20:11	260n8
20:25–26	288
23:29–30	291
23:31	308n60
23:33	271
29:14	299
33:7	299
34:13	271

Leviticus
4:12	299
4:21	299
6:11	299
8:17	299
9:11	299
10:4	299
11:9–12	306n54
11:41–47	306n54
13:46	299
14:40–41	299
14:45	299
16:27	299
19:14	259n6
19:32	259n6
24:14	299
24:23	299
25:17	259n6
25:36	259n6
25:43	259n6
26:1	271
26:12	170

Numbers
5:3–4	299
15:35–36	299
19:3–9	299

365

366 Index of Ancient Texts

Numbers (*continued*)
25:1–2	60n106, 138
25:1–9	184n41, 187, 241
25:8–9	138
31:8	183n39
31:16	60n106, 138, 187
32:17	292
33:52–53	292
33:55	292

Deuteronomy
3:2	151
4:2	319
5:6–7	162, 322
5:6–9	160, 171
6:2	259n6
6:4	63, 71, 159
6:5–6	159
6:24	259n6
8:19	171
10:10	259n6
11:16	171
11:24	308n60
13:1–5	243, 243n30, 322
13:4	259n6
17:19	259n6
19:15	223n89
28:59	301
29:19–20	319
30:17	171
31:12–13	259n6
32	300
32:4 (LXX)	302, 302n41
32:36	164
32:43 (LXX)	304

Joshua
1:4	308n60
1:13	131n46
23:16	171

Judges
4:15	309
5:2–31	151
5:19	309
7:1	309

1 Samuel
31:1–6	309
44:6–24	160

2 Samuel
7:12–16	167
7:14	170

1 Kings
4:21	308n60
4:24	308n60
17:1	224
18:3–4	140n68
18:13	140n68
18:38–40	203n37
19:18	224
21:23–24	140n68
22:19–20	166n58

2 Kings
1:10	224
2:11	224
9:7	140n68
9:22 (LXX)	138
9:27–28	309
17:9–18	160
17:35–38	259n6
19:15	260n8
23:29	309

1 Chronicles
24:4–6	196n9

2 Chronicles
9:26	308n60

Nehemiah
9:6 (LXX)	260n8, 302

Psalms
1	164
1:1–5	275n52
1:4	298n33
2:7	199
2:8–9	245
2:9	199
13:1–2	164
13:3 (LXX)	223n89
14:1	148
21:8 (LXX)	223n89
22	173n69
23	288n3
32:1–4	275n51
34:10 (LXX)	201
34:19	164
35:5	298n33
35:24–26	164
41:1–3	275nn50, 51
68:25 (LXX)	305n50
70:19 (LXX)	202
77:44 (LXX)	306n53
78	162
78:3 (LXX)	304
78:10 (LXX)	304
79	164
85 (LXX)	301
85:8 (LXX)	202n29
85:9 (LXX)	302
85:9–10 (LXX)	301, 303
86:8–10	151
86:9	76
88:9 (LXX)	202n29
89:15	275nn50, 51
93:1–2	165
94:1–6	164
96	160n46
96:1–9	160
96:2	160n46
96:3	160n46
96:5	160, 160n46
96:7	160n46
96:7–8	76
96:7–9	160n46
96:10	160n46, 167
96:13	160n46, 167
97:1	165
97:2 (LXX)	167, 302
97:6–7	160
98:1–2	151
98:9	167
99:1	165, 167
99:4	167
103:20–21	166
104:4	97n12
105	162
106	162
110:1	167, 253
110:2 (LXX)	301, 301n40
112:1	259n6
112:1–3	275nn50, 51
115:3–11	160
118:137 (LXX)	304
127:5	275n51
128:1–2	275n51
135:13–21	160
135:14	164
138:14 (LXX)	301, 301n40
144:17 (LXX)	302, 302n41
148:2	166

Proverbs
1–9	292
3:1–11	164
3:11	253n46
3:12	191n57, 252, 253n46

Index of Ancient Texts 367

3:13–14	275n49	65:17–18	170	27:28–36	310n69
8:34–35	275n49	65:19	170	27:32b–36	45n47
8:34–36	275n52	66:23	302, 303	27:35–36	45n47
16:6	259n6			28:2	310n69
28:14	275n52	**Jeremiah**		28:5	310n69
		1:1–3	9	28:17–18	310n69
Ecclesiastes		1:14–16	309	34	288n3
12:13	259n6	2:2	236n22	37:27	170, 171
		3:6–10	204n41	37:28	171
Isaiah		6:22–26	309	38:22–23	302
1:1	9, 119	10:1–10	302	40–48	171, 171n63
1:17	73, 74	10:1–11	160	48:30–35	171n62
1:21	204n41	10:5–8	302n42		
6	196n10	10:6–7a	151	**Daniel**	
6:1–6	166	10:6–7	151	2	206
6:2–3	97	10:7	302	2:20–21	108
8:7–8	309	10:11	260n8	2:21	206
11:2–3	97n12	10:25	305n50	2:35	298n33
12:1–6	151	17:10	128, 244, 244n32	2:36–45	108
14:14 (LXX)	202	23:5–6	167	3	173
17:13	298n33	25:9–11	309	3:6	173, 173n69
21:9	269	25:15	155n36	3:17–18	336
23	161	28:33 (LXX)	298n33	3:27 (LXX)	302, 302n41, 304, 305
23:2–3	310n69	46:6–10	309		
23:8	310n69	47:2	309	4	206
23:15–18	310n69	51	108, 152, 161	4:17	108
23:16–17	204n41	51:7	155n36	4:25–27	108
23:17	155n36, 205n44	51:7–8	269	4:32	108, 206
24:8	213n73	51:13	155n36	5:18–28	108
25:8	170, 288n3	51:33	76, 298n33	7	35, 105, 124n27, 168
29:5	298n33	51:49	208		
29:13 (LXX)	223n89			7:2–8	168
31:9–10	275n49	**Ezekiel**		7:3–7	39
35:8	172	1	124n27, 196n10	7:9–14	102
37:16 (LXX)	260n8, 302	1–2	122	7:13	110, 129, 148, 168, 180n27, 297
40:3–5	162	1:4–28	166		
43:16–19	162	1:5–11	97	7:21	199n17
44:24–45:6	309	1:26–28	131	7:25a	202n32
44:27	309	2	132n48	7:27	168
46:6–7a	202n29	2:8–3:6	131	8:9–14	202n32
47	152, 161	3:12	123, 124n27	10	122, 124, 124n27
49:2	309	4:4–6	3	10:5–6	123, 131
49:10	217, 288n3	11:20	170, 172	10:9	131
49:25	309	11:21	172	11:36	202n32
52:1–6	162	16:15–22	204n41	12:1	127, 307n56
52:11	172	20:3–26	162	12:3	173n69
57:1–2	278	23:1–49	204n41	12:9	4
60:3–5	171	23:25–29	207n50		
60:14	249	26–27	108, 152, 161	**Hosea**	
62:2	169	26:13	213n73	1:1	119
62:4–5	169	26:16–18	45n47	2:14–20	169
63:1–3	76n36	26:27	45n47	4:12–13	204n41
63:2–6	110, 299	27:12–24	310n69	5:3	204n41

Index of Ancient Texts

Hosea (continued)
6:11 — 76
13:3 — 298n33

Joel
1:1 — 119
2:10 — 290n8
2:30–31 — 290n8
3:13 (LXX) — 76n36, 110, 298, 298n34

Amos
3:13 (LXX) — 301
4:13 (LXX) — 301

Jonah
3:4 — 11
3:10 — 11
4:5 — 11

Micah
1:1 — 119
4:12–13 — 76, 298n33

Nahum
3:4 — 155n36, 204n41, 205n44

Habakkuk
3:12 — 76

Zephaniah
1:1 — 119
3:8 — 305n50

Zechariah
2:11 — 170
2:11–12 — 171
4:1–14 — 154
12:10 — 129, 130n42, 148
12:14 — 129
14:16 — 302

Malachi
1:1 (LXX) — 119
3:2 — 216

APOCRYPHA/DEUTEROCANONICAL BOOKS

Tobit
4:21 — 259n6
12:12 — 289n6
12:15 — 97n12, 196n9, 289n6
12:22 — 301
13:16 — 276n49

Greek Esther
15:13–15 — 195

Wisdom
1:16–5:23 — 164
3:1–3 — 278
10:15–11:20 — 162
11:15–16 — 163
11:17–19 — 218
12:8–10 — 243n31
12:8–11 — 75
12:9–10 — 291
12:23–27 — 162
13–15 — 103n25, 160
13:1–14:31 — 271
14:12 — 59n106
15:18–19:22 — 162
16:15–16 — 163
18:14–16 — 242

Sirach
10:19 — 259n6
19:20 — 259n6
21:15 — 155n33
23:27 — 259n6
28:19–20 — 276nn49, 50
39:6 — 123n23
48:11 — 276n49
50:28–29 — 276nn49, 51
56:1 — 276n51

Baruch
4:4 — 276nn49, 50, 51
4:6–7 — 43

Letter of Jeremiah
— 103, 271

Prayer of Azariah
1:4 — 302, 304, 305
1:15 — 13n36

Song of the Three
31–32 — 166

1 Maccabees
4:46 — 13n36
14:41 — 13n36

2 Maccabees
4:18–20 — 56
6–7 — 240
7 — 102n21, 164

2 Esdras
See 4 Ezra; 5 Ezra

4 Maccabees
1:1 — 103
1:2 — 80
1:8 — 80
1:10 — 80
3:19 — 80, 295n29
5–13 — 240
5:1–18:24 — 102n21
9:8–9 — 164
9:32 — 164
10:11, 15 — 164
12:11–12 — 164
13:13b–15 — 273
15:2–3, 8 — 273n39
17:4–6 — 164
17:15 — 240n28
18:1–2 — 20n54
18:9 — 276n49

NEW TESTAMENT

Matthew
3:12 — 76, 298n33
4:17 — 238
5:3–10 — 275n49
5:3–11 — 277n56
5:10–11 — 277n56
10:28 — 240, 247n35, 274
10:32 — 238
11:3 — 105n32
11:15 — 106n33, 238, 238n26
13:9 — 106n33, 238, 238n26
13:16 — 275n49
13:24–30 — 298n33
13:37–43 — 298n33
13:41–42 — 173
13:41–43 — 173, 173n69
13:42 — 173
13:43 — 106n33, 238, 238n26
16:17 — 275n49
17:24 — 56
18:10 — 127
22:1–14 — 170
22:44 — 253n47
24:12 — 236n22
24:15 — 105n32
24:29–30 — 290n8
24:30 — 129, 148
24:36 — 133n55

24:42	238, 247n35,	21:27	105n32	**1 Corinthians**	
	300n35	22:69	253n47	1:7	120
24:42–44	300n35	**John**		1:26–27	52n79
24:43	247n35, 280n59	4:35–36	298n33	8:1–13	61n111
25:13	238, 300n35	4:35–38	76	8:4	61
25:29	238n26	8:44	55	9:25	240n28
25:41–45	173	8:51	238	10:1–22	61n111
26:64	105n32, 253n47	13:31–35	237n24	10:14–21	43
Mark		15:12–14	237n24	10:14–22	271
4:9	238n26	19:37	130n42	10:19–20	99
4:23	238n26			12:4–11	10n32
4:29	76, 298n33	**Acts**		13	237n24
7:6	223n89	2:14–21	10n32	14	144
7:15	61	2:20	290n8	14:1–40	10n32
7:16	238n26	2:34–35	253n47	14:6	120
8:34–35	240	5:29	240, 274	14:26	12
12:28–34	237n24	7:54–8:3	57	14:29	145
12:36	253n47	9:1–2	57	14:29–33	33n8, 144,
13:14	105n32	10–11	171		144n84
13:19	307n56	12:1–3	57	14:31	144
13:26	105n32	12:15	127	15:8	11
13:32	133n55	13:48–52	57	15:25	253n47
13:35	238, 247n35,	14:19–20	57	15:33	148n2
	300n35	14:27	248n38	15:44	5
13:37	238, 247n35,	15	171	15:50	5
	300n35	16:14	61	16:9	248n38
14:57–59	223n89	17:28	148n2	**2 Corinthians**	
14:62	105n32, 253n47	18	58n99	1	20
16:19	253n47	18:12–17	58n99	1:15–2:4	81, 87
		20:31	300n35	1:20	249
Luke		21:10–14	10n33	2	20
1:8–10	289n6	24:10b–21	87	2:12	248n38
1:11–20	289n6	24:28	87	4:16–18	273n39
1:19	97n12			5:9	236
1:32	167	**Romans**		5:9–10	279n58
1:45	275n49	1:1	131	5:10	236
3:1–6	171	1:3–4	167	6:16–18	170
3:17	76, 298n33	1:18–23	210, 271	7:5–16	87
6:20–21	275n49	1:18–32	59n106, 271	7:8–12	81
6:20–22	277n56	1:24–32	272	10–13	32
8:8	238n26	2:4	243n31	11:2–3	170
12:8	247n35	2:6–11	272, 279n58	12:1	11, 120
12:21	238n26	3:9–10	148	12:1–10	32
12:37	280n59	6:1–11	240	12:4	11
12:39	280n59	8:34	253n47	12:7	120
13:3	238	13:8–10	237n24		
13:5	238	14:1–3	61n111	**Galatians**	
13:9	238n26	15:1	61n111	1:1	131
14:14	275n49	15:7–13	77, 171	1:6–9	144, 158
14:35	238n26	16:23	60	1:12	11, 120
18:7–8	289	22:10	77	1:15–16	11
20:42–43	253n47	22:11	77	1:22–24	57
21:4	238n26	22:12	77	2:2	120

Index of Ancient Texts

Galatians (continued)	
3:1–4:7	171
3:14	249
5:13–14	237n24
5:19–21	271

Ephesians	
3:1–6	171
5:1–2	237n24
5:3–6	210
5:22–32	170
5:25–33	327

Philippians	
1:1	131
2:5–11	223n91
3:10–11	240
3:21	349

Colossians	
4:3	248n38

1 Thessalonians	
1:9	271
1:10	57
2:13–16	57
3:1–6	54
5:2	247n35
5:2–4	300n35
5:3	107n37
5:6	300n35
5:19–22	144

2 Thessalonians	
1:3–9	54

2 Timothy	
2:11–12	240
4:8	240n28

Titus	
1:1	131

Hebrews	
1:3	253n47
1:7	97n12
1:13	253n47
3:12	298n33
4:14–16	290n7
6:1–2	272n38
7:7	52n79
8:1	253n47
10:12	253n47
10:32–34	54
11:6	279n58
11:11–16	349
11:34	105n32
12:2	240
12:4–11	191n57, 253, 253n46
13:1	237n24
13:3	54
13:13–14	349

James	
1:1	131
1:12	240n28, 275nn49, 51
2:8	237n24

1 Peter	
1:7	120
1:11	240
1:13	120
1:22	237n24
2:4–10	171
2:11–12	54
2:12	99
2:13–17	199
2:17	237n24
2:18–25	54
2:21	240
2:21–25	223n91
3:8	237n24
3:13–17	54
3:14	277n56
4:1–4	54
4:3	271
4:3–4	44n43, 59n106, 60n106
4:12–19	54
4:14	275n49, 277n56
5:4	240n28
5:8	300n35

2 Peter	
1:1	131
1:16–18	31
2:4–8	288n4
2:9	288n4
3:8–9	243n31
3:10	300n35

1 John	
1:1–4	158
2:6	223n91
2:18	55
3:8–10	55
3:11–18	237n24
4:1–3	158
4:1–4	144
5:21	271

Jude	
1:1	131
8	125, 145

Revelation	
1	122, 124
1:1	4, 11, 53, 119, 129, 130, 130n45, 131, 132, 136, 143, 143n82, 154, 180, 286, 296, 317
1:1–2	32, 128
1:1–3	9, 32n8, 119, 143n82, 181n29
1:1–20	25, 118
1:2	71, 120, 132, 132n51, 136, 224
1:3	4, 10, 86, 110, 118, 120, 129, 134, 136, 153, 154, 180, 222, 231, 234n19, 258, 275, 275n49, 282, 283, 317, 319
1:3b	10
1:4	9, 32n8, 97n12, 109, 119, 126, 132, 178, 180, 181n28, 196n9
1:4–6	110
1:4–8	9
1:5	71, 132, 224
1:5–6	128, 162, 186, 281, 283, 347
1:7	110, 129, 148, 149n5, 153, 154, 155, 168, 196n8, 202n29, 236
1:7–8	110n45, 180n26
1:8	109, 125, 180, 181n28
1:9	32, 33, 71, 126, 132, 180, 210, 224, 317
1:9–20	110n45, 131
1:10	121, 123
1:11	65, 131
1:12	121n14
1:12–13	182
1:12–15	123
1:12–16	102, 111, 128, 152, 152n21, 155, 158, 181
1:12–20	122, 176n6, 180n26, 181, 183, 198, 235, 237

1:13	134	2:10d	239	2:24	142n77, 247
1:15	134	2:11	106n33, 110, 186,	2:24–25	184, 187,
1:17	121, 121n14,		189, 192n61, 224,		244, 254
	182, 209n62		238, 240, 254, 281	2:24a	244
1:17–20	125	2:11b	70n16, 83, 184	2:24b	244
1:18	196n8	2:12	126, 131, 183,	2:24c	244
1:19	4, 10, 131,		183n38	2:25	186n45, 244, 245
	286, 296	2:13	49, 53, 71, 85, 107,	2:26	224
1:20	111, 182		132, 142n77, 165,	2:26–27	169, 245
2	126		185, 186, 187, 210,	2:26–28	70n16, 186,
2–3	4n8, 30, 54, 176,		224, 242, 254		192n61
	182, 193	2:13–14	241	2:28a	245
2:1	111, 126, 127,	2:14	50, 114, 160, 188,	2:29	106n33, 189, 238
	131, 182		188n46, 230, 241	3	126
2:1–3:22	10, 125,	2:14–15	50, 59, 86, 138,	3:1	85, 126, 131,
	137, 180		183, 187, 191n60,		190, 191, 247,
2:2	32, 49, 114, 145,		241, 254		254, 279
	158, 279	2:14b	59n105	3:1–3b	86
2:2–3	85	2:15	59n105, 187, 241,	3:1b	248n36
2:2a	185		254	3:1c	245
2:2b	49n67	2:16	111, 180n26,	3:1d	245
2:3	49, 53, 185		181n30, 183, 188,	3:2	52n79, 230, 238,
2:4	62n113, 236, 254		230, 238, 254,		246, 280n60
2:4–5	70, 74, 186,		280n59, 330n44	3:2–3a	83
	191n60, 246	2:16a	241	3:2–3	247n35
2:5	82, 111, 180n26,	2:16b	183nn35, 38;	3:2a	127, 245
	182, 186n45, 230,		241, 242, 254	3:2b	245
	238, 254	2:17	106n33, 186, 189,	3:3	183, 186n45, 238,
2:5a	236, 237		192n61, 224, 238		246, 247n35, 280n60
2:5b	183nn35, 38;	2:17b	70n16	3:3a	190, 245
	236, 254	2:18	10n34, 126, 131	3:3b	83, 127, 183nn35,
2:5c	237	2:19	49, 53, 54, 74, 19,		38; 245, 246n34, 254
2:6	49, 49n67, 59,		185, 186, 191n60,	3:4	190, 247, 254
	187, 191n60		273n40, 279	3:4–5	70n15, 83, 380n60
2:7	106n33, 127, 186,	2:20	32, 50, 59, 114,	3:4a	247
	189, 192n61,		131, 139, 140,	3:4b	247
	224, 238		160, 187, 188,	3:4c	247
2:7b	70n16, 82		243, 254, 264	3:5	58n100, 70n16,
2:8	57n98, 102, 126,	2:20–21	86		110, 172, 186, 191,
	131, 240	2:20–22	139, 188		192n61, 224, 238,
2:8b	184	2:20–23	59, 67n8		247n35, 247
2:9	49, 50, 54, 55, 56,	2:21	69, 139, 183n37,	3:5b	127
	59, 85, 114, 137,		188, 244, 264	3:6	106n33, 189, 238
	142, 142n77, 185,	2:21–23	183	3:7	126, 131, 249
	186, 187, 191, 239	2:22	83, 138, 230n5,	3:7–8	184
2:10	49, 53, 101, 112,		238, 243,	3:8	49, 53, 85, 185,
	115, 127, 165, 184,		244, 330n44		230, 230n5, 238,
	230n5, 250n41,	2:22–23	111, 139, 172,		249, 254, 279
	253n46, 254, 277		183, 244,	3:8–9	247
2:10–11	57n98		245, 254	3:8–10	254
2:10a	184, 239, 240	2:23	128, 189, 244,	3:8a	248
2:10b	102, 239, 240		246, 252, 279	3:8b	59, 185, 248
2:10c	83, 239	2:23b	184, 245	3:8c–e	248

Revelation (*continued*)
3:9 49, 55, 56, 142, 142n77, 172, 185, 187, 230n5, 248
3:10 49, 185, 230, 238, 248
3:10a 249
3:10b 249
3:11 4, 110, 180n26, 181n30, 185, 186n45, 250, 254, 280n59
3:11a 250
3:11b 250
3:11c 250
3:12 70n16, 186, 192n61, 224, 249n38
3:13 106n33, 189, 238
3:14 71, 126, 131
3:15 85, 248n36, 251, 279
3:15–16 254
3:15–18 253n46
3:15b–16 190
3:16 172, 191, 230
3:16–18 251n42
3:16a 251
3:16b 251
3:17 50, 59, 114, 128, 190, 191, 244, 251, 252n44, 346
3:17–18 46, 67, 70n15, 252n44
3:17a 67
3:17b 67
3:18 83, 191, 251, 254, 280n60
3:18b 190
3:19 67, 230, 238, 253n46
3:19–20 252, 252n44
3:19a 252, 253n46
3:19b 191, 222, 252
3:19b–20 253n46
3:20 111, 191, 230n5, 253
3:21 67, 70n16, 102, 167, 169, 186, 192n61, 224, 253
3:21a 253
3:21b 253
3:22 106n33, 189, 238

4 98, 124n27
4–5 86, 99, 100, 194, 201, 204, 258, 260, 263
4:1 4, 53, 97, 121n14, 196n8, 286, 296
4:1–5:14 181, 198, 210
4:1–22:5 24
4:2 97, 165, 196n8
4:3 134, 196, 196n8
4:4 97
4:5 97n12, 196
4:5b 97
4:6 134, 196n8
4:6–8 97
4:7 134, 196n8
4:8 99n17
4:9 165
4:10 165
4:11 86, 197, 198, 258, 260, 264n20, 289
4:22 48
5 98
5:1 121n14, 165
5:1–6 197, 261
5:1–14 167
5:2 121n14
5:3 100
5:3–4 182, 198, 262
5:4 209n62
5:5 167, 196n8, 224
5:5–6 101
5:6 112, 121n14, 167, 196n8
5:7 165
5:9 4n8, 101, 112, 113, 198, 201, 201n24, 261n14, 337
5:9–10 86, 98, 171, 197, 197n13, 224, 258, 260, 262, 281, 283, 289, 347
5:10 102n20, 112, 162
5:11 97, 121n14
5:12 86
5:13 97, 98, 165, 196, 198, 201, 216, 262
6 285, 287
6–9 219, 226, 290
6:1 121n14
6:1–8 101, 347
6:2 121n14, 196n8
6:5 121n14, 196n8

6:5–6 46
6:5–17 175n2
6:6 37n26, 209n58
6:7–8 74n28
6:8 121n14, 196n8
6:9 53, 71, 121n14, 132, 224, 289, 303
6:9–11 37, 54, 125, 165, 165n57, 207, 210, 277, 278, 290, 303n45, 304, 320
6:10 165, 250n41, 304
6:11 53, 55
6:11b 109, 207
6:12 121n14, 218
6:12–14 98, 290n8
6:12–17 101, 110, 290
6:14 216
6:15 73, 74, 216
6:15–16 162n49, 216
6:15–17 111, 217
6:16 165, 209
6:16–17 217
6:17 209, 217
7 305n5, 316, 318
7–9 286, 289
7:1 121n14
7:1–3 101, 287
7:1–8 85, 163
7:1–17 217
7:2 121n14
7:2–3 201
7:2–8 226
7:3 131
7:4–8 287
7:9 4n8, 113, 121n14, 171, 196n8, 217
7:9–10 217
7:9–12 98, 287
7:9–17 217, 287
7:13–17 85, 112, 185n43, 217, 283, 296, 339, 348
7:14–15 287, 287n3
7:14b 109
7:15 99n17
7:15–17 258
7:15b 217
7:16 217
7:16–17 287, 288n3
7:17 167
7:17a 217
8 98, 218

Index of Ancient Texts

8–9	285, 287
8:1–5	37, 289n5
8:1–6	100
8:1–9:21	148n4, 296
8:2	97n12, 121n14, 196n9
8:2–5	290
8:3	289
8:3–5	303n45
8:4	289
8:5	289
8:6–11	287
8:7	4
8:7–9:19	101
8:13	121n14, 218, 250n41
9	98, 218
9:1	121n14
9:4	85, 112, 163, 218, 250n41, 287
9:7	134
9:7–10	218
9:10	134
9:12	196n8
9:17	121n14
9:17–19	218
9:19	134
9:20	142, 287
9:20–21	43, 75, 85, 98, 99, 142, 160, 163, 203n37, 210, 210n63, 225, 290
10	131n48, 132n48
10:1	121n14
10:1–11	131
10:4	121, 133
10:5	121n14
10:6	181n30, 215n79
10:7	130n45, 153
10:11	113
11	140, 223, 224n94, 225
11:1	134
11:1–2	37
11:3–12	283
11:3–13	71, 86, 292
11:4	154, 155
11:5	223n89, 224
11:6	223n89, 224
11:6–7	223n89
11:7	107, 210, 223n89
11:7–8	101
11:7–10	53
11:9	113, 199n18, 223n89
11:9–10	199n18
11:10	76n33, 199n18, 250n41, 266
11:11–13	220
11:12	224
11:13	76, 218, 224, 225
11:13b	113
11:14	196n8
11:15	167
11:15–18	110, 258, 259n7, 263, 290
11:15–19	148n4
11:16–18	168
11:17–18	297
11:18	102, 111, 130n45, 154, 165, 209, 218
11:19	37
12	104, 224n94
12–13	198, 203
12:3	196n8
12:4	113, 199
12:5–6	199
12:7–8	199
12:9	104, 114, 139, 142, 199, 203
12:10–11	53
12:10–12	70n16, 105, 283
12:11	71, 85, 86, 102, 224, 224n93
12:12	105
12:12c	201
12:17	69, 71, 101, 105, 132, 160, 199, 210, 219, 277, 319
13	106n34, 155n34, 204, 227, 258
13–16	154
13:1	105, 106, 112, 121n14, 202, 210
13:1–2	39
13:1–7	199
13:1–8	272
13:1–10	141, 168
13:1–18	86, 160, 227
13:1–14:13	272
13:2	104, 121n14, 134, 199
13:2–4	114
13:2b	201
13:3	35, 39, 106, 200n20, 206nn48, 49
13:3–4	262
13:3a	112
13:3b	206
13:3b–4a	43
13:3b–4	112, 201, 202
13:4	39, 85, 99, 104, 106, 107, 141, 201, 205, 206n49, 226
13:5–6	105, 202, 210
13:5b	201
13:6	202
13:7	38, 39, 101, 107, 109, 113, 198, 199, 201, 210, 219, 261n14
13:7b–8	112
13:8	39, 85, 106, 113, 201n24, 206, 226, 250n41, 277
13:9	106
13:10	107, 273n40
13:11	121n14, 134, 202
13:11–18	114, 163
13:12	35, 106, 226, 250n41
13:13–14	203, 203n37, 203
13:14	35, 39, 106, 114, 139, 141, 142, 250n41
13:14–15	114, 203
13:15	203
13:15–17	48, 53, 55, 85, 101, 109, 112, 141, 165, 219, 272, 273, 277, 278
13:16	73, 73n27, 114, 201
13:16–17	203
13:17	203
13:18	36, 230
14	106n34, 258n2
14:1	114, 121n14, 196n8, 226
14:1–5	76, 86, 114, 223, 224, 226n98, 227, 283, 331
14:3	114, 226
14:4	114, 265n22
14:4–5	226
14:4a	226
14:4b	226
14:5	114, 226
14:6	84, 113, 121n14, 168n59

Index of Ancient Texts

Revelation (*continued*)

14:6–7	4n8, 85, 113, 160, 160n46, 171, 225, 259, 272	15	300	16:10–11	101
		15–16	285, 290	16:11	75, 142, 163, 210, 291, 307
		15:1	121n14, 206n48, 209, 290, 301	16:12	309
14:6–11	258	15:1–4	296	16:12–16	215n79, 308
14:6–13	76, 125, 160n46, 173, 231, 257, 258, 289	15:2	36n23, 121n14	16:13	121n14, 306
		15:2–4	70n16, 85, 113, 125n30, 163, 165, 185n43, 223, 258, 300	16:14	111
				16:15	86, 110n46, 125n32, 196n8, 215n79, 222, 231, 247n35, 248n36, 258, 279, 280n60, 283, 300n35
14:7	83, 160n46, 210, 231, 259, 259n7, 264n20, 273, 298n33, 308, 345	15:3	151, 153, 154, 162n50, 165, 206n48, 304, 304n47		
14:7b	259			16:15–17	207
14:8	85, 139, 204n39, 263, 264, 264n20, 269	15:3–4	86, 151, 152n23, 158, 259n7, 263	16:17	290
				16:17–21	101
		15:3b	300, 301	16:17–19:8	310
14:9–10	270	15:3c	300, 302	16:18	218, 307
14:9–11	84, 85, 113, 114, 163, 173, 219, 227, 237, 259n7, 263, 274, 278	15:4	76, 302	16:19	209, 310
		15:4a	300, 301, 302	16:21	163, 210, 291, 306, 307
		15:4b	300, 302		
14:9–12	270	15:4c	301, 302	17	269, 310, 311, 325, 326
14:10	209, 271, 272n36, 310	15:4d	301		
		15:5	37, 121n14	17–18	45, 45n47, 139n68, 160, 203, 205, 264, 269
14:11	271, 272n36, 278	15:5–8	100		
14:12	85, 112, 154, 155, 160, 190n56, 217, 220, 227, 273, 273n40, 274, 277, 303, 317, 319	15:6	37	17:1	205, 292
		15:7	209, 210	17:1–6	152, 152n21, 155n36, 158
		15:8	37		
		16	300, 305, 310	17:1–18:24	86, 207
		16:1	37, 209, 305n50	17:2	205, 250n41
14:12–13	227, 279, 281	16:1–21	263, 273, 296	17:2–3	85
14:13	86, 125, 125n32, 131, 222, 231, 258, 274, 275n49, 277, 277n56, 278, 279, 280n61, 283, 290	16:2	85, 163, 219, 306	17:3	121n14, 205
		16:3	306	17:3–6	306n51
		16:4	306	17:3–18	292
		16:4–5	163	17:4	208, 294
		16:5–6	53, 125n30, 163, 165, 210, 303n45	17:5	139, 205
14:14	121n14, 134, 196n8, 297, 298	16:5–7	85, 86, 107, 125, 207, 210, 220, 289, 300, 303, 305n50	17:6	53, 54, 71, 85, 107, 121, 121n14, 140n68, 165, 206n49, 207, 210, 212
14:14–16	298n33				
14:14–20	76, 110, 237, 263, 273, 297, 298n33, 299	16:5b	303		
		16:6a	303, 304	17:6–8	222
		16:6b	303	17:6b	206, 209n62
14:14–16:21	297	16:7	125n30, 165, 303n45, 304, 304n47, 305, 320	17:7	209n62
14:15	37, 298, 298n33			17:7a	206
14:16	298			17:8	206, 206nn48, 49; 250n41
14:17	37, 298	16:7b	304		
14:18	303n43	16:8	306n55	17:9	35, 38, 230
14:18–19	298	16:8–9	291	17:9–10	35
14:19	209, 298	16:9	75, 142, 163, 210, 307	17:11	106
14:19–20	76n36, 219, 299			17:12–13	310
14:19a	298				
14:20	299	16:10	219, 306	17:15	113, 198, 261n14

Index of Ancient Texts   375

17:16	140n68, 294, 326	18:21	212	20:4–6		53, 85, 86,
17:16–17	206	18:21–23a	85			113, 169, 283
17:17	101	18:21–24	101, 213n73,	20:5		281
17:18	38, 306n51, 326		258, 265, 267,	20:6		86, 125n32,
18	38, 73, 141n73,		268, 268n26			130n45, 231, 258,
	162n49, 204n42,	18:22	213n73			277, 281, 283
	211, 265, 269,	18:22–23a	213	20:7–10		101, 202
	294n21, 310, 311	18:22–23	212	20:8		114, 203
18:1	121n14	18:23	114, 139, 142	20:10		114, 173,
18:1–24	125, 152,	18:23–24	204n39,			203, 272n36
	158, 219		265, 269	20:11		121n14
18:2	204n39, 206, 213,	18:23b–24	85, 107, 207,	20:11–15		263, 273
	264, 264n20,		209, 213	20:11–22:5		263
	265, 326	18:23c–24	267	20:12		121n14
18:2–3	85, 264, 265	18:24	53, 107,	20:12–13		279
18:2–8	258, 265, 269		140n68, 165,	20:14–15		173, 281
18:3	205, 208, 208n55,		209n59, 210, 212	20:15		85, 319
	264, 265, 268n26	19:1–2	168, 268	21		315n5
18:4	39n29, 71, 84, 89,	19:1–8	258, 259n7	21–22		294n23
	140, 231, 235n21,	19:2	53, 85, 86,	21:1		121n14
	258n5, 266, 269,		131, 140n68,	21:1–4		281
	294, 312		204n39, 210	21:1–8		85
18:4–5	265	19:2–5	125n30	21:1–22:5		163, 296, 339
18:4–8	163, 268	19:3	85	21:1–22:19		294n23
18:5	208	19:5	131	21:2		121n14, 170
18:5–6	209	19:6	168	21:3		196n8
18:6	204n39, 209n60,	19:6–8	86	21:3–4		136, 170, 172,
	266, 279	19:6b–9	170			221, 282
18:6–7b	266n24	19:7–8	281, 294	21:4		157, 220, 348
18:6–8	266	19:8	347	21:5		131, 136, 196n8
18:6b	267	19:9	86, 121, 125,	21:5a		125
18:7	45, 204n39, 266		125n32, 131, 136,	21:5b		125
18:7–8	85, 206, 212,		231, 232, 258, 283	21:6		221
	252n44, 346	19:10	71, 132, 135,	21:6–8		125
18:7b	67		234, 316	21:7		170, 221
18:8	67, 212, 267	19:11	121n14, 196n8	21:7–21		221
18:9	45, 212, 326	19:11–21	110, 220	21:8		76, 86, 86n59,
18:9–20	212, 265,	19:11–20:15	237			172, 173, 222,
	310n69	19:13	132			283, 348
18:10	212, 306n51	19:15	110, 209	21:9		134, 170, 292
18:11	212	19:17	121n14	21:9–22:5		136, 294,
18:11–13	45, 310n69	19:17–18	111			294n21
18:12–13	208	19:17–21	101	21:10–22:5		292
18:13	45n45, 46, 74	19:18	73, 74	21:11		134
18:14	212	19:19	121n14, 280,	21:12		32
18:15	212		280n61	21:12–14		171n62
18:16	306n51	19:20	107, 114, 139,	21:14		32, 347
18:17	212		173, 219, 272n36	21:15		283
18:18	205, 326	20:1	121n14	21:18		134
18:19	212, 306n51	20:2	121n14	21:22		121n14, 171
18:20	207, 211n66	20:3	114, 203	21:22–23		221, 282
18:20–24	269	20:4	71, 133, 224, 281	21:23		76

Revelation (continued)		22:21	180	8:36	279
21:24	171			8:59–61	197
21:25	220, 348	**PSEUDEPIGRAPHA**		10	170n66
21:25–27	282	*Apocalypse of Abraham*	12	11–12	155n34
21:27	172, 173, 220,	29–30	306	11:39–12:1	214
	221, 348	29:15	300n36	11:40–46	161
22:1	221	30:1–8	300n36	12:11–12	39, 161
22:2	221, 282, 348			12:17–18	36n22
22:3	131, 220	*2 Baruch*	12, 48, 73, 120,	12:23–25	214
22:3–4	221		214, 269, 300	13:9–11	242
22:3–5	282	13:11–12	214	13:27–28	242
22:5	97	14:12–13	279	13:37–38	242
22:6	69, 131, 134,	21:6–7	196n10		
	136, 181n30,	22:1–2	121n15	*5 Ezra*	
	286, 296	23:4–5a	165n57	2:38–38	316
22:6–21	118	24:1–2	279	*Jubilees*	
22:6–22	25	29:2–3	217n80	35:17	127
22:6a	136	36:8	214		
22:6b	10, 136	37:1	214	*Letter of Aristeas*	
22:6b–7	136	39:5–7	39, 214	152	59n106
22:7	4, 10, 70n16, 86,	71:1	217n80	*Psalms of Solomon*	
	110, 116, 118,	*1 Enoch*	12, 100, 120,	2:10	302
	125n32, 134, 153,		124, 125, 165n57	2:15	304
	154, 181n30,	1–5	99	4:23	276nn50, 51
	190n56, 196n8,	1:9	219	5:16	276nn50, 51
	231, 234, 258,	5:2	99	6:1–2	276nn50, 51
	282, 283, 317,	6–16	127	8:8	302
	319, 346	20:1–8	196n9	8:23	304
22:8	121	20:7	97n12	10:1	276n51
22:8b–9	135	47:1–2	289n6	17:10	304
22:9	32, 69, 135, 136,	47:4	165n57	**Pseudo-Philo**	
	143, 153, 154, 234	56:5–7	309n62	*Biblical Antiquities*	
22:10	4, 10, 181n30	62:1–9	162n49	32	151
22:11	75	63:1, 12	162n49		
22:12	4, 10, 110,	67:8	162n49	*Sibylline Oracles*	12, 214
	111, 181n30,	97:8–9	252n45	3:350–352	46n56, 214n78
	196n8, 279	99:3	289n6	4:137–139	46n56, 214n78
22:13	202n29	100:3	76n36	4:145–148	46n56, 214n78
22:14	86, 125n32,	100:3–4	110, 299		
	231, 258, 283	*2 Enoch*	12	*Testaments of*	
22:14–15	221, 282			*The Twelve Patriarchs*	
22:15	76, 86, 172,	*4 Ezra*	12, 35, 48, 66, 73,	*T. Reuben*	
	173, 222, 283		120, 125, 153, 161,	4:6	59n106
22:16	32n8, 143		214, 258, 269,	*T. Levi*	12
22:17	170		300, 318	2–5	166, 196n10
22:18	10, 135	4:35–37	165n57	2	196n9
22:18–19	61n111, 135,	7:21–24	197, 272	3:4–5	97n12
	143, 317n7, 318	7:77	279		
22:19	10	7:78–87	272n35	**DEAD SEA SCROLLS**	
22:20	4, 10, 110, 135,	7:79	210n64	*The Seductress* (4Q184)	
	136, 181n30	7:81, 83, 87	210n64		293n20
22:20b	135	8:32	279		

Index of Ancient Texts   377

Exhortation to Seek Wisdom
(4Q185)   293n20
The New Jerusalem
(4Q554–555)   171n63
Temple Scroll (11QT)
                     171n63, 172
Thanksgiving Hymns
(Hodayoth)
1QH 2 [10].22   55
War Scroll
1QM 4.9   55

JOSEPHUS
War
1.13.1–9 §§248–270
                     309n62
1.13.2 §250   310n66
2.10.4 §197   56n87
2.14.9 §§305–308   56n90
2.17.2 §409   56n87
4.9.2 §502   36n22
5.1.1–5 §§1–38   306n51
7.6.6 §218   56

PHILO
Sacrifices
20–35   293n15
Special Laws
1.315–317   243n30

RABBINIC LITERATURE
B. Abodah Zarah
1.8a   56
1.11b   56
1.13b   56
1.14b   56
Exodus Rabbah
14.3   306n52
Leviticus Rabbah
6.6   306n52
Mekilta de Rabbi Ishmael
Beshallah 5.15   300n37
Midrash Psalms
22.3   306n52
27.1   306n52
136.7   300n37

GRECO-ROMAN
LITERATURE
Aelius Aristides
Orations
26.3   38
26.11–13   38, 208n55
Aeschylus
Agamemnon
1080–86   104n29
Aristotle
Nicomachian Ethics
8.14.4   260n11
Politics
1.4   44
Rhetoric   15, 16–17,
                     17n48, 18
1.1.10   297n30
1.2.3   22n59
1.2.4   22, 117
1.2.5   22
1.2.8   270n28
1.2.18   263n19, 305n49
1.3.1   90
1.3.1–6   79n43
1.3.3   83
1.3.5   20n56, 81n49
1.4–2.26   21n57
1.4.9   270n28, 305, 308
1.5.4   252
1.7.1–2   272
1.7.16   272
1.7.26   272
1.7.30   272
1.8.6   117
1.9.16–17   197n14,
                     261nn12, 13
1.9.19   197n14,
                     261nn12, 13
1.9.25   278
1.9.34   275
1.9.35–36   80, 275
1.9.38   87n63, 197,
                     262n15
1.9.40   23n66, 239,
                     270n28, 307
1.10   79n45
1.10.18   272
1.15   79n45
2.1.2   22
2.1.3   22n60, 117, 118

2.1.4   22
2.1.5   22n60, 117
2.1.8   22
2.1.9   192
2.2–11   22, 176
2.2.1   272
2.2.3   210
2.2.8   272
2.2.17   210
2.2.22   186
2.2.23   210
2.3.5   188n49, 210
2.4.2   186, 187, 199
2.4.4   187, 199
2.4.5   186, 199
2.4.6–7   187, 199
2.4.14   185, 186
2.4.16   186
2.4.17   186, 191
2.4.19   185, 186
2.4.27   186
2.4.29   186, 199
2.5.1   181, 274n41
2.5.1–15   195
2.5.2   181
2.5.3   183
2.5.4   218
2.5.5   183
2.5.8   219
2.5.10   216
2.5.14   181, 183n37
2.5.15   219
2.5.16   181, 185,
                     217, 220, 221
2.5.17   184, 221, 217
2.5.18   184, 220
2.5.21   184, 221
2.6.12   190n54
2.6.14–15   189n52
2.6.24   189n53
2.7   176
2.7.2   197, 261n12,
                     262n15
2.7.5   208n56
2.8.2   212
2.9.1   188n48, 200
2.9.5   200
2.9.9–10   202n31
2.9.11   188n48, 200,
                     201n24, 210
2.11.1   190, 222
2.11.3   190, 222

Index of Ancient Texts

Rhetoric (continued)
2.11.7 191, 224n92
2.18–19 23n65
2.18–26 79n45
2.20 23n65, 287
2.20.2 308
2.20.6 287
2.20.8 239, 270n28, 286, 287, 307
2.21 23n67
2.21.2 22, 232
2.21.6 234n19, 259
2.22 23n63
2.23–26 23n64
2.23.1 242
2.23.12 270n28, 310
2.23.14 270n30
2.23.19 242
2.23.21 278n57
2.23.25 305n48
2.24.1–10 231n6
3.1.5 214n77
3.9.8 252
3.14 24
3.14.6–7 109, 118n3
3.14.12 109, 118n3, 129
3.16.11 84n56, 286, 296
3.17.4 270n30, 307n57
3.17.16 124, 137n61
3.19 24
3.19.1 118n3, 137n61

Virtues and Vices
5.2 258n4

Athenaeus
Deipnosophistae
12.510 293n15

Aulus Gellius
Attic Nights
7.14.2–4 272n38

Cicero
Ad Atticum
6.5 38

De Inventione 17, 18
1.53.101 201n28, 202n33
1.53.101–1.56.109 177
1.53.102 203n36
1.55.107 211, 212

1.55.108 212

De Officiis
1.32.118 293n15

De Oratione 17n48

De Oratore 18
2.43.182 137n61
2.45.189–2.47.197 177, 182n33, 209n61, 216
2.51.205–2.52.211 177
2.51.206 186, 188, 197, 208n56, 261n12
2.51.208 188, 208n56
2.53.215–216 177, 194

Topica
55–56 233n13

Demetrius
On Style
5.292 140

Dio Cassius
Roman History
66.19.3 37n24

Dio Chrysostom
Orations 15
1.66–84 293n15
29.21 20n54
31 190n55
48.15–16 23

Dionysius of Halicarnassus
Epistulae 17n48

Epictetus
Diatribai
3.7.29 252n45

Hermogenes
Progymnasmata 17

Herodotus
History
1.189–191 309

Hesiod 23

Homer 23

Inscriptions
I. Eph.
18d.11–14 42n38, 195n6

Julian
Orations
2.57 293n15

Longinus
On the Sublime
15.1–2 177

Lucian
Alexander 133

Bis Accusatus
21 293n15

Hercules
4 206n49

Hermotimus
22–28 293n15

De Mercede Conductis
42 293n15

Nigrinus 45

Peregrinus 133

Vitarum Auctio 133

Rhetorum Praeceptor
6–7 293n15

Somnium
6 293n15

Livy
History of Rome
1.44 221

Martial
Epigrams
4.64 38

Maximus of Tyre
Orations
14.1 293n15

Nicolaus of Damascus
Life of Augustus
1 41, 196

Pausanius
Description of Greece
10.12.10 110

Philostratus
Vita Apollonii
4.38 200, 200n20
6.10 293n15

Index of Ancient Texts   379

Plato		6.2.24	213, 214n77	1.5.8	137n61
Gorgias		6.2.26	177, 209n61	1.6.9	22n61
526D–527A	273n39	6.2.26–30	216	1.10.18–1.15.25	235
Pliny the Younger		6.2.29–30	177	2.1.1–2.19.30	79n45
Epistles		6.2.29–32	180	2.30.48	201n28,
10.34	60n108	6.2.32	177		202n33
10.96	44n43	9.2.36	293n15	2.30.48–2.31.50	177
10.96–97	78n41	*Res gestae divi Augusti*		3.2.2–3.4.9	19n53,
Panegyric	51, 80		198n15, 261, 262		79n44
		34	262	3.2.3	88, 259
Plutarch		*Rhetorica ad Alexandrum*		3.3.4	84n54, 88, 197,
Moralia	108	1421b18–20	80		258n4, 259n8,
317	39	1421b21–1422b12	248		260n11
548–68	243n31	1421b21–1423a12	19n53,	3.3.5	239
1102C–D	62		79n44	3.8.15	20n56, 81n49
1125D–E	62	1421b28–31	80	3.10.18	21n58
Sertorius		1421b36–40	258n4	3.17.4	82n51
13–14	47, 267n25	1421b37–1422a2	197,	4.15.21	252
			259n8,	4.17.25–4.18.26	233n13
Pseudo-Isocrates			260n11	4.28.38	270n32
Ad Demonicum		1424b36–40	268	4.39.51	270
13	62	1425a2–4	268	4.50.63	203
Pseudo-Libanius		1425b38–41	80	4.53.66	203
Epistolary Styles		1426a22–23	197n14,	4.55.68	177
46	20n56		261n13,	**Silius Italicus**	
92	20n56		268n26	*Punica*	
		1426b25–28	89n71	15.1–132	293n15
Quintilian		1427b12–15	243	**Statius**	
Institutes	15, 17, 19	1427b31–35	20n56, 81n49	*Silvae*	
3.4.1–16	79n43	1428b12–17	23n66,	4.3.128–129	41
3.4.6	90		270n28,		
3.7.6–9	86n61		297n30,	**Suetonius**	51
3.7.7	260n9		307n57	*Nero*	
3.7.16	261n12, 262n15	1429a25–28	23nn65, 66;	57.2	37n24
3.7.28	80n47, 275		270n28, 308	*Domitian*	
3.8.7	118n3	1430a27–34	23n63	4	38n28
3.8.12	194n2	1430a40–1430b7	23n67	7.2	37n26
3.8.13	22n60, 117	1432a33–37	215n79	14.2	37n26
3.8.36	23n66	1434a35–37	232		
3.9–11	79n45	1436a33–37	118nn1, 3	**Tacitus**	
4.1.14–15	137n61	1436b8–12	118nn1, 2	*Agricola*	
4.1.28	202, 212	1437b18–21	139	30	44, 214
5.10.1–3	233	1439b15–18	194n2	*Annals*	
6.1.14	188n49, 210	1440a30–35	199	14.15	195n6
6.1.15	188n50, 202,	1440a30–39	188n47	*Histories*	
	205, 207	1440a34–39	200n23	1.11	36n22
6.1.18	177, 194, 207n52	*Rhetorica ad Herennium*		4.64.3	47, 267n25
6.1.20	177, 194		17, 18, 177	**Theon**	
6.1.23	211	1.2.2	79n43	*Progymnasmata*	17
6.1.46	177, 194	1.4.7	24, 118		
6.2.5	214, 214n77				

Thucydides		De Doctrina Christiana		Gospel of Thomas	238n26
History		1.36.40	159		
2.44	20n54	1.36.40–41	158	**Irenaeus**	
		1.36.41	158–59	Adversus Haereses	
Virgil				4.14.1	31
Aeneid	43, 105,	De Principiis		5.26.1	31
	108	2.11.2–5	5n16	5.30.3	37n25
1.236–237	38	**Clement of Alexandria**		**Justin Martyr**	
4.232	38	Paedagogus		Dialogue	
6.782	38	2.10.110	293n16	81.4	31
6.851–853	39	***Didache***		Second Apology	
Eclogae		10.7	10n32	11	293n16
4.1–10	105	11–13	32, 145		
Xenophon		11.3–13.7	10n32	**Martyrdom of Polycarp**	
Memorabilia		***Epistle to Diognetus***		12.2	58n99
2.1.21–22	293n14	5.1–5	349	13.1	58n99
		Eusebius		**Minucius Felix**	
EARLY CHRISTIAN LITERATURE		Ecclesiastical History		Octavius	
		2.20	33	6	38
Augustine		3.18.1–4	51n70	**Tertullian**	
City of God		3.28.1–2	32	Apology	
20	5n17	4.26.5–11	51n70	5.3–4	51n70

Index of Modern Authors

Applebaum, S., 56n9
Armstrong, Herbert W., 175n2, 217, 217n81, 218
Aune, David E., 13n38, 14n39, 17n48, 22n62, 32n8, 33n8, 34n13, 37n24, 38n27, 44n42, 52n79, 55n86, 57n98, 58nn99, 101; 97n12, 104n28, 108n41, 110n44, 121n13, 122n90, 130n45, 143, 143n82, 144n84, 162n49, 171nn63, 64; 172n68, 178, 178nn16, 17, 18; 179, 179nn19, 20, 24; 181n28, 185n43, 186n45, 189n51, 196n10, 199n17, 200n19, 201n25, 202nn29, 30, 32, 34; 203nn35, 37; 204nn40, 41; 205nn44, 46; 206n49, 207n50, 208n55, 209n60, 212n71, 213n74, 233, 233nn11, 14, 15, 17; 234n18, 236n22, 237n25, 238nn26, 27; 240n28, 243n30, 244n32, 247n35, 248n37, 38; 250n41, 252n45, 258n2, 262n17, 265n23, 285n1, 298n33

Balch, David L.,104, 104n30
Barnett, Paul, 41n33, 262n18
Barr, D. L., 3n5, 5n17, 123n21, 178n14, 199n18, 224n93, 225n96
Bartsch, S., 206n49
Bauckham, Richard, 46nn51, 56; 48n65, 76nn34, 35, 36, 37; 102n20, 150n12, 151, 151nn15, 16, 17, 18; 152n23, 153, 153n30, 156n38, 160n46, 163n53, 171n61, 200n20, 201n27, 202n29, 213n76, 214n78, 223n90, 226n100, 270n29, 283n68, 289n6, 298n33, 300, 300n38
Beale, G. K., 34n13, 55n86, 58n99, 150n12, 185n43, 236n22, 248n36, 249n38, 294n24, 295n27, 298n33, 300nn36, 37; 306nn52, 54
Beasley-Murray, G. R., 203n35

Becker, G. S., 274n41
Beckwith, I. T., 211n67, 277n55
Bell, A. A., Jr., 34nn13, 15
Berger, P. L., 66n2, 332n51, 334n59, 335, 335nn60, 61, 62; 337n65, 342, 342nn69, 70
Bertram, G., 125n32, 275n42, 277n56
Betz, Hans Dieter, 24n70
Bieder, W., 281n64
Biguzzi, G., 44n42
Bitzer, Lloyd F., 29, 29n2, 232n10, 233n16
Bloomquist, L. Gregory, 24n69
Blount, Brian, 8n28, 225n96
Böcher, Otto, 122n20, 281n64
Boesak, Allen, 7, 8n28, 324, 324n20
Bousset, Wilhelm, 38n29, 277n55
Brent, Allen, 37n26, 42nn36, 38; 44n42, 51n70, 58n100, 195n6, 196n10
Buchanan, G. W., 306n51, 309n62, 310n66

Caird, G. B., 61n110, 211n67, 283n67, 308n60
Cambier, J., 294n24
Carey, Greg, 8n30, 15n41, 57n97, 66n4, 75nn31, 32; 77, 77n38, 120n10, 121n11, 125nn29, 30; 126nn35, 36; 127n40, 130nn43, 44; 132n50, 133n52, 54; 135n57, 137n61, 138, 139nn64, 67; 140n69, 141nn73, 74; 142n76, 143,143n81, 153, 153n28, 154, 154n31, 180n25, 200n21, 201, 201n26, 211nn65, 66; 212n69, 230, 230n2, 264n21, 316, 316n6, 317, 317nn8, 9; 321, 322n17, 323, 323n18
Casey, Jay, 162n52, 163nn53, 54, 55, 56
Classen, C. Joachim, 178n13
Clemen, C., 122n17

381

Cohen, Shaye, 262, 262n16
Collins, Adela Yarbro, 33n10, 34n13, 43n40, 50n69, 51n71, 63n114, 69n13, 104n28, 121n13, 126n33, 175n3, 194n1, 200n23, 205, 205n45, 207, 208nn54, 55; 209n60, 211nn67, 68; 212n70, 219n82, 223, 223n90, 289n5
Collins, J. J., 13, 13n37, 94n5, 95n8
Conley, Thomas M., 232n10, 233n16
Cooper, John M., 177n9, 195n5
Corbett, E., 233n12
Cruz, V. P., 277n55, 281n64
Cushman, Philip, 334nn56, 57, 58
Cuss, Dominique, 202n30, 203n35, 295n25

Danker, F. W., xiii, 272n37
deSilva, D. A., 12n35, 15n41, 20n55, 34nn13, 17; 41n34, 50n69, 52n76, 77; 54n84, 59n105, 60n106, 62n112, 66nn1, 3; 72n19, 77n39, 81n48, 83n53, 86n60, 89n71, 91n72, 94n4, 95n8, 106n34, 119n4, 121nn13, 14; 123n24, 125n30, 135n58, 139n66, 140n69, 141n75, 142n78, 160n46, 175n3, 177n11, 178n17, 189n52, 191n57, 194n3, 195n4, 196n11, 197n12, 200nn19, 21, 22; 203n37, 206n47, 207n53, 220n84, 222n88, 223n91, 225n97, 258nn2, 3, 4; 259n8, 260n10, 261n14, 264n21, 269n27, 271n33, 272n37, 275n43, 284n69, 286n2, 291n10, 295nn25, 26; 321n16
Diefenbach, Manfred, 17n49
Downing, F. G., 34nn14, 16; 35n21
Drury, John, 2, 2n1
Duff, Paul B., 15n41, 48n63, 49n67, 50n69, 52n78, 53n81, 59nn103, 104, 105, 106; 60, 60nn106, 107; 61nn109, 110; 62n113, 66, 66nn4, 7; 67, 67n9, 68, 68n12, 69, 72nn19, 21; 73, 73nn22, 23; 74, 77n40, 78n42, 109n42, 112n47, 119n4, 139nn65, 68; 140nn68, 69, 70, 71, 72; 143, 143n80, 178n17, 184n41, 191n59, 203n37, 204n43, 252n44, 264n21

Elliott, John H., 25n74, 260n10
Engberg-Pedersen, Troels, 179nn23, 24; 183n35
Engelmann, H., 45n49
Engels, F., 35n18

Fee, Gordon D., 24n69
Fekkes, Jan, 122n20, 124n28, 150, 150nn12, 13; 152, 156n38, 294n24, 295n27
Finley, Moses I., 60n108
Foerster, W., 123n21
Ford, Josephine M., 61n110, 271n34
Frey, Jörg, 38n29, 42n39, 43n40, 103n24, 235n21, 258nn3, 5
Friesen, Steven, 42n36, 194n3, 203n35, 295n25

Furnish, V. P., 133n53

Gager, J. G., 66n2
Gammie, John G., 179n24
Garrow, A. J. P., 35, 35n20
Geertz, Clifford, 94n6, 95, 95n7, 96, 96n11, 98nn14, 15; 100n18, 101, 101n19, 102, 102n22, 115n53, 116nn54, 55, 56
Giessen, Heinz, 125n31, 276n45, 277n55, 280n61, 281n64, 282n65, 283n67
Glancy, Jennifer A., 45n45, 74n29
Glassman, R. M., 106n35
Glasson, T. F., 211n67
Grassi, Ernesto, 232n9
Gregg, Steve (ed.), 3nn2, 7, 8; 4nn10, 11; 7n25
Griffin, Miriam, 52n77
Guroian, Vigen, 332n52, 333
Gwyther, Anthony, 34n12, 41n34, 46nn54, 55; 47nn57, 60; 48n66, 71n17, 74n30, 203n38, 213n73, 267n25, 313n1, 342n71, 345n79

Hall, Robert G., 121n12
Hanson, K. C. (1996), 222n87, 275n43
Hanson, P. D. (1976), 66n2
Harrington, Wilfrid, 184n41, 277n55
Harris, Michael A., 260n9
Hartlib, Samuel, 2, 2n1
Harvey, Barry A., 332, 333, 333nn53, 54, 55; 336n64, 338n68, 343n72, 346n80
Hauck, F., 125n32, 274n42, 277n56
Havel, Václav, 345, 345n77
Hayes, John H., 56n87
Hemer, Colin J., 6n21, 30n4, 33n11, 34n13, 37n26, 42n36, 43nn40, 41; 55n86, 56n88, 57n98, 58nn99, 100; 61n110, 122n20, 124, 124n26, 127n39, 178n14, 236n22, 251n43, 295n25
Hengel, Martin, xi, 48n64
Hermansen, G., 60n108
Hollander, John, 295n27
Horsley, G. H. R., 60n108
Howard-Brook, Wes, 34n12, 41n34, 46n54, 55; 47nn57, 60; 48n66, 71n17, 74n30, 203n38, 213n73, 267n25, 313n1, 342n71, 345n79
Hurley, P. J., 233n12
Hylen, Susan E., 8, 8n29, 45n46, 204nn39, 40; 206n50, 326n28, 330n46

Janzen, E. P. (1994), 48n64
Janzen, W. (1965), 275n43
Johanson, Bruce C., 177n11
Johns, Loren L., 17n49, 86n62, 88n67, 89n69, 102n20, 103n24, 108n40, 138n62, 175n4, 176n5, 224n94
Jörns, Klaus-Peter, 196n10
Jung, C. G., 175n1

Keck, Leander E., 176n7
Kee, Howard C., 25n74
Keener, Craig, 55n86, 58n99, 251n43, 337n67
Kennedy, G. A., 14n40, 18n52, 68n11, 232, 232nn8, 9; 233n12, 236n23, 246n33, 280, 280n62
Kiddle, M., 211n67
Kim, Jean K., 328, 328n39
Kirby, John T., 82, 82n50, 85, 86n57, 110n45, 126n33, 128n41, 131n47, 132n51, 149n7, 178, 178n15, 179n21, 181, 181n32, 182, 230, 230nn4, 5; 255
Klauck, H.-J., 37n24
Knibbe, D., 45n49
Knight, J. M., 53n80, 71n17, 72n19, 107n39, 120n7, 126nn33, 37
Koester, Craig, 3n6, 224n95
Kraft, H., 277n55
Kraftchick, Steven J., 177nn9, 10; 178n12, 181n31
Kraybill, Nelson, 33nn8, 11; 40n31, 42n38, 45nn49, 50; 46nn51, 52, 53, 55; 47nn58, 59, 61, 62; 48n64, 50, 50n68, 53n80, 56, 56nn88, 89, 90, 92, 93, 94; 59n102, 60n108, 152, 152n22, 161, 161n47, 195n6, 203n38, 208n55, 209n59, 213n75, 221n85, 222n86, 283n66, 310nn67, 68, 69; 343n73
Krodel, Gerhard A., 184n41

Lawrence, D. H., 8n30, 172, 172n66, 175n1, 194n1, 200n23, 324
Lee, Michelle V., 95n9
LeGrys, A., 61n110
Leon, Harry J., 57n96
Levison, John R., 123n23
Lewis, I. M., 123n25
Lilje, Hans, 211n67
Lipinski, Eugene, 31n5, 35n18, 275n43, 276nn46, 48, 49
Llewelyn, S. R., 60n108
Lohmeyer, E., 283n67
Lohse, Eduard, 31n7, 174, 174n70, 236n22, 237n25, 248n38, 294n24
Loisy, Alfred, 236n22, 237n25, 242n29, 248n38, 251n42
Longenecker, Bruce W., 15n41, 66n3
Luckmann, Thomas, 332n51

Mack, Burton L., 18n52
Magie, David, 204n40
Malherbe, A. J., 20n56, 185n44, 186n45, 191n58
Mandell, Sara R., 56n87
Marcussen, A. Jan, 314, 314n3
Martin, Clarice, 74n29
Martin, Troy W., 177n9
Mede, Joseph, 2, 2n1

Meeks, W. A., 94n1
Mellor, R., 40n32
Moore, B. R., 15n41
Morton, Russell, 97n13, 195n7, 196n10, 260n9
Mounce, Robert H., 3n2, 5n18, 6n23, 31n6, 61n110, 277n55, 281n64
Moxnes, Halvor, 260n10
Moyise, Steven, 156n41, 157n42, 161n48, 294n24, 295nn25, 27
Mueller, Ekkehardt, 223n89
Mulligan, C. B., 274n41
Murphy, Frederick J., 236n22, 237n25, 242n29, 248n38, 249n39, 250n41, 251n42, 253n46, 273n40

Newport, Kenneth G. C., 3nn3, 4, 7; 5nn13, 15; 16n47
Nikolakopoulos, C., 15n41

Oehler, Klaus, 262n16
Olbricht, Thomas H., 177n11, 178n13, 195n5
Olbrechts-Tyteca, Lucie, 80n46, 130n43, 178n13, 219n83
O'Leary, S. D., 16n47, 105n31, 112n48, 126n33, 314, 314n2

Patte, Daniel, 152n24
Paulien, Jon, 148nn3, 4; 152n21, 155n36, 156n40, 295n27
Perdue, Leo G., 179n24
Perelman, Chaim, 80n46, 130n43, 178n13, 219n83
Peterson, Eugene H., 124n28, 158, 158n43, 229, 229n1, 230, 346n81
Pieters, Albertus, 7n24
Pippin, Tina, 8, 8n29, 206nn48, 50; 226n98, 292n12, 294n21, 324, 324nn21, 22; 325, 325nn23, 24, 25, 26, 27; 326nn28, 33; 327, 327nn35, 37; 329n43, 331nn48, 49, 50; 347n83
Popkes, Wiard, 179nn23, 24; 183n35
Price, S. R. F., 41n35, 106n34, 189n53, 194n3, 195n6, 196n11
Prigent, Pierre, 236n22, 237n25, 246n34, 250n41, 251n42, 253n46, 273n40, 277n55, 281n64, 283n67

Ramsay, W. M., 30n4, 57n98, 178n14, 295n25
Reid, Ronald F., 16n47
Resseguie, James L., 290, 290n9
Robbins, V. K., 231nn6, 7; 295, 295n28
Roberts, Keith A., 94n4
Robinson, J. A. T., 34n15
Roloff, Jürgen, 34n13, 184n41, 271n34, 281n64
Ross, M. K., 211n67

Rossing, Barbara R., 15n41, 25n73, 204n42, 285n1, 292, 292n13, 293, 293nn15, 17, 18, 19, 20; 294nn21, 22; 326, 326n34
Rowland, Christopher, 34n13
Royalty, Robert, 17nn49, 50; 24n72, 25n73, 45nn47, 48, 50; 46n50, 50n69, 57n97, 59nn102, 105; 61n111, 62n113, 66, 66nn4, 5, 6; 67, 67n8, 68, 68n10, 73, 73nn25, 26, 27; 74, 84n55, 86nn58, 59; 87n63, 94n3, 109n42, 122, 122n19, 125n30, 126nn33, 38; 131n46, 132n49, 140n69, 141n73, 142n77, 143, 143n79, 149nn5, 6; 150n10, 152, 152nn19, 20; 153, 153nn25, 26, 27; 154, 154n32, 155, 155nn34, 35, 36, 37; 156, 172, 172n65, 173n69, 174, 176n5, 179nn20, 22; 181n29, 200n19, 207n51, 211, 276n53, 285n1, 294n23, 318, 318n10, 319, 319nn11, 12; 320, 320n13, 321, 321n15
Ruiz, Jean Pierre, 72n20, 133n54, 150n10, 156n41, 294n24
Ryan, E., 233nn14, 16

Saffrey, H. D., 33n11
Scherrer, Steven J., 203n37
Schnelle, Udo, 38n27
Schüssler Fiorenza, Elisabeth, 5n12, 6nn19, 20; 7n27, 8, 8nn28, 29, 30; 15, 15nn42, 43, 44; 16nn45, 46; 18n51, 25n73, 29n1, 30, 30n3, 33n8, 43n40, 49n67, 51n70, 56n91, 57n97, 61nn110, 111; 67n8, 72n20, 76n33, 86n61, 87, 94, 94n2, 95n10, 102n23, 104n29, 107, 107n38, 114nn50, 51, 52; 119n4, 120nn5, 6, 8, 9; 122, 122nn16, 18; 124, 126n33, 132n49, 133n55, 137n61, 143nn82, 83; 150, 150nn9, 10, 11; 151, 151n14, 153n29, 156, 156n39, 163n54, 175n4, 176n5, 178nn17, 18; 181n29, 195n7, 197n13, 198n16, 200n19, 201n24, 209n58, 213n76, 217n80, 226, 226n99, 227, 227n101, 261n13, 281n64, 291n10, 308n59, 321n14, 324, 324nn19, 20; 326, 326nn28, 29, 30, 31, 32; 327n36, 328, 328nn38, 40; 329nn41, 42; 330nn45, 46, 47
Schütz, A., 332n51
Scobie, C. H. H., 295n25
Shea, William H., 309, 309nn61, 64, 65
Slater, T. B., 53n82, 54n84
Smallwood, E. M., 56n88
Smith, Ian (2002), 274n41
Smith, P. Christopher (1998), 176n4

Snyder, Lee (2000, 2004), 71n18, 91n72, 133n56
Stamps, Dennis L., 15n41
Starr, James, 179nn23, 24; 183n35, 185n44, 186n45
Stauffer, Ethelbert, 295n25
Strecker, Georg, 38n27, 276n47
Stringfellow, William, 344, 344n74, 345nn75, 76, 78
Sumney, Jerry L., 177n11, 178n12
Swartley, Willard, 223n91
Sweet, J. P. M., 275n44, 280n63
Swete, H. B., 147n1

Talbert, C. H., 61n110, 160n45
Thompson, James W. (2001), 363
Thompson, Leonard L. (1986, 1990), 33, 33nn9, 11; 41n34, 42n37, 44n42, 51, 51nn71, 72, 73, 74, 75; 52, 103n26, 295n25
Thuren, Lauri, 176n4

Ulrichsen, J. H., 35n19

van Henten, Jan Willem, 104nn28, 29
Vanhoye, A., 295n27
van Kooten, George H., 34n13, 36nn22, 23; 37nn24, 25
Vos L. A., 238n27

Wainwright, Arthur W., 3nn3, 5; 4n9, 5nn13, 14; 6n22, 16n47
Walvoord, John F., 5n12, 7n26
Watson, Duane F., xii, 18n52, 24n69, 177n11
Wengst, K., 46n55
Wettstein, Joannes Jacobus, 6n22
White, C. Dale (1998), 313n1
White, Ellen G. (1950), 223n89
Wilcock, M., 249n38
Wilder, Amos N., 122, 122n20
Wilson, J. Christian (1993), 34n13
Wilson, R. R. (1981), 66n2
Windisch, H., 276n47
Wink, Walter, 313n1
Witherington, Ben, III, 24n71, 34n12, 38n28, 41n33, 52nn77, 79; 53n79, 58n99, 59n105, 86n61, 87, 87n63, 88, 88nn64, 65, 66, 68; 89nn69, 70; 104nn27, 29; 106n36, 124n28, 131n48, 150nn8, 12; 175n4, 179n20, 184n41, 188n46, 189n51, 195n6, 196n9, 200n19, 206n47, 225n96, 230, 230n3, 235, 235n20, 285n1, 289n5, 291n10, 337n66

Index of Subjects

abyss, 2, 12, 94, 104n29
accommodation, 30, 49–50, 58–63, 112, 132, 157, 187, 194, 225–26, 242, 243n30, 277, 289, 320, 322, 340, 349
advantage, 5, 19–20, 22, 24n68, 30, 52–53, 57, 60n108, 78, 83, 85, 89, 89n69, 101–3, 139, 186, 235–37, 239–41, 247, 252, 253, 258–59, 259n8, 269, 273–75, 279–80, 282, 286, 290, 308, 311
agriculture, 46
alienation, 44n43, 85, 315, 333–37, 339, 341, 345
alliance, 83, 84n54, 85, 108, 114, 139, 161, 205, 205n44, 220–21, 258, 265, 268–69, 274, 280. *See also* allies; topics, argumentative: allies
allies, 101, 184–85, 206, 220, 265, 268, 289, 294, 309n62. *See also* alliance; topics, argumentative: allies
ally, 35n19, 101, 184–85, 199, 215, 221, 228, 268, 272, 277, 329, 331
amplification, 19, 87n63, 109–10, 129–30, 135, 135n57, 237, 244, 261–62, 262n16, 270, 270n32, 298
analogy, 65, 287. *See also* argumentation: from analogy
angel, angels, 1, 12, 32, 76–77, 83–84, 97–98, 100–101, 104–5, 107, 113, 119, 121, 123, 124n27, 125–28, 130, 134–37, 143–44, 153–54, 160n46, 165–66, 168n59, 171, 173, 181, 195–96, 206–7, 209, 209nn60, 62; 210, 215, 218, 220, 225, 231–32, 234, 238, 247, 258–60, 263–65, 267–74, 280–81, 289, 289n6, 292, 298–301, 303–4, 306n51, 307, 324n21, 352
Antipas, 49, 52–54, 90, 102, 107, 132–33, 137–38, 219, 224, 240n28, 242, 242n29
Apollo, 104, 104n29
apostle, apostles, 10–11, 31–33, 49, 49n67, 67n8, 74, 81, 114, 137, 145, 158, 171n62, 207, 227, 254, 269, 332, 339, 343, 347
approaches to interpretation, 2–8
   contemporary-historical, 6–8, 14–16
   feminist, 8
   idealist, 5–6, 7
   liberationist, 7–8
   as predictive prophecy, 2–5, 7, 10–11
      futurist, 3–4, 6
      historicist, 3
      preterist, 5, 7
   rhetorical-critical, 14–18
argumentation
   from analogy, 7, 23, 26, 82, 247n35, 251–54, 276n52, 287, 308, 311
   from consequences, 10, 23, 76, 79, 82–85, 87, 89–90, 129, 156, 184, 215, 222, 227, 233, 235–36, 239–47, 250–52, 254, 258, 259n7, 262n15, 263, 265, 267, 270–73, 274n41, 276, 278, 280–81
   from contrary, 26, 84, 233, 236–38, 241–42, 244–46, 254, 276, 283
   from historical precedent, 23, 59n105, 82, 102, 152, 156, 183n39, 225, 235, 240–41, 245, 253, 269–70, 282, 286–87, 297, 305–12, 343

argumentation (*continued*)
  rationales, 22, 160n46, 164, 171, 230, 232–34, 236, 239–40, 245–49, 251–52, 259–60, 261n13, 263–64, 266–68, 273, 276, 278–80, 281–82, 288, 298
  from revelation of contradictions, 242–43, 254
  See also enthymeme; topics, argumentative
arrangement, rhetorical, 15n41, 18, 24–25, 83.
  See also exordium; peroration
Artemision. *See* Temple of Diana
Asia Minor, 5–9, 14, 17n49, 31, 33–34, 37n24, 39–41, 44, 46n53, 47–48, 52, 56–57, 61, 63, 65–66, 68, 70, 103, 105–6, 143n83, 144, 194–95, 203n38, 205, 208n57, 215, 220, 225, 259, 272n38, 308, 319, 354, 359–60
Augustus, 35, 40–42, 44n44, 105–6, 195n6, 196, 198, 203n35, 261–62
  ideology of, 40–43 (*see also* Roman imperialism: emperor)
authoritarianism, 8n30, 69, 142–45, 174, 180, 255, 315–17, 340
authorship, 31–34
awe, arousal of, 36, 111, 121, 128, 181–82, 194–96, 198, 203, 205–6, 209n62, 222, 227, 235, 341

Babylon, 5, 25, 34, 37–38, 39n29, 45, 46n50, 53, 59, 67–68, 70n15, 71, 72n21, 74, 76, 78, 84–85, 87, 89, 101, 107–8, 113–14, 116, 121, 125, 137, 139–40, 141n73, 152, 162nn49, 51; 163, 192, 198, 200nn19, 23; 202, 204–7, 209–14, 219, 222, 226, 235n21, 250n41, 258, 258n5, 261n14, 263–69, 282, 292–94, 298, 300, 305, 306n51, 308–12, 315, 324–28, 328n38, 330–31, 336–39, 342–49, 360, 363
Balaam, 50, 59n105, 60n106, 138, 140, 183, 187–88, 188n46, 217, 225, 241–42
beast from the land, 37, 106, 112–14, 202, 203n35
beast from the sea, 35, 37, 104–6, 112–14, 199, 200n19, 203. *See also* imperial cult; Roman imperialism: emperor; worship: of the beast; worship: of the emperor
beatitude. *See* macarism.
benefaction, 41, 56, 83, 196–97, 232–33, 249–50, 260–61, 271–73. *See also* benefactor; beneficence; favor; grace; patronage
benefactor, 23, 41, 84, 190n55, 196–97, 199–200, 208, 233, 249, 260–61, 272. *See also* benefaction; beneficence; favor; grace; patronage

beneficence, 99, 104, 187, 197–99, 210, 214, 233, 249, 260n10, 261–62. *See also* benefaction; benefactor; favor; grace; patronage
Book of Life, 58, 85, 106, 110, 113, 206, 220, 247, 281
boundaries, group, 16, 57, 62, 75, 78, 135, 138, 140, 157, 187, 194, 314, 317–18, 331–35, 340, 346, 348
Branch Davidians, 16
bride, 2, 60n106, 114n49, 169–70, 213, 226n98, 264n21, 280–81, 292–94, 325–27, 330n47, 331, 346–47, 361

Caligula, 35n19, 52
cause, 23, 33, 38, 44, 60, 84n55, 88, 105, 121, 140, 165–66, 206, 219n82, 223, 249, 251n42, 257, 264, 267, 276, 276n51, 287, 290, 305n48, 312. *See also* topics, argumentative: similar causes
censure, 1, 20, 80–81, 81n49, 86–87, 186, 188, 231–32, 251n42, 268n26
Cerinthus, 32
character delineation, 203
civil wars, 36, 39–41, 107, 216, 310n68. *See also* Year of the Four Emperors
colonialism, 7–8, 49, 316, 321, 323, 336
commandments (of God), 70, 72, 85, 102, 111, 112, 132, 144, 154–55, 160, 164–65, 173, 175n2, 190n56, 197, 210, 212, 220, 227, 241, 259–60, 271, 273–74, 277, 279, 296, 303, 317, 319–20, 340, 346–47
compromise, 55–56, 58–59, 69, 82, 90, 128, 160, 199, 222, 241–42, 264, 279–80
conclusion, 23, 43, 72n21, 75, 89n70, 136, 154, 161–62, 179, 207, 223n89, 226n98, 231n6, 232, 236–37, 238n27, 245, 252–53, 273
confidence, 68, 164, 279, 341
  arousal of, 22, 129, 176, 181–82, 184–85, 192–94, 217, 220–22, 225, 228
conquering. *See* overcoming
consequences. *See* argumentation: from consequences
contradiction. *See* argumentation: from revelation of contradictions
contrary. *See* argumentation: from contrary
courage. *See* topics, argumentative: courage
covenant, 7, 10, 55, 78, 161–62, 164, 166, 170, 186, 273, 289
creation, 1, 12, 110, 112, 125, 160n46, 198, 214, 271, 307n56, 328, 348
crisis, focal, 109–12, 280, 297–300
critical distance, 69–71, 78, 90, 115, 204–5, 228, 268, 332, 335, 341–42
curse, 134–35, 137, 143, 187, 220, 223, 317–19

date, 34–37
Dea Roma, 204, 327. See also Dea Roma coin
Dea Roma coin, 38n27, 108, 204n40
deinosis, 213–15, 341
delay of divine vengeance, 165n57, 207, 243
deliberation, 80, 89n70, 215n79, 239, 241, 246–47, 251, 268, 275–76, 297. See also deliberative rhetoric
deliberative rhetoric, 19–21, 23–24, 78–85, 87–91, 117, 129, 194, 231, 235, 239, 248, 250, 254, 258–59, 260n8, 264–65, 269–70, 275, 284, 286, 294, 296, 296n29, 297n30, 307, 307nn57, 58; 311. See also deliberation
Dionysius of Alexandria, 31–32
disadvantage, 30, 85, 237, 273, 280
disgrace, 20n56, 85, 210, 225, 237, 252, 280. See also dishonor; shame
dishonor, 265, 268, 271, 273
disincentive, 222, 238, 266
disloyalty, 128, 273
dispensationalism, 4
divi filius, 105, 194, 202
domination systems, 8, 69, 74, 77–78, 135, 139, 160–62, 203, 206, 208, 228, 268, 311–12, 313n1, 320–21, 323, 328–39, 341, 343–49
Domitian, 7n26, 33–37, 40–42, 49, 51–53, 100, 104n29, 195, 310
dragon, 1–2, 12, 37, 43, 86, 95, 102, 104–6, 112–14, 139, 198–99, 201–3, 206n49, 210, 223, 258, 262, 272, 325, 342, 344, 348
dualism, 13, 112–15

economic exploitation, 46n50, 48, 51, 57, 59, 68, 73–74, 204n39, 205, 214, 265, 329, 343–44
economic justice, 73–74. See also economic exploitation
ecstasy, ecstatic experience, 11, 120–24, 131, 144, 152n21, 156, 180n27, 229, 232
Eden, 2, 12, 346
elite, 34, 39, 47, 73–74, 267, 294, 325–26, 328
emulation, 20, 80, 86, 190–92, 194, 222–27, 245, 247, 341
enmity, 176, 187–89, 192–94, 199–200, 202–3, 205, 207, 211, 213–14, 227, 269, 341
enthymeme, ix, 22–23, 197, 210, 230–34, 242, 254, 257–58, 260, 262n15, 263–64, 267, 270, 276, 278, 280, 284, 287n3, 305, 312
  definition of, 232–34
Ephesus, 32, 40, 42, 45, 47, 49, 54n85, 62n113, 63, 69–70, 99, 137, 144, 187, 190n54, 191n60, 195, 204, 237n25, 238

oracle to, 3n8, 53, 63n113, 82, 182–83, 186–87, 189, 235–38, 246, 252n44, 254, 279
Epicureans, 62
epideictic rhetoric, 20–21, 24, 24n68, 78–81, 81n49, 85–87, 88n67, 90–91, 231, 264, 275, 284, 296
eschatology, 105, 354, 361
ethos, appeals to, 15n41, 17, 22, 26, 33, 62n113, 66n4, 87, 96, 116–74, 177n9, 179–80, 196n8, 235, 297, 315–24, 339–40
  and amplification, 129–30
  and apocalyptic genre, 119–21
  authentication of Revelation, 134–37
  critique of John's, 142–45, 315–24
  deconstruction of rival voices, 137–42
  and John's role as "prophet," 130–34
  prejudice, creating and dispelling, 21–22, 24, 67n8, 77, 118, 137, 139, 296
  and testing prophets, 143–45, 158–74
  and "voice" in Revelation, 119–21, 124–29, 178–80, 238
  See also authoritarianism
ethos (social-scientific term), 103, 111, 222, 234, 260n10, 314
evangelism, 4n8, 5, 168, 213. See also witness
Exodus, 7, 108, 161–64, 218, 288, 290–92, 300, 306–8
new Exodus, 102n20, 162–64, 172, 291
exordium, exordia, 24–25, 109–10, 118, 129, 144
expediency. See topics, argumentative: expediency; topics, argumentative: relative expediency

faithfulness, 7, 14, 26, 68n12, 75, 85, 103, 111–12, 126, 132, 158, 159n44, 160n45, 222, 268, 273n40, 277–78, 283, 322, 340, 343. See also loyalty
favor (grace), 11, 14, 39, 47, 51–52, 63, 117, 128, 132, 134–36, 176, 184, 197, 215, 217, 222, 232, 234, 253n46, 272, 274–82, 321, 346. See also benefaction; benefactor; beneficence; grace; ingratitude; patronage
fear, 36, 62, 72n19, 76–77, 83, 111, 113, 130n45, 151, 160, 162n49, 168, 195, 221, 225, 227, 239–40, 244, 259, 271n34, 273, 279, 296, 300, 302, 318–19, 341, 345
  arousal of, 22, 110, 128–29, 175n2, 181–84, 192–94, 200n23, 209n62, 215–220, 228, 341
feasible. See topics, argumentative: feasibility
feminist criticism, 8, 326, 330, 358, 364
fiscus Iudaicus. See temple tax
Flavian dynasty, 36–37, 51–52, 214

forensic (judicial) rhetoric, 19–21, 24, 57, 78–79, 79n45, 81–82, 85, 87–89, 177, 188n49, 214, 215n79, 235, 240n28, 268–69, 286–87, 296, 302, 305, 307n58
friendship, 132, 176, 185–87, 189, 192–93, 199, 235

Gaius (Christian author), 31–32
Galba, 35–36
genre, literary, 9–14
  apocalypse, 11–14, 70–71, 84, 93–97, 119–21, 336–39
    Revelation as apocalypse, 97–116
  letter, 9–10, 14
  prophecy, 10–11, 14
genre, rhetorical, 19–21, 78–91
  deliberative, 19–21, 23–24, 78–85, 87–91, 117, 129, 194, 231, 235, 239, 248, 250, 254, 258–59, 260n8, 264–65, 269–70, 275, 284, 286, 294, 296, 296n29, 297n30, 307, 307nn57, 58; 311 (see also deliberation)
  epideictic, 20–21, 24, 24n68, 78–81, 81n49, 85–87, 88n67, 90–91, 231, 264, 275, 284, 296
  forensic (judicial), 19–21, 24, 57, 78–79, 79n45, 81–82, 85, 87–89, 177, 188n49, 214, 215n79, 235, 240n28, 268–69, 286–87, 296, 302, 305, 307n58
  mixed, 20–21
  Revelation as deliberative, 82–85
  Revelation as epideictic, 85–87
  Revelation as forensic, 87–89
good news, 40–41, 160n46
grace, 9, 106, 119, 132, 178, 195. See also benefaction; benefactor; beneficence; favor; ingratitude; patronage
gratitude, 23, 41–42, 60, 63, 84n54, 98, 106, 141, 173, 176n8, 186, 189, 193–94, 196–98, 200, 203, 205, 208, 210, 215, 227, 249, 259n8, 260, 261n12, 271–74, 341

heaven, heavens, 11–12, 45n50, 53, 87, 94, 97–98, 105, 121n15, 139–40, 166, 170, 265–66, 320, 330, 335
heavenly beings, 1, 2, 12, 97, 99, 104, 114, 125, 127–28, 131, 133, 137, 166, 181, 196n9, 207, 220, 266
heavenly worship, 1, 53, 114–15, 195n7, 196n10, 204, 210, 224, 262, 268, 271, 305. See also worship of God
Hebrew Bible. See Old Testament
honor, 20, 23, 41–42, 60n108, 71, 76–78, 80–81, 83, 86, 89–90, 97, 113, 133–34, 141, 160n46, 164, 173, 189nn52, 53; 190–91, 196–97, 202, 205, 210, 214, 220, 222, 224–25, 227, 232–33, 244, 259–60, 262, 271–72, 274–84, 311, 338, 340. See also, topics, argumentative: honor
honorable, topic of the, 19, 23, 79, 88, 89n70, 102–3, 190–92, 225, 227, 235, 244, 246–47, 252–53, 257–58, 265, 271, 273–84. See also honor
Horus, 104
Hydra, 105, 200n20

idolatry, 43, 44n43, 47–49, 59–60, 68, 71, 72nn19, 21; 78, 85, 90, 99, 103, 111, 114, 137, 139–41, 154, 157, 159–61, 173, 192, 194, 203, 205, 219, 227, 235n21, 241–42, 266, 271–74, 289, 296, 302n42, 303, 305, 320, 322–23, 343–44, 346. See also worship: of idols
idols, food sacrificed to, 59–63, 72n19, 140, 160, 184n41, 194, 241–42, 332
image of the beast, 36, 36n23, 42, 198, 200, 203, 242, 354. See also worship: of the beast
imitation of Christ, 102, 223, 240, 245, 253, 342–43
imminence, 4–5, 10, 109–110, 129, 135, 148, 153, 180–85, 215, 218, 234, 239, 250, 259, 265, 276, 282
imperial cult, 30, 36–37, 39–44, 47–49, 54n85, 55, 67, 71, 99, 106, 106n34, 114, 141, 160, 182, 189, 193–96, 196n10, 198, 200, 202n31, 203, 203n35, 271–72, 274, 274n41, 278, 281, 284, 295n25, 296, 353–54, 356, 358, 360–62, 364
imperial edict, 178n18, 179
incentive, 5, 222, 238, 240, 250, 253, 273
indignation, 22, 125, 138, 176–77, 187–89, 193–94, 198, 200–211, 213–14, 227, 266n24, 292n11, 341
inexpedience, 88, 241, 250, 264–65, 269–70, 273, 307n57. See also topics, argumentative: expediency
ingratitude, 210, 271–72, 278
injustice, 48, 71–75, 88, 201, 203–8, 211n66, 218, 264–65, 270, 289, 308, 328n38, 330n47, 343
inspiration, 7n24, 33n8, 121n12, 128, 145, 148, 152n21, 155n34, 166, 243n30, 316
intertexture, viii, xii, 26, 123, 148, 249, 270, 285–86, 288n3, 294–95, 295nn25, 27; 297, 299–300, 305–8, 310–12, 355, 364
invention, rhetorical, 15, 17n50, 21–23, 27, 79n45, 130, 149, 156n38
Isis, 47, 104

Index of Subjects 389

Israel, 7, 11, 50, 55, 60, 73, 77–78, 102–3, 119, 127, 138–39, 159, 161, 167, 169, 171, 187, 188n46, 203n37, 204n41, 217n80, 241–42, 249, 260n8, 262, 277, 288, 301–3, 305, 308–9, 311, 323, 327, 347

Jerusalem, 37, 119, 169–70, 200n19, 204n41, 206n50, 304, 306n51, 309n62, 322, 347
 destruction of, 5, 12, 37, 219n82
Jesus
 death of, 113, 128, 197, 201, 224n93, 227, 261, 283, 287n3, 331, 342, 344
 sayings of, 155, 172–74, 238, 246–47, 257, 280n59, 286, 298n33, 300n35, 317
Jewish revolt, 44, 57, 332
Jezebel, 32, 50, 59–63, 66, 67n8, 68–70, 72, 72n21, 77–78, 83, 86, 86n59, 114, 116, 119, 132, 137–40, 140n69, 142n77, 158, 183–84, 184n41, 187–89, 194, 217, 225–26, 243–45, 264, 264n21, 289, 294, 300, 317, 319–22, 325, 328, 330, 330n44, 332–33, 339–40
Joachim of Fiore, 3
Jonah, 11
Judgment, Last, 2–3, 12–13, 76–77, 83–84, 100–101, 107, 109–12, 115, 130, 162n49, 168, 172–74, 197, 216, 219, 234, 236–37, 254, 259, 261, 263–64, 266, 271, 279, 282, 286, 297–300, 308, 343–44
judgment, vindication, 11, 14, 43, 75–77, 82–84, 87–89, 98, 100–101, 107–8, 111–12, 125, 130, 141n73, 151, 160n46, 164–68, 173, 184, 186, 197, 205, 207, 210–12, 215–16, 219, 224n93, 225, 234, 237, 245–46, 250n41, 254, 259, 261, 263–64, 266, 268–69, 271, 282, 287–92, 296, 300–305, 307–8, 310–12, 330, 343–44, 347–48. *See also* Judgment, Last
Jupiter Capitolinus, 56–57
justice, 53, 72–75, 82, 84n54, 86, 88–89, 107–8, 165, 167–68, 188n48, 200, 203–8, 213–14, 240, 258, 263–64, 268–69, 281, 289n5, 300–305, 308, 312, 320, 323–25, 330n47, 334, 337, 341, 344, 347. *See also* topics, argumentative: justice
juxtaposition, 24, 98, 112–14, 184, 204, 216–18, 225–27, 278, 292–94

kingdom of God, 2–3, 4n8, 33, 68n12, 75–76, 85, 102, 105, 107, 112–13, 128, 132, 162, 163n53, 167–68, 171–73, 197, 201n24, 261, 281, 283, 290, 297, 334, 337, 346–47. *See also* Reign of God
Koinon Asias, 40, 41n34, 52, 105, 203n35

lake of fire, 2, 12, 85, 107, 172, 204n39
Lamb, 1–2, 24, 53, 75–76, 85–86, 88n67, 97–98, 99n17, 100–102, 106, 109–10, 112–15, 163, 167–68, 171, 182n33, 194, 196–98, 201, 209n62, 210, 216–17, 220–21, 223, 224n93, 226–28, 232, 261–62, 270–71, 277, 280–81, 283, 287n3, 289–90, 292, 294, 300, 331, 334, 338, 342, 344
 as symbol, 101–2, 224n94 (*see also* imitation of Christ)
Laodicea, 31, 40–41, 50, 54n83, 59, 63, 67–70, 93, 128, 144, 190–91, 194, 205, 244, 320, 333–34, 344, 346
 oracle to, 3n8, 46, 59n102, 62n113, 67, 83, 111, 190–92, 236, 245, 248n36, 250–54, 280n60, 344
legitimation, 11, 13, 32n8, 37–48, 55, 61n110, 72, 74, 78, 94, 96, 103, 107, 114, 121, 125n30, 141, 149n5, 158, 161, 166, 195, 198n15, 203, 215, 219, 226–27, 261–62, 264, 274, 311, 315, 321, 326–27, 332, 337, 343, 347–48
Leto, 104
liberationist, 7–8
liturgy, 72, 98, 104, 143, 160, 164–67, 210, 260, 289, 315, 318, 340
logos, appeals to, 17, 22–23, 26, 229–312, 342–43
 and Christian worldview, 236–38, 240, 242, 244, 246, 253–54, 279
 enthymematic elaboration, 230–34, 235–55, 287n3 (*see also* enthymeme)
 and intertexture, 294–312
 in macarisms, 274–84
 markers of argumentative texture, 230–31, 234
 narrative logic, 230, 235, 286–94
 radical rhetoric, 232, 235–37, 246, 252, 254, 280
 stasis, 110n45, 235, 236, 239, 245, 247, 250–51, 254
 in the seven oracles, 235–55
 in the visions, 257–84
 See also argumentation; topics, argumentative
love, 62n113, 67, 70, 73–74, 82, 111, 128, 158–59, 161, 167, 172, 177, 183, 186–89, 191, 236–38, 248, 252–53, 255, 321, 327, 342–43
loyalty, 41, 47–48, 52, 54, 56, 59n106, 63, 69, 83, 86, 90, 110, 126, 128, 138, 141, 159, 161, 164, 168, 173, 194, 228,

loyalty (continued)
  240, 248–50, 273–74, 277–79, 283, 289, 332. See also faithfulness
luxury, 37, 45, 47, 71n18, 108, 161–62, 208, 264, 266–67, 335, 341, 343

macarisms, 86, 125n32, 134–37, 222, 231, 234, 258, 274–84, 319
martyrs, 1, 31, 36n23, 52, 52nn78, 79; 53, 53n79, 55, 58n99, 107, 125n30, 132, 165, 207, 211, 211n66, 225, 228, 240n28, 269, 277, 277n55, 281, 283, 289–90, 295n29, 303n45, 304, 314, 320, 332, 336, 342, 358–59
maxim, 22, 233–34, 259
merchants, 45–47, 56, 71, 73, 162n49, 204n39, 208, 212, 264, 267, 310–11
millennium, 3, 5, 5n14, 360
mortal wound, 35–36, 106, 112, 201

narration, narrative, viii, 9, 11–13, 24, 54, 58, 71n18, 75, 84, 84n56, 85, 87–90, 93–94, 100–101, 110, 110n45, 112, 115, 123, 137, 149–50, 154, 165, 173n69, 180, 198, 204n39, 208–9, 211, 213, 216, 230, 235, 243, 248, 261–63, 270, 281, 285–86, 289–90, 292, 294–96, 298, 303–9, 312, 325, 361–62
necessary sign, 263, 305
neōkoros, 41–42, 189n53
new earth, 2–3, 13, 170
new heaven, 2–3, 13, 170
new Jerusalem, 2, 5, 12, 25, 59, 68, 76–78, 87, 113n49, 134, 136, 140, 143, 168–72, 204, 220–22, 226n98, 248n38, 282–83, 292–94, 319, 328n38, 331, 339, 341, 342n71, 346–49
Nicolaitans, 49–50, 59–63, 66, 67n8, 70, 72, 83, 86, 114, 119, 132, 137–40, 182, 187–90, 191n60, 194, 225, 241–42, 272n38, 289, 294, 300, 315, 319–20, 330n44, 333, 339

Old Testament (Hebrew Bible), 147–74, 294–312
  anthological versus exegetical use in Revelation, 149–52, 158–59
  critique of John's use of, 153–58
  explicit references to, 153–54, 156
  John's alignment with, 158–74
  See also intertexture
orbis terrarum, 38, 45, 54, 106
Osiris, 104
overcoming, 70–71, 82, 85–86, 100–102, 107–8, 115, 161, 169–70, 191, 192n61, 206n48, 221, 223–24, 240, 245, 247, 249n38, 253, 277, 300, 303, 305, 316, 342, 344

parody, 43n41, 112–14, 201, 204, 258, 260n8
partnership, 71, 115, 139, 141, 204–5, 232, 264–65, 267–69, 296, 312, 329, 348
Passover, 101, 102n20, 163, 261n13
pathos, appeals to, 17, 22, 26, 96, 117, 175–228, 341
  awe, 36, 111, 121, 128, 181–82, 194–96, 198, 203, 205–6, 209n62, 222, 227, 235, 341
  confidence, 22, 129, 176, 181–82, 184–85, 192–94, 217, 220–22, 225, 228
  deinosis, 213–15, 341
  emulation, 20, 80, 86, 190–92, 194, 222–27, 245, 247, 341
  enmity, 176, 187–89, 192–94, 199–200, 202–3, 205, 207, 211, 213–14, 227, 269, 341
  fear, 22, 110, 128–29, 175n2, 181–84, 192–94, 200n23, 209n62, 215–20, 228, 341
  friendship, 185–86
  gratitude, 63, 141, 189, 193, 196–98, 200, 203–8, 210, 215, 227, 261n12, 341
  identifying, 176–78
  imminence, topic of, 109–10, 129, 180–85, 215, 218, 250, 282
  indignation, 22, 125, 138, 176–77, 187–89, 193–94, 198, 200–211, 213–14, 227, 266n24, 292n11, 341
    against emperor, 200–203
    and God's anger, 209–11
    against Rome, 203–9, 214–15
  pity, 22, 176–77, 205, 207n52, 211–13
  in seven oracles, 175–92
  shame, 22, 176, 189–93
  in visions, 193–228
Patmos, 29n1, 33, 33n11, 132, 351, 355, 361
patriarchs, 32, 171n62
patriarchy, 8, 329, 331
patronage, 23, 41n34, 54, 60n108, 61, 104, 138, 141, 187, 232–33, 249–50, 260, 271–73. See also benefaction; benefactor; beneficence; grace; ingratitude
Paul, 5, 9, 10n33, 11, 17n48, 20, 32, 33n8, 54, 54n85, 57, 58n99, 60–61, 61nn110, 111; 65–66, 69, 73, 77, 81, 87, 107n37, 119–20, 133n53, 143–44, 148, 170, 176n7, 236, 271, 349, 351, 353–55, 358–60, 363–64
pax Augusti. See Roman peace.
pax Romana. See Roman peace.
Pergamum, 40–43, 49, 52n78, 53, 55, 59n105, 63, 70, 83, 137, 183, 187, 188nn46, 47; 189, 191n60, 195n6, 204, 272, 330n44, 333, 346
  oracle to, 3n8, 50, 52n78, 59n105, 183, 186–89, 192, 205, 236, 241–43, 246, 252n4
peroration, 24, 110, 118, 181n30

Index of Subjects   391

persecution, 3n8, 29n1, 34, 49–55, 57, 65–66, 70, 107, 109n42, 219n82, 250n41, 277n56, 314, 354
personification, 203, 204n42, 268, 293
Philadelphia, 41, 49, 53, 55, 58n100, 59, 63, 69–70, 137, 187
  oracle to, 3n8, 83, 184–85, 187, 192, 247–50
pity, 22, 176–77, 205, 207n52, 211–13
Pliny the Younger, 34, 44n43, 60n108, 78n41, 80, 99
Pontifex maximus, 106
postcolonialism, 47, 321
poverty, 30, 50, 54, 59, 185, 191, 222, 239, 329, 344
praise, 1, 20, 80, 81, 81n48, 86, 87n63, 88n67, 97, 107, 113, 125, 141, 166, 185–86, 189, 191n60, 195n6, 196, 198, 224, 231–32, 242, 260n9, 261n12, 275, 294n23, 361
prayer, 289–90, 304, 332, 345
precedent. *See* argumentation: from historical precedent
prejudice, 99, 123, 143–44, 318, 330n47
  creating and dispelling, 21–22, 24, 67n8, 77, 118, 137, 139, 296 (*see also* ethos)
premise, 2–3, 5–6, 17n49, 66, 165, 197, 232–33, 236–37, 241, 244–45, 249, 249n40, 252–54, 260–61, 268, 270n28, 279, 288, 303–4, 312
Priene inscription, 40, 105, 105n31
progymnasmata, 15n41, 17, 17n49, 254
prophecy, 4, 7, 13n36, 14, 37, 45, 67, 116, 120, 128, 134–36, 148, 153–54, 174, 190n56, 232, 234, 276, 282–83, 316, 318–19, 343, 346
  early Christian, 10–11, 33, 50, 63, 145, 238n27, 264, 286, 296, 317n7
prophet, prophets, 10–11, 18, 32–33, 48, 50, 52n78, 59nn102, 105; 61n110, 63, 66–69, 73–74, 107, 109, 111, 114, 119, 121, 130–32, 135–40, 142–45, 149n5, 153–54, 157–59, 161–63, 165, 167–70, 172, 174, 184, 187–88, 200n19, 202, 207, 209, 224–28, 236, 238n27, 243, 264, 267, 303–5, 311, 316–17, 320, 322–23, 330, 332, 334, 338–40, 343
prophetic school, 32n8, 69, 143–44
  power struggle between, 48, 59n102, 66–69, 113n62, 130
  testing of, 49, 69, 120–21, 144–45, 158, 174, 340
prosōpopoiia, 293
Providence, *Providentia*, 40–41, 43, 104–5, 108
prudence, 19
pseudonymity, 13n36, 31n5, 32, 125–26, 126n35, 138

public discourse, 17n50, 27, 39–40, 43–44, 70, 74, 104–6, 106n34, 108, 199, 203, 205–6, 262
Python, 104

Qumran, 12, 55, 171, 202n29, 302n42

radical rhetoric, 232, 235–37, 246, 252, 254, 280
Rapture, 4–5
rationale, 22, 160n46, 164, 171, 230, 232–34, 236, 239–40, 245–49, 251–52, 259–60, 261n13, 263–64, 266–68, 273, 276, 278–80, 281–82, 288, 298
recapitulation, 111, 290
Reign of God, 165–72, 346–49. *See also* kingdom of God.
religio licita, 58
repentance, 10–11, 83, 163, 188, 243, 290–92. *See also* witness: and conversion
resurrection, 5, 225, 281, 283, 342
  of Christ, 35n19, 102, 128, 182, 240, 342
return of Christ, 3, 5, 57, 100, 110, 126, 129, 133n55, 182, 234, 237, 250, 280, 283. *See also* Judgment, Last
rhetorical criticism
  overview of theory, 18–25
  and Revelation, 14–18, 25–27
  See also argumentation; arrangement, rhetorical; *ethos*, appeals to; exordium; genre, rhetorical; invention, rhetorical; *logos*, appeals to; *pathos*, appeals to; peroration; rhetorical situation; topics, argumentative
rhetorical situation, 29–30, 42, 48–50, 54, 62–63, 63n113, 70, 81, 315, 323–24, 330n47, 341, 352, 354
Roma Aeterna, 108, 116, 206, 268, 327. *See also* Roman imperialism and ideology
Roma et Augusti, 43, 49, 177n9, 195–96, 204. *See also* Roman imperialism and ideology
Roman economy, 31, 38–40, 45–49, 56–63, 68–71, 72n21, 83, 85–86, 89–90, 107, 160–61, 194, 205, 208–9, 214, 226, 263–70, 294, 311, 325–26. *See also* luxury; Roman imperialism and ideology
Roman imperialism and ideology, 37–48, 71–74, 102–16, 140–42, 160–62, 198–215, 263–70, 311–12
  emperor, 40–43, 51–52, 104–6, 141–42, 196, 198–203, 270–74
Roma, ideology of Rome, 38–40, 108–9, 116, 141, 196, 203–15, 263–70, 327
  See also Roman economy; Roman peace
Roman peace, 40, 44–45, 106–8, 199

safety, 36, 60n108, 74, 84–85, 138, 184–85, 188n47, 215, 217, 244, 259, 299, 311–12, 314, 332. *See also* topics, argumentative: security; security
Sardis, 52n79, 54n83, 58n100, 63, 69–70, 90, 194, 252n44, 280n60, 333
  oracle to, 3n8, 52n79, 58n100, 67, 83, 86, 183, 190–92, 236, 245–47, 248n36, 254, 280n60, 344
Satan, 43, 43n41, 48n63, 49, 53, 55–56, 101, 103–5, 107, 113, 139–40, 142, 173, 179n18, 187, 198–99, 201–3, 218, 224n93, 244, 248, 272n36, 364
Second Coming. *See* return of Christ; Judgment, Last.
security, 39, 44, 54, 63, 83, 107n37, 108, 139, 221–22, 252, 265, 269, 271, 282, 287n3, 289, 320, 345. *See also* topics, argumentative: security; safety
Septuagint, 23, 119, 162n50
Seth, 104
seven letters. *See* seven oracles
seven oracles, 3n8, 4, 10, 30–31, 48–63, 70, 82–83, 85, 88, 106n33, 116, 122, 126, 128, 172, 224, 229–34, 255–58, 280n60, 284
  appeals to *logos* in, 235–55
  appeals to *pathos* in, 175–92
  and epistolary parenesis, 178–80
  and genre of oracle, 178–80
  See also Ephesus: oracle to; Smyrna: oracle to; etc.
seven spirits, 97n12, 196n9
shame, 22, 164, 176, 189–93, 246, 251, 279–80
slander, 49, 53n81, 54–55, 57–58, 137, 142, 202, 210
slave, slaves, 22, 32, 42, 44, 45n45, 74, 111, 119, 130–32, 135–36, 143, 143n82, 153–54, 161–62, 162n49, 168, 188, 216, 221, 232, 234, 243, 267–68, 280n59, 287, 304, 326, 328, 334, 336n63, 356
Smyrna, 40, 49, 53, 54n83, 55, 57, 58n100, 59, 63, 69–70, 93, 102, 137, 187, 191, 204, 222, 272
  oracle to, 3n8, 82, 184–87, 239–40, 245, 250n41, 254, 344
social justice, 72–75
social location, 8n28, 34, 313, 323, 337, 340
sociology of religion, 18, 93–97, 354, 364
South Africa, 7, 74, 324
spirit, the, 10, 13n36, 120–21, 123n23, 125–27, 144, 155n34, 189, 277, 316
stasis, 110n45, 235, 236, 239, 245, 247, 250–51, 254
steno-symbol, 6, 95, 326
suffering, 57n98, 102, 170, 211, 245, 253n56, 254, 289, 349, 352

syllogism, 22–23, 230, 232–34
symbolic universe, 94–96, 100, 103
synagogue, 17n49, 20, 48–50, 53n81, 55–58, 58n100, 63, 69, 80, 82, 109, 137, 142, 147, 162n5, 185, 185n42, 239, 241, 248, 332
synkrisis (comparison), 24, 87, 243

temperance, 208
temple, heavenly, 37, 224, 289
Temple, Jerusalem, 55–56
Temple of Diana, 40, 42, 47, 49, 54n85, 177n9, 195
temple tax, 56, 58
tensive symbol, 6, 95
throne vision, 97–98, 165–69, 194–98, 260–63
Thyatira, 32, 41, 53, 59n105, 61n110, 63, 67–68, 70, 134, 137–40, 191n60, 205, 225, 236, 333, 346
  oracle to, 3n8, 49–50, 59n105, 83, 138–40, 183–84, 186, 188–89, 192, 243–47, 252n44, 254, 344
Tiberius, 40, 42, 57
topics, argumentative
  allies, 84n54, 184–85, 199, 265, 268–69, 290
  amplification, 19, 87n63, 109–10, 129–30, 135, 135n57, 237, 244, 261–62, 262n16, 270, 270n32, 298
  courage, 19, 20n54, 173, 239–40, 242n29, 254
  expediency, 19, 20n56, 23, 79–80, 89, 250, 252, 254, 258, 264, 272, 274, 276, 281–82, 312 (*see also* relative expediency)
  feasibility, 19, 23, 79, 114, 248, 250, 254, 290, 310
  honor, 19, 23, 79, 88, 89n70, 102–3, 190–92, 225, 227, 235, 244, 246–47, 252–53, 257–58, 265, 271, 273–84
  inexpediency, 88, 241, 250, 264–65, 269–70, 273, 307n57
  justice, 19, 20n56, 23, 84n54, 88, 188n48, 200, 240, 249–50, 258–61, 264 (*see also* justice)
  relative expediency, 240, 254, 272–74, 277–79, 281, 312
  security, 83, 89n70, 221, 252, 257–59, 265, 271, 276
  similar causes, 239, 241, 254, 269–70, 305, 308
  two women topos, 292–94, 326
  universal consensus, 262
trade, 34, 39, 45, 45nn45, 50; 46–48, 54n85, 56, 60, 60n108, 73–74, 108, 205n44, 208, 215, 329
  and idolatry, 47–48
  See also Roman economy

Trajan, 34, 37, 51–52, 60, 78n41, 80, 308n60
transfiguration, 1, 128
tribulation, 5, 33, 75, 127, 132, 239, 244, 250n41, 283, 287n3, 288n3, 307n56, 348, 363
twenty-four elders, 97, 99n17, 196n9, 260
two women topos, 292–94, 326
Typhon, 104–5

Vespasian, 36, 36n22, 40, 310n66
vindication, 54, 76, 100–102, 125, 138, 164–65, 169, 171, 209n60, 211n66, 220, 225, 245, 249, 289, 303n45, 304–5, 343–44. *See also* judgment; Judgment, Last
violence, 8, 26, 44, 46n50, 47–48, 57, 71, 72n21, 73n24, 107, 161, 165, 174, 203, 204n39, 205, 207, 209, 214–15, 263, 266–68, 270, 294, 303, 305, 305n49, 311, 314–15, 318, 320–21, 325–26, 329–30, 342–45, 347–48, 357–58
vivid description (*ekphrasis*), 87, 129, 173, 206n49, 219, 270, 274n41, 285, 292, 293
voice, ix, 9–10, 13n36, 21, 26, 30, 39, 42, 46, 48, 61n111, 62–63, 69, 71–74, 82, 89, 114, 119–21, 123n23, 124–28, 131–34, 137–38, 141–43, 145, 149–50, 153–58, 160, 165, 169–70, 174, 180, 187, 194, 207, 211, 214–15, 235, 246, 258, 264–67, 276–78, 280n61, 281, 299, 303, 315n5, 316–17, 319–22, 325, 332–33, 338–40, 349

wealth, 5, 20, 22, 30–31, 45–47, 50, 59, 68, 73, 83, 108, 160, 194, 203, 205, 214n78, 232, 251–52, 267, 333–34, 336, 338, 341, 344, 346, 361
witness, 8, 11, 16, 33, 49, 53–54, 56, 60, 63, 69–72, 73n24, 74–78, 89–90, 102–3, 107–9, 113, 132–33, 135–38, 140, 154, 189, 199n18, 203, 205, 207, 209n60, 212–15, 220, 222–28, 234, 236n22, 240, 246, 248n38, 250n41, 267, 274, 277–78, 282–83, 292, 305, 316, 320–21, 324, 330–36, 340–41, 348, 363
and conversion, 75–78, 213, 224
See also evangelism
witnesses, two, 53, 86, 102, 140, 154, 223–25, 231, 266, 342
women in Revelation, 8, 26, 67n8, 69, 114, 204n39, 226, 294n21, 315, 324–31
worldview, 16, 88n67, 94n4, 96, 100, 103–4, 108–12, 114–16, 116n54, 123, 159n44, 179, 234, 272n38, 284, 314, 336n63, 337, 342
worship, 97–100, 112–14, 151, 194–203, 258–63, 287–89
of the beast, 24, 39, 42–43, 53, 75–76, 84–85, 87, 106, 112–14, 125n30, 169, 195, 200–204, 206n49, 210, 219, 226, 242, 258, 262, 270–74, 277–78, 281 (*see also* imperial cult)
of emperor, 36, 41–43, 51, 106, 195–96, 205 (*see also* imperial cult; worship of the beast)
of God, 14, 24, 69, 71, 76–77, 83, 85–87, 97–98, 100–101, 112–16, 142, 154, 159–60, 163, 166, 195–98, 201, 204, 210, 218, 220–21, 234, 243, 258–60, 277, 287, 289, 301–2, 319, 339, 341, 345
of idols, 43–44, 59–63, 71, 72n19, 75, 98–99, 101, 111, 138, 142, 154, 160, 173, 195, 210, 220, 241–43, 266, 287, 291, 302, 322, 336 (*see also* idolatry; imperial cult; worship, of beast)
of Lamb, 24, 97–98, 112–13, 197–98, 210, 221, 258, 260–63, 277, 289

Year of the Four Emperors, 34, 36, 36n22, 216

Zealots, 48n64, 55, 357
Zeus, 38, 43, 49, 55, 110, 177n9, 180, 195
altar of, 43, 49, 177n9, 195

www.ingramcontent.com/pod-product-compliance
Lightning Source LLC
Chambersburg PA
CBHW031402290426
44110CB00011B/237